T0338613

Handbook of Research on Natural Language Processing and Smart Service Systems

Rodolfo Abraham Pazos-Rangel
Tecnológico Nacional de México, Mexico & Instituto Tecnológico de Ciudad Madero, Mexico

Rogelio Florencia-Juarez
Universidad Autónoma de Ciudad Juárez, Mexico

Mario Andrés Paredes-Valverde
Tecnológico Nacional de México, Mexico & Instituto Tecnológico de Orizaba, Mexico

Gilberto Rivera
Universidad Autónoma de Ciudad Juárez, Mexico

A volume in the Advances in Computational Intelligence and Robotics (ACIR) Book Series

Published in the United States of America by
    IGI Global
    Engineering Science Reference (an imprint of IGI Global)
    701 E. Chocolate Avenue
    Hershey PA, USA 17033
    Tel: 717-533-8845
    Fax: 717-533-8661
    E-mail: cust@igi-global.com
    Web site: http://www.igi-global.com

Copyright © 2021 by IGI Global. All rights reserved. No part of this publication may be reproduced, stored or distributed in any form or by any means, electronic or mechanical, including photocopying, without written permission from the publisher. Product or company names used in this set are for identification purposes only. Inclusion of the names of the products or companies does not indicate a claim of ownership by IGI Global of the trademark or registered trademark.

Library of Congress Cataloging-in-Publication Data

Names: Pazos-Rangel, Rodolfo Abraham, 1951- editor.
Title: Handbook of research on natural language processing and smart
  service systems / Rodolfo Abraham Pazos-Rangel, Rogelio
  Florencia-Juarez, Mario Andrés Paredes-Valverde, Gilberto Rivera,
  editors.
Description: Hershey, PA : Engineering Science Reference, an imprint of
  IGI Global, [2020] | Includes bibliographical references and index. |
  Summary: "This book is a collection of innovative research on the
  integration and development of intelligent software tools and their
  various applications within professional environments"-- Provided by
  publisher.
Identifiers: LCCN 2019058351 (print) | LCCN 2019058352 (ebook) | ISBN
  9781799847304 (hardcover) | ISBN 9781799847311 (ebook)
Subjects: LCSH: Natural language processing (Computer science) | Natural
  language generation (Computer science) | Computational linguistics.
Classification: LCC QA76.9.N38 H3645 2020 (print) | LCC QA76.9.N38
  (ebook) | DDC 006.3/5--dc23
LC record available at https://lccn.loc.gov/2019058351
LC ebook record available at https://lccn.loc.gov/2019058352

This book is published in the IGI Global book series Advances in Computational Intelligence and Robotics (ACIR) (ISSN: 2327-0411; eISSN: 2327-042X)

British Cataloguing in Publication Data
A Cataloguing in Publication record for this book is available from the British Library.

All work contributed to this book is new, previously-unpublished material. The views expressed in this book are those of the authors, but not necessarily of the publisher.

For electronic access to this publication, please contact: eresources@igi-global.com.

Advances in Computational Intelligence and Robotics (ACIR) Book Series

Ivan Giannoccaro
University of Salento, Italy

ISSN:2327-0411
EISSN:2327-042X

MISSION

While intelligence is traditionally a term applied to humans and human cognition, technology has progressed in such a way to allow for the development of intelligent systems able to simulate many human traits. With this new era of simulated and artificial intelligence, much research is needed in order to continue to advance the field and also to evaluate the ethical and societal concerns of the existence of artificial life and machine learning.

The **Advances in Computational Intelligence and Robotics (ACIR) Book Series** encourages scholarly discourse on all topics pertaining to evolutionary computing, artificial life, computational intelligence, machine learning, and robotics. ACIR presents the latest research being conducted on diverse topics in intelligence technologies with the goal of advancing knowledge and applications in this rapidly evolving field.

COVERAGE

- Artificial Life
- Automated Reasoning
- Evolutionary Computing
- Natural Language Processing
- Computational Logic
- Intelligent control
- Heuristics
- Cognitive Informatics
- Fuzzy Systems
- Computational Intelligence

IGI Global is currently accepting manuscripts for publication within this series. To submit a proposal for a volume in this series, please contact our Acquisition Editors at Acquisitions@igi-global.com or visit: http://www.igi-global.com/publish/.

The Advances in Computational Intelligence and Robotics (ACIR) Book Series (ISSN 2327-0411) is published by IGI Global, 701 E. Chocolate Avenue, Hershey, PA 17033-1240, USA, www.igi-global.com. This series is composed of titles available for purchase individually; each title is edited to be contextually exclusive from any other title within the series. For pricing and ordering information please visit http://www.igi-global.com/book-series/advances-computational-intelligence-robotics/73674. Postmaster: Send all address changes to above address. Copyright © 2021 IGI Global. All rights, including translation in other languages reserved by the publisher. No part of this series may be reproduced or used in any form or by any means – graphics, electronic, or mechanical, including photocopying, recording, taping, or information and retrieval systems – without written permission from the publisher, except for non commercial, educational use, including classroom teaching purposes. The views expressed in this series are those of the authors, but not necessarily of IGI Global.

Titles in this Series

For a list of additional titles in this series, please visit:
http://www.igi-global.com/book-series/advances-computational-intelligence-robotics/73674

AI-Based Services for Smart Cities and Urban Infrastructure
Kangjuan Lyu (SILC Business School, Shanghai University, China) Min Hu (SILC Business School, Shanghai University, China) Juan Du (SILC Business School, Shanghai University, China) and Vijayan Sugumaran (Oakland University, USA)
Engineering Science Reference • © 2021 • 330pp • H/C (ISBN: 9781799850243) • US $195.00

Intelligent Computations Applications for Solving Complex Problems
Naveen Dahiya (Maharaja Surajmal Institute of Technology, New Delhi, India) Zhongyu Lu (University of Huddersfield, UK) Vishal Bhatnagar (Ambedkar Institute of Advance Communication Technologies & Research, India) and Pardeep Sangwan (Maharaja Surajmal Institute of Technology, New Delhi, India)
Engineering Science Reference • © 2021 • 300pp • H/C (ISBN: 9781799847939) • US $225.00

Artificial Intelligence and the Journey to Software 2.0 Emerging Research and Opportunities
Divanshi Priyadarshni Wangoo (Indira Gandhi Delhi Technical University for Women, India)
Engineering Science Reference • © 2021 • 150pp • H/C (ISBN: 9781799843276) • US $165.00

Practical Applications and Use Cases of Computer Vision and Recognition Systems
Chiranji Lal Chowdhary (Vellore Institute of Technology, India) and B.D. Parameshachari (GSSS Institute of Engineering and Technology for Women, India)
Engineering Science Reference • © 2020 • 300pp • H/C (ISBN: 9781799849247) • US $195.00

Machine Learning Applications in Non-Conventional Machining Processes
Goutam Kumar Bose (Haldia Institute of Technology, Haldia, India) and Pritam Pain (Haldia Institute of Technology, India)
Engineering Science Reference • © 2020 • 300pp • H/C (ISBN: 9781799836247) • US $195.00

Handbook of Research on Smart Technology Models for Business and Industry
J. Joshua Thomas (UOW Malaysia KDU Penang University College, Malaysia) Ugo Fiore (University of Naples Parthenope, Italy) Gilberto Perez Lechuga (Autonomous University of Hidalgo State, Mexico) Valeriy Kharchenko (Federal Agroengineering Centre VIM , Russia) and Pandian Vasant (University of Technology Petronas, Malaysia)
Engineering Science Reference • © 2020 • 491pp • H/C (ISBN: 9781799836452) • US $295.00

Advancements in Computer Vision Applications in Intelligent Systems and Multimedia Technologies
Muhammad Sarfraz (Kuwait University, Kuwait)
Engineering Science Reference • © 2020 • 324pp • H/C (ISBN: 9781799844440) • US $225.00

701 East Chocolate Avenue, Hershey, PA 17033, USA
Tel: 717-533-8845 x100 • Fax: 717-533-8661
E-Mail: cust@igi-global.com • www.igi-global.com

Editorial Advisory Board

Giner Alor-Hernández, *Instituto Tecnológico de Orizaba, Mexico*
Luis Omar Colombo-Mendoza, *Instituto Tecnológico Superior de Teziutlán, Mexico*
Verónica Pérez-Rosas, *University of Michigan, USA*
María del Pilar Salas-Zárate, *Instituto Tecnológico Superior de Teziutlán, Mexico*
Alejandro Rodríguez González, *Universidad Politécnica de Madrid, Spain*
Miguel Ángel Rodríguez-García, *Universidad Rey Juan Carlos, Spain*
Rafael Valencia García, *Universidad de Murcia, Spain*

List of Contributors

Table of Contents

Section 1
Smart Interactive Systems

Chapter 1
    Rodolfo A. Pazos-Rangel, Tecnológico Nacional de México, Mexico & Instituto Tecnológico de Ciudad Madero, Mexico
    Gilberto Rivera, Universidad Autónoma de Ciudad Juárez, Mexico
    José A. Martínez F., Tecnológico Nacional de México, Mexico & Instituto Tecnológico de Ciudad Madero, Mexico
    Juana Gaspar, Tecnológico Nacional de México, Mexico & Instituto Tecnológico de Ciudad Madero, Mexico
    Rogelio Florencia-Juárez, Universidad Autónoma de Ciudad Juárez, Mexico

Chapter 2
    Marcos E. Martinez, Universidad Autónoma de Ciudad Juárez, Mexico
    Francisco López-Orozco, Universidad Autónoma de Ciudad Juárez, Mexico
    Karla Olmos-Sánchez, Universidad Autónoma de Ciudad Juárez, Mexico
    Julia Patricia Sánchez-Solís, Universidad Autónoma de Ciudad Juárez, Mexico

Chapter 3
    Sanah Nashir Sayyed, Dr. Babasaheb Ambedkar Marathwada University, India
    Namrata Mahender C., Dr. Babasaheb Ambedkar Marathwada University, India

Section 2
Text Analytics Systems

Section 3
Text Mining Systems

Detailed Table of Contents

Section 1
Smart Interactive Systems

Chapter 1

Rodolfo A. Pazos-Rangel, Tecnológico Nacional de México, Mexico & Instituto Tecnológico de Ciudad Madero, Mexico

Gilberto Rivera, Universidad Autónoma de Ciudad Juárez, Mexico

José A. Martínez F., Tecnológico Nacional de México, Mexico & Instituto Tecnológico de Ciudad Madero, Mexico

Juana Gaspar, Tecnológico Nacional de México, Mexico & Instituto Tecnológico de Ciudad Madero, Mexico

Rogelio Florencia-Juárez, Universidad Autónoma de Ciudad Juárez, Mexico

This chapter consists of an update of a previous publication. Specifically, the chapter aims at describing the most decisive advances in NLIDBs of this decade. Unlike many surveys on NLIDBs, for this chapter, the NLIDBs will be selected according to three relevance criteria: performance (i.e., percentage of correctly answered queries), soundness of the experimental evaluation, and the number of citations. To this end, the chapter will also include a brief review of the most widely used performance measures and query corpora for testing NLIDBs.

Chapter 2

Marcos E. Martinez, Universidad Autónoma de Ciudad Juárez, Mexico

Francisco López-Orozco, Universidad Autónoma de Ciudad Juárez, Mexico

Karla Olmos-Sánchez, Universidad Autónoma de Ciudad Juárez, Mexico

Julia Patricia Sánchez-Solís, Universidad Autónoma de Ciudad Juárez, Mexico

The interaction between humans and machines has evolved; thus, the idea of being able to communicate with computers as we usually do with other people is becoming increasingly closer to coming true.

Nowadays, it is common to come across intelligent systems named chatbots, which allow people to communicate by using natural language to hold conversations related to a specific domain. Chatbots have gained popularity in different kinds of sectors, such as customer service, marketing, sales, e-commerce, e-learning, travel, and even in education itself. This chapter aims to present a chatbot-based approach to learning English as a second language by using computer-assisted language learning systems.

Chapter 3

Summarization is the process of selecting representative data to produce a reduced version of the given data with a minimal loss of information; so, it generally works on text, images, videos, and speech data. The chapter deals with not only concepts of text summarization (types, stages, issues, and criteria) but also with applications. The two main categories of approaches generally used in text summaries (i.e., abstractive and extractive) are discussed. Abstractive techniques use linguistic methods to interpret the text; they produce understandable and semantically equivalent sentences with a shorter length. Extractive techniques mostly rely on statistical methods for extracting essential sentences from the given text. In addition, the authors explore the SACAS model to exemplify the process of summarization. The SACAS system analyzed 50 stories, and its evaluation is presented in terms of a new measurement based on question-answering MOS, which is also introduced in this chapter.

Chapter 4

Databases and corpora are essential resources to evaluate the performance of Natural Language Interfaces to Databases (NLIDB). The Geobase database and the Geoquery corpus (Geoquery250 and Geoquery880) are among the most commonly used. In this chapter, the authors analyze both resources to offer two elaborate resources: 1) N-Geobase, which is a relational database, and 2) the corpus Geoquery270. The former follows the standard normalization procedure, then N-Geobase has a schema similar to enterprise databases. Geoquery270 consists of 270 queries selected from Geoquery880, preserving the same kind of natural language problems as Geoquery880, but with more challenging issues for an NLIDB than Geoquery250. To evaluate the new resources, they compared the performance of the NLIDB using Geoquery270 and Geoquery250. The results indicated that Geoquery270 was the harder corpus, while Geoquery250 is the easier one. Consequently, this chapter offers a broader range of resources to NLIDB designers.

Chapter 5

Ossiel Villanueva-Mendoza, Universidad Autónoma de Ciudad Juárez, Mexico
Martha Victoria González, Universidad Autónoma de Ciudad Juárez, Mexico
Maritza Varela, Universidad Autónoma de Ciudad Juárez, Mexico
Lucero Zamora, Universidad Autónoma de Ciudad Juárez, Mexico

Conversation practice is essential for second-language acquisition and necessary for learners to reach an acceptable communicative level. In an ideal scenario, students should regularly hold conversations with native speakers of the target language, but this is often not possible. Although the teachers use the target language during the classes, they cannot offer a continuous conversation with each student, and they are usually not available wherever and whenever the student requires them to practice. This chapter presents the development and use of a mobile application to hold conversations in the Japanese language. The objective is to provide a software tool to improve the level of communicative competence (both inside and outside a classroom environment). So, the authors created and used a conversational agent (chatbot) using Dialogflow (a Google API), which is connected to the application's interface through the Internet using a client access token to give responses to user inputs in real time.

Chapter 6

Jesús Fernández-Avelino, Tecnológico Nacional de México, Mexico & Instituto Tecnológico de Orizaba, Mexico
Giner Alor-Hernández, Tecnológico Nacional de México, Mexico & Instituto Tecnológico de Orizaba, Mexico
Mario Andrés Paredes-Valverde, Tecnológico Nacional de México, Mexico & Instituto Tecnológico de Orizaba, Mexico
Laura Nely Sánchez-Morales, Tecnológico Nacional de México, Mexico & Instituto Tecnológico de Orizaba, Mexico

A chatbot is a software agent that mimics human conversation using artificial intelligence technologies. Chatbots help to accomplish tasks ranging from answering questions, playing music, to managing smart home devices. The adoption of this kind of agent is increasing since people are discovering the benefits of them, such as saving time and money, higher customer satisfaction, customer base growing, among others. However, developing a chatbot is a challenging task that requires addressing several issues such as pattern matching, natural language understanding, and natural language processing, as well as to design a knowledge base that encapsulates the intelligence of the system. This chapter describes the design and implementation of a text/speech chatbot for supporting health self-management. This chatbot is currently based on Spanish. The main goal of this chapter is to clearly describe the main components and phases of the chatbot development process, the methods, and tools used for this purpose, as well as to describe and discuss our findings from the practice side of things.

Alexander Gelbukh, Instituto Politécnico Nacional, Mexico

José A. Martínez F., Tecnológico Nacional de México, Mexico & Instituto Tecnológico de Ciudad Madero, Mexico

Andres Verastegui, Tecnológico Nacional de México, Mexico & Instituto Tecnológico de Ciudad Madero, Mexico

Alberto Ochoa, Universidad Autónoma de Ciudad Juárez, Mexico

In this chapter, an exhaustive parser is presented. The parser was developed to be used in a natural language interface to databases (NLIDB) project. This chapter includes a brief description of state-of-the-art NLIDBs, including a description of the methods used and the performance of some interfaces. Some of the general problems in natural language interfaces to databases are also explained. The exhaustive parser was developed, aiming at improving the overall performance of the interface; therefore, the interface is also briefly described. This chapter also presents the drawbacks discovered during the experimental tests of the parser, which show that it is unsuitable for improving the NLIDB performance.

Alberto Ochoa, Universidad Autónoma de Ciudad Juárez, Mexico

Roberto Contreras-Masse, Tecnológico Nacional de México, Mexico & Instituto Tecnológico de Ciudad Juárez, Mexico

Jose Mejia, Universidad Autónoma de Ciudad Juárez, Mexico

Diego Oliva, Universidad de Guadalajara, Mexico

This research describes an intelligent tool based on a karaoke system to represent the linguistic resources related to a social network for music and songs associated with a cultural bulwark: Otomí (a language spoken in México). This system employs a representation of the Dublin Core metadata standard for document description, composed by XML standard to describe profiles and provide recommendations to a group of persons associated with this social network. The novel idea of this research is the analysis (with an improved methodology) of each search to provide a recommendation based on petitions of each user in this social network, reducing the human efforts spent on the generation of a specific profile. In addition, this chapter presents and discusses some experiments to corroborate the impact of this research, based on quantitative and qualitative evaluations. This chapter introduces an innovative idea of how to help this type of ethnic group.

José A. Martínez F., Tecnológico Nacional de México, Mexico & Instituto Tecnológico de Ciudad Madero, Mexico

Juan Javier González-Barbosa, Tecnológico Nacional de México, Mexico & Instituto Tecnológico de Ciudad Madero, Mexico

German Castillo, Tecnológico Nacional de México, Mexico & Instituto Tecnológico de Ciudad Madero, Mexico

Currently, there exist tools for query composition that can be used by users who are not skillful in a DB query language such as SQL. Many tools are difficult to use, and others cannot answer some queries that inexperienced users would like to formulate. This chapter describes the new functionality developed for a query composition interface, which allows inexperienced users to compose queries that involve one, two, or three subqueries without the need to have any knowledge of neither SQL nor the database schema. The experimental tests showed that users could easily compose queries that involve one subquery. Furthermore, the new functionality preserves the domain independence of the previous version of the interface. Additionally, like the earlier version, the latest release offers language independence; that is, it can be configured for other languages similar to Spanish, for example English, French, Italian, and Portuguese.

Section 2
Text Analytics Systems

Chapter 10

Alejandro Requejo Flores, Universidad Autónoma de Ciudad Juárez, Mexico
Alejandro Ruiz, Universidad Autónoma de Ciudad Juárez, Mexico
Abraham López, Universidad Autónoma de Ciudad Juárez, Mexico
Raul Porras, Universidad Autónoma de Ciudad Juárez, Mexico

The primary objective of this chapter is to analyze the content retrieved from an RSS newspaper report written in the Spanish language and determine if it describes a traffic incident. The real-world case study occurs in a Mexican city with 1.5 million inhabitants, and its purpose is to offer an application to inform in real-time about traffic incidents that happen in the town, gathering its information from the reports published by a local newspaper. However, to do so, the authors first need to classify the articles and ignore those whose content does not imply any kind of road accident.

Chapter 11

Iqra Ameer, Instituto Politécnico Nacional, Mexico
Grigori Sidorov, Instituto Politécnico Nacional, Mexico

The automatic identification of an author's demographic traits (e.g., gender, age group) from their written text is termed as author profiling. This problem has become an essential problem in fields like linguistic forensics, marketing, and security. In recent years, online social setups (e.g., Twitter, Facebook, blogs, hotel reviews) have extended remarkably; however, it is easy to provide fake profiles. This research aims to predict the traits of the authors for a benchmark existing corpus, based on Twitter, hotel reviews, social media, and blogs' profiles. In this chapter, the authors have explored four sets of features, including syntactic n-grams of part-of-speech tags, traditional n-grams of part-of-speech tags, combinations of word n-grams, and combinations of character n-grams. They used word unigram and character three-gram as a baseline approach. After analyzing the results, they concluded that the performance improves when the combination of word n-grams is used.

Roberto Contreras-Masse, Tecnológico Nacional de México, Mexico & Instituto Tecnológico de Ciudad Juárez, Mexico
Juan Carlos Bonilla, Universidad Autónoma del Estado de Morelos, Mexico
Jose Mejia, Universidad Autónoma de Ciudad Juárez, Mexico
Alberto Ochoa, Universidad Autónoma de Ciudad Juárez, Mexico

Nowadays, the internet has an astonishing amount of useful material for personality mining; nevertheless, many companies fail to exploit the information and screen job candidates using personality tests that fail to grasp the very information they are trying to gather. This research aims to highlight and compare the different machine learning classifiers that can be used to predict the personality of a Spanish-speaking job applicant based on the written content posted on their social networks. The authors conduct experiments considering the most critical measures (such as accuracy, precision, and recall) to evaluate the classification performance. The results show that the random-forest classifier outperforms the other classifiers. It is of utmost importance to correctly assess the resumes to determine the most qualified people in a smart manufacturing position.

Joaquín Pérez Ortega, Tecnológico Nacional de México, Mexico & CENIDET, Mexico
Nelva Nely Almanza Ortega, Tecnológico Nacional de México, Mexico & Instituto Tecnológico de Tlalnepantla, Mexico
Andrea Vega Villalobos, Tecnológico Nacional de México, Mexico & CENIDET, Mexico
Marco A. Aguirre L., Tecnológico Nacional de México, Mexico & Instituto Tecnológico de Ciudad Madero, Mexico
Crispín Zavala Díaz, Universidad Autónoma del Estado de Morelos, Mexico
Javier Ortiz Hernandez, Tecnológico Nacional de México, Mexico & CENIDET, Mexico
Antonio Hernández Gómez, Tecnológico Nacional de México, Mexico & CENIDET, Mexico

In recent years, the amount of texts in natural language, in digital format, has had an impressive increase. To obtain useful information from a large volume of data, new specialized techniques and efficient algorithms are required. Text mining consists of extracting meaningful patterns from texts; one of the basic approaches is clustering. The most used clustering algorithm is k-means. This chapter proposes an improvement of the k-means algorithm in the convergence step; the process stops whenever the number of objects that change their assigned cluster in the current iteration is bigger than the ones that changed in the previous iteration. Experimental results showed a reduction in execution time up to 93%. It is remarkable that, in general, better results are obtained when the volume of the text increase, particularly in those texts within big data environments.

    Alonso García, Universidad Autónoma de Ciudad Juárez, Mexico
    Martha Victoria González, Universidad Autónoma de Ciudad Juárez, Mexico
    Francisco López-Orozco, Universidad Autónoma de Ciudad Juárez, Mexico
    Lucero Zamora, Universidad Autónoma de Ciudad Juárez, Mexico

Recent technological advances have allowed the development of numerous natural language processing applications with which users frequently interact. When interacting with this type of application, users often search for the economy of words, which promotes the use of pronouns, thereby highlighting the well-known anaphora problem. This chapter describes a proposal to approach the pronominal anaphora for the Spanish language. A set of rules (based on the Eagle standard) was designed to identify the referents of personal pronouns through the structure of the grammatical tags of the words. The proposed algorithm uses the online Freeling service to perform tokenization and tagging tasks. The performance of the algorithm was compared with an online version of Freeling, and the proposed algorithm shows better performance.

    Carlos Manuel Ramirez López, Universidad Politécnica de Aguascalientes, Mexico
    Martín Montes Rivera, Universidad Politécnica de Aguascalientes, Mexico
    Alberto Ochoa, Universidad Autónoma de Ciudad Juárez, Mexico
    Julio César Ponce Gallegos, Universidad Autónoma de Aguascalientes, Mexico
    José Eder Guzmán Mendoza, Universidad Politécnica de Aguascalientes, Mexico

This research presents the application of Empirical Bayesian Kriging, a geostatistical interpolation method. The case study is about suicide prevention. The dataset is composed of more than one million records, obtained from the report database of the Emergency Service 911 of the Mexican State of Aguascalientes. The purpose is to get prediction surfaces, probability, and standard error prediction for completed suicide cases. Here, the variations in the environment of suicide cases are relative to and dependent on economic, social, and cultural phenomena.

    Alejandro Requejo Flores, Universidad Autónoma de Ciudad Juárez, Mexico
    Alejandro Ruiz, Universidad Autónoma de Ciudad Juárez, Mexico
    Ricardo Mar, Universidad Autónoma de Ciudad Juárez, Mexico
    Raúl Porras, Universidad Autónoma de Ciudad Juárez, Mexico

Around the world, cities suffer from a large variety of problems. One of them is urban mobility, and the most common cause is related to traffic incidents, which unexpectedly provoke delays to people and produce losses to businesses. Through natural-language-processing methods, this chapter proposes a way to inform people about events that could have happened on the road. The proposed application takes information from news reports (published by a local newspaper) that have been previously classified as 'traffic incidents'; the app tries to extract the location where these events occurred. These data are then served on a web application, which shows a map that marks all the recent incidents. In this way, the authors offer an alternative to allow citizens to be informed about this kind of event so they can take preventive actions.

Chapter 17

Namrata Kumari, National Institute of Technology, Hamirpur, India
Pardeep Singh, National Institute of Technology, Hamirpur, India

Text summarization is a compressing technique of the original text to form a summary which will provide the same meaning and information as provided by the original version. Summarizer helps in saving time and increasing efficiency. This chapter gives the full insight of text summarizers, which can be categorized based on methodology, function and target reader, dimension, and language. Various researches have been conducted in the field of text summarization using different approaches. Consequently, the chapter aims to provide an overview of how text summarizers work with different methods and state their domain-oriented applications. Additionally, the authors discuss multi-lingual text summarization in detail. This chapter focuses on showing the effectiveness and shortcomings of text summarization approaches by comparing them.

Chapter 18

Irvin Raul Lopez Contreras, Universidad Autónoma de Ciudad Juárez, Mexico
Alejandra Mendoza Carreón, Universidad Autónoma de Ciudad Juárez, Mexico
Jorge Rodas-Osollo, Universidad Autónoma de Ciudad Juárez, Mexico
Martiza Concepción Varela, Universidad Autónoma de Ciudad Juárez, Mexico

The quantity of information in the world is increasing every day on a fast level. This fact will be an obstacle in some situations; text summarization is involved in this kind of problem. It is used to minimize the time that people spend searching for information on the web and in a lot of digital documents. In this chapter, three algorithms were compared; all of them are an extractive text summarization algorithm. Popular libraries that influence the performance of these kinds of algorithms were used. It was necessary to configure and modify these methods so that they work for the Spanish language instead of their original one. The authors use some metrics found in the literature to evaluate the quality and performance of these algorithms.

Section 3
Text Mining Systems

Chapter 19

Jose L. Martinez-Rodriguez, Universidad Autónoma de Tamaulipas, Mexico
Ivan Lopez-Arevalo, CINVESTAV Tamaulipas, Mexico
Jaime I. Lopez-Veyna, Tecnológico Nacional de México, Mexico & Instituto Tecnológico de Zacatecas, Mexico
Ana B. Rios-Alvarado, Universidad Autónoma de Tamaulipas, Mexico
Edwin Aldana-Bobadilla, Conacyt, Mexico & Cinvestav Tamaulipas, Mexico

One of the goals of data scientists and curators is to get information (contained in text) organized and integrated in a way that can be easily consumed by people and machines. A starting point for such a goal is to get a model to represent the information. This model should ease to obtain knowledge semantically (e.g., using reasoners and inferencing rules). In this sense, the Semantic Web is focused on representing the information through the Resource Description Framework (RDF) model, in which the triple (subject, predicate, object) is the basic unit of information. In this context, the natural language processing (NLP) field has been a cornerstone in the identification of elements that can be represented by triples of the Semantic Web. However, existing approaches for the representation of RDF triples from texts use diverse techniques and tasks for such purpose, which complicate the understanding of the process by non-expert users. This chapter aims to discuss the main concepts involved in the representation of the information through the Semantic Web and the NLP fields.

Chapter 20

Rafael Jiménez, Universidad Autónoma de Ciudad Juárez, Mexico
Vicente García, Universidad Autónoma de Ciudad Juárez, Mexico
Abraham López, Universidad Autónoma de Ciudad Juárez, Mexico
Alejandra Mendoza Carreón, Universidad Autónoma de Ciudad Juárez, Mexico
Alan Ponce, Universidad Autónoma de Ciudad Juárez, Mexico

The Autonomous University of Ciudad Juárez performs an instructor evaluation each semester to find strengths, weaknesses, and areas of opportunity during the teaching process. In this chapter, the authors show how opinion mining can be useful for labeling student comments as positives and negatives. For this purpose, a database was created using real opinions obtained from five professors of the UACJ over the last four years, covering a total of 20 subjects. Natural language processing techniques were used on the database to normalize its data. Experimental results using 1-NN and Bagging classifiers shows that it is possible to automatically label positive and negative comments with an accuracy of 80.13%.

Chapter 21

Karina Castro-Pérez, Tecnológico Nacional de México, Mexico & IT Orizaba, Mexico
José Luis Sánchez-Cervantes, CONACYT, Mexico & Instituto Tecnológico de Orizaba, Mexico
María del Pilar Salas-Zárate, Tecnológico Nacional de México, Mexico & ITS Teziutlán, Mexico
Maritza Bustos-López, Tecnológico Nacional de México, Mexico & Instituto Tecnológico de Orizaba, Mexico
Lisbeth Rodríguez-Mazahua, Tecnológico Nacional de México, Mexico & Instituto Tecnológico de Orizaba, Mexico

In recent years, the application of opinion mining has increased as a boom and growth of social media and blogs on the web, and these sources generate a large volume of unstructured data; therefore, a manual review is not feasible. For this reason, it has become necessary to apply web scraping and opinion mining techniques, two primary processes that help to obtain and summarize the data. Opinion mining, among its various areas of application, stands out for its essential contribution in the context of healthcare, especially for pharmacovigilance, because it allows finding adverse drug events omitted by the pharmaceutical companies. This chapter proposes a hybrid approach that uses semantics and machine learning for an opinion mining-analysis system by applying natural-language-processing techniques for the detection of drug polarity for chronic-degenerative diseases, available in blogs and specialized websites in the Spanish language.

Chapter 22

Rafael Jiménez, Universidad Autónoma de Ciudad Juárez, Mexico
Vicente García, Universidad Autónoma de Ciudad Juárez, Mexico
Karla Olmos-Sánchez, Universidad Autónoma de Ciudad Juárez, Mexico
Alan Ponce, Universidad Autónoma de Ciudad Juárez, Mexico
Jorge Rodas-Osollo, Universidad Autónoma de Ciudad Juárez, Mexico

Social networks have moved from online sites to interact with your friends to a platform where people, artists, brands, and even presidents interact with crowds of people daily. Airlines are some of the companies that use social networks such as Twitter to communicate with their clients through messages with offers, travel recommendations, videos of collaborations with YouTubers, and surveys. Among the many responses to airline tweets, there are users' suggestions on how to improve their services or processes. These recommendations are essential since the success of many companies is based on offering what the client wants or needs. A database of tweets was created using user tweets sent to airline accounts on Twitter between July 30 (2019) and August 8 (2019). Natural language processing techniques were used on the database to preprocess its data. The latest classification results using Naive Bayes show an accuracy of 72.44%.

Foreword

When I was invited to write the foreword for the *Handbook of Research on Natural Language Processing and Smart Service Systems* (edited by Professors Dr. Rodolfo Abraham Pazos Rangel, Dr. Rogelio Florencia Juárez, Dr. Mario Andrés Paredes Valverde, and Dr. Gilberto Rivera Zárate), I was quite excited because the topics covered in this handbook are cutting-edge topics.

I would like to point out that due to the large amount of digital information on the Internet, the need for software applications capable of automatically processing this large volume of data has been highlighted in many research studies. This fact has motivated the scientific community to develop Natural Language Processing algorithms to improve human-computer interaction. Natural Language Processing (NLP) is a field of Computer Science whose purpose is to develop algorithms that provide computers with the ability to understand human language.

From my perspective, at present, there is a growing number of institutions, organizations, and companies, which are finding a way to take advantage of the development of smart solutions based on NLP to improve the experience of their users. The current trend in this area is to incorporate NLP algorithms in software applications for the processing of structured and unstructured data generated in their businesses, social networks, or the Internet. These NLP algorithms, in combination with Machine Learning algorithms and Artificial Intelligence, become Smart Analytics applications, capable of generating knowledge that can be vital for decision making.

This handbook is a handy tool in this perspective. It is well organized and aims to collect the latest algorithms in the field of NLP, for both structured and unstructured information, focused on improving commercial services related to Sentiment Analysis, Suggestion Mining, Natural-Language Interfaces, Chatbots, Text Classification, among other topics related to NLP. Therefore, I believe that those of us who are interested in any of these topics will benefit from this handbook. I can say that this handbook helps practitioners and students know how to get started implementing these algorithms, and with this, start developing Smart Analytics applications.

Finally, I consider that this handbook has enough elements to motivate its readers to implement these technologies and to advance towards a Smart Business environment, as well as to encourage researchers to continue contributing to this field.

Grigori Sidorov
Instituto Politécnico Nacional, Mexico

Preface

Natural Language Processing (NLP) is an area of Artificial Intelligence (AI) whose purpose is to develop software applications that provide computers with the ability to understand human language. NLP includes essential applications such as machine translation, speech recognition, text summarization, text categorization, sentiment analysis, suggestion mining, question answering, chatbots, and knowledge representation. All these applications are critical because they allow developing smart service systems, i.e., systems capable of learning, adapting, and making decisions based on data collected, processed, and analyzed to improve its response to future situations.

In the age of knowledge, the NLP field has gained increased attention both in the academic and industrial scenes since it can help us to overcome the inherent challenges and difficulties arising from the drastic increase of offline and online data. NLP is useful for developing solutions in many fields, including business, education, health, marketing, education, politics, bioinformatics, and psychology. Academics and practitioners use NLP to solve almost any problem that requires to understand and analyze human language either in the form of text or speech. Nowadays, people use NLP without even realizing it. For example, they interact with mobile devices and services like Siri, Alexa or Google Home to perform daily activities (e.g., search the Web, order food, ask directions, shop online, turn on lights). Businesses of all sizes are also taking advantage of NLP to improve their business; for instance, they use this technology to monitor their reputation, optimize their customer service through chatbots, and support decision-making processes, to mention but a few. This book aims to provide a general overview of novel approaches and empirical research findings in the area of NLP.

This book is intended for researchers, computer scientists, engineers, and teachers seeking for novel applications of NLP technologies and resources on domains such as education, second language acquisition, smart cities, health self-management, preservation of cultural heritage, and suicide data analysis. The primary beneficiary of this book will be the undergraduate, graduate, and postgraduate community who have just stepped into the NLP area and is interested in designing, modeling, and developing cross-disciplinary solutions based on NLP. This book helps them to discover the particularities of the applications of this technology for solving problems from different domains.

Handbook of Research on Natural Language Processing and Smart Service System is organized into three different sections that provide comprehensive coverage of relevant topics such as smart interactive systems, text analytic systems, and text mining systems. The following paragraphs provide a summary of the importance of the contents.

Section 1, named "Smart Interactive Systems", features nine chapters connected to three major fields:

(1) Question Answering (QA). The Computer Science discipline concerned with building systems that can get questions and answer them in natural language.

(2) Chatbots. Computer programs that simulate human conversation through voice commands or text chats or both, allowing humans to interact with digital devices.

(3) Recommender Systems. They suggest relevant items to users such as documents, products, videos, news, among others, becoming a part of our daily lives.

Chapter 1, "Natural Language Interfaces to Databases: A Survey on Recent Advances", presents a survey of Natural Language Interfaces to Databases (NLIDBs) based on three relevance criteria: performance (percentage of correctly answered queries), soundness of experimental evaluation, and the number of citations. This survey helped to identify current challenges in this domain, such as developing domain independent NLIDBs whose accuracy is above 95%, databases with design anomalies, and determining if a natural language expression is grammatical, i.e., if it satisfies the rules of grammar.

Chapter 2, "Mispronunciation Detection and Diagnosis through a Chatbot", is dedicated to the engineering of a chatbot that integrates a mispronunciation detection module for providing second language students with descriptive feedback about this habit. To achieve this goal, the system combines a Natural Language Understanding module, a Natural Language Generation module, and a dialogue manager. The advantage of this tool is that it allows users to access this service at any time, something that is not possible or practical when we are working with human language teachers.

Chapter 3, "Story Summarization Using a Question-Answering Approach", explains the types, stages, issues, criteria, and applications of text summarization procedures, which consists of selecting essential data and presenting them in the form of summary. To demonstrate the process of summarization, the authors explore the use of SACAS, a model based on story summarization that consists of six main phases namely story, preprocessing, Named Entity Recognition (NER), anaphora resolution, conceptual dependency (i.e., the association between noun and verb), and summary generation.

Chapter 4, "Two New Challenging Resources to Evaluate Natural Language Interfaces to Databases Generated Based on Geobase and Geoquery", contributes to the field of NLIDBs by analyzing and offering two elaborate resources: N-Geobase, which is a relational database, and the corpus Geoquery270, which consists of 270 queries selected from Geoquery880. To evaluate these resources, the N-Geobase performance was compared using Geoquery270 and Geoquery250. The results indicated that Geoquery270 is the most challenging corpus for an NLIDB.

Chapter 5, "Chatbot for the Improvement of Conversational Skills of Japanese Language Learners", describes the development of a chatbot for supporting Japanese language learning. This chatbot is capable of holding conversations in such language, thus helping college students to improve their oral communicative competence (speaking and listening). To this end, this chatbot uses speech-to-text technology to transform voice input into hiragana, katakana, or kanji, three character sets of the Japanese language. Once the text is recognized, the system selects a response and provides it to the user by using Text-to-Speech technology.

Chapter 6, "Developing Chatbots for Supporting Health Self-Management", describes the main components and phases of the chatbot development process, a generic architecture of chatbots, as well as different software tools for its development such as Chatfuel, ManyChat, Conversica, Pandora bot, and Dialogflow, among others. Furthermore, the authors exemplify this process by describing the design and implementation of a text/speech Spanish chatbot for the automatic generation of user interfaces for health self-management mobile applications.

Chapter 7, "Issues in the Syntactic Parsing of Queries for a Natural Language Interface to Databases", presents an exhaustive parser that aims to be used on NLIDBs. This parser is based on three layers of analysis, namely lexical analysis, syntactic parsing, and semantic analysis, as well as on a set of algorithms for consecutive peer reduction, loading of phrase rules, reduction of sub-expressions, and path generation. This parser was evaluated in terms of processing time by using the Geoquery 880 corpus, obtaining encouraging results.

Chapter 8, "Preservation of Cultural Heritage in an Ethnic Minority Using Internet of Things and Smart Karaoke", contributes to the preservation of Otomi, a Mesoamerican language spoken in Central Mexico, through an intelligent system that recommends songs in such dialect. This system adopts a content-based approach; therefore, all users must provide their music preferences, which are stored in an XML-based user profile. This profile is used to recover the song's lyrics and distribution lists. A marked feature of the developed system is that it can also be used to translate songs in Otomi.

Chapter 9, "Interface for Composing Queries That Include Subqueries for Complex Databases", describes a natural language interface that allows non-expert people to generate SQL-based queries composed by one, two, or three subqueries without the need to have any knowledge of neither SQL nor the database schema. This interface is now designed for Spanish; however, it offers language independence, i.e., the feasibility for configuring it for other languages such as English, French, Italian, and Portuguese.

Section 2, "Text Analytics Systems", is organized into nine chapters that provide comprehensive coverage of NLP areas such as text categorization, information extraction, and text summarization. Text categorization is the task of automatically assigning predefined categories to natural language texts. This task facilitates organizing and finding information across a massive collection of documents, reports, and emails, to mention but a few. Information Extraction aims at automatically locating specific facts inside natural language text. Text summarization consists of generating a shorter version of an input document that contains the main pieces of information, thus allowing users to obtain the main ideas with much shorter reading time.

Chapter 10, "News Classification to Notify About Traffic Incidents in a Mexican City", contributes to the development of smart cities by proposing an NLP-based algorithm for classifying news articles that imply any kind of traffic incident, thus allowing people to take an alternative road when a street is blocked, or its traffic is moving slowly. Furthermore, this chapter presents a case study that required obtaining news from a local newspaper from Ciudad Juárez called "El Diario". Although there are studies that address the same problem, they are focused on non-Spanish languages.

Chapter 11, "Author Profiling Using Texts in Social Networks", addresses the problem of automatic identification of the author's demographic traits, which is present in different fields such as linguistic forensics, marketing, and security. The authors used word unigram and character three-gram as a baseline approach for predicting the traits of the authors for an existing corpus that integrates information from Twitter, hotel reviews, social media, and blog's profiles. The proposed approach was compared with the baseline and state-of-the-art results by using the accuracy measure. Results showed that the performance of this approach improved when the combination of word n-grams was used.

Chapter 12, "A Comparison of Personality Prediction Classifiers for Personnel Selection in Organizations Based on Industry 4.0", presents a comparison of machine learning classifiers that can be used to predict the personality of a Spanish-speaker job applicant based on the written content posted in their social networks. The performance of the analyzed classifiers was evaluated through accuracy, precision, and recall. The results show that the random forest classifier outperforms the others. This research could be useful to many companies that just screen job candidates by using personality tests and do not consider meaningful personality information coming from social networks.

Chapter 13, "Improving the K-Means Clustering Algorithm Oriented to Big Data Environments", proposes an improvement of the k-means algorithm in the convergence step that consists of stopping the process whenever the number of objects that change their assigned cluster in the current iteration is larger than the ones that change in the previous iteration. Experimental results depicted that the proposed improvement helps to reduce execution time up to 93%. Furthermore, it was observed that, in general, better results were obtained in Big Data environments.

Chapter 14, "Pronominal Anaphora Resolution on Spanish Text", describes a rule-based algorithm to approach the pronominal anaphora, one of the most frequent types of anaphora in Spanish, and a current challenge in the NLP field due to the ambiguity existing at all levels of processing. The set of rules was designed to identify the referents of personal pronouns through the structure of the grammatical tags of the words. The performance of the algorithm was compared to an online version of Freeling, an open-source multilingual language processing library. The results show that the proposed algorithm outperforms the Freeling library.

Chapter 15, "Geospatial Situation Analysis for the Prediction of Possible Cases of Suicide Using EBK: A Case Study in the Mexican State of Aguascalientes", represents a research effort for analyzing the phenomenon of suicide which impacts multiple sectors including public health and economy. To this end, the authors applied the Empirical Bayesian Kriging (EBK) method for obtaining prediction surfaces, probability, and standard error prediction, for completed suicide cases in the State of Aguascalientes (Mexico), collected from the database of reports of the Emergency Service 911 of that State. From this analysis, the authors detected that suicide is more present in the east zone of the city, where the socioeconomic level is medium-low.

Chapter 16, "Location Extraction to Inform a Spanish-Speaking Community About Traffic Incidents", presents a Web application that allows citizens to be informed about any kind of road incidents that could slow down the traffic so they can take preventive actions such as taking other routes or preparing earlier. For this purpose, this application implements NLP-based extraction rules for analyzing news reports published by a local newspaper and extract the location of the event. Then, it provides users with a map that marks all the recent incidents. This system was evaluated with a corpus of Spanish-written news reports from a local newspaper from Ciudad Juárez, obtaining encouraging results.

Chapter 17, "Text Summarization and its Types: A Literature Review", introduces readers to the field of text summarization using real-life examples that clear the picture of this area. This chapter describes the types of text summarization: based on input, based on language, and based on approach, which in turn are subclassified in different kinds. On the other hand, the authors discuss in detail the architecture of multilingual summarization. This strategy can be used to depict the day to day trend analysis on social networks aiming to know about a trending topic, the most wanted product in the market, or monitor what people say about their brand, among others. Such information could help support decision making in organizations from a broad range of domains.

Chapter 18, "Extractive Text Summarization Methods in the Spanish Language", presents a comparison of three extractive text summarization algorithms that were configured and adapted to work with Spanish texts from the Computer Science field. These algorithms were developed by Usman Malik, Shivangi Sareen, and Anannya Uberoj using Python Version 2. For comparison purposes, precision, recall, and f-measure were used to evaluate the effectiveness of each algorithm. The algorithm developed by Shivangi Sareen obtained the best performance.

Section 3, "Text Mining Systems", consists of four chapters that describe research efforts on knowledge representation, sentiment analysis, and suggestion mining technologies for solving problems in the medical, education, and airline domains.

Regarding knowledge representation, which is vital to develop and promote the development of new knowledge, Chapter 19, "NLP and the Representation of Data on the Semantic Web", provides readers with the theoretical foundations (definitions and techniques) of NLP technology involved in the task of representing data extracted from the Semantic Web. Meticulously, it describes the traditional flow of procedures and activities involved in the construction of knowledge graphs, which can be defined as models of knowledge that provide a standard interface to de data and enables the establishment of multilateral relations throughout different knowledge bases. Knowledge graphs have been adopted by prominent organizations such as Google and Microsoft to develop applications focused on data integration and analytics, semantic search and question answering, and other cognitive services.

Chapter 20, "Opinion Mining for Instructor Evaluations at the Autonomous University of Ciudad Juarez", shows how opinion mining is used to rapidly evaluate the opinions given by students in the form of comments regarding their teachers. This information could help identify strengths, weaknesses, and areas of opportunity in the teaching-learning process. The authors present a case study for which a database of real opinions from professors at the Autonomous University of Ciudad Juarez in four years was collected. Experimental processes were carried out, obtaining a high rate of accuracy for the 1-NN and the bagging classifier.

Chapter 21, "An Opinion Mining Approach for Drug Reviews in Spanish", presents a solution proposal for the detection of drug polarity for chronic-degenerative diseases on Spanish opinions available in blogs and specialized websites. This proposal aims to provide health care professionals with information that helps them to identify the view of patients regarding the drugs they prescribe. To perform this process, the proposal uses web scraping techniques for acquiring poorly structured data and convert it into a format that can be used for machine learning purposes.

Finally, Chapter 22, "Identifying Suggestions in Airline-User Tweets Using Natural Language Processing and Machine Learning", addresses some of the core concepts of suggestion mining, which can be defined as the automatic extraction of suggestions from unstructured text, for collecting and analyzing recommendations provided to airlines through Twitter. Nowadays, user tweets are valuable because, through them, organizations may discover areas of opportunity and create strategies to improve their products or services. Therefore, this work could be important for people in charge of decision-making bodies.

The chapters included in this book report detailed literature surveys on NLP applications and resources as well as novel and original research that aims at solving problems from different domains through NLP-based solutions. It is expected that this book represents a door open to discussion, conversation, and reflection about the impact and potential of NLP for addressing everyday and emerging needs. Also, we hope that readers find this book (or any of its chapters) highly informative and useful, inspiring them to conduct productive research that benefits society through the production of new knowledge and smart solutions that consider not only the NLP field but also other related disciplines.

Rodolfo Abraham Pazos-Rangel
Tecnológico Nacional de México, Mexico & Instituto Tecnológico Ciudad Madero, Mexico

Rogelio Florencia-Juárez
Universidad Autónoma de Ciudad Juárez, Mexico

Mario Andrés Paredes-Valverde
Tecnológico Nacional de México, Mexico & Instituto Tecnológico Orizaba, Mexico

Gilberto Rivera
Universidad Autónoma de Ciudad Juárez, Mexico

Acknowledgment

The editors sincerely thank all the authors and reviewers for their motivation, and their constant and tireless efforts, without whom this handbook would not have been possible. Moreover, our gratitude goes to Dr. Grigori Sidorov for the foreword of this handbook, and to our Editorial Advisory Board members for their valuable recommendations and great support demonstrated from the very beginning.

The editors would like to express their gratitude to IGI-Global for agreeing to publish *Handbook of Research on Natural Language Processing and Smart Service Systems*, despite the daunting challenge caused by the COVID-19 pandemic.

Also, the editors would like to thank the UACJ/DMCU for the freedom to work on research that we have found to be exciting and rewarding. We recognize that the UACJ/DMCU is much more than an average center located at an institution of higher education, and we fully appreciate the opportunity to be part of this "big family" that allows us to address Artificial Intelligence issues that are urgent today. Our gratitude goes to the head of division—Enrique Anchondo López—and our academic coordinator—Amaelvi Arce Ponce—for their broad support for our project. We also are grateful for the engineering students who have played a part in this book development (Abel Alejandro Ruiz Rivera, Maria Isabel Herrera Rojas, and Jaqueline Gandarilla Luna).

Finally, we would like to thank the ITCM and ITO for the flexibility and opportunities offered to complete this project.

Section 1
Smart Interactive Systems

Chapter 1
Natural Language Interfaces to Databases:
A Survey on Recent Advances

Rodolfo A. Pazos-Rangel
Tecnológico Nacional de México, Mexico & Instituto Tecnológico de Ciudad Madero, Mexico

Gilberto Rivera
https://orcid.org/0000-0002-2365-4651
Universidad Autónoma de Ciudad Juárez, Mexico

José A. Martínez F.
Tecnológico Nacional de México, Mexico & Instituto Tecnológico de Ciudad Madero, Mexico

Juana Gaspar
https://orcid.org/0000-0002-9762-2660
Tecnológico Nacional de México, Mexico & Instituto Tecnológico de Ciudad Madero, Mexico

Rogelio Florencia-Juárez
https://orcid.org/0000-0002-5208-6577
Universidad Autónoma de Ciudad Juárez, Mexico

ABSTRACT

This chapter consists of an update of a previous publication. Specifically, the chapter aims at describing the most decisive advances in NLIDBs of this decade. Unlike many surveys on NLIDBs, for this chapter, the NLIDBs will be selected according to three relevance criteria: performance (i.e., percentage of correctly answered queries), soundness of the experimental evaluation, and the number of citations. To this end, the chapter will also include a brief review of the most widely used performance measures and query corpora for testing NLIDBs.

DOI: 10.4018/978-1-7998-4730-4.ch001

Copyright © 2021, IGI Global. Copying or distributing in print or electronic forms without written permission of IGI Global is prohibited.

INTRODUCTION

In the last decades, the volume of information has grown exponentially. For manipulating such vast amounts of information, databases have been widely used by businesses and organizations. For accessing database information, different types of software tools have been developed. One type of such tools are database query languages; for example, SQL, which allows users to access data with ample flexibility, because of the high expressiveness of SQL. Unfortunately, SQL is a computer language that is difficult to utilize by users that are not computer professionals.

In order to facilitate casual and inexperienced users accessing database information, graphical form-based applications have been developed. These tools are very easy to use; however, they do not offer flexibility for accessing information in ways different from those for which they are developed.

Natural language interfaces to databases (NLIDBs) are software applications that allow inexperienced users to formulate queries in natural language for obtaining information stored in databases. NLIDBs have the advantages of both types of database querying tools: they are easy to use and offer high flexibility for accessing information.

Several surveys on NLIDBs have been published; some of the most important and recent are the following:

1. Natural language interfaces to databases - An introduction by Androutsopoulos (1995).
2. Natural language interface for database: A brief review by Nihalani (2011).
3. A survey of natural language interface to database management system by Sujatha (2012).
4. Natural language interfaces to databases: An analysis of the state of the art by Pazos (2013).
5. Natural language interface to databases: A survey by Tyagi (2014).

The purpose of this chapter is to describe the most relevant advances in NLIDBs of this decade. Unlike many surveys on NLIDBs, for this chapter, the NLIDBs have been selected according to three relevance criteria: performance (i.e., percentage of correctly answered queries), soundness of the experimental evaluation, and the number of citations. To this end, the chapter will also include a brief review of the most widely used query corpora for testing NLIDBs. The focus of this chapter is on approaches that translate queries in natural language to SQL expressions; so, other database query languages are out of the scope (e.g., Porras, Florencia-Juárez, Rivera & García, 2018).

BACKGROUND

NLIDBs are software applications that allow users to formulate queries in natural language for obtaining information stored in databases. This is accomplished by translating a natural language expression into an SQL statement. Unfortunately, the translation from a natural language query to SQL is an extremely complex problem. This difficulty explains the slow development of NLIDB technology, which is summarized next.

Chomsky (1957) published a monograph titled *Syntactic Structures*, which has been considered a landmark of modern linguistics. He proposed a formal approach to natural language syntax, which consists of symbols and rules and is the origin of the constituency grammar approach. In the decades of the 60s and 70s, the first natural language querying systems were developed, and they were basically interfaces for expert systems implemented for specific domains. Some of the most famous are BASEBALL (Green, Wolf, Chomsky, & Laughery, 1961) and LUNAR (Woods, Kaplan, & Webber, 1972). Most of those NLIDBs were developed for a particular database, and consequently, they could not be easily modified for querying different databases. These systems are called domain-dependent NLIDBs, and many of them achieved good results: accuracy (percentage of correctly translated queries) of around 95%.

The development of an NLIDB for a specific database was time consuming, and it was similar to developing an information system before database management systems were available. Therefore, the next step in NLIDB technology was to develop domain-independent systems, i.e., NLIDBs that can be used for querying many different databases. LADDER (Hendrix, Sacerdoti, Sagalowicz, & Slocum, 1978) is considered one of the first systems that could be configured for querying different databases. It was until 1990 that IBM introduced SAA LanguageAcess (its first commercial NLIDB), which was withdrawn from marketing in 1993. In 2000 Microsoft included English Query in SQL Server 2000, which had a similar fate because it was no longer included in SQL Server 2005. Developing domain-independent systems has proven to be very difficult: they still have deficiencies in the translation process and have attained accuracies in the interval of 80-90%.

NATURAL LANGUAGE INTERFACES TO DATABASES

This section includes brief descriptions of the most relevant NLIDBs developed from 2010 to 2019. Descriptions are grouped according to the approach used for the interfaces: neural networks, syntax based, semantic grammar, and pattern matching, as well as systems for languages different from English. Additionally, the performance obtained (mainly accuracy or precision) and the databases/benchmarks used for testing are mentioned. Additionally, for each approach, the systems are ordered from the most recent to the oldest.

Neural network NLIDBs use deep neural networks (based on recurrent neural networks), which are powerful machine learning techniques that have been used for natural language processing. In particular, a type of deep neural networks, called sequence-to-sequence recurrent neural networks, has been used for translating from a natural language query to SQL. It is important to mention that, like statistical approaches, interfaces based on neural networks have to be trained with very large datasets (tens of thousands of sentences for training the neural network and hundreds of thousands for testing).

Syntax-based systems use a grammar that consists of symbols and rules, which are applied to a natural language expression for determining its structure and grouping syntactically related words. The following is an example of a simple grammar for parsing *Which river passes through Illinois?* (Pazos et al., 2013):

$S \rightarrow WQ\ VP$
$Wh \rightarrow$ "what" | "which"
$WQ \rightarrow Wh$ "river" | Wh "state"
$VP \rightarrow V\ ValN$
$V \rightarrow$ "passes through" | "borders"
$ValN \rightarrow$ "Illinois" | "Missouri" | "Indiana"

Semantic grammar systems are similar to syntax based systems, except that nonterminal symbols may be different from syntactic concepts (noun phrases, prepositional phrases). The following is an example of a semantic grammar (Pazos et al., 2013):

S → *River_question Flow_through*
River_question → "which river"
Flow_through → "passes through" *State*
State → "Illinois" | "Missouri" | "Indiana"

Pattern matching uses a simple technique based on patterns or rules that are applied to the user query. The following is an example of a rule that could be used:

"Which river passes through" <*State*>

The corresponding SQL statement (see Figure 3) is

SELECT *State.state_name*
FROM *State*, *RiverState*, *River*
WHERE *State.abreviation = RiverState.abreviation*
AND *RiverState.river_id = River.river_id*
AND *State.state_name = <State>*

Neural Network Systems

NADAQ System

NADAQ is an NLIDB that combines deep learning and traditional techniques of SQL parsing (Xu et al., 2019). To this end, the system adds to the decoding phase new dimensions of schema-understanding bits and includes new neurons controlled by a finite state automaton for supervising the grammatical states in the decoder part. Additionally, the NLIDB includes a technique that allows the neural network to reject user queries that are irrelevant for the database domain and suggests candidate queries in natural language.

NADAQ consists of three major modules, which are described next:

1. **Data Storage:** This module includes MySQL as a database management system, from which it extracts table metadata for training the translation model, and which processes SQL statements for presenting results to the users.
2. **Model Management:** This module constitutes the NLIDB kernel, which uses several models for bidirectional translation between natural language and SQL, as well as models for rejecting irrelevant user queries. The module provides information from the models to the User Interface module.
3. **User Interface:** This module consists of the interfaces for user-computer interaction.

The most important module of NADAQ is the User Interface, which performs most of the translation processes. The main components are explained next:

1. **Speech Recognition:** The task of this component is converting a spoken user query into text. To this end, it uses the voice-to-text translator iFlytek. Additionally, it provides manual correction so that the user can review the translator output to adapt it to his/her intention.

2. **Translation:** This component uses a machine learning model based on a recurrent neural network coder-decoder, which is a state-of-the-art technique for machine translation. The innovation of this component consists in the integration of hidden states to the model by using a finite state machine for supervising the grammar states for SQL parsing. These hidden states are useful for discarding invalid output words in the decoder part and providing useful suggestions for improving neural-network training.

3. **Rejection:** This component allows NADAQ to reject incoherent user questions. In order to determine the relevance of user queries to the database, the system includes a rejection model in addition to the translation model. Rejection decisions are made based on the uncertainty of the translation model when choosing tables, columns, and search conditions for the SQL statements.

4. **Recommendation:** This component increases the effectiveness of the interface by providing candidate queries to the user for refinement and selection. For helping users without SQL knowledge, the interface translates the candidate queries to natural language, so that users can easily understand the exact meaning (according to the database domain) of the candidate queries and improving the effectiveness of the user-computer interaction.

NADAQ was evaluated using three databases: MAS (Microsoft Academic Search), IMDb, and Geobase. The tests involved the comparison of three methods: convolutional neural network machine, attention-based sequence-to-sequence machine translation, and semantic parsing model with feedback. The NLIDB obtained F1 scores of 83.9% for Geobase and greater than 80% for IMDb.

Cross-Domain NLI Based on Adversarial Text Method

The NLIDB uses a general-purpose question tagging method and a multi-lingual neural network translation model that allows obtaining domain independence (Wang, 2019). For question tagging, each domain is treated equally by using a recurrent neural network. An approach is proposed where different types of natural language queries and different domains share the same components. To this end, the NLIDB performs a preprocessing that consists in separating the domain-specific information from the query.

Given an NL-SQL pair, the key approach consists in inserting predesigned symbols and annotating DB elements (tables, columns, values, keywords, etc.) mentioned in the question for treating each sample (of different domains and types) uniformly. The approach used by the NLIDB is described next:

1. The NLIDB includes a binary classifier BC, which detects elements for predicting if a data element e is present in a question q corresponding to an SQL statement p according to the semantic meaning of the question. The classifier takes q and e, without referencing p.

2. The system looks for the most influential phrase in the query by using gradient-based adversarial text methods.

3. Symbols are inserted in question q for annotating phrases that describe DB elements, which are denoted by q'.

4. A multi-lingual cross-domain sequence-to-sequence (seq2seq) model is constructed for translating q' to p', where p' denotes a query where the DB elements are replaced by SQL symbols inserted in q.

5. The symbols inserted are replaced by DB elements for generating the original query; i.e., conversion from p' to p.

This NLIDB has an encoder that uses a stacked bi-directional multi-layer recurrent neural network. It uses a prefix symbol for dealing with different types of queries and treating each type equally.

Experiments were carried out for this NLIDB using the WikiSQL, OVERNIGHT, and Geoquery880 datasets. The metrics used were query-match accuracy denoted by Acc_{qm}, and the execution results Acc_{ex}. For WikiSQL, the interface obtained an Acc_{qm} of 74.5% and an Acc_{ex} of 82.7%, for OVERNIGHT attained an Acc_{qm} of 76.8%, and for Geoquery880 obtained an Acc_{qm} of 84.1%.

DBPal System

DBPal is based on deep learning models for achieving more robust natural language query understanding in two ways (Utama, 2018). First, DBPal uses a deep model for translating NL questions to SQL, making the translation process more robust to wording variations. DBPal provides a learned auto-completion model that suggests partial extensions of queries to users when formulating questions. Second, DBPal has two important features that are based on neural network models: robust query translation and interactive auto-completion.

DBPal consists of two major components, which are explained next.

1. **Neural query translation:** For achieving robust query translation, DBPal proposes a translation method based on a sequence-to-sequence recurrent neural network model. The robustness of the translation process allows to effectively map natural language varying expressions to predefined relational database operations. An important challenge for NLIDBs that use neural networks is to select a comprehensive training set. The main innovation of this NLIDB is a synthetic generation approach, which takes as input the database schema with minimal annotations and generates a large set of natural language questions and their translation to SQL statements. The generation of the training set consists of two steps: generator and augmentation. The first step uses the database schema and a set of base templates that describe NL-SQL pairs and slot-filling dictionaries for generating from 1 to 2 million pairs. The second step automatically increases the initial set of NL-SQL pairs, using existing language models for automatically modifying the NL part of each pair by using different linguistic variations.

2. **Interactive auto-completion:** DBPal provides a real-time auto-completion tool and question suggestion for helping users that are not familiar with the database schema, thus helping them to write complex queries.

For comparing DBPal versus other approaches, the Geoquery benchmark was used, which has been utilized for evaluating other NLIDBs. Additionally, for testing linguistic variations, another benchmark was generated called Patients, which is a database of hospital patients, which consists of one table and 290 queries. Also, a comparison versus NaLIR and NSP was conducted. The accuracies attained by DBPal for the Patients and Geoquery benchmarks were 75.93% and 48.9%, respectively.

Syntax-Based Systems

NaLIR System

NaLIR (Natural Language Interface to Relational database) is an interactive NLIDB that explains the user how the interface interprets his/her question step by step (Li, 2017). When ambiguities are detected, the interface shows the user various interpretations with explanations for the user to choose from, which allows to solve ambiguities by interacting with the user. A training example is collected each time the user makes a choice and confirms its interpretation.

This system consists of three components, which are described next:

1. **Query interpretation:** This component includes a parse tree node mapper and a structure adjustor, which performs the interpretation of the natural language query and the representation of the interpretation as a query tree.
2. **Interactive communicator:** The task of this component is to handle the interaction with the user in order to make sure that the resulting interpretation is correct.
3. **Query tree translator:** This component carries out the translation of a query tree to an SQL statement and sends the SQL query to a database management system.

More specifically, the query interpretation component consists of three modules, which are explained next:

1. **Dependency parser:** The system uses a dependency parser (Stanford Parser) for generating a parse tree from the natural language query. In this tree, each node represents a word/phrase in the query, and each edge is a linguistic dependency relationship between two words/phrases.
2. **Parse tree node mapper:** This module identifies the tree nodes that can be mapped to SQL components and tokenizes them. Additionally, several nodes may have various mappings, which causes ambiguities when interpreting these nodes. For such nodes, the parse tree node mapper sends the best mapping to the parse tree structure adjustor and transmits all candidate mappings to the interactive communicator.
3. **Parse tree structure adjustor:** This module verifies the correctness of the parse tree, specifically, if the tree is coherent with the database schema and there are no ambiguities in the interpretation. In case the parse is incoherent or ambiguous, the system adjusts the tree structure in two steps. In the first step, the tree nodes are reformulated to make the tree coherent with the semantic coverage of the NLIDB. If there exist several correct candidate trees, the best one is selected for the second step. In this step, the selected parse tree is semantically analyzed, and implicit nodes are inserted to make it more semantically coherent. This process is performed under user supervision.

NaLIR was evaluated using 98 queries of the Microsoft Academic Search dataset, and it achieved an accuracy of 89.79% (88 correct answers).

NLI Based on Layered Architecture

This NLIDB is based on an approach that uses a layered architecture (Pazos et al., 2016). The election of this method originates from the following premise: *translation from a natural language query to an SQL statement is an extremely complex problem.* Systems whose design is based on functionality layers (like the OSI model for communication networks) provide the flexibility and modularity for implementing more complex processing strategies than systems designed otherwise. A layered architecture is recommended for dealing with complex problems; therefore, in this NLIDB, each functionality layer deals with a different problem in the translation process.

The Semantic Information Dictionary (SID) is the keystone of the NLIDB since it stores the information necessary for the interface to interpret a query. Initially, the system carries out an automatic configuration, which populates the SID based on the descriptions of DB tables and columns and the information of relations between tables, which are stored in the data dictionary of the DB management system. Additionally, the SID can keep information on words and phrases that refer to tables, columns, relations between tables, imprecise values, alias values, which allows to have the necessary information and facilitates query interpretation.

The core of the interface consists of three layers, whose description is the following:

1. **Lexical Analysis:** The task of this layer is to divide the user query into tokens, search query words in the lexicon and assign (one or more) POS tags to the words found. In case a word is not found in the lexicon, it is considered as a possible search value.
2. **Syntactic Analysis:** This layer consists of a shallow parser that uses a heuristics for determining one syntactic category for those words with multiple categories and ignoring irrelevant words.
3. **Semantic Analysis:** This is the most important layer, and it performs several tasks for understanding the user query and translating it to SQL.

The Semantic Analysis layer is constituted by five sub-layers that are described next:

1. **Treatment of imprecise and alias values:** This sub-layer detects and deals with words that denote imprecise values (i.e., words that represent value ranges, such as afternoon, evening) and aliases (i.e., words for referring to search values, such as noon, couple, fifth, or Philly instead of Philadelphia). To this end, the process scans each word of the input question and searches the SID to determine if the word is declared as an imprecise or alias value.
2. **Identification of tables and columns:** This sub-layer is responsible for identifying the DB tables and columns referred to by words/phrases in the user query, which can be nominal, verbal, adjectival, or prepositional. Specifically, this sub-layer scans each word/phrase of the input question and searches the SID to determine if the word is associated to a table or column.
3. **Identification of the Select and Where phrases:** From the identification of tables, columns, and search values, this sub-layer uses a heuristics for determining the segments of the question that constitute the Select and Where phrases. To this end, each search value is associated to a column according to the proximity and coincidence of data type. The pairs column-search value constitute the WHERE clause of the SQL statement and the remaining columns constitute the SELECT clause.
4. **Treatment of aggregate functions and grouping:** The task of this sub-layer is to identify and deal with the words/phrases of the query used for referring to aggregate functions and grouping

(Group By); for example, words such as average, how many, minimal, maximal, smallest, largest, first, best, for each, etc. This process is carried out by scanning each word of the input question and searching the SID to determine if the word/phrase is associated with an aggregate function or grouping clause. Since the values stored in different columns may be of different natures, different words/phrases are associated to each column.

5. **Determining implicit joins:** For constructing the SQL statement, it is necessary that the graph consisting of the tables involved in the query and the join conditions (search conditions constituted by a column in one table and a column in another table) be a connected graph. When the graph does not satisfy this condition, this sub-layer generates a connected graph by using a heuristics that adds a minimal number of join conditions. Once a connected graph is constructed, the generation of the SQL statement is straightforward.

An experimental evaluation of this NLIDB was conducted using 71 queries for the ATIS database, and it achieved an accuracy of 90% when configured by the implementers (Pazos et al., 2016). Additionally, comparative tests were performed versus ELF and C-Phrase and using the Geoquery250 benchmark; the accuracies obtained were 56.4% for the NLIDB, 35.6% for ELF, and 56.4% for C-Phrase. There are very few publications that report NLIDB performance when the interfaces are not configured by the implementers. An experiment was carried out with two groups of undergraduate students, who configured the interface for the ATIS database, and the accuracies attained were 44.69% for one group and 77.05% for the other. Finally, a Wizard was developed for semi-automatically fine-tuning the configuration. An experiment was performed with another two groups of undergraduate students, who used the Wizard, and the accuracies obtained were 80.53% and 84.82%.

NALI System

NALI is an NLIDB which uses methods for simplifying the configuration without reducing linguistic coverage and accuracy (Mvumbi, 2016). To this end, it uses two authoring frameworks for reducing the work needed for configuring the system for querying different databases.

The first authoring framework is called top-down, and it uses an unannotated corpus of sample natural language queries for extracting lexical terms for simplifying the NLIDB configuration. This strategy reduces the work for configuring the interface by automatically including the semantic information for verbs in negative form, comparative and superlative adjectives in the configuration model.

The second authoring framework is called bottom-up, and it examines the possibility of constructing a configuration model without manual intervention using the information from the database schema and a dictionary.

NALI uses SQL as output language and English as input language. This system assumes that natural language queries are written without spelling and grammatical errors. The syntactic parser is based on a symbolic method for analyzing natural language queries.

The process for translating a question to SQL consists of four main phases, which are described next:

1. **Lexical analysis:** The task of this phase is to scan the question tokens and perform POS tagging, lemmatization, and named entity recognition.
2. **Syntactic analysis:** This phase uses a dependency parser (Stanford Parser) for generating a parse tree from the natural language query.

3. **Semantic analysis:** This phase is responsible for translating the question to an intermediate representation language, which uses first-order logic to express the question meaning.
4. **SQL translation:** This phase constructs the SQL statement from the logical query.

NALI was evaluated using Geoquery250 and attained an accuracy of 74.5% and a precision of 77.4%.

Ontology-Based NLI to Relational DBs

This NLIDB is based on a generic system that consists of several phases and uses an ontology implemented for a customer database (Sujatha, Raju, & Viswanadha, 2016). This system allows accessing information independently of the underlying database. Additionally, the design of the interface allows the scalability and robustness of the system. Word sense disambiguation is performed by using n-grams.

The proposed approach of this NLIDB takes a natural language query and translates it to an SQL statement by using six phases, which are described next.

1. **Stop word removal:** This phase removes stop words from the natural language query according to a predefined list of stop words.
2. **Stemming:** The task of this phase is to determine the root words of the remaining words.
3. **Content word extraction:** This phase assigns POS tags to words by using a natural language toolkit.
4. **Syntactic analysis:** This phase is responsible for parsing the question using a top-down parser. Parsing is performed by applying syntactic rules expressed in Backus-Naur Form.
5. **Semantic analysis:** This phase uses an ontology and n-grams. The ambiguity of a word meaning is resolved by using n-grams and the ontology constructed from the database schema.
6. **Candidate query formulation:** This phase uses the EFFECN algorithm, which performs the division of the natural language question, joining of tables, and selection of multiple tables and columns according to the search conditions specified in the question.

This NLIDB was evaluated using a set of 100 queries to a customer database, and it obtained an accuracy of 84% and a precision of 86%.

Query Builder Based on Dependency Parsing

The main objective of this NLIDB is to allow users to access information stored in a database, without the need of learning a database query language (Kokare & Wanjale, 2015). Constituency and dependency parsing are two techniques widely used in natural language processing. The NLIDB uses dependency parsing for extracting POS tags and typed dependencies. In dependency parsing, the parse tree connects words according to the relation among words. Each node in the tree represents a word, and the children of a node are words that depend on the parent. The labels of the arcs describe the relationship between parent and child.

The translation of a natural language query to SQL is described next:

1. **Lexical analysis:** The task of this phase is to scan the user question for detecting stop words and punctuation marks, which are discarded. Next, the question is separated into tokens.

2. **Syntactic analysis:** This phase uses a dependency parser (Stanford Parser) for generating a parse tree from the user query. Nouns, adjectives, etc. are related pairwise for constituting the arcs of the dependency tree. Additionally, POS tags and typed dependencies are determined.
3. **Semantic analysis:** This phase is responsible for analyzing the typed dependencies for determining the meaning of the question; specifically, the tokens and nouns are mapped to database tables, columns, and search values. Next, a logic query is generated by including the tables, attributes, and search values.
4. **Translation:** This phase translates the natural language query to SQL using the tables, columns, and values previously determined. Finally, the SQL statement is sent to the database management system for returning the results to the user.

Additionally, the NLIDB uses a buffering strategy that stores user questions and the corresponding SQL translations, so that when a previously processed question is detected, the NLIDB uses the stored SQL statement for avoiding all the translation process.

The accuracy reported for this NLIDB is 91.66%. However, the benchmark used for the evaluation is not specified.

Restricted NL Querying of Clinical DBs

The NLIDB uses an approach based on the Top-k algorithm for translating queries in restricted natural language to SQL (Safari & Patrick, 2014). This interface was designed for querying a specific purpose database of a Clinical Information System (CIS) by using a special-purpose language (CliniDAL) for clinical data analytics, which has six classes of query templates. The mapping and translation algorithms are generic, and therefore, they can be used for querying clinical databases designed in any of the three data models: Entity-Relationship (ER), Entity-Attribute-Value (EAV) and XML.

This NLIDB allows a user to compose a question using the CliniDAL restricted natural language, without requiring any knowledge of the CIS database schema, SQL or XML. CliniDAL is a generic query language, and its associated processes for parsing, mapping, translation, and interpretation of temporal expressions are generic and do not depend on the CIS.

The main components of the NLIDB are explained next:

1. **Query Processor:** This component takes a query expressed in CliniDAL as input and processes it by using its sub-components (Parser, Categorizer and Optimizer) for generating a parse tree of the query. Afterward, the parse tree is processed by the Query Translator.
2. **Query Translator:** This component translates the parse tree of a CliniDAL query to SQL, and it consists of four sub-components. The first subcomponent is Mapper, which tries to map the tokens detected in the CliniDAL query to CIS database elements (tables and columns) using the similarity-based algorithm Top-k along with some NLP tools that include tokenization, abbreviation expansion and lemmatization for preparing information for the automatic mapping. The Translator sub-component performs two classes of translations related to the general CIS data model. If the CIS uses an EAV or ER data model, the CliniDAL query is translated to SQL, while if the CIS stores XML documents, the query is translated to XML. The Temporal Analyzer finds and maps the temporal entity (database table) corresponding to the mapped terms of the query to the data elements of the CIS model.

The NLIDB was evaluated using a database of a Clinical Information System and a corpus of 108 queries, and it obtained an accuracy above 84%.

AskMe System

AskMe is a domain-independent NLIDB that uses previously proposed approaches, such as an ontology for describing the database schema, a template-based method for the dynamic generation of the lexical analyzer, syntactic parser and semantic analyzer (Llopis & Ferrández, 2013). Additionally, it provides an innovative characteristic: services for generating queries that reduce the learning time for users. The design of AskMe allows it to be automatically reconfigurable for multiple domains while achieving accuracy comparable to domain-specific NLIDBs.

AskMe consists of two main components, which are described next:

1. **Ontology builder:** After connecting to a database, AskMe looks in the ontology repository for an ontology that describes the database schema. The repository consists of a dictionary that contains ontology references for any pair <server, database> for which the interface has been used. If the ontology for the database is not in the repository, then the system automatically extracts information on tables, columns, and relations from the database schema for building the ontology.
2. **Dynamic parser generator:** This component automatically creates the lexical, syntactic parser, and semantic analyzer, which allows to interpret natural language queries and to translate them into SQL statements for being executed by the database management system. This component has three sub-components: Lexicon, Syntactic parser, and Semantic Analyzer. The lexicon consists of the set of words/phrases that are used in questions for referring to database tables and columns. The NLIDB uses a Link Grammar Parser for parsing operations. The semantic parser uses semantic templates that are filled with the concepts defined in the database ontology.

AskMe was evaluated using the ATIS database and a set of the 448 queries in the ATIS "Scoring Set A". The NLIDB achieved an accuracy of 94.8%.

Semantic Grammar Systems

Intelligent System for Relational DBs

The NLIDB has a general architecture for an intelligent database system, including an implementation that provides domain independence (Gunjal, Rathod, & Pise, 2017). Another feature of this system is that it can be easily configured. The interface uses a semantic matching technique for converting a natural language query to SQL using a dictionary and a set of production rules. The dictionary consists of semantic sets for tables and columns. The SQL query generated by the NLIDB is executed, and the result is presented to the user. This interface was tested using the Northwind database and a Suppliers-Parts database.

The NLIDB is domain independent, which is achieved by an automatic configuration process. Additionally, the interface can be easily configured; to this end, it uses a set of metadata and a semantic set for tables and columns. The system has an intelligent layer that allows to query any database. The layer carries out the processing of information and allows to answer a large variety of questions.

The main functionality is based on semantic sets and rules, which can be modified by the database administrator. The proposed system consists of two modules, which are explained next:

1. **Preprocessor:** The task of this module is to generate the domain dictionary, which is built automatically, and it also generates rules, which are used by a semantic parser, The rules are based on the database schema, WordNet and feedback from the database administrator. The administrator can add, modify, and delete rules.
2. **Run time processor:** This module uses the rules and tries to match words of the user question to predefined data structures, tables, and columns of the database schema. The rules describe the relations between the table and its attributes.

This NLIDB was evaluated using the Northwind database and the Suppliers and Parts database, and a group of five students was asked to formulate queries in English for the two databases. The query sets consisted of 40 questions for Northwind and 20 questions for Suppliers and Parts. The results from the evaluation were: accuracy of 70% for Northwind and accuracy of 75% for Suppliers and Parts.

Pattern-Matching Systems

nQuery System

nQuery is a domain-independent NLIDB that is based on an approach that focuses on incorporating complex natural language requests (questions and data manipulation operations) together with simple requests (Sukthankar, Maharnawar, Deshmukh, Haribhakta, & Kamble, 2017). The interface allows to process requests that involve aggregate functions, multiple conditions in the Where clause, and clauses such as Order by, Group by and Having. The system has been developed for the MySQL database management system.

nQuery translates requests to SQL before retrieving data from the database. This system focuses on retrieving data, but it also allows the translation of other data manipulation operations (Insert, Delete, and Update). However, the interface translates requests that can be processed by MySQL in order to reduce the complexity of the database requests.

The NLIDB takes as input a natural language request, which is translated to SQL through several phases, which are explained next:

1. **Tokenize and tag:** This phase divides the request into tokens and assigns them POS tags by using the NLTK tokenizer package.
2. **Analyze tagged tokens:** This phase scans the tagged tokens and generates a noun map and a list of verbs. Additionally, the type of SQL statement (Select, Insert, Delete, and Update) is determined.
3. **Map to table names and attributes:** This phase uses the noun map and verb list for generating the table set, which specifies the tables that will be needed for building the SQL statement. This strategy is based on the observation that table names are usually referred to by nouns and verbs in requests. Furthermore, the noun map is used to determine the table columns that are needed in the SQL expression.

4. **Filter redundancy and finalize clause mapping:** This phase obtains information for the Group by and Having clauses from information from previous phases and the basic rules of SQL. In addition, redundant tables and attributes are removed using some filter algorithms.
5. **SQL formation:** This phase selects the appropriate SQL statement template according to the type of SQL statement determined in the second phase. Finally, the SQL statement is generated by filling in the selected template the information on the clauses previously gathered and tables and columns stored in the table and attribute map.

nQuery was evaluated using a corpus of synthetic requests to a bank database and a university database, which respectively have 11 and 6 tables. The NLIDB performance was assessed with 75 requests for the university DB and 50 requests for the bank DB, and it obtained approximately an accuracy of 86%.

Aneesah System

Aneesah is an NLIDB based on the combination of a pattern matching approach and dialog interaction with the user for dealing with natural language complexities and ambiguities for dynamically generating SQL statements (Shabaz, O'Shea, Crockett, & Latham, 2015). The NLIDB has conversational capabilities for providing an interactive and friendly environment to help users to access information in relational databases.

The NLIDDB architecture was designed using a pattern matching technique. Additionally, Aneesah implements a conversational agent based on a scripting language, a knowledge base, and an SQL query engine. The interface has a modular architecture that provides flexibility for querying databases of different domains by configuring the NLIDB. The architecture consists of three components, which are explained next:

Component 1: This component is constituted by a Conversation Manager, User Interface, Temporary Memory, and Conversational Agent (constituted by Controller, Pattern Matching Engine, Pattern Matching Scripting Language, and Response Analyzer). The Controller plans and conducts the interaction with the user for guiding him/her in specifying the information the user wants from the database. The Pattern Matching Engine determines the coincidence of user questions with the scripts in the system knowledge base. Additionally, the NLIDB uses a Pattern Matching Scripting Language that allows dialog with the user.

Component 2: This component consists of a Knowledge Base, which allows Aneesah to interact with the database to be queried (a sales history database), and it can be configured for interacting with different databases.

Component 3: This component consists of an SQL Query Engine, which is constituted by an SQL Configurator, SQL Execution, and SQL Analyzer. This component retrieves information from the database.

This NLIDB was evaluated using a sales history database. In the experiments, two groups of participants were used: group A consisted of participants without SQL skills, while group B consisted of participants familiar with SQL. The overall accuracy was 85.01%, and the overall precision was 92.96%.

Systems Based on Other Approaches

Transfer-Learnable NLIDB

This work proposes an NLIDB that is domain independent and transferable to other databases, which is achieved by learning one model that can be applied to any other relational database (Wang, Tian, Xiong, Wang, & Ku, 2018). The approach adopts the principle of separating data and database schema and adding support for the particularities and complexity of natural language. Specifically, the strategy consists in separating the idiosyncrasy of natural language and focusing on the semantics of SQL queries in order to develop a domain-independent and transferable NLIDB.

For obtaining this objective, the information is separated into specific components: the database schema and the use of natural language specific to the schema. The approach used consists of three stages: conversion of a natural language question q to its annotated form q_a, use of a sequence-to-sequence (seq2seq) model for translating q_a to an annotated SQL statement s_a, and conversion of the annotated SQL statement s_a to a normal SQL statement s.

The annotation of the natural language query is performed for detecting words/phrases in the question for referring to DB elements (tables, columns, and values). However, sometimes words/phrases for referring to DB elements depend largely on the context, and sometimes they are not explicitly specified (semantic ellipsis).

The NLIDB uses the information of the database metadata: database schema, database statistics of each column, and natural language expressions specific for a database, a column, and column values.

This NLIDB was trained and evaluated using the WikiSQL dataset that contains 87,673 natural language queries and their respective translations to SQL and 26,521 tables. The interface attained an accuracy of 82%. For evaluating the transferability aspect, the NLIDB was tested using the OVERNIGHT dataset after being trained with WikiSQL. For this test, the query accuracy was 60% (a reduction of 22%).

NLI Based on Semantic Representations Using Ontologies

This NLIDB is based on a proposed approach that uses semantic representations to model the knowledge of the NLIDB using the Ontology Web Language (OWL). The semantically modeled knowledge allows the system to deal with discourse (a sequence of related questions) and to be used for querying databases of different domains (González et al., 2015).

The most important component of this system is the Customization Module. The configuration of the NLIDB is performed in two phases, which are described next:

1. **Database Schema Extraction:** Knowledge is automatically generated by a configuration module, which extracts metadata from the database schema and identifies the elements that integrate the structure of a relational database, such as table names, column names, data type of the columns and existing relations between tables. To generate the NLIDB knowledge, the database administrator must only indicate to the configuration module the connection parameters to his/her relational database. Subsequently, the configuration module automatically models the knowledge and stores it in an ontology, which is a .owl file.
2. **NLIDB Customization:** Once these elements have been identified, the Customization Module analyzes the name of each of them to generate the vocabulary of the NLIDB, which is extended

using lemmas and synonyms. All these elements are modeled by the Customization Module using the proposed semantic representations.

In order to improve the performance of the NLIDB, the configuration module allows the database administrator to manage the knowledge generated, i.e., add, delete, or update knowledge. In addition, it allows the administrator to define the use of superlatives. Specifically, the configuration process consists of the following steps:

1. Associate language words to database tables and columns, which may occur in user questions for referring to tables and columns.
2. Define superlative words, as well as an indication of whether they refer to a maximal or minimal value and the columns to which the superlative can be applied.
3. Indicate which database columns store information that could be used by users as search values in natural language queries.

Classes, object properties, and data properties were defined to design the proposed semantic representations. Classes to model the name of tables and the name of columns extracted from the relational database were defined. Object properties to semantically relate each of the tables to their respective columns were defined, as well as the relations among tables (for representing referential integrity). Finally, data properties to store the data type of each of the columns were defined. In this way, semantic modeling based on the relational schema of the database is generated.

In order to model the relations between natural language and the semantic schema, classes and object properties were also defined. A class to identify the vocabulary words was defined, as well as an object property to relate each word to the elements of the semantic schema it refers to. A class to model superlative words was also defined. Additionally, data properties to indicate the columns of the database on which the superlative can be used and to define the aggregate function to be applied (max or min) were also defined. In this way, all the semantic knowledge of the NLIDB is generated.

The ontology generated by the configuration module is used by the NLIDB to interpret user queries expressed in natural language, as well as to generate the corresponding SQL query, with which the information requested by the user is extracted from his/her relational database.

An experimental evaluation of this NLIDB was conducted using the Geoquery250 benchmark, which also included other NLIDBs (ELF, NLP-Reduce, and FREyA). The results obtained indicate that the proposed semantic representations, used to model the knowledge of the NLIDB, allowed the interface to obtain a good performance, specifically, an accuracy of 85.2%.

NLI Concordant with Knowledge Base

The NLIDB uses an approach for translating natural language questions to a formal language query by using a graph-based knowledge base, i.e., an ontology (Han, Park, & Park, 2016). This method considers a subgraph of the knowledge base as a formal query. The method is based on the principle that a natural language expression (answerable question) has a one-to-one mapping to a formal query; therefore, the natural language question is translated to a formal query by comparing the question to NL expressions and finding the most adequate. If the confidence level of this comparison is not high enough, the interface rejects the question and does return an answer.

This NLIDB performs the translation of a natural language question to a formal query in two phases, which are explained next.

1. **Generation of system-interpretable expressions from a knowledge base:** This phase prepares all the NL expressions that will be compared to the natural language question. These NL expressions are generated from an ontology. The ontology was designed in such a way that allows each subgraph of the ontology to be expressed in natural language, and at least one NL expression can be generated for each subgraph. For each expression, a sequence of NL tokens is generated for being compared to natural language questions. The sequence is called normalized expression.

2. **Translation of user questions into formal queries by using the generated expressions:** In this phase of the process, a natural language question is translated to a formal query. To this end, the normalized expression that is equivalent to the question is determined. First, for a natural language question, one or more normalized expressions are generated, because of various possible interpretations of the question. Next, pairs of normalized expressions are generated, where one element of the pair is generated from the knowledge base and the other element is derived from the question. Afterward, the meaning of the question is determined by selecting the adequate pair of normalized expressions. Finally, a formal query is generated by using the selected pair.

The NLIDB was evaluated using the Geoquery880 and the Geoquery250 benchmarks and the performance metrics precision and accuracy. For Geoquery880, the interface attained an accuracy of 83.2% and a precision of 86.6%, and for Geoquery250, it achieved an accuracy of 86.6% and a precision of 90.6%.

Question Translation with Generative Parser

This NLIDB takes advantage of the database schema for generating a set of candidate SQL queries, which are classified by an SVM-ranker based on tree kernels (Giordani & Moschitti, 2012). In the generation phase, the system uses lexical dependencies and the database schema for constructing a set of SELECT, FROM, and WHERE clauses and also joins. Additionally, clauses are combined by applying rules and a heuristic weighting mechanism, which generates a list of sorted candidate SQL statements. This method can be recursively applied for processing complex queries that involve nested SELECT statements. Finally, a reranker is used for reordering the list of pairs of questions and candidate SQL statements, where both members are represented by syntactic trees.

Ambiguity and errors may affect the interpretation of the user query; however, information of the database schema can be used for verifying the correctness of the selected interpretation. The strategy consists in generating all the possible SQL queries by using information from the database schema (for example, primary keys, foreign keys, data types, etc.) for selecting the most likely using a ranking method.

The NLIDB translates natural language queries that involve nested SQL queries and complex natural language questions that have subordinate phrases, conjunctions, and negations. To this end, an algorithm is used that is based on coincidences between lexical dependencies and SQL structure, which allows to generate a viable set of queries.

This interface gets the lexical relations of a question by using the Stanford Dependency Parser, which obtains the set of binary word relations between a governor and a dependent (gov, dep), where gov and dep denote a parent node and child node in the parse tree.

This NLIDB was evaluated using three subsets of Geoquery and attained an accuracy of 87.2%, a precision of 82.8%, and an F-measure of 85%.

Systems for Languages Different from English

Hindi NLIDB

This is a domain-specific NLIDB that uses natural language processing techniques (Nichante, Giripunje, Nikam, Arsod, & Sonwane, 2017). The input for this interface is a natural language request (question or data manipulation operation) in Hindi. This request is translated to English using a semantic matching technique. Next, a semantically equivalent SQL statement is generated from the English request, which is sent to a database management system, and the result is presented to the user in the Hindi language. The interface is a domain-specific NLIDB that facilitates access to data, insertion, updating, and deletion of information of a transport database.

The approach used for translating a natural language request to SQL consists of the following steps:

1. Generation of a transport database, which stores information on transport services.
2. Identification of the type of request (select, insert, delete, update, and aggregate functions).
3. Mapping of tokens of the Hindi question to database elements (tables and columns).
4. Generation of SQL statements by mapping input requests with the assistance of stored values in the database.
5. Execution of the SQL statement and presenting the result in the Hindi language.

This NLIDB has two databases: a Compiler Database and a Transport Database. The system also has four important modules: Tokenizer, Mapper, SQL Query Generator, and database management system. The process performed by these modules is explained next:

1. The Tokenizer divides the Hindi language request into tokens and stores these tokens in an array. These Hindi tokens are stored in the lexicon (system dictionary) with their corresponding English words.
2. The Mapper sequentially compares the extracted tokens with tokens stored in the lexicon (system dictionary), where the mapping is performed. Those tokens that match the corresponding English words are saved together with their type, and all the remaining tokens are discarded as useless.
3. With the table and column names, the SQL statement is generated.
4. The generated SQL instruction is executed in the database management system and the answer is presented to the user.

There are no experimental results reported for this NLIDB; the article only mentions that it was tested with a transport database designed by the NLIDB implementer.

GANLIDB System

GANLIDB is an NLIDB that translates queries in the Arabic language to SQL; it is domain independent and can improve through experience its knowledge base (Bais, Machkour, & Koutti, 2016). This NLIDB allows users to access data stored in a database by answering queries in Arabic. The interface uses natural language processing techniques for translating queries into SQL statements. The most important advantage of this system is that it is independent of language, content, and model of the database.

The operation of this interface uses an approach based on an intermediate representation language, which translates a natural language query to a logical query in XML. Expressing the logical query in XML allows the interface to operate independently of language, content, and model (relational, object-oriented, relational-object, XML) of the database.

The architecture of GANLIDB consists of three modules, which are explained next:

1. **Linguistic component:** This module performs several analyses (morphological, syntactic, and semantic) of the natural language query and generates the logical interpretation of the question in an XML expression.
2. **Database knowledge component:** This module translates the logical query resulting from the first module to an SQL statement. Next, the SQL statement is sent to the database management system for generating the result in tabular form. The strategy of separating the database knowledge component from the linguistic component allows the interface to query different domain databases.
3. **Natural language query definition:** This module helps the interface to reuse previously processed queries for reducing translation time.

The NLIDB was evaluated using a corpus of 1,300 synthetic questions. The interface answered correctly 1,166 questions, which is equivalent to an accuracy of 95.1%.

Vietnamese NLIDB

This NLIDB has two main components: Question Analysis module y Result Computing module (Nguyen, Hoang, & Pham, 2012). The first component determines the type of user query and extracts information from it. The second component identifies the information requested by the user y calculates query statistics. This is a domain-specific interface for a survey database for individuals and businesses that want to know economic information from economic surveys.

The NLIDB has two main components, which are explained next:

1. **Question Analysis Component:** In the application domain of the NLIDB, a typical natural language query consists of three parts: question term indicates the type of question, question type specifies the statistical measure that users are interested in, and question information is the type of information requested and that will be used for determining the corresponding table columns that store the information. The purpose of this component is to determine Question Term, Type of Question and Question Information from a user question. Considering that user questions not only specify the requested information, but they include special words and phrases, the NLIDB uses JAPE (Java Annotation Patterns Engine) rules for detecting question terms and integrates the results into a Vietnamese word segmentation VNTokenizer so that the question terms are correctly identified as words. There exist many types of questions in Vietnamese; some of the types are Yes/No, Calculate, Give Reason (Why) y Comparing; therefore, for treating these types, the system uses a statistical question answering system that satisfies user's need of information stored in the database.

2. **Result Computing Component:** This component determines the database columns that correspond to the question information part of the user query. This system analyzes the survey questionnaires and sorts the information of each question of the survey; this process is called Relevant Data Retrieval. This system has a synonym dictionary for the economic and statistical domain.

This NLIDB was evaluated using a database of economic surveys. The corpus of queries consists of 500 questions formulated by users, 300 of these questions were used for training the system and 200 questions were used for evaluation. Out of the 200 questions, 157 were correctly answered, which is equivalent to an accuracy of 78.5%.

COMMERCIAL NATURAL LANGUAGE INTERFACES TO DATABASES

Available Commercial Natural Language Interfaces

Access ELF

Access ELF is an existing commercial NLIDB for translating natural language queries to SQL for Access databases (ELF, 2009). It is considered one of the best commercial interfaces. It is important to mention that, since ELF can only be used for Access, it cannot be used for large databases. It has several important characteristics:

1. **Domain independence:** Once ELF is installed on a computer, it is able to interact with any database (after configuring the interface).
2. **Automatic configuration:** The system can automatically obtain the structure of the database; therefore, its initial configuration is easy and simple. The automatic configuration examines the words in the names of tables and columns, and it uses them for generating the dictionary. These words are called synonyms and are used by ELF as references for tables and columns when they occur in natural language queries. The automatic configuration also stores for each column its data type and the table it belongs to.
3. **Configuration edition:** The configuration is performed by assigning new synonyms to tables and columns or by assigning synonyms to the words that have already been related to tables and columns.
4. **Database semantics:** During the analysis of the user query, ELF examines the terms (called synonyms) used for describing database tables and columns, and it uses its dictionary for trying to predict the synonyms used in questions.

The evaluation described by Conlon, Conlon and James (2004) involved users who are human resource professionals (administrators and staff). The success rate reported (presumably recall) was 70–80%. Additionally, ELF was evaluated using the Northwind database and achieved 91% of accuracy (Githiari, 2014).

EasyAsk

EasyAsk is an existing commercial NLIDB that is used for querying eCommerce databases (FinancesOnline, 2019). This is a software search tool that integrates natural language technology (Quiri) and analyses. Users can utilize keywords or terms to filter search results. This system provides product concepts, which yield specific groups of products that match the description of user requests. Additionally, this interface provides assistance when formulating queries by offering options to users when writing their questions.

The most important features are semantic processing that relates various text descriptions to concepts, automatic word stemming and spell-correction, automatic association of attributes to product concepts, and relaxation (ignoring irrelevant or unknown words).

A major component of EasyASk is Quiri, which is a natural language technology that combines linguistic processing with the understanding of data. Quiri divides a user question into words, and then it groups them into phrases and normalizes the content for interpreting the question. Additionally, it provides spell correction, stemming, and synonyms.

EasyAsk was evaluated using the Northwind database and attained an accuracy of 31% and a precision of 48.4% (Githiari, 2014).

Prototype Natural Language Interfaces

ATHENA

ATHENA is a prototype NLIDB developed by IBM, whose main feature is the ability to process complex nested SQL queries for business applications (Sen et al., 2019). The system uses domain ontologies that describe the semantic entities and their relationships in a domain. This system does not need user training nor feedback.

For processing a user question that involves several nested queries, this interface uses the following components:

1. **Evidence Annotator:** This component scans all the tokens of the natural language query and gathers evidence that one or more ontology elements (concepts, properties, and relations between concepts) have been referred to in the user question. Tokens that are mapped to some ontology elements are called entities (database tables and columns).
2. **Nested Query Detector:** A reasoning submodule obtains information from a linguistic analyzer and semantic annotators for identifying a possible nested query.
3. **Subquery Formation:** In the case of a nested query, this component uses lexicon-based techniques to divide the user question into two segments: the first segment for the outer query, and the second for the inner query. Specifically, this component determines the correct sets of tokens associated to each query by using a set of rules applicable to the query, which use the annotator outputs and domain elements. The result of this component is two queries expressed in Ontology Query Language (OQL).
4. **Subquery Join Condition:** For a nested query, this component generates the join condition that involves the inner and outer queries for constructing the complete query in OQL. Join generation depends on linguistic analysis and domain reasoning.
5. **Query Translator:** The task of his component is to convert an OQL query into an SQL statement.

ATHENA was tested using a FIBEN dataset that contains realistic business intelligence queries and combines data from two different financial sub-domains: SEC (Securities and Exchange Commission) dataset and TPoX (XML transaction processing benchmark). No performance results (accuracy or precision) are reported for this test.

Discontinued Natural Language Interfaces

English Query

English Query (developed by Microsoft) is commercial software that includes a set of tools, which database administrators can use for setting up an NLIDB (Microsoft, 2010). This interface was no longer included in SQL Server 2005. English Query applications allow users to formulate ad hoc questions to a database using English expressions. This system provides an environment for developing an English Query model. However, since databases are different and users formulate a large variety of questions, defining a model for answering user queries can be a complex process.

The task of the English Query engine is to perform the translation from a natural language query to SQL. The engine uses a domain file that contains the database model. The model contains specific information of the database to be queried, specifically, the database schema, a semantic abstraction layer constructed on top of the schema, and a mapping between them. In the model, database tables and columns are represented by entities, and joins are represented by relations. Entities and relations defined in a model allow English Query to translate a question to SQL.

English Query has a wizard that helps to configure the interface by automatically defining some entities and relations based on the structure of the database. Database administrators can define other entities and relations by using the development environment. The environment allows defining joins and change/define entity properties; for example, associated words, entity type, field, help text.

The evaluation of English Query described by Conlon et al. (2004) involved users who are human resource professionals (administrators and staff). The success rate reported (presumably recall) was 70–80%. Additionally, it was evaluated using the Northwind database and obtained an accuracy of 39% and a precision of 46.1% (Githiari, 2014).

SAA LanguageAccess

In 1990 IBM introduced SAA LanguageAccess (IBM, 1990). This interface uses other tools developed by IBM, such as Application System (AS) and Query Management Facility (QMF) for showing results to users. These results are shown in different ways: a pie chart, a table or a histogram. This NLIDB was withdrawn from marketing in 1993.

This interface is based on the use of grammar and dictionaries for translating a natural language query to an SQL statement. To this end, it consists of three main components, which are described next:

1. **Query Interface:** This component is based on AS or QMF, which allows the user to formulate queries in natural language. Additionally, the system uses these tools for showing results to the user.
2. **Natural Language Engine:** The task of this component is to syntactically parse the user question, interpret its meaning, and ensure accurate answers. This component involves the following ele-

ments/aspects. Lexicons or dictionaries for storing basic and domain-specific vocabulary. Syntax or grammar for taking into account the structure of the user question, which is used for performing a syntactic parsing and verifying the correct grammatical form of a question. Semantics for helping to understand the exact meaning of the natural language query; for example, determining the adequate meaning of a word with several meanings. Pragmatics for solving situation-dependent interpretation of the user question; for example, for identifying the references of pronouns in the question.

3. **Customization Tool:** This tool is used for defining the vocabulary utilized by users when formulating questions. Typically, this tool is used by the database administrator, since he/she knows the database structure and the vocabulary used in the organization by specific users. Specifically, it is used for including in the lexicon specific terms and acronyms likely to be used in user questions for referring to database elements (tables and columns).

EVALUATION BENCHMARKS

ATIS Database

ATIS (Air Travel Information Services) database is a relational database that has information on flights, flight fares, aircraft, airlines, airports, and cities in the USA, and ground services. From 1990 to 1994, SRI International used this database for conducting annual evaluations for research sponsored by DARPA for spoken natural language (SRI International, 2019).

The ATIS database contains information obtained from the Official Airline Guide, which is organized as a relational database. The database consists of 28 tables and a total of 125 columns, and its schema is shown in figure 1. The most used corpus to query ATIS for evaluating NLIDBs is the ATIS0 Pilot, which was designed in 1990 by SRI and consists of 2884 of queries. This corpus is available at https://catalog.ldc.upenn.edu/docs/LDC93S4B/trn_prmp.html.

Geobase Database

Geobase is a database that contains geographical information of the United States of America, and it is used by many NLIDBs as a test benchmark since the 90s. It includes information on cities, states, mountains, rivers, lakes, and highways. Originally, Geobase was used by the Geobase system, which was an application example included in the Prolog commercial system, mainly in Turbo Prolog 2.0 version distributed by Borland International (Borland, 1988). It first appeared in 1988 as a deductive database implemented in Prolog, which was complemented with a natural language interface for querying the database.

The schema of the original Geobase is the following:

state(name, abbreviation, capital, area, admit, population, city, city, city, city)
city(state, abbreviation, name, population)
river(name, length, statestringlist)
border(state, abbreviation, statelist)
highlow(state, abbreviation, point, height, point, height)

Figure 1. ATIS database schema

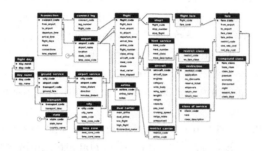

mountain(state, abbreviation, name, height)
lake(name, area, statelist)
road(number, statelist)

Since the 90s, Geobase (sometimes referred to as Geoquery) has been used for evaluating many NLIDBs; some of the most recent are C-Phrase, Precise, and WASP. Therefore, many researchers have adapted Geobase to the relational model.

Unfortunately, there exist different versions of the relational schemas, which differ from the original schema; for example, the addition of an extra column *density* to table *state*, the division of table *highlow* into tables *high* and *low*, the elimination of the four city columns from table *state*. Additionally, most of the versions lack a foreign key from column *capital* to table *city*, which is necessary because every state capital is a city. This situation complicates comparing the performance reported for different NLIDBs, despite being evaluated using Geobase. Figure 2 shows a database schema for Geobase proposed by the authors.

Figure 2. The proposed relational schema for Geobase

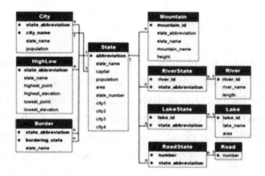

There exist two query corpora for testing: Geoquery880 and Geoquery250, which were designed by Mooney for training a system for semantic analysis. These corpora are available at http://www.cs.utexas.edu/users/ml/nldata/geoquery.html.

Northwind Database

Figure 3. Northwind database schema

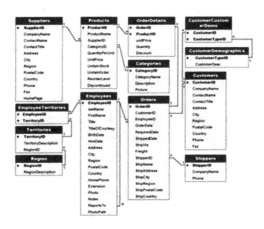

Northwind is a database used by Microsoft for showing the features of some of its products, including SQL Server and Microsoft Access. The database contains information on sales of the Northwind Traders company, a food import, and export company. This database has 13 tables, as shown in **Figure 3** (Borker, 2006).

Spider Dataset

Spider is a text-to-SQL dataset for large scale semantic analysis and contains complex and cross-domain queries. It was developed at Yale University with the participation of 11 computer science students. It consists of 10,181 natural language questions and 5,693 complex queries on 200 databases with multiple tables that span 138 different domains (Yu et al., 2018).

The query corpus comprises a large variety of clauses and operations: SELECT, WHERE, GROUP BY, HAVING, ORDER BY, LIMIT, JOIN, INTERSECT, EXCEPT, UNION, NOT IN, OR, AND, EXISTS, LIKE, as well as subqueries. Spider is an extensive query corpus designed for training neural networks used in NLIDBs. The corpus comprises 200 databases covering 138 different domains, 10,181 questions, and 5,693 complex SQL queries. This dataset is available at https://github.com/taoyds/spider.

IMDb Database

The Internet Movie Database (IMDb) is an online database that stores information on movies, directors, producers, actors, television shows, and series. IMDb makes available for public access subsets of IMDb data at https://datasets.imdbws.com/. Each dataset is in tsv format and can be accessed using a spreadsheet. Because the information is not compatible with the relational model, some relational database versions have been developed, which vary in the number of tables and columns. One of these is available at https://relational.fit.cvut.cz/dataset/IMDb.

WikiSQL Database

WikiSQL is a dataset published in 2017 by Zhong, Xiong and Socher (2017) for training Seq2SQL, an NLIDB based on deep neural networks. WikiSQL consists of 80,654 annotated natural language queries and SQL queries involving 24,241 tables from Wikipedia. It is important to mention that the WikiSQL database has no foreign keys, and each domain has only one table. This database is available at https://github.com/salesforce/WikiSQL.

SOLUTIONS AND RECOMMENDATIONS

As mentioned before, the slow development of NLIDB technology, from 1961 to 2019, shows that translating a natural language query to SQL has proven to be very difficult. In particular, developing domain-independent systems that achieve accuracies above 95% is an extremely complex problem.

The accuracies reported for neural network NLIDBs are below 85%, which is still far from 95%. The best results for syntax-based interfaces are in the range of 90% to 95% for accuracy. The accuracy obtained by a semantic grammar system is 75%, which is very far from 95%. For pattern-matching interfaces, the accuracies reported are around 85%. The best accuracies obtained by systems based on other approaches is 87%. Finally, the best performance reported for commercial NLIDBs is 80%, which is far from 95%.

The results summarized in the previous paragraph show that more work is needed for increasing the effectiveness of NLIDBs, particularly for neural network systems, which is a new approach for translating from natural language to SQL.

The descriptions of NLIDBs show that there are no widely accepted benchmarks for evaluation, which makes it very difficult to compare the performance of different systems. Although Geobase is one of the most used databases, unfortunately, there exist several versions of the relational schema. Therefore, figure 2 shows a proposed schema for Geobase.

There exist several metrics for measuring NLIDB performance: accuracy (also called recall), precision, and F1. One of the most widely used metrics is precision, which is defined as the percentage of correctly answered queries with respect to the number of translated queries. However, end users are more interested in accuracy, which is the percentage of correctly answered queries with respect to all the input queries. Unfortunately, several systems do not report accuracies, which makes it difficult to compare the performance of NLIDBs that only report precision and/or F1. Therefore, it is recommended that accuracy be always reported.

FUTURE RESEARCH DIRECTIONS

After almost 60 years of development of NLIDB technology, the challenge for achieving accuracies close to 100% still remains. Most of the problems found in translating from natural language are linguistic; for example, modifier attachment, conjunction and disjunction, and semantic ellipsis.

The following example illustrates the problem of modifier attachment: *Which Delta flights depart to Washington at night?* In this sentence, *at night* could be considered as a modifier of *Washington*, which is syntactically correct, but semantically incorrect, because it should be a complement of the verb *depart*. The word *and*, which is a conjunction, is often used to denote logical disjunction, whose meaning is usually difficult to determine. Ellipsis is the omission of important words (in the wording of a natural language query) that are necessary for an NLIDB to understand the query fully. The following query for the ATIS database illustrates this problem: *How many engines does an M80 have?* In this query, a value *M80* is specified; however, no table name is mentioned nor a column name associated to the specified value.

Other problems are related to database schemas and usability. The evaluations reported are for NLIDBs that have been configured by the implementers, who are the experts. However, for practical applications, it is more important the performance obtained when the interface is configured by database administrators. Unfortunately, very few NLIDBs report results of systems configured by users different from the implementers; therefore, more work is needed for addressing this problem.

CONCLUSION

The current challenge for domain-independent NLIDBs consists of developing systems whose accuracy is above 95% and that can be easily configured for obtaining this accuracy.

The development of domain-independent NLIDBs has proven to be more difficult than initially thought. By way of comparison, it has been shown that the problem of determining if a natural language expression is grammatical (i.e., it satisfies the rules of grammar) is an NP-complete problem (Koller & Striegnitz, 2002). Therefore, the syntactic parsing of natural language is an NP-hard problem, whose exact solution requires an algorithm whose computational complexity is exponential.

In order to improve NLIDB performance, the authors propose a layered approach, which is recommended for dealing with complex problems. Systems whose design is based on functionality layers provide the flexibility and modularity for implementing more complex processing strategies than systems designed otherwise. Complex systems that have been developed using a layered architecture are communication networks that use the seven-layered architecture of the OSI model, and database management systems that use the three-level ANSI-SPARC architecture.

The architecture of the NLIDB described by Pazos et al. (2016) has allowed to include more layers for dealing with additional problems. For example, a Wizard for semi-automatically fine-tuning the configuration, which allowed undergraduate students to configure the system for obtaining accuracies in the range of 80.53% to 84.82%.

Another layer has been recently developed for dealing with a difficult semantic ellipsis problem that involves Boolean columns. These are columns that can only store two possible values: true/false, yes/no, 1/0. Natural language queries that involve Boolean columns do not specify search values; for example, consider the following query to the ATIS database *Which flights are in wide body airplanes?* Table *aircraft* has a column *wide_body*, whose values are *YES* or *NO*, but the search value *YES* is not specified in the query.

Finally, a new layer is being developed for querying databases that have design anomalies, such as the absence of primary and foreign keys, use of surrogate keys instead of primary keys, columns for storing aggregate function calculations, repeated columns in two or more tables, tables that are not in second normal form, and tables not in third normal form. Dealing with this problem is important because there are many databases that have design anomalies; therefore, many NLIDBs do not perform correctly with a large number of databases that have this problem.

REFERENCES

Androutsopoulos, I., Ritchie, G. D., & Thanisch, P. (1995). Natural language interfaces to databases – An introduction. *Journal of Natural Language Engineering*, *1*(1), 29–81. doi:10.1017/S135132490000005X

Bais, H., Machkour, M., & Koutti, L. (2016). An independent-domain natural language interface for relational database: Case Arabic language. In *Proceedings of 2016 IEEE/ACS 13th International Conference of Computer Systems and Applications* (pp. 1-7). Agadir. Morocco: IEEE. 10.1109/AICCSA.2016.7945786

Borker, S. (2006). Business intelligence data warehousing an open source approach (Report). Kansas State University, Manhattan, KS.

Borland International. (1988). *Turbo Prolog 2.0 reference guide*. Scotts Valley, Borland International.

Chomsky, N. (1957). Syntactic Structures (463-480). The Hage: Mouton & Co.

Conlon, S. J., Conlon, J. R., & James, T. L. (2004). The economics of natural language interfaces: Natural language processing technology as a scarce resource. *Decision Support Systems*, *38*(1), 141–159. doi:10.1016/S0167-9236(03)00096-4

FinancesOnline. (2019). *EasyAsk review*. Retrieved on December 16, 2019, from https://reviews.financesonline.com/p/easyask/

Giordani, A., & Moschitti, A. (2012). Translating questions to SQL queries with generative parsers discriminatively reranked. In *Proceedings of the International Conference on Computational Linguistics (COLING)* (pp. 401-410). Mumbai, India: Academic Press.

Githiari, L. M. (2014). *Natural Language Access to Relational Databases: An Ontology Concept Mapping (OCM) Approach*. PhD dissertation.

González, J. J., Florencia-Juarez, R., Fraire, H. J., Pazos, R. A., Cruz-Reyes, L., & Gómez, C. (2015). Semantic representations for knowledge modelling of a natural language interface to databases using ontologies. *International Journal of Combinatorial Optimization Problems and Informatics*, *6*(2), 28–42.

Green, B. F., Wolf, A. K., Chomsky, C., & Laughery, K. (1961). BASEBALL: An automatic question answerer. In *Proceedings of the Western Joint Computer Conference* (pp. 207-216). Los Angeles, CA: Academic Press.

Gunjal, U. P., Rathod, V., & Pise, N. N. (2017). An intelligent system for relational databases. *International Journal of Scientific Research (Ahmedabad, India)*, *6*(3), 1546–1550.

Han, Y. J., Park, S. B., & Park, S. Y. (2016). A natural language interface concordant with a knowledge base. *Computational Intelligence and Neuroscience*, *2016*, 1–15. doi:10.1155/2016/9174683 PMID:26904105

Hendrix, G. G., Sacerdoti, E. D., Sagalowicz, D., & Slocum, J. (1978). Natural language interfaces to databases – An introduction. *ACM Transactions on Database Systems*, *3*(2), 105–147. doi:10.1145/320251.320253

IBM. (1990). *IBM SAA LanguageAccess: A straighter way to your information*. Retrieved December 16, 2019, from https://archive.org/details/TNM_IBM_SAA_Language_Access_-_IBM_20171017_0041

International, S. R. I. (2019). *Air Travel Information Service (ATIS)*. Retrieved December 2, 2019, from http://www.ai.sri.com/natural-language/projects/arpa-sls/atis.html

Tyagi, M. (2014). Natural Language Interface to Databases: A Survey. *International Journal of Scientific Research (Ahmedabad, India)*, *3*(5), 1443–1445.

Kokare, R., & Wanjale, K. (2015). A natural language query builder interface for structured databases using dependency parsing. *International Journal of Mathematical Sciences and Computing*, *1*(4), 11–20. doi:10.5815/ijmsc.2015.04.02

Koller, A., & Striegnitz, K. (2002). Generation as dependency parsing. In *Proceedings of the 40th Annual Meeting of the Association for Computational Linguistics* (pp. 17-24). Philadelphia, PA: Academic Press.

Li, F. (2017). *Querying RDBMS using natural language* (Doctoral dissertation). University of Michigan, Ann Arbor, MI.

Llopis, M., & Ferrández, A. (2013). How to make a natural language interface to query databases accessible to everyone: An example. *Computer Standards & Interfaces*, *35*(5), 470–481. doi:10.1016/j.csi.2012.09.005

Microsoft. (2010). *Chapter 32 - English Query Best Practices*. Retrieved December 16, 2019, from http://technet.microsoft.com/es-mx/library/cc917659(en-us,printer).aspx

Mvumbi, T. (2016). *Natural language interface to relational database: A simplified customization approach* (Master thesis). University of Cape Town. Cape Town, South Africa.

Nguyen, D. T., Hoang, T. D., & Pham, S. B. (2012). A Vietnamese natural language interface to database. In *Proceedings of 2012 IEEE Sixth International Conference on Semantic Computing* (pp. 130-133). Palermo, Italy: IEEE. 10.1109/ICSC.2012.33

Nichante, R., Giripunje, S., Nikam, A., Arsod, S., & Sonwane, N. (2017). Hindi language as a graphical user interface to relational database for transport system. *International Research Journal of Engineering and Technology*, *4*(3), 349–353.

Nihalani, N., Silakari, S., & Motwani, M. (2011). Natural language interface for database: A brief review. *International Journal of Computer Science Issues*, *8*(2), 600–608.

Pazos, R. A., Aguirre, M. A., González, J. J., Martínez, J. A., Pérez, J., & Verástegui, A. A. (2016). Comparative study on the customization of natural language interfaces to databases. *SpringePlus*, *5*(553), 1–30. doi:10.118640064-016-2164-y

Pazos, R. A., González, J. J., Aguirre, M. A., Martínez, J. A., & Fraire, H. J. (2013). Natural Language Interfaces to Databases: An Analysis of the State of the Art. In *Recent Advances on Hybrid Intelligent Systems* (pp. 463–480). Springer-Verlag. doi:10.1007/978-3-642-33021-6_36

Porras, J., Florencia-Juárez, R., Rivera, G., & García, V. (2018). Interfaz de lenguaje natural para consultar cubos multidimensionales utilizando procesamiento analítico en línea. *Research in Computing Science*, *147*(6), 153–165. doi:10.13053/rcs-147-6-12

Safari, L., & Patrick, J. D. (2014). Restricted natural language based querying of clinical databases. *Journal of Biomedical Informatics, 52*, 338–353. doi:10.1016/j.jbi.2014.07.012 PMID:25051402

Sen, J., Ozcan, F., Quamar, A., Stager, G., Mittal, A., Jammi, M., ... Sankaranarayanan, K. (2019). Natural Language Querying of Complex Business Intelligence Queries. In *Proceedings of the 2019 International Conference on Management of Data, SIGMOD Conference* (pp. 1997-2000). 10.1145/3299869.3320248

Shabaz, K., O'Shea, J. D., Crockett, K. A., & Latham, A. (2015). Aneesah: A conversational natural language interface to databases. In *Proceedings of the World Congress on Engineering* (pp. 227-232). London, UK: Academic Press.

Software, E. L. F. (2009). *ELF Software Documentation Series*. Retrieved December 16, 2019, from http://www.elfsoft.com/help/accelf/Overview.htm

Sujatha, B., & Raju, S. V. (2016). Ontology based natural language interface for relational databases. *Procedia Computer Science, 92*, 487–492. doi:10.1016/j.procs.2016.07.372

Sujatha, B., Raju, S. V., & Shaziya, H. (2012). A Survey of Natural Language Interface to Database Management System. *International Journal of Science and Advanced Technology, 2*(6), 56–60.

Sukthankar, N., Maharnawar, S., Deshmukh, P., Haribhakta, Y., & Kamble, V. (2017). nQuery - A natural language statement to SQL query generator. In *Proceedings of the 55th Annual Meeting of the Association for Computational Linguistics, Student Research Workshop* (pp. 17-23). 10.18653/v1/P17-3004

Utama, P., Weir, N., Basık, F., Binnig, C., Cetintemel, U., Hättasch, B., ... Usta, A. (2018). *DBPal: An end-to-end neural natural language interface for databases*. Retrieved from https://arxiv.org/abs/1804.00401

Wang, W. (2019). A cross-domain natural language interface to databases using adversarial text method. In *Proceedings of the Very Large Data Bases PhD Workshop*. Los Angeles, CA: Academic Press.

Wang, W., Tian, Y., Xiong, H., Wang, H., & Ku, W. (2018). *A transfer-learnable natural language interface for databases*. Retrieved from https://arxiv.org/abs/1809.02649

Woods, W. A., Kaplan, R. M., & Webber, B. N. (1972). The lunar sciences natural language information System (BBN Report 2378). Bolt Beranek and Newman Inc.

Xu, B., Cai, R., Zhang, Z., Yang, X., Hao, Z., Li, Z., & Liang, Z. (2016). NADAQ: Natural language database querying based on deep learning. *IEEE Access: Practical Innovations, Open Solutions*. Advance online publication. doi:10.1109/access.2019.2904720

Yu, T., Zhang, R., Yang, K., Yasunaga, M., Wang, D., Li, Z., ... Radev, D. R. (2018). *Spider: A large-scale human-labeled dataset for complex and cross-domain semantic parsing and text-to-SQL task*. Retrieved from https://arxiv.org/abs/1809.08887

Zhong, V., Xiong, C., & Socher, R. (2017). *Seq2SQL: Generating structured queries from natural language using reinforcement learning*. Retrieved from https://arxiv.org/abs/1709.00103

Chapter 2
Mispronunciation Detection and Diagnosis Through a Chatbot

Marcos E. Martinez
https://orcid.org/0000-0002-9777-6395
Universidad Autónoma de Ciudad Juárez, Mexico

Francisco López-Orozco
Universidad Autónoma de Ciudad Juárez, Mexico

Karla Olmos-Sánchez
https://orcid.org/0000-0002-9145-6761
Universidad Autónoma de Ciudad Juárez, Mexico

Julia Patricia Sánchez-Solís
Universidad Autónoma de Ciudad Juárez, Mexico

ABSTRACT

The interaction between humans and machines has evolved; thus, the idea of being able to communicate with computers as we usually do with other people is becoming increasingly closer to coming true. Nowadays, it is common to come across intelligent systems named chatbots, which allow people to communicate by using natural language to hold conversations related to a specific domain. Chatbots have gained popularity in different kinds of sectors, such as customer service, marketing, sales, e-commerce, e-learning, travel, and even in education itself. This chapter aims to present a chatbot-based approach to learning English as a second language by using computer-assisted language learning systems.

INTRODUCTION

During day-to-day activities, human beings make use of natural language. Something that characterizes natural language is its ambiguity, especially when it is expressed in written format. Hence, Artificial Intelligence (AI) community has been extensively researched and developed techniques, algorithms, and tools in order to improve the human-computer interaction. Natural Language Processing (NLP) arises in

DOI: 10.4018/978-1-7998-4730-4.ch002

Copyright © 2021, IGI Global. Copying or distributing in print or electronic forms without written permission of IGI Global is prohibited.

1950 from the need to interact with computers in a natural manner and extract information from human speeches (Kamath, Liu, & Whitaker 2019). Since then, various computer applications have been developed to accomplish this task. An example of these applications is chatbots, which are computer programs that use NLP to imitate human behavior to the point of making them believe that they are interacting with other humans (Roos, 2018). Chatbots are frequently used in areas such as customer service, marketing, sales, e-Commerce, travel, and even in education (Zumstein & Hundertmark, 2018).

The advantage of implementing a chatbot is that it allows users to access services at any time. In addition, the implementation of chatbots in education is of great potential since they can be appropriate partners for learning (Shawar, 2017). Also, they can be used to learn a second language through *Computer Assisted Language Learning* (CALL) systems. Pronunciation is usually the skill that causes most problems during second language learning. Diverse factors such as shyness, lack of practice, or bad feedback can affect the development of this skill. *Computer-Assisted Pronunciation Training* (CAPT) is a CALL sub-area which aims to help develop speech skills. These systems use *Automatic Speech Recognition* (ASR) and *Mispronunciation Detection and Diagnosis* (MDD) algorithms to detect pronunciation errors. Equip a chatbot with an MDD algorithm could emulate a second language teacher that provides pronunciation error feedback. Currently, there are some systems with these characteristics; however, they are focused on teaching vocabulary in isolated words (Heil, Wu, Lee, & Schmidt, 2016), depriving students' opportunities to create their own sentences.

The aim of this chapter is to introduce a proposal integrating automatic speech recognition, chatbots, and mispronunciation detection and diagnosis in order to improve second language learners' pronunciation skills. The purpose of using a chatbot is to achieve a conversation with a character emulating a real person. The structure of this chapter is as follows. First, the Background section provides a review of the literature on NLP, as well as some of its applications and techniques. Second, the Main Focus section describes the interest of this research, which is to integrate a mispronunciation detection module in a Chatbot. Additionally, a description of Computer-Assisted Language Learning Systems and Computer-Assisted Pronunciation Training is presented. The Solutions section shows one of the possible algorithms that could be used in the development of this research proposal. Finally, future trends are described, and a discussion of the partial results obtained is presented.

BACKGROUND

Natural Language Processing

The NLP emerged with the aim of allowing the interaction between humans and computers in a natural way, i.e., the capacity of understanding, interpreting, and generating human language. In the beginning, simple tasks such as the translation of words from Russian to English were carried out by a translation machine. Later, problems that involved the way the language is structured were detected (Nadkarni, Ohno-Machado, & Chapman, 2011).

In 1957, the Noam Chomsky's book on Syntactic Structure was published, in which the importance of syntax for understanding the language is discussed. The set of grammatical rules proposed by Chomsky helped to structure and label different characteristics in sentences. That contribution influenced not only NLP but also other areas of Artificial Intelligence (AI) (Liddy, 2001). Since then, research on NLP has been carried out in relation to what was proposed by Chomsky. The way in which the language is structured helped to generate new research, as well as systems that applied this new knowledge. Soon after, question-answer systems began to emerge, integrating the natural language understanding and logic-based systems.

Later, in the 1990s, statistical language processing became popular and generated new ideas about data generation and manipulation. Text corpus began to be used for the linguistic process based on the word occurrences and the creation of probabilistic models. A large amount of data in different languages was presented through the World Wide Web, which caused a great deal of research on machine translators, text summarization, and classification. In addition, at that time, there was a noticeable improvement in the memory used in computers, allowing NLP-related systems to work in the real world (Kamath, Liu, & Whitaker, 2019).

With the arrival of Deep Learning and Artificial Neural Networks (ANN), statistical models were able to introduce new approaches in the NLP field. Deep Learning methods were used on many of the NLP tasks, such as text classification, question-answer systems, text generation, character recognition, and even speech recognition (Fahad & Yahya, 2018). All these tasks were accomplished with different Deep Neural Networks (DNN) applications, such as Recurrent Neural Networks (RNN) or Convolutional Neural Networks (CNN) (Young, Hazarika, Poria, & Cambria, 2018)

Text Analysis

An NLP system is divided into two areas: Natural Language Understanding (NLU) and Natural Language Generation (NLG). NLU processes the incoming text and gives it meaning, while NLG looks to communicate a text with appropriate meaning. In other words, NLU processes inputs, and NLG provides outputs. For reasons of this work, the main interest is focused on the use of NLU, which can be divided into text analysis and audio analysis. Nowadays, text generation grows rapidly. Occasionally, it may contain useful information that can be used for certain purposes. From the text analysis, it is possible to find some elements that give it meaning or even generate new information. Khurana et al. (2017) propose a series of steps to achieve text analysis, which is described below:

Steps to perform text analysis:

a. Lexical analysis: Firstly, the text is segmented into words, sentences, or paragraphs. Each segment is structured in a format that will be used in syntactic analysis.
b. Syntactic analysis: Each segmentation is analyzed so that the order and a relationship between the words are found.
c. Semantic analysis: Possible meanings of words within the segmentation are determined based on the interactions among them.
d. Discourse: The meaning of a sentence depends on the relationship it has with previous or subsequent sentences.
e. Pragmatics: External characteristics that involve knowing aspects of the real world.

One of the most used techniques for text analysis is Word Embedding, where texts are represented by numerical vectors. The dimension of a vector is given by the number of occurrences of each word in a text. The central idea of *Word Embedding* is that the meaning of a word is given by others that frequently appear near the first. The goal is to learn a joint probability for a sequence of words that will occur throughout the text. The higher the probability, the sequence is more commonly used (Li & Yang, 2017). Word Embedding encodes semantic and syntactic word information, where semantic information must be related to of meaning of words, while semantic information refers to the roles that words play in vocabulary structure. It is assumed that in a similar context, the words should have a similar meaning. The existing Word Embedding methods are:

1. **Frequency-based Embedding**
   a. Count Vectors
   b. TF-IDF
   c. Co-Occurrence Matrix
2. **Prediction-based Embedding**
   a. CBOW
   b. Skip-Gram

The most common method to perform this task is Word2Vec, which is formed by two neural network layers processing vectors representing words. Word2Vec has a large text corpus in which each word is represented by a vector. Later the vector is traversed using a central word and context words. The similarity between vectors is used to calculate the word-context probability in the central word. This process continues until the probability is increased. To increase the method efficiency, common words that do not represent context variance are discarded. This helps to improve the times for modeling and training. **Figure 1** shows the central word and the context words.

Figure 1. Representation in Word2vec
Source: (Umezawa, 2018)

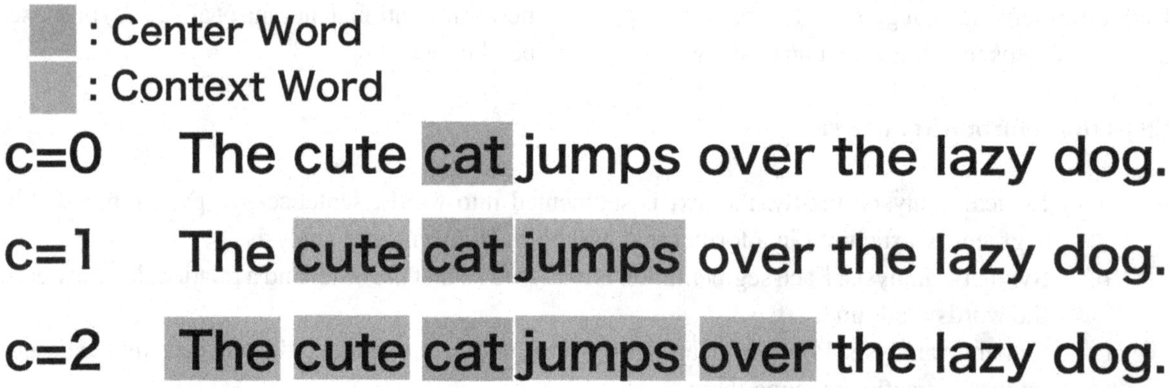

■ : Center Word
■ : Context Word

c=0   The cute cat jumps over the lazy dog.

c=1   The cute cat jumps over the lazy dog.

c=2   The cute cat jumps over the lazy dog.

Mikolov et al. (2013) proposed a neural architecture set that could compute continuous word representations on large data sets. The difference with other neural network models is that these new architectures allowed to handle even a billion words vocabularies. The proposed architectures consist of a *Continuous Bag of Words* (CBOW) model and the *Skip-Gram* model. To achieve text analysis, it is possible to implement two approaches: *rules-based* or *machine learning* techniques. As we have seen, text can be segmented into words, sentences, or paragraphs. The term *token* is usually used to refer to these textual units. *Tokenization* is defined as word segmentation, where tokens are useful words. An NLP task requires the input texts to be tokenized into individual words before being processed (Jettakul et al., 2018). From this modeling, it is possible to apply certain rules which are manually constructed by linguistic or grammatical experts. Some machine translation systems often use a rule-based approach.

Machine Learning (ML) is another approach used in NLP. Algorithms are used to understand the terms in the documents. ML for NLP involves a set of statistical techniques to identify certain aspects of texts. The advantage of this is that the algorithm "learns", and it is not necessary to manually code the required rules. ML techniques can be classified into three categories: *supervised learning*, *semi-supervised learning*, and *unsupervised learning*. Supervised learning is currently the dominant technique to use in NLP. Machine Learning supervised models automatically induces the rules from a training data set (Khan, Daud, Nasir, & Amjad, 2016).

Audio Analysis

The automatic speech recognition approach is used to audio analysis in the NLP field, which aims to transform the audio signal from voice to text. There exist features useful to carry out this task, these are:

Voice analysis

  a. Phonetics: Assignment of a specific sound to a phoneme.
  b. Phoneme: Minimal articulation of a sound, each language has its phonemes set.
  c. Prosodic: External characteristics of speech like tone, stress, and intonation.

Automatic Speech Recognition

Automatic Speech Recognition (ASR) has gained popularity in the NLP field. Many of the tools and applications that are developed today have the option to detect the voice, some as cognitive assistants or automatic translators. Although the subject has become widely studied in recent years, its first research emerged in 1950. Bell Laboratories created a system that could recognize digits pronunciation from zero to nine by a single speaker using the voice spectrum frequency format (Juang & Rabiner, 2004). In the 60s, small vocabularies were used, and acoustic phonemes were investigated with techniques based on frequency analysis. IBM Shoebox was able to recognize words such as arithmetic operators as well as digits and thus be able to do mathematical operations with them.

In the following decade, new techniques such as *Pattern Recognition* and the *Hidden Markov Model* (HMM) were developed, which are some of the most widely used nowadays. The HMM method uses probability and transitions between states. With the introduction of the neural networks in speech recognition modules in 1980, the HMM method began to be used for improving state prediction, being capable of handling the nature of an ongoing conversation.

In the 2000s, advances in ML research continued towards the development of new techniques that presented improvements in speech recognition. *Deep Belief Networks* were applied for phonemes recognition. These networks have an unsupervised learning algorithm, which is used to represent audio in spectral characteristics form (Banerjee et al. 2018). Advances in Deep Neural Networks continued in the 2000s, the research on hybrid models DNN / HMM became dominant in the literature. Since 2012, Deep Learning has been applied in ASR development, even replacing HMM.

Feature extraction

Feature extraction looks to provide an audio signal numerical representation. They are obtained after processing the raw audio. The *Mel-Frequency Cepstral Coefficients* (MFCC) are the features most used in automatic speech recognition systems. They are based on human ear behavior. To extract the MFCCs coefficients, the audio signal is segmented in equal frames, usually 20ms, since the time required to identify phonemes. For each segment, a feature vector is calculated and will be used later to create an acoustic model (Das & Sharma, 2016).

Steps to calculate MFCC:

1. Pre-emphasis: A filter is applied to audio to eliminate high and low frequencies.
2. Framing: Segment the audio signal into frames.
3. Hamming windowing: Reduces sharp changes near edges of each frame that can be caused during segmentation.
4. Fast Fourier Transform: Converts signal from the time domain to the frequency domain. A spectrogram is a visual form of this.
5. Mel filter bank processing: Signal does not follow a linear behavior; thus, filters are applied to act logarithmically at high frequencies and linearly at low frequencies.
6. Discrete Cosine Transform: Assigns Mel scale features to the time domain. The output of this conversion is the MFCC. Each audio segment becomes a feature vector.

Hidden Markov Model

HMM approach is generally used in automatic speech recognition tasks. It has not changed much since its inception. An HMM is finite-state stochastic automation, which is made up of a state set connected by transitions where the sequence of states is hidden (Muhammad, Nasrun, Setianingsih, & Murti, 2018).

HMM Parameters:

1. A state set. $S = \{s_1, s_2, \ldots, s_n\}$
2. Transition probabilities between states, where $\{a_{ij}\}$ represents the transition probability from the ith state to the jth state.
3. Observation sequence.

An HMM model can be used with linguistic units such as phonemes, words, or sentences. For continuous speech recognition, the linguistic unit used is the phoneme. That said, the phoneme set can be used to concatenate them and thus create words. In phonetic models, each state represents a phoneme, and the state change is made based on the transition probabilities (Gales & Young, 2007).

Computer-Assisted Pronunciation Training

CALL systems are part of a subarea named Computer-Assisted Pronunciation Training. These systems are based on Automatic Speech Recognition, used to detect sentences that the user is saying. The system oversees and evaluates the said pronunciation and, if required, providing feedback to the user (Su, Wu, & Lee, 2015). Some of these systems have the characteristics of being a game with scores; thus, it may seem attractive to users. A CALL system is made up of several components where feedback is one of the most important to carry the language process. It is necessary for a CALL system to show the user the correct pronunciation form, and for this, digital voice synthesizers that correctly pronounce the words are commonly used.

Computer-Assisted Pronunciation Training (CAPT) applications using ASR for the assessment of non-native pronunciation should evaluate learners in the same way as a human expert would, detecting those problems that impose difficulties. An ideal CAPT system should recognize everything the user says, point out those areas that are most problematic, and explicitly provide feedback on how to improve (González, 2015).

The implementation of this technology might facilitate second language acquisition. Compared to a second-language human teacher, a CAPT system is not fatigued and can be used at any time, regardless of workload. This is beneficial for second-language learners because it helps them build more confidence while they speak, and it allows them to practice as many times as they wish, improving pronunciation. The errors in these are mainly produced by non-native speakers (Leung, Liu, & Meng, 2019). This is due to the cognitive scheme developed is based on native speakers; so, it tends to interpret words and their meaning and pronunciation in the same way when applied to language learners.

CAPT systems focus on *Mispronunciation Detection and Diagnosis* (MDD). To a certain context, MDD can have a greater difficulty degree than an ASR, which is only responsible for generating text through voice (Li, Qian, & Meng, 2017). ASR engines generate a language model which generates the word sequence to be transcripted. However, this operation does not apply in the same way in the detection and diagnostic systems. Also, the ASR's effectiveness significantly decreases when dealing with non-native speakers, and ASR ratings do not always correlate with those by human raters.

An MDD needs to differentiate from correct to incorrect pronunciation for a CAPT system function properly (Li et al., 2017). There are different approaches that are used within a CAPT system. One of them is the *Hidden Markov Model* (HMM). An ASR system is used to provide confidence scores for error detection or to diagnose the mispronunciation (Chen & Li, 2017). These systems can develop pronunciation obtaining higher scores, but they are limited since they do not provide correct pronunciation error feedback.

Chatbots

A chatbot is a program that uses AI to simulate a conversation to the point of giving the impression that it is human interaction (Zemčík, 2018). Until a few years ago, the use of the term 'chatbot' was related to applications for conversation via writing, but this changed with the speech recognition development and its implementation in them. NLP is the main tool for chatbot construction, which began to develop in 1960. Among the first chatbots developed can be mentioned Eliza. This system had a basic operation basic, had a simple pattern mechanism, and preloaded responsive templates to simulate conversation (Dale, 2016). Later, in 1972, PARRY was developed, which simulated a schizophrenia patient. It was developed by Kenneth Mark Colby, a psychiatrist and computer scientist (Deshpande, Shahane, Gadre, Deshpande, & Joshi, 2017). PARRY's design appeared to have conversations with paranoid people.

Later, ALICE was developed, which used the AIML language developed by Richard Wallace in 1995. AIML language is an XML adaptation; it is a series of classified patterns of stimuli and responses contained in the document. Mostly, a user starts a conversation by greetings or general questions. AIML is defined with templates of greetings and general queries (Thomas, 2016). The greatest contribution is the automatic knowledge extrapolation process based on previously processed information.

More complex AIML techniques have been developed in recent years, involving probability-based techniques and decision trees. As machine learning techniques are developed, the skills of chatbots improve. With larger knowledge corpora, it is possible to create more robust chatbots that give linguistically stronger responses (Garcia Brustenga, Fuertes Alpiste, & Molas Castells, 2018).

Mitsuki was developed in AIML using a rule-based approach. AIML structure is built by categories to route user input. When the bot is unable to find the best match to return a suitable answer, it will be redirected to a default category. Supervised machine learning is used to learn data, such as personal details about the user. These data are sent and reviewed by a human manager. Only verified data is incorporated into the application (Nuruzzaman & Hussain, 2018).

Some machine learning techniques have been applied to chatbots to increase their operation and performance. Recurrent Neural Networks (RNN) was used by Muangkammuen, Intiruk, and Saikaew (2018) to develop a Frequently Asked Questions system. One of the reasons for choosing RNN was due to the input capacity retain over a long period. This same foundation was applied by Mao, Su, Yu and Luo (2019) with the purpose of creating a chatbot that gives the best response in a multi-turn context.

MAIN FOCUS OF THE CHAPTER

Pronunciation is usually the skill that causes most problems during second language learning. Diverse factors such as shyness, lack of practice, or bad feedback can affect the development of skills. Computer Assisted Language Learning systems are used to teach a second language without the need for a classroom or a teacher. These systems include lessons and exercises to improve language skills, such as grammar, vocabulary, even pronunciation. Computer-Assisted Pronunciation Training (CAPT) is a CALL sub-area which aim is to help to improve pronunciation. However, many of these systems use isolated words without context. This impedes students could follow a fluent conversation. Nevertheless, learners could hardly improve pronunciation by just listening to conversations and words. Then, it is necessary for a language application to evaluate them and provide meaningful feedback.

Correct feedback is vital to increase correct pronunciation. If it is not carried out correctly, learning will be affected and poorly constructed. For this reason, it is necessary to detect the pronunciation error made. To accomplish this task, an MDD algorithm is used. With its integration to a chatbot, it is possible to imitate a personal teacher's behavior who performs feedback on pronunciation errors. *Goodness of Pronunciation* (GOP) is one of the algorithms that use MDD. GOP calculates the probability that a phoneme corresponds to phoneme that that should have been pronounced (Kanters, Cucchiarini, & Strik, 2009).

SOLUTIONS AND RECOMMENDATIONS

The proposal of this research is to integrate a module for detecting mispronunciation in a chatbot, which could be an option to mitigate some problems that may be prevented by practicing enough. As mentioned above, the areas where chatbots can be implemented are very diverse. The results of Haristiani (2019) found advantages in using a chatbot for learning Japanese grammar.

A chatbot that processes audio to detect mispronunciation errors and, in turn, provides accurate feedback on them is a good option for practicing pronunciation. To accomplish this, a module for mispronunciation detection and diagnosis will be integrated into a chatbot architecture. One of the most used algorithms for that task is the GOP algorithm. Below, its functionality and implementation are described.

Goodness of Pronunciation

The GOP algorithm measures or scores each sentence phoneme. When calculating this measurement, it is assumed that orthographic transcription is known, as well as the HMM model is capable of determining observations sequence (Witt & Young, 2000). The above approach has been used in many studies in the recent last years since then. For example, Wang et al. 2019 developed a system to improve Chinese pupils' pronunciation, where the main technology used was a DNN-HMM acoustic model and GOP scoring. Another example is presented by Luo et al. 2019, where was implemented GOP algorithm for English speaking tests.

The GOP algorithm workflow is shown in **Figure 2**. Feature extraction is necessary to converts the speech waveform to MFCC coefficients, and these are used in two recognition steps. The first is the speech recognition phase, where the most likely known phoneme sequence from input audio is determined. This is performed by an acoustic model trained with MFCC features. The second is the forced alignment phase, which is similar to the above process, but it differs in a major aspect. The ASR system is provided with an exact audio orthographic transcription. Then, the system aligns the transcription with the audio speech, identifying which time segments in the speech data corresponds to a particular word in the transcription data. Forced alignment task is realized by a toolkit called TextGrid (Hendrik Buschmeier, 2013). The two above steps get phonemes in two different ways. The next step is calculating the absolute difference value between log probability for each phoneme (Pellegrini, Fontan, Mauclair, Farinas, & Robert, 2014). The result is the GOP score applied to each phoneme. Finally, by means of a threshold defined by a human expert, phonemes that were mispronounced are rejected (Witt and Young 2000). The scores given by the GOP algorithm depends on the generated acoustic model quality.

DNN-HMM has better performance over HMM models, therefore, better quality. This is because the DNN-HMM model has a significant improvement in the Word Error Rate (WER), which is a score to measure sentence recognition performance. It is calculated by the sum of substitutions (S), insertions (I), and deletions (D). If there are (N) words in the transcript, then WER is calculated as follows:

$$W = \frac{I + D + S}{N}$$

To test the GOP algorithm, a GMM-HMM model was generated by training a *LibriSpeech* corpus subset. The complete set contains 1,000 hours of English audio voice sampled at 16 kHz (Panayotov, Chen, Povey, & Khudanpur, 2015). Kaldi, an automatic speech recognition open-source toolkit, written in C++, was used to generate the model (Povey, Boulianne, Burget, Motlicek, & Schwarz, 2011). This toolkit is actively maintained and has been used in several ASR systems. When the model was generated, the GOP algorithm was used by Tu et al. (2018) to generate scores for each sentence phoneme.

Figure 2. GOP algorithm workflow
Source:(Witt & Young, 2000)

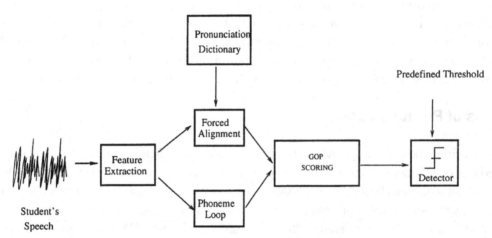

Also, in that work was implemented both the native language and non-native language acoustic models to extract features for automatic pronunciation evaluation.

Table 1 shows results obtained from the forced alignment that was generated from audio samples whose orthographic transcription is: "NORTHANGER ABBEY". As mentioned above, the forced alignment task is to find an audio segment where phonemes occur. The complete sentence has 1.95 duration seconds. The audio signal is segmented in intervals where a phoneme is found. Each interval has a minimum and maximum duration time that is phoneme duration in sentence audio signal. Table 2 shows the GOP score obtained for each phoneme after applying the algorithm. In this case, intervals with "SIL" and "B" have a negative score, which means they are mispronounced phonemes.

Table 1. Forced alignment of an audio sample

Interval	1	2	3	4	5	6	7	8	9	10	11	12	13
Min	0.00	0.56	0.68	0.76	0.81	0.91	1.05	1.12	1.19	1.30	1.48	1.53	1.77
Max	0.56	0.68	0.76	0.81	0.91	1.05	1.12	1.19	1.30	1.48	1.53	1.77	1.95
Phoneme	SIL	N	AO	R	TH	AE	NG	ER	SIL	AE	B	IY	SIL

A module for mispronunciation detection was developed. As part of the proposal, the intention is to integrate that module in a chatbot architecture in order to help second language learners to develop their

Table 2. GOP Score

Phoneme	SIL	N	AO	R	TH	AE	NG	ER	SIL	AE	B	IY	SIL
GOP Score	0	0	0	0	0	0	0	0	-5.3	0	-1.3	0	0

pronunciation skills. The chatbot emulates a conversation to practice the second language, increasing speaking ability, and offering feedback.

Figure 3. Proposal chatbot architecture

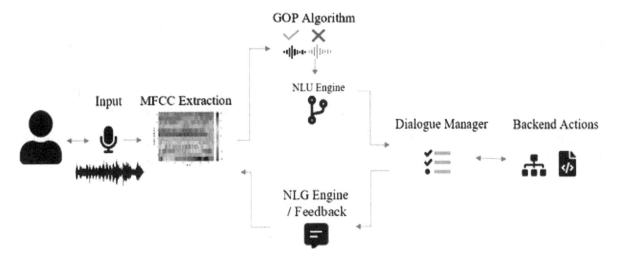

Figure 3 shows the proposal chatbot architecture. The user interacts with the system through an interface, giving a voice input signal. The speech audio signal is converted to MFCC coefficients to be used by the acoustic model and forced alignment system. The GOP algorithm process the text obtained and verify if there exists a pronunciation error or if the utterance has been well pronounced. Then, the NLU engine process that text and send it to the Dialogue Manager. That module decides what is the correct response to give back to the user. If there is not mispronunciation, an answer is given to follow the conversation; contrarily, mispronunciation feedback is given to the user. Finally, the NLG generates the appropriate response to the user.

DISCUSSION AND FUTURE WORK

Chatbot applications in education areas, specifically in second language learning, have been well received for second language learners. Developing pronunciation skills requires constant practice. Thus, a chatbot is an option to do it. There are different ways to mispronunciation detection and diagnosis that could be applied. The GOP algorithm was reviewed, and its simplicity was showed. However, the use of this algorithm limits the chatbot functionality because, in the forces alignment phase, it is necessary to give an orthographic transcription to ASR, meaning that the user is mandatory to practice pronunciation with defined sentences.

Another kind of ASR engine has been developed without the drawback (train each component separately) presented in DNN-HMM models. End-to-end Connectionist Temporal Classifier (CTC) ASR uses only raw speech to train the model using RNN (Ke Li, Li, Ye, Zhao, & Gong, 2019). A CTC-ASR model was studied by Niu et al. (2018) with the aim of using a pronunciation error detector. Thus, it is possible to replace the DNN-HMM ASR model and GOP algorithm for a CTC-ASR model to do mispronunciation detection and diagnosis in order to have a more fluent conversation with the chatbot.

REFERENCES

Abdul-Kader, S., & Woods, J. (2015). Survey on Chatbot Design Techniques in Speech Conversation Systems. *International Journal of Advanced Computer Science and Applications*, 6(7), 72–80. doi:10.14569/ijacsa.2015.060712

Banerjee, A., Dubey, A., Menon, A., Nanda, S., & Chand Nandi, G. (2018). *Speaker Recognition using Deep Belief Networks*. Retrieved from https://arxiv.org/ftp/arxiv/papers/1805/1805.08865.pdf

Buschmeier, H., & Wlodarczak, M. (2013). TextGridTools: A TextGrid Processing and Analysis Toolkit for Python. In Tagungsband Der 24. Konferenz Zur Elektronischen Sprachsignalverarbeitung (ESSV 2013) (pp.152–157). Academic Press.

Chen, N. F., & Li, H. (2017). Computer-assisted pronunciation training: From pronunciation scoring towards spoken language learning. In *2016 Asia-Pacific Signal and Information Processing Association Annual Summit and Conference, APSIPA 2016* (pp. 1–7). doi:10.1109/APSIPA.2016.7820782

Das, R., & Sharma, U. (2016). Extracting acoustic feature vectors of South Kamrupi dialect through MFCC. In *2016 3rd International Conference on Computing for Sustainable Global Development, IN-DIACom 2016* (pp.2808–2811). Academic Press.

Deshpande, A., Shahane, A., Gadre, D., Deshpande, M., & Joshi, P. M. (2017). A Survey of Various Chatbot Implementation Techniques. *International Journal of Computer Engineering and Applications*, *11*, 7. Retrieved from www.ijcea.com

Fahad, S. K. A., & Yahya, A. E. (2018). Inflectional Review of Deep Learning on Natural Language Processing. In *2018 International Conference on Smart Computing and Electronic Enterprise, ICSCEE 2018*, (pp. 1–4). 10.1109/ICSCEE.2018.8538416

Gales, M., & Young, S. (2007). The application of hidden Markov Models in speech recognition. *Foundations and Trends in Signal Processing*, *1*(3), 195–304. doi:10.1561/2000000004

Galitsky, B. (2019). Chatbot Components and Architectures. In Developing Enterprise Chatbots (pp. 13–47). doi:10.1007/978-3-030-04299-8_2

Garcia Brustenga, G., Fuertes Alpiste, M., & Molas Castells, N. (2018). *Briefing paper: chatbots in education*. doi:10.7238/elc.chatbots.2018

González, J. (2015). Trends and Directions in Computer-Assisted Pronunciation Training. In Investigating English Pronunciation (pp. 314–342). doi:10.1057/9781137509043

Haristiani, N. (2019). Artificial Intelligence (AI) Chatbot as Language Learning Medium: An inquiry. *Journal of Physics: Conference Series*, *1387*(1), 012020. Advance online publication. doi:10.1088/1742-6596/1387/1/012020

Heil, C. R., Wu, J. S., Lee, J. J., & Schmidt, T. (2016). A review of mobile language learning applications: Trends, challenges and opportunities. *The EUROCALL Review*, *24*(2), 32. Advance online publication. doi:10.4995/eurocall.2016.6402

Jettakul, A., Thamjarat, C., Liaowongphuthorn, K., Udomcharoenchaikit, C., Vateekul, P., & Boonkwan, P. (2018). A Comparative Study on Various Deep Learning Techniques for Thai NLP Lexical and Syntactic Tasks on Noisy Data. In *2018 15th International Joint Conference on Computer Science and Software Engineering* (pp.1–6). 10.1109/JCSSE.2018.8457368

Juang, B. H., & Rabiner, L. R. (2004). Automatic Speech Recognition – A Brief History of the Technology Development. Elsevier Encyclopedia of Language and Linguistics, 50(2), 637–655.

Kamath, U., Liu, J., & Whitaker, J. (2019). *Deep Learning for NLP and Speech Recognition*. doi:10.1007/978-3-030-14596-5

Kanters, S., Cucchiarini, C., & Strik, H. (2009). The goodness of pronunciation algorithm: a detailed performance study. *Speech & Language Technology in Education -SLaTE*, (2), 2–5. Retrieved from http://www.eee.bham.ac.uk/SLaTE2009/papers%5CSLaTE2009-33.pdf

Khan, W., Daud, A., Nasir, J. A., & Amjad, T. (2016). A survey on the state-of-the-art machine learning models in the context of NLP. *Kuwait Journal of Science*, *43*(4), 95–113.

Khurana, D., Koli, A., Khatter, K., & Singh, S. (2017). *Natural Language Processing: State of The Art, Current Trends and Challenges*. Retrieved from https://arxiv.org/abs/1708.05148

Leung, W. K., Liu, X., & Meng, H. (2019). CNN-RNN-CTC Based End-to-end Mispronunciation Detection and Diagnosis. In *ICASSP 2019-IEEE International Conference on Acoustics, Speech and Signal Processing* (pp. 8132–8136). 10.1109/ICASSP.2019.8682654

Li, K., Li, J., Ye, G., Zhao, R., & Gong, Y. (2019). Towards Code-switching ASR for End-to-end CTC Models.In *ICASSP 2019-IEEE International Conference on Acoustics, Speech and Signal Processing* (pp.6076–6080). 10.1109/ICASSP.2019.8683223

Li, K., Qian, X., & Meng, H. (2017). Mispronunciation Detection and Diagnosis in L2 English Speech Using Multidistribution Deep Neural Networks. *IEEE/ACM Transactions on Audio, Speech, and Language Processing*, *25*(1), 193–207. doi:10.1109/TASLP.2016.2621675

Li, Y., & Yang, T. (2017). Word Embedding for Understanding Natural Language : A Survey. In S. Srinivasan (Ed.), *Guide to Big Data Applications* (pp. 83–104)., doi:10.1007/978-3-319-53817-4

Liddy, E. D. (2001). Natural Language Processing. In *Encyclopedia of Library and Information Science* (2nd ed., pp. 1–15). Marcel Decker, Inc.

Luo, D., Xia, L., Zhang, C., & Wang, L. (2019). Automatic Pronunciation Evaluation in High-states English Speaking Tests Based on Deep Neural Network Models. In *2019 2nd International Conference on Artificial Intelligence and Big Data, ICAIBD* (pp.124–128). 10.1109/ICAIBD.2019.8836976

Mao, G., Su, J., Yu, S., & Luo, D. (2019). Multi-Turn Response Selection for Chatbots With Hierarchical Aggregation Network of Multi-Representation. *IEEE Access: Practical Innovations, Open Solutions*, *7*, 111736–111745. doi:10.1109/ACCESS.2019.2934149

Mikolov, T., Chen, K., Corrado, G., & Dean, J. (2013). Efficient estimation of word representations in vector space. In *1st International Conference on Learning Representations, ICLR 2013 - Workshop Track Proceedings* (pp.1–12). Academic Press.

Muangkammuen, P., Intiruk, N., & Saikaew, K. R. (2018). Automated Thai-FAQ chatbot using RNN-LSTM. In *2018 22nd International Computer Science and Engineering Conference* (pp. 1–4). 10.1109/ICSEC.2018.8712781

Muhammad, H. Z., Nasrun, M., Setianingsih, C., & Murti, M. A. (2018). Speech recognition for English to Indonesian translator using hidden Markov model. In *2018 International Conference on Signals and Systems, ICSigSys* (pp.255–260). 10.1109/ICSIGSYS.2018.8372768

Nadkarni, P. M., Ohno-Machado, L., & Chapman, W. W. (2011). Natural language processing: An introduction. *Journal of the American Medical Informatics Association, 18*(5), 544–551. doi:10.1136/amiajnl-2011-000464 PMID:21846786

Niu, C., Zhang, J., Yang, X., & Xie, Y. (2018). A study on landmark detection based on CTC and its application to pronunciation error detection. In *2017 Asia-Pacific Signal and Information Processing Association Annual Summit and Conference (APSIPA ASC)* (pp. 636–640). doi:10.1109/APSIPA.2017.8282103

Nuruzzaman, M., & Hussain, O. K. (2018). A Survey on Chatbot Implementation in Customer Service Industry through Deep Neural Networks. In *2018 IEEE 15th International Conference on e-Business Engineering (ICEBE)* (pp. 54–61). 10.1109/ICEBE.2018.00019

Panayotov, V., Chen, G., Povey, D., & Khudanpur, S. (2015). Librispeech: An ASR corpus based on public domain audio books. In *2015 IEEE International Conference on Acoustics, Speech and Signal Processing (ICASSP)* (pp. 5206–5210). 10.1109/ICASSP.2015.7178964

Pellegrini, T., Fontan, L., Mauclair, J., Farinas, J., & Robert, M. (2014). The goodness of pronunciation algorithm applied to disordered speech. In *Proceedings of the Annual Conference of the International Speech Communication Association, INTERSPEECH* (pp.1463–1467).

Povey, D., Ghoshal, A., Boulianne, G., Burget, L., Glembek, O., Goel, N., …Vesely, K. (2011). The Kaldi Speech Recognition. *IEEE 2011 Workshop on Automatic Speech Recognition and Understanding.*

Qian, X., Meng, H., & Soong, F. (2012). The use of DBN-HMMs for mispronunciation detection and diagnosis in L2 english to support computer-aided pronunciation training. In *13th Annual Conference of the International Speech Communication Association 2012 INTERSPEECH,* (Vol. 1, pp.774–777).

Roos, S. (2018). *Chatbots in education: A passing trend or a valuable pedagogical tool?* Retrieved from http://www.diva-portal.org/smash/record.jsf?pid=diva2%3A1223692&dswid=879

Shawar, B. A. (2017). Integrating CALL Systems with Chatbots as Conversational Partners. *Computación y Sistemas, 21*(4), 615–626. doi:10.13053/CyS-21-4-2868

Su, P.-H., Wu, C.-H., & Lee, L.-S. (2015). A recursive dialogue game for personalized computer-aided pronunciation training. *IEEE/ACM Transactions on Audio, Speech, and Language Processing, 23*(1), 127–141. doi:10.1109/TASLP.2014.2375572

Thomas, N. T. (2016). An e-business chatbot using AIML and LSA. In *2016 International Conference on Advances in Computing, Communications and Informatics (ICACCI)* (pp.2740–2742). 10.1109/ICACCI.2016.7732476

Tu, M., Grabek, A., Liss, J., & Berisha, V. (2018). Investigating the role of L1 in automatic pronunciation evaluation of L2 speech. In *Proceedings of the Annual Conference of the International Speech Communication Association, INTERSPEECH* (pp.1636–1640). 10.21437/Interspeech.2018-1350

Umezawa, K. (2018). *Word2Vec: Obtain word embeddings.* Retrieved from https://medium.com/@keisukeumezawa/word2vec-obtain-word-embeddings-885716a56270

Wang, H., Xu, J., Ge, H., & Wang, Y. (2019). Design and implementation of an english pronunciation scoring system for pupils based on DNN-HMM. In *2019 10th International Conference on Information Technology in Medicine and Education (ITME)* (pp. 348–352). 10.1109/ITME.2019.00085

Witt, S. M., & Young, S. J. (2000). Phone-level pronunciation scoring and assessment for interactive language learning. *Speech Communication, 30*(2), 95–108. doi:10.1016/S0167-6393(99)00044-8

Young, T., Hazarika, D., Poria, S., & Cambria, E. (2018). Recent trends in deep learning based natural language processing. *IEEE Computational Intelligence Magazine, 13*(3), 55–75. doi:10.1109/MCI.2018.2840738

Zemčík, T. (2018). A Brief History of Chatbots. *Perception, Control. Cognition.* Advance online publication. doi:10.12783/dtcse/aicae2019/31439

Zumstein, D., & Hundertmark, S. (2018). Chatbots : an interactive technology for personalized communication and transaction. *International Journal on WWW/Internet, 15*(1), 96–109.

Chapter 3
Story Summarization Using a Question–Answering Approach

Sanah Nashir Sayyed
Dr. Babasaheb Ambedkar Marathwada University, India

Namrata Mahender C.
Dr. Babasaheb Ambedkar Marathwada University, India

ABSTRACT

Summarization is the process of selecting representative data to produce a reduced version of the given data with a minimal loss of information; so, it generally works on text, images, videos, and speech data. The chapter deals with not only concepts of text summarization (types, stages, issues, and criteria) but also with applications. The two main categories of approaches generally used in text summaries (i.e., abstractive and extractive) are discussed. Abstractive techniques use linguistic methods to interpret the text; they produce understandable and semantically equivalent sentences with a shorter length. Extractive techniques mostly rely on statistical methods for extracting essential sentences from the given text. In addition, the authors explore the SACAS model to exemplify the process of summarization. The SACAS system analyzed 50 stories, and its evaluation is presented in terms of a new measurement based on question-answering MOS, which is also introduced in this chapter.

1. INTRODUCTION

Visualizing any text summarizer system which briefs about the whole document in such a way that clears every essential requirement needed to understand the text, that too in a short time and shorter in size as compared with the original text is possible as many such systems are available, but their performance is not up to the expectation. In a wide variety of domains, summarization is needed; its applications are also very crucial, like medical history summarization, research document summarization in law case history summarization, official document summarization, search information summarization, and many more interesting applications can be made. So let's first understand the concept of summarization, its categories, and components.

DOI: 10.4018/978-1-7998-4730-4.ch003

Copyright © 2021, IGI Global. Copying or distributing in print or electronic forms without written permission of IGI Global is prohibited.

Summarization is the procedure of selecting essential data, which includes important information of the whole set and gives the result in the form of a summary. A broad categorization of summarization is the following:

- **Text summarization:** Text summarization is a procedure of production of summaries by selecting important sentences without changing the meaning of the original document (Bhatia & Jaiswal, 2016).
- **Image summarization:** In image summarization, images are summarized to get the accurate impression of the original scene, e.g., image summarization are picture collages, 3D collages, etc. (Chen, Cafarella, & Adar, 2011).
- **Video summarization:** The video summarization is the production of a short video by selecting the visual data from the main video. Applications of video summarizations are video browsing, action recognition, or the creation of a visual diary (Lee, Ghosh, & Grauman, 2012).
- **Speech summarization:** Speech summarization is the procedure of extracting vital sentences from spoken document considering the linguist aspect of the spoken language (McKeown, Hirschberg, Galley, & Maskey, 2005).

The focus of this chapter is on the text summarization; here, an extractive technique based on the SACAS model is used for story summarization, we discuss and highlight the major criteria and challenges encountered. A new Question-based MOS measuring technique is also specified.

2. Text Summarization, Types and Components

Text summarization is the art of presenting the gist of the given text by selecting important aspects or concepts from the text without changing its form, context, and meaning, in a manner that the derived text is clearly readable and understandable. The work on automated summarization actually started from 1950 still today; it's a dream of many researchers. There are a lot of elementary tasks, which makes automated text summarization an unresolved challenge. Some important points are listed here: (Okumura, Fukushima, & Nanba, 2001)

i. The main challenge is to decide which information is relevant.
ii. The system needs to understand the context of the text prior to summarizing
iii. Sentence revision that emphasizes elimination, combination, or substitution.
iv. Sentence fusion is to consider more than one sentence with some overlapping information too.
v. Generation of text (rather than just extracting to brief the essential information).
vi. Even summarization depends on the requirement of the user; e.g., A company's annual report does not seem to provide the same information to each user or category of employees as the marketing/ sales requirement is different from the production team, although there are some common requirements among them. The main highlight is each requirement is totally different, even if the content is the same and the aims are also same (the company should have more sales, for more profit); thus the challenge is the same pieces of text should be briefed according to the needs of each user.
vii. Evaluation metrics should be developed for judging summaries.
viii. No standard benchmark to assess the performance or accuracy of summarization.

As text summarization comes under the view of NLP, with the above challenges, it also has to face NLP related issues like anaphora resolution, syntactic and semantic analysis, discourse analysis for proper interpretation, pragmatic analysis for better understanding, etc. Text summarization challenges also depend on the source, whether it is a single document or multiple, or only one or more languages are used. Generally, based on languages used in the text, sources of getting text and approaches applied, the text summarization process is classified into various categories. These are discussed briefly in Section 2.1.

2.1 Types of Text Summarization

Text Summarization can be classified based on various aspects or views, like depending on the source: single or multi-document, depending on the language of the text: monolingual/bilingual/multilingual and depending on the approaches, i.e., abstraction or extraction (Basiron, Kumar, Goh, Ngo, & Suppiah, 2016).

A) **Depending on the source**
   i. **Single document:** Only a single document is considered for the generation of summary
   ii. **Multi-document:** Several documents are considered for the generation of summary.
B) **Depending on the language of source text**
   i. **Monolingual:** The contents of the document are written only in the same language; for example, documents in the English language.
   ii. **Bilingual:** The materials are written in two different languages. It is difficult because it requires language translation and supportive pragmatic and discourse analysis of the given text for better performance of summarization.
   iii. **Multilingual:** The content of the document is in three or more languages; such systems are too complex.
C) **Depending on the approaches**
   i. **Extractive summarization:** It gives emphasis on extracting important sentences in the document.
   ii. **Abstractive summarization:** It gives attention to the generation of sentences, which express the perspective of the main document in brief.

A detailed explanation of these approaches is given in Section 3.

2.2 Important Component of Text Summarization System

There are three main steps used for summarizing documents. Eduard Hary and Chin-Yewlin in 1999 gave three stages

i. Topic identification
ii. Interpretation
iii. Summary generation
   "Summarization =Topic identification + Interpretation +Generation."

In this chapter, these three basic stages are followed (topic identification, interpretation, and summary generation).

2.2.1 Topic Identification

The main aim of this phase is to determine the central theme of the text document.
The features used are generally

i.   Positional criteria: the location in the text holds significant content such as title, heading, first paragraph, etc.
ii. Cue phrases indicator: most of the sentences contain significant words, and such words have great associations with heading or subtitles.
iii. Word and phrase frequency: high-frequency words contained by sentences are considered for summary generation
iv. Query and title overlap: any sentence having correspondence with the title or responses to queries are extracted.

2.2.2 Interpretation

In this step, the required information is combined to form the general content. There is always a need to include new words for making a sentence, which does not have a similarity with the main text. However, these words link the abstractive aspect of the main text.

2.2.2.1 General Features Considered Under Interpretation

i) **Concept generalization**
e.g., "Ram ate bananas, grapes, and mangoes", can be generalized as "Ram ate fruits".

ii)   **Script identification**

This real feature event is identified with the term of topic signature. Here, the actual event happened is identified; it is also termed as a topic signature, e.g., "He downloaded the app, checked the menus, ordered, and loved the sandwich". In this simple script, the description will be "He ordered sandwich online and like it".

2.2.3 Summary Generation

The main aim of this is to generate the final output in the form of a summary.

3. APPROACHES OF TEXT SUMMARIZATION

3.1 Extractive Text Summarization

An extractive text summarization technique gives emphasis on the selection of important sentences and paragraphs from the document and combines them for the generation of a shorter summary. The important sentences are based on statistical and linguistic features. This technique avoids the redundancy of data, and it is easier than the abstractive text summarization techniques (Basiron et al., 2016). The commonly used features in extractive methods are

a) **Title/headline word:** Sentences that contain the word in the heading or title are considered an important sentence.
b) **Sentence position:** If the sentence comes first or last in the paragraph are considered as a significant sentence.
c) **Term weight:** A word that occurs many times in the document is treated as a significant sentence, which is added in the summary.
d) **Sentence length:** Short length sentence contains less information, while the longer sentences are less significant to include in the summary.
e) **Proper noun feature**: Sentences containing proper nouns such as name, location, organization, etc. these sentences get more priority to be part of the summary.
f) **Cue phrase feature:** Cue phrase feature is used to indicate the flow of the document structure, and it is vital while selecting the sentence. Cue phrases are such as "information", "because", "summary", "develop", etc., are mostly added in the summary.
g) **Biased word feature:** The sentences that consist of biased words are considered as vital. The biased words may belong to specific domains, they are important as they represent the theme of the document. e.g., "illegal immigrants" and "undocumented immigrants", etc.
h) **Upper case word feature:** The sentences that contain upper case words are considered important for making a final summary, e.g., UNICEF (Moratanch, & Chitrakala, 2017)

The extractive methods include the following main steps

Step 1: the first step is the pre-processing step, which includes sentence tokenization, word tokenization, POS tagging, stop word removal, computation of frequently occurring words, stemming, etc.
Step 2: In this step, a score is assigned to a particular word or sentence; the highest score is assigned to the most important word, and in sentence scoring, the score of the sentence depends upon the feature such as the position of a sentence in the document and similarity of the sentence to the title. A score-based graph represents the link or relationship between the sentences.

Most of the time, general techniques are used for calculating the score of words, such as word frequency, lexical similarity, proper noun, and upper case word. Common features are used for calculating scores of sentences such as length of sentence and similarity of the sentence to the title and cue phrases, for example, "significantly", "investigation", "in conclusion", etc. and the graph considers scoring methods such as aggregate similarity, text rank, etc.

Step 3: In this step, those sentences having the highest score are selected and sorted them with a specific order, and then the final summary is produced if it is single-document summarization. In the case of multi-document summarization, there is a long procedure; here, each document produces a summary and a clustering technique is used to group the significant sentences from each summary of the document to generate the final summary (Asa, Akter, Uddin, Hossain, Roy, & Afjal, 2017).

There are a few important extraction methods which are discussed below:

3.1.1 Latent Semantic Analysis (LSA)

The SVD is an influential mathematical tool, mainly used to find principal orthogonal dimensions of multidimensional data. It is mostly used in the Latent semantic analysis, the motive behind the name LSA is because SVD is used in the document (Zamanifar, Minaei-Bidgoli,& Sharifi, 2008;Wang, M., Wang, X., & Xu, 2005).

The major advantages of the LSA method are:

1)   It automatically captures the conceptual relationships in the human brain
2)   LSA algorithm captures the words, patterns, and trends of all documents.

And the major disadvantages of the LSA method are:

1)   As it is a distributional model, it is dense and difficult to index depending upon the dimension.
2)   It is a linear model, so it does not provide a good solution for nonlinear dependencies.
3)   The model debug is possible by finding the same words in latent space; however, it is too difficult to interpret it.

3.1.2 Concept Obtained Approach

This approach mainly used Hownet to get the concepts of words and use that concept like features, the alternative of a word, by using the conceptual vector space model. This method produces rough summarization, and then, for eliminating its redundancy, finds the degree of semantic similarity of sentences. The final summary of sentences is generated after eliminating redundancy (Suanmali, Binwahlan, & Salim, 2009).

3.1.3 Fuzzy Logic-Based Approach

In this approach, the features of the text are considered as input to the fuzzy system. Some common features are the length of the sentence, the presence of keywords, etc. Rules of the knowledge are required for generating a summary. The values are assigned to the sentences from zero to higher numbers depending upon the features of text and the rules in the knowledge base. The final summary is obtained from the important sentence, which depends upon the value of sentences. The membership functions consist of insignificantly low values, very low, medium, significant values, high, and very high. IF-THEN rules are mainly used for extracting important sentences depending upon the features (Das & Martins, 2007).

3.1.4 Term Frequency-Inverse Document Frequency Method (TF-IDF)

It is a numerical statistic method that returns the significant words in a document; if a word is found a number of times, then the value of TF-IDF also increases. This method is mainly applicable to the weighted term frequency and inverse term frequency. Similarly, the number of sentences is 'sentence frequency'. The sentences with the highest score are considered in making the summary; these sentences should include a definite word to be considered as significant sentences, mostly the important words are the nouns; here, DF means the number of times a word appears in the document (Babar & Patil, 2015).

3.1.5 Clustering-Based Method

In a cluster-based approach, all similar documents are clusterized, and then each document cluster contains sentences that are clustered into sentence clusters. The highest score sentence cluster is considered for the generation of summary (Deshpande & Lobo, 2013).

3.2 Abstractive Text Summarization

According to Atif Khan et al. (2014), abstractive text summarization requires a deeper knowledge of the text and their interpretation and depends on linguistic methods. It produces new words that were not in the main text and avoids redundant words; summaries produced by the abstractive techniques are more relevant and short. Abstractive techniques are more complicated but more powerful than extractive techniques because of their capabilities such as paraphrasing, and knowledge of the text. The summary generation of a moral story requires a full understanding of the whole story and, depending upon interpretation, expresses it in the form of new phrases and in a shorter form.

The commonly used features in abstractive methods are:

a. **Position features:** The features that calculate the distance among tokens and their relative position.
b. **Lexical features:** The lexical features include lemma, stem word, POS tag.
c. **Syntactic features:** The features representing the syntactic path among actions, identifying the actions that syntactically control other actions.
d. **Modiðer features:** The features that represent the modals, auxiliary verbs, including negation (Li et al., 2016).

The abstractive methods include the following main steps:

1) **Input document:** In this step, the input document is considered in the form of text.
2) **Pre-processing:** The main purpose of pre-processing is to filter the unwanted data (like punctuation marks, preposition, etc.) and generate the rich semantic graph of sentences. In this step, the following tasks are performed.
   2.1 POS tagging: It is referred to as assigning the tags to the words.
   2.2 Stop word removal: This step removes the stop words. Stop words are those words that are not important, e.g., "a", "an", "in", etc.
   2.3 Stemming: In this step, a stemming algorithm is used to find the word to their root. For e.g., running- run.
3) **Rich Semantic Sub Graph Generation:** after pre-processing, each sentence consists of an order of words, and each word is signified as a triple sequence, words=[S, TG, D] where S denotes the stem word, TG denotes the tags of words, and D denotes the typed dependency relation.
4) **Rich Semantic Graph Generation:** This step produces a final rich semantic graph from the highly ranked rich semantic subgraphs of the sentences in the document.
5) **Reduction Phase of Rich Semantic Graph (RSG):** In this step, heuristic rules are used; a heuristic rule of sentences consists of three nodes that are a subject-noun node, a main-verb node, and an object-noun node. These rules reduce the final rich semantic graph by adding, removing, or combining graph nodes.

6) **Generation of the summary:** This step produces the abstractive summary from the reduced rich semantic graph, this step understands the semantic representation in the form of RSG and produces the summary. To accomplish this task, the step uses the domain ontology and wordnet. Domain ontology includes the information required in a similar domain of semantic graph to produce the ultimate texts. Wordnet is used for producing text, depending on the synonym of the word (Yeasmin, Tumpa, Nitu & Palash, 2017).

Abstractive summarization techniques are broadly classified into two categories: Structure-based approach and Semantic-based approach, and both are briefly discussed below:

3.2.1 Structure-Based Approach

Genest and Lapalme (2011) used a structure-based approach to encode significant sentences of the text by using cognitive methods such as a rule-based method, template-based method, and ontology-based method.

3.2.1.1 Template-Based Method

The template-based method given by Harabagiu and Lacatusu (2002) uses a template to represent the topic that takes out data from one or more documents, including slots and fillers.

3.2.1.2 Ontology-Based Method

Many researchers use an ontology-based method to enhance the processes of NLP (Lee, Jian & Huang, 2005; Porras, Florencia-Juárez, Rivera, & García, 2018). The model by Lee et al. (2005) represents the online documents that are domain-related, which are considered the same type of data or event, because each domain may have their own information structure, it can be better resolve with fuzzy ontology because it depicts the domain knowledge for resolving uncertainty reasoning problems.

3.2.1.3 Tree-Based Method

Barzilay, McKeown and Elhadad (1999) apply dependency trees for representing the document text. Diverse content-selection algorithms are used for producing the summary. A theme-selection algorithm is used to identify the essential theme of the two or more documents. Sentences are rearranged by clustering algorithms, and this approach mainly uses the language-generator algorithms for producing summaries.

3.2.1.4 Rule-Based Method

The rule-based method by Genest and Lapalme (2012) represents documents in the form of classes and aspects. For producing sentences, this method uses a rule-based information extraction module, patterns, and content selection patterns. Nouns and verbs are recognized to generate extraction rules. Several candidate rules are passed to the summary generation module.

3.2.2 Semantic-Based Approach

The approach by Saggion and Lapalme (2002) pays attention to noun and verb phrases by using linguistic data; the approach consists of different methods, which are discussed below.

3.2.2.1 Multimodal Semantic Model

Greenbacker (2011) applied the multimodal semantic model to capture concepts and their relationships to represent multi-document content, depending upon the significant measures in them. The concepts are scored, selective concepts are conveyed as sentences for the generation of summary. The result of this approach is brilliant because it consists of the textual and graphical content of the whole document. The advantage of this framework is that it produces an abstractive summary, whose coverage is excellent because it includes salient text and graphical content from the entire document. Manual evaluation is the main disadvantage of this approach.

3.2.2.2 Information Item Based Method

In the study of Genest and Lapalme (2011), main highlights are given to produce the summary from an abstract illustration of source document instead of the sentence of the document source. The abstract representation is an information item, which is the smallest number of elements of logical information in a text. The advantage of this method is to generate little, logical, and minimum redundant summaries. The disadvantage of this approach is to discard many information items because of the complexity of generating significant and grammatically correct sentences, and because of inaccurate parses, the linguistic quality of summary is poor.

3.2.2.3 Semantic Graph-Based Method

The method of Moawad and Aref (2012) creates a semantic graph called Rich Semantic Graph from the original document; it reduces the produced semantic graph and produces the final abstractive summary from the reduced graph. The main advantage of this system is to produce logical and less irrelevant summaries. This method is applicable only to single abstractive document summarization. To address the challenges of NLP, we develop a summarization system applied to a case study, which is discussed in detail in the next section.

4. A CASE STUDY ON SUMMARIZATION

We are clear with the idea that summarization is nothing but providing a briefing of a given text. A question arises on what parameters should the briefing to be done. There are a few important criteria followed while writing a manual summary, i.e., they can be taken as base or parameters while designing the automated summarizer.

The criteria are:

1. A summary should contain significant information.
2. A summary should remove redundant information.

3.   A summary should be coherent and maintain the order and readability.
4.   If the summary is answering a query, then its sentences should provide relevant information about the query.

The case study which is discussed in this chapter is "Question-answering based on story summarization", that means the domain of text is stories. The first thing comes up is "why story summarization?". Stories are important because each story contains some useful instruction or information. From ancient time stories have been used by many great leaders or philosophers as a tool to help their followers or disciples to overcome their problems. Stories play an important role in our life, which amaze us, inspire us, and make us feel puzzled. From childhood to now, we are learning so many things through stories. In school, teachers explain many concepts through stories, helping children to enhance ideas. Our elders tell us stories to develop moral principles in us. Stories are also majorly classified into seven categories by the writer Christopher; those are overcoming the monster, rags to riches, the quest, voyage and return, comedy, tragedy, and rebirth (Booker, 2004). To start with the process for text summarization, the first thing needed is to know the domain of the text, its source, i.e., single or multiple documents, the language of the text (which helps the designers of the system to select the approach, suitable for summarizing). To explain the overall requirement of text summarization, the "Story Anaphoric Conceptual Association Summarization" (SACAS) model is explored in detail. It is a Question-answering based on a summarization system of stories, which are the input to the system (Sayyed, Aurangabad & Mahender, 2020).

Figure 1. The workflow diagram of the SACAS model (Sayyed, Aurangabad & Mahender, 2020)

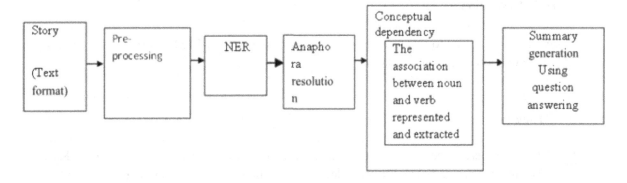

Step 1: The first stage in the model is to provide stories for processing

Fifty stories are chosen as input; its description log is generated, and the content of the story is used further for summarization. **Figure 2** shows the original story inputted sample of one story to the system, and Table 1 shows the overall description of the sample story. Form the fifty stories analyzed in the description, and the log output states that the minimum length of the story is six, and the maximum length of the story is 12.

Step 2: Once the log is created, the next step is to pre-process the given text

Figure 2. The input text is an original story

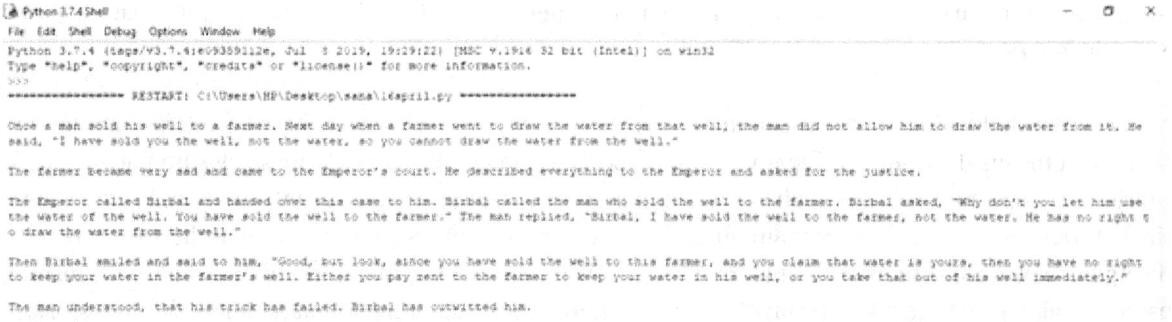

```
Python 3.7.4 Shell
File  Edit  Shell  Debug  Options  Window  Help
Python 3.7.4 (tags/v3.7.4:e09359112e, Jul  8 2019, 19:29:22) [MSC v.1916 32 bit (Intel)] on win32
Type "help", "copyright", "credits" or "license()" for more information.
>>>
=============== RESTART: C:\Users\HP\Desktop\sana\16april.py ===============

Once a man sold his well to a farmer. Next day when a farmer went to draw the water from that well, the man did not allow him to draw the water from it. He
said, "I have sold you the well, not the water, so you cannot draw the water from the well."

The farmer became very sad and came to the Emperor's court. He described everything to the Emperor and asked for the justice.

The Emperor called Birbal and handed over this case to him. Birbal called the man who sold the well to the farmer. Birbal asked, "Why don't you let him use
the water of the well. You have sold the well to the farmer." The man replied, "Birbal, I have sold the well to the farmer, not the water. He has no right t
o draw the water from the well."

Then Birbal smiled and said to him, "Good, but look, since you have sold the well to this farmer, and you claim that water is yours, then you have no right
to keep your water in the farmer's well. Either you pay rent to the farmer to keep your water in his well, or you take that out of his well immediately."

The man understood, that his trick has failed. Birbal has outwitted him.
```

Here we have removed stop words, "Stop words" are the most common words in a language like "the", "a", "on", "is", "all". These words do not add important meaning and are usually removed from the texts. In the SACAS model, the following steps are applied for pre-processing.

a)   **Sentence Tokenization**

   Sentence tokenizer is applied to split the story into sentences, and each sentence is arranged into a row on a new line. **Figure 3** shows the sentence-level tokenization of the sample story.

b)   **Word Tokenization**

   Word tokenizer is used to tokenize sentences of story into words. **Figure 4** shows the word-level tokenization of the sample story.

c)   **POS Tagging**

   POS Tagging is performed to assign a tag to each word in the row-wise sentences (Jahangiri, Kahani, Ahamdi & Sazvar, 2011). **Figure 5** depicts the sample story with POS tagging.

Step 3: Performing NER and Anaphora resolution

Table 1. Overall description of the sample story

Story Name	Actual length of Story	Minimum length sentence the in story	Max. length of sentence in story
Farmers Well & Witty Birbal	11	4	39

Story accessed from https://www.moralstories.org/farmers-well-witty-birbal/

Figure 3. Sentence tokenization of sample story

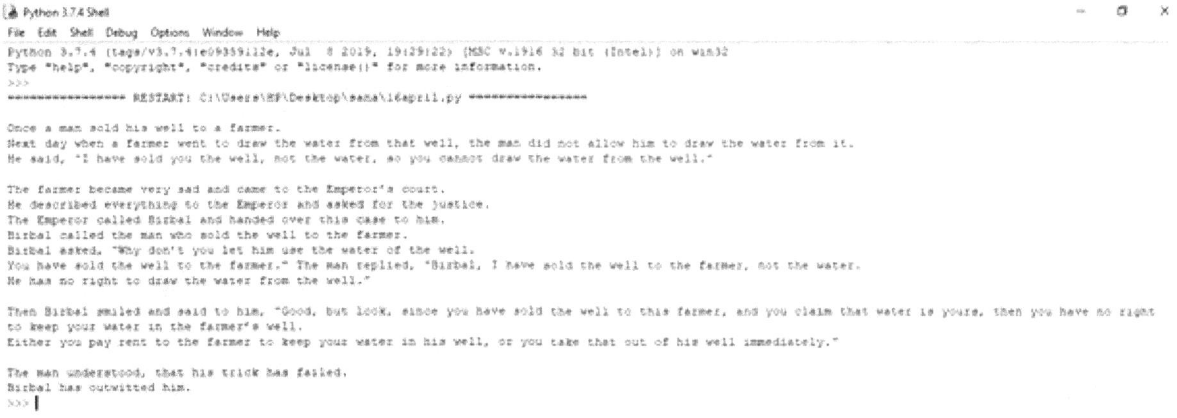

a)   **Named Entity Recognition**

To the pre-processed data, NER and anaphora resolution are performed. Let's understand first what is NER and anaphora resolution, and why they are applied. NER has a wide range of applications in the field of NLP. NER, —a.k.a entity identification, entity chunking, and entity extraction— is a sub-task of information extraction that seeks to locate and classify named entities in text into pre-defined categories such as the names of persons, organizations, locations, expressions of time, quantities, monetary values, percentages, etc.

The tagged data was temporarily tokenized, and the Stanford NER (Kamath & Wagh, 2017) was deployed to get the names, date, location, or place. The hurdle in stories uses a common noun, like a farmer man as an individual; thus, farmer NN and man NN tags have to be redefined as a proper noun. For this, at present work, we intended the rules for nouns, which treats common nouns as a proper noun; e.g., farmer NN PERSON, man NN PERSON, Birbal NNP PERSON, court NN LOCATION, etc.

Figure 4. Word tokenization of the sample story

Figure 5. POS tagging of the sample story

```
=============== RESTART: C:\Users\HP\Desktop\sana\14april.py ===============
[('Once', 'RB'), ('a', 'DT'), ('man', 'NN'), ('sold', 'VBD'), ('his', 'PRP$'), ('well', 'NN'), ('to', 'TO'), ('a', 'DT'), ('farmer', 'NN'), ('.', '.')]
[('Next', 'JJ'), ('day', 'NN'), ('when', 'WRB'), ('a', 'DT'), ('farmer', 'NN'), ('went', 'VBD'), ('to', 'TO'), ('draw', 'VB'), ('the', 'DT'), ('water', 'NN'), ('from', 'IN'), ('that', 'DT'), ('well', 'NN'), (',', ','), ('the', 'DT'), ('man', 'NN'), ('did', 'VBD'), ('not', 'RB'), ('allow', 'VB'), ('him', 'PRP'), ('to', 'TO'), ('draw', 'VB'), ('the', 'DT'), ('water', 'NN'), ('from', 'IN'), ('it', 'PRP'), ('.', '.')]
[('He', 'PRP'), ('said', 'VBD'), (',', ','), ("'", "''"), ('I', 'PRP'), ('have', 'VBP'), ('sold', 'VBN'), ('you', 'PRP'), ('the', 'DT'), ('well', 'RB'), (',', ','), ('not', 'RB'), ('the', 'DT'), ('water', 'NN'), (',', ','), ('so', 'IN'), ('you', 'PRP'), ('can', 'MD'), ('not', 'RB'), ('draw', 'VB'), ('the', 'DT'), ('water', 'NN'), ('from', 'IN'), ('the', 'DT'), ('well', '.'), ('.', ''), ('The', 'DT'), ('farmer', 'NN'), ('became', 'VBD'), ('very', 'RB'), ('sad', 'JJ'), ('and', 'CC'), ('came', 'VBD'), ('to', 'TO'), ('the', 'DT'), ('Emperor', 'NNP'), ("'", 'NNP'), ('s', 'JJ'), ('court', 'NN'), ('.', '.')]
[('He', 'PRP'), ('described', 'VBD'), ('everything', 'NN'), ('to', 'TO'), ('the', 'DT'), ('Emperor', 'NNP'), ('and', 'CC'), ('asked', 'VBD'), ('for', 'IN'), ('the', 'DT'), ('justice', 'NN'), ('.', '.')]
[('The', 'DT'), ('Emperor', 'NNP'), ('called', 'VBD'), ('Birbal', 'NNP'), ('and', 'CC'), ('handed', 'VBN'), ('over', 'RP'), ('this', 'DT'), ('case', 'NN'), ('to', 'TO'), ('him', 'PRP'), ('.', '.')]
[('Birbal', 'NNP'), ('called', 'VBD'), ('the', 'DT'), ('man', 'NN'), ('who', 'WP'), ('sold', 'VBD'), ('the', 'DT'), ('well', 'NN'), ('to', 'TO'), ('the', 'DT'), ('farmer', 'NN'), ('.', '.')]
[('Birbal', 'NNP'), ('asked', 'VBD'), (',', ','), ("'", 'NNP'), ('Why', 'WRB'), ('don', 'NN'), ("'", 'NN'), ('t', 'IN'), ('you', 'PRP'), ('let', 'VBP'), ('him', 'PRP'), ('use', 'VB'), ('the', 'DT'), ('water', 'NN'), ('of', 'IN'), ('the', 'DT'), ('well', 'NN'), ('.', '.')]
[('You', 'PRP'), ('have', 'VBP'), ('sold', 'VBN'), ('the', 'DT'), ('well', 'NN'), ('to', 'TO'), ('the', 'DT'), ('farmer', 'NN'), ("'", 'VBZ'), ('The', 'DT'), ('man', 'NN'), ('replied', 'VBD'), (',', ','), ("'", "''"), ('Birbal', 'NNP'), ('I', 'PRP'), ('have', 'VBP'), ('sold', 'VBN'), ('the', 'DT'), ('well', 'NN'), ('to', 'TO'), ('the', 'DT'), ('farmer', 'NN'), (',', ','), ('not', 'RB'), ('the', 'DT'), ('water', 'NN'), ('.', '.')]
[('He', 'PRP'), ('has', 'VBZ'), ('no', 'RB'), ('right', 'JJ'), ('to', 'TO'), ('draw', 'VB'), ('the', 'DT'), ('water', 'NN'), ('from', 'IN'), ('the', 'DT'), ('well', '.'), ('.', ''), ('NNP'), ('Then', 'RB'), ('Birbal', 'NNP'), ('smiled', 'VBD'), ('and', 'CC'), ('said', 'VBD'), ('to', 'TO'), ('him', 'PRP'), (',', ','), ("'", 'RB'), ('Good', 'JJ'), (',', ','), ('but', 'CC'), ('look', 'NN'), (',', ','), ('since', 'IN'), ('you', 'PRP'), ('have', 'VBP'), ('sold', 'VBN'), ('the', 'DT'), ('well', 'RB'), ('to', 'TO'), ('this', 'DT'), ('farmer', 'NN'), (',', ','), ('and', 'CC'), ('you', 'PRP'), ('claim', 'VBP'), ('that', 'IN'), ('water', 'NN'), ('is', 'VBZ'), ('yours', 'RB'), (',', ','), ('then', 'RB'), ('you', 'PRP'), ('have', 'VBP'), ('no', 'DT'), ('right', 'NN'), ('to', 'TO'), ('keep', 'VB'), ('your', 'PRP$'), ('water', 'NN'), ('in', 'IN'), ('the', 'DT'), ('farmer', 'NN'), ("'", 'NN'), ('s', 'RB'), ('well', 'RB'), ('.', '.')]
[('Either', 'CC'), ('you', 'PRP'), ('pay', 'VBP'), ('rent', 'VB'), ('to', 'TO'), ('the', 'DT'), ('farmer', 'NN'), ('to', 'TO'), ('keep', 'VB'), ('your', 'PR
P$'), ('water', 'NN'), ('in', 'IN'), ('his', 'PRP$'), ('well', 'NN'), (',', ','), ('or', 'CC'), ('you', 'PRP'), ('take', 'VBP'), ('that', 'DT'), ('out', 'IN
'), ('of', 'IN'), ('his', 'PRP$'), ('well', 'NN'), ('immediately.', 'RB'), ("'", 'VBZ'), ('The', 'DT'), ('man', 'NN'), ('understood', 'NN'), (',', ','), ('t
hat', 'IN'), ('his', 'PRP$'), ('trick', 'NN'), ('has', 'VBZ'), ('failed', 'VBN'), ('.', '.')]
[('Birbal', 'NNP'), ('has', 'VBZ'), ('outwitted', 'VBN'), ('him', 'PRP'), ('.', '.')]
>>>
```

b)   Anaphora Resolution

Anaphora resolution mainly used for pronoun resolution is the problem of resolving references to previous or next items in the context. The etymology of anaphora:

Ana: Back, upstream, back upstream.
Phora: Act of Caring.
Anaphora: Act of Caring back.

It has two elements.

1)   **Anaphor:** The reference that points to the previous item.
2)   **Antecedent:** The entity to which the anaphor refers.

After pre-processing, the paragraphs are broken down into sentences using the stop words "Full stop". Each sentence of the text is assumed to be a separate sentence that is due to the existence of pronouns in the sentence. It's very difficult to resolve anaphoras if two or more antecedents have the same gender.

Example:
Shivaji was king.
He was very loyal to *his* people.
They love *him* very much.

Here, in the previous sentences, the underlined words (i.e., the pronouns "he" and "they") are not possible to know what they refer to if each sentence is considered as an independent sentence; thus, anaphora resolution is applied before splitting the paragraph into sentences. In this example, "he", "his", "him" refers to Shivaji, and "they" refers to people.

Thus, after anaphora resolution is made, the above example looks like:

Shivaji was king.
Shivaji was very loyal to Shivaji's people.
People love Shivaji very much.

The text of the story used for NER is manually annotated for anaphora resolution. **Figure 6** shows the manually annotated text of the story "Farmers Well & Witty Birbal".

Figure 6. Manually annotated anaphora resolution of sample story Farmers Well & Witty Birbal

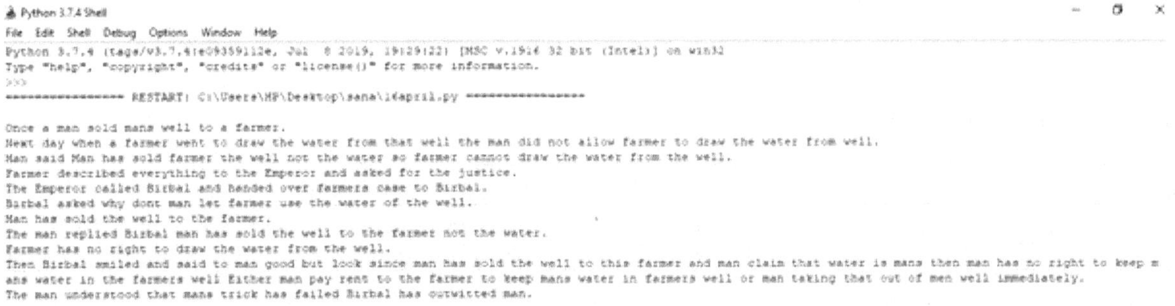

```
Python 3.7.4 Shell
File Edit Shell Debug Options Window Help
Python 3.7.4 (tags/v3.7.4:e09359112e, Jul  8 2019, 19:29:22) [MSC v.1916 32 bit (Intel)] on win32
Type "help", "copyright", "credits" or "license()" for more information.
>>>
================ RESTART: C:\Users\HP\Desktop\sana\16april.py ================

Once a man sold mans well to a farmer.
Next day when a farmer went to draw the water from that well the man did not allow farmer to draw the water from well.
Man said Man has sold farmer the well not the water so farmer cannot draw the water from the well.
Farmer described everything to the Emperor and asked for the justice.
The Emperor called Birbal and handed over farmers case to Birbal.
Birbal asked why dont man let farmer use the water of the well.
Man has sold the well to the farmer.
The man replied Birbal man has sold the well to the farmer not the water.
Farmer has no right to draw the water from the well.
Then Birbal smiled and said to man good but look since man has sold the well to this farmer and man claim that water is mans then man has no right to keep m
ans water in the farmers well Either man pay rent to the farmer to keep mans water in farmers well or man taking that out of men well immediately.
The man understood that mans trick has failed Birbal has outwitted man.
```

Step 4: Applying Conceptual Dependency

In stories, the important sentences will be those sentences showing some event or action happening in association with nouns. These events or actions are accordingly important because they are the happening statements in stories, which can be considered while making summaries; thus, conceptual dependencies are applied in the SACAS model.

Conceptual dependency is used to represent the natural language statement, and it depends upon a few primitive acts, which are discussed below. The main concept of conceptual dependency is that, if two statements have the same meaning, they should have the same CD representation (Schank, 1977).

The Primitive acts of conceptual dependency (CD)

- **ATRANS:** The transfer of an abstract relationship, such as possession rights or has power over. ATRANS needs a participant actor, an object, and a recipient; e.g., give, sell, and buy.
- **PTRANS:** It transmits the physical location of an object. PTRANS requires an actor, an object, and a direction, e.g., go, fly.
- **PROPEL:** The application of a physical force is applied to the object, e.g., push, pull, and kick.
- **MOVE:** It represents the movement of body parts, e.g., raise your hand, scratch, etc.
- **GRASP:** It represents the act of grasping or holding an object, e.g., hold, grabs, let go, and throw, etc.

- **INGEST:** The ingesting of an object into the body by drinking or eating, e.g., eat, drink, smoke, breathe, etc.
- **EXPEL:** It represents the expulsion of something out of the body, e.g., cry, sweat.
- **MTRANS:** It represents the transmission of information between or within entities, e.g., forget, read, tell, and see, etc.
- **MBUILD:** It represents the building of new information from old information, e.g., decide, conclude, imagine, and consider, etc.
- **SPEAK:** This represents actions that generate sounds, e.g., say, play music, purr, scream, etc.
- **ATTEND:** Focusing on an object using the senses, e.g., listen, see, etc.
- **CONC:** It represents thinking about something, e.g., consider, think, etc. (Schank,1975).
    a)   **Extraction of nouns**

Nouns are extracted from the stories, noun illustrates actor, and the extracted nouns are shown in Table 2.

Table 2. Extracted Nouns

Story name	Extracted nouns
Farmers Well & Witty Birbal	court, everything, cheat, justice, try, day, look, case, man, trick, water, right, Birbal, farmer, well, water, understood, Emperor

b)   **Extraction of verbs**

Verbs are extracted from the stories; a verb illustrates action or event. Extracted verbs are shown in Table 3.

Table 3. Extracted Verb

Story name	Extracted verbs
Farmers Well & Witty Birbal	called, claim, went, draw, came, sold, end, described, failed became, think, smiled, allow, draw, paying, keep, pay, handed, use

And Table 4 presents the words and their CD-primitive representation.

Step 5: Summary Generation
The final step is the summary generation for which the following two approaches are used
    a.   Priority ranking.
    b.   Question and Answering.
        a)   **Priority ranking**

Table 4. Words and its CD primitives forms

Verb	CD primitives
Replied, asked, Said, called	SPEAK
Draw	MOVE
Take, smiled	ATRANS
Claim	MBUILD
Went, came	PTRANS
Look	ATTEND
Think	CONC

Only highly scored sentences are considered for inclusion in the summary. The score considers which sentences contain the maximum number of verbs and nouns. They are sorted in descending order, and only half of those are considered for the generation of the summary, which is arranged into ascending order of the story.

b)   Question and Answering

QA systems are designed systems that try to answer a question or query posed in natural language for a given text, paragraph, or document. It tries to resemble the question-answering process humans do. This section discusses the components of QA systems and issues related to it.

i.   Question

Questions are those quotes which are raised basically under the following conditions:

- More information is required.
- There is nothing understood.
- To clarify what has already been understood.

ii.   Knowledgebase

Question answering access the knowledge base to give a correct and exact answer by using facts stored in the original database. But, firstly, it requires putting the conversion in natural language questions into structural queries.

iii.   Answer

The answer is that piece of relative information generated in the form of response to the identified focus of a given question. Its response generally depends on the type and needs (present in the question). The responses can be generally categorized into three types.

i.   Confirmative (agree/disagree).
ii.   Interpretive/reflective.

iii.   Analytic/Evaluative.

In SACAS, the prioritized sentences are considered for the question generation; for example, "In the village of Vijaynagar, there was a poor farmer?". Queries are generated following the way in which many questions, in reality, can be generated: "In which village the poor farmer lived?", "Who lived in Vijaynagar?", and "Where does the poor farmer live?".

One of the major limitations of the SACAS model is that questions were manually selected after generation and few questions where directly fed to the system like:

Q1) What is the title of the story?
Q2) How many actors/players are introduced in the story?
Q3) Is any location/place name given importance to?
Q4) Enlist the important events in the story.
Response to Q1) Farmers Well and Witty Birbal
Response to Q2) Farmer, Emperor, Birbal
Response to Q3) Well
Response to Q4) Sold, Justice, case, trick.

However, finding the answer to Q4 is a difficult case because all verbs are selected as events. Thus, Q4 has adhered to much effort. Final generated output is rearranged in such a manner that before the last question sentence, are added TITLE: Farmers Well & Witty Birbal. The current system produces sentences from verbs and nouns. Table 5 shows the total length of the story from the extracted unique sentences in the form of a summary. The original length of the story is 11, and the length of the summarized story is six.

Figure 7. The system's output for the story "Farmers Well & Witty Birbal"

```
Python 3.7.4 Shell                                                    -  o  x
File  Edit  Shell  Debug  Options  Window  Help
Python 3.7.4 (tags/v3.7.4:e09359112e, Jul  8 2019, 19:29:22) [MSC v.1914 32 bit (Intel)] on win32
Type "help", "copyright", "credits" or "license()" for more information.
>>>
=============== RESTART: E:\my project\finalascendingSapril.py ===============
[2, 4, 'Next day when a farmer went to draw the water from that well the man did not allow farmer to draw the water from well.']
[3, 3, 'Man said Man has sold farmer the well not the water so farmer cannot draw the water from the well.']
[5, 4, 'The Emperor called Birbal and handed over farmers case to Birbal.']
[6, 4, 'Birbal asked why dont man let farmer use the water of the well.']
[8, 5, 'The man replied Birbal man has sold the well to the farmer not the water.']
[10, 25, 'Then Birbal smiled and said to man good but look since man has sold the well to this farmer and man claim that water is mans then man has no right
to keep mans water in the farmers well Either man pay rent to the farmer to keep mans water in farmers well or man taking that out of men well immediately.'
]
>>> |
```

Experiments are performed on 50 stories; the overall results of reduction in stories are shown in Table 6; also, the reduction can be seen from the original story. Table 6 gives the summarized report of all fifty stories used during the experiment.

Table 5. Shows the description of the summarized story

Story Name	The total length of the story	Minimum length in the story	Max. length of the story
Farmers Well & Witty Birbal	6	11	39

The comparison from Table 6 indicates that the overall compression ratio on an average was found to be 51.8%. The SACAS model is an extractive method; so, it was unable to answer the question "what is the moral of the story?" because it requires conceptual understanding and self-generation of sentences. Although 51.8% compression looks good, a lot of effort is required beyond size, i.e., understanding and self-generative sentences to provide a brief, thus text summarization has more challenges for budding researchers in various domains.

Step 6: Intelligibility test by MOS

Here, a mean position score test is conducted. MOS is the arithmetic mean of all the individual scores. To check the accuracy of the given summary, we have made a questionnaire that contains 250 questions based on the original story, and ten persons were selected to answer the summary. If persons are able to answer the maximum number of questions (four or five), then the quality of the summary is excellent. If the persons are able to answer an average number of questions (two or three), then the quality of the summary is good. If the persons are able to answer a minimum number of questions (one or none), then the quality of the summary is bad. The MOS specification is given in Table 7.

Table 7 shows that 28 summaries were good, and 15 summaries were excellent, which indicates that 43 stories were able to be understood from summaries; only seven stories were not clearly explainable through summarization. The overall compression ratio on an average was found to be 56% through MOS, which is good, and the SACAS system can be further improved by enhancing it to abstractive methods.

5. APPLICATIONS

5.1 Media Monitoring

The information is widely spread on the internet because automatic text summarization is possible to compress a stream of information into a shorter form.

5.2 Search Marketing and SEO (Search Engine Optimization)

When estimating search results for queries, it is difficult to analyze what participants talked about the contents. For multi-document summarization will be an influential technique to examine search results promptly and comprehend the significant points and provide a summary.

Table 6. Evaluation of Summary

Sr. No	Story Names	The actual length of the story	Total no. of sentences in the summarized story	Ratio in percentage
1	The crystal ball	10	5	50%
2	The jackal and the drum	7	4	57%
3	The tale of two fishes and a frog	8	4	50%
4	The loyal mongoose	8	4	50%
5	Goats and jackal	6	3	50%
6	Elephants and hares	8	4	50%
7	Fisherman and the little fish	7	4	57%
8	Bundle of sticks	11	6	54%
9	The crows and the cobra	8	4	50%
10	The cave that talked	12	6	50%
11	The lion and the jackal	76	38	50%
12	The two goats	6	3	50%
13	The monkey and the crocodile	16	8	50%
14	The tortoise and the geese	7	4	57%
15	Two Cats and a Monkey	5	3	60%
16	The story of the blue jackal	24	12	50%
17	The dog and the shadow	5	3	60%
18	The talkative tortoise	10	5	50%
19	The lazy donkey	7	4	57%
20	The mouse and the saint	6	3	50%
21	The stork and the crab	14	7	50%
22	The goat	6	3	50%
23	An ass in lion's skin	6	3	50%
24	The evil snake	6	3	50%
25	Fox and the grapes	4	2	50%
26	The elephants and the mice	14	7	50%
27	The bird with two heads	10	5	50%
28	The lion and the boar	7	4	57%
29	The monkey and the wedge	8	4	50%
30	The boy who cried wolf	12	6	50%
31	The proud rose	9	5	55%
32	The hermit and the mouse	10	5	50%
33	The bear and the two friends	18	9	50%
34	The fox without a tail	7	4	57%
35	The golden touch	8	4	50%
36	Of crows and owls	8	4	50%
37	The ugly duckling	9	5	55%
38	The lion and the camel	11	6	54%
39	The milkmaid and her pail	10	5	50%
40	The cow's bell	4	2	50%
41	The lion that sprang to life	10	5	50%
42	Counting wisely	8	4	50%
43	The tale of the pencil	9	5	55%
44	The roaring lion	6	3	50%
45	The ant and the grasshopper	6	3	50%
46	The musical donkey	8	4	50%
47	The king and the foolish monkey	7	4	57%
48	Four friends and a hunter	8	4	50%
49	When adversity knocks	11	7	63%
50	Farmers Well & Witty Birbal	11	6	54%

Table 7. The intelligibility MOS score

MOS	Quality	Total number of stories answered by users from a total of five questions for each story
Maximum questions can be answered	Excellent	15
Average questions can be answered	Good	28
Minimum questions can be answered	Bad	7

5.3 Internal Document Workflow

Companies continuously generate large amounts of information stored in their unstructured databases and files. Companies require such a tool to help them to get a notion of the outstanding relations in their information systems. Summarization can become a powerful tool to allow analysts to understand what the company already has and recover all important documents together.

5.4 Financial Research

It is difficult for financial analysts to read each and every news regarding market and news reports, summarization can be useful for the analysts by helping them to understand and get market signals from the multiple reports.

5.5 Legal Contract Analysis

Summarization is a powerful tool to analyze legal documents.

5.6 Question Answering and Bots

The summarization is an influential tool to question answering, which gathers relevant documents for a particular question, and generates an appropriate summary in the form of a multi-document summary.

5.7 Helping Disabled People

Voice to text process is beneficial to a person with hearing disability. The summarization procedure would also be helpful for getting relevant content.

5.8 Meetings and Video-Conferencing

Video-meetings have been increased, and there is a need to get important content from the conversations, systems which convert the voice to text, and then generate summaries from the text are needed.

5.9 E-Learning and Class Assignments

Most of the time, teachers have to provide their case studies in the form of an outline for lecturers; summarization will be helpful to teach by quickly making a summary of the case studies.

5.10 Programming Languages

A code summarizer will be helpful for a programmer to get a good picture of the complete project.

6. CONCLUSION

Summary generation is the most needed unit for many applications. Automatic summarization, even today, has not reached to mark where compressed and well-framed sentences are generated for a given paragraph, even it's still a difficult aspect to understand the context of a given text. These issues make summarization a difficult task. Topic identification, interpretation, and text generation are the basic building blocks of the automatic summarization systems. The most important criterion for summarization is to preserve important information, which should be short and easy to understand. This chapter has the emphasis on question-based summarization, and the domain discussed is on stories, because stories are the most easily adaptable as highlighting the most difficult and important issues in NLP, required during summarization. The SACAS model for summarization is explained in detail. The components of the SACAS model are input (story), pre-processing, NER, anaphora resolution, association, and representation using conceptual dependency, and the final stage is the priority based on the answer-based generation of summaries, the evaluation of the accuracy of the summarized story. The compression ratio of summarized stories was found to be 51.8% on average, and the MOS test gave an overall 56% of comprehension, on average.

ACKNOWLEDGMENT

The authors would like to acknowledge, and thanks to CSRI DST Major Project sanctioned No.SR/CSRI/71/2015(G), Computational and Psycholinguistic Research Lab Facility supporting this work and Department of Computer Science and Information Technology, Dr. Babasaheb Ambedkar Marathwada University, Aurangabad, Maharashtra, India.

REFERENCES

Asa, A. S., Akter, S., Uddin, M. P., Hossain, M. D., Roy, S. K., & Afjal, M. I. (2017). A Comprehensive Survey on Extractive Text Summarization Techniques. *American Journal of Engineering Research*, *6*(1), 226–239.

Babar, S. A., & Patil, P. D. (2015). Improving performance of text summarization. *Procedia Computer Science*, *46*, 354–363. doi:10.1016/j.procs.2015.02.031

Barzilay, R., McKeown, K., & Elhadad, M. (1999). Information fusion in the context of multi-document summarization. In *Proceedings of the 37th annual meeting of the Association for Computational Linguistics* (pp. 550-557). 10.3115/1034678.1034760

Basiron, H., Kumar, Y., Goh, S., Ngo, H. C., & Suppiah, C. (2016). A review on automatic text summarization approaches. *Journal of Computational Science*, *12*(4), 178–190. doi:10.3844/jcssp.2016.178.190

Bhatia, N., & Jaiswal, A. (2016,). Automatic text summarization and it's methods-a review. In 2016 6th International Conference-Cloud System and Big Data Engineering (Confluence) (pp. 65-72). IEEE. doi:10.1109/CONFLUENCE.2016.7508049

Booker, C. (2004). *The seven basic plots: Why we tell stories*. Continuum International Publishing Group.

Chen, S. Z., Cafarella, M. J., & Adar, E. (2011). Searching for statistical diagrams. Frontiers of Engineering, National Academy of Engineering, 69-78.

Das, D., & Martins, A. F. (2007). *A Survey on Automatic Text Summarization*. Academic Press.

Deshpande, A. R., & Lobo, L. M. R. J. (2013). Text summarization using Clustering technique. *International Journal of Engineering Trends and Technology*, *4*(8), 3348–3351.

Genest, P. E., & Lapalme, G. (2011). Framework for abstractive summarization using text-to-text generation. In *Proceedings of the 49 th Annual Meeting of the Association for Computational Linguistics* (pp. 64-73). Academic Press.

Genest, P. E., & Lapalme, G. (2012, July). Fully abstractive approach to guided summarization. In *Proceedings of the 50th Annual Meeting of the Association for Computational Linguistics* (pp. 354-358). Academic Press.

Greenbacker, C. F. (2011, June). Towards a framework for abstractive summarization of multimodal documents. In *Proceedings of the ACL 2011 Student Session* (pp. 75-80). Portland, OR: Association for Computational Linguistics.

Harabagiu, S. M., & Lacatusu, F. (2002). Generating single and multi-document summaries with gistexter. In *Document Understanding Conferences* (pp. 11-12). Academic Press.

Jahangiri, N., Kahani, M., Ahamdi, R., & Sazvar, M. (2011). A study on part of speech tagging. *5th Symposium on Advance and Science and Technology*.

Kamath, S., & Wagh, R. (2017). Named entity recognition approaches and challenges. *International Journal of Advanced Research in Computer and Communication Engineering*, *6*(2), 259–262.

Khan, A., & Salim, N. (2014). A Review on Abstractive Summarization Methods. *Journal of Theoretical and Applied Information Technology, 59*(1), 64–72.

Lee, C. S., Jian, Z. W., & Huang, L. K. (2005). A fuzzy ontology and its application to news *summarization. IEEE Transactions on Systems, Man, and Cybernetics. Part B, Cybernetics, 35*(5), 859–880. doi:10.1109/TSMCB.2005.845032 PMID:16240764

Lee, Y. J., Ghosh, J., & Grauman, K. (2012, June). *Discovering important people and objects for egocentric video summarization. In 2012 IEEE conference on computer vision and pattern recognition.* IEEE.

Li, W., He, L., & Zhuge, H. (2016, December). Abstractive News Summarization based on Event Semantic Link Network. In *Proceedings of COLING 2016, the 26th International Conference on Computational Linguistics: Technical Papers* (pp. 236-246). Academic Press.

McKeown, K., Hirschberg, J., Galley, M., & Maskey, S. (2005, March). From text to speech summarization. In *Proceedings (ICASSP'05) IEEE International Conference on Acoustics, Speech, and Signal Processing, 2005 (Vol. 5*, pp. v-997). IEEE.

Moawad, I. F., & Aref, M. (2012, November). Semantic graph reduction approach for abstractive Text Summarization. In *2012 Seventh International Conference on Computer Engineering & Systems (ICCES)* (pp. 132-138). IEEE. 10.1109/ICCES.2012.6408498

Moratanch, N., & Chitrakala, S. (2017, January). A survey on extractive text summarization. In *2017 International Conference on Computer, Communication and Signal Processing (ICCCSP)* (pp. 1-6). IEEE.

Okumura, M., Fukushima, T., & Nanba, H. (2001). Text Summarization Challenge 2/Text Summarization Evaluation at NTCIR Workshop3. In *Proceedings of the third NTCIR Workshop Meeting* (pp. 1-7). Academic Press.

Porras, J., Florencia-Juárez, R., Rivera, G., & García, V. (2018). Interfaz de lenguaje natural para consultar cubos multidimensionales utilizando procesamiento analítico en línea. *Research in Computing Science, 147*(6), 153–165. doi:10.13053/rcs-147-6-12

Saggion, H., & Lapalme, G. (2002). Generating indicative-informative summaries with sumUM. *Computational Linguistics, 28*(4), 497–526. doi:10.1162/089120102762671963

Sayyed, S.N., Aurangabad, B.A., & Mahender, C.N.(2020). Conceptual Dependency to Extract the important event from story to enhanced Summarization. *International Journal of Scientific & Technology Research, 9*(3), 6797-6801.

Schank, R. C. (1975). The primitive ACTs of conceptual dependency. Theoretical issues in natural language processing. doi:10.3115/980190.980205

Schank, R. C., & Abelson, R. P. (1977). *Scripts, plans, goals, and understanding: An inquiry into human knowledge structures.* Lawrence Erlbaum Associates.

Suanmali, L., Binwahlan, M. S., & Salim, N. (2009, August). Sentence features fusion for text summarization using fuzzy logic. In *2009 Ninth International Conference on Hybrid Intelligent Systems* (Vol. 1, pp. 142-146). IEEE. 10.1109/HIS.2009.36

Wang, M., Wang, X., & Xu, C. (2005, October). An approach to concept-obtained text summarization. In *IEEE International Symposium on Communications and Information Technology, 2005. ISCIT 2005* (Vol. 2, pp. 1337-1340). IEEE.

Yeasmin, S., Tumpa, P. B., Nitu, A. M., Uddin, M., Ali, E., & Afjal, M. (2017). Study of Abstractive Text Summarization Techniques. *American Journal of Engineering Research*, 6(8), 253–260.

Zamanifar, A., Minaei-Bidgoli, B., & Sharifi, M. (2008, August). A New Hybrid Farsi Text Summarization Technique Based on Term Co-Occurrence and Conceptual Property of the Text. In *2008 Ninth ACIS International Conference on Software Engineering, Artificial Intelligence, Networking, and Parallel/ Distributed Computing* (pp. 635-639). IEEE Computer Society. 10.1109/SNPD.2008.57

Chapter 4
Two New Challenging Resources to Evaluate Natural Language Interfaces to Databases Generated Based on Geobase and Geoquery

Juan Javier González-Barbosa

Tecnológico Nacional de México, Mexico & Instituto Tecnológico de Ciudad Madero, Mexico

Juan Frausto Solís

Tecnológico Nacional de México, Mexico & Instituto Tecnológico de Ciudad Madero, Mexico

Juan Paulo Sánchez-Hernández

Universidad Politécnica del Estado de Morelos, Mexico

Julia Patricia Sanchez-Solís

Universidad Autónoma de Ciudad Juárez, Mexico

ABSTRACT

Databases and corpora are essential resources to evaluate the performance of Natural Language Interfaces to Databases (NLIDB). The Geobase database and the Geoquery corpus (Geoquery250 and Geoquery880) are among the most commonly used. In this chapter, the authors analyze both resources to offer two elaborate resources: 1) N-Geobase, which is a relational database, and 2) the corpus Geoquery270. The former follows the standard normalization procedure, then N-Geobase has a schema similar to enterprise databases. Geoquery270 consists of 270 queries selected from Geoquery880, preserving the same kind of natural language problems as Geoquery880, but with more challenging issues for an NLIDB than Geoquery250. To evaluate the new resources, they compared the performance of the NLIDB using Geoquery270 and Geoquery250. The results indicated that Geoquery270 was the harder corpus, while Geoquery250 is the easier one. Consequently, this chapter offers a broader range of resources to NLIDB designers.

DOI: 10.4018/978-1-7998-4730-4.ch004

Copyright © 2021, IGI Global. Copying or distributing in print or electronic forms without written permission of IGI Global is prohibited.

INTRODUCTION

An NLIDB (Natural Language Interface to Database) is a system that can be used to access information in a database by typing sentences in a natural language such as English, French, or any other (Androutso-poulos, Ritchie, & Thanisch, 1995). For example, the sentence on the left side of **Figure 1** is the query "Show all the employees called Laura and the customers whose orders have been generated by these employees"; for this sentence, the NLIDB on the right side of this figure will generate an equivalent query in SQL (Structured Query Language) to extract the information demanded by the user.

Figure 1. A simple query processed with a Natural Language Interface to Database (NLIDB)

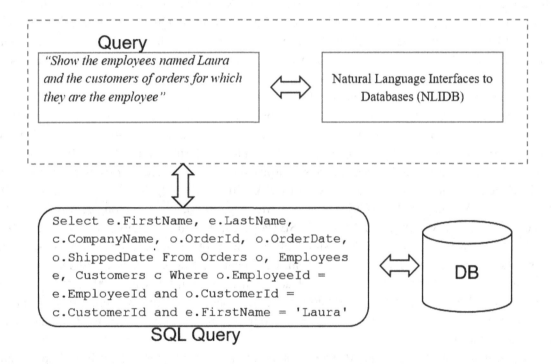

Notable success on modern techniques to translate queries in natural language to SQL has been developed. From the 1960s to the 1990s, the first applications of NLIDBS were published, examples follow:

- In 1961, BASEBALL was introduced for a database about baseball games (Green Jr, Wolf, Chomsky, & Laugh, 1961).
- In 1972, LUNAR was applied for lunar rocks and soil composition (Woods, Kaplan, & Nash-Webber, 1972).
- In the 1980s, CHAT-80 was implemented in Prolog, and its database integrated by facts (true sentences in Prolog) relating to 150 of the world's countries (Warren, 1981).
- In 1987, TEAM used a database that comprises geographic data (Grosz, Appelt, Martin, & Pereira, 1987).

- In 1989, PARLANCE was applied to different versions of a large Navy database (Bates, 1989).
- In 1990, JANUS was used for US Navy applications (Bobrow, Resnik, & Weischedel, 1990).

In the 1990s some spoken language understanding systems appeared: CMU (Ward, 1991), MIT (Seneff et al., 1991), SRI (Murveit et al., 1991), BBN Byblos (Kubala et al., 1992), and AT&T (Tzoukermann, 1991). All these systems were evaluated in relational databases, making the performance comparisons between NLIDBs. The database used by these systems was ATIS, of which some corpora of natural language queries are available in the literature (ATIS0 Complete, ATIS0 Pilot, ATIS0 Read, ATIS0 SD Read, ATIS2, ATIS3 Training Data, ATIS3 Test Data) (Consortium, 2019). The ATIS database consists of data obtained from the Official Airline Guide, organized under a relational schema. This guide contains information about flights, fares, airlines, cities, airports, and ground services (Hemphill,n.d.). Also, in the late 1990s and at the beginning of the next decade, NLIDBs as English Wizard was used using the Northwind database (Technology, 1997), two of them are English Query (Bhootra & Parker, 2004) and ELF (ELF software, 2002). Northwind is a relational database with information about a shipping company. Unlike ATIS, there is no corpus of natural language queries in the literature for Northwind. However, in several works, we can find small sets of queries that have been used (Tan, Lane and Rijanto, 2019; Bhootra and Parker, 2004; Nihalani, Motwani & Silka, 2011). At this time, the NLIDB, named NLPQC (Stratica, Kosseim, & Desai, 2005), was explicitly designed for the Cindi Virtual Library.

In the 2000s, NLIDBs using Learning Semantic Parsing (the process of mapping a natural language sentence into a complete formal meaning representation or logical form) was used; also, they mostly used Geobase (Borland International, 1988) which is a corpus of natural language queries. Some examples are CHILL (Zelle & Mooney, 1996), COCKTAIL (Tang & Mooney, 2001), WOLFIE (Thompson, 2003), KRISP (Kate & Mooney, 2006), SCISSOR (Ge & Mooney, 2005), WASP (Wong & Mooney, 2006), Giordani (Giordani & Moschitti, 2009), PRECISE (Popescu, Armanasu, Etzioni, Ko, & Yates, 2004), and C-PHRASE (Minock, Olofsson, & Näslund, 2008). On the other hand, some interfaces use ontologies as a database, such as GINSENG (Bernstein, Kaufmann, & Kaiser, 2005), QUERIX (Kaufmann, Bernstein, & Zumstein, 2006), NLP-REDUCE (Kaufmann, Bernstein, & Fischer, 2007), PANTO (Wang, Xiong, Zhou, & Yu, 2007) and FREyA (Damljanovic, Agatonovic, & Cunningham, 2010). In addition to these interfaces to ontologies, ORAKEL queries geographical facts about Germany (Cimiano, Haase, & Heizmann, 2007).

Recently, interfaces that are using different databases and a set of queries have been implemented, which does not allow comparing the performance of NLIDBs (e.g., Porras, Florencia-Juárez, Rivera & García, 2018). Jaydeep (2019) used financial ontologies and proposed a set of queries for its data; also Sujatha (2016) proposed a generic NLIDB that uses ontologies to be constructed; in the last reference is mentioned that this NLIDB can be used in any data set and it gives results even without test data. Also, an NLIDB model is presented by Bais (2016), which uses queries generated using a program.

Table 1 shows the databases used to evaluate NLIDBs and the availability of the corpus of natural language queries in the literature. In **Table 1**, we can observe there are only a few resources available in the literature that can be used to evaluate and to compare the performance between NLIDBs. Besides, as we remarked before, Geobase and Geoquery are among the most used resources for NLIDBs. Thus, we have the following questions:

1. Are Geobase and Geoquery suitable for use in the evaluation of NLIDBs?
2. If Geobase and Geoquery could be improved, how would this be done?

Table 1. Databases commonly used to evaluate NLIDBs

NLIDB	Date	Database	Is the corpus available?
CMU	1990	ATIS	Yes
MIT	1990	ATIS	Yes
SRI	1991	ATIS	Yes
BBN Byblos	1992	ATIS	Yes
AT&T	1994	ATIS	Yes
CHILL	1996	Geobase	Yes
ENGLISH WIZARD	1997	Northwind	Yes
COCKTAIL	2001	Geobase	Yes
ELF	2002	Northwind	Yes
ENGLISH QUERY	2002	Northwind	Yes
NLPQC	2002	Cindi Virtual Library	No
WOLFIE	2003	Geobase	Yes
PRECISE	2004	Geobase, ATIS	Yes
GINSENG	2005	Geobase	Yes
KRISP	2006	Geobase	Yes
QUERIX	2006	Geobase	Yes
SCISSOR	2006	Geobase	Yes
WASP	2006	Geobase	Yes
NLP-REDUCE	2007	Geobase, Restaurants	Yes
ORAKEL	2007	Geographical facts about Germany	No
PANTO	2007	Geobase, Restaurants, Jobs	Yes
C-PHRASE	2010	Geobase	Yes
FREyA	2010	Geobase	Yes
GIORDANI	2010	Geobase	Yes

In this paper, Geobase and Geoquery resources (Geoquery250 and Geoquery880) are analyzed to design two new resources: a) N-Geobase, which is a normalized relational database, and b) a corpus of natural language queries named Geoquery 270. The complexity of N-Geobase was evaluated by comparing the performance of our NLIDB on both, the N-Geobase versus the other relational schemas. This paper is structured as follows: Section 2 describes the Geobase database and the formalization of Geoquery 270. In Section 3, N-Geobase and its normalization are presented. Section 4 presents the Geoquery corpus and some natural language problems. Section 5 presents Geoquery 270 corpus, which is structured from Geoquery880 with the same kind of problems but using only just 270 queries. Section 6 shows the experimental results, and Section 7 presents the conclusions.

Geobase Database

Geobase is a system that is supplied as a sample application with Turbo Prolog 2.0. This system has a database containing about 800 Prolog facts about USA states, including population, area, the capital cities of every state, neighboring states, major rivers, major cities, and highest and lowest points along with their elevation. This database is described in the following subsection.

Description of the Geobase Database

Geobase is a deductive database designed in Prolog. The structure of Geobase is built with predicates in Prolog and is shown in **Table 2**. These predicates are used to represent states, cities, rivers, neighboring states, highest and lowest points, mountains, roads, and lakes (lines 01-08, respectively).

Table 2. Prolog predicates used to define the structure of Geobase

Line	Prolog predicate
01	state(name, abbreviation, capital, population, area, state_number, city1, city2, city3, city4)
02	city(state, state_abbreviation, name, population)
03	river(name, length, [states through which it flows])
04	border(state, state_abbreviation, [states that border it])
05	highlow(state, state_abbreviation, highest_point, highest_elevation, lowest_point, lowest_elevation)
06	mountain(state, state_abbreviation, name, height)
07	road(number, [states it passes through])
08	lake(name, area, [states it is in])

Next, we explain the attributes of **Table 2**:

- The attributes that define a state are shown in line 1, and they are the next: name, abbreviation, capital name, population, area, state_number, and the name of its four best cities (city1, city2, city3, and city4). Besides, the capital and the four best cities defined for each state should also be defined as cities according to line 02 in **Table 2**.
- In line 2, the attributes that define a city are the next: the name of the state to which it belongs (state), the abbreviation of that state, the name of the city, and its population.
- In line three, the attributes that define a river are defined as the following: name, length, and a list of the states through which it flows. The last information is required because a river flows through different states of the United States.
- In line four, the attributes for the neighboring states of a specific state are established as follows: the name of the state, state_abbreviation, and a list of neighboring state names.
- In line five, the highest and lowest points are stored. In this case, the attributes are the following: state, state_abbreviation, the name of the highest point, its highest_elevation, the lowest_point, and its lowest_elevation.

- In line six, the features of the mountains of a state are defined; to do that, each mountain is described with the following attributes: the state where the mountain is located, state_abbreviation, the mountain's name, and its height.
- In line seven, the attributes that define a road of every state are defined with these attributes: the number of the road, and a list of states through which the road passes.
- Finally, in line eight, the attributes of the lakes of the states are defined with the following attributes: name, area, and states where the lake is located.

The facts about the above entities were stored in Geobase. This was also done by using predicates of Prolog, as is shown in **Table 3**, where we only present two examples of each entity (state, city, river, road, and so on). Notice that **Table 3** has the same structure as **Table 2**. The states of the country are represented by 51 similar facts to those specified in lines 01 and 02 of **Table 3**. For instance, a state is defined in **Table 2** as follows:

state (name, abbreviation, capital, population, area, state_number, city1, city2, city3, city4)

While the example given in the first line of **Table 3** is:

state ('alaska','ak','juneau',401.8e+3,591.0e+3,49,'anchorage','fairbanks','juneau','sitka').

In other words, Alaska (represented by "alaska" in the later predicate), has the abbreviation "ak"; the capital of Alaska State is Juneau (represented in the predicate as "juneau"), has a population of 401800 inhabitants, the territorial extension of Alaska is 591 (represented in the predicate as 591.0e+3). Also, this predicate continues saying that Alaska is the State number 49, and the four main cities of Alaska are 'anchorage', 'fairbanks', 'juneau', and 'sitka'.

Similarly, we can examine the other predicates in **Table 3**:

- the cities by 386 similar facts to those specified in lines 03 and 04;
- the rivers by 46 similar facts to those specified in lines 05 and 06;
- the neighboring states by 51 similar facts to those in lines 07 and 08;
- the highest and lowest points by 51 similar facts to those in lines 09 and 10;
- the mountains by 50 similar facts to those in lines 11 and 12; the roads by 40 similar facts to those in lines 13 and 14; and
- the lakes by 22 similar facts to those in lines 15 and 16.

Analyzing these facts, we identify the following inconsistencies:

1. There are some states whose capital is not defined as a city; for instance: Annapolis, Augusta, Bismarck, and Carson City.
2. There are some states where some of their best cities are not defined as cities, for example, Aberdeen, Auburn, Bangor, Bennington, and Biloxi.

Because deductive databases as Geobase are used less frequently than relational databases, then Geobase has been migrated to different relational databases. Moreover, Geobase has even been migrated

Table 3. Examples of Prolog predicates for defining the facts stored in Geobase

Line	Prolog predicate
01	state('alaska','ak','juneau',401.8e+3,591.0e+3,49,'anchorage','fairbanks','juneau','sitka').
02	state('arizona','az','phoenix',2718.0e+3,114.0e+3,48,'phoenix','tucson','mesa','tempe').
03	city('alabama','al','birmingham',284413).
04	city('alabama','al','mobile',200452).
05	river('arkansas',2333,['colorado','kansas','oklahoma','arkansas']).
06	river('canadian',1458,['colorado','new mexico','texas','oklahoma']).
07	border('alabama','al',['tennessee','georgia','florida','mississippi']).
08	border('alaska','ak',[]).
09	highlow('alabama','al','cheaha mountain',734,'gulf of mexico',0).
10	highlow('alaska','ak','mount mckinley',6194,'pacific ocean',0).
11	mountain('alaska','ak','mckinley',6194).
12	mountain('alaska','ak','st. elias',5489).
13	road('29',['north dakota','south dakota','iowa','missouri']).
14	road('65',['indiana','kentucky','tennessee','alabama']).
15	lake('superior',82362,['michigan','wisconsin','minnesota']).
16	lake('huron',59570,['michigan']).
17	country('usa',307890000,9826675).

to different platforms like XML and OWL. Among these different platforms, we are interested in the relational databases, since they are related to our research. For this reason, some relational database schemas, migrated from Geobase, are described in the following subsection.

Description of Relational Database Schemas Migrated from Geobase

Geobase has been migrated to different relational databases, such as those used by Chandra (Chandra & Mihalcea, 2006), and Elf (ELF software, 2002). The Chandra schema is composed of 10 tables, 37 columns, and 9 table relationships (**Figure 2a**). The ELF schema is composed of 9 tables, 8 table relationships, and approximately 41 columns (**Figure 2b**). The Lakes and Road tables, defined in Geobase by lines 07, and 08 in **Table 2**, are not considered in the schema used by ELF (ELF software, 2002). Both schemas are acyclic schemas; that means there is only one path between each pair of tables. Thus, no cycles are formed.

Normalization and Table Relationships

The normalization includes relationships among tables and according to the rules designed for both, to protect the data and make the database more flexible. This is done by eliminating redundancy and inconsistent dependencies. As is well known, the relational databases are normalized to accomplish the following features:

Figure 2. Schema of Geobase migrated to other databases

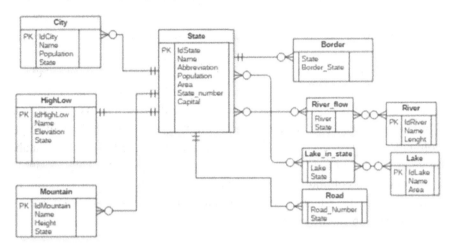

Figure 2a. Chandra Schema

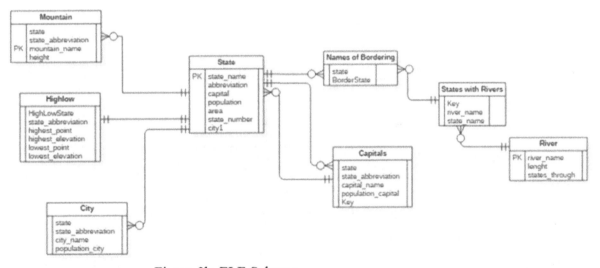

Figure 2b. ELF Schema

1. avoid data redundancy,
2. reduce problems updating the data in tables, and
3. protect the integrity of the data.

Considering the normalization (Codd, 1972), we can see that all tables of both schemas are in their first normal form (1NF) because all columns contain atomic values (i.e., they store a single value). However, from **Figure 2**, we can notice that the next tables are not in their second normal form (2NF):

*   In Chandra schema: City, Highlow, Mountain, and Borders tables.
*   In ELF schema: City, Highlow, Mountain, Capitals, and River.

The later situation occurs because there is a functional dependency between the State and State_abbreviation columns. For this reason, we consider the state_abbreviation column is defined redundantly in both schemas, as was mentioned above. We observe that redundancy should be avoided when a database is standardized.

Let us now consider the table relationships. Notice that the main columns used to relate tables in both schemas are defined in type columns that store descriptive information for users. This situation is not common when relational databases are designed because one of the situations, as time passes, may need to be updated with data stored in any of these main columns, and this could involve updating the information in all columns related to this one. For this reason, in the normalization of a database, main columns are generally defined in numeric type columns (**Figure 3**) as primary keys. A single primary key is just a single attribute or a column that uniquely identifies a row. Primary keys are commonly used in the database design to ensure the integrity of the information of the user stored in the database. Therefore, duplicated information should not be stored.

Figure 3. Possible primary key defined for the State table

Primary key

	IdCity	Name	Population	State
1	343	abilene	98315	44
2	311	abingdon	59084	39
3	283	akron	237177	36
4	79	alameda	63852	5
5	128	albany	74425	11
6	262	albany	101727	33
7	256	albuquerque	331767	32

Capitals and the Neighbouring States

Let us now analyze the situation between capitals and states in a country. Because the capital of a state is also a city, the information about capitals should be stored in the City table in both schemas. However, in the Chandra schema (Chandra & Mihalcea, 2006), the capital name of a state is stored in the State. capital column; still, there is not a relationship between the State and City tables to enable a domain-independent NLIDB to retrieve specific information from a capital (for instance, the population of the capital which should be stored in the City.Population column), since the only definite relationship between these tables is used to identify which cities belong to which state (see **Figure 4**). In the schema used by ELF (ELF software, 2002), the information from capitals is stored in a table named Capitals, which is independent of the City table. In this way, it is possible to directly query the Capitals table to extract information easily from capitals (see **Figure 2b**). However, this information is redundant since it is a subset of the data stored in the City table.

Figure 4. City and State tables relationship

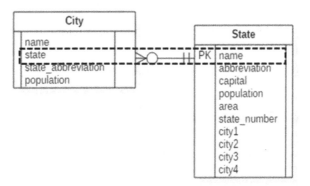

As the capitals of a state, a similar situation occurs in the neighboring states of a state. In the Chandra schema, the names of the neighboring states of a state are stored in the Border.border_state column. However, as is shown in **Figure 5**, there is no relationship between the Border and State tables to enable a domain-independent NLIDB to retrieve specific information from neighboring states (for instance: area, population, and major cities) (Chandra & Mihalcea, 2006).

Highest and Lowest Points

Chandra and Elf schema are similar in a particular issue: both schemas have a table named Highlow used to store information about the highest and lowest points in each state. This information is stored in the following columns: Highlow.highest_point and Highlow.highest_elevation store the highest point name and its elevation respectively; Highlow.lowest_point and Highlow.lowest_elevation store the lowest point name and its elevation respectively, as is shown on the table Highlow of **Figure 2**. This table is designed to store only these two points per state in a single record. **Figure 2** has the columns needed to store the information of the highest and lowest points. As a matter of fact, this situation facilitates an NLIDB to identify these points. Notice that this table could be designed to store more than two points per state. Then each of these points is stored in different records. This situation would involve an NLIDB, identifying the highest or lowest point among the points stored.

Figure 5. State and Border table relationship

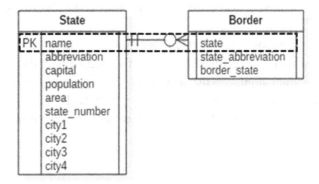

Major Cities

In a similar case to the above subsection, the names of the four major cities of a state are defined in the State.city1, State.city2, State.city3, and State.city4 columns. We can access these columns from the State table in **Figure 2**, as we have marked in the box in **Figure 6**.

Figure 6. Four major cities defined in the State table

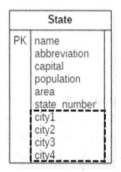

It is noteworthy that storing the four major cities in this manner causes the State table not to be in 2NF. Moreover, the idea of storing the names of the four major cities would have to be applied to rivers, mountains, and lakes to identify the major rivers, mountains, and lakes. We may observe that this idea is not always feasible since this data could change over time, which involves updating the information manually in each of these columns, a tedious task. Therefore, we consider that instead of statically storing the four major cities, an NLIDB must be able to automatically identify this information by sorting them in ascending order by city population. Thus, based on this idea, an NLIDB should also be able to automatically identify a certain number (greater than one) of major cities, mountains, rivers, and so on. We can do that by designing any criteria specified by users in their queries.

Remarks

To conclude this section, we state that there is no relational schema migrated from Geobase to be considered as a standard in the evaluation of NLIDBs and that the existing relational models differ from each other. We also identified that these schemas present issues that can be improved. These issues may indirectly allow NLIDBs to achieve good performance. Therefore, the reported results of some NLIDBs could be misleading.

For this reason, we aim to propose a relational schema to be considered as a standard in the literature. The relational schema proposed was designed following the standards in database normalization. The normalization makes its schema similar to the schema of databases used by enterprises. Therefore, it should be more challenging than other relational database schemas also migrated from Geobase. In this paper, we named this relational schema N-Geobase, and we will describe it in the following section.

The N-Geobase Database

N-Geobase was designed following the standards in database normalization described by Codd (1972) and based on the Prolog predicates described in **Table 2**. The names of these predicates (state, city, river, border, highlow, mountain, road, and lake) were used to name the tables in our schema, and the structure of these predicates let us define the structure of our tables.

Unlike relational schemas described in Subsection 2.2, primary keys were defined on integer type columns (as regularly used in schemas of databases used by enterprises) in our main tables. **Figure 7** has the tables defined and the primary keys added (State.IdState, City.IdCity, HighLow.IdHighLow, Mountain.IdMountain, River.IdRiver, and Lake.IdLake).

Figure 7. Tables of N-Geobase

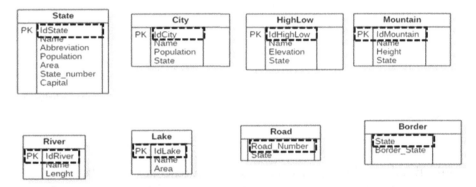

Normalization

Because all columns in all tables store atomic values, we observe that tables are in 1NF. Because in Geobase, a river and a lake could pass through different states, and a state could be crossed by different rivers and lakes, we have what is known in the relational model as an N:M relation in data. This relation can be represented by adding two new tables named in **Figure 8** as River_Flow and Lake_in_states. In this way, all three tables State, Lake, and River, are all of them in 2NF because their columns depend on

Figure 8. Normalization of the River and Lake tables

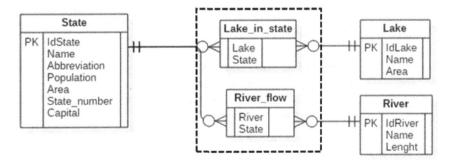

their respective primary keys. We observe that these tables are also in 3NF since there exists no transitive functional dependency among columns.

A similar situation to the previous one exists in the neighboring states (in an N:M relation). To model the neighboring states of a state, a new relationship between the Border and State tables was added in addition to the existing relationship between both tables, but now through the Border.border_state and State.IdState columns, as is shown in **Figure 9**. In this manner, the State and Border tables are in 2NF and, since there exists no transitive functional dependency in columns, we may also say that these tables are also in 3NF.

Figure 9. Normalization of the State and Border tables

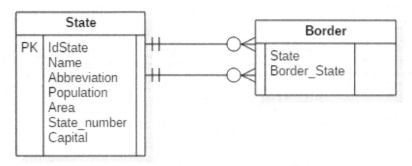

It is noteworthy that the addition of this new relationship generates a circular reference between the State and Border tables. For this reason, to enter data into these tables, the referential integrity in SQL Server was disabled for this new relationship (see **Figure 10**). A circular reference is a set of references where the last object references the first, resulting in a closed loop. Referential integrity protects the defined relationships between tables when records are created, modified, or eliminated. Enforced referential integrities prevent a user from entering a value into the referencing table that does not exist in the referenced table.

Figure 10. Referential integrity in SQL Server 2008

Due to the circular reference, an NLIDB must join both tables twice to retrieve the neighboring states of a state: one through the State.IdState−Border.State columns and the other through the Border. Border_State−State.IdState. For this reason, the NLIDB must be able to identify that both columns of Border table are foreign keys related to the same primary key, State.IdState. For example, the SQL query to retrieve the neighboring states of Alabama can be similar to the next code on SQL (Query 1):

Query 1:
Select c.Name
From State a, Border b, State c
Where a.IdState = b.State and a.Name = 'alabama' and b.Border_State = c.IdState

A similar situation to the previous one is in the Capital of every State. Instead of storing the capital name in the State.Capital column, a new relationship between the State and City tables was added, for which, the State.Capital column is used as a foreign key related to the primary key City.IdCity (see **Figure 11**). However, this new relationship generates a circular reference between both tables. Therefore, the referential integrity in SQL Server was disabled for this new relationship.

Figure 11. The new relationship between the State and City tables

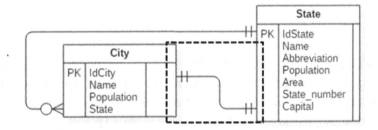

Modifications Made to Some Tables of Geobase

To design N-Geobase, we made minor modifications to Geobase, mainly in the HighLow table:

1. removing the four columns that store the name and elevation of the highest and lowest points per state, shown in **Figure 5,** and
2. adding only two columns to store the name and elevation of any point. The HighLow table modified is shown in **Figure 12**.

Figure 12. Modification of the Highlow table

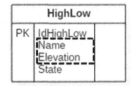

Figure 13. The Highest and the lowest points. a) The highest and lowest points in Montana are stored in Chandra Model; b) The same points are stored in our Schema.

state	state_abbreviation	highest_point	highest_elevation	lowest_point	lowest_elevation
massachisetts	ma	mount greylock	1064	atlantic ocean	0
michigan	mi	mount curwood	604	lake erie	174
minnesota	Mn	eagle mountain	701	lake superior	183
mississippi	ms	woodall mountain	246	gulf of mexico	0
missouri	mo	taum sauk mountain	540	st. francis river	70
montana	mt	granite peak	3901	kootenai river	549
nebraska	ne	johnson township	1654	southeast corner	256

a)

IdHighLow	Name	Elevation	State
25	woodall mountain	246	25
76	gulf of mexico	0	25
77	st. francis river	70	26
26	taum sauk mountain	540	26
27	granite peak	3901	27
78	kootenai river	549	27
79	southeast corner	256	28

b)

Figure 13a shows how information about the highest and lowest points in Montana could be stored in the Chandra schema. In this schema, both points are stored in only one record. **Figure 13b** shows how the same information is stored in our schema. Notice that in our schema, each point is stored in different records, which allows the possibility to store more than two points. In this example, the records containing the value 27 in the Highlow.State column corresponds to the state of Montana (Chandra & Mihalcea, 2006).

To retrieve information about the lowest or highest point in Montana, an NLIDB must be able to solve superlative queries by using the MIN() and MAX() aggregation functions in a SQL query. For example, the SQL query to retrieve the highest point in Montana could be similar to the following:

Figure 14. Modification of the State table

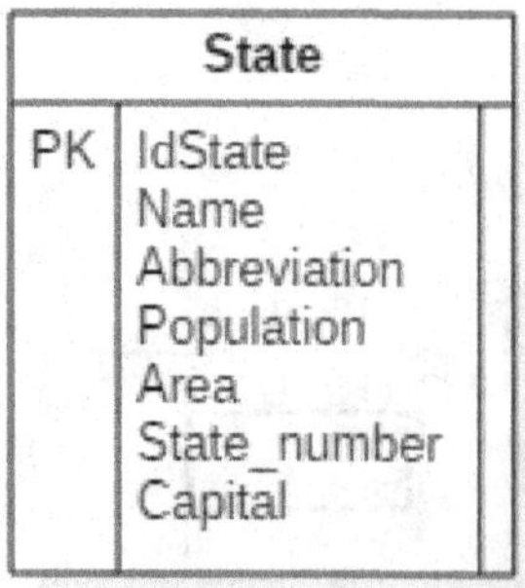

State		
PK	IdState	
	Name	
	Abbreviation	
	Population	
	Area	
	State_number	
	Capital	

Query 2:
Select a.Name, a.Elevation
From HighLow a, State b
Where a.State = b.IdState and b.Name ='montana' and a.Elevation = (**Select** MAX(a.Elevation)
From HighLow a, State b
Where a.State = b.IdState and b.Name = 'montana')

As can be seen, the modification made to the structure of the Highlow table implies an NLIDB identifying the highest or lowest point among the records corresponding to Montana. In a similar way to what we did in the Highlow table, the State table was modified. The city1, city2, city3, and city4 columns (shown in **Figure 6**) were deleted from this table. The State table modified is shown in **Figure 14**.

Figure 15. Relational schema of N-Geobase

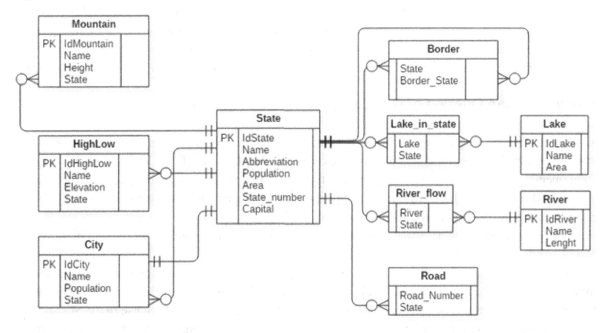

To retrieve information about the major cities of a state, an NLIDB must be able to automatically identify the information about cities by sorting in ascending order by city population. Based on the modifications described in this section, the relational schema of N-Geobase is composed of 10 tables, 11 table relationships, and 33 columns. The relational schema of N-Geobase is shown in **Figure 15**, and it was implemented in SQL Server 2008.

The Geoquery Corpus

Zelle and Mooney (1996), at the University of Texas, provided the Geoquery corpus. The corpus is based on a series of questions gathered from undergraduate students over an example US geography database named Geobase (described in Section 2). The corpus consists of natural language queries and equivalent logical formulas in Prolog. As we described before, there are two popular versions of Geoquery in the literature: Geoquery250 and Geoquery880, of which Geoquery250 is the most used. A small corpus is preferred to evaluate NLIDBs because it is desirable to manually enter all queries from the corpus in each NLIDB to be evaluated. Also, it is also necessary to check which queries were correctly answered for each NLIDB. For these reasons, the evaluation of NLIDBs is a very tedious task. However, Geoquery880 has more complex queries than Geoquery250 (Tang & Mooney, 2001). Although Geoquery880 has a larger number of queries, many of these have similar patterns. For example, the queries "How big is Alaska", "How big is New Mexico" and "How long is Rio Grande" have similar patterns. The difference between the first two queries is the referred state. The difference between these two queries concerning the third is that the first queries refer to the area or (the number of inhabitants of a state) while the third refers to the length of a river.

Queries with similar patterns are suitable to train NLIDBs based on techniques such as Learning Semantic Parsing, before interacting with users. However, this situation is indifferent to the NLIDBs based on knowledge about the relationship between the natural language and the database schema because they do not require training. It is noteworthy that if an NLIDB based on knowledge can correctly answer a query, it is probable that it can also correctly answer queries with similar patterns. As a consequence, it is possible that the performance of the NLIDB could be high. In the following subsections, we present the results of an analysis carried out in response to the queries of Geoquery250 and Geoquery880.

Analysis of the Queries of Geoquery250 and Geoquery880

To answer a natural language query, an NLIDB based on knowledge must be able to interpret or understand the query. To interpret a natural language query, the NLIDB must first identify database schema components implicitly mentioned by the user in the query (tables, columns, and values). Subsequently, the NLIDB must solve the natural language problems of the query to give semantic meaning to the components identified and to use them to build the SQL query.

Among these components, values are the most difficult to identify, since a query is no more than a bag of words without any sense for an NLIDB. For this reason, an NLIDB must have a mechanism to determine which word or words should be considered as a value. The identification of values is very important to generate the SQL query. This is because the values are used for filtering the information requested by the user. For this reason, values are directly part of the WHERE clause in the SQL query. When a value is not correctly identified or when it is wrongly processed, this could lead to displaying incorrect answers or showing additional information to the user, which could adversely affect their

Table 4. Value types in queries from Geoquery250 and Geoquery880

Characteristic	Geoquery250		Geoquery880	
	# queries	% queries	# queries	% queries
Any value	184	73.60%	578	65.68%
Simple value	158	63.20%	505	57.39%
Compound value	26	10.40%	73	8.30%
Different contiguous values	8	3.20%	30	3.41%

decisions. We consider as a value the words or sequences of words that are stored in any column in the database and are used by the user to formulate queries.

For this reason, with the aim of identifying, quantifying, and classifying the values, an analysis of each query of Geoquery250 and Geoquery880 was performed. This information is summarized in **Table 4**.

As can be seen in **Table 4**, most of the queries from both corpora contain at least one value (73.60% in Geoquery250 and 65.68% in Geoquery880). We define the three types of values identified as follows:

1. **Simple value.** It is a unique value in a query, and it is represented by a single word. For example, in the query "What states border Montana?", Montana is a value that is stored in the State.Name column. This type of value is found in 63.20% of the queries from Geoquery250 and 57.39% from Geoquery880.
2. **Compound value.** It is a unique value in a query, and it is composed of two or more contiguous words. This condition complicates the identification of values, since the NLIDB, apart from identifying that both words are values, must determine that both words should be considered as a single value. For example, in the query "What is the largest city in Rhode Island?" the Rhode and Island words should be considered as a single value, which is stored in the City.Name column. This type of value is found in 10.40% of the queries from Geoquery250 and 30% from Geoquery880.
3. **Different contiguous values.** These are different contiguous values in a query, and they are composed of one or more contiguous words. In this case, the NLIDB must identify the word or words representing each value and that they are different from each other. For example, in the query "What is the population of Springfield Missouri?" Springfield and Missouri are different values because Springfield is stored in the City.Name column and Missouri in the State.Name column. In this case, both values are represented by one word (i.e., the word "Springfield Missouri").

Types of Natural Language Problems

The queries from Geoquery250 and Geoquery880 were analyzed to identify the types of natural language problems that they have. The types of problems identified were the following: (a) ellipsis, (b) superlatives, (c) ambiguities, (d) aggregation operators, (e) reasoning, (f) negation operator, (g) calculating, and (h) comparison.

1. Ellipsis is the absence of information in a query. For example, in the query "Name the rivers in Arkansas" the user does not specify that Arkansas is a state; however, it is important to mention that an NLIDB could solve this problem based on the identification of values, identifying that Arkansas is a value stored in the State.Name column (as shown in **Figure 16**).

Figure 16. Ellipsis problem in Natural language

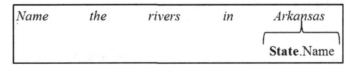

2. A superlative, in the context of NLIDBs, expresses the characteristic of a column in its maximum degree. For example, in the query "What is the highest mountain in Alaska?" the word "highest" is a superlative referring to the mountain with the largest numeric value is stored in the Mountain. Height column (as shown in **Figure 17**).

Figure 17. Superlative

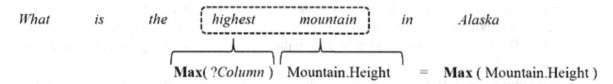

3. In Natural Language Processing, we say that "An ambiguity" occurs where there exists the possibility of interpreting an expression in two or more distinct ways. For example, in the query "What rivers run through New York?" New York is a value stored in the City.Name column and in the State.Name column (as shown in **Figure 18**), causing ambiguity. To disambiguate this situation, an NLIDB might display a clarification dialogue to the user to disambiguate.

Figure 18. Ambiguity in natural language queries. In this case, to answer a simple query about the rivers that through New York, an ambiguity occurs because, for SQL, there are two possible interpretations: New York as a city or as a state.

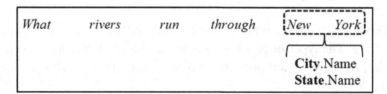

4. In Natural Language and particularly in NLIDBs, aggregation operators are defined as words that imply summarization based on the given information. Examples of these operators are counts, totals, and averages. For example, in the query "What is the total population of the states that border

Figure 19. Aggregation operator schema

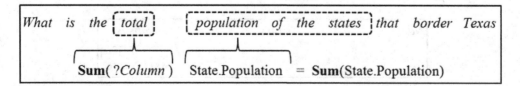

Texas?" the total word implies performing a sum of the populations of the states surrounding Texas (as shown in **Figure 19**).

5. We observe that a query requires reasoning when the interface must build the SQL query in a certain order. For example, in the query "What is the highest point of the state with the largest area?" the NLIDB must first determine what the state with the longest area is, and subsequently, it must determine the highest point in that state (**Figure 20**).

Figure 20. The reasoning process for the query "What is the highest point of the state with the largest area?". In this case, the NLIDB firstly determines the State in the USA with the largest area. Then, for this state, the highest point is determined.

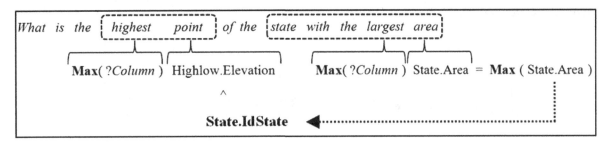

6. A negation has two possible implications for an NLIDB in Geoquery:
    a. To describe the first one, let us examine the next phrase: The query "Which is the highest peak not in Alaska?". In this case: We have the not negation represented by the word "not". This not negation establishes that Alaska value should be excluded from the answer to the query. This negation is easy to solve because, in Geobase, a point (either the highest or lowest point) belongs to one state. To answer this query, a SQL query similar to any of these (**Query 3 and 4**) is sufficient:
        Query 3:
        Select * From HighLow **Where** highest_elevation=(Select **MAX**(highest_elevation) **From** HighLow **Where** State <> 'alaska')
        Query 4:
        Select Top 1 * **From** Highlow **Where** State <> 'alaska' **Order By** highest_elevation **DESC**
    b. Let us explain the second implication of the negation operator with the next example: The query: "What is the longest river that does not run through Texas?". Here we found a "not negation" represented by the words "does not." A not negation as in this query is difficult to solve. In this example, the affirmative sentence deals with the words: "a river flows through different states". In this case, the red, Canadian, Rio Grande, Pecos, and Washita rivers flow through Texas, but these same rivers also flow through other states (e.g., the Canadian river also flows through the states of New Mexico and Oklahoma). Then, to answer this query, a SQL query similar to any of the previous SQL queries is wrong because only the records of these rivers flowing through Texas are discarded, but not the records of these same rivers

flowing through other states. So, incorrectly, these rivers are also part of the answer to the above query anyway. To correctly answer this query, the not negation defines that these rivers must be discarded; thus, a SQL query similar to the following is needed (**Query 5**):

Query 5:

Select * **From** River **Where** Name **Not in** (**Select** Name **From** River_flow **Where** State = 'texas' **Order By** Length **DESC**

7. In some queries, it is required to perform a calculation to obtain the requested information. The last situation occurs when the information requested is not directly stored in any column in the database. For example, in the query "What is the population density of Wyoming?", population density is a fact that does not exist in Geobase. However, this fact can be calculated by dividing the population of the state by its area (as shown in **Figure 21**). It is noteworthy that a domain-independent NLIDB must allow a user to define such calculations as part of its configuration on a database.

Figure 21. Calculation of Population Density

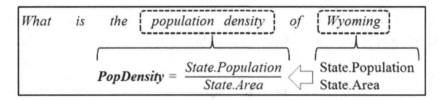

8. To answer a query involving a comparison, it requires identifying the comparison factor correctly, the point of comparison and the entity to be compared. For example, in the query "How many rivers in Texas are longer than the Red?"; the words "longer than" denote a comparison. The word "longer" indicates that the comparison factor is the size or length of both entities. The "red river length" is the point of comparison, and the" rivers in Texas" are the entities to be compared (**Figure 22**).

Figure 22. Comparison of two entities

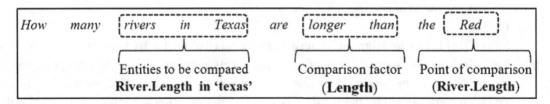

In **Table 5**, a classification of the queries of Geoquery250 and Geoquery880, according to the above-described problems, is presented.

As we can observe in **Table 5**, the distribution of queries for Geoquery250 and Geoquery880 is quite similar for each type of identified problems for both corpora. The difference is that Geoquery880 has a higher number of queries in each type of problem. Thus, Geoquery880 has more complex queries than

Table 5. Classification of natural language problems for the queries of Geoquery880 and Geoquery250

Type of natural language problem	Geoquery250		Geoquery880	
	# queries	%	# queries	%
Aggregation operator	30	12.20%	130	14.77%
Ambiguity	49	19.92%	143	16.25%
Calculating	1	0.41%	8	0.91%
Comparison	1	0.41%	8	0.91%
Ellipsis	154	62.60%	482	54.77%
Negation	1	0.41%	13	1.48%
Reasoning	13	5.28%	127	14.43%
Superlative	113	45.93%	443	50.34%

Geoquery250 because the former has a greater variety of queries than the second (Tang & Mooney, 2001). For this reason, we planned to develop a corpus of queries that preserves the same type of problems than Geoquery880 with the aim of offering a greater challenge than Geoquery250. In the following section, the criteria used to form the proposed corpus, named Geoquery270, are shown.

Geoquery270 Corpus

Geoquery270 is a subset of 270 queries extracted from Geoquery880. As we described and showed before in **Table 5**, Geoquery880 has a wider range of queries, and they are more complex for each type of problem than Geoquery250 (Tang & Mooney, 2001). Among this variety of queries, Geoquery270 was formed by selecting representative queries from each type of problem. To select the queries, these were filtered during different phases:

- The first phase consists of filtering repeated queries syntactically. At this stage, only the queries "Give me the cities in Virginia", "Name all the rivers in Colorado", "Name the rivers in Arkansas" were repeated, so it was only possible to filter three queries of the 880.
- The second phase consists of filtering the remaining queries according to the database components (tables, columns, and values) implicitly mentioned in each query and according to the types of problems that each query has (superlative, negation, aggregation, etc.). To this end, each word

Figure 23. Example of replaced queries

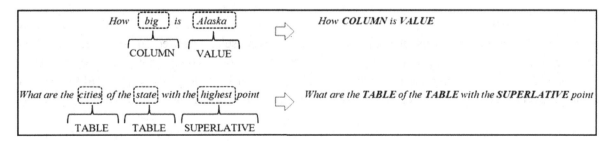

representing any database component or any problem was replaced with the name of the database component or of the type of problem that it represents (**Figure 23**).

For example, in the first query shown in **Figure 24**, "How big is Alaska?", the big word is replaced with the COLUMN word since the big word refers to a column (State.Area), and the Alaska word is replaced with the VALUE word since Alaska is a value stored in the State.Name column. In this way, all database components and all types of problems were manually replaced in all queries of Geoquery880. Subsequently, the repeated replaced queries were filtered. For example, queries in **Table 6** are repeated, so only some of them were selected, and the remaining queries were filtered.

Table 6. Repeated replaced queries

Original query	Replaced query
how *big* is *Alaska*	how *COLUMN* is *VALUE*
how *big* is *new Mexico*	how *COLUMN* is *VALUE*
how *tall* is *mount McKinley*	how *COLUMN* is *VALUE*
how *large* is *Alaska*	how *COLUMN* is *VALUE*
how *long* is *Rio Grande*	how *COLUMN* is *VALUE*
how *high* is *Guadalupe peak*	how *COLUMN* is *VALUE*

Although in this second phase the number of queries was reduced to 451, there were still too many queries. Some of them have the same structure, although they syntactically differ in some words that we consider will not affect their interpretation. **Table 7** shows three queries that have the same structure TABLE-TABLE-SUPERLATIVE (TTS considering the initials of each component). However, they are different in the following: in the first query, the words "are" and "the" appear. In the second, only the word "is" appears. In the third query, the word "is" is followed by the word "the".

Table 7. Replaced queries with the same components but syntactically different

Query	Components
what *are* the *TABLE* of the *TABLE* with the *SUPERLATIVE* point	TTS
what *is* *TABLE* of the *TABLE* with the *SUPERLATIVE* point	TTS
what is the *TABLE* of the *TABLE* with the *SUPERLATIVE* point	TTS

Therefore, the third and final phase consists of ordering all replaced queries based on the initials of its components. Subsequently, some queries from each group were selected based on our criterion. In this way, we aim to preserve the structure and all types of problems from Geoquery880 in our corpus. After this last phase, the remaining queries were selected to form our Geoquery270 corpus. **Table 8** shows a comparison of the percentages of the three corpora. Columns two and three show again the percentages of Geoquery250 and columns four and five the percentages of Geoquery880 (shown in **Table 5**). Columns six and seven show the percentages corresponding to our corpus.

Table 8. Classification of the types of natural language problems in the queries of our corpus Geoquery270.

Type of natural language problem	Geoquery250		Geoquery880		Geoquery270	
	# queries	%	# queries	%	# queries	%
Superlative	113	45.93%	443	50.34%	92	47.92%
Ellipsis	154	62.60%	482	54.77%	89	46.35%
Reasoning	13	5.28%	127	14.43%	40	20.83%
Aggregation operator	30	12.20%	130	14.77%	40	20.83%
Ambiguity	49	19.92%	143	16.25%	30	15.63%
Negation	1	0.41%	13	1.48%	4	2.08%
Comparison	1	0.41%	8	0.91%	3	1.56%
Calculating	1	0.41%	8	0.91%	3	1.56%

As we can see in **Table 8**, Geoquery270 preserves the same structure and types of problems than Geoquery880 in just 270 queries.

Experimentation

Since, in this paper, two resources are proposed: (a) the normalized relational database N-Geobase, and (b) the Geoquery270 corpus, this section is divided into two subsections.

Then, in Subsection 6.1, we present the evaluation of N-Geobase and, in Subsection 6.2, we present the evaluation of Geoquery270.

N-Geobase Evaluation

Due to the fact that the normalization of N-Geobase makes its schema similar to the schema of databases used by enterprises, we can obviously suppose that N-Geobase is more complex (for a particular NLIDB) than the schemas described in Section 2.2. To prove this statement and validate the design of N-Geobase, we compared the performance of our NLIDB by configuring it on N-Geobase and also on one of the two schemas previously described in Subsection 2.2. In this step, we used the Chandra schema for the next reasons:

1. Chandra schema has the best normalization, and
2. Chandra schema is most similar to the original structure of Geobase (described in **Table 2**).

For using Chandra Schema, we implemented it on a SQL Server 2008 database based on the entity-relationship diagram (**Figure 2a**). We used SQL Server 2008 because our NLIDB has been evaluated before in this Database Management System. We observe that both databases contain the same information (migrated directly from the original version of Geobase); in fact, the only difference between them is the structure of each relational schema.

The evaluation made in this work basically consisted of introducing our NLIDB on the Chandra schema (Chandra & Mihalcea, 2006) and, subsequently, all the queries of GeoQuery250. To measure the performance, we considered the percentage of queries correctly answered by the NLIDB. Among the precision and recall metrics in the literature, we used the recall formula to measure performance, which is expressed in equation (1).

$$Recall = \frac{Number\ of\ correctly\ answered\ queries}{Total\ number\ of\ queries} * 100 \# \tag{1}$$

We used the recall metric because it measures the real effectiveness of an NLIDB since it considers the number of correctly-answered queries by an NLIDB concerning the total number of introduced queries.

The results obtained from the evaluation are shown in **Table 9**, which shows the number of correctly-answered queries, incorrectly-answered queries, and the percentage of recall obtained by our NLIDB in each database used.

Table 9. Performance of our NLIDB on both Schema: N-Geobase and Chandra

Database	Correctly Answered	Incorrectly Answered	Recall (in %)
Chandra	216	34	86.40
N-Geobase	136	114	54.40

As we can observe in **Table 9**, our NLIDB obtained an 86.40% success rate on the Chandra model and 54.40% on N-Geobase. This significant decrease is due to the performance of our NLIDB, which was affected (as shown in **Table 10**) by the modifications described in Section 3.

Table 10. Causes affecting the performance of the NLIDB

Details	Normalization					Modified tables	
	State/Border	State/Capital	Lake	Road	River	Highlow	Major cities
Queries	24	40	0	0	0	0	10
Percentage	32.43	54.05	0	0	0	0	13.51

As we show in **Table 10**, the performance of the NLIDB on N-Geobase was not affected by the modifications made to the tables, described in Subsection 3.2, because our NLIDB can solve superlatives. Otherwise, their performance may be even lower. However, the main cause that adversely affected the performance was the normalization of the Border and State tables (described in Section 3.1), since the NLIDB was not able to answer queries like:

- "What states border Montana?", "What is the biggest city in Georgia?".
- "What is the population of Seattle Washington?", "What is the capital of Washington?".
- "What are the major cities in Texas?", "Which state has the largest city?".

Based on the performance of our NLIDB (**Table 9**) and on the causes that affected its performance (**Table 10**), we can say that the normalization and the modifications described in Section 3 makes the N-Geobase schema more complex than the existing in the literature and similar to the schemas of databases used by enterprises. Therefore, N-Geobase could be used as a standard resource in the evaluation of NLIDBs, since it could give a clearer idea of the real performance of an NLIDB on relational databases used by enterprises.

Geoquery270 Evaluation

Since Geoquery270 preserves the same structure and types of problems as Geoquery880, Geoquery270 should be more challenging than Geoquery250. To prove this statement and validate our corpus, we compared the performance of our NLIDB using our corpus and using the Geoquery250 corpus. The database schema used was the Chandra schema (Chandra & Mihalcea, 2006). The evaluation consisted of introducing to our NLIDB all queries of our corpus and all queries of Geoquery250. In the same way, as in Subsection 6.1, we considered the percentage of queries correctly answered by the NLIDB and the recall formula as a metric to measure the performance.

The results obtained from the evaluation are shown in **Table 11**, presenting the number of queries correctly and incorrectly answered and the percentage of recall obtained by our NLIDB in each corpus used.

Table 11. Performance of our NLIDB using Geoquery270 and using Geoquery250

Corpus	Correctly Answered	Incorrectly Answered	Recall (in %)
Geoquery250	216	34	86.40
Geoquery270	142	128	52.59

According to **Table 11**, our NLIDB obtained a 52.59% success rate using our corpus and 86.40% using Geoquery250. This significant decrease is due to the fact that Geoquery270 integrates more complex queries than Geoquery250. Based on these results, we can say that our corpus is more challenging than Geoquery250. Therefore, Geoquery270 could be used as a standard resource in the evaluation of NLIDBs.

CONCLUSION

The first challenge of NLIDBs is to take a query in natural language and translated it into a well-formed query in SQL. In practice, the researchers are using different strategies to achieve them. The second challenge is how to test the improvement in efficiency and performance among NLIDBs systems. In this sense, it is important to have well-designed databases and a corpus of queries that, without being excessive, are complex for the scientific community to test their systems. Also, databases and query corpus are resources widely recognized and indispensable to evaluate the performance of Natural Language Interfaces to Databases. However, there are few resources available in the literature because, in many cases, the resources are designed for specific uses, and they are not available to the scientific community on NLIDBs. For this reason, it is difficult to find resources considered as a standard in the literature. As a consequence, the evaluation and comparison between NLIDBs are difficult to perform.

Among the existing resources in the literature, the deductive database, Geobase, and its corpus, Geoquery, are resources commonly used to evaluate NLIDBs. Because deductive databases such as Geobase are much less used than relational databases, Geobase has been migrated to different relational schemas. These schemas differ from each other, and they present some issues that can be improved. These issues could indirectly lead to NLIDBs getting a good performance from them. For this reason, we propose N-Geobase to be considered as a standard to evaluate the performance of Natural Language Interfaces to Databases. N-Geobase is a relational database migrated from Geobase following the standards of normalization of databases. The normalization of N-Geobase makes its schema similar to the schema of databases used by enterprises, making it more complicated than the relational schemas.

To validate the complexity of N-Geobase, we compared the performance of our NLIDB on N-Geobase, and the relational schema migrated from Geobase previously published and described in the paper. The difference between both schemas is the normalization of each of them since both contain the same information. The results indicate that N-Geobase is the most complex because the performance of our NLIDB significantly decreased in this schema. On the other hand, referring to the two versions of Geoquery, Geoquery250 is the most common corpus used to evaluate NLIDBs; this is because Geoquery250 has fewer queries than Geoquery880. Then this condition is desirable to make less tedious the evaluation of NLIDBs. However, as was known, Geoquery880 includes more complex queries than Geoquery250. For this reason, we propose Geoquery270, which was designed with the aim of preserving the same types of natural language problems as Geoquery880 and offering a greater challenge than Geoquery250 in just 270 queries. We compared the performance of our NLIDB using Geoquery270 and Geoquery250. The results indicate that Geoquery270 is the most complex because the performance of our NLIDB significantly decreased using this corpus.

As the final reflections, we state the following:

1. The schema of a database is an important factor affecting the performance of an NLIDB. This was tested with the experiment described in the paper with data from Geoquery250 and Geoquery270. These two databases have the same information, and the only difference between them is their normalization.

2. As is shown in the experimentation section, the proposed resources, N-Geobase and Geoquery270 offer a greater challenge to NLIDBs. Thus, they could be considered as standard resources in the evaluation of NLIDBs. Evaluate an NLIDB in N-Geobase could provide an idea of its performance

on databases used by enterprises. Also, Geoquery270 would allow evaluating an NLIDB in all types of problems of Geoquery880 with fewer queries.

Data Availability

The Geoquery270 data used to support the findings of this study have been deposited in the Dropbox repository (https://drive.google.com/open?id=1Jz5uUhYwFkQldHSLYCWj2W4YyFpp1GRr).

Conflicts of Interest

The authors declare that they have no competing interests.

ACKNOWLEDGMENT

We acknowledge the financial support from CONACYT Mexico and the National Technological of Mexico.

REFERENCES

Androutsopoulos, I., Ritchie, G. D., & Thanisch, P. (1995). Natural language interfaces to databases–an introduction. *Natural Language Engineering*, *1*(1), 29–81. doi:10.1017/S135132490000005X

Bais, H., Machkour, M., & Koutti, L. (2016). A Model of a Generic Natural Language Interface for Querying Database. *International Journal of Intelligent Systems and Applications*, *8*(2), 35–44. doi:10.5815/ijisa.2016.02.05

Bates, M. (1989). Rapid porting of the parlance natural language interface. *Proceedings of the workshop on Speech and Natural Language*, 83-88. 10.3115/100964.100966

Bernstein, A., Kaufmann, E., & Kaiser, C. (2005). Querying the semantic web with ginseng: A guided input natural language search engine. *15th Workshop on Information Technologies and Systems*, 112-126.

Bhootra, R. A., & Parker, L. (2004). *Natural language interfaces: comparing english language front end and english query* (Doctoral dissertation). Virginia Commonwealth University.

Bobrow, R. J., Resnik, P., & Weischedel, R. M. (1990). Multiple underlying systems: Translating user requests into programs to produce answers. *Proceedings of the 28th annual meeting on Association for Computational Linguistics*, 227-234. 10.3115/981823.981852

Borland International. (1988). *Turbo Prolog 2.0 Reference Guide*. Scotts Valley.

Chandra, Y., & Mihalcea, R. (2006). Natural language interfaces to databases. Masters Abstracts International, 45(4).

Cimiano, P., Haase, P., & Heizmann, J. (2007). Porting natural language interfaces between domains: an experimental user study with the orakel system. *Proceedings of the 12th international conference on Intelligent user interfaces*, 180-189. 10.1145/1216295.1216330

Codd, E. F. (1972). Further normalization of the data base relational model. *Data Base Systems*, 33-64.

Consortium, L. D. (2019). *Linguistic Data Consortium.* Retrieved from https://catalog.ldc.upenn.edu/

Damljanovic, D., Agatonovic, M., & Cunningham, H. (2010). Natural language interfaces to ontologies: Combining syntactic analysis and ontology-based lookup through the user interaction. *Extended Semantic Web Conference*, 106-120.

Ge, R., & Mooney, R. J. (2005). A statistical semantic parser that integrates syntax and semantics. *Proceedings of the ninth conference on computational natural language learning*, 9-16. 10.3115/1706543.1706546

Giordani, A., & Moschitti, A. (2009). Semantic mapping between natural language questions and SQL queries via syntactic pairing. In *International Conference on Application of Natural Language to Information Systems*, (pp. 207-221). Springer.

Green, B. F., Jr., Wolf, A. K., Chomsky, C., & Laugh, K. (1961). Baseball: an automatic question-answerer. *Papers presented at the May 9-11, western joint IRE-AIEE-ACM computer conference*, 219-224. 10.1145/1460690.1460714

Grosz, B. J., Appelt, D. E., Martin, P. A., & Pereira, F. C. (1987). TEAM: an experiment in the design of transportable natural-language interfaces. *Artificial Intelligence, 32*(2), 173–243. doi.org/10.1016/0004-3702(87)90011-7

Hemphill, C., Godfrey, J., & Doddington, G. (n.d.). *The ATIS Spoken Language Systems Pilot Corpus.* Retrieved from: https://catalog.ldc.upenn.edu/docs/LDC93S4B/corpus.htmlhttps

Jaydeep, S., Oscan, F., Quamar, A., Stager, G., Mittal, A., Jammi, M., …Sankaranarayanan, K. (2019). Natural Language Querying of Complex Business Intelligence Queries. In *SIGMOD'19 Proceedings of the 2019 International Conference on Management of Data* (pp. 1997–2000). 10.1145/3299869.3320248

Kate, R. J., & Mooney, R. J. (2006). Using string-kernels for learning semantic parsers. *Proceedings of the 21st International Conference on Computational Linguistics and the 44th annual meeting of the Association for Computational Linguistics*, 913-920.

Kaufmann, E., Bernstein, A., & Fischer, L. (2007). NLP-Reduce: A naive but domain independent natural language interface for querying ontologies. *4th European Semantic Web Conference (ESWC).*

Kaufmann, E., Bernstein, A., & Zumstein, R. (2006). Querix: A natural language interface to query ontologies based on clarification dialogs. *5th International Semantic Web Conference (ISWC 2006)*, 980-981. 10.1007/11926078_78

Kubala, F., Barry, C., Bates, M., Bobrow, R., Fung, P., Ingria, R., ... Stallard, D. (1992). BBN Byblos and HARC February 1992 ATIS benchmark results. *Proceedings of the workshop on Speech and Natural Language*, 72-77. 10.3115/1075527.1075544

Minock, M., Olofsson, P., & Näslund, A. (2008). Towards building robust natural language interfaces to databases. In *International Conference on Application of Natural Language to Information Systems*, (pp. 187-198). Springer. 10.1007/978-3-540-69858-6_19

Murveit, H., Butzberger, J., & Weintraub, M. (1991). Speech Recognition in SRI's Resource Management and ATIS Systems. *Proceedings of the workshop on Speech and Natural Language (HTL'91),* 94-100. Retrieved from: https://www.aclweb.org/anthology/H91-1015.pdf

Nihalani, N., Motwani, M., & Silaka, S. (2011). Natural language interface to database using semantic matching. *International Journal of Computers and Applications, 31*(11), 29–34.

Popescu, A. M., Armanasu, A., Etzioni, O., Ko, D., & Yates, A. (2004). Modern natural language interfaces to databases: Composing statistical parsing with semantic tractability. *Proceedings of the 20th international conference on Computational Linguistics.* 10.3115/1220355.1220376

Porras, J., Florencia-Juárez, R., Rivera, G., & García, V. (2018). Interfaz de lenguaje natural para consultar cubos multidimensionales utilizando procesamiento analítico en línea. *Research in Computing Science, 147*(6), 153–165. doi:10.13053/rcs-147-6-12

Seneff, S., Glass, J., Goddeau, D., Goodine, D., Hirschman, L., Leung, H., & Zue, V. (1991). Development and Preliminary Evaluation of the MIT ATIS System. *Speech and Natural Language: Proceedings of a Workshop Held at Pacific Grove.* 10.3115/112405.112417

Software, E. L. F. (2002). *Demo Gallery.* Retrieved from http://www.elfsoft.com/help/accelf/Overview.htm

Stratica, N., Kosseim, L., & Desai, B. C. (2005). Using semantic templates for a natural language interface to the Cindi virtual library. *Data & Knowledge Engineering, 55*(1), 4–19. doi:10.1016/j.datak.2004.12.002

Sujatha, B., & Raju, S. (2016). Ontology based natural language interface for relational databases. *Procedia Computer Science, 92,* 487–492. doi:10.1016/j.procs.2016.07.372

Tan, J. J., Lane, H., & Rijanto, A. (2019). *Report on NLIDBs.* Retrieved from http://www.elfsoft.com/Resources/References.htm

Tang, L. R., & Mooney, R. J. (2001). Using multiple clause constructors in inductive logic programming for semantic parsing. In *European Conference on Machine Learning,* (pp. 466-477). Springer. 10.1007/3-540-44795-4_40

Technology, L. (1997). *English Wizard – Dictionary Administrator's Guide.* Linguistic Technology Corp.

Thompson, C. (2003). Acquiring word-meaning mappings for natural language interfaces. *Journal of Artificial Intelligence Research, 18*(1), 1–44. doi:10.1613/jair.1063

Tzoukermann, E. (1991). The use of a commercial natural language interface in the ATIS task. *Speech and Natural Language: Proceedings of a Workshop Held at Pacific Grove,* 134-137. 10.3115/112405.112425

Wang, C., Xiong, M., Zhou, Q., & Yu, Y. (2007). Panto: A portable natural language interface to ontologies. In *European Semantic Web Conference,* (pp. 473-487). Springer. 10.1007/978-3-540-72667-8_34

Ward, W. (1991). Evaluation of the CMU ATIS System. *Speech and Natural Language: Proceedings of a Workshop,* 19-22.

Warren, D. H. (1981). Efficient processing of interactive relational data base queries expressed in logic. *Proceedings of the seventh international conference on Very Large Data Bases,* 272-281.

Wong, Y. W., & Mooney, R. J. (2006). Learning for semantic parsing with statistical machine translation. *Proceedings of the main conference on Human Language Technology Conference of the North American Chapter of the Association of Computational Linguistics*, 439-446. 10.3115/1220835.1220891

Woods, W. A., Kaplan, R. M., & Nash-Webber, B. (1972). T*he lunar sciences natural language information system.* BBN Report.

Zelle, J. M., & Mooney, R. J. (1996). Learning to parse database queries using inductive logic programming. *Proceedings of the national conference on artificial intelligence*, 1050-1055.

Chapter 5

Chatbot for the Improvement of Conversational Skills of Japanese Language Learners

Ossiel Villanueva-Mendoza
Universidad Autónoma de Ciudad Juárez, Mexico

Martha Victoria González
(iD) https://orcid.org/0000-0002-9366-9998
Universidad Autónoma de Ciudad Juárez, Mexico

Maritza Varela
Universidad Autónoma de Ciudad Juárez, Mexico

Lucero Zamora
Universidad Autónoma de Ciudad Juárez, Mexico

ABSTRACT

Conversation practice is essential for second-language acquisition and necessary for learners to reach an acceptable communicative level. In an ideal scenario, students should regularly hold conversations with native speakers of the target language, but this is often not possible. Although the teachers use the target language during the classes, they cannot offer a continuous conversation with each student, and they are usually not available wherever and whenever the student requires them to practice. This chapter presents the development and use of a mobile application to hold conversations in the Japanese language. The objective is to provide a software tool to improve the level of communicative competence (both inside and outside a classroom environment). So, the authors created and used a conversational agent (chatbot) using Dialogflow (a Google API), which is connected to the application's interface through the Internet using a client access token to give responses to user inputs in real time.

DOI: 10.4018/978-1-7998-4730-4.ch005

Copyright © 2021, IGI Global. Copying or distributing in print or electronic forms without written permission of IGI Global is prohibited.

INTRODUCTION

The Japanese language occupies the second place in being the fastest language in the world, just below Spanish (CourseFinders, 2017). This is why the domain of the conversational area (both spoken and heard) becomes really important to obtain an optimal communicative competence for the exchange of ideas in this language.

The main problem discussed here is that, in the specific case of the Japanese classes of the Subdirección de Lenguas Extranjeras de la Universidad Autónoma de Ciudad Juárez, the conversation is one of the areas that is least practiced, there are even cases where this is not evaluated or is given very little importance. Due to this, it is determined as the objective of this document, the creation and implementation of the chatbot previously mentioned, which will be used as a teacher support tool and does not intend to replace them.

A chatbot is a software that simulates a real person and can hold conversations with users for various purposes. These have been used for teaching a second language on several occasions, clear examples of this are the use of chatbot "SoyDiego" for teaching Spanish in Sweden, as well as the use of the chatbot "Lucy" for teaching English in China.

This paper describes the implementation of a chatbot in a mobile application capable of holding conversations in the Japanese language. The chatbot was designed as a support tool so that, through their interaction, the Japanese language students have the possibility of increasing their level of communicative competence. Its knowledge base was modeled from the contents of the books *Minna no Nihongo: Shokyu II* and *Minna no Nihongo: Chukyu I.*

BACKGROUND

It is estimated that around 7,000 different languages are spoken worldwide. 90% of these are spoken by less than 100,000 people, such as those from tribes or populations with different dialects. From 150 to 200 languages are spoken by one million people, while 46 types of language are spoken by only one individual (BBC, 2014).

With around 128 million speakers, of which 127 million are native, Japan occupies the eleventh place worldwide. As you can see, it is a language that is around 99% concentrated in its country of origin, but whose importance remains in the fact that it is currently positioned as the third world power and is expected to continue in that position in the following years (Portillo, 2019).

Due to the globalization that has been generated in recent decades and the need for communication that this represents, technologies have been developed to facilitate the learning of a foreign language or that directly facilitate communication between people who do not speak the same language. Although chatbots (or chatterbots) have been used for different purposes for several years, little has been said about their participation as assistants for the practice of a foreign language, especially through the use of inputs and outputs using voice.

In the work of Angga, Fachri, Angga, Suryadi, and Agushinta (2015), it is mentioned that text inputs generated by users to interact with chatbots are considered inefficient because the conversation becomes unnatural and uninteresting for the user. Based on this, the author proposed the use of a voice interface, which uses technologies such as the recognition and generation of spoken language to obtain the inputs and generate the appropriate outputs. A third-dimensional avatar was integrated, capable of generating different facial expressions in real-time to give the user experience closer to a conversation with a human being. The author proposes the use of webcams in future designs as an additional tool to analyze the emotions and reactions of the user. It should be noted that this design was focused on the customer service area and not on teaching.

Wang (2008) emphasizes the idea of chatbots as a tool for learning a foreign language because they are useful to practice conversation, but do not intend to take the place of the teacher. The study is supported using Lucy software, a digital English language tutor. This system uses, as seen in the design of Angga et al. (2015), voice recognition and a graphical interface. It is worth mentioning that the author did not deeply explain how it was created or what programming tools were used. To validate his study, the author performed interaction tests between Lucy and five students of Chinese origin. The results revealed that students feel more confident during a conversation in which they are not being evaluated or when their mistakes are not pointed out directly. This freedom allows them to feel more relaxed when engaging in a real conversation in the target language, in addition to the fact that students usually correct their mistakes by imitating the way the chatbot speaks.

The work of Fryer (2006) explains the functionality of Jabberwacky, a chatbot predecessor of Cleverbot, who learns after the interaction he has with users, so the amount of conversation patterns he knows depends not only on the programmer but also on the individuals it interacts with. Because of this, Jabberwacky gives the opportunity for the user to create and train their own bot, so that it is even possible to teach him to respond to grammatical or spelling mistakes. Although the methods that were used for its creation are not mentioned, there is an emphasis on the fact that, unlike other chatbots already existing at the time of its development, it is not created using Artificial Intelligence Markup Language (AIML). Fryer mentions that, because the chatterbots were created with the purpose of engaging in conversations with native speakers, their use in the teaching of a foreign language is more useful for more experienced students. Based on this, the author proposes some ways in which this type of software can be included as another learning tool in the classroom. One of his most important arguments points out that much of the content seen in class is often not reviewed again, so using chatbots to recapitulate specific topics can boost knowledge retention through practice. On the other hand, as a solution to the problem of not having a method of direct evaluation when using this technology, Fryer proposes to use the transcription of audio to text that some systems such as Jabberwacky offer, so that the teacher can review and give feedback regarding the conversation. However, this idea can reduce the level of confidence that the students may have when talking to the chatbot, since they would know that everything they say will be read and evaluated by their teacher.

One of the problems that Löwgren (2013) points out regarding the teaching of a second language is that, commonly, students do not speak the target language within the classroom if the teacher does not. Even if they did, just listening to the language in class is not enough to acquire it, since this represents a few hours a week, in addition to not necessarily implying that the student is involved in a real conversation. Löwgren's study is based on the use of SoyDiego for teaching Spanish as a foreign language in Sweden (although it should be noted that this software was not created specifically for this purpose). SoyDiego, created by the company Botgens, uses a common interface in which the inputs and outputs are through text, but the latter is accompanied by a robotic voice that simulates the character. This study was conducted by presenting this system as a tool for second language acquisition to several Spanish teachers in Swedish universities. After allowing them to do tests, they were conducted a survey, in which it was revealed that 90% of them believe that a chatbot could be a good tool to develop students' communicative competence. It is also mentioned that, when working with current technologies, because they cannot create a perfect simulation, certain suggestions should be followed to get the most out of them, such as:

- That the teachers explain to their students the limitations of the system.
- Ask the chatbot questions about their likes, personal data, personality, etc.
- Ask about topics that interest them.
- Try to keep the conversation as long as possible.
- Try to use the most advanced topics that have been seen in class.

On the other hand, the creation of chatbots for teaching English in China has also been explored. Jia (2009) developed a software called Computer Simulation for Educational Communication (CSIEC). The author proposes the use of Natural Language Markup Language (NLML), to create bots that not only match the user's words to give an answer but also be able to mark and analyze grammatical elements (phrases), their relationship with other linguistic information (words, type, context, etc.), as well as factors such as the mood. Jia proposed the use of three different databases in MySQL Server, which help the software to be able to retain information about the user, about general issues or common sense, and about its own personality. In this way, CSIEC addresses the problem that chatbots are commonly designed to interact with humans, but not to interact as humans. In other words, by giving it a personality, its responses become more human. Unfortunately, this particular system only integrates interaction through text, so, unlike the design proposed by Angga et al. (2015), it moves further away, in that sense, from being able to have a conversation as close to reality as possible. To measure the quality of the conversations that students had with CSIEC, Jia uses the duration of the conversation, which takes into account the number of rounds of each user, as well as the time spent on them; being considered a round every time there is an input provided by the user and its corresponding output by the chatbot. On the other hand, as expected, it was revealed that 66% of users preferred to do so without receiving corrections regarding grammar or spelling. CSIEC was tested at universities and colleges in China, where students indicated that their use could help them with course reviews, improve their listening skills, and boost their interest in English language learning. It should be noted that 60.5% of the students stated that they would continue to use the system after school, even without their teacher's request.

It can be noted that chatbots that have been designed directly for the teaching of a foreign language normally lack an interface that communicates through audio. On the other hand, although there are currently systems such as Cleverbot (Hill, Ford, & Ferreras, 2015), which has learned conversational patterns of the Japanese language through its interaction with users of this language; or Rinna (McKirdy, 2015) from Microsoft, a bot entirely in Japanese and with the purpose of simulating the thought model of the human brain; no artificial intelligence that functions as an assistant for learning that language has been found in the literature review.

This chapter is focused on the development of conversational skills of the students, so it would be convenient to discuss some of the techniques used for language learning. Learning strategies are steps taken by the learner to aid the acquisition, storage, and retrieval of information (Rigney, 1978). Strategies are referred to as learning techniques, behaviors, or actions; or learning-to-learn, problem-solving, or study skills. No matter what they are called, strategies can make learning more efficient and effective (Oxford & Crookall, 2014).

Some of the most common strategies for conversational skills improvement are interviews and thinking aloud. Instead of observing or intuiting, some researchers have asked the learner to explain or describe how he or she uses strategies. One way to do this is to interview learners; another is to listen to learners as they think aloud; yet another is to combine the two procedures.

In the studies made by Naiman, Frohlich and Todesco (1975), a group of Toronto was interviewed with a structure divided into two parts: a biographical interview and a discussion of strategies that participants would use in hypothetical language learning situations. The researchers listed six strategies as keys to success:

1. finding a set of learning preferences and selecting language situations that allow those preferences to be used;
2. becoming actively involved in the language learning process;
3. developing an awareness of language both as a formal system of rules and as a means of communication;
4. constantly extending and revising the individual understanding of the target language system;
5. gradually developing the new language into a reference system and learning to think in it;
6. addressing the affective demands of language learning.

Cohen and Hosenfeld (1981) offered a useful model for interviewing, which can be used to gather data on mentalistic or unobservable processes. The three dimensions of this model are:

-   Activities: thinking aloud, in which the subjects verbalize thoughts freely (a sort of stream of consciousness) and self-observation, in which the subjects analyze their own thoughts to some degree.
-   Time: Different amounts of time can elapse between the use of a strategy and its verbalization. The smallest time-lapse is with think-aloud data. For self-observation data, verbalized analysis of the strategy can be immediate (introspection), or it can take place later (retrospection) and is then subject to some forgetting of detail.
-   Content: i.e., the topic of the interview (often influenced by the researcher).

Wenden (1985) employed a semi-structured interview to assess the strategies of her students. Before the interview, she gave students a list of topics to be covered in the interview. Students completed a grid of their daily activities (e.g., watching TV, talking to friends) and the kind of strategies they used in each one. During the interview, the learners focused on the information in the grid, using a form of retrospection. In one instance, Wenden interviewed a young Spanish economist who was learning English; as the young man talked, Wenden clustered his strategies into cognitive, communication, global practice, and metacognitive categories.

These strategies, although sometimes can be combined with others like note-taking, tend to need a conversational partner or an evaluator, since they need someone to interact within the target language. It is here where a chatbot can be useful in an environment where there are no native speakers.

MAIN FOCUS OF THE CHAPTER

One of the best ways to learn a foreign language is through dialogue with native speakers (Jia, 2009), which is often not possible. Currently, there are technologies that allow communication between people from all over the world, and that are often even specifically for learning a foreign language. Unfortunately, factors as simple as time difference, student shyness or fear of being judged make this method quite difficult.

The lack of practice of the conversation of a foreign language causes that the students do not reach an optimal level of communicative competence (Löwgren, 2013). Teachers, no matter how much they use the target language during classes, cannot offer a continuous conversation with each of the students (Fryer, 2006), and even if they did, the amount of weekly practice time is very low (Löwgren, 2013). Many teachers choose to make the students talk to each other, but this is usually a slow process, without grammar evaluation or pronunciation, not very interactive due to predefined structures, and that is only carried out for a few moments or, at best of the cases, during the time assigned for the class (Fryer, 2006).

USING A CHATBOT FOR JAPANESE LANGUAGE PRACTICE

Being Japan the place with the best tourism in Asia and the fourth-best in the world (World Economic Forum, 2017), it is a place that arouses the interest of millions of people around the globe.

In addition, considering the good relationship that it has maintained with México over the years, and its positive position on the idea of receiving more foreigners to work there from April 2019, growth opportunities have been increasing (International Press en Español, 2018). But, as expected for those seeking adventure on the other side of the world, mastery of the Japanese language is essential to work in the country, at least in places outside the tourist areas. This is because there are currently relatively few Japanese people who really get significant benefits from being able to speak English, so there is little reason for them to acquire that language (Yamagami & Tollefson, 2011).

The purpose of the development of this chatbot is to offer Japanese language students an alternative to improve their conversation level. For this, it is proposed an artificial intelligence that cannot get bored of repeating the same topic countless times until the user dominates it, that it is available at any time, and that is able to generate confidence and strengthen their fluency at the time of maintaining a real dialogue with a native speaker or another person who speaks that language. It is planned to become another tool in the classroom, being a support for the teacher, which may not be available to start conversations with their students at any time. For this reason, the chatbot can be used as a resource to be assigned as homework or even for practice after each of the lessons in the books.

NAOKA'S DEVELOPMENT

The system is constituted as follows: the inputs are received by the user through the microphone of the device and are transformed through voice to text technology directly to *hiragana*, *katakana* and/or *Kanji*. During this process, a connection is made between the user interface and the Dialogflow API through a client access token. Thus, once the text is recognized, an adequate response is sought in the knowledge base, which was manually shaped to cover the variants that the input may have. In this way, the response is selected and sent to the interface. Finally, the response obtained in the form of text is transformed into a synthetic voice using text-to-speech technology and is transmitted to the user through the audio outputs of the device in order to simulate a real conversation. In case the chatbot cannot recognize the content of the received entry, it will try to lead the user to talk about a different topic. The proposed chatbot architecture is presented in **Figure 1**.

Figure 1. Diagram of the chatbot's internal operation

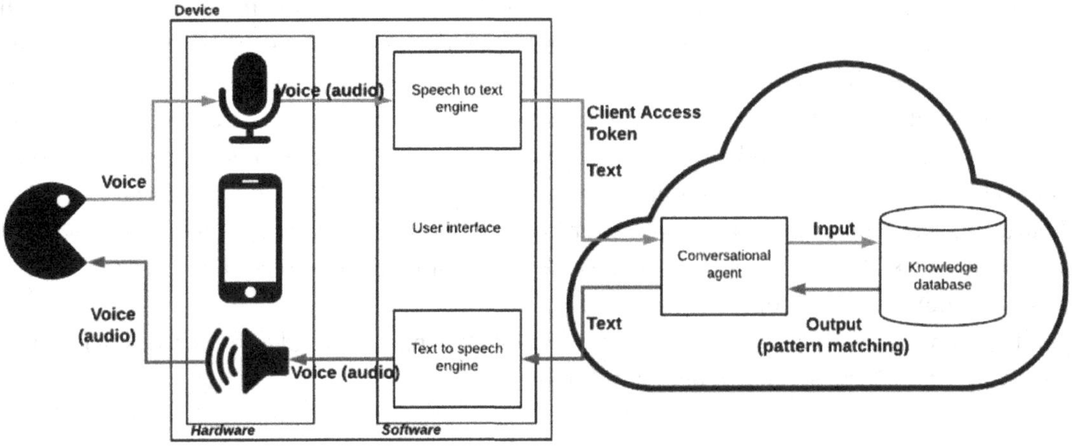

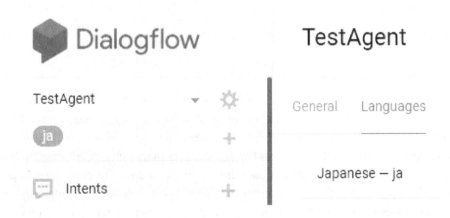

An initial conversational agent was developed in Dialogflow for testing. For this, it was necessary to develop a basic interface capable of receiving inputs by voice and display in text format the response obtained by the chatbot.

Using the Dialogflow interface, a new conversational agent named TestAgent was created, functional for the Japanese language, as shown in **Figure 2**.

Figure 2. Creation of the initial chatbot called TestAgent

The creation of this agent only means that a new empty project has been created, but it has some initial configuration. Before explaining this configuration, it is necessary to define the functionality and way to use a specific element of the interface that will have an important impact on the development of the chatbot.

The conversation flow in Dialogflow works in such a way that an entry is provided, the conversational agent analyzes it, and thus shows a coherent response to the user. To define the type of conversations that the chatbot will be able to maintain, it is necessary to use intents. These, as the name implies, compile the examples of phrases or statements that the user could use with the same intention, and allows the association of corresponding responses to them. A typical agent has different intents declared, which are identified with a name provided by the developer and represent a variety of possible entries that the user could use. It also has different declared answers, of which one will be selected randomly. The training phrases, in addition to functioning as triggers for the intents, can be used to extract information and offer a more complete and/or empathic response to the user. Similarly, Dialogflow automatically expands these phrases to associate them with similar ones that can be introduced by the user. As an example, you could have an agent who engages in conversations about sports, so if the user says something like "My favorite sport is basketball," the agent associates the entry with the corresponding intent and shows one of the answers defined within of it (Google, 2019).

With this in mind, every new agent created in Dialogflow has an initial configuration with two pre-configured intents, which are shown below in **Figure 3**.

Figure 3. Pre-configured intents on the initial agent

The Default Welcome Intent contains patterns of basic welcome phrases and greetings since a "Hello" or similar phrases are usually the first interaction between the user and the chatbot. It is necessary to mention that the input phrases and the pre-configured answers in this intent are completely configurable by the developer. Likewise, the Default Fallback Intent provides different configurable phrases for the agent to respond in case of receiving any input that does not match or is not like any of the training phrases defined in other intents. Because of this, the Default Fallback Intent does not have its own input phrases. It should be noted that, as in any other intent, the selection between the responses established in each one is completely random.

It is important to mention that the Dialogflow console allows you to test the agent's responses by sending text or audio, so tests were performed with the pre-configured intents.

As previously stated, the software was created using the Android Studio IDE. When starting the project, it was necessary to define it to work on devices that have Android 5.0 (Lollipop) or higher. As can be seen in **Figure 4**, Android Studio shows that, by choosing this system as the minimum, the application works on 85.0% of the devices at the date of creation of this document.

Figure 4. Project creation

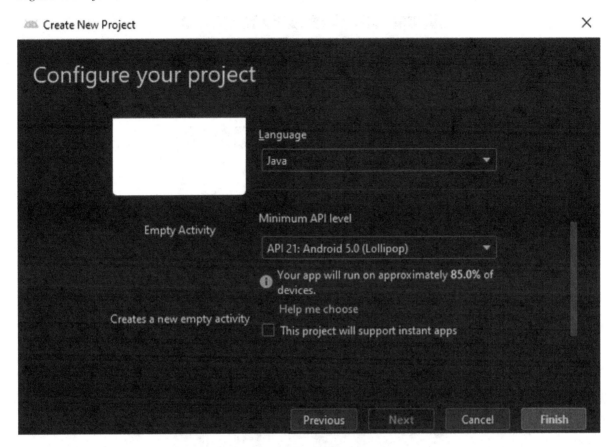

The interface was initially configured with two TextView elements. The first one shows the input received from the user, while the second one provides the response offered by the agent. Likewise, a button with the legend "Press here!" was added, which fulfills the function of initiating the reception of audio using the microphone of the device when it is pressed. The design of the initial interface can be seen in **Figure 5**.

All the internal logic of the software was developed in a single main activity. When it is created, the activity calls two functions consecutively, as shown in **Figure 6**.

The first one, called validateOS, is responsible for validating that the operating system in which the application is trying to run is Android 5.0 (Lollipop) or higher, and then it makes the request to access the Internet. On the other hand, the function called assistantConfig is responsible for defining Japanese as the language in which the application text is displayed, as well as the configuration for the connection between it and the Dialogflow API. In this function, it is necessary to include the client access token of the agent, which allows both to define the agent to be used, and to have access to all its configuration. This key consists of an alphanumeric character string, which is obtained from the agent configuration in the Dialogflow console, as shown in **Figure 7**.

Then, the logic of a function called onResult was defined, which is activated each time a response is received from the conversational agent. This defines that the result of the query is transformed to text and is displayed in the second TextView of the interface.

Figure 5. Initial chatbot interface

Finally, a function called onError was used to define how the software acts in case of an error. In order to prevent the user from losing the sensation of having a conversation with another person, explicit error messages were avoided, and it was decided to make the interface show specific responses, thus simulating that the chatbot is still active. For this, two main errors were taken into account: when the device does not detect any audio input, and the lack of Internet connection. In the first case, the interface shows "I'm sorry, I couldn't hear you", while in the second one, "I'm sorry, I can't think very well when I don't have access to the Internet". Of course, both in the Japanese language. For any other error, it was decided that the interface simply shows "Sorry, I did not understand."

Figure 6. Diagram of the initial functions of the main activity

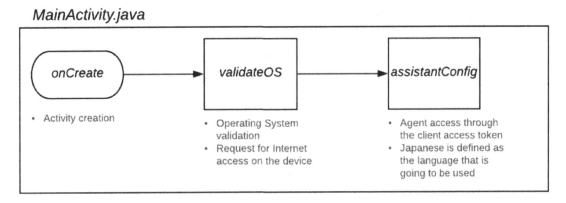

Figure 7. TestAgent's client access token

API KEYS (V1)

Client access token   65b9064866c141ee9eadfb9c57287f82

Figure 8 shows the operation of these functions after the software has been initialized.

Once the connection with the agent is already established, the implementation of voice recognition was necessary to begin giving inputs to the chatbot. For this purpose, it is necessary to use the button previously located at the bottom of the interface, for which modifications were made to the previously mentioned functions. In validateOS the request for permission to use the device's microphone and audio recording was added. This, unlike the Internet access request, is explicitly shown to the user when installing the application, as can be seen in **Figure 9**.

On the other hand, the assistantConfig function was modified in such a way that the system's voice recognition engine was defined as the one that would be used for the conversational agent. In addition, it was defined that the button would work in such a way that, once pressed, the audio recording does not stop until it stops receiving voice inputs. For this, a new function called onLongClick was created, which is activated by pressing the button, and allows the conversational agent to hear the user's voice.

This engine recognizes words in Japanese and transforms them into text written in *hiragana*, *katakana* and/or *Kanji*, whether or not they are within the database of the conversational agent's knowledge. That is, if the user were making pronunciation or intonation errors, the engine could recognize words other than the intended ones.

During the development of this first cycle, and to save resources on the equipment in which the corresponding programming was carried out, a cell phone was used for testing. The objective of the tests was that, through the designed interface, the chatbot could perform the same actions as in the Dialogflow console. The intention of this is that the agent receives the entries by voice, shows them in *hiragana*, *katakana* and/or *Kanji* in the first TextView, and at the same time shows the response received in the second one.

Figure 8. Diagram of the functions of the main activity after its initialization

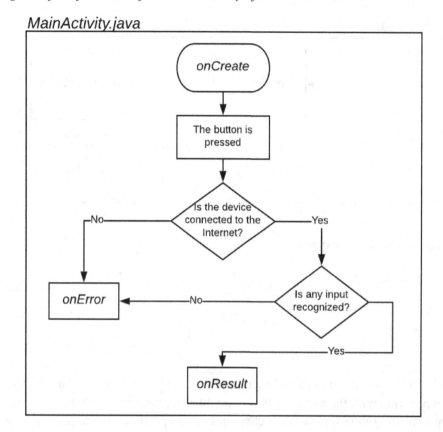

During the design and programming, there were only minimal syntax errors, but the Android Studio IDE has very useful functionalities and recommendations, so the solution of these was quite fast and efficient. On the cell phone used for testing, the chatbot worked as expected. However, when compiling the APK (Android Application Package, for its acronym) and testing it on other devices, only those with Android 9.0 (Pie) could use the application correctly. Table 1 shows the devices where these tests were performed.

As a result of this problem, a device with Android 5.1.1 (Lollipop) was used to perform tests until verifying that the software worked correctly on devices with older operating systems.

After arduous research on the problem, it was determined that the biggest conflict was in the compilation configurations of the APK. At the time of compilation, it was necessary to select both option V1 (Jar Signature), and V2 (Full APK Signature), as shown in **Figure 10**.

Once the compilation was performed, and its operation was tested on the selected device, tests were performed again with the previous devices, thus confirming its correct operation.

As a final part of the development of this cycle, it was decided to add some elements to the interface for user convenience. Two labels showing "Listened" and "Response" were included respectively to differentiate each of the existing TextViews, as can be seen in **Figure 11**.

For the implementation of the text-to-speech engine, the NeoSpeech API was considered, since it supports up to 23 languages, and has different voices and accents. However, the limitations within its free version and the little existing documentation for its implementation with Android applications were

Figure 9. Explicit request for audio recording

key points to be quickly discarded. Thus, it was decided to use Google's text-to-speech engine, which is quite convenient, since it does not need to make a connection with an external API. In addition, being the engine that is commonly used in Android devices, the amount of documentation is abundant and updated. It should be noted that this engine has a female voice by default, which cannot be replaced, but features such as tone or speech speed can be modified.

Google's text-to-speech engine is usually preinstalled and selected by default on devices with Android operating systems. Due to this, it is only necessary to initialize it when starting the application, that is, in the onCreate function. For this, a new object of type Text to Speech is created, and its status is evaluated. If the initialization is successful, Japanese is defined as the language to be used and, if for some reason it is not available on the device for the text-to-speech engine, the button that activates the voice recording will remain disabled.

Table 1. Devices used for initial tests

Device	Operative System
HTC One M8	Android 6.0 (Marshmallow)
Xiaomi Redmi Note 7	Android 9.0 (Pie)
Samsung Galaxy S8	Android 9.0 (Pie)
Sony Xperia AX1 Ultra	Android 8.0 (Oreo)
Samsung Galaxy Grand Prime	Android 5.1.1 (Lollipop)
Moto G5 Plus	Android 6.0 (Marshmallow)
Samsung Galaxy S9 Plus	Android 9.0 (Pie)

Then, in the onResult function, it was necessary to take the text shown in the second TextView (that is, the chatbot response) and pass it as a parameter to the speech function of the Text to Speech object.

Figure 10. Chatbot's APK compilation

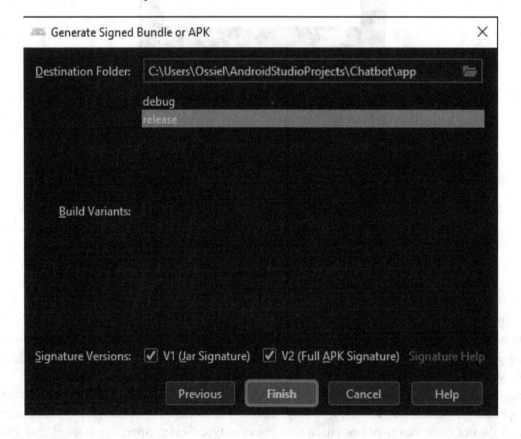

Figure 11. Inclusion of labels in the interface design

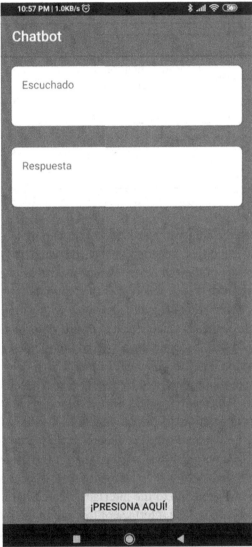

In this way, the text-to-speech engine is told what it has to say. Also, when calling this function the attribute QUEUE_ADD is used, which creates a queue and tells the object to which it is associated (in this case, the Text to Speech object) to add its output to it, in order to prevent that an answer gets reproduced before the previous one has concluded.

In the onError function, it was necessary to include the object's speech function in each of the error responses described in the previous cycle. This was done for the same purpose those responses were proposed in the first place: to prevent the user from losing the sensation of engaging in a real conversation.

Finally, every time an Android application is closed, it is necessary to include an onDestroy function, even if it is empty. Because the Text to Speech object was initialized when the application started, it needs to be stopped and turned off in the onDestroy function, so the logical sequence of the software would be as shown in **Figure 12**.

Figure 12. The logical sequence of the chatbot

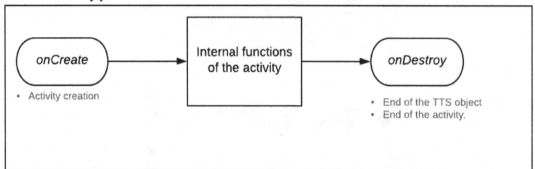

Once the chatbot already had the ability to speak, it was time to include a bar that allows the user to adjust the playback speed of the responses. The tone and speed are the two main characteristics that must be considered for the configuration of the synthesized voice used. These characteristics are modifiable through decimal values ranging from 0 to 2, where 1 is the value that represents the standard pitch or speed. It was defined that the conversational agent had a voice with a tone with a value of 1.2, which is enough to distinguish it from the standard voice, but it keeps its deformation to a minimum.

For the inclusion of the speed bar, it was necessary to add to the design an object of type SeekBar, as well as its respective description label, as shown in **Figure 13**.

The values of this bar, unlike those requested by the Text to Speech object, range from 0 to 100, so, at the time of receiving this information, it was necessary to divide it by 50. Thus, it was defined that the bar would always start at position 50, which generates a value of 1 for the synthesized voice, which means that the value of the standard speed is generated. In the onResult function, in addition to performing the division mentioned before, it was defined that, if the value were less than 0.1, it would automatically equal 0.1, since, if the speed had a value of 0, the response would never get reproduced.

Before the implementation of the engine to the interface created in the first cycle, its functionality was tested through a simple application. The interface of this prototype receives through text what will be reproduced by the engine and allows you to configure both the tone of the voice and its speed, as shown in **Figure 14**.

Once successful results were obtained, the same logic was used with the chatbot, and that is where the idea of allowing users to modify the playback speed came from.

The tests of the product obtained in this second cycle were performed on the same devices as in the first. This time there was a problem specifically with Samsung devices since, in these, the button to talk to the agent appeared disabled. As mentioned at the beginning of this phase, this button was set to disable if the Japanese language for the text-to-speech engine is not available. After research on why this happened specifically on these devices, it was found that this brand includes its own engine, which is commonly selected as default. This Samsung engine does not include the Japanese language, so to solve this problem, it was necessary to enter the text-to-speech configuration of the devices and change the engine preferred by Google, as shown in **Figure 15**.

Once this problem was solved, it was concluded that the software worked correctly on all the devices on which it was tested.

Figure 13. Chatbot interface after the inclusion of the speed bar

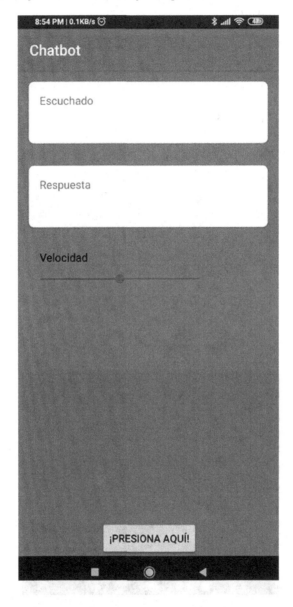

At this point in the development, almost all the modifications were made directly in the Dialogflow console, so it was only necessary to reinstall the software on the test devices once again. The necessary intents were created to minimize the number of entries that could lead the chatbot to use its Default Fallback Intent.

As described by Morales, Nguyen and Chin (2017), a chatbot with a lack of personality and identity is not very convincing for the user, causing him to get bored quickly and stop using it. In addition, Jia (2009) addresses the problem that chatbots are commonly designed to interact with humans, but not to act like them. Because of this, it was necessary to create the next conversational agent as a fictional character with which users could empathize.

On the identity side, the following characteristics were defined:

Figure 14. The prototype used to test the text-to-speech engine. In the text entered, the word "Hello!" can be read in the Japanese language

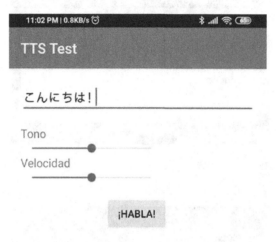

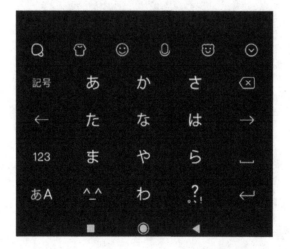

Name: Naoka
Age: 21 years old
Gender: Female
Nationality: Japanese
Occupation: University student

Both the name and the nationality were defined in this way so that the user has the feeling of having a conversation with a real Japanese person. On the other hand, age and occupation were thus done to empathize with the students of the Subdirección de Lenguas Extranjeras de la UACJ, who are mostly

Figure 15. Preferred engine settings on a Samsung Galaxy S8 device

active students and are around that age. Finally, the gender of the agent was defined based on the voice implemented in the second cycle.

Thus, a new conversational agent was created in Dialogflow with the name Naoka, in the same way, that the TestAgent was created in the first cycle. Consequently, this new chatbot has a different client access token, so it was necessary to update this information in the assistantConfig function of the Android Studio project, compile the APK once more, and reinstall the software on the test devices. This update was used to change the top label of the software to the name of the new agent, as shown in **Figure 16**.

Once this was updated, all the following changes were made directly in the Dialogflow console.

On the other hand, Naoka was defined with a kind, energetic personality and always willing to help, which is reflected in her way of speaking, expressing herself, and responding to user input. This is so that they feel comfortable when engaging in a conversation with the agent.

Small talk in human conversation commonly serves to kill time and avoid awkward silences. However, when it comes to the design of a conversational agent, it seeks to avoid unnecessary fallbacks, in order to provide it with human qualities, which creates an invaluable connection with the user (Harlowe, 2019).

Small talk entries are some of the most common messages the chatbot will receive. Users often test agents by trying to push their knowledge to the limit. It is necessary that the chatbot is able to answer

Figure 16. Interface name change

these types of questions, or else it will feel quite flat, ending the conversation every time it is tested. An agent that can answer "I'm fine, thanks" instead of an "I'm sorry, I didn't understand you", feels like it is really listening to the user (Harlowe, 2019).

Harlowe's work (Harlowe, 2019) was used as the basis for the creation of Naoka's first small talk intents since it shows forty examples of essential phrases that a conversational chatbot should be able to answer appropriately. These phrases are divided into four categories: essential greetings, funny phrases, phrases that can occur if the user is not happy and phrases to test the chatbot, of which the most relevant were taken.

Conveniently, Dialogflow has some pre-configured conversational agents. One of these, simply called Small-Talk, has fifty-six intents of, as the name says, small talk. These have their respective input phrases, but the agent's responses must be configured by the developer for the intent to be functional. In addition, these intents can easily be exported to another project, so the most relevant ones were used to complement Naoka's small talk knowledge.

For the inclusion of the themes of the books *Minna no Nihongo: Shokyu II* (Elementary Level II) and *Minna no Nihongo: Chukyu I* (Intermediate Level I), the vocabulary and grammar explained in them were considered. Each of the lessons in these books has a section where different grammar pieces are explained, in addition to a conversation where they are used. Thus, the main phrases of the conversations of each lesson were extracted, where the grammar pieces explained in it were used. However, these phrases include specific topics and, therefore, the phrases that the chatbot could recognize would be quite limited. Because of this, knowledge about these same phrases was expanded; that is, intents were created that recognized phrases with the same structure but covered different topics to create a larger knowledge database.

The phrases used in this section commonly have the objective (unlike those of small talk) to transmit information between the user and the agent. Due to this, the structure of the intents is somewhat different, and it is convenient to know certain concepts to build them better and so that the user feels a more empathic connection.

For the identification and extraction of useful data from natural language inputs, Dialogflow mechanisms called entities are used. These mechanisms are used for the specific selection of information provided by the user, from addresses to dates or place names. Like the intents, these mechanisms also require a name to identify them, which works also to define the type of entity the system is working with. Likewise, the entity's entries provide a set of words or phrases that are considered equivalent. Thus, if you have an entity of type "Ice cream flavors", the respective entries of this would be words like "pistachio", "chocolate", "cookies and cream", and so on. Similarly, synonyms can be defined if the input requires it. It should be noted that Dialogflow also has the so-called system entities, which are already predefined and do not require any additional configuration. These types of entities include common data such as dates, time periods, languages, telephone numbers, currency type, etc. **Figure 17** shows the operation of this element within an intent.

Figure 17. Information extraction using entities (Google, 2019)

On the other hand, one of the best options to control the flow of the conversation is the use of contexts. These represent the current state of the dialogue and allow the conversational agent to carry information from one intent to another. Once a certain intent is activated, an output context can be defined, which will be active for the number of rounds the developer chooses, also called "context life". In this way, you can define intents that are only accessible when that context is active. That is, your input context will be the output context of the initial intent. Following this logic, you could have a conversation like the following:

User: *"How are you?"* - The intent that has an output context with a two-round life is activated.

Agent: *"Pretty good! And you? "*- The output context is activated.
User: *"Very good!"* - Round 1.
Agent: *"How good."* - Round 1.
User: *"What is your favorite color?"* - Round 2. The context is deactivated.

If, for example, the user had said, "Very good!" Without having activated the context, the agent would not have understood or activated a different intent.

In this way, Naoka can make decisions about when the use of certain intents is valid and can extract information to answer in a much more personalized way, giving the user the feeling of being heard.

The conversation tests were mainly performed after the inclusion of each of the intents. Once Naoka's conversation architecture was already in a state that included the points mentioned above, general conversation tests were performed with the same devices used in the first cycle.

During the validation period to obtain results, the feedback was received from the Japanese language students of the Subdirección de Lenguas Extranjeras, mainly about recommendations of topics that they would like to talk about with Naoka, but that was not within the knowledge database. All these recommendations fell within the scope of the small talk, so it was easy to include new intents with the topics that the students wanted to practice. Thanks to this, greater immersion is achieved, and better results are expected.

Some phrases that could generate ambiguities and activate other intents were found, so it was necessary to improve the input phrases using synonyms or adding another type of vocabulary. An example of this is the intent called "The user wants attention", in which one of the input phrases is "shitsumon ga arimasu" (which translates as "I have a question"). One of the answers defined for this intent is "hai" (literally "yes") since this word can be used in Japanese to imply that the interlocutor is being heard. During some of the tests with the students, one of them used the phrase "mirai ni itta koto ga arimasu ka" (which translates as: "have you ever traveled to the future?"), which was not found as a phrase of entry for no intent. However, instead of the phrase activating the Default Fallback Intent, the user surprisingly received "hai" as a response, because the machine learning of Dialogflow expands within the existing intents, so, by finding the word "arimasu" in both sentences, it assumed that they had the same intention. Thus, it was necessary to create an intent in which the entry phrase was "mirai ni itta koto ga arimasu ka", to avoid this confusion.

Once Naoka already had enough knowledge to start conversations, the development process was terminated. However, the amount of intents that would be necessary to cover to have a chatbot with an impeccable conversational capacity is quite large, so new ones are often added, especially when they are direct requests from users who want to start conversations on specific topics. In this way, Naoka remains in the process of continuous improvement.

RESULTS

Battery Consumption and Data Usage

For the measurement of battery consumption and data of the proposed software, it was used in different devices continuously for one hour. Table 2 shows the records obtained after the tests.

It can be seen that the battery consumption is very variant since it depends on the type of hardware of the device. On the other hand, data consumption was quite similar among all devices.

Table 2. Battery and data consumption after using Naoka for one hour

Device	Android Version	Battery consumption	Data consumption
Xiaomi Mi 9 SE	9.0 (Pie)	5%	1236.6KB
HTC One M8	6.0 (Marshmallow)	11%	1255.2KB
Xiaomi Redmi Note 7	9.0 (Pie)	5%	1121KB
Samsung Galaxy S8	9.0 (Pie)	6%	1257.66KB
Sony Xperia AX1 Ultra	9.0 (Oreo)	3%	1235KB
Samsung Galaxy Grand Prime	5.1.1 (Lollipop)	10%	1188KB
Moto G5 Plus	6.0 (Marshmallow)	4%	1176KB
Samsung Galaxy S9 Plus	9.0 (Pie)	6%	1222.6KB
Samsung J7 Prime	6.0 (Marshmallow)	10%	1167KB
Samsung Galaxy A7	9.0 (Pie)	7%	1204.8KB
Sony Xperia XZ	8.0 (Oreo)	3%	1231KB
Moto Z2 Play	8.0 (Oreo)	4%	1161KB
Samsung J5 Prime	6.0 (Marshmallow)	11%	1173KB

Thus, it was obtained that, on average, 6.53% battery and 1202.22KB of data are consumed. This indicates that, after one hour of continuous use, only a little more than 1MB of data (1024KB) is consumed, which is quite efficient when compared to a commonly used application such as Facebook, which consumes on average 1MB per minute (Mamani, 2018).

Conversational Level Improvement

In order to evaluate the usefulness of the chatbot, an exam was designed to measure the conversational level of the students. This was carried out with the support of Mr. Iori Sugiyama, an Information Science Master's Degree graduate from the University of Fukui in Japan, and Prof. Omar Velazquez Gutierrez, one of the teachers of the Japanese language of the Subdirección de Lenguas Extranjeras, who also has N3 level certification on the Japanese Language Proficiency Test (JLPT). In addition, with the help of Prof. Vanessa Gómez Ávila from the Bachelor of English Teching of the Universidad Autónoma de Ciudad Juárez, a rubric was designed to measure different elements of the conversational area.

The exam was applied individually in a controlled group of 12 intermediate students with the support of Prof. Velazquez, after which only half of them were given access to the software. After 36 days in which the selected students were interacting daily with the chatbot, the test was applied again to the whole group without prior notice, in order to verify the difference between the progress of the students who had access to Naoka, and those who didn't. Although the system does not focus on perfecting specific areas of the conversational level of users, it was expected that different conversational aspects would be improved after daily use.

The exam consists of three different situations based on the conversations in Lessons 29, 35, and 39 of the book *Minna no Nihongo Shokyu II* (Elementary Level II). The evaluation procedure is that each student was randomly assigned one of the three situations, and a roleplay conversation with the evaluator was developed from it. The objective was that the situation was acted as if it were being lived in real life, in order to measure the student's performance in different categories of the conversational area. Before beginning the roleplay, the student was given time to read and understand the situation. For the second evaluation, the student was assigned a different situation from the one presented in the first test.

A simple way to represent the results obtained by each student is to compare the scores of both exams. For this, it is convenient to use a color code, which is shown in Table 3 below.

Table 3. Interpretation of the score obtained in each category

Score	Color
5	Red
10	Orange
15	Yellow
20	Green

Each of the categories has a value of up to 20 points depending on the student's performance, thus giving the possibility of obtaining a maximum of 100 points in the exam. For convenience, from this point on, the group that did not have access to Naoka will be named as "Group 1", while the group that did have access will be named as "Group 2". Table 4 and Table 5 show, respectively, the results obtained by Group 1 and Group 2 in the first exam, as well as in each of the categories evaluated.

Table 4. Grades obtained in the first test by Group 1

Student	Vocabulary	Grammar	Fluency	Communication	Pronunciation	Total
1A	Red	Orange	Orange	Yellow	Yellow	55
2A	Red	Red	Red	Red	Orange	30
3A	Orange	Yellow	Orange	Orange	Yellow	60
4A	Red	Red	Orange	Orange	Orange	40
5A	Red	Red	Red	Red	Red	25
6A	Orange	Orange	Red	Yellow	Orange	50

It can be noted that the grades of both groups are similar before the use of Naoka. Next, Table 6 and Table 7 show, respectively, the results obtained by Group 1 and Group 2 in the second exam.

There was a considerable improvement in the results of Group 2, while those of Group 1 remained similar to those of the first review. **Figures 18** and **19** show a comparison of the scores obtained in both exams by Group 1 and Group 2, respectively.

Table 5. Grades obtained in the first test by Group 2

Student	Vocabulary	Grammar	Fluency	Communication	Pronunciation	Total
1B	Orange	Orange	Yellow	Yellow	Yellow	65
2B	Orange	Orange	Red	Orange	Orange	45
3B	Yellow	Orange	Yellow	Yellow	Yellow	70
4B	Red	Red	Orange	Orange	Red	35
5B	Red	Red	Red	Red	Yellow	35
6B	Orange	Orange	Red	Orange	Orange	45

Table 6. Grades obtained in the second test by Group 1

Student	Vocabulary	Grammar	Fluency	Communication	Pronunciation	Total
1A	Yellow	Yellow	Yellow	Yellow	Yellow	50
2A	Red	Red	Red	Orange	Red	30
3A	Orange	Orange	Orange	Orange	Orange	50
4A	Red	Red	Orange	Orange	Orange	40
5A	Red	Red	Red	Red	Red	25
6A	Red	Orange	Orange	Red	yellow	45

Table 7. Grades obtained in the second test by Group 2

Student	Vocabulary	Grammar	Fluency	Communication	Pronunciation	Total
1B	Yellow	Green	Green	Green	Green	95
2B	Orange	Orange	Yellow	Yellow	Orange	60
3B	Yellow	Green	Yellow	Green	Green	90
4B	Red	Orange	Orange	Yellow	Yellow	55
5B	Orange	Red	Orange	Yellow	Orange	50
6B	Orange	Orange	Orange	Red	Orange	45

In these graphs, the difference in grades in the second exam (blue bars) becomes much more evident, thus showing that the improvement obtained by Group 2 is greater than that obtained by Group 1. To show the results in a way even clearer, **Figures 20** and **21** show the difference in scores obtained between the first and second exams of both groups using line graphs.

In Group 1, half of the students obtained a lower grade in the second exam due to lack of practice, while the other half did not present any change. In Group 2, 83.3% of the students obtained a significant improvement between both exams, while only 16.6% remained unchanged, although it should be noted that there was no decrease in their grades.

To observe the difference in the results in another context, the average grades obtained by both groups in the first and second exams, respectively, are shown in Table 8.

Thus, while in Group 1, the average grades decreased by 3.33%, in Group 2, they increased by 16.67%.

Figure 18. Group 1 results comparison

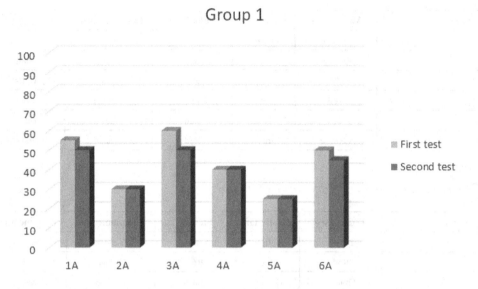

Figure 19. Group 2 results comparison

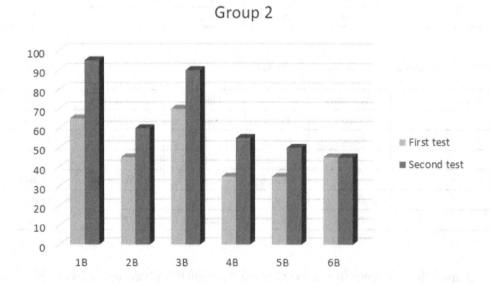

On the other hand, it is also important to highlight the main areas of improvement for the group that had access to Naoka. Thus, it was possible to obtain the average grades obtained in each of the conversational areas of both exams, as shown in Table 9.

To observe the change in a better way, **Figure 22** shows the difference in average between both exams graphically, that is, the values resulting from subtracting the averages obtained in the first exam from those obtained in the second one.

It can be noted that the areas that had the greatest impact were grammar, fluency, and communication, in which an improvement of 4.17 points on average was obtained.

Figure 20. Group 1 results comparison using a line chart

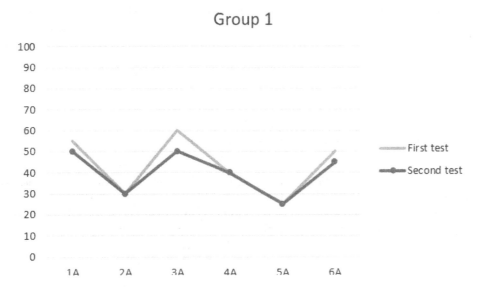

Figure 21. Group 2 results comparison using a line chart

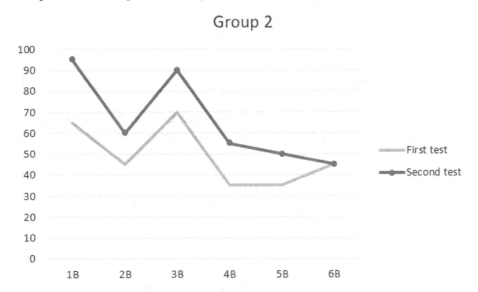

DISCUSSION

The results obtained from both groups clearly reflect the usefulness of the proposed software. At this point, it is necessary to discuss how the inclusion of Naoka impacts in the conversational studies of the students of the Subdirección de Lenguas Extranjeras de la UACJ.

As expected initially, the group that had access to Naoka had better improvement than the one obtained by the group that did not. All students in Group 2, except for student 6B, obtained a significant improvement in the results of the second exam. As stated at the beginning of this article, the practice of conversation is a fundamental piece for learning a second language (Jia, 2009). This is reflected in the

Table 8. Average score obtained by both groups in both tests

Test Group	First	Second
1	$\bar{X} = 43.33$	$\bar{X} = 40$

Table 9. Average scores obtained by Group 2 in each area of the first and second tests

Area Test	Vocabulary	Grammar	Fluency	Communication	Pronunciation
First	$\bar{X} = 9.16$	$\bar{X} = 8.33$	$\bar{X} = 9.16$	$\bar{X} = 10.83$	$\bar{X} = 11.66$
Second	$\bar{X} = 10.83$	$\bar{X} = 12.5$	$\bar{X} = 13.33$	$\bar{X} = 15$	$\bar{X} = 14.16$

Test Group	First	Second
2	$\bar{X} = 49.16$	$\bar{X} = 65.83$

tests carried out, where students with more practice developed in a better way in just 36 days after the daily use of a chatbot.

Likewise, the results obtained by Group 1 are related to the fact that the lack of practice of the conversation of a foreign language causes that the students do not reach an optimum level of communicative

Figure 22. Improvement in the average points obtained by Group 2 in each area

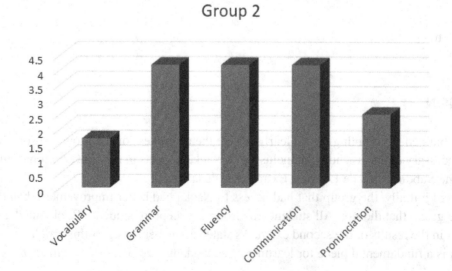

competence (Löwgren, 2013). In this specific case, the lack of practice of the conversation affected the students of Group 1 in such a way that half of them obtained a decrease in their grades.

It should be noted that, regardless of the conversational level that was demonstrated by Group 2 in the first exam, the improvement was significant in most of its students. A clear example is students 4B and 5B, who, despite having obtained in the first exam some of the lowest grades, improved enough to exceed the average obtained in both exams by Group 1. Because these students form part of the 50% that practiced with the software for 2 to 6 hours a day, it can be said that this had a direct impact on their results.

As shown earlier, the fields where there was a greater improvement are grammar, fluency, and communication. This is mainly due to the type of interaction that students should use with Naoka, where fluency is essential for the chatbot to recognize what they are trying to say because if the speech to text engine detects very long pauses, it takes the sentence as finished. On the other hand, grammar and communication go together; students improve their grammar by practicing the contents of the books they already know and, at the same time, this improves their ability to express what they really mean so that Naoka understands and can continue talking with them. The vocabulary and pronunciation areas show less progress mainly due to two reasons: the vocabulary used by Naoka is based on lessons from the book that students already know, and, on the other hand, the pronunciation of the Japanese language is very similar to that used in Spanish.

During the period Group 2 was assigned to use Naoka, although students' progress and feedback were being monitored, the use of the software was not mandatory for their class, but it was recommended. As mentioned above, in Group 2, it was observed that one of the students did not present improvements or a decrease in their grade. However, it should be noted that, although his score remained the same in both exams, there was a variation within the results of each specific area, where his fluency improved, but his communication worsened five points. On the other hand, one of the students did not practice with Naoka during the assigned period, being this one the 6B student, which explains his lack of improvement in the second exam.

The use of Naoka proposes a solution to the problem indicated by Löwgren (2013) regarding that students do not speak the target language within the classroom if the teacher does not, and that, even if they did, this does not necessarily mean the student is involved in a real conversation. In addition, the results of this author revealed that 90% of the professors who were involved in their study consider that a chatbot could be a good tool to develop students' communicative competence.

On the other hand, within the results obtained by Jia (2009), it is mentioned that 60.5% of the students involved in their study stated that they would continue to use the system after school, even without their teacher's request.

CONCLUSION

This chapter has been written around a general objective, which is about the development of a chatbot capable of holding conversations in the Japanese language that allows improving the level of communicative competence of the students of the Subdirección de Lenguas Extranjeras de la UACJ. Now that Naoka is working and the tests have yielded positive results, it can be said that this goal has been successfully achieved.

Likewise, the specific objectives were reached until reaching the current state of the software. An initial agent was designed for testing, which was presented as TestAgent. Next, an interface was created for interaction with Android users, and the necessary engines were implemented so that the interaction with the chatbot was as human as possible. Afterward, the agent who now is presented as Naoka and it was created was given a personality, identity, and knowledge necessary for the practice of the students. Finally, the performance of the system was evaluated, as shown in the previous part of this chapter. In this way, it can be said that these objectives have also been successfully achieved.

From the beginning, the use of the books *Minna no Nihongo: Shokyu II* (Elementary Level II) and *Minna no Nihongo: Chukyu I* (Intermediate Level I) was proposed, being the first one that mainly helped to structure the knowledge base by use phrases that appear in his conversations, as well as his vocabulary and grammar pieces. The use of this kind of book as a source implies the inclusion of knowledge that students have already studied in class and, therefore, requires practice and review. However, although the inclusion of knowledge based on traditional books works for the Japanese language, this method may differ for other languages. In addition, according to what was pointed out by Fryer (Fryer, 2006), there is still a long way to reach a level of development of chatbots in which they are useful for all types of students.

At this point, it is necessary to consider what was described by Wang (2008), who emphasizes that chatbots work as a means to practice the conversation, but do not intend to take the place of the teacher. Surveys of students after the use of Naoka show a positive response to the idea of using the software as homework or even as an activity within the class, where each student can have their own conversational partner. Finally, this is consistent with the argument made by Fryer (2006) that much of the content seen in class is often not reviewed again, so its inclusion as an after-homework assignment can help students retain knowledge.

Thus, although there is still a long way to go in terms of adopting these types of conversational agents for all levels of learning, it is concluded that this tool will have a great impact and will be quite useful in teaching foreign languages in the future.

REFERENCES

Angga, A., Fachri, E., & Angga, E., Suryadi, & Agushinta, D. (2015). Design of Chatbot with 3D Avatar, Voice Interface, and Facial Expression. In *International Conference on Science in Information Technology* (pp. 326-330). Yogyakarta, Indonesia. IEEE. 10.1109/ICSITech.2015.7407826

BBC. (2014). *Languages of the world - Interesting facts about languages*. Retrieved from http://www.bbc.co.uk

Ciechanowski, L., Przegalinska, A., Magnuski, M., & Gloor, P. (2019). In the shades of the uncanny valley: An experimental study of human-chatbot interaction. *Future Generation Computer Systems*, *92*, 539–548. doi:10.1016/j.future.2018.01.055

Cobos, J. (2013). *Integración de un chatbot como habilidad de un robot social con gestor de diálogos* (Master's thesis). Madrid: Universidad Carlos III de Madrid.

Cohen, A. & Hosenfeld, C. (1981). *Some Uses of Mentalistic Data in Second Language Acquisition*. Academic Press.

Collobert, R., Weston, J., Buttou, L., Karlen, M., Kavukcuoglu, K., & Kuksa, P. (2011). Natural Language Processing (Almost) from Scratch. *Journal of Machine Learning Research, 12*, 2493–2537.

Corrales, K. (2009). Construyendo un segundo idioma. *Zona Próxima, 10*, 156–167.

Cortez, A., Vega, H., Pariona, J., & Huayna, A. (n.d.). Procesamiento de lenguaje natural. *Revista de Investigación de Sistemas e Informática, 6*, 45–54.

CourseFinders. (2017). *¿Cuál es el idioma más rápido del mundo?* (CourseFinders) Retrieved from https://coursefinders.com/blog/es/5637/espanol-cual-es-el-idioma-mas-rapido-del-mundo

Ellis, R., Allen, T., & Tuson, A. (2007). *Applications and Innovations in Intelligent Systems XIV.* Springer-Verlag. doi:10.1007/978-1-84628-666-7

Fariño, G. (2011). *Modelo en Espiral de un proyecto de desarrollo de software.* Universidad Estatal de Milagro. Retrieved https://es.ryte.com

Ferguson, C. A. (1975). Toward a Characterization of English Foreigner Talk. *Anthropological Linguistics, 17*, 1–14.

Fryer, L., & Carpenter, R. (2006). Bots as Language Learning Tools. *Language Learning & Technology, 20*, 8–14.

Google. (2019). *Actions on Google.* Retrieved from https://developers.google.com

Google. (2019). *Productos de IA y aprendizaje automático.* Retrieved from https://cloud.google.com/dialogflow/docs/

Google. (n.d.). *Android Studio - Conoce Android Studio.* Retrieved from https://developer.android.com

Google. (n.d.). *Dialogflow - Agents Overview.* Retrieved from https://dialogflow.com

Gottlieb, N. (2009). The Rōmaji Movement in Japan. *The Royal Asiatic Society, 20*, 75–88.

Harlowe, H. (2019). *40 Small Talk Questions Your Chatbot Needs To Know (And Why It Matters).* Retrieved from https://medium.com

Hill, J., Ford, W. R., & Ferreras, I. G. (2015). Real conversations with artificial intelligence: A comparison between human–human online conversations and human–chatbot conversations. *Computers in Human Behavior, 49*, 245–250. doi:10.1016/j.chb.2015.02.026

Holmquist, L. E., Redström, J., & Ljungstrand, P. (1999). Token-Based Access to Digital Information. In *International Symposium on Handheld and Ubiquitous Computer.* Springer. 10.1007/3-540-48157-5_22

Hoya. (n.d.). *NeoSpeech.* Retrieved from https://neospeech.com

Huang, J., Zhou, M., & Yang, D. (2006). Extracting Chatbot Knowledge from Online Discussion Forums. *IJCAI (United States), 7*, 423–428.

IBM. (n.d.). *Watson - Speech To Text.* Retrieved from https://www.ibm.com/watson

International Press en Español. (2018). *Abe: Japón quiere comenzar a recibir más trabajadores extranjeros desde abril.* Retrieved from https://internationalpress.jp

Jacques, F. (1999). *Multi-Agent System: An Introduction to Distributed Artificial.* Academic Press.

Jelinek, F. (1997). *Statistical Methods for Speech Recognition.* Massachusetts Institute of Technology.

Jia, J. (2009). CSIEC: A computer assisted English learning chatbot based on textual knowledge and reasoning. *Knowledge-Based Systems, 22*(4), 249–255. doi:10.1016/j.knosys.2008.09.001

Jutte, B. (2012). *Project Risk Management Handbook.* Academic Press.

Kawabata, K. J., Twomey, T., Parker, O., Seghier, M. L., Haji, T., Sakai, K., & Devlin, J. T. (2013). *Inter- and Intrahemispheric Connectivity Differences When Reading Japanese Kanji and Hiragana* (Vol. 24). Cerebral Cortex. Oxford University Press.

Konsynski, B. R., Kottemann, J. E., Nunamaker, J. F. Jr, & Stott, J. W. (1984). plexsys-84: An Integrated Development Environment for Information Systems. *Journal of Management Information Systems, 1*(3), 64–104. doi:10.1080/07421222.1984.11517710

Krashen, S. D. (1982). Principles and Practice in Second Language Acquisition. Academic Press.

Litwin, E. (1995). *Tecnología educativa: Política, historias, propuestas.* Paidós SA.

Litwin, E. (2005). *Tecnologías educativas en tiempos de Internet.* Amorrotu.

Long, M. H. (1981). Input, Interaction and Second Language Acquisition. [Pennsylvania.]. *Annals of the New York Academy of Sciences, 379*(1), 259–278. doi:10.1111/j.1749-6632.1981.tb42014.x

Löwgren, M. (2013). Chatbot como recurso didáctico en la enseñanza de español como lengua extranjera. Academic Press.

Mamani, R. (2018). *Internet: ¿Cuántos megas consumen las redes sociales?* Retrieved from https://larepublica.pe

Marukawa, K., Koga, M., Shima, Y., & Fujisawa, H. (1993). A Post-Processing Method for Handwritten Kanji Name Recognition Using Furigana Information. In *Proceedings of 2nd International Conference on Document Analysis and Recognition* (pp. 218-221). IEEE. 10.1109/ICDAR.1993.395745

McKirdy, A. (2015). *Microsoft says Line's popular Rinna character is new way to engage customers.* Retrieved from https://www.japantimes.co.jp

Méndez, E. M., & Moreiro, J. A. (1999). Lenguaje natural e Indización automatizada. *Ciencias de la Información, 30,* 11–24.

Microsoft. (2017). *Visual Studio - Edición del código.* Retrieved from https://visualstudio.microsoft.com

Morales, D., Nguyen, H., & Chin, T. (2017). *A Neural Chatbot with Personality.* Stanford University.

Naiman, N., Frohlich, M., & Todesco, A. (1975). The Good Second Language Learner. *TESL Talk, 6,* 58–76.

Nakayama, T., Patterson, K. E., & Humphreys, G. W. (1993). Phonologically Mediated Access to Meaning for Kanji. *Journal of Experimental Psychology, 3,* 491–514.

Noda, I., & Stone, P. (2003). The RoboCup Soccer Server and CMUnited Clients: Implemented Infrastructure for MAS Research. *Autonomous Agents and Multi-Agent Systems*, *7*(1/2), 101–120. doi:10.1023/A:1024128904944

Oxford, R., & Crookall, D. (2014). Research on language learning strategies: Methods, Findings, and Instructional issues. *The Modern Language*, *73*(4), 404–419. doi:10.1111/j.1540-4781.1989.tb05321.x

Pilato, G., Augello, A., & Gaglio, S. (2011). AModular SystemOriented to the Design of Versatile Knowledge Bases for Chatbots. *ISRN Artificial Intelligence*, *2012*, 1–10. doi:10.5402/2012/363840

Portillo, J. (2019). *¿Cuáles son las mayores economías del mundo?* Retrieved from https://cincodias.elpais.com

Rigney, J. (1978). Learning Strategies: A Theoretical Perspective. In Learning Strategies (pp. 165-205). Academic Press.

Riley, P. F., & Riley, G. F. (2003). Spades - A Distributed Agent Simulation Environment with Software-in-the-loop execution. In *Proceeding of the 2003 Winter Simulation Conference*. IEEE. 10.1109/WSC.2003.1261500

Rivero, I., Gómez, M., & Abrego, R. (2013). Tecnologías educativas y estrategias didácticas: Criterios de selección. *Educational Technology*, *3*, 190–206.

Sasanuma, S. (1975). Kana and Kanji Processing in Japanese Aphasics. *Brain and Language*, *2*, 369–383. doi:10.1016/S0093-934X(75)80077-0 PMID:1182502

Savington, S. J. (1991). Communicative Language Teaching: State of the Art. *TESOL Quarterly*, *25*(2), 261–278. doi:10.2307/3587463

Spector, J. M. (2001). An Overview of Progress and Problems in Educational Technology. *IEM*, *3*, 27–37.

Statista. (2019). *Los idiomas más hablados en el mundo (hablantes y hablantes nativos, en millones)*. Retrieved from https://es.statista.com

Tamaoka, K., Leong, C. K., & Hatta, T. (1992). Effects of Vocal Interference on Identifying Kanji, Hiragana and Katakana Words by Skilled and Less Skilled Japanese Readers in Grades 4-6. [Matsuyama.]. *Psychologia*, *35*, 33–41.

Taylor, P. (2009). *Text-to-Speech Synthesys*. Cambridge University Press. doi:10.1017/CBO9780511816338

Trincado, B. (2019). *Evolución de las mayores economías del mundo*. Retrieved from https://www.cincodias.elpais.com

Wang, Y. (2008). *Designing Chatbot Interfaces for Language Learning: Ethnographic Research into Affect and Users' Experience* (Doctoral Dissertation). Vancouver.

Wenden. (1985). Helping Language Learners Think about Learning. *ELT Journal, 40*, 3-12.

Winograd, T. (1972). Understanding Natural Language. *Cognitive Psychology*, *3*(1), 1–191. doi:10.1016/0010-0285(72)90002-3

World Economic Forum. (2017). *Travel and Tourism Competitiveness Report 2017*. Retrieved from http://reports.weforum.org

Wu, Y., Wang, G., Li, W., & Li, Z. (2008). Automatic Chatbot Knowledge Acquisition from Online Forum via Rough Set and Ensemble Learning. In *2008 IFIP International Conference on Network and Parallel Computing* (pp. 242-246). Chongqing: IEEE. 10.1109/NPC.2008.24

Wydell, T., Patterson, K. E., & Humphreys, G. W. (1993). Phonologically Mediated Access to Meaning for Kanji:Is a rows still a rose in Japanese Kanji? *Journal of Experimental Psychology. Learning, Memory, and Cognition, 19*(3), 491–514. doi:10.1037/0278-7393.19.3.491

Yamagami, M., & Tollefson, J. (2011). Elite discourses of globalization in Japan: The role of Enflish. In *English in Japan in the Era of Globalization* (pp. 15–37). Palgrave Macmillan. doi:10.1057/9780230306196_2

Chapter 6
Developing Chatbots for Supporting Health Self-Management

Jesús Fernández-Avelino
Tecnológico Nacional de México, Mexico & Instituto Tecnológico de Orizaba, Mexico

Giner Alor-Hernández
iD https://orcid.org/0000-0003-3296-0981
Tecnológico Nacional de México, Mexico & Instituto Tecnológico de Orizaba, Mexico

Mario Andrés Paredes-Valverde
iD https://orcid.org/0000-0001-9508-9818
Tecnológico Nacional de México, Mexico & Instituto Tecnológico de Orizaba, Mexico

Laura Nely Sánchez-Morales
Tecnológico Nacional de México, Mexico & Instituto Tecnológico de Orizaba, Mexico

ABSTRACT

A chatbot is a software agent that mimics human conversation using artificial intelligence technologies. Chatbots help to accomplish tasks ranging from answering questions, playing music, to managing smart home devices. The adoption of this kind of agent is increasing since people are discovering the benefits of them, such as saving time and money, higher customer satisfaction, customer base growing, among others. However, developing a chatbot is a challenging task that requires addressing several issues such as pattern matching, natural language understanding, and natural language processing, as well as to design a knowledge base that encapsulates the intelligence of the system. This chapter describes the design and implementation of a text/speech chatbot for supporting health self-management. This chatbot is currently based on Spanish. The main goal of this chapter is to clearly describe the main components and phases of the chatbot development process, the methods, and tools used for this purpose, as well as to describe and discuss our findings from the practice side of things.

DOI: 10.4018/978-1-7998-4730-4.ch006

Copyright © 2021, IGI Global. Copying or distributing in print or electronic forms without written permission of IGI Global is prohibited.

INTRODUCTION

Communicating with systems based on natural language is very much appealing and of growing interest and importance also for industry. Artificial intelligence techniques have been increased the capacity of chatbots for accomplishing daily tasks of users. Designing and implement easy and natural interaction modalities is a primary research field in the Human-Computer Interaction Domain. A chatbot is an artificial service that can handle complex interactions with human partners in their natural language. Voice-enabled chatbots, today, are considered as classical yet innovative interfaces for natural language interaction with machines. In addition, devices with small screens (such as watches) and no screens (such as the Amazon Echo and Google Home) are becoming more popular, and voice is often the preferred—or the only—way to interact with them.

The main purpose of this paper is to provide a general overview about chatbots, firstly, a description of what chatbots are is presented, then a related work section is presented about the current status in healthcare, chatbots, and mobile healthcare. After, it describes the different types of chatbots that exist. Also, this chapter considers a generic architecture for building a chatbot; afterward, examples of chatbots implemented in a healthcare context are described to have a better idea of what chatbots are important for performing daily users' activities. Moreover, this chapter describes a group of licensed, open, and free tools for developing chatbots. Finally, a prototype for the automatic generation of medical user interfaces using voice recognition is presented as a study case.

BOTS THROUGH CHATBOTS

At a very basic level, bots are a new user interface. This new user interface lets users interact with services and brands using their favorite messaging apps.

Bots are a new way to expose software services through a conversational interface. Bots are also referred to as chatbots, conversational agents, conversational interfaces, chat agents, and more.

Why do we need these bots? Why would we want to expose a service through a conversation? Why not just build a web page (or a mobile app), like we have been doing for the last 20 years or so? Isn't that much easier than building bots?

The answer is that things have changed in the software industry and in user behavior, and these changes are making bots more and more compelling to software companies. Here are some key developments (Bouras et al., 2018):

1. In the last few years, most users have adopted mobile devices, and it has become harder and more expensive to impress and engage with them through the web. This has made a lot of software providers turn to create native mobile apps (apps that run natively on your phone, for example, Instagram or Google Maps) and exposing these mobile apps through app stores.
2. The mobile apps ecosystem quickly became saturated, making it harder and more expensive to compete. In addition, users became tired of installing and uninstalling mobile apps, and only a very few apps prevailed.
3. Surprisingly, the apps that prevailed and became very common were the messaging apps. Most modern users have three or more of these apps on their phones.

4. The user mind share has stuck with messaging apps. Users spend most of their time in these apps; this is even a growing trend with young users who do not have the "old" notion of the web and spend most of their time in chat. Messaging and the ubiquity of connectivity mean that people are more available and responsive via messaging than the alternative, indirect modes of communication.

5. These new apps opened up the ability to expose services, products, and brands on these chat platforms. Slack and Kik launched their platforms in 2015, followed by Facebook, Skype, and Apple in 2016.

6. In conjunction with these user and industry trends, technology has made a leap in natural language processing, making it easier (though not easy) to build and construct conversational interfaces.

As can be seen, the increased use of mobile devices such as cellphones, watches, and virtual assistants has been an important piece in the emergence of voice user interfaces, since they provide significant benefits to perform tasks on mobile devices.

VOICE USER INTERFACES

The youngest users of smartphones today are incredibly adept at two-thumbed texting, multitasking between chat conversations, Instagram comments, Snapchatting, and swiping left on Tinder photos of men posing with tigers. Why add another mode of communication on top of that?

Voice has some important advantages:

- **Speed:** A recent Stanford study showed speaking (dictating) text messages was faster than typing, even for expert texters.
- **Hands-free:** Some cases, such as driving or cooking, or even when you're across the room from your device, make speaking rather than typing or tapping much more practical (and safer).
- **Intuitiveness:** Everyone knows how to talk. Hand a new interface to someone and have it asks that person a question, and even users who are less familiar with technology can reply naturally.
- **Empathy:** How many times have you received an email or text message from someone, only to wonder if they were mad at you or maybe being sarcastic? Humans have a difficult time understanding tone via the written word alone. Voice, which includes tone, volume, intonation, and rate of speech, conveys a great deal of information.

Voice user interfaces improve aspects for users depending on the context; nevertheless, it is important to know which advantages and issues people face to implement them and use them. The following section presents related work about mobile healthcare, chatbots, and chatbots in healthcare; this section is useful for knowing important aspects to be considered.

MOBILE HEALTHCARE RELATED WORK

Mobile health (mhealth) is a rapidly expanding field in the digital health sector, providing healthcare support, delivery, and intervention via mobile technologies such as smartphones, tablets, and wearables. Whilst mhealth refers to all mobile devices which can transmit data; mobile phones are currently the most popular platform for mhealth delivery. The term mhealth can be used to describe a range of healthcare activities in both clinical and non-clinical populations. For example, thousands of popular smartphone apps are available to download under 'health' categories to help individuals improve their fitness, count calories, and monitor their sleep. However, recent research has shown that many of these apps, including both clinical and non-clinical mhealth technologies, do not contain evidence-based content, and do not adhere to clinical guidelines. A major problem for the mhealth industry is how to improve the quality of technologies to incorporate current research and scientific evidence (Kumar et al., 2013).

The following is a summary of the most important related work regarding mobile healthcare, which allowed obtaining reliable information related to this work.

Debon et al. (2019) performed a systematic literature review between November 2017 and May 2018 on the Virtual Health Library's interface. A total of 816 records were identified. In the selection process, 24 studies met inclusion criteria for analysis. Study characteristics were extracted and synthesized. They identified applications with similar functionalities, such as the use of reminders and medical monitoring. Most of them addressed the treatment of conditions related to an already diagnosed chronic disease, including Diabetes Mellitus, Hypertension, Cardiovascular Diseases, Asthma, Neoplasms, and chronic conditions in general. The main lifestyle changes were the reduction of body weight, promotion of healthy eating, and adherence to the regular practice of physical exercises. They concluded that technology could facilitate health care with simple messages and alerts that aid in adherence to treatment. Benefits may be even greater if more applications address the importance of prevention and not just treatment. Banbury et al. (2019) designed and evaluated a health literacy intervention for older people with chronic disease delivered by telehealth. The Telehealth Literacy Project (THLP) was a mixed-method, quasi-experimental, non-randomized trial nested within a telehealth remote monitoring study. An intervention group participated in five weekly videoconference group meetings lasting for 1.5 hours, and a control group received remote monitoring only. Outcomes were measured using the nine-scale Health Literacy Questionnaire (HLQ) and two scales of the Health Education Impact Questionnaire (heiQ). Semi-structured interviews and focus group data were thematically analyzed. They identified small effects in the intervention group only, with improved health literacy behaviors (five HLQ scales) and self-management skills (two heiQ scales). ANOVA of HLQ scales indicated no significant differences between the two groups over time, indicating a contributing effect of the remote monitoring project. Intervention participants reported an improved perception of companionship, emotional, and informational support. Finally, they concluded that The THLP delivered with telemonitoring indicates the potential to improve social support and some health literacy factors in older people. On the other hand, Bouras et al. (2018) provide a solution for self-managing diabetes mainly type two diabetes and prevent pre-diabetes by using gamification and social networking platform. The proposed solution is based on improving social support and help patients with diabetes, and those that are at high risk of diabetes learn more about their condition in an interactive way. The solution is named myTrybeCare; it is a holistic user-centered app that aims to connect between social networking and gamification capabilities so as to encourage and empower its users to interact with each other. Among designated features are setting challenges and activities that can help members' self-manage their goals. Moreover, Yuan Huang (2019) analyzed the development of iWMS (*Intelligent Weight Management System*) and contours the future plan for the clinical trial. They concluded that the development app supports user to collect and transmit the objective data in real-time. iWMS app collects the date-stamped information for further analysis of self-monitoring. Compared with the traditional paper diary, no additional coding time is required for transferring the food and drink data collected on iWMS to nutrient output. iWMS differs from some researcher-developed apps and commercially available apps in that it takes an energy balance approach and contains some usability features, such as a function to allow users to record the food choice verbally and then search and pull the nutrition and ingredient information from the food database, which makes the meal logging easier, an official Taiwan-specific food database used for estimating the daily caloric intake, as well as a web-based interactive dashboard. Also, Farzandipour et al. (2017) reviewed the functionalities and effects of patient self-management of asthma using mobile health applications. The aim of the systematic review was to summarize the evidence regarding the effects of mobile health applications (mHealth apps) for self-management outcomes in patients with asthma and to assess the functionalities of effective interventions. They systematically searched Medline, Scopus, and the Cochrane Central Register of Controlled Trials. Also, they included English-language studies that evaluated the effects of smartphone or tablet computer apps on self-management outcomes in asthmatic patients. The characteristics of these studies, the effects of interventions, and features of mHealth apps were extracted. Outcomes that were assessed in the included studies were categorized into three groups (clinical, patient-reported, and economic). mHealth apps improved asthma control (five studies) and lung function (two studies) from the clinical outcomes. From the patient-reported outcomes, quality of life (three studies) was statistically significantly improved, while there was no significant impact on self-efficacy scores (two studies). Effects on economic outcomes were equivocal so that the number of visits (in two studies) and admission and hospitalization-relevant outcomes (in one study) statistically significantly improved; and in four other studies, these outcomes did not improve significantly. mHealth apps features were categorized into seven categories (inform, instruct, record, display, guide, remind/ alert, and communicate). Eight of the ten mHealth apps included more than one functionality. Nearly all interventions had the functionality of recording user-entered data, and half of them had the functionality of providing educational information and reminders to patients. According to the review performed, multifunctional mHealth apps have good potential in the control of asthma and in improving the quality of life in such patients compared with traditional interventions. Further studies are needed to identify the effectiveness of these interventions on outcomes related to medication adherence and costs. Winterlich et al. (2017) developed an infrastructure for e-health self-management tools, which will provide the infrastructure for mobile health self-management tools including patient education, wearable sensors and supporting applications and services so that people with type one or type two diabetes 'do the right thing at the right time' to self-manage their condition. The Diabetes Digital Coach test bed will focus specifically on implementing interconnected digital innovations in health and social care. Data collected from the testbed will be further analyzed and evaluated to inform policymakers, potentially improving workforce planning and enabling a more stratified approach to patient care.

CHATBOTS RELATED WORK

A chatbot is artificial intelligence (AI) software that can simulate a conversation (or a chat) with a user in natural language through messaging applications, websites, mobile apps, or through the telephone. Why are chatbots important? A chatbot is often described as one of the most advanced and promising expressions of interaction between humans and machines. However, from a technological point of view, a chatbot only represents the natural evolution of a Question-Answering system leveraging Natural Language Processing (NLP). Formulating responses to questions in natural language is one of the most typical examples of Natural Language Processing applied in various enterprises' end-use applications. A summary of chatbots work-related is presented in order to have a better idea about the context.

Cerezo et al. (2019) implemented a chatbot for expert recommendation tasks. The chatbot expertise recommendation system that they presented increases the communication quality by giving open-source developers the ability to know who they can contact when facing issues. Also, they conducted a preliminary study, where interactions were analyzed, and also conducted interviews and an emotion test. The results show that while participants are open to the potential of an expert recommendation system based on a chatbot, significant work is necessary to increase its acceptance. In particular, participants expected the chatbot to be able to conduct a conversation with them, rather than simply answer queries. Another chatbot implementation was performed by Galitsky (2019). He described a chatbot performing advertising and social promotion to assist in the automation of managing friends and other social network contacts. This agent employs a domain-independent natural language relevance technique that filters web mining results to support a conversation with friends and other network members. This technique relies on learning parse trees and parses thickets (sets of parse trees) of paragraphs of text such as Facebook postings. Also, they proposed an algorithm for CASP (*Chatbot Advertising Social Promotion*) to make a translation into multiple languages plausible as well as a method to merge web mined textual chunks. Finally, they observed that a substantial intelligence in information retrieval, reasoning, and natural language-based relevance assessment is required so that members of the social network retain an interest in communication with CASP. Otherwise, the result of social promotion would be negative, and the host would lose friends instead of retaining them. The implementation demonstrated that a properly designed social promotion chatbot could indeed relieve its human host from the efforts on casual chatting with her least important friends and professional contacts. Similarly, Chung et al. (2018) implemented a chatbot in order to analyze whether luxury fashion retail brands can adhere to their core essence of providing personalized care through e-services rather than through traditional face-to-face interactions. Then, they used customer data to test a five-dimension model measuring Chatbot for customer perceptions of interaction, entertainment, trendiness, customization, and problem-solving. The study reveals that Chatbot e-service provides an interactive and engaging brand/customer service encounters. Marketers and managers in the luxury context can adapt the instrument to measure whether e-service agents provide desired outcomes and to determine whether they should adopt Chatbot virtual assistance. Cui et al. (2017) presented SuperAgent, a customer service chatbot that leverages large-scale and publicly available e-commerce data. Distinct from existing counterparts, SuperAgent takes advantage of data from in-page product descriptions as well as user-generated content from e-commerce websites, which is more practical and cost-effective when answering repetitive questions, freeing up human support staff to answer much higher value questions. We demonstrate SuperAgent as an add-on extension to mainstream web browsers and show its usefulness to the user's online shopping experience. Otherwise, Augello (De Pietro et al., 2016) proposed a model of a social chatbot able to choose the most suitable dialogue plans according to what in sociological literature is called a "social practice". The proposed model is discussed considering a case study of a work in progress aimed at the development of a serious game for communicative skills learning. They concluded that the architecture puts social practice at the heart of the deliberative process of an agent, allowing for a more accurate interpretation of user sentences. As future work, they will contain a more developed implementation of the agent with particular attention to the semantic understanding of the conversation.

CHATBOTS IN HEALthCARE RELATED WORK

Technology is reshaping the healthcare industry. While doctors and researchers push the boundaries of medicine, advances in technology are changing the way patients and doctors communicate and how care is administered. Chatbots and artificial intelligence are two revolutionary technologies that are leading the way in transforming the industry. The following summary is about how chatbots are important for healthcare.

Sheth et al. (2019) talked about how patient-chatbot experience is extending with IoT (*Internet Of Things*) and background knowledge. In this article, they shared a perspective on how contemporary chatbot technology can be extended towards a more intelligent, engaging, context-aware, and personalized agent. Furthermore, the importance of contextualization, personalization, and abstraction with the use of domain-specific as well as patient-specific knowledge, and present examples of three healthcare applications. They described how to augment existing health strategies by extending patient-chatbot experience that relies on three types of input knowledge:

1) A background Health Knowledge Graph (HKG) that comprises of the domain and disease-specific knowledge which may be manually developed or extracted from Web of Data that includes a rich source of structured medical and life science data;

2) An evolving Patient Health Knowledge Graph (PHKG) that incorporates Patient-Generated Health Data (PGHD) from sensors and IoT devices and structured knowledge extracted from a patient's Electronic Medical Record (EMR) as well as environmental data, for example, pollen and air quality, from public web services. The PHKG continues to grow by expanding informative pieces of knowledge from continuous patient interactions with the chatbot; and

3) is refined by the healthcare provider's feedback on predictions and analytics. In another interesting work (Roca et al., 2019), a chatbot architecture was introduced for chronic patient support grounded on three pillars: scalability by means of microservices, standard data sharing models through HL7 FHIR and standard conversation modeling using AIML (*Artificial Intelligence Markup Language*). The goal is facilitating the interaction and data gathering of medical and personal information that ends up in the patient health records. To align the way people interact with each other using messaging platforms with chatbot architecture. To conclude, it is worth highlighting that the chatbot architecture proposed in this work covers the necessities of mHealth scenarios. The security measurements are addressed, as well as data storage and FHIR-AIML automation. Moreover, the proposed architecture has been designed for inter-operability with any communication channel, such as messaging platforms or web interfaces, thanks to the proxy translator that is able to convert from the specific formats of communication channels into the general data format used within the chatbot architecture. Also, a knowledge-enabled personalized chatbot system called kBot was designed by Kadariya et al. (2019) for health applications and adapted to help pediatric asthmatic patients (ages 8 to 15) to control their asthma better. Its core functionalities include continuous monitoring of the patient's medication adherence and tracking of relevant health signals and environment data. kBot takes the form of an Android application with a frontend chat interface capable of conversing in both text and voice, and a backend cloud-based server application that handles data collection, processing, and dialogue management. It achieves contextualization by piecing together domain knowledge from online sources and inputs from clinical partners. The personalization aspect is derived from patient answering questionnaires and day-to-day conversations. kBot's preliminary

evaluation focused on chatbot quality, technology acceptance, and system usability involved eight asthma clinicians and eight researchers. For both groups, kBot achieved an overall technology acceptance value of greater than eight on the 11-point Likert scale and a mean System Usability Score (SUS) greater than 80. They performed an evaluation and it shows great acceptance of kBot among domain and non-domain experts as a system for asthma self-management. The next step is to conduct a pilot study on a group of pediatric asthma patients. Finally, Brixey et al. (2018) presented the implementation of an autonomous chatbot named SHIHbot, deployed on Facebook, which answers a wide variety of sexual health questions on HIV/AIDS (*Human Immunodeficiency Virus/Acquired Immunodeficiency Syndrome*). The chatbot's response database is compiled from professional medical and public health resources in order to provide reliable information to users. The system's backend is NPCEditor, a response selection platform trained on linked questions and answers; this is the first retrieval-based chatbot deployed on a large public social network.

Table 1. Comparative table between the related work with the present paper

Article	A	B	C	D	E
Debon et al. (2019)	N/A	√	N/A	√	√
Banbury et al. (2019)	N/A	√	N/A	√	√
Bouras et al. (2018)	N/A	√	N/A	√	√
Huang et al. (2019)	√	√	N/A	√	√
Farzandipour et al. (2017)	N/A	√	N/A	√	√
Winterlich et al. (2017)	N/A	√	√	√	N/A
Cerezo et al. (2019)	N/A	N/S	√	N/A	√
Galitsky (2019)	N/A	N/A	√	N/A	√
Chung et al. (2018)	N/A	N/A	√	N/A	√
Cui et al. (2017)	N/A	N/A	√	N/A	√
De Pietro et al. (2016)	N/A	N/A	N/A	N/A	√
Sheth et al. (2019)	N/A	√	N/A	√	√
Roca et al. (2019)	N/A	√	√	√	√
Kadariya et al. (2019)	√	√	√	√	√
Brixey et al. (2018)	N/S	√	√	√	√

A) Voice recognition implementation, **B)** Mobile-oriented, **C)** IoT-oriented, **D)** Healthcare-oriented, **E)** Research work
N/S: Not specified
N/A: Not Available

Table 1 shows a comparative table among related studies and this research, the table indicates the domain for which the work is focused.

As can be seen in Table 1, the related work with this paper shows some implementations of chatbots focused on business, home automation, and healthcare, to mention but a few. These works have been presented excellent results for accomplishing user's tasks using chatbots, the automatization of workflows decrease performing time and improve user satisfaction to use a service. Nevertheless, voice recognition is not implemented in the most related work; the English language is the commonly supported language; due to this, there is an opportunity to support other languages such as Spanish. Otherwise, the implementation of chatbots on mobile applications in the healthcare context is increasing, especially in chronic diseases.

There is a great variety of chatbots implementation; however, it is important to keep in mind what aspects are important depending on the approach. The following section describes the types of chatbots according to the knowledge domain, service provided, goals, and input processing, and response generation method.

TYPES OF CHATBOTS

Figure 1. Classification of Chatbots

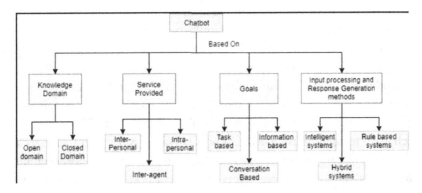

Based on the knowledge a chatbot has or accesses, Nimavat and Champaneria (2017) classified into two kinds: open domain and closed domain. As can be seen in **Figure 1**, also chatbots are classified using other parameters too, such as level of interaction and method of response generation.

A. Knowledge domain
B. Service Provided
C. Goal
D. Response generation method

A. Knowledge Domain

In this classification, the chatbots are based on the knowledge they access or the amount of data they are trained upon. The classes are as follows:

1) Open Domain: Such bots can talk about general topics and respond appropriately

2) Closed Domain: Such bots are focused on a particular knowledge domain and might fail to respond to other questions. For example, a restaurant booking bot won't tell you the name of the first black president of America. It might tell you a joke or respond to how your day is, but it isn't expected to do so since its job is to book a table and give you information about the restaurant.

B. Service Provided

The bots are classified based on the proxemics like classification, but instead of physical proximity, it is based on the sentimental proximity of the bot to the user, the amount of intimate interaction that takes place, and hence is also dependent upon the task the bot is performing.

1) **Interpersonal:** Chatbots that lie in the domain of communication that belongs to the in the Social or Personal distance range in the Proxemics chart fall under this category; bots that provide services such as Restaurant booking, Flight booking, FAQ bot, to mention but a few. These chatbots are not supposed to be companions of the user, and they are supposed to get information and pass them on to the user, they are just enablers. They can have a personality and can be friendly and will probably remember information about the user, but they are not obliged or expected to do so.

2) **Intrapersonal:** These chatbots will exist within the personal domain of the user, such as chat apps like messenger, slack, and WhatsApp, and perform tasks that are lying in the personal domain of the user. Managing calendar, storing the user's opinion, and others. They will be companions to the user and will understand the user like a human does. These might not be dominant in the current scenario, but as natural language understanding progresses, they will soon emerge.

3) **Inter-agent:** Bots like this will be prevalent in IoT dominant areas. These two systems communicate with each other to accomplish a task. As bots become omnipresent, all bots will require some inter-bot communication possibilities. The need for protocols for inter-bot communication will soon emerge. While a bot cannot be a completely inter-agent bot, but it can be a service that handles other bots or handles communication making it easier for developers and users to integrate different services in the conversational ecosystem. Alexa-Cortana integration is an example of inter-agent communication.

C. Goals

Here the bots are classified based on the primary goal they aim to achieve.

1) **Informative:** These bots are designed to provide the user with information that is stored beforehand or is available from a fixed source. Usually, they are information retrieval algorithm based and would either fetch the result of a query from the database or would perform string matching. Very often, they will refer to a static source of information such as a site's FAQ page or a warehouse database with inventory entry.

2) **Chat-based/conversational:** These bots talk to the user, like another human being. Their goal is to respond correctly to the sentence they've been given. Hence, they are often built with the purpose of continuing conversation with the user based on techniques like cross-questioning, evasion, and deference. Example: Siri, Alexa, Mitsuku, Jenny, Tay, Xaoice.

3) **Task-based:** They perform one certain task, such as booking a flight or helping you browse a store. The majority of the times, the actions needed in order to perform a task are predetermined; the flow of events, including exceptions, is decided as well. The bots are intelligent in the context of asking for information and understanding the user's input.

D. Input Processing and Response Generation Method

This classification takes into account the method of processing inputs and generating responses.

Truly intelligent systems generate responses and use natural language understanding to understand the query. These systems are used when the domain is narrow and ample data is available to train a system.

Rule-based systems use pattern matching and prove to be rigid. These are used when the number of possible outcomes is fixed, and scenarios are imaginable in number.

1) **Hybrid:** These systems are a mix of rules and machine learning. An example would be a system that uses a flow chart for managing the direction of conversation but provides responses that are generated using natural language processing.

Bots do not have to belong to one category or other exclusively. These categories exist in each bot in varying proportions. For example, all bots will require some kind of chat capabilities, perhaps a bot for a store will need to use information extraction when it comes to FAQs and search the site when it comes to giving product results. A service that the bot provides hence can include all three kinds of algorithms. Taking another example, a bot will be closed domain but will be programmed for small talk or a bot will be open domain and intrapersonal such as a productivity bot, but it will also be extremely focused on conversations related to productivity.

This classification helps tell the user what to expect and build an image of the bot in the user's mind reducing the gap between user expectations and the delivered bot (Nimavat & Champaneria, 2017).

A GENERIC ARCHITECHTURE OF A CHATBOT

A chatbot consists of four stages sequential or modules, as shown in Figure 2, the input is taken and processed into an appropriate format. Next, named entities are extracted, and intent is discovered. These are used to generate multiple possible responses, select the most appropriate, and present it to the user.

Chunking, Sentence Boundary Detection, Sentence Parsing, Part of Speech Tagging are some basic input processing algorithms that always take place. As one uses libraries, these tasks get masked in functions. Next, Named Entity Extraction, Intent detection, ambiguity detection, context detection, sentiment analysis, query classification, concepts, and synonym detection, etc. take place for understanding the input. Once the query or input is structured into the desired form, the response is generated. It can be generated through a predefined format or via machine learning. Summarization and simplification techniques can also be used if the response is fetched from a text source. Once there is a set of candidate responses, the responses can be checked for relevancy, and a suitable response can be returned (Nimavat & Champaneria, 2017).

Chatbots are of two kinds based on what action they perform in response generation:

Figure 2. Chatbot pipeline

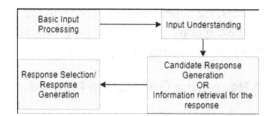

1) **Retrieval based models:** The ones that are rule-based or fetch responses from a predetermined set of responses. Retrieval Based models can be used when the data is limited, and the conversation domain is constricted to a few conversation scenarios. Hence, if all the possible conversations for a use case with the bot are imaginable, a retrieval-based model works well. Also, when the bot is not expected to display intelligence in all scenarios but can afford to deny knowing the answer, such retrieval-based models work well. Booking systems, FAQ systems, or any other systems that fetch information could work well even with a retrieval-based bot.

2) **Generative models:** These systems intend to maintain the hierarchical structure of underlying meanings of the language, can be used when a large amount of data is available, and the system can be trained on that data. They often use NLP and NLU algorithms to process input and generate sentences. Artificial Neural Networks, sequence models, Generative algorithms are some algorithms that are used in this model. Currently, there are not purely generative models, even the most advanced systems such as Alexa, Siri, and Cortana are semi-rule based.

CHATBOTS IN HEALTHCARE

SLOWbot is a research project conducted via a collaboration between Iaso health and FBK (Fondazione Bruno Kessler). It is an innovative chatbot and app that enables a user to follow a 14-day "healthy longevity" meal plan. The diet has recipes containing "longevity foods" and a group provides support and resources via a closed Facebook group. The chatbot focuses on increasing the participants' health literacy through the use of motivational and educational messages during the 14-day period. It will also reinforce the users' reasons for undergoing the dietary change by sending positive messages that are linked to specific personal health benefits as articulated by the user during their onboarding process. (Gabrielli et al., 2018).

Another example is a solution called "Smart Wireless Interactive Healthcare System" (SWITCHes) is developed to facilitate objective data reception and transmission in a real-time manner. Based on the user data acquired from SWITCHes app and the auxiliary data from medical instruments, not only SWITCHes app can engage the user with tailored feedback in an interactive way, in terms of artificial intelligence-powered health chatbot, but the healthcare professional provides the more accurate medical advice to the user also. **Figure 3** illustrates the operational concept of SWITCHes. SWITCHes app is developed to keep track of the individual's weight, dietary intake, and physical activity, on the basis of the energy balance equation, as follows:

$$E_s = E_1 - E_e$$

where E_s, E_1, E_e represent energy storage, energy intake, and energy expenditure, respectively. E_1 consists of the chemical energy from the food and fluids individual daily consumes. E_e reflects body maintenance needs, fuels metabolized for growth, physical activity, and some other processes. (Huang et al., 2019).

Figure 3. The operational concept of SWITCHes

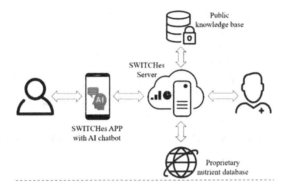

On the other hand, a chatbot-based healthcare-service framework is implemented for the provision of fast treatment in response to accidents that may occur in everyday life, and also in response to changes in the conditions of patients with chronic diseases. This framework is composed as follows: data layer, knowledge layer, information layer, and service layer. To establish and analyze big data on the basis of a variety of collected knowledge and to provide data for users conveniently, a service is offered in each of these four layers. In the service layer, a customized UI/UX offers the service, as can be seen in **Figure 4**.

Figure 4. The initial screen of the development of a chatbot for searching health services

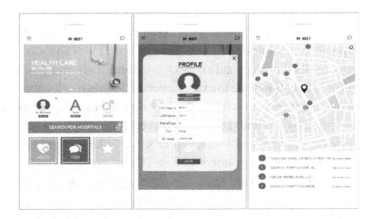

Figure 5 shows the chatbot-based healthcare-service framework. The data layer comprises data processing and storage components that are for the processing and storage of the data that are obtained from multiple sensors, including a wireless body area network (WBAN) sensor. In real-time, the data-

Figure 5. Chatbot-based healthcare-service Framework

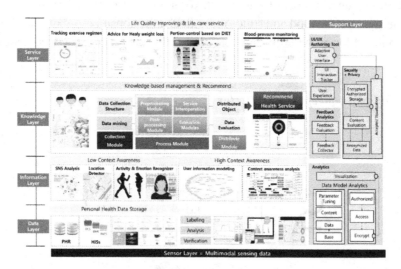

processing module performs data collection, data labeling and analysis, and data filtering depending on the type of data collection.

TOOLS FOR DEVELOPING CHATBOTS

The next section is a set of APIs for named entity extraction and intent detection:

1) **Recast.ai:** It allows the user to create custom queries and train the bot on them. Apart from providing machine learning services to extract entities and intent, it provides everything from templates to analytics for deployed bots. It provides hosting and bot integration across various platforms. One can also add external integrations and create custom logic in the bot. It has built-in support for sentiment analysis and multiple languages. On top of allowing to add custom queries, it also has a drag and drop interface for designing the conversation flow. (*SAP Conversational AI*, n.d.).

2) **Wit.ai:** Wit.ai helps classify the intent and extract named entities from a given input. It then returns the labels to the app or bot. It allows one to extract information such as location, time, date, weather, and also allows one to create one's own intents. It parses the user input into structured data and also helps in conversation by sending the text. However, for performing actions on the structured data, the output of wit.ai must be sent to the app or server whose response wit.ai then returns to the conversation platform such as messenger or Kik. (*Wit.ai*, n.d.)

3) **Dialogflow:** It is an end-to-end, build-once deploy-everywhere development suite for creating conversational interfaces for websites, mobile applications, popular messaging platforms, and IoT devices. It is used for building interfaces (such as chatbots and conversational IVR) that enable natural and rich interactions between users and businesses. (*Dialogflow*, n.d.).

The following is a group of tools for generating story flow-based and rule-based chatbots:

1) **Chatfuel:** It provides a drag and drop interface for making a rule-based bot. Its artificial intelligence module lets you train the bot to map input statements to output, but in comparison to recast.ai and other modules, it is quite rigid in terms of conversation flows. It also allows response prompts and integration with services such as email and IFTTT (*If This Then That*). It also allows a JSON integration for accommodating custom logic into the bot. The most attractive point of the service is that it is extremely simple to build a rule-based bot that is suitable for small businesses. It also allows the user to opt-in or out for mailing lists and can send broadcast messages. It only needs integration with the Facebook page and does not need any other setups (*Chatfuel*, n.d.).

2) **Pandora bot:** Pandora bots provide Artificial intelligence as a service along with a platform to build bots. It also makes custom bots on a paid basis. It uses AIML (*Artificial Intelligence Markup Language*) and provides an IDE (*Integrated Development Environment*) for building bots as well as AIaaS (*Artificial Intelligence as a Service*) API. It allows coding in AIML wherein the developer is supposed to mention the input out responses as a framework. The model can then be trained on data and used.

3) **Text Processing Platforms:** Apart from that, various Cloud platforms such as Amazon, IBM, Google, Microsoft have released their own conversational APIs that allow developers to analyze data, convert speech to text and vice versa and generate appropriate responses even. The benefit of using these platforms lies in the fact that it is easier to integrate them with an already existing cloud infrastructure.

These models are built upon massive amounts of data and employ powerful deep learning capabilities giving these platforms the kind of accuracy that a developer can't achieve with simple resources. Example: Microsoft bot framework, LUIS, Amazon Lex and Poly, IBM Watson, Google Speech API, Google Natural Language API.

4) **For training on your own data:** One can also build their prototype models from scratch and test them on the dataset. They can be trained using platforms such as TensorFlow and Weka. The model can then be scaled using either one's own server or the machine learning services provided by platforms such as Amazon, Google, and the others mentioned above.

Otherwise, there are business-oriented platforms for building chatbots and conversational agents to improve the user experience:

1) ManyChat is a great platform for people without any coding skills. Its primary market is the digital marketing specialist that has no coding skill or a limited coding skill capacity. However, if your business wants flexible AI apps, this is not the way to go. User-friendly, free plan, great Marketing tools are some advantages of this platform. Nevertheless, the lack of flexibility for custom coding and the lack of community resources are the main disadvantages of it. (*ManyChat – Chat Marketing Made Easy*, n.d.).

2) Conversable is the enterprise-class software-as-a-service (SaaS) platform for designing, building, and distributing AI-enhanced messaging and voice experiences across multiple platforms, including Facebook Messenger, Twitter, SMS, Amazon Echo, Google Home, and many others. This platform is an excellent option for big companies and for integrations to conversation channels (*About : Conversable*, n.d.).

3) Comm.ai is an omnichannel API cloud communications platform that revolutionizes the way in which customers and developers can embed programmable digital telephony and cross-channel messaging within their web applications. This tool provides the API cloud communications platform that enables customers and developers to embed programmable digital telephony and cross-channel messaging within web applications. Answer phone calls with JavaScript, program proactive SMS & Add to apps, and automated texting, are some examples for implementing comm.ai (*Integrate voice or text with API for developers - comm.ai*, n.d.).

4) Conversica is a leading provider of Intelligent Virtual Assistants for business, helping organizations attract, grow, and retain customers. The flagship Conversica® Sales AI Assistant helps companies find and secure customers more quickly and efficiently by autonomously contacting, engaging, qualifying, and following up with leads via natural, two-way conversations. Reaching out to over 100 million people on behalf of thousands of companies, Conversica's Intelligent Virtual Assistants are built on a proven and patented platform integrating natural language understanding (NLU), natural language generation (NLG), autonomous action chains and deep learning capabilities that engage prospects over multiple communication channels and in multiple languages (*Conversica*, n.d.).

5) Botsify lets you create AI chatbots on your website or Facebook messenger without any coding knowledge. Botsify is integrated with several services, including WordPress, Shopify, Slack, Alexa, Google Sheets, RSS Feed, JSON API, ZenDesk. The easy-to-use drag and drop interface helps you with a template design for your chatbot. Lots of big brands use Botsify to design their chatbots, including Apple and Shazam (*Botsify - Create Automated Chatbots Online For Facebook Messenger or Website*, n.d.).

DESCRIPTION OF THE PROCESS FOR AUTOMATIC GENERATION OF MEDICAL USER INTERFACES USING VOICE RECOGNITION

The process proposed in this work is divided into two phases, which consist of a set of steps where different programming languages, frameworks, and voice recognition technologies can be implemented. The interaction between these phases is described below in **Figure 6**.

1. **Voice recognition.** In this phase user's speech is recorded and save it as an audio file in order to turn it into word sequence, which is analyzed to detect user intention. NLP (Natural Language Processing) and Semantic technologies are used to identify elements of user intention such as application type, layout, user interface design patterns, platform, and information of user and application. When user intention is not completed, the dialog management module asks the user for missing elements that help to clarify user intention. For this purpose, the dialog management module uses speech synthesis technologies to improve user interaction. This process is iterative until user intention is completed, i.e., when all aforementioned elements were identified. Once the user's intention is completed, an XML-based document is generated. This document describes the features of the application to be generated by the project generation phase.

2. **Project generation.** This phase analyses the XML-based document generated in the previous phase. Then, the project configuration module selects all elements that will be integrated into a software application. Finally, the source code of this application is generated.

Figure 6. Process for automatic generation of medical user interfaces using voice recognition

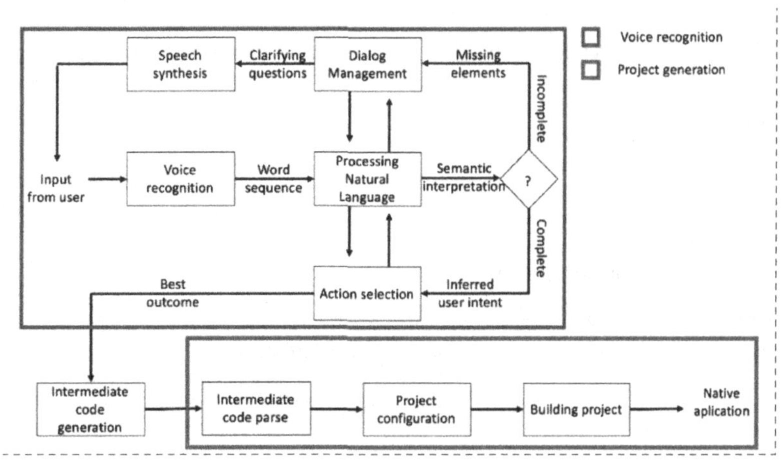

The main modules of the phases are described below with more details.

- **Voice recognition**: In this module, speech is processed to analyze word sequence and turn into text. This text will be processed to determine its semantic.
- **Natural Language Processing**: Semantic text is determined in this module to detect user intentions. Whether user intention is completed, then it will be submitted to the action selection module. Otherwise, the dialog management module is notified to ask the user for missing elements by using speech synthesis technology.
- **Action selection**: This module selects action according to user intention. An XML-based document is generated to describe all features of the software application. This document is submitted to the phase of project generation to generate the software application.
- **Dialog management**: The goal of this module is to ask the user for the missing elements when the NLP module does not have all elements to detect user intention.
- **Speech synthesis**: The main function of this module is to convert questions as a text file from the dialog management module into an audio file. Then this module plays an audio file to make a question or give a result to the user.
- **Intermediate code generation**: In this module, semantic and syntactic validation of the XML-based document is performed to configure the final project.
- **Project configuration**: The project's features are defined in this module. This configuration depends on the XML-based document's description.
- **Project building**: Finally, in this module, the software application is built according to specified features through the process proposed.

Study Case

As a proof-of-concept, a Web-based application prototype with voice recognition was developed to segment the process. This prototype helps to have a better idea for developing an agent conversational that will provide a better user experience. Technologies such as AngularJS and PHP were implemented for front-end and back-end in this prototype, respectively.

In order to develop this prototype, a workflow was organized into seven steps:

1) Selection of application type.
2) Specification of user interface layout.
3) Selection of patterns design.
4) Specification of platforms.
5) Description of user and application information.
6) Project information summary, finally.
7) The download of the application, as can be seen in **Figure 7**.

Figure 7. Prototype's workflow

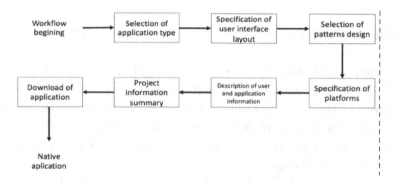

The workflow is guided by a virtual assistant that works with voice recognition to improve user performance. NER (Named Entity Recognition) is a technique implemented in this prototype for knowing what users want to intent. Also, machine learning is used to understand what users are saying.

Figure 8A depicts the first step. In this step, available medical applications are displayed; the virtual assistant asks the user for the application type. Depending on the context of use and kind of user, there are two types of medical apps:

1) apps for health professionals, and
2) apps for the citizens.

The user selects an application type by using voice recognition; then, a medical application is selected automatically. Afterward, a layout of application elements must be specified; a carrousel of different layout templates is displayed, as can be seen in **Figure 8B**. After the selection of layout template, a set of user interfaces design patterns according to the type of application is displayed. The most used user interface design patterns in medical apps are, Datalist, Login, Gallery, Video, Splashscreen, Map, Form and Menu, to name a few. Each UIDP (User Interface Design Pattern) is used according to the characteristics and functionality that the application has. For example, in applications to locate medical services the most used UIDPs are the Maps and Datalist. The Maps have support to the geolocation, and the Datalist allows listing the health services units. Another example is the use of Search, Gallery and Dashboard patterns in health encyclopedias apps, where Search allows searching information about a particular pathology or medication, the gallery shows sets of images, and Dashboard presents the corresponding information. Next, in **Figure 8C** is depicted as the selection of platforms for the software application. User has to use voice commands to specify the platforms. As can be seen in **Figure 8D**, information about user and software is specified, e.g., author name, company name, author email and author's website, application's title, application's short name, and application's version.

Figure 8. Web application prototype: A) Selection of application type; B) Selection of layout template; C) Selection of devices and platforms; D) Specification of user and application information

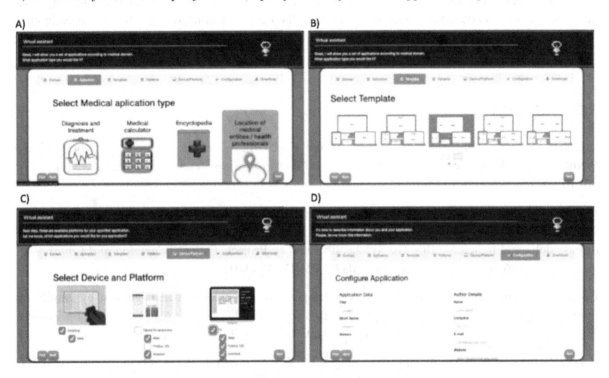

Before proceeding project generation, the prototype displayed a modal with a summary of the application's information. Finally, the building process of the application is executed. When the building process has finished, the software project is downloaded automatically.

CONCLUSION AND FUTURE WORK

The software development process has iterative activities that can be automated to optimize the time of development; thus, involved people will invest time and effort in activities such as business rules, analysis, and design. Voice recognition is an innovative user interface to have better interaction with users.

Chatbots will not be limited to the messenger window. The architecture mentioned above can be generalized for all systems of interaction. Bots are the beginning of an interface between humans and artificial general intelligence. The architecture and the tools that are surveyed help one has an idea of the kind of bot to be built for a system, what to expect from the bot and what tools to use to build it.

Looking for methods and techniques to improve the software development process, this paper suggests a support process by a workflow in order to generate native projects of different platforms by using voice recognition. This approach applies engineering software techniques and natural language, processing which permits to hide some technical aspects to final users by a friendly user interface. Furthermore, medical applications have taken on great importance today, especially in healthcare. Due to this, it is important to investigate the use of these applications in order to develop appropriate graphical user interfaces for this domain.

As future work, we are considering developing an agent conversational to improve user experience. Likewise, research will study additional user interface design patterns and increase compatibility with other devices to promote application development in the field of healthcare. Finally, we are evaluating to include more medical applications that allow generating other user interface design patterns in the medical domain.

REFERENCES

Augello, A., Gentile, M., Weideveld, L., & Dignum, F. (2016). A Model of a Social Chatbot. In G. De Pietro, L. Gallo, R. Howlett, & L. Jain (Eds.), *Smart Innovation, Systems and Technologies, 55* (pp. 5–7). doi:10.1007/978-3-319-39345-2

Banbury, A., Nancarrow, S., Dart, J., Gray, L., Dodson, S., Osborne, R., & Parkinson, L. (2019). Adding value to remote monitoring: Co-design of a health literacy intervention for older people with chronic disease delivered by telehealth - The Telehealth Literacy Project. *Patient Education and Counseling, 103*(3), 597–606. doi:10.1016/j.pec.2019.10.005 PMID:31744701

Bouras, A., Usop, K., & Popescu, M. (2018). Empowering diabetes self-management by gamifying intelligent system: MyTrybeCare concept. In *2018 IEEE 4th Middle East Conference on Biomedical Engineering, MECBME* (pp.137–140). doi:10.1109/MECBME.2018.8402421

Brixey, J., Hoegen, R., Lan, W., Rusow, J., Singla, K., Yin, X., Artstein, R., & Leuski, A. (2018). SHIH-bot: A Facebook chatbot for Sexual Health Information on HIV/AIDS. In *Proceedings of the 18th annual SIGdial meeting on discourse and dialogue* (pp. 370–373).doi: 10.18653/v1/w17-5544

Cerezo, J., Kubelka, J., Robbes, R., & Bergel, A. (2019). Building an expert recommender chatbot. In *Proceedings - 2019 IEEE/ACM 1st International Workshop on Bots in Software Engineering (BotSE)* (pp. 59–63). 10.1109/BotSE.2019.00022

Chatfuel. (n.d.). Retrieved from: https://chatfuel.com/

Chung, M., Ko, E., Joung, H., & Kim, S. J. (2018). Chatbot e-service and customer satisfaction regarding luxury brands. *Journal of Business Research*, 1–9. doi:10.1016/j.jbusres.2018.10.004

Cui, L., Huang, S., Wei, F., Tan, C., Duan, C., & Zhou, M. (2017). Superagent: A customer service chatbot for E-commerce websites. In *ACL 2017 - 55th Annual Meeting of the Association for Computational Linguistics, Proceedings of System Demonstrations*, (pp.97–102). 10.18653/v1/P17-4017

Debon, R., Coleone, J. D., Bellei, E. A., & De Marchi, A. C. B. (2019). Mobile health applications for chronic diseases: A systematic review of features for lifestyle improvement. *Diabetes & Metabolic Syndrome*, *13*(4), 2507–2512. doi:10.1016/j.dsx.2019.07.016 PMID:31405669

Farzandipour, M., Nabovati, E., Sharif, R., Arani, M. H., & Anvari, S. (2017). Patient self-management of asthma using mobile health applications: A systematic review of the functionalities and effects. *Applied Clinical Informatics*, *8*(4), 1068–1081. doi:10.4338/ACI-2017-07-R-0116 PMID:29241254

Gabrielli, S., Marie, K., & Corte, C. (2018). SLOWBot (chatbot) lifestyle assistant. In *Proceedings of the 12th EAI International Conference on Pervasive Computing Technologies for healthcare* (pp. 367–370). 10.1145/3240925.3240953

Galitsky, B. (2019). A Social Promotion Chatbot. Developing Enterprise Chatbots. doi:10.1007/978-3-030-04299-8_12

Google Cloud. (n.d.). *Dialogflow*. Retrieved from https://cloud.google.com/dialogflow/?hl=en

Huang, C. Y., Yang, M. C., Huang, C. Y., Chen, Y. J., Wu, M. L., & Chen, K. W. (2019). A Chatbot-supported Smart Wireless Interactive Healthcare System for Weight Control and Health Promotion. In *IEEE International Conference on Industrial Engineering and Engineering Management* (pp. 1791–1795). doi: 10.1109/IEEM.2018.8607399

Kadariya, D., Venkataramanan, R., Yip, H. Y., Kalra, M., Thirunarayanan, K., & Sheth, A. (2019). KBot: Knowledge-enabled personalized chatbot for asthma self-management. In *Proceedings - 2019 IEEE International Conference on Smart Computing (SMARTCOMP)* (pp. 138–143). doi: 10.1109/SMARTCOMP.2019.00043

Nimavat, K., & Champaneria, T. (2017). Chatbots: An Overview Types, Architecture, Tools and Future Possibilities. *International Journal of Scientific Research and Development*, *5*(7), 1019–1026.

Roca, S., Sancho, J., García, J., & Alesanco, Á. (2019). Microservice chatbot architecture for chronic patient support. *Journal of Biomedical Informatics*, *102*, 103305. doi:10.1016/j.jbi.2019.103305 PMID:31622802

SAP Conversational AI. (n.d.). *Automate Customer Service With AI Chatbots*. Retrieved January 26, 2020, from https://cai.tools.sap/

Sheth, A., Yip, H. Y., Shekarpour, S., & Sheth, A. (2019). Extending Patient-Chatbot Experience with Internet-of-Things and Background Knowledge: Case Studies with Healthcare Applications. *IEEE Intelligent Systems*, *34*(4), 24–30. doi:10.1109/MIS.2019.2905748

Winterlich, A., Stevenson, I., Waldren, A., & Dawson, T. (2017). Diabetes Digital Coach: Developing an Infrastructure for e-Health Self-Management Tools. *2016 9th International Conference on Developments in ESystems Engineering, DeSE*, 68–73. doi:10.1109/DeSE.2016.56

Wit.ai. (n.d.). *Natural Language for developers*. Retrieved from https://wit.ai/

ADDITIONAL READING

Banbury, A., Nancarrow, S., Dart, J., Gray, L., Dodson, S., Osborne, R., & Parkinson, L. (2019). Adding value to remote monitoring: Co-design of a health literacy intervention for older people with chronic disease delivered by telehealth - The Telehealth Literacy Project. *Patient Education and Counseling*, (August). Advance online publication. doi:10.1016/j.pec.2019.10.005 PMID:31744701

Bouras, A., Usop, K., & Popescu, M. (2018). Empowering diabetes self-management by gamifying intelligent system: MyTrybeCare concept. *Middle East Conference on Biomedical Engineering, MECBME, 2018-March*, 137–140. 10.1109/MECBME.2018.8402421

Brixey, J., Hoegen, R., Lan, W., Rusow, J., Singla, K., Yin, X., Artstein, R., & Leuski, A. (2018). *SHIH-bot: A Facebook chatbot for Sexual Health Information on HIV/AIDS. August*, 370–373. doi:10.18653/v1/w17-5544

Pietro, G., Gallo, L., Howlett, R. J., & Jain, L. C. (2016). A Model of a Social Chatbot. *Smart Innovation. Systems and Technologies*, 55, v–vii. doi:10.1007/978-3-319-39345-2

Chapter 7
Issues in the Syntactic Parsing of Queries for a Natural Language Interface to Databases

Alexander Gelbukh

https://orcid.org/0000-0001-7845-9039

Instituto Politécnico Nacional, Mexico

José A. Martínez F.

Tecnológico Nacional de México, Mexico & Instituto Tecnológico de Ciudad Madero, Mexico

Andres Verastegui

Tecnológico Nacional de México, Mexico & Instituto Tecnológico de Ciudad Madero, Mexico

Alberto Ochoa

https://orcid.org/0000-0002-9183-6086

Universidad Autónoma de Ciudad Juárez, Mexico

ABSTRACT

In this chapter, an exhaustive parser is presented. The parser was developed to be used in a natural language interface to databases (NLIDB) project. This chapter includes a brief description of state-of-the-art NLIDBs, including a description of the methods used and the performance of some interfaces. Some of the general problems in natural language interfaces to databases are also explained. The exhaustive parser was developed, aiming at improving the overall performance of the interface; therefore, the interface is also briefly described. This chapter also presents the drawbacks discovered during the experimental tests of the parser, which show that it is unsuitable for improving the NLIDB performance.

DOI: 10.4018/978-1-7998-4730-4.ch007

Copyright © 2021, IGI Global. Copying or distributing in print or electronic forms without written permission of IGI Global is prohibited.

INTRODUCTION

Linguistics is the science that studies the origin, evolution, and structure of human language. For the human being, it is easy to acquire and master language, as well as is genetically and socially predisposed to acquire it naturally. The scientific study of human language is a complicated task mainly because of the variability in language, which complicates the construction of a general theory that describes the function of language.

In computer science, there exist two types of languages: *Formal Language* and *Natural Language* (NL).

Formal language is a set of strings of symbols formed according to a certain rule or rules that determine how the symbols in a given collection can be combined (Lexico, 1920). Formal language is created by the human being, who has formally created rules for its construction and use. Some examples of formal languages are programming languages and mathematical logic. In contrast, *NL* is a language that has been created in a natural way and it has not been designed by humans (Lexico, n.d.). NLs are those that are generated spontaneously by human society to communicate with each other. Some examples of NL are English, Russian, and Spanish. One of the main differences between both languages is variability. Formal languages have a limited variability because they are subject to very precise rules to avoid understanding problems. On the contrary, NLs have a lot of variabilities. NL variability is a communicative advantage because it allows the generation of the large variability of information, but from the computational point of view, it is a very challenging problem for a computer to understand this information.

In Computer Science, Artificial Intelligence aims at developing systems that mimic human intelligence. Natural Language Processing (NLP) is a sub-area of the Artificial Intelligence field, and specifically in Computational Linguistics. NLP studies the interaction between computers and humans though NL (written or spoken) aiming at the implementation of systems that ease human-computer communication, to make it as simple as the communication among people. A subarea in NLP is Natural Language Interfaces to Databases. A Natural Language Interfaces to Databases (NLIDBs) is a system that allows the user to access information stored in a database by typing requests expressed in some natural language (Androutsopoulos, Ritchie, & Thanisch, 1995).

Nowadays, a huge amount of information is stored in databases (DBs). In order to obtain information stored, generally in relational databases, database query languages can be used. A relational database is an auto descriptive collection of interrelated tables (Kroenke & Auer, 2012). An intuitive definition of a relational database is as follows: a relational database is a database type that complies with the relational model. It allows the establishment of interconnections or relations among data stored in tables, and through those connections, relate the data of the tables. To access the information stored in a relational database, the commonly used query language is SQL (Structured Query Language). SQL, originally property of IBM, is an international standard used by almost every relational database. It is used to query, define data structures, modify data, and specify security restrictions in a database (ISO, 1989). Unfortunately, querying a database using SQL requires technical knowledge and expertise in SQL; therefore, it is complicated for a casual and inexperienced user to formulate queries in SQL. The vast majority of users that formulate queries in SQL are information technology professionals. To make information stored in databases accessible to anyone, NLIDBs were developed, whose purpose is to allow inexperienced users to formulate queries to databases in natural language, without having to use SQL. An NLIDB translates NL queries into SQL queries to extract the information stored in a database and shows the information requested to the user.

BACKGROUND

An intuitive definition of an NLIDB is the following: an NLIDB is a system that translates a natural language query into a database query. The only function of the interface is to translate the query. To obtain the information stored in the database, a database management system is used, for example, Access, PostgreSQL, etc. The data flow of an NLIDB is depicted in Figure 1.

Figure 1. The flow of an NLIDB

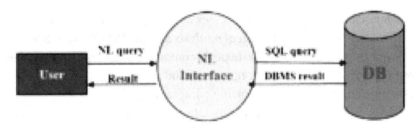

The first NLIDBs were domain-dependent interfaces. These interfaces were developed in the decades of the 60s and 70s for querying a particular database. Some of the most famous interfaces are BASE-BALL (Green, Wolf, Chomsky, & Laughery, 1961) and LUNAR (Woods, Kaplan, & Webber, 1972). Domain-dependent NLIDBs are usually very effective. They achieve accuracies (percentage of correctly translated queries) of around 95%. This high accuracy can be obtained because the software is designed for the particular characteristics of the database and the queries usually formulated for the DB. Since this type of interface is developed for a particular database, it cannot be easily modified for querying different databases. For this reason, domain-independent interfaces were developed for querying many different databases. LADDER (Hendrix, Sacerdoti, Sagalowicz, & Slocum, 1978) is considered one of the first systems that could be configured for querying different databases. The accuracies achieved by this type of interfaces are usually lower than those for domain-dependent NLIDBs; specifically, the best accuracies are in the range from 85% to 90%.

The vast majority of problems present in NLIDBs are linguistic problems. These problems are not only a matter of algorithms and the ability to develop complex software systems, but they are caused by the extreme complexity of NL, which complicates the development of NLIDBs that are highly effective: close to 100% of correctly translated queries.

There are different types of NLIDBs. The most important types, such as *template-based, pattern matching, semantic grammar* (semantic parsing), *neural networks*, and *syntax-based,* are described in the following paragraphs.

Template-based interfaces like NLPQC use domain-specific templates for generating the SQL query. The main disadvantage is that, in order to increase the performance of the interface, it is necessary to increase the number and complexity of the templates. However, if the number and complexity of the templates are increased, then the precision might decrease. This happens because by increasing the number of templates, the probability of choosing the wrong template increases.

Pattern matching interfaces like Aneesah (Shabaz, O'Shea, Crockett, & Latham, 2015) use a pattern matching technique to generate SQL queries. Unfortunately, this method has very low performance in domain-independent interfaces, mainly because it is very difficult to design patterns that are adequate for every case. The pattern matching technique is also prone to semantic problems as the patterns are created as a substitute for syntactic parsing.

Semantic grammar interfaces use a semantic parsing technique, which creates a logical form of the input query before creating the SQL query. There are two types of semantic parsing: *shallow semantic parsing* that identifies entities and the role they play in the input query and *deep semantic parsing* that is a more complex parsing, which fills the slots left in the input query when analyzing the composition.

Neural networks based interfaces have reported a performance above 90%. An interface that uses this technique is NADAQ (Xu et al., 2016). Unfortunately, neural networks need tens of thousands of queries to be trained (Goldberg, 2017).

In *syntax-based* interfaces, three general processes are considered necessary: *lexical analysis, syntactic parsing*, and *semantic analysis*. The *lexical analysis* assigns POS (Part of Speech) tags to words, which can be retrieved from the lexicon (the lexicon contains all the words of the language ideally). The *syntactic parsing* generates relations among words, and the *semantic analysis* must understand the query. The processes are described in the following paragraphs.

The three processes have linguistic and computational problems that complicate the translation process. In the *lexical analysis*, one of the most important problems is the words that have more than one syntactic category, for example, the word *ship,* which can be a vessel (noun) or the action of sending or transporting something (verb). In *syntactic parsing*, a very common problem is the generation of word groupings that are semantically incoherent, i.e., have no sense. And the last one, the *semantic analysis* has problems in the identification of search values in the query. These are only some of the problems that exist in the most important processes of NLIDBs. In general, of the three processes, the two processes that pose the greatest problems are *syntactic parsing* and *semantic analysis*. This chapter focuses on syntactic parsing.

Syntactic parsing is the part of linguistics that studies the way words are combined to generate more complex information. The study of syntactic parsing is important since the correct interpretation and understanding of texts greatly depends on an adequate parsing. *Syntactic parsing* has as its basic unit the word, as an intermediate point the phrase, and as an endpoint the sentence. The word, also called *token*, is the basic unit that represents information.

Syntactic Parsers

The rest of this section is devoted to briefly describing syntactic parsers and their implementation. Two types of syntactic parsers can be distinguished: *shallow parser* and *full parser*. In a shallow parser, the isolated syntactic constituents are identified. No syntactic relations are established among the constituents; therefore, the computational cost is low, at the expense of reducing the deepness of the analysis in the sentence. A full parser, in contrast, rejects any sentence that it is not able to analyze fully. Nevertheless, it yields a lot more information and more valuable since it establishes functional links among the different syntactic elements that constitute the sentence (Saiz, 2003).

Syntactic parsers are mainly based on two methods: *top-down* and *bottom-up*. Both methods analyze one symbol at a time from the left, using the rules of a formal grammar. *Top-down* syntactic parser examines the initial symbol that represents the sentence and, based on the production rules, generates a structure that represents the decomposition of the sentence into the sequence of words that constitute the input sentence. The process is visualized as a tree, where partial structures are built one by one from the initial symbol and continue downwards until the appropriate syntactic structure is found for the input sentence. *Bottom-up* syntactic parser examines each word that constitutes the input sentence and marks it as a leaf of the tree to be built. This method knows the right part of the production rules and tries to replace it with the left part that the rule indicates. After explaining the basic methods followed by syntactic parsers for their implementation, it is necessary to specify the rules that are described next, so that they are linguistically correct. Since phrases are grammatical sequences, they must obey certain grammatical rules.

Designing methods that determine only the correct grammatical sequences in the linguistic processing of texts has been the objective of the grammatical formalisms of Computational Linguistics. There have been considered two main approaches to describe the grammaticality of sentences.

- **Constituency Approach:** The constituents and the assumption about the sentence structure, suggested by Leonard Bloomfield in 1933. It is the approach that analyzes sentences through a segmentation and classification process (Galicia, 2007). The sentence is segmented into its constituent parts, which are classified as syntactic categories. Next, the process is repeated for each part by dividing it into sub-constituents, and so on until the parts are the indivisible parts of the word in the grammar (morphemes) (Galicia, 2007) as shown in Figure 2.

Figure 2. Constituent approach

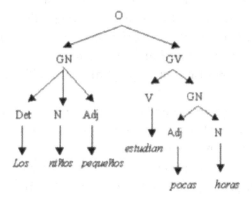

- **Dependency Approach:** The first real attempt to construct a theory that describes the dependency grammar was the work by Lucien Tesnière in 1959. Dependencies are established between pairs of words, where one is the governor and the other is dependent on the first. If each word in the sentence has its own guiding word, the whole sentence is seen as a hierarchical structure of different levels, as a dependency tree. The only word that is not dependent on another is the root of the tree (Galicia, 2007), as shown in Figure 3.

Now some of the different grammars that can be used to implement a parser will be described. It is important to make clear that the term grammar used in this section refers to the type of parsing to be carried out on a sentence in order to construct the syntax tree, unlike the usual concept of grammar of a specific language.

Figure 3. Dependencies approach

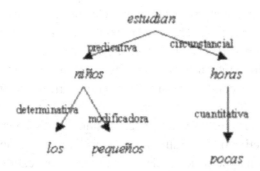

- **Generalized Phrase Structure Grammar (GPSG):** It proposes only a syntactic level of representation, which corresponds to the surface structure, and rules that are not sentence structure, in the sense that they are not in direct correspondence with parts of the tree (Galicia, 2007).
- **Grammar of Functional Lexicon (LFG):** It considers that there is in syntax more than what can be expressed with sentence structure trees, but it also considers the sentence structure as an essential part of the grammatical description (Galicia, 2007).
- **Head-driven Phrase Structure Grammar (HPSG):** It considers the importance of the information coded in the lexical h-cores of the syntactic phrases; more specifically, the preponderance of the use of the *head* mark in the main *child* sub-constituent (Galicia, 2007). HPSG is based on the following key principles: an architecture based on linguistic signs; organization of linguistic information using types, type hierarchies, and restriction inheritance; phrasal projection using general principles from rich lexical information; organization of this lexical information using a system of lexical types; and factoring phrase properties in specific constructions and more general constraints.
- **Categorial Grammar:** The central idea of Categorial Grammar is that an enriched conception of syntactic categories can eliminate the need for many of the constructs used in other grammatical theories (for example, transformations) (Galicia, 2007).
- **Constraint Grammar (CG):** The main goal of Constraint Grammar is surface-oriented syntactic parsing based on the morphology of unrestricted texts. It is considered surface syntax, and not deep syntax, because no syntactic structure is assigned that is not in direct correspondence with the lexical components of the word forms that are in the sentence (Galicia, 2007).
- **Dependency Grammar (DG):** The fundamental basis of this model is to consider not only the lexical elements that constitute the syntactic structure but also the relations among them. According to this theory, there is a link that relates the ideas expressed by words to form an organized thought (Galicia, 2007).
- **Text Meaning Theory (MTT):** It is built for a language in which the word order is more flexible. Syntactic parsing separates word order dependencies differently. The word order constitutes the surface syntax, and the dependencies the deep syntax (García, 2008).

Related Work

An exhaustive survey of the literature on recent syntax-based NLIDBs and relevant syntactic parsers was carried out. Table 1 summarizes information on the most important systems. The third column indicates if a parser is a general-purpose software, and for NLIDB it indicates if the interface uses a general-purpose or specific-purpose parser.

Table 1. Syntax-based NLIDBs and syntactic parsers

Project	NLIDB or Syntactic Parser	Type of use
Goldberg´s parser	Parser	General purpose
FreeLing	Parser	General purpose
NLPWin	Parser	General purpose
Stanford Parser	Parser	General purpose
Chander's NLIDB	NLIDB	General purpose
NaLIR	NLIDB	General purpose
Sujatha's NLIDB	NLIDB	Specific purpose
Bais' NLIDB	NLIDB	Specific purpose

Goldberg´s parser is based on a recurrent neural network to generate syntax trees with an accuracy of 99% (Goldberg, 2017). The book mentions that it uses tens of thousands of sentences to train the neural network and a total of hundreds of thousands of test sentences. The parser is for general-purpose applications and is not mentioned if it has been used to query databases (DBs).

FreeLing is an open-source syntactic parser (Atserias et al., 2006). Its objective is to be used by developers who work in NL, so it is independent of the domain, and it is a general-purpose. Uses a dependency parser to relate the tokens of the query with their modifiers. This allows you to generate more complete syntax trees. For example, in *cats eat slowly*, *slowly* modifies *eat*. LAS2 (syntactic function labeling) accuracy of 83% to 86% is reported for FreeLing (Lloberes, Castellón, & Padró, 2015).

NLPWin was a Microsoft project that intended that Windows could understand written NL (Vanderwende, 2015). The process consists of two parts: the first phase takes stored phrases and the second builds a general tree where the relations among the tokens are labeled. The important thing to note is that NLPWin reports that the tree is syntactically and semantically valid. NLPWin uses two dictionaries, the Logan Dictionary of Contemporary English and the American Heritage Dictionary, to refine the generated tree.

The Stanford parser is a probabilistic based parser implemented in Java versions that have been made for other languages such as Chinese, German, Arabic, etc. (Stanford NLP Group, 2019). Substantial improvements have been made to this parser since a reduced version and a version with neural networks have been created. The lexicalized probabilistic parser implements a factored product model. The parser provides universal dependency and Standford dependencies as well as phrase structure trees. An accuracy of 86.6% has been reported for the Stanford Parser.

Chander proposes the IIRS (Intelligent Information Retrieval System), which is the technique implemented in this project (Chander, Soundarya, Priyadharsini, & Bharathi, 2018). The IIRS is a package with three components: Semantic building, MR generation stage, and query generation stage, which are described next.

1. **Semantic building:** A RDBMS (Relational Database Management System) is an organized set of tables connected to each other with a vast amount of data in them. The semantic builder carries out its work on a *semantic layer*. A *semantic map* for a particular database is created once. It consists of table information, the relations, and the lexicons.
2. **MR generation:** MR consists of one or more tokens and the relations between them, i.e., a coincidence. DB column-column token and DB value-value token must be compatible and related. Each relation token must correspond to an attribute token or value token. A mapping that satisfies the above constraints is a valid mapping. IIRS uses an open-source NLP or Stanford parser to parse the questions and extract the relations among the tokens from the parse tree.
3. **Query generation:** Query generator generates the SQL query by establishing the relation between the MR map and the semantic information. While mapping the synonyms of irrelevant words can be found using WordNet. For example, the set {every, pupil} {entire, seekers} will produce the same amplified set {all, students} in which *students* is the token that will be mapped to the DB column *student*, and *all* is the token that will be considered as a reserved keyword and can be utilized later.

NaLIR (Natural Language Interface to Relational database) is a template-based and generic interactive NL interface for querying relational databases (Li, 2017). One of the main features of NaLIR is that it explains to the user how the interface interprets the input question step by step. NaLIR can accept a logically complex English language sentence as an input query. This query is first translated into an SQL query, which may include aggregate functions, nesting, and various types of joins, among other things, and then processed by an RDBMS. The NLIDB consists of three main parts: query interpretation, interactive communicator, and query tree translator. The query interpretation part includes parsing tree node mapper and structure adjustor. It is responsible for interpreting the user query and representing the interpretation as a query tree. The Stanford parser is used to generate the parse tree. The task of the interactive communicator is to interact with the user to ensure that the interpretation process is correct. The function of the query tree translator is to translate the tree into a SQL statement and send it to an RDBMS.

Sujatha's NLIDB is a generic NLIDB that uses an ontology for disambiguation of meanings (Sujatha, & Raju, 2016). The interface uses a top-down parser using first-order logic, which transforms NL into a formal system of relations among tokens, aided by the normal Backus form to represent first-order logic. In addition, it is mentioned that the system is flexible and adaptable to any database management system and any relational database. Accuracies of 84% and 86% are reported for a corpus of queries to CPVbase (a customer database). Another ontology-based interface is proposed by Porras, Florencia-Juárez, Rivera & García (2018) to compose queries in natural language and translate them into MDX expressions to query OLAP cubes.

Bais' NLIDB uses two types of syntactic rules (Bais, Machkour, & Koutti, 2016). In the first type, the rules for non-terminal symbols are designed using extended context-free grammar, which is independent domain rules. The second type of rules are for terminal symbols, are domain-dependent, and are automatically generated by a rule generator. The semantic analysis uses a set of independent domain rules; therefore, they are general purpose, but each semantic rule has its corresponding syntactic rule. The authors mention that the NLIDB obtains an accuracy of 89%. The tests were performed with a corpus of artificial queries generated by the program.

EXHAUSTIVE SYNTACTIC PARSER

In NLIDBs, syntactic parsing is one of the three main pillars for query translation. The NLIDB described in (Pazos et al., 2016) is based on three layers of analysis: lexical analysis, syntactic parsing, and semantic analysis.

In the lexical analysis, each token of the query is analyzed, looking for the syntactic category in the NLIDB lexicon, which ideally contains all the words of the language. If the syntactic category of the token is not found, then it is assumed that it might be a search value and gets a *false* tag, which means that it might be irrelevant.

The syntactic parsing layer performs a shallow parsing eliminating irrelevant words such as articles and prepositions, as well as determining one syntactic category for tokens that have two or more syntactic categories.

Finally, the semantic analysis is the core of the interface. It is responsible for understanding the meaning of the query. The analysis is performed by examining the query tokens and searching for them in the semantic information dictionary, which contains the descriptors of the DB tables and columns. Once the tables and columns specified in the NL query are detected, they are tagged with the corresponding phrases Select or Where. From there, it is possible to generate the SQL statement using the information collected.

The syntactic parsing layer, being a shallow parser, did not perform the syntactic reductions that are necessary for an effective semantic analysis; therefore, to increase the percentage of correctly answered queries, it was decided to replace the shallow syntactic parser by a full exhaustive parser. An exhaustive syntax parser is capable of generating all possible syntactic reductions from the query entered.

Phrases are syntactic constituents formed from tokens that are grouped based on a syntactic core. The integration of phrases is not performed randomly since the phrases have rules for generating them. There are five types of lexical phrases: noun phrase, prepositional phrase, verb phrase, adjectival phrase, and adverbial phrase. They are called lexical phrases since this type of phrase has a core that gives its name to the phrase. Therefore, a noun phrase is based on a noun; a prepositional phrase is based on a proposition, and so on. If a sentence is syntactically correct, reductions can be generated from the tokens, which constitute phrases that, in turn, are reduced to reach a syntactically correct sentence finally.

The operation of a general parser is detailed below. A parser uses production rules and symbols (terminal and non-terminal). The production rules indicate the order and syntactic category of the tokens that are reduced. For example, NouP → article noun. This indicates that the rule for noun phrases (NouP) can be applied when an article exists, followed by a noun. Similarly, a phrase can be reduced by production rules. For example, a prepositional phrase is formed by a preposition and a noun, PreP → preposition noun. Additionally, a prepositional phrase can also be generated by reducing a preposition and a noun phrase, PreP → preposition, NouP.

Elements that cannot be divided are called terminal symbols; in this case, syntactic categories are terminal symbols since they cannot be broken down into more tokens. Phrases are non-terminal symbols since a phrase can be composed of several syntactic categories or even other phrases. It is important to mention that the rules of production are based on generative grammar, developed by Noam Chomsky.

This theory promotes the hypothesis that any syntactically correct sentence can be described by a finite set of production rules. Based on this theory, the production rules for the exhaustive syntactic parser were developed.

Syntactic parsing, as previously mentioned, tries to reduce tokens using production rules, which are based on language grammar. Unfortunately, language variability complicates the design of the rules. Syntactic parsing is crucial for understanding NL queries since syntactic reductions facilitate understanding the meaning of the query by grouping tokens that are semantically related, for example, column names of a database and search values in a query,

Two classes of syntactic parsers can be distinguished: partial or shallow parser and full parser. Isolated syntactic constituents are identified in the shallow parser. No syntactic relations are established among them, so the computational cost is low, at the cost of decreasing the depth of analysis in the sentence. A full parser, in contrast, rejects any sentence that is not able to analyze globally. However, it provides much more valuable information since it establishes functional links among the different syntactic elements that constitute the sentence (Faili, 2009). Table 1 presents information on recent NLIDBs and parsers detected during a thorough literature search.

In order to increase the accuracy of the NLIDB, which is currently 90%, it was considered convenient to use a new syntactic parser, which must have an accuracy greater than 90%. The use of a general-purpose parser has several drawbacks: FreeLing has an accuracy of 86%, and recursive neural networks require training with thousands of sentences, as mentioned in the Related Work section. Additionally, although there are NLIDBs that report an accuracy of 84% to 92%, unfortunately, these values are not significant, because the tests were not performed using well-known query corpora (ATIS or Geobase). Therefore, it was decided to develop a specific-purpose parser that considers the particularities of queries and domain information.

Computational Complexity of Syntactic Parsing

It has been shown that the problem of determining if an expression in LN is grammatical (i.e., it complies with the rules of grammar) is an NP-complete problem (Koller, & Striegnitz, 2002); therefore, the generation of a syntax tree of an expression (given a grammar) is a problem at least as complex as the previous one and is formally considered NP-hard. This implies that the only way to perform a syntactic parsing without errors of expression in NL is using an exhaustive algorithm whose computational complexity is exponential, i.e., $O(a^n)$ where n denotes the number of words in the expression and a is a constant.

The main reason why this problem arises is due to the syntactic complexity of NL. Syntactic variability is a linguistic problem that complicates processing from a computational point of view: there are a lot of variations that are syntactically correct. Below are a sentence and several syntactic variations of it.

- The dog swims behind Jonny in the lake.
- In the lake the dog swims behind Johnny.
- Behind Johnny swims the dog in the lake.

As noted, the three sentences are semantically equal; in other words, they mean the same. However, they are syntactically different, which means they were built differently. This implies that grammatical rules must allow the inherent variability of NL. In this regard, it is important to mention that in Spanish, the grammar allows greater variability than in English. In order to obtain all the syntax trees of a sentence, an exhaustive syntactic parser was designed.

Description of the Exhaustive Parser

The parser works after carrying out the lexical analysis. Once the terminal symbols (tokens) have been tagged with their syntactic category (or categories), it is possible to perform the syntactic parsing.

Algorithm 1: Coding of syntactic categories of tokens.

Because of the convenience of dealing with numbers instead of alphanumeric strings, it was decided to code the syntactic categories (terminal symbols), phrases (non-terminal symbols), and production rules. This way is easier and faster for the parser algorithms to process the production rules. Therefore, the task of Algorithm 1 is to code the syntactic categories of all the tokens in the input expression (NL query). To this end, the algorithm examines the syntactic category of each token and replaces it by its numeric code (Table 7).

Algorithm 2: Reduction of consecutive peers.

There are expressions in which two consecutive symbols have the same syntactic category, for example, *Ann Mary* (two proper nouns). In these cases, it is unnecessary to analyze both symbols separately; since they have the same syntactic category, it does not affect the integration of phrases (this principle applies for phrases too). This algorithm scans the expression for detecting if there are two or more identical consecutive symbols (terminal or non-terminal); if so, it reduces the identical symbols to just one, reducing the size of the expression. Therefore, the processing time is reduced without affecting the final result.

Algorithm 3: Loading of phrase rules.

As mentioned in Algorithm 1, it was decided to code the production rules in numerical form. Table 8 presents the production rules, and Table 9 shows the corresponding coded rules. It is important to mention that the rules have 1, 2, or 3 symbols on the right-hand side of the rule (Tables 7 and 8). Table 2 shows a sample of the original and the coded rules. The table consists of 3 columns. The second column shows that the symbol on the left is the result of the combination of the symbols on the right, and the third column shows the coded rule, where each symbol (terminal and non-terminal) is substituted by its numeric code (Table 7). For example, the first row shows that a verb phrase is composed of a verb phrase, a noun phrase, and an adjectival phrase. The second row shows that a noun phrase is composed of an article and a noun. To identify the elements, a blank space is used to separate them.

In order to be able to add, delete or modify the production rules, without the need to modify the parser programs, it was considered convenient to store the coded rules in two text files (reductions of 3 elements and reductions of 2 elements). Algorithm 3 simply reads the rules (Table 9) and stores them in two bi-dimensional arrays so that they can be easily located during the processing.

Algorithm 4: Reduction of sub-expression

Table 2. Sample of production rules for building phrases

Type of Phrase	Production Rule	Rule Coding
Verb phrase	VerP → VerP NouP AdjP	12 → 12 10 11
Noun phrase	NouP → art nou	10 → 1 2

Using the reduction rules (Algorithm 3), Algorithm 4 receives a sub-expression and simply determines if there is a rule whose right-hand side matches the sequence of symbols in the sub-expression. If it exists, the algorithm returns the symbol (numeric code) on the left-hand side of the rule. In case the analyzed sub-expression cannot be reduced by any rule, the algorithm returns -1, which indicates that the subexpression could not be reduced.

Algorithm 5: Reduction

The process of exhaustive syntactic parsing (i.e., trying to apply to an expression all the possible reductions that the grammar rules allow) can be represented by a tree, see Figure 4. The root of the tree (denoted by a 0) represents the entire expression (sentence or phrase) NL. Note: although the syntactic parsing is implemented as a depth-first traversal of the tree, the explanation will be made assuming that it is a breadth-first traversal.

From the complete expression, the algorithm tries to make all possible reductions of 3 symbols, then all possible reductions of 2 symbols, and finally all the possible reduction of 1 symbol. The child nodes of the root node represent these reductions and are denoted as follows: 1.1, 1.2, ..., 1.m. Nodes with a continuous line circumference represent successful reductions, while nodes with a segmented line represent impossible reductions. Each success node has a reduced expression associated, i.e., an expression that is obtained from the expression of the parent, in which 3, 2 or 1 symbols have been replaced by a single symbol. In addition, each success node can be reduced further if it has two or more symbols, which is denoted in the figure as arcs to other nodes in the lower level. In contrast, each failure node should not continue to be reduced since the expression associated with this node is the same as that of the parent. Each node of this type will be called fathomed, similar to the branch and bound algorithm.

Figure 4. Processing tree with root node and 1st level nodes

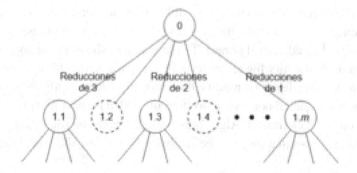

From each success node that is a child of the root node, reductions can be made, performing the same process described in the previous paragraph. The process of reducing node $1.i$ is shown in Figure 5.

Note that the reduction process is finite, since, following any path that begins at the root node to the lower levels of the tree (in such a way that at each node the path continues to only 1 of its children), the number of symbols of the expression associated with each node is generally reduced to 1 or a fathomed node is reached.

Figure 5. Processing tree with one node of 1st level and nodes in the second level

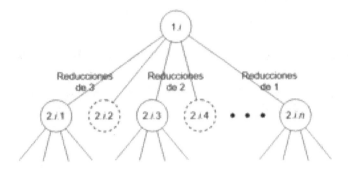

From the reasoning described in the previous paragraph, it follows that the maximum number of levels (including the root) that the tree can have is $f(n) = n$, where n denotes the number of tokens.

Additionally, the number of children that each node can have is finite, which, together with the deduction from the previous paragraph, leads to the conclusion that the maximum number of nodes the tree can have is finite; and therefore, the reduction process is finite.

As previously mentioned, the syntactic parsing is carried out by a depth-first traversal of the tree. The process begins with the expression associated with the root node, to which the algorithm tries to apply a reduction of 3 (i.e., considering three contiguous symbols). If this reduction is impossible, a fictitious node is generated (such as 1.2 in Figure 4), to which no process is applied; otherwise, if this reduction is feasible, a child node (such as 1.1) is generated, to which the same process as that of the root is applied; more precisely, a complete depth-first traversal is performed of the subtree that is rooted in this child node. In any of the two cases: either the reduction was impossible, or it was feasible, and the entire subtree path generated by this reduction was made; an attempt is made to apply another reduction of 3 to which the process described above is applied; then another reduction of 3 is tried, and so on until the algorithm has tried all reductions of 3. The process continues, trying all the reductions of 2 and finally all the reductions of 1.

The high-level pseudocode of the exhaustive syntactic parsing of an expression in NL is described next.

Input: let E_{act} be the current expression to reduce, i.e., a sequence of terminal and non-terminal symbols.

1.   Perform all reductions of 3.
     a.   Let R3 be the set of all candidate reductions of 3 considering the expression E_{act}.
     b.   For each candidate reduction in R3, determine whether the reduction is feasible or not. If this reduction is feasible:

i. Obtain the new E_{new} expression from E_{act} in which three symbols are replaced by the symbol to which these symbols are reduced.

ii. If the number of symbols in E_{new} is greater than 1, make an exhaustive reduction of E_{new}.

iii. If the number of symbols in E_{new} is equal to 1, return E_{new} as a result of the reduction.

2.   Perform all reductions of 2.

    a.   Let R2 be the set of all candidate reductions of two considering the expression E_{act}.

    b.   For each candidate reduction in R2, determine whether the reduction is feasible or not. If this reduction is feasible:

i. Obtain the new E_{new} expression from E_{act} in which two symbols are replaced by the symbol to which these symbols are reduced.

ii. If the number of symbols in E_{new} is greater than 1, make an exhaustive reduction of E_{new}.

iii. If the number of symbols in E_{new} is equal to 1, return E_{new} as a result of the reduction.

3.   Perform all reductions of 1.

    a.   Let R1 be the set of all candidate reductions of 1 considering the expression E_{act}.

    b.   For each candidate reduction in R1, determine whether the reduction is feasible or not. If this reduction is feasible:

i. Obtain the new E_{new} expression from E_{act} in which one symbol is replaced by the symbol to which this symbol is reduced.

ii. If the number of symbols in E_{new} is greater than 1, make an exhaustive reduction of E_{new}.

iii. If the number of symbols in E_{new} is equal to 1, return E_{new} because of the reduction.

This algorithm is recursive since, in steps 1.b.ii, 2.b.ii and 3.b.ii, the algorithm is executed taking E_{new} as input. In addition, it is important to note that for the fathomed nodes, no process is performed, as observed in steps 1.b, 2.b, and 3.b.

Algorithm 5 stores the results in a matrix. A fragment of the matrix is shown in Table 3, which shows the parsing of the query *muestra las aerolíneas que son empresa dual* (show the airlines that are dual carrier). Each row of the matrix corresponds to a node generated during the process. Each node is identified by an integer number (1, 2, 3, etc.); incidentally, the labels in the nodes shown in Figure 4 and Figure 5 are only for explanation purposes. The matrix has four columns: the first column shows the node number, the second column indicates the parent node, the third column shows the entire sequence of symbols that the node receives for reduction, and the fourth column indicates if the node is a leaf, which indicates that the initial expression has been successfully reduced. In the third column, the curly braces are used for indicating the symbols that will be reduced at each step of the process.

Algorithm 6: Generate Path.

Once the reduction process has been completed, and the nodes are stored in the matrix, the syntax trees are generated. The matrix shown in Table 3 is used as input for this process. The task of this algorithm is to generate all existing paths from the leaf nodes to the root node.

Table 3. Matrix for results of parsing

Node	Parent	Expression	Leaf Node
0	--	5 1 2 4 5 2 3 (ver {art nou} pro ver nou adj)	No
1	1	5 10 4 5 2 3 ({ver NouP} pro ver nou adj)	No
2	2	12 4 5 2 3 (VerP pro ver {nou adj})	No
3	3	12 4 5 10 (VerP pro {ver NouP})	No
4	4	12 4 12 (VerP {pro} VerP)	No
5	5	12 4 12 (VerP {NouP VerP})	No
6	6	12 17 ({VerP} DecS)	No
7	7	15 17 (ImpS DecS)	Yes

The process consists of an outer *for* cycle that scans the entire matrix in search of leaf nodes. When a leaf node is detected, a variable (*row*) stores the row where that leaf node was found. Therefore, when the path of that leaf node is completed, the cycle can resume from this row.

The outer *for* cycle has an inner *while* cycle, which searches the matrix looking for all the nodes of the path from the detected leaf node to the root node. Initially, a variable *node* (which indicates the current node) is set equal to *row*. The *while* cycle calls a Search() method, which receives two parameters: *matrixElements* and *matrixElements*(*node*, 1), where the first parameter is the matrix of Table 3, and the second parameter is the position of the parent of *node*. The method returns the position of the parent node in the variable *node*. When the *while* cycle is iterated again, it is positioned at the row of the new node (formerly the parent node). The process continues until the *while* cycle reaches the root node (*node* = 0). When the root node is reached, the *while* cycle ends, and the process for collecting the path nodes concludes. After the inner *while* cycle ends, the outer *for* cycle resumes scanning the matrix at *row*+1, looking for more leaf nodes, until the last row of the matrix.

Experimental Results

Tests were performed on the exhaustive parser to assess its usefulness for the NLIDB, in particular the processing time, considering that its complexity is exponential. The results of the tests performed with the Geoquery880 corpus (Machine Learning Research Group, 2001) are presented in Table 4.

369 of the 880 queries that constitute the Geoquery corpus were used for the test. The parser found that 152 are grammatically correct, and 202 are not. In addition, 15 queries had problems at the time of

Table 4. Test results of the exhaustive syntactic parser

Results for queries	Number of queries
Grammatical queries	152
Non-grammatical queries	202
Troublesome queries	15
Total number of queries	369

processing, 13 of the 15 queries with problems overflowed the data structure of the parser, and two had extremely large processing times, so it was necessary to interrupt them.

Although most queries were processed in a reasonable time (seconds), there are queries whose processing time can reach minutes or hours; there were even cases in which the process had to be interrupted since the processing time was excessive. The average processing time was 60 seconds, which is undesirable considering that parsing is only one phase of the overall translation process, and it still remains to perform the semantic analysis and the translation to SQL.

A serious problem detected is the overproduction of syntax trees, which is the result of the syntactic variability mentioned above. Table 5 shows two examples.

Table 5. Overproduction of syntax trees

Query	Time in Seconds	No. of Syntax Trees
Cuáles estados en los United States tienen una ciudad Springfield What states in the United States have a city of Springfield	92.30	3,633
Cuál es la densidad de población de cada estado de US What are the population densities of each US state	69.50	2,759

As Table 5 shows, the first query generated 3,633 syntax trees (all syntactically correct), which constitute all the possible syntactic variations of the query. Additionally, it has been detected that many of the trees generated are syntactically equivalent to other trees or are semantically incoherent. The number of generated syntax trees is excessive for obtaining a result in a reasonable time since large amounts of run-time are necessary for discarding redundant and incoherent trees. The difficulty for selecting from a large number of trees significantly increases the overall processing time of a query.

Another problem detected was data overflow, which occurs when the data generated during parsing exceeds the capacity of the data structure of the parser. As expected, as the size of the structure was increased, the number of non-grammatical queries decreased; however, there are queries for which 50,000 reductions were generated, an extremely large number for one query. This problem is a consequence of the overproduction of trees.

Semantic incoherence is perhaps the most important problem of all since the overproduction of trees and processing time could be reduced using more powerful hardware. However, semantic incoherence is a problem that may prevent the correct translation of a query regardless of whether the processing time is short or large. Semantic incoherence occurs when a query is parsed correctly according to the production rules, but the word groupings determined by the production rules generated by the parsing are not semantically correct, i.e., they make no sense. The following example illustrates this problem: *Which Delta flights depart to Washington at night?* In this example, the following rule NouP → NouP PreP could be applied to *Washington at night*; therefore, at *night* would be a modifier of *Washington*, which is syntactically correct, but semantically incorrect, because it should be a complement of the verb *depart*. This situation complicates the semantic analysis of the query since at *night* refers to a flight departure, not to a characteristic of *Washington*.

SOLUTIONS AND RECOMMENDATIONS

The overproduction of trees occurs because there are many possible sequences in which the production rules can be applied. Table 6 shows three different parses for the query *muestra las aerolíneas que son empresa dual* (show the airlines that are dual carrier), whose parsing process is shown in Table 3. The second column of Table 6 shows the same sequence of reductions in Table 3. The third column presents a different sequence of application of the production rules; for example, at step 2, the last two symbols are reduced instead of the first two; however, the final result is the same. The last column shows an incoherent parse; specifically, at step 5, the rule VerP → VerP NouP allows to reduce the first two symbols, which is semantically incoherent because the resulting verb phrase is the reduction of *muestra las aerolíneas que* (show the airlines that).

Table 6. Different results of parsing

Step	Correct Parse	Alternate Parse	Incoherent Parse
0	ver {art nou} pro ver nou adj	ver {art nou} pro ver nou adj	ver {art nou} pro ver nou adj
1	{ver NouP} pro ver nou adj	ver NouP pro ver {nou adj}	{ver NouP} pro ver nou adj
2	VerP pro ver {nou adj}	{ver NouP} pro ver NouP	VerP pro ver {nou adj}
3	VerP pro {ver NouP}	VerP pro {ver NouP}	VerP pro {ver NouP}
4	VerP {pro} VerP	VerP {pro} VerP	VerP {pro} VerP
5	VerP {NouP VerP}	VerP {NouP VerP}	{VerP NouP} VerP
6	{VerP} DecS	{VerP} DecS	{VerP} VerP
7	ImpS DecS	ImpS DecS	ImpS {VerP}
8			ImpS DecS

When constructing the parse trees for the second and third columns of Table 6, it is evident that the two parses are the same, the only difference is that the production rules have been applied in a different order. A variant of the exhaustive parser described before could be designed using dynamic programming, which would also be exhaustive, but it would eliminate parses that are equivalent, i.e., those that only differ in the order of the application of rules.

For avoiding the generation of semantically incoherent parses, it is necessary to develop a syntactic parser that involves semantic information for preventing the application of the rule that allows to reduce VerP NouP because the noun phrase is a reduction of the word *que* (that), which is a pronoun. Therefore, it is necessary to design reduction rules that involve semantic information. For example, the noun phrase that results (step 5) from reducing the pronoun should be distinguished from other noun phrases for precluding the application of the rule VerP → VerP NouP.

FUTURE RESEARCH DIRECTIONS

The current challenge for domain-independent NLIDBs consists of developing systems whose accuracy is above 95%. As mentioned in the Background section, the best accuracies of this type of interfaces are in the range from 85% to 90%. The reason for their low effectiveness is that it is very difficult to design general algorithms that can deal with all the particular characteristics of many different DBs and all the problems that are involved in all the possible queries that can be formulated.

For syntax-based NLIDBs, the information generated by syntactic parsers is crucial for semantic analysis, specifically word groupings (phrases). Therefore, in order to develop an NLIDB with an accuracy above 95%, it is necessary to use a syntactic parser with an accuracy above 95%. Unfortunately, general-purpose parsers such as Stanford and Freeling (as mentioned in the section Related Work) achieve accuracies below 90%, and neural network parsers need tens of thousands of sentences for training the network.

In Stratica et al. (2005), the authors mention that the schema of the DB to be queried can be used as an additional resource for improving the interpretation of a query by taking advantage of the limitation of its domain (i.e., the DB to be queried). Therefore, for an NLIDB, it is convenient to implement a specific-purpose parser that takes advantage of the particularities of queries (for example, the presence of search values) and domain information for generating word groupings adequate for the subsequent semantic analysis, instead of using a general-purpose parser.

CONCLUSION

The experimental results obtained for an exhaustive syntactic parser described in this chapter, show that it has two major disadvantages: the generation of a large number of syntax trees and the semantic incoherence of many of the syntax trees. The overproduction of syntax trees can be reduced by using dynamic programming; however, semantic incoherence raises a problem that is practically impossible to solve using only syntactic rules.

From the problems found, it was discovered that lexical, syntactic, and semantic analysis should share information to generate correct results. Therefore, a new syntactic-semantic parser has been developed that uses a different set of production rules, which combine syntactic and semantic information.

REFERENCES

Androutsopoulos, I., Ritchie, G. D., & Thanisch, P. (1995). Natural language interfaces to databases – An introduction. *Journal of Natural Language Engineering, 1*(1), 29–81. doi:10.1017/S135132490000005X

Atserias, J., Casas, B., Comelles, E., González, M., Padró, L., & Padró, M. (2006). FreeLing 1.3: Syntactic and semantic services in an open-source NLP library. In *Proceedings of the Fifth International Conference on Language Resources and Evaluation (LREC'06)* (pp. 48-55). Genoa, Italy: Academic Press.

Bais, H., Machkour, M., & Koutti, L. (2016). A Model of a generic natural language interface for querying database. *International Journal of Intelligent Systems and Applications, 2*(8), 35–44. doi:10.5815/ijisa.2016.02.05

Chander, S., Soundarya, J., Priyadharsini, R., & Bharathi, B. (2018). Data analysis of natural language querying using NLP interface. *International Journal of Applied Engineering Research, 13*(8), 5792–5795.

Faili, H. (2009). From partial toward full parsing. In *Proceedings of the International Conference RANLP-2009* (pp. 71-75). Borovets, Bulgaria: Academic Press.

Fei-Fei, L. (2017). *Querying RDBMS using natural language* (Doctoral dissertation). University of Michigan, Ann Arbor, MI.

Galicia, S. (2002). Análisis sintáctico conducido por un diccionario de patrones de manejo sintáctico para lenguaje español. *Computación y Sistemas, 6*(2), 143–152.

García, O. (2008). Gramática contrastiva computacional: MTT vs. HPSG. *Proceedings of VIII congreso de Lingüística General*. Retrieved from http://www.lllf.uam.es/ clg8/actas/index.html

Goldberg. (2017). Neural network methods for natural language processing. *Synthesis Lectures on Human Language Technologies, 10*(1).

Green, B. F., Wolf, A. K., Chomsky, C., & Laughery, K. (1961). BASEBALL: An automatic question answerer. In *Proceedings of the Western Joint Computer Conference* (pp. 207-216). Los Angeles, CA: Academic Press.

Hendrix, G. G., Sacerdoti, E. D., Sagalowicz, D., & Slocum, J. (1978). Developing a natural language to complex data. *ACM Transactions on Database Systems, 3*(2), 105–147. doi:10.1145/320251.320253

ISO. (1989). *ISO/IEC 9075:1989 International standard. Information processing systems – Database language SQL with integrity enhancement* (2nd ed.). ISO/IEC.

Koller, A., & Striegnitz, K. (2002). Generation as dependency parsing. In *Proceedings of the 40th Annual Meeting of the Association for Computational Linguistics* (pp. 17-24). Philadelphia, PA: Academic Press.

Kroenke, D. M., & Auer, D. (2012). *Database processing: Fundamentals, design and implementation*. Pearson Education, Inc.

Lexico. (1920). *Formal language*. Retrieved from https://www.lexico.com/en/ definition/formal_language

Lexico. (n.d.). *Natural language*. Retrieved from https://www.lexico.com/en/ definition/natural_language

Lloberes, M., Castellón, I., & Padró, L. (2016). Enhancing FreeLing rule-based dependency grammars with subcategorization frames. In *Proceedings of the Third International Conference on Dependency Linguistic*s (pp. 201-210). Uppsala, Sweden: Academic Press.

Machine Learning Research Group. (2001). *Geoquery Data*. Retrieved from http://www.cs.utexas.edu/ users/ml/nldata/geoquery.html

Pazos, R. A., Aguirre, M. A., González, J. J., Martínez, J. A., Pérez, J., & Verástegui, A. A. (2016). Comparative study on the customization of natural language interfaces to databases. *SpringePlus, 5*(553), 1–30. doi:10.118640064-016-2164-y

Porras, J., Florencia-Juárez, R., Rivera, G., & García, V. (2018). Interfaz de lenguaje natural para consultar cubos multidimensionales utilizando procesamiento analítico en línea. *Research in Computing Science, 147*(6), 153–165. doi:10.13053/rcs-147-6-12

Saiz, M. (2003). Procesamiento del lenguaje natural: Presente y perspectivas futuras. In *Proceedings of IX Jornadas Iberoamericanas de Informática, Ingeniería de Software en la Década del 2000* (pp. 191-226). Cartagena, Colombia: Academic Press.

Shabaz, K., O'Shea, J. D., Crockett, K. A., & Latham, A. (2015). Aneesah: A conversational natural language interface to databases. In *Proceedings of the World Congress on Engineering* (pp. 227-232). London, UK: Academic Press.

Sleator, D. D. K., & Temperley, D. (1995). *Parsing English with a link grammar*. Retrieved from https://arxiv.org/pdf/cmp-lg/9508004v1.pdf

Stanford Natural Language Processing Group. (2019). *The Stanford parser: A statistical parser*. Retrieved from https://nlp.stanford.edu/software/lex-parser.shtml

Stratica, N., Kosseim, L., & Desai, B. C. (2005). Using semantic templates for a natural language interface to the CINDI virtual library. *Data & Knowledge Engineering*, *55*(1), 4–19. doi:10.1016/j.datak.2004.12.002

Sujatha, B., & Raju, S. V. (2016). Ontology based natural language interface for relational databases. *Procedia Computer Science*, *92*, 487–492. doi:10.1016/j.procs.2016.07.372

Vanderwende, L. (2015). *NLPwin – an introduction* (no. MSR-TR-2015-23). Retrieved from https://www.microsoft.com/en-us/research/publication/nlpwin-an-introduction/

Woods, W. A., Kaplan, R. M., & Webber, B. N. (1972). The lunar sciences natural language information System (BBN Report 2378). Bolt Beranek and Newman Inc.

Xu, B., Cai, R., Zhang, Z., Yang, X., Hao, Z., Li, Z., & Liang, Z. (2016). NADAQ: Natural language database querying based on deep learning. *IEEE Access: Practical Innovations, Open Solutions*, *7*. Advance online publication. doi:10.1109/access.2019.2904720

APPENDIX

This appendix presents the alphabetical coding of the symbols, numerical coding and the production rules designed for the exhaustive parser. Grammatical categories, phrases and types of sentences are coded numerically to facilitate reductions and standardize the elements for facilitating algorithm implementation. The production rules of the grammar are shown in Table 8.

The production rules coded to generate syntactic reductions are presented in Table 9. The rules are coded according to the coding numbers shown in Table 7.

Table 7. Terminal and non-terminal symbols of the grammar

Terminal and Non-terminal Symbols	Description of Symbols	Numeric Code
art	Article	1
nou	Noun	2
adj	Adjective	3
pro	Pronoun	4
ver	Verb	5
adv	Adverb	6
pre	Preposition	7
con	Conjunction	8
int	Interjection	9
NouP	Noun phrase	10
AdjP	Adjectival phrase	11
VerP	Verb phrase	12
AdvP	Adverbial phrase	13
PreP	Prepositional phrase	14
ImpS	Imperative sentence	15
IntS	Interrogative sentence	16
DecS	Declarative sentence	17

Table 8. Production rules of the grammar

Noun Phrases			
NouP → art nou adj	NouP → art nou NouP	NouP → art nou AdjP	NouP → art nou PreP
NouP → art nou	NouP → nou adj	NouP → nou con	NouP → nou NouP
NouP → nou AdjP	NouP → nou PreP	NouP → nou	NouP → adj nou
NouP → adj NouP	NouP → pro nou	NouP → pro NouP	NouP → pro AdjP
NouP → pro PreP	NouP → pro	NouP → con art nou	NouP → con nou
NouP → con NouP	NouP → NouP AdjP	NouP → NouP PreP	
Verb Phrases			
VerP → ver art nou	VerP → ver adj nou	VerP → ver adv	VerP → ver NouP
VerP → ver PreP	VerP → ver	VerP → adv ver	VerP → con ver adv
VerP → con ver	VerP → con adv ver	VerP → VerP NouP AdjP	VerP → VerP NouP
VerP → VerP PreP	VerP → PreP VerP		
Adjectival Phrases			
AdjP → adj PreP	AdjP → adv adj PreP	AdjP → adv adj	AdjP → AdjP NouP
Prepositional Phrases			
PreP → pre art nou	PreP → pre nou adj	PreP → pre adj nou	PreP → pre nou
PreP → pre adj	PreP → pre NouP	PreP → pre AdjP	PreP → pre VerP
PreP → pre AdvP	PreP → pre PreP	PreP → con pre	PreP → PreP NouP
Adverbial Phrases			
AdvP → adv nou	AdvP → adv NouP	AdvP → adv PreP	AdvP → adv
AdvP → AdvP NouP	AdvP → AdvP PreP		

Table 9. Coding of production rules

Noun Phrases			
10 → 1 2 3	10 → 1 2 10	10 → 1 2 11	10 → 1 2 14
10 → 1 2	10 → 2 3	10 → 2 8	10 → 2 10
10 → 2 11	10 → 2 14	10 → 2	10 → 3 2
10 → 3 10	10 → 4 2	10 → 4 10	10 → 4 11
10 → 4 14	10 → 4	10 → 8 1 2	10 → 8 2
10 → 8 10	10 → 10 11	10 → 10 14	
Verb Phrases			
12 → 5 1 2	12 → 5 3 2	12 → 5 6	12 → 5 10
12 → 5 14	12 → 5	12 → 6 5	12 → 8 5 6
12 → 8 5	12 → 8 6 5	12 → 12 10 11	12 → 12 10
12 → 12 14	12 → 14 12		
Adjectival Phrases			
11 → 3 14	11 → 6 3 14	11 → 6 3	11 → 11 10
Prepositional Phrases			
14 → 7 1 2	14 → 7 2 3	14 → 7 3 2	14 → 7 2
14 → 7 3	14 → 7 10	14 → 7 11	14 → 7 12
14 → 7 13	14 → 7 14	14 → 8 7	
Adverbial Phrases			
13 → 6 2	13 → 6 10	13 → 6 14	13 → 6
13 → 13 10	13 → 13 14		

Chapter 8
Preservation of Cultural Heritage in an Ethnic Minority Using Internet of Things and Smart Karaoke

Alberto Ochoa

https://orcid.org/0000-0002-9183-6086
Universidad Autónoma de Ciudad Juárez, Mexico

Roberto Contreras-Masse
Tecnológico Nacional de México, Mexico & Instituto Tecnológico de Ciudad Juárez, Mexico

Jose Mejia
Universidad Autónoma de Ciudad Juárez, Mexico

Diego Oliva
Universidad de Guadalajara, Mexico

ABSTRACT

This research describes an intelligent tool based on a karaoke system to represent the linguistic resources related to a social network for music and songs associated with a cultural bulwark: Otomí (a language spoken in México). This system employs a representation of the Dublin Core metadata standard for document description, composed by XML standard to describe profiles and provide recommendations to a group of persons associated with this social network. The novel idea of this research is the analysis (with an improved methodology) of each search to provide a recommendation based on petitions of each user in this social network, reducing the human efforts spent on the generation of a specific profile. In addition, this chapter presents and discusses some experiments to corroborate the impact of this research, based on quantitative and qualitative evaluations. This chapter introduces an innovative idea of how to help this type of ethnic group.

DOI: 10.4018/978-1-7998-4730-4.ch008

Copyright © 2021, IGI Global. Copying or distributing in print or electronic forms without written permission of IGI Global is prohibited.

INTRODUCTION

Nowadays, there are large amounts of digital songs available for users in open music format via the Web. Most of these songs can be used by a device called Karaoke, an electronic instrument invented in Japan by Daisuke Inoue in the past century, that displays the lyrics of a song and the music track. The main advantage of open music is the minimization of promotion turnaround. Therefore, the Digital Libraries (DLS) have become the main repositories of digital documents, links, and associated metadata (Baeza-Yates, Ribeiro-Neto, 1999). A recommender system makes decisions by personalized information associated with users in order to learn by first-hand the references of a community and how recommendations are perceived. Customization is associated with the way in which content and services can be tailored to meet the specific needs of a user or a group of individuals through a social network. The system's feasible and objective recommendations based on the needs associated with a specification-centered human demand are not easy tasks. Everyone can experience this difficulty in trying to find a new song in a good indexing and retrieval system in a native language such as Otomi.

To create a proper search and conceptualize specific requirements based on specific restrictions is complicated, coupled with an extensive list of user requirements together with the requirements that must possess these requests, including long waiting times associated with query validation. A very low proportion of users are suitable to spend a few hours searching, finding new songs, where the target language appears. This functionality, the query specification, can be achieved by analysis of user activities, history, or claims information, to mention a few factors. In this chapter, a set of recommendations of karaoke music associated with a young community who spoke Otomi is proposed; the recovered songs are associated with a karaoke playlist. The main contribution of this paper is to provide a mechanism for user-based recommendation reducing human effort invested in profile generation. The chapter is organized as follows: We started to give an overview of the literature and concepts background, then the recommendation system and detail of its architecture and techniques. Finally, some quantitative and qualitative experiments to test and validate our system, along with a discussion of results and conclusions of our research are presented. Although in Mexico the official language is Spanish, about 57 dialects are mainly spoken by ethnic minorities throughout the country, as is shown in **Figure 1**. This means a lack of opportunities for people being monolingual, so the federal government has tried to safeguard minorities to try to give the same opportunity to spread their culture and gain new speakers to their language groups.

There are different efforts to achieve assimilation of ethnic minorities through their language, but there are no media in the oral part of the same, which is why new speakers do not have a large vocabulary of his mother tongue. One of the few alternatives is the use of books with stories, fables, and legends printed to textbooks for infants in the native language along with Spanish translation, as is shown in **Figure 2**. However, you cannot hear the correct pronunciation. We propose Web Radio and, in turn, a Smart Karaoke with the purpose of expanding knowledge of spoken dialect by indigenous groups.

Theoretical Foundations

The technologies associated with the semantic Web are characterized by providing efficient and intelligent access when you want to interact with digital documents on the Web. The standard-based metadata is used to describe information objects, and in turn, have two main advantages: the first is related to the computational efficiency in the process of gathering information and interoperability between distribution lists (DL) associated with the repositories of information. The second advantage is due to

Figure 1. Distribution of ethnic dialects in Mexico

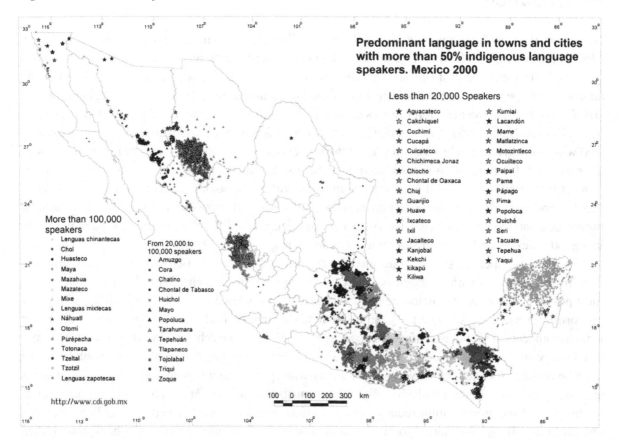

the increasing use of the Dublin Core (DC) metadata standard (DCMI, 2005) obtained as a result of the OAI (Open Archive Initiative, 2005) initiative. This metadata standard DC was conceived with the goal of defining a minimum set of metadata that could be used to describe the resources of a DL available. This standard defines a set of 15 metadata items (Dublin Core Metadata Initiative, 2005) associated with each characteristic of one of the kinds and the source of the data. The main objective of the OAI is to create a standard form of communication associated with information retrieval, allowing distribution

Figure 2. Indigenous Language book related to cultural minority children in Mexico

lists worldwide to interoperate as a federation of repositories (Open Archives Initiative, 2019; Sompel, 2000). The process of collecting metadata DL is achieved by OAI-PMH (Open Archives Protocol, 2019), which defines how the transfer of metadata between two entities, data and service providers, is done. The data provider acts by searching the database metadata to generate in this way the availability associated with the service provider, which uses the data collected to provide specific services related to information content. The core of a recommendation system is associated with the personal information of a group of individuals with similar characteristics as it can be a community. It is critical to use and evaluate existing considerations associated with each user's tastes. For our research, the user profile is obtained from a social network like the one used by Laustanou, (2007), but one should consider that there are three different methodologies used to characterize a Recommendation System, to generate an appropriate recommendation (Huang et al., 2005):

(i) Based on the context of the application domain, which recommends starting classification according to the profile of the user and the options generated by the most proactive users;
(ii) Collaborative filtering, which is based on the similarity of common interests of different users;
(iii) Hybrid approach, combining both models' prerequisites to take advantage of all benefits.

In our work, the context-based approach is used, once the user information is taken from the members of the social network associated with the Otomi dialect karaoke. This referral process can be perceived as a process of information retrieval, in which each of the relevant contexts associated with songs associated with each user must be recovered, and the recommendation may be performed to determine its value assessed. Therefore, to make viable and credible recommendations, we can use the classical models of information retrieval, such as the Boolean model, the vector space model (VSM), or the probabilistic model. In this paper, VSM was selected because it provides satisfactory results with a suitable computational effort. In this model, the songs and queries are represented by items associated with vectors. The terms are words or expressions extracted from documents (song lyrics or the context in which they develop) and queries that can be used for identification and representation of pertinent content. Each term has a weight associated with it to provide distinctions between each of the songs in the repository of information according to its importance and value. According to Salton (1988), weight may vary continuously between 0 and 1 (the threshold associated with the objectivity of being convenient. Values closer to 1 are more important, while values closer to 0 are irrelevant.

The VSM uses an n-dimensional space to represent the terms, where n is the number of different terms for each document or associated song, and the query represents the weight associated with the vector of coordinates in the corresponding dimension. VSM principle is based on the inverse correlation between the distance (angle) between the vectors of contextualization in space and the similarity between the songs they represent. To calculate a similar score, cosine (Equation 1) can be used. The resulting value indicates the degree of relevance between a query (Q) and a document (song) (D), where w represents the weights of the terms contained in Q and D respectively, and t represents the number of terms (size associated with the vector). This equation provides an output of recovery classified based on the order of similarity values recovery classified according to the decrease of its value, as proposed in Salton (1988).

$$sim\left(d_k,q\right) = \frac{\sum_{j=1}^{n}\sum_{i=1}^{n}w_{i,k}*w_{j,q}*t_i\bullet t_j}{\sqrt{\sum_{i=1}^{n}w_{i,k}^2}*\sqrt{\sum_{i=1}^{n}w_{i,q}^2}} \tag{1}$$

We propose the use of the same equation, which is widely used to compare and evaluate the similarity among songs, and their respective similarity by other authors (e.g., Wong 1985; Slamet et al., 2018; Watanabe and Goto, 2019). In our research, Q represents the user profile associated with social networking and D the document descriptors (lyrics and the principal components of music associated with this song) that are harvested from the DL. The term weighting scheme is very important to guarantee an effective retrieval process.

The similarities among songs and items consist of documents within the available catalog, and each of them is represented as a multi-dimension vector. In VSM is required to define:

- Set of words know as Vocabulary, which forms the vector space;
- Set of weights *Wij* corresponding to query *j* per item *i*;
- The document query vector *dj = (W1, W2, ..., Wtj) | j = {1, 2, ..., n}*

In VSM, the documents are represented by a term-document matrix or term-frequency matrix. Each cell in the matrix is according to the weight given by a term in a document. If the value equals zero, it means that the term is not present in the document. As VSM has been around for a long time, readers can rely on literature to research details on in this topic (Lee, Chuang, & Seamons, 1997)

The results depend crucially on the choice of weighting system and assessment associated with each term considered; also, the selection of query terms is essential for a recommendation according to user's needs and if this may be the first to be displayed as the application domain suggest like we are looking for the concept of "A forest of China" to recover the equivalent of a legend and not a fable. Our research focuses on selecting and weighting query terms to obtain and to generate a ranking of assessment before recovery. Anyone within the social network that requires to recover music (song) can assess the complexity of the process and the difficulty in finding the most suitable search context lyrics. The central idea is to develop an automated recovery and music recommendation system where the cost of user effort is limited to the presentation of a group of existing preferences associated with similar queries to those used in specialized Broadcasting Otomi (a sort of Web radio). An important aspect of our research is that it can be used to translate songs in Otomi and enrich the possibilities of using a wider variety and modernize the sample of the songs used by potential listeners in a Web radio named "Tibetan Avenue" followed by ethnic Tibetan speakers who need a Radio in their original language obtaining future followers of Tibetan Language, whom now represent 27% of all new speakers of this language.

In addition to this, the Internet of Things (IoT) is nowadays an incredible asset to provide not only telemetry but work as an actuator for a system. IoT or Industrial IoT (IIOT) requires an architecture and commercial provider selection; this decision is preferably supported by multi-criteria decision methodology (Contreras-Masse, R. et al., 2020). As IIOT is evolving with sensors, the other important area is actuators. A variant of this is to provide to a thing (e.g., appliance, houseware, wearable devices, doors) certain degree of intelligence. A karaoke system can be summarized as a simple machine that will receive input from the user and will execute the selected music. By embedding a recommender system into the karaoke device, it receives a certain degree of intelligence, converting it into an IoT-device that can make decisions under a certain degree based on historical data and user input.

AN INTELLIGENT RECOMMENDER SYSTEM ASSOCIATED WITH A LINGUISTIC COMMUNITY

Our system focuses on the recommendation of songs associated with a karaoke system and its respective social network using this information. The source of information for recommendations is the database associated with this system Karaoke (lyrics and music of each song), while the user profile is obtained from the profile associated with the respective database and its respective subset of records. However, any metadata repository provides DC DL and can be supported by the OAI-PMH protocol, which can be used as a primary source of disambiguation. An alternative to the user profile generation is under development to distinguish the duplication of the same user. This alternative approach is made for the information retrieval system to collect data from other music sources, which may include versions in different musical styles. A musical repository stores the digital songs (either on the Web or in a physical format) and the respective metadata with the content. DL data provider allows an agent associated with the search and retrieval of documents with metadata through the OAI-PMH. Our system takes care of the songs described in an XML format as the standard DC is analyzed by Laustanou, (2007).

Proposal Recommendation System Architecture: An Overview

This section presents the components associated with the architecture of our system and their respective functions (**Figure 3**). To start the process, users must have all their preferences in the XML format version linked to the system. Each time a new user registers in the system sends its respective list of preferences. XML module links a procedure with documents, respectively, and each of the songs. Information on the user's interest is stored in the database named local user profile; then, the metadata-collecting module is activated to update the local database associated with the songs incorporated as metadata. This module makes a request to a DL data provider to collect documents associated with specific metadata. Subsequently, receives an XML document in response to this request, and local XML DC to DB module is activated to retrieve the most appropriate song to the search performed. It also generates a ranking associated with the same preferences for this active user all the time a query occurs. This module extracts the relevant metadata to make the recommendation XML document and stores it in the local database of songs called metadata format. Once the user profile and the metadata associated with songs are available in the local database, the recommendation module can be activated and begins to perform the matching process associated with the model Grand Prix. The aim is to recover the song's lyrics and a distribution list to evaluate and find the best matches for the user profile that can be described through the profile of each user within a social network related Karaoke System. A similar notion was proposed for a particular social network (Lavranos et al., 2015).

Figure 3. The recommender system architecture and its principal features

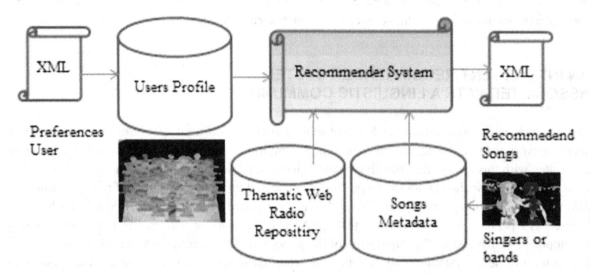

A PROPOSAL RECOMMENDATION MODEL TO OUR INTELLIGENT APPLICATION

As stated previously, each recommendation is based on our proposed VSM model, which was the better option analyzed. The query vector is represented and built with the term parsed from the title of the song, keywords which are descriptors of musical style, performing singer or band, published album, and date of the first sell. The parser ignores stop-words as in CLEF (2005) (a list of common or general representation terms that are not used to realize the information retrieval process and is very important in organizing topics, e.g., prepositions, conjunctions, and articles not are used). The parser considers each term as if this will be represented by a single word. On the other hand, the terms are taken integrally, as single expressions to recover specific thematic topics such as "sky", "forest" or "wind". The query vector term weights are built up according to Equation 2. This equation considers the kind of term (keyword or title), the native language, or their translation to other variants of this same language and the year of the first air data (a more complicated situation because many of these songs are related to legends). Keyword terms are considered more important than the titles because they make the correct matching of each song and have more reading proficiency with even more valorized weights (higher weight), and the terms obtained from the most recent album played by more famous singers or bands, cover artist or bands, including cameos and contributions with another singers or bands in unplugged records are assigned with a more important weight than the less recent ones to better organize the correct search of each song each time.

$$W_t = W_{KeywordOrTitle} \times W_{Language} \times W_{Year} \qquad (2)$$

The weights $W_{KeywordOrTitle}$, $W_{Language}$, W_{Year} are calculated with Equation 3.

$$W_i = 1 - (i-1)\left(\frac{1-W_{min}}{n-1}\right) \tag{3}$$

In this equation, W_i varies according to the kind of weight we want to compute. To illustrate with greater detail this, in the experimental evaluation (Section 4), for $W_{KeywordOrTitles}$ W_{min} was 0.95, and i is 1 if the language-skill level is "good", 2 for "reasonable" and 3 for "few". For W_{Years} W_{min} was 0.55, and i varies from 1 to n, where n is the interval of years considered, begin 1 the highest and n the lowest. In our experimental evaluation proposed, it was considered as the interval of songs produced in a Web Radio from Otomi Community between 2008 and 2015. This is a longitudinal study related to a Community that speaks this language. It is critical to use a Musical repository with real songs naturally associated to requests and preferences of each user's profile; every single song is linked with beliefs of song's meaning to each person in the Social Networking; the desire to listen to again in a specific situation and finally, the intention to be scheduled in a playlist to keep in the future. However, if the interval is omitted, it will be considered as between the present year and the less recent year associated with the first song when it was aired (the smallest between *artist:first-album* and *artist:last-album*).

If w_{min} is not informed, the default value will be used to evaluate the importance of this query and the evaluation of correspondent matching (presented in Equation 4). In the situation, Equation 3 is reduced to Equation 5.

$$W_{min\,default} = \frac{1}{n} \tag{4}$$

$$W_i = \frac{n-i-1}{n} \tag{5}$$

Once the *query vector* is built and evaluated, the songs vector associated with recommendation terms and their respective weights must be defined when all patterns related to the song are evaluated. The adopted approach was (*tf * idf*), i.e., the product of each term associated with the frequency and the inverse document frequency, as is suggested in Salton, (1988). This approach allows automatic evaluation of term weights assignment for the song's retrieval and the real opportunity of being used by different users. The term frequency (*tf*) corresponds to the number of occurrences of a term in a document related to each song. The *inverse document frequency* (*idf*) is a factor that varies inversely with the number of songs n to which evaluate a term, which is assigned in a collection of N songs related to a Musical Repository (typically computed as *log(N/n)*). Best terms related to the identification of content are those who can distinguish individual songs related to better ones from the remainder collection, as is proposed in Salton, 1988. Thus, the best terms correspond to songs related to better qualifications, with high term frequencies (*tf*) and low overall collection frequencies (high *idf*). To calculate the values of *tf * idf*, the system uses DC metadata *dc:title* and *dc:description* to represent the song's content with lyrics and a description of symbology associated with the music of each song. Moreover, as the system deals with different variants of the same language or with beginner people on this language, the total number of songs will vary accordingly with different cultural patterns. After building a correct and individual query associated with song vectors, the system can calculate correct function similarities values among the songs and the query established according to Equation 1.

EXPERIMENTAL EVALUATION

In order to evaluate our proposed music recommendation system, preferences have been evaluated in a social network based on the values set with different terms associated with each of the different musical genres such as ballads, pop, instrumental music or songs interest's poetic. In response, a group of 24 people helped with our study to send their wish list; the information was loaded into the repository Songs represented as related to the construction of the local database associated with Karaoke System metadata. The songs represented as metadata and included in a local database were loaded into the user profile of the local database, respectively related to their social network associated with the community that speaks, writes, and listens to the Otomi language. This database has data up to January 2015, and it has been generated with the intention of understanding the cultural representation of a linguistic community, totaling 116 songs of 11 singers or bands in 16 albums. The Intelligent System produced twenty recommendations that were generated by the system for each song related to Karaoke's performance, considering many patterns associated with the individual's profile and their categories preferences, including cultural patterns associated with religion, ethnicity, or another language spoken. This information was obtained using each profile of the user database related to social networking.

The evaluation was a major aspect of our research, which is why two evaluations were performed. The first one is based on the hypothesis that the best songs to describe the profile of a user must be produced by themselves. As we had information on the songs of each user, we could match those recommended for those elements. This evaluation is carried out with the selection of a song and propose a measuring accuracy, which is a standard evaluation strategy for information retrieval systems. The withdrawal of the related material allows users to choose from a range of musical possibilities and is used to measure the percentage of relevant songs returned in relation to the number of songs that should have been recovered from repository content. For these songs should be to categorize, the metric can be revoked if a song has been selected erroneously and is used to measure the percentage of songs that are right to be classified in relation to the number of songs to be sorted. The accuracy is used to measure the percentage of recovered songs properly; that is, the number of songs properly obtained divided by the number of songs recovered.

As the profiles of each user can be seen as classes and the songs as items in them to be classified in these profiles to generate a more specific weight-related to a more considered profile, we can verify the number of items from each author that are correctly identified in the group of recommendations (i.e., classified) by the user profile. As we have many users associated with different kinds of recommendations (i.e., many classes), it is necessary to combine the results obtained. The *macro average* presented in Equation 6 was designed by Lewis,(1991), to perform this specific combination ("the unweighted mean of effectiveness across all categories –in our case is the group of songs") and was applied by the evaluation of classification algorithms and techniques associated with the correct return of ideal songs.

$$macroaverage = \frac{\sum_{i=1}^{n} X_i}{n} \tag{6}$$

In equation 6, X_i is represented as the recall or the precision, depending on the metric we want to evaluate, of each individual class (user in our social networking to our research case), and n is the number of classes (users). Thus, the *macro average recall* is the arithmetic average of each one of these recalls obtained for everyone through the user profile, and the *macro average precision* is the arithmetic average of the precisions of returning an ideal song in a correct performance which is obtained for each individual evaluation on time.

Because users are not interested in their own favorite songs, but recommendations of the group of users, other evaluation that considers only the items of other users is performed. Then, 15 recommendations were presented to everyone, ranking in a relative degree of relevance generated by the system itself. In this range, the songs with the highest degree of similarity to the user profile are established as 100% relevant, and the others were adjusted to a lesser value. In this case, each person was asked to evaluate the generated recommendations for them and to assign one of the following items (following five-point Likert scale and as a definition of a concept); "Adequate", "Bad", "Normal", "Good" and "Excellent" including to comment on the results through a narrative script. The following sections present the results.

PROPOSAL DESIGN OF EXPERIMENTS

To evaluate our Intelligent System correctly, we proposed the first experiment. It was designed to evaluate the capability of the system to correctly identify different user profiles (i.e., to represent their preferences accurately) since we believe that the best songs related to user profiles are those selected by themselves in the function of symbolic capital and their desire to listen to them, as stated before. To perform such evaluation, we organized a technique to identify each song related to each user and was used at the Karaoke System to support the representation of the cultural capital of this linguistic community. After that, we employed a recall metric to evaluate how many of the number of articles were recovered for each singer and combined then with the micro average equation explained before to organize a correct ranking model.

We have found an average macro recall of 43.25%. It is important to state that each user received twenty recommendations from other people in the same social networking. This is an acceptable value, compared with our literature review, because the query construction was made automatically without human intervention, a very important goal in our research. However, it happened to be lower than expected. An option would be to use more songs (maybe by accessing to the Otomi Community Radio Broadcasting, which has a broad range of songs in different musical styles); however, the problem is the limited number of songs by singer or band to be representative. Another important consideration is that the recommendation ranking was generated with a depreciation degree to determine the importance of a group of songs that were dependent on the promotion year, a particular situation because this language is not spoken in all states in Mexico. As the considered time-slice corresponds to a small part of the full period stored (a snapshot on the time) in the database related to the Karaoke System, not all songs are good recommendations since the preferences change on the time or exist in different circumstances related to cultural celebrations where songs are used by more people, similar at proposed by Ochoa (2009). For the assessment to allow us to generate adequate and reliable narrative script, we proposed the use of an avatar that features user preferences and determine if there were any more preferences associated with the gender of the person who performed the recommendation and groups recommending users consider any relevant aspect including ethnicity and religion, in order to make a more objective

Figure 4. User's evaluations of the recommendations organized by avatars related to Profiles Users

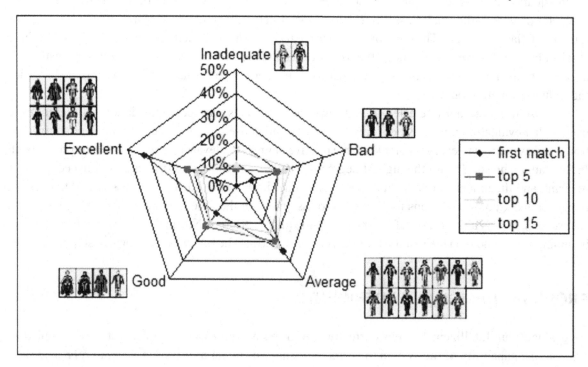

analysis of the different user groups together with the personality in terms of musical preferences and recommendation to each individual user.

An innovative idea represented in **Figure 4** is to show the results of our second part of the experiment design, which is based on a qualitative assessment by linking each of the songs recommended to a user. In this experiment, each user of the social network received fifteen recommendations, and they were evaluated using a Likert scale and associated with different concepts linked to key assertion such as "inadequate for the profile", "misrepresentation of the song", "media in accordance with the outlines of the user", "good to be heard at different times" and "excellent even to dance with it." The results were grouped into different categories the "first matching for the matching song", "top 5", "top 10" and "top 15", as it can be seen in its representation in **Figure 5,** showing even the type of group that received certain category.

Analyzing these three different results, we can see that follow a recommendation realized by a single user is not sufficient to generate a ranking of songs, so it should be considered the first song as the most accurate (the "first matching"), the number of items that were rated as "excellent" value had a greater occurrence than others associated with its significance values (i.e., a value of 42.86%) and none of these were classified as "inappropriate" by the people receiving the recommendation. This strengthens the ability of the system to make recommendations tailored to different gender preferences present in the interests of each cluster of users. All groups have also generated associated concepts of "good" and "excellent" in a category called "positive recommendation" and to concepts of "bad" and "wrong" in a group associated with the concept of "negative recommendation" so that we could get better representation in visualized form for further understanding of each of the results, as it can be seen in (**Fig. 5**).

Figure 5. Grouped user's evaluation

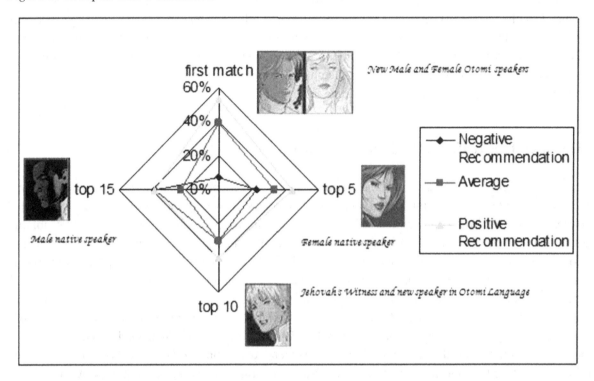

We could see that the positive recommendations could always be the majority, considering that only the "first match", are mostly higher (57.14%) compared with negative recommendations (7.14%). The same behavior can be seen in the categories "top 5" and "top 10", the recommendations had a negative assessment only in the "top 15" and that probably occurred because as the number of recommendations grows more difficult is to only assess its impact, and should make a ranking to improve as the number of correct recommendations therefore decreases. Clearly, the automated method in our research proposed to adopt is suitable for a system of warning and forecast recommendation to change the user group. Our proposal is to add the Karaoke system an automatic alert that periodically sends the user a list of the most important songs that have been heard recently on the Web Radio Otomi for seven or more weeks, which could be a "trend topic", something very common in Google Scholar and recently reputation algorithms to measure suggestions by the research community ResearchGate. Furthermore, in our tests of the users who have changed the search parameters during the last three months, they have qualified negatively for the recommendations made previously. In the following experiments, a threshold variable time and different depreciation values are used, and the time component will be analyzed comprehensively to measure whether the time together with age and gender determines changes in musical preferences with respect to the time where the song was heard. An innovative aspect of our research was to consider avatar groups associated with clusters (a group of users with high similitude) and presented in **Figure 5,** somewhat surprisingly, was thereby determined that new Otomi speakers accepted receiving the first recommendation even they were not experts in the language. What was best for them usually were the sound and the musical arrangement over lyrics; for the group of native language women the best recommendations established a pattern with respect of time; meanwhile for native language men was only important the duration as they used it in work, so that group preferred music lasting much longer in a playlist. Finally, the men of Jehovah's Witnesses religion, with a greater capacity for languages because mnemonic techniques are used by their religion to establish ideas in complete sentences of the Bible, preferred songs with poetic lyrics. They found more emotional aspects with consideration of the Supreme Being. These relationships helped identify the cluster as possible, even predict viably new songs in a playlist, something innovative for our research.

CONCLUSION AND FUTURE RESEARCH

This research proposes a music recommendation system for users of a system related to Karaoke lyrics, and music of many songs in the Otomi language. Nowadays, in which the retrieval of relevant digital information on the Web is a complex task, such systems are of great value to minimize the problems associated with the phenomena of information overload, minimizing the time spent to access the right information, and using IoT to improve an Intelligent Karaoke as is shown in **Figure 6.** The main contribution of this research is the strong use of an innovative automated music recommendation system and the use of metadata set in the Digital Library (DL) format to make recommendations in a timely manner. The system was evaluated by BDBComp but is designed to work with digital library open OAI-PMH, then it can easily be extended to work with any DL that supports this mechanism. The same applies to the format of songs related to the song, but it can be extended to support other formats or to analyze user information stored in tools like a Web radio or a Radio Station of the Otomi Community. Alternatively, the operational prototype offers users the possibility to upload the lyrics electronically. Analyzing the evolution of this music will be our future research as proposed by Kostagiolas, (2015).

The developed system will have many applications. One is the song recommendation to support a social network related to a type of music to relax or to perform daily activities. Thus, the user can log on to a specific distance or electronic environment Karaoke System supported by this system and receive song recommendations containing updates to complement his current musical selection.

A decision to investigate in the future may be to establish specific content for different subgroups of the community and what is done in digital systems followers of Eurovision as is proposed in Ochoa, et al., (2008), where some countries have participated with more than 50 songs in time while other countries like Australia and Morocco only have participated once, this could create an unbalanced playlist to load a priority style of an era in which the French dominated the music of this international event, for instance. The intelligent system can generate a "Pot" for grouping factor that determines a musical category allowing an adequate balance in the playlist, as is shown by Ochoa et al. (2007), reducing the monotony of the listener and making an interesting music selection. In our future research, we propose the use of an intelligent diorama that allows reorganizing the value of each of the recommendations in the social network and visually verify the use of colors nodes that provide a greater number of recommendations, including what you can see in **Figure 7**, from experience in similar research communities of Java programmers who are women of Asia, providing a greater amount of open source to help while there are also men of the same continent that perform greater code problem monitoring associated to other early or inexperienced programmers. This would confirm our hypothesis that the cultural aspects have greater strength in recommendations as we try to help others in our social group towards a reputation model rather than argumentation or negotiation drivers.

Figure 6. Ideal representation using IoT to an Intelligent Karaoke

Figure 7. Proposal Reactive Diorama to represent the source of each musical recommendation

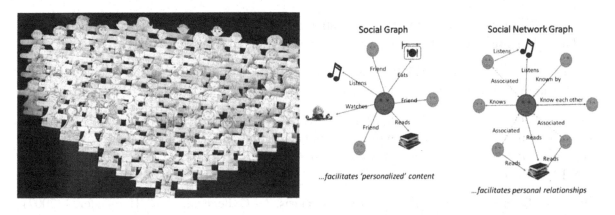

REFERENCES

Baeza-Yates, R., & Ribeiro-Neto, B. (1999). *Modern Information Retrieval*. Addison-Wesley.

Contreras-Masse, R., Ochoa-Zezzatti, A., García, V., Elizondo-Cortés, M., & Pérez-Dominguez, L. (2020). Implementing a Novel Use of Multicriteria Decision Analysis to Select IIoT Platforms for Smart Manufacturing. *Symmetry, 12*(3), 368. doi:10.3390ym12030368

Dublin Core Metdata Initiative (DCMI). (2005). *DCMI*. Retrieved from Dublin Core Metdata Initiative: https://www.dublincore.org/

Huang, Z., Chung, W., Ong, T., & Chen, H. (2002). A Graph-based Recommender System for Digital Library. JCDL'02. doi:10.1145/544220.544231

Kostagiolas, P. A., Lavranos, C., Korfiatis, N., Papadatos, J., & Papavlasopoulos, S. (2015). Music, musicians and information seeking behaviour: A case study on a community concert band. *The Journal of Documentation, 71*(1), 3–24. doi:10.1108/JD-07-2013-0083

Laustanou, K.(2007). *MySpace Music*. Academic Press.

Lavranos, C., Kostagiolas, P., Korfiatis, N., & Papadatos, J. (2015). Information seeking for musical creativity: A systematic literature review. *Journal of the Association for Information Science and Technology, 67*(9), 2105–2117. doi:10.1002/asi.23534

Lee, D. L., Chuang, H., & Seamons, K. (1997). Document ranking and the vector-space model. *IEEE Software, 14*(2), 67–75. doi:10.1109/52.582976

Lewis, D. D. (1991). Evaluating text categorization. In *Proceedings of Speech and Natural Language Workshop*. Defense Advanced Research Projects Agency, Morgan Kaufmann. 10.3115/112405.112471

Ochoa, A., González, S., Esquivel, C., Matozzi, G., & Maffucci, A. (2009). Musical Recommendation on Thematic Web Radio. *Journal of Computers, 4*(8), 742–746. doi:10.4304/jcp.4.8.742-746

Ochoa, A., Hernádez, A., Sánchez, J., Muñoz-Zavala, A., & Ponce, J. (2008). Determining the ranking of a new participant in eurovision using cultural algorithms and data mining. In *18th International Conference on Electronics, Communications and Computers. (CONIELECOMP)*. IEEE. 10.1109/CONIELECOMP.2008.27

Ochoa, A., Tcherassi, A., Shingareva, I., Padméterakiris, A., Gyllenhaale, J., & Hernández, J.(2007). Italianitá: Discovering a Pygmalion effect on Italian communities using data mining. *Advances in Computer Science and Engineering, 57*.

Open Archives Initiative. (2019). *Open Archives Initiative (OAI)*. Retrieved from Open Archives Initiative: http://openarchives.org/

Salton, G., & Buckley, C. (1988). Term-Weighting Approaches in Automatic Text Retrieval. *Information Processing and Management an International Journal, 24*(5), 513–523. doi:10.1016/0306-4573(88)90021-0

Slamet, C., Atmadja, A. R., Maylawati, D. S., Lestari, R. S., Darmalaksana, W., & Ramdhani, M. A. (2018). Automated text summarization for indonesian article using vector space model. IOP Conference Series: Materials Science and Engineering, 288(1). doi:10.1088/1757-899X/288/1/012037

Sompel, H., & Lagoze, C.(2000). The Santa Fe Convention of the Open Archives Initiative. *D-Lib Magazine, 6*(2).

Watanabe, K., & Goto, M. (2019). Query-by-Blending: a Music Exploration System Blending Latent Vector Representations of Lyric Word, Song Audio, and Artist. In *Proceedings of ISMIR* (pp. 144-151). Academic Press.

Wong, S. K. M., Ziarko, W., & Wong, P. (1985). Generalized vector spaces model in information retrieval, In *Proceedings of the 8th annual international SIGIR ACM conference on Research and development in information retrieval* (pp 18-25). 10.1145/253495.253506

KEY TERMS AND DEFINITIONS

Data Mining: Process that attempts to discover behavior patterns hidden in large volumes of data sets.

Decision Support System: Collection of integrated software applications and hardware to help decision makers compile useful information from raw data, documents, personal knowledge, and/or business models to identify and solve problems and make decisions.

Otomi Dialect (Language): Dialect spoken in México principally in Queretaro State with unique vocals and pronunciation which requires using a specific keyword, for this reason many people has an incorrect birth certificate.

Public Policy: Public policies are the answers that the government provides for the needs of the governed, in the form of rules, institutions, services, public goods or services. It involves decision making and advance a process of analysis and valuation of these needs.

Strategic Planning: Process whereby the statement of the overall goals and objectives, analyze the situation, establishing strategic objectives and formulating strategies and strategic plans necessary to achieve those objectives.

Web Radio: Digital repository of Thematic Music related to a Community related to ethnicity, religion or language.

Chapter 9
Interface for Composing Queries That Include Subqueries for Complex Databases

José A. Martínez F.
Tecnológico Nacional de México, Mexico & Instituto Tecnológico de Ciudad Madero, Mexico

Juan Javier González-Barbosa
Tecnológico Nacional de México, Mexico & Instituto Tecnológico de Ciudad Madero, Mexico

German Castillo
Tecnológico Nacional de México, Mexico & Instituto Tecnológico de Ciudad Madero, Mexico

ABSTRACT

Currently, there exist tools for query composition that can be used by users who are not skillful in a DB query language such as SQL. Many tools are difficult to use, and others cannot answer some queries that inexperienced users would like to formulate. This chapter describes the new functionality developed for a query composition interface, which allows inexperienced users to compose queries that involve one, two, or three subqueries without the need to have any knowledge of neither SQL nor the database schema. The experimental tests showed that users could easily compose queries that involve one sub-query. Furthermore, the new functionality preserves the domain independence of the previous version of the interface. Additionally, like the earlier version, the latest release offers language independence; that is, it can be configured for other languages similar to Spanish, for example English, French, Italian, and Portuguese.

DOI: 10.4018/978-1-7998-4730-4.ch009

Copyright © 2021, IGI Global. Copying or distributing in print or electronic forms without written permission of IGI Global is prohibited.

INTRODUCTION

Nowadays, information is very important, and accessing information is important for businesses and organizations of all sizes: small, medium, or large. For medium and high-ranking officers, obtaining adequate and timely information is crucial for decision making. One alternative to access information stored in databases (DBs) is to have professionals that are experts in a database query language. Unfortunately, most users are not able to formulate queries in a query language that allows them to access the information they need. Currently, there exist tools for query composition that can be used by users who are not skillful in a DB query language such as SQL.

Many query composition tools are difficult to use (as mentioned in the Section Related Work), and others cannot answer some queries that inexperienced users would like to formulate. To facilitate the formulation of queries to databases, several graphical interfaces have been developed, which help inexperienced users to formulate queries. However, some interfaces do not have the functionality to easily access information that can only be obtained by queries that include subqueries and aggregate functions. Therefore, new functionality for subqueries was designed, implemented and integrated to an existing query composition interface (QCI) (Pazos, Aguirre, Aguirre & Martínez, 2015), in order to prepare the interface for aggregate functions (count, sum, average, maximum and minimum) in the near future.

This book chapter describes the new functionality developed for the QCI, which allows inexperienced users query composition that includes one, two, or three subqueries without the need to have any knowledge of neither SQL nor the database schema. This interface guides the user in the process of fragmenting a natural language query using the QCI to generate an SQL query that includes one, two, or three subqueries in a transparent way for the user, i.e., without the need to have any knowledge of the database schema.

Finally, the experimental tests show that users can easily formulate queries that include subqueries. Additionally, the new functionality preserves the domain independence of the previous version of the interface, i.e., the possibility to configure the QCI for querying different databases. Furthermore, like the previous version, the new version offers language independence, i.e., the feasibility to configure the interface for other languages similar to Spanish, for example, English, French, Italian, and Portuguese.

BACKGROUND

This section describes some terminology and basic concepts to understand better the interface and the systems presented in the following section.

As mentioned previously, the need to access information stored in databases has been a decisive motivation for developing different computer applications, among them, query composition interfaces. These tools use different methods for query composition to generate a query in some database query language, such as SQL (e.g., Pazos et al., 2015) and MDX (e.g., Porras, Florencia-Juárez, Rivera & García, 2018), in order to obtain from the database the information specified by the user.

The following list includes the most common methods used by some interfaces for query composition:

- QBE (Query by Example) for query composition.
- Dropdown lists to select elements for query composition.
- Drag and drop to select tables and columns of the database schema.

- Menu-based interface to carry out the query composition.
- Predefined templates to perform query composition.

Domain independence is the term used to refer to interfaces that can be used to query different databases (ideally, any database). Domain-independent interfaces need an initial configuration process before the final users can introduce their queries.

RELATED WORK

The interfaces presented in this section use different methods to carry out the query composition. An important aspect is that they have been designed to be used by inexperienced users, i.e., they have no knowledge of a DB query language such as SQL.

Table 1 shows a summary of the most important interfaces for query composition. The second column indicates if the interface is domain-independent. The third column mentions the method used for query composition. The fourth column indicates if the interface allows formulating queries that include subqueries. The last column shows the degree of knowledge required for using the interface. The last row of the table shows the information of the interface presented in this chapter.

Table 1. Features of the most important interfaces for query composition

Interface	Domain Independence	Composition Method	Subqueries Allowed	Knowledge of DB Query Language
Microsoft Access (Microsoft, 2010)	Yes	QBE	Yes	Much
Structured Advanced Query Page – SAQP (Latendresse & Karp, 2010)	Yes	Lists	Yes	None
Blended Browsing and Querying – BBQ (Munroe & Papakonstantiou, 2000)	?	Drag and drop	No	Little
Visual Composition of Complex Queries (Pessina, Masseroli & Canakoglu, 2013)	No	Menus	No	Little
Query Builder (Little, de Ga, Özyer & Alhajj, 2004)	Yes	NL, menus	No	None
Query Composition Interface (Pazos et al., 2015)	Yes	Selection	Yes	None

Some of the interfaces shown in Table 1 require some knowledge of database concepts and the DB schema. Additionally, only two interfaces allow query composition that includes subqueries. Microsoft Access allows users to formulate such queries. Unfortunately, to include a subquery in a search condition ('Where' clause), it is necessary to formulate it as an SQL query. SAQP allows including subqueries; however, the interface design does not prevent the possibility of an error because of a malformed composed query.

QUERY COMPOSITION INTERFACE

The functionality that has been integrated into the QCI aims at allowing inexperienced users to formulate queries that include subqueries for complex databases without knowing the database schema. To this end, the interface guides the user through different windows to carry out the query composition from a natural language description of the query.

Levels of Subqueries Processable by the Interface

Three types of queries have been considered based on an exhaustive analysis of the queries in the ATIS corpus (Linguistic Data Consortium, 1990). Examples of the three types of queries are presented in Table 2, which shows queries that include one, two, and three subqueries.

Table 2. Types of queries processable by the QCI

Type of Query	Natural Language Query	Translation into SQL	No. of Subqueries
1	¿Qué tipo de avión tiene el vuelo No. 301? What type of aircraft has flight number 301?	SELECT aircraft_type FROM aircraft WHERE aircraft_code IN (SELECT aircraft_code FROM flight WHERE flight.flight_number = 301)	1
2	Dame la tarifa de viaje sencillo del vuelo No. 140 Give me the one-way fare of flight No. 140	SELECT one_way_cost FROM fare WHERE fare_code IN (SELECT fare_code FROM flight_fare WHERE flight_code IN (SELECT flight.flight_code FROM flight WHERE flight.flight_number = 140))	2
3	Dame la lista de transporte en la ciudad de ATLANTA Give me the list of transport in the city of ATLANTA	SELECT transport_desc FROM transport WHERE transport_code IN (SELECT transport_code FROM ground_service WHERE city_code IN (SELECT city_code FROM airport_service WHERE city_code IN (SELECT city.city_code FROM city WHERE city.city_name = 'ATLANTA')))	3

Figure 1. Example of fragmentation into an external query and one subquery

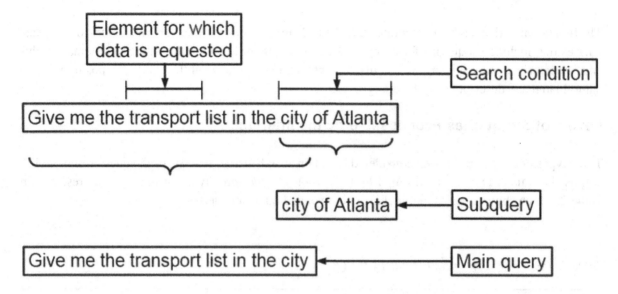

Figure 2. Example of fragmentation into an external query and two subqueries

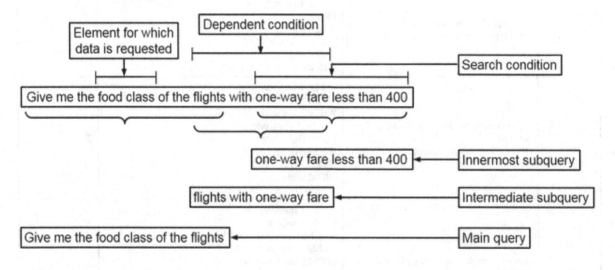

Manual Fragmentation of Queries

Before formulating a query using the interface, the user must first write the natural language query and then fragment it into several parts. Each part is one of the subqueries or the outer query. For performing this process, it is necessary to apply the following steps to perform the fragmentation.

1. To fragment a query, the user must first identify the search condition, which will be considered a subquery.

2. In case there exists a search condition that depends on the result of the subquery of the preceding step, then the query that includes the said condition will be considered a subquery of the immediate outer level; otherwise, the process continues to the following step.

3. The remaining query elements that specify the requested information by the user will constitute the external (main) query.

Figures 1 and Figure 2 show examples of the fragmentation of queries that include subqueries. The first example is *Dame la lista de transporte in the city of Atlanta* (Give me the transport list in the city of Atlanta) and the second example is *Dame la clase de comida de los vuelos con tarifa de viaje sencillo menores que 400* (Give me the food class of the flights with one-way fare less than 400).

Table 3. Basic concepts for query composition that include subqueries

Concept	Description
Fragmentation of query.	The process to fragment a natural language query into several natural language queries, specifically, one y several subqueries and the main query.
Topic of interest.	The topic (i.e., a database table) from which the user wants to retrieve information (in a query or subquery).
Search condition.	The element or elements that restrict the search of information.
Result of the internal subquery.	Result returned by a subquery generated internally by the interface.
Search condition for the result of a subquery.	Definition of the search condition, which is defined by choosing one of two options: "*is in*" or "*is not in*" the set of values returned by a subquery.
Elements of interest.	Specific elements of the topic (DB table) of interest, from which the user wants to retrieve information.

Figure 3. The window for fragmentation of natural language queries

Concepts for Query Composition that Includes Subqueries

Even though it is not necessary for a user to know the database schema or a DB query language, it is necessary that they know some basic concepts to use the QCI. Table 3 describes some basic concepts about the windows the user must employ for query composition that includes subqueries.

After understanding the concepts described in Table 3 that are needed to use the QCI, the user can utilize the interface to perform the query composition that includes subqueries.

Fragmentation of Natural Language Queries

Figure 3 shows a window in which the user must fragment the natural language query into several fragments, as explained in the Section Manual Fragmentation of Queries. Table 4 presents a description of the components that constitute this window, where each number in the first column indicates the number that identifies a component in Figure 3.

Table 4. Components of the window for fragmentation of queries in NL

Component	Description
1. Original query.	This text box is used to write the original natural language query.
2. Main query.	This text box is employed to write the most external query (the query that includes the elements of interest) according to the manual fragmentation of the query (Figure 1 and Figure 2).
3. Number of subqueries.	From the dropdown list, the number of subqueries (1, 2, or 3) is selected, which are determined in the manual fragmentation of the query.
4. Subqueries.	Each text box is used to write one subquery. These subqueries are obtained from the manual fragmentation of the original query, taking the subqueries from left to right (Figure 2), excluding the main subquery.
5. "*Continuar*" (continue) button.	After writing all the subqueries in the text boxes, the user must click the button to start the phases for query composition.
6. Menu bar.	This bar contains the options "*Archivo*" (file), "*Herramientas*" (tools), and "*Ayuda*" (help). The first option is used to cancel the composition process, the second option is used by the DB administrator to configure the interface, and the third option displays the user manual.

Figure 4. The window for selection of the topic of interest

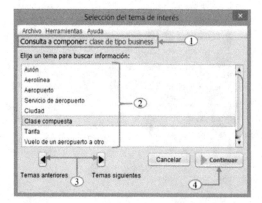

It is important that the user has correctly identified each fragment of the natural language query since the phase of query fragmentation is crucial for the interface to guide the user step by step through the process of composing the main query and the subqueries.

Selection of the Topic of Interest for a Subquery

Figure 4 shows a window where the user selects the topic (i.e., a database table), which will be used for query/subquery composition. Table 5 describes the components that constitute this window, where each number in the first column corresponds to the number that identifies a component in Figure 4.

The topics that are shown in the window (Figure 4) are textual descriptions of the database tables. The tables are shown ordered from the most to the least relevant for query composition, and they are classified into the following types: base tables, catalogs, *M* to *N* relations, and satellite tables (Pazos et al., 2015).

Table 5. Components of the window for selection of the topic of interest

Component	Description
1. Query to be composed.	The interface shows in blue the subquery to be composed at the current step of the process.
2. List of topics.	This list shows the topics (DB tables) of the database from which the user can select one topic for query composition.
3. Browsing for examining more topics.	The buttons can be used for browsing through all the topics, i.e., all the tables of the database. The topics are ordered from the most to the least relevant. This functionality is useful for databases constituted by many tables.
4. *"Continuar"* (continue) button.	After selecting the topic of interest, the user must click the button to proceed to the next phase of the process.

Figure 5. The window for the specification of search conditions

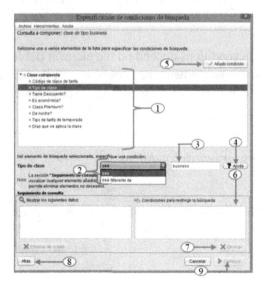

Specification of Search Conditions

Figure 5 shows one of the most important windows for query composition that includes subqueries. Since, to start the composition of this type of query, it is necessary to define conditions for restricting the search of information, especially for the innermost subquery, because, for this subquery, it is necessary to define a search condition.

Table 6 presents a description of the components that constitute this window, where each number in the first column indicates the number that identifies a component in Figure 5.

Table 6. Components of the window for the specification of search conditions

Component	Description
1. Tree of topic elements.	This structure shows the elements (table columns) of the topic (DB table) previously selected. One or more search conditions can be specified, one at a time. For each condition, one element must be previously selected.
2. List of comparison operators for the element selected.	This list shows N different operators (in textual form) that can be chosen to define a search condition, where N can be 2, 3, 4, 5 or 6, and depends on the element. The possible operators are equal to (=), less than (<), greater than (>), less than or equal to (<=), greater than or equal to (>=), and different from (<>).
3. Value of the·search condition.	This text box, together with the list of comparison operators, (2) allow the user to specify the intended condition for restricting the search.
4. "*Ayuda*" (help) button.	This button allows the user to obtain directions on how to specify a search condition.
5. Add search condition.	After specifying a condition, the user must click the button to add the condition to the list of conditions (6).
6. List of search conditions for the query/subquery.	This box shows all the conditions that have been specified in this window.
7. "*Eliminar*" (eliminate) button.	This button can be used to eliminate a condition from the list of conditions (6).
8. "*Atrás*" (back) button.	This button can be used to go back to the previous window if it is necessary to make a correction.
9. "*Continuar*" (continue) button.	After adding all the conditions necessary for the query/subquery, the user must click the button to continue to the next phase of the process.

The options to specify search conditions depend on the element (table column) selected. Therefore, adequate comparison operators for an element are retrieved from the semantic information dictionary (SID), which is depicted in Figure 6. To this end, the SID had to be previously configured by the database

Figure 6. Comparison operators for search conditions

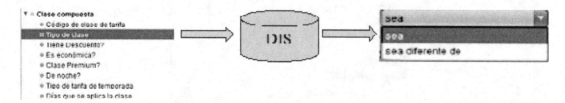

administrator. The comparison operators displayed are expressed in textual form. For example, for element *Tipo de clase* (class type), the operators displayed are *sea* (is) and *sea diferente de* (is different from).

Display of Results of Internal Subquery

The window shown in Figure 7 is simply used to show to the user the results obtained by the SQL query, which is automatically generated by the interface, though the user is not aware of this generation. The result of the subquery is displayed as feedback for the user, so they can verify if the subquery has been correctly composed.

Table 7 shows a description of the components that constitute this window, where each number in the first column corresponds to the number that identifies a component in Figure 7.

The purpose of the window shown in Figure 7 is to serve as feedback for the user, so they can see the results returned by the interface to verify if they are the ones expected. Therefore, the user can only click the "*Continuar*" button to proceed to the next phase of the process or click the "*Back*" button to go back to the previous window for making a correction.

Specification of Search Condition for the Result of a Subquery

Figure 8 shows a window to define the search condition of the main query (outermost query) or another subquery of the immediate outer level that includes the results that an inner subquery will retrieve. For the search condition, there are only two options: *sea igual a alguno(s) de* (is equal to some of) or *sea*

Figure 7. The window for the display of results of the internal subquery

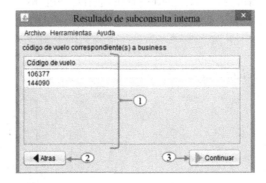

Table 7. Components of the window for the display of results of the subquery

Component	Description
1. Preview of results.	This area consists of a table that shows a preview of the results that are obtained by the subquery at the current phase of the process. Note: the current subquery may include one or two internal subqueries.
2. "*Atrás*" (back) button.	This button can be used to go back to the previous window if it is necessary to make a correction.
3. "*Continuar*" (continue) button.	After the user has seen the result returned by the subquery, they must click the button to proceed to the next phase of the process.

Figure 8. The window for the specification of the search condition for the result of a subquery

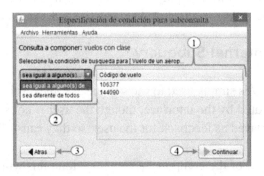

Table 8. Components of the window for the specification of search condition for the result of a subquery

Component	Description
1. Table of results.	This area consists of a table that shows the results returned by the database management system for the subquery.
2. List of comparison operators.	This list shows two possible operators that can be chosen to define a search condition: • Sea igual a alguno(s) de (is equal to some of). • Sea diferente de todos (is different from all).
3. "*Atrás*" (back) button.	This button can be used to go back to the previous window if it is necessary to make a correction.
4. "*Continuar*" (continue) button.	After defining the search condition for the result of a subquery, the user must click the button to continue to the next phase of the process.

diferente de todos (is different from all). The first option corresponds to the operator *IN* of SQL, and the second one corresponds to *NOT IN*.

Figure 9. Construction of the Select and From clauses of the SQL query

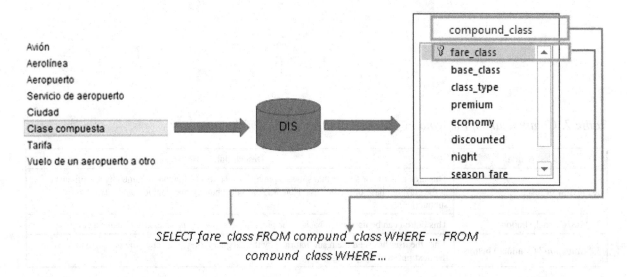

Table 8 presents a description of the components that constitute this window, where each number in the first column indicates the number that identifies a component in Figure 8.

If there exists a subquery that is not the innermost, the interface retrieves from the SID the name and the primary key of the table that corresponds to the topic selected by the user in the phase *Selection of the topic of interest* (described in the Section Selection of the Topic of Interest), as depicted in Figure 9. The interface internally constructs the *Select* and *From* clauses of the SQL query using the information obtained from the SID. The *Where* clause is complemented with the search condition specified in the window shown in Figure 8 and the subquery previously composed, i.e., the subquery of the immediate inner level.

Figure 10. The window for selection of elements of interest for the main query

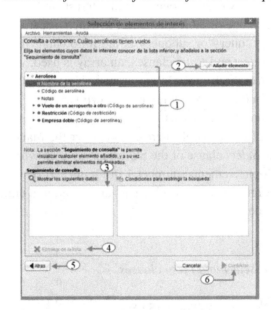

Table 9. Components of the window for selection of elements of interest for the main query

Component	Description
1. Tree of topic elements.	This structure shows the elements (table columns) of the topic (DB table) previously selected. One or more elements can be selected one at a time.
2. "*Añadir elemento*" (add element) button.	After selecting an element from the tree (1), it can be added to the list of selected elements (3).
3. List of selected elements.	This box shows the elements of the topic from which the user wants to retrieve information.
4. "*Eliminar elemento*" (eliminate element) button.	This button can be used to eliminate an element from the list of elements selected (3).
5. "*Atrás*" (back) button.	This button can be used to go back to the previous window if it is necessary to make a correction.
6. "*Continuar*" (continue) button.	After selecting all the elements from which the user wants to retrieve information, they must click the button to proceed to the next phase of the process.

Selection of Elements of Interest for the Main Query

Figure 10 shows a window in which the user can select one or more elements of interest (table columns) from which they want to retrieve information. The elements are selected one by one, which will constitute the Select clause of the main query (outermost query) of the SQL query. Table 9 includes a description of the components that constitute this window, where each number in the first column corresponds to the number that identifies a component in Figure 9.

Construction of SQL Queries that Include Subqueries

One of the main tasks of the interface is the generation of SQL queries that include subqueries. The SQL query is constructed differently depending on the levels of the subqueries.

First, for a query that includes one or more subqueries, the user must start the process by composing a subquery. To this end, it is necessary to select one topic of interest, and next, select from the tree of topic elements (number 1 in Figure 5) one or more elements for which a search condition must be defined.

The basic syntax of an SQL query or subquery is the following: SELECT *columns* FROM *table* WHERE *conditions*. For the *Select* and *From* clauses, an array is used, which is filled in the phase described in the Section Selection of the Topic of Interest for a Subquery. In this phase, the interface obtains the name of the table (corresponding to the topic) and the primary key. Figure 11 shows an example of the construction of the *Select* and *From* clauses.

The window for selection of elements of interest is used for the main query (outermost query), so the interface can construct the *Select* clause of the SQL query, which will include the elements that the user selects from the tree of topic elements (number 1 in Figure 10). The selected elements are shown in the text box (number 3 in Figure 10). These elements are stored in a unidimensional array, so it can be used to generate the SQL query.

Figure 11. Construction of the Select and From clauses

SELECT *flight_code* FROM *flight* WHERE			
Array Select			
Table description	**Table name**	**Primary key**	**Type**
Flight form an airport to another	flight	flight_code	normal

The construction of the *Where* clause for the innermost subquery is carried out considering the search condition to each element of interest described in the Section Specification of Search Conditions. To this end, an array is used that contains information on the topic and the element of interest selected by the user and another array that contains information on the comparison operators for the elements of interest. Figure 12 shows an example of the construction of the *Where* clause.

The construction of the *Where* clause for a subquery that is not the innermost subquery is performed considering only one search condition, which is described in the Section Specification of Search Condition for the Result of a Subquery. To this end, an array is used that contains information on the topic and element of interest (Figure 12).

Figure 12. Construction of the Where clause

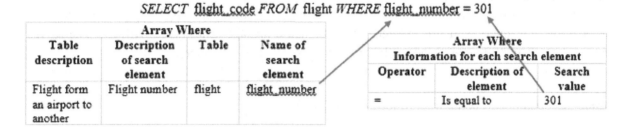

SELECT flight_code FROM flight WHERE flight_number = 301

Array Where			
Table description	Description of search element	Table	Name of search element
Flight form an airport to another	Flight number	flight	flight_number

Array Where Information for each search element		
Operator	Description of element	Search value
=	Is equal to	301

To construct the main query (outermost query), the user must select one or more elements of interest from which they want to retrieve information. Next, the user must define the search condition for the result of the subquery (described in the Section Specification of Search Condition for the Result of a Subquery). Additionally, the user can specify search conditions for other topics and elements of interest.

The interface constructs the *Select* and *From* clauses for the main query (outermost query) by generating arrays like those shown in Figure 11. Each array corresponds to an element that the user selected from the tree of topic elements in the phase described in the Section Selection of Elements of Interest for the Main Query.

The construction of the *Where* clause for the main query is explained next. For the main query for which the interface has to generate the SQL subquery necessary to complete the SQL query statement, the construction of the SQL search condition for the result of a subquery is carried out like the construction of the *Where* clause for a subquery (previously described). In case the user-specified additional search conditions, the construction of each SQL search condition is performed like the construction of

Figure 13. The window for preview and results

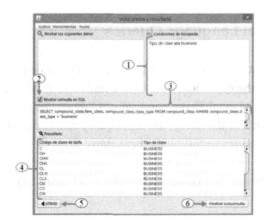

the *Where* clause for the innermost subquery (previously explained). Finally, all the SQL search conditions are combined using AND operators.

Preview and Results

Figure 13 shows a window that displays the results of the main query or subquery composed by the user. Table 10 includes a description of the components that constitute the window, where each number in the first column indicates the number that identifies a component in Figure 13.

After the user ends the subquery composition or the entire query, the interface generates the corresponding SQL query, which is executed in the database management system (DBMS). The results returned are displayed in this window (Figure 13), as well as the SQL query.

Table 10. Components of the window for preview and results

Component	Description
1. List of search conditions	This box shows the search conditions defined by the user.
2. Checkbox.	This checkbox allows the user to view the generated SQL query.
3. Translation.	This text box shows the generated SQL query.
4. Result table.	This area consists of a table that shows the results returned by the database management system.
5. "*Atrás*" (back) button.	This button can be used to go back to the previous window if it is necessary to make a correction.
6. "*Finalizar*" (end) button.	"*Finalizar consulta*" (end query) is used to finish query composition. In contrast, the "*Finalizar subconsulta*" (end subquery) allows the user to finish subquery composition and continue the composition of the immediate outer subquery or the main query.

QUERY COMPOSITION EXAMPLE

The process of query composition that includes subqueries is described in the following example:

¿Cuáles aerolíneas tienen vuelos con clase de tipo business?
Which airlines have flights with a class 'business'?

Fragmentation of Natural Language Queries

The first step is the fragmentation of natural language queries. Prior to starting a query composition process, the user must analyze the query and identify the main query and the subqueries by applying the steps described in the Section Manual Fragmentation of Queries. In the window shown in Figure 14, the user must type the fragments of the query: the main query and two nested subqueries for the current example. To this end, it is necessary to follow the next steps.

1.   The user must write in the text box (indicated by No. 1 in Figure 14) the entire query that they want to compose.

Figure 14. Fragmentation of queries in NL

2. Next, the user must identify the innermost subquery and write it in the text box (No. 2).
3. Additionally, the user must identify the middle subquery and write in the text box (No.3).
4. The user must write the main query in the text box (No. 4).
5. Finally, the user must click the *"Continuar"* (continue) button (No.5) to start the query composition process.

Selection of the Topic of Interest of the Innermost Subquery

Next, the interface displays the window (Selection of the topic of interest) shown in Figure 15. In this window, the user must select the topic (DB table) from which they want to retrieve information for the subquery. To this end, the next steps must be followed.

1. The user might notice that the interface shows the subquery to be composed (indicated by No. 1 in Figure 14), which for this example is *clase de tipo business* (class of type business).
2. The interface displays a list that shows the topics of interest (DB tables) of the database, from which the user can retrieve information, i.e., for subquery composition mentioned in the previous paragraph. From the list, the user must select just one topic to compose the subquery (No. 2) mentioned in the previous paragraphs. For this example, the user must select *Clase compuesta* (compound class).
3. Finally, the user must click the *"Continuar"* (continue) button to proceed to the next phase.

Specification of Search Conditions

Afterward, the interface displays the window (Specification of search conditions) shown in Figure 16. This window is used to specify a search condition for the topic selected in the previous window. For

Figure 15. Selection of the topic of interest for the innermost subquery

this example, it is necessary to specify the following condition: *clase de tipo business* (class of type business). The next steps must be followed to specify the condition.

1.   Initially, the user must select the element of interest *Tipo de clase* (class of type) from the list of elements (No. 1).
2.   Next, the interface displays a list of two comparison operators (No. 2), which are the only possible operators that are adequate for the element selected. From this list, the user must select the operator *sea* (is).
3.   Afterward, the user must write a search value that is suitable for the element of interest *Tipo de clase* (class of type), which for this example is *business* (No. 3).
4.   After defining the search condition, the user must click the button "*Añadir condición*" (add condition) to add the search condition (No. 4) to the box *Condiciones para restringir la búsqueda* (conditions to restrict the search), which is shown in Figure 16.

Figure 16. Specification of search conditions for the innermost subquery

5.   Finally, the user must click the button *"Continuar"* (continue) to finish the specification of the search condition and proceed to the next phase of the process.

Preview and Results of the Innermost Subquery

Next, the interface displays the window (Preview and results). Figure 17 shows a window that displays the results of the subquery composed in previous phases, as well as the SQL query that the interface has generated for the subquery. Once the user has finished subquery composition, the interface executes the SQL query in the DBMS to obtain the results for the subquery. The results returned by the DBMS are displayed, so the user receives feedback, and they can verify if the subquery has been correctly composed. The following steps describe the actions that the user must perform in this window.

1.   First, the user has the option to view or not the SQL query generated in the previous phases. For this example, the user clicks the checkbox (No. 1) with the label *"Mostrar consulta en SQL"* (show SQL query).
2.   After examining the results returned by the interface, the user must end the subquery composition by clicking the button (No. 2) *"Finalizar subconsulta"* (end subquery), to proceed to the composition of the intermediate subquery.

Selection of the Topic of Interest

Subsequently, the interface displays the window (Selection of the topic of interest) shown in Figure 18 in which the user must select the topic from which they want to retrieve information for the intermediate subquery. To this end, the user must follow the steps described next.

Figure 17. Preview and results of the innermost subquery

1. The user might notice that the interface shows the subquery to be composed (No. 1 in Figure 18), which for this example is *vuelos con clase* (flights with class).
2. Next, for subquery composing mentioned in the previous paragraph, the user must select the topic on which they want to retrieve information. For this example, the user must select the element *Vuelo de un aeropuerto a otro* (flight from one airport to another) from the list of topics (DB tables) displayed (No. 2).
3. Finally, the user must click the button *"Continuar"* (continue) to finish this phase.

Display of Results of the Innermost Subquery

Next, the interface detects that it is necessary to define the search condition for the intermediate subquery. Therefore, the interface displays the window (Results of internal subquery) shown in Figure 19, so the user receives feedback to verify if the results returned by the innermost subquery are coherent with the nature of the search condition for the intermediate subquery.

The window (Results of internal subquery) shows the results returned by the innermost subquery. In this window, the user can only review the results of the innermost subquery, and then they must click the button *"Continuar"* (continue) to proceed to the definition of the search condition.

Figure 18. Selection of the topic of interest for the intermediate subquery

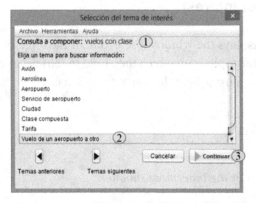

Figure 19. Results of the innermost subquery for the intermediate subquery

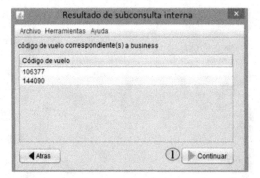

Specification of Search Condition for the Result of the Innermost Subquery

Subsequently, the interface displays the window (Specification of search condition for subquery) shown in Figure 20. This window is used to define a search condition for the subquery. For this example, it is necessary to specify the following condition: *sea igual a alguno(s) de* (is equal to some of) the results obtained by the innermost query. The following steps describe the actions that the user must perform in this window.

1.   First, the user must select from the list shown in Figure 20 (No. 1) the right comparison operator for the intended purpose. The list shows two operators, which correspond to the SQL operators IN and NOT IN, which are the only possible for the results returned by a subquery. For this example, the user selects *sea igual a alguno(s) de* (is equal to some of).
2.   Finally, the user must click the button "*Continuar*" (continue) to finish the specification of the search condition. Next, the system will ask the user if they want to define additional search conditions (not shown in Figure 20). For this example, the user must click the option "*No*" to proceed to view the results returned by the intermediate subquery.

Preview and Results of the Intermediate Subquery

Figure 20. Specification of search condition for the result of the innermost subquery

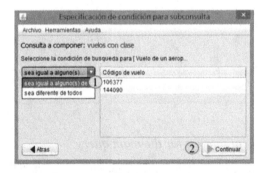

Afterward, the interface displays the window (Preview and results) shown in Figure 21. This window displays the results of the intermediate subquery composed in previous phases, as well as the SQL query that the interface has generated for the subquery. Once the user has finished subquery composition, the interface executes the SQL query in the DBMS to obtain the results for the subquery, which are shown in the window. The results are intended to provide feedback to the user, so they can verify if the subquery has been correctly composed. The following two steps describe the actions that the user must carry out for this example.

1.   First, the user has the option to view or not the SQL query generated in the previous phases. For this example, the user clicks the checkbox (No. 1) with the label "*Mostrar consulta en SQL*" (show SQL query).

2.   After examining the results returned by the interface, the user may end the composition of the intermediate subquery by clicking the button (No 2) "*Finalizar subconsulta* (end subquery) to proceed to the composition of the main query.

Selection of the Topic of Interest for the Main Query

Subsequently, the interface displays the window (Selection of the topic of interest) shown in Figure 22. In this window, the user must select the topic (DB table) from which they want to retrieve information for the main query. To this end, the next steps must be followed.

Figure 21. Preview and results of the intermediate subquery

Figure 22. Selection of the topic of interest for the main query

1. The user might notice that the interface shows the query to be composed (No. 1 in Figure 21), which for this example is *Cuáles aerolíneas tienen vuelos* (which airlines have flights).
2. The user must select the topic from which they want to retrieve information (No. 2), i.e., for query composition mentioned in the previous paragraph. For this example, the user must select the topic *Aerolínea* (airline) from the list of topics (DB tables) displayed (No. 2).
3. Lastly, the user must click the button "*Continuar*" (continue) to finish the specification of the selection of the topic to proceed to the selection of the elements of interest.

Selection of Elements of Interest for the Main Query

Next, the interface displays the window (Selection of elements of interest) shown in Figure 23. In this window, the user must select the elements (table column) from which they want to retrieve information for the query. For this example, the user must select one element: *Nombre de la aerolínea* (name of the airline). To this end, the user must follow the next steps.

1. The user must add the element to the box "*Mostrar los siguientes datos*" (show the following data) by clicking the button (No. 2) "*Añadir elemento*" (add element).
2. After selecting the element of interest (No. 1), the user must add the element to the box "*Mostrar los siguientes datos*" (show the following data) by clicking the button (No. 2) "*Añadir elemento*" (add element).
3. If the user would want to retrieve information from other elements of interest, they should repeat the operation described in the preceding paragraph. For this example, the user would end this phase by clicking the button "*Continuar*" (continue) to proceed to the definition of the search condition for the results returned by the intermediate subquery.

Figure 23. Selection of elements of interest for the main query

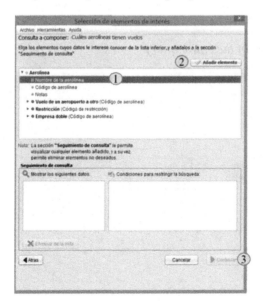

Specification of Search Condition for the Result of the Intermediate Subquery

Afterward, the interface displays the window (Specification of search condition for subquery) shown in Figure 24. In this window, the user must define the search condition for the results returned by the intermediate subquery. For this example, it is necessary that they specify the following search condition: *el vuelo sea igual a alguno(s) de* (the flight is equal to some of) the flights returned by the subquery. To this end, the user must perform the operations described next.

1. The user must select from the list sown in Figure 24 (No. 1) the right comparison operator for the intended purpose. The list shows two operators that correspond to the SQL operators IN and NOT IN, which are the only possible for the results returned by a subquery. For this example, the user selects from the list *sea igual a alguno(s) de* (is equal to some of).
2. Finally, the user must click on "*Continuar*" (continue), and the system will ask if they want to specify more search conditions (not shown in Figure 23), in addition to the one defined for the results of the subquery. For this example, the user must click the option "*No*" to proceed to view the results returned by the entire query.

Figure 24. Specification of search condition for the result of the intermediate subquery

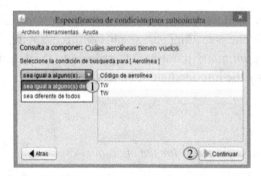

Figure 25. Preview and results of the entire query

Preview and Results of the Entire Query

Finally, the interface displays the window (Preview and results) shown in Figure 25. This window shows the results of the entire query and its corresponding SQL query. After the user has finished the composition of the main query, the interface executes the SQL query in the DBMS to retrieve the results of the entire query to show the results in this window (Figure 25). The following steps describe the operations that the user must perform.

1. First, the user has the option to view or not the SQL query generated in the previous phases. For this example, the user clicks the checkbox (No. 1) with the label "*Mostrar consulta en SQL*" (show SQL query).
2. After the user has examined the results returned by the system, the user may end the query composition by clicking the button (No 2) "*Finalizar*" (end). In this step, the process for query composition that includes subqueries is ended.

EXPERIMENTAL RESULTS

For the tests that are described next, a group of 14 undergraduate students was used as test subjects. The purpose of the test was to assess how friendly the new version of QCI is. Specifically, the purpose of the usability tests was to measure the easiness of operation of the interface, which includes the new functionality that allows users to query composition that includes subqueries.

The features that were evaluated in these tests for query composition that include from 1 to 4 subqueries in their translation into SQL are the following:

- The time that it takes a user for query composition that includes subqueries.
- The number of attempts made by a user for query composition (correctly or incorrectly).

Description of the Experimental Setting

The tests were carried out in a single session of two hours with a group of 14 students majoring in engineering in Computer Science. A user guide was given to students two days before the tests. The guide explains the components of the windows that constitute the QCI, as well as an example for composing each type of query mentioned in the Section Levels of subqueries processable by the interface.

At the beginning of the tests, a brief explanation was given to the students to carry out the manual decomposition of natural language queries into the main query and the nested subqueries. The steps are described in the Section Manual fragmentation of queries.

At the outset of the tests, the students were given a document with 20 natural language queries whose translation into SQL requires nested subqueries. The queries were ordered from the least to the most difficult to compose. Additionally, the queries were divided into two groups of 10 queries each. The first group consisted of queries that include one or two subqueries in their translation into SQL, and the second group was constituted of queries that required three or four subqueries.

The test queries were selected from the ATIS corpus (Linguistic Data Consortium, 1990). Several queries were modified by eliminating aggregate functions because the current version is not able to process queries that include aggregate functions, as mentioned in Section Introduction. It is important to emphasize that the students were not given the ATIS schema nor the correct translation of the test queries. They only received the natural language queries and the results that had to be obtained for each query.

To collect the information on the queries composed by the users (students) and the results obtained by the queries, a program was developed and integrated to the interface to monitor and store in a database the compositions carried out by the users. The monitoring process for the QCI is depicted in Figure 26.

The process described in Figure 26 starts showing a list of queries that the users have not yet composed. Therefore, if there are queries pending to be composed, the user selects the query that they want to compose, and the interface displays the windows for query composition that includes subqueries. After carrying out the composition, the system verifies if the query was correctly composed and stores the information of the composition of the query, the results obtained by the query, and the number of attempts for composing the query, which initially is 1. In case the query has not been composed correctly, the monitoring program asks the user if they want to make a new attempt to compose the query. In case the user answers *yes*, then the system displays the windows for composing the same query again. In case the user answers *no*, the system shows a list of queries pending to be composed. In case there are no pending queries, the system concludes the test.

Figure 26. Process for monitoring the query composition

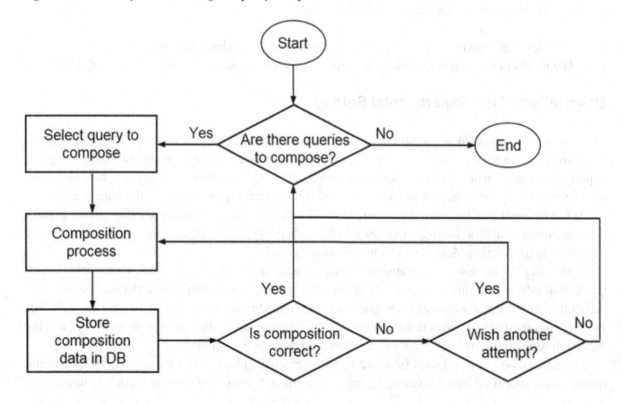

Experimental Results

Table 11 shows the results of using the interface when users made the composition of the 20 queries that include subqueries. The results show the number of attempts and the time spent by the users for the composition of only the queries that were correctly composed. Figure 27 shows the same results as a bar plot.

Table 11. Results of the use of the QCI

Query No.	Min. Attempts	Max. Attempts	Average Attempts	Min. Time (sec.)	Max. Time (sec.)	Average Time (min)	No. of Users that Composed Correctly
1	1	2	1.25	117	1061	8.66	12
2	1	2	1.28	52	505	3.37	14
3	1	3	1.21	70	702	2.92	14
4	1	7	2.42	76	1272	6.05	14
5	1	2	1.07	52	231	1.82	14
6	1	2	1.14	70	359	2.84	14
7	1	2	1.08	59	249	2.55	12
8	2	2	2	400	400	6.66	1
9	1	6	2.57	50	1152	7.35	7
10	1	2	1.08	72	287	2.97	12
11	1	2	1.16	48	369	2.32	12
12	1	1	1	45	146	1.6	11
13	1	3	1.16	51	376	1.73	12
14	1	1	1	45	157	1.34	12
15	1	8	4.6	119	886	9.97	5
16	1	2	1.5	56	220	2.68	4
17	1	3	1.33	78	285	2.29	9
18	1	5	1.71	71	293	2.35	7
19	1	3	1.5	84	358	2.8	6
20	1	1	1	62	128	1.49	6
Average			1.55			3.68	

Table 11 presents for each query correctly composed the following data: the minimal, the maximal, and the average number of attempts shown in the second, third, and fourth columns, respectively. The minimal, the maximal, and the average time for query composition are presented in the fifth, sixth, and seventh columns, respectively. The number of users who correctly composed each query is shown in the last column.

The results obtained show that 1.55 attempts are performed for composing one query. It is noteworthy that the average time for composing the query number 1 is 8.66 minutes, which is significantly higher than the average time of 3.68 minutes for all the queries. The reason for this difference is that users are faced with the interface for the first time. Therefore, the first query allows users to learn how to use the

Figure 27. Results of the use of the QCI

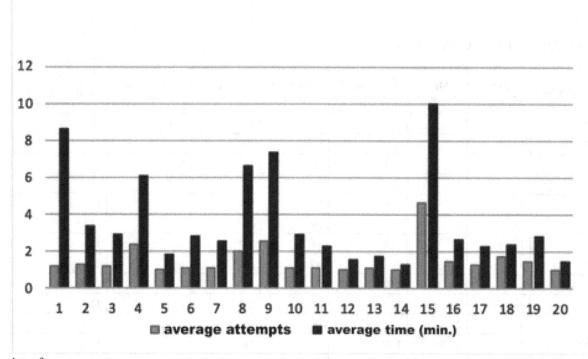

interface.

It is also remarkable that for query number 8, just one user was able to compose it. The explanation of this difficulty is the complexity of the ATIS schema. The query is the following:

¿Cuál es el nombre del aeropuerto de destino del vuelo número 140?
What is the name of the destination airport of flight number 140?

For this query, the user was asked to obtain the name of *aeropuerto de destino* (destination airport). Therefore, the user tries to find this element of interest in the topic of interest *aeropuerto* (airport). However, the searched element is in the topic *vuelo de un aeropuerto a otro* (flight from one airport to another), and the interest element is in the topic *aeropuerto de destino* (destination airport). Since the users could not find the element of interest in the topic *aeropuerto* (airport), most of them did not consider the possibility that the element of interest could be in another topic.

The first group of ten queries (those that include one or two subqueries) was correctly composed by most of the users in three or four minutes in 1.5 attempts, approximately. For the second group of queries (those that include one or two subqueries), there were no problems for composing the first five queries. However, the last five are the more complex, because, for these queries, it is necessary to manually decompose the natural language queries into the main query and two subqueries.

As can be seen, most of the queries could be composed by most of the users, with the exception of queries 8, 15, 16, 19, and 20. Query number 8 was the most complicated due to the problem explained in the previous paragraph. For the rest of the queries that could not be composed by most of the users, the reason is that their manual decomposition requires two subqueries.

SOLUTIONS AND RECOMMENDATIONS

Knowing the opinion of the users at the end of the tests was important because it provides the perspective of the user, and it helps to identify those parts of the interface that can be improved. Therefore, at the end of the test, users were asked to respond to five questions. The following question was the one in which most of the users agreed: *what phase of the composition was more difficult and why?*

Most of the users agreed that looking for elements of interest in the tree of topic elements (Table 9) was difficult because they did not know what elements were in each topic. This can be explained because ATIS is a complex database that consists of 28 tables and 125 columns. Therefore, they erroneously assumed that an element was in some topic, which occurred with query number 8, described in Section Experimental results. This problem can be solved by adding a finder of elements of interest and developing a tutoring module so the users can learn how to compose queries that include subqueries.

FUTURE RESEARCH DIRECTIONS

According to the results obtained by the QCI in the usability tests, it was shown that inexperienced users could use this interface to obtain database information by query composition that includes subqueries. Specifically, the results show that most users were able to compose 15 queries correctly. For the five incorrect queries, the explanation of the observed results is that they require manually decomposing the natural language query into a query that includes two subqueries. Therefore, there are improvements that can be made to the interface.

1. Add the functionality of query composition that includes aggregate functions to the new version, which would allow us to retrieve information that cannot be obtained with the version proposed in this chapter.
2. Add a finder of elements of interest which can facilitate the location of the topic of interest that includes a given element.
3. Develop a tutoring module so the users can learn how to compose queries that include subqueries, mainly, the manual decomposition of natural language queries.
4. Develop a module that translates the SQL query generated by the interface into natural language, so the user can receive feedback on how the interface interpreted the query.

Regarding the functionality for query composition that includes aggregate functions, it is important to notice that SAQP (Latendresse & Karp, 2010), which has most of the features of QCI (Table 1), mentions the following: basic statistics (e.g., averages) cannot be performed within the SAQP.

CONCLUSION

Nowadays, information is very important, and accessing information is important for businesses and organizations of all sizes: small, medium, or large. For medium and high-ranking officers, obtaining adequate and timely information is crucial for decision making. One alternative to access information stored in databases is to have professionals that are experts in a database query language. Unfortunately, most users are not able to formulate database queries that allow them to access the information they need.

Therefore, there exist different applications that can be used to access information stored in databases. Many of them are DBMS, which require users with skills in a database query language like SQL, to formulate the necessary queries to retrieve the requested information.

To facilitate access to the information stored in a database, different graphical interfaces have been developed to help inexperienced users to query databases. However, some interfaces do not offer functionality to facilitate access to information that could only be accessed by using database queries that include subqueries. Therefore, the functionality for query composition that includes subqueries was developed and integrated into a previous version that allowed query composition that includes joins, but not subqueries.

The new functionality allows inexperienced users query composition that includes from one to three subqueries without the need to have any knowledge of SQL. This interface guides the user in the query composition process, which is based on fragmenting a natural language query into the main query and one, two, or three subqueries.

By using this fragmentation, the interface guides the user through different windows to carry out query composition by parts, i.e., from the innermost subquery, through intermediate subqueries, up to the main query (the outermost).

The experimental tests showed that users could easily compose queries that include one subquery. Furthermore, the new functionality preserves the domain independence of the previous version of the interface. Additionally, like the previous version, the new version offers language independence, i.e., it can be configured for other languages like Spanish, for example, English, French, Italian, and Portuguese.

According to the results obtained from the experimental usability test, it was shown that inexperienced users could use the interface to access database information using queries that include subqueries.

REFERENCES

Latendresse, M., & Karp, P. D. (2010) An Advanced Web Query Interface for Biological Databases. *Database - The Journal of Biological Databases and Curation*.

Linguistic Data Consortium. (1990). *The 2884 ATIS0 speaker-dependent training prompts*. Retrieved from https://catalog.ldc.upenn.edu/docs/LDC93S4B/trn_prmp.html

Little, J., de Ga, M., Özyer, T., & Alhajj, R. (2004). Query builder: A natural language interface for structured databases. In *International Symposium on Computer and Information Sciences* (pp. 470-479). Springer. 10.1007/978-3-540-30182-0_48

Microsoft. (2010). *How to Navigate & use the Query by Example (QBE) interface in Microsoft Access 2007*. Retrieved from https://ms-office.wonderhowto.com/how-to/navigate-use-query-by-example-qbe-interface-microsoft-access-2007-398173/

Munroe, K. D., & Papakonstantiou, Y. (2000). BBQ: A visual interface for integrated browsing and querying of XML. In *Working Conference on Visual Database Systems* (pp. 277-296). Springer. 10.1007/978-0-387-35504-7_18

Pazos, R. A., Aguirre, A. G., Aguirre, M. A., & Martínez, J. A. (2015). Interface for composing queries for complex databases for inexperienced users. In E. Onieva, I. Santos, E. Osaba, H. Quintián, & E. Corchado (Eds.), *Hybrid Artificial Intelligent Systems. HAIS 2015* (pp. 61–72). Springer. doi:10.1007/978-3-319-19644-2_6

Pessina, F., Masseroli, M., & Canakoglu, A. (2013). Visual composition of complex queries on an integrative Genomic and Proteomic Data Warehouse. *Engineering (London)*, *5*(10, 10B), 94–98. doi:10.4236/eng.2013.510B019

Porras, J., Florencia-Juárez, R., Rivera, G., & García, V. (2018). Interfaz de lenguaje natural para consultar cubos multidimensionales utilizando procesamiento analítico en línea. *Research in Computing Science*, *147*(6), 153–165. doi:10.13053/rcs-147-6-12

Section 2
Text Analytics Systems

Chapter 10
News Classification to Notify About Traffic Incidents in a Mexican City

Alejandro Requejo Flores
Universidad Autónoma de Ciudad Juárez, Mexico

Alejandro Ruiz
https://orcid.org/0000-0002-7913-5682
Universidad Autónoma de Ciudad Juárez, Mexico

Abraham López
Universidad Autónoma de Ciudad Juárez, Mexico

Raul Porras
https://orcid.org/0000-0002-6772-5351
Universidad Autónoma de Ciudad Juárez, Mexico

ABSTRACT

The primary objective of this chapter is to analyze the content retrieved from an RSS newspaper report written in the Spanish language and determine if it describes a traffic incident. The real-world case study occurs in a Mexican city with 1.5 million inhabitants, and its purpose is to offer an application to inform in real-time about traffic incidents that happen in the town, gathering its information from the reports published by a local newspaper. However, to do so, the authors first need to classify the articles and ignore those whose content does not imply any kind of road accident.

DOI: 10.4018/978-1-7998-4730-4.ch010

Copyright © 2021, IGI Global. Copying or distributing in print or electronic forms without written permission of IGI Global is prohibited.

INTRODUCTION

All cities generate a massive amount of news through different media. In our modern society, newspapers always have something to report; there is always news. However, almost no newspaper website offers a precise classification of their information; most times, they give vague categories that fit many of their reports at once. Additionally, due to the globalization of the information, local newspapers show articles about things happening in other countries and even continents, so, in order to classify their data, it is pertinent to consider that we may need to filter out news that are not relevant to the area taken into consideration.

It is interesting to detect articles that include traffic incidents; in this way, we could identify when a street is blocked, or its traffic is moving slowly, and, with this information, notify the citizens so they can take an alternative road. However, due to the high number of information newspapers generate, especially online newspapers, it is easy for some reports to pass unnoticed even if we consistently and manually check the website. This chapter presents a way to solve this problem by automatizing the classification of reports that imply any kind of traffic. The way this is done is by applying a process that involves different techniques and algorithms on different stages based in areas of Natural Language Processing.

This application of Natural Language Processing is a contribution to the development of a smart city. In the literature, we find many different definitions of what a 'smart city' is: Washburn et al. (2010) described it with an emphasis on the use of smart computing technologies to serve society in a fast and efficient manner; it is expected from Smart Computing to get more involved in aspects like city administrations, education, healthcare, transportation, and utilities.

Our proposal aims to enhance these aspects of the development of a smart city, improving the quality of transportation. In order to do so, it is necessary to have a good source of reports that informs about incidents. By having such a source, we would be able to extract the information, organize it, and serve it in a simple application that the public could easily use.

Taking into consideration everything that was introduced before, we present a real-world application that enables a shared understanding of what is happening in the city and improves transportation through it. The case study occurs in Ciudad Juárez, which is located in the Mexican state of Chihuahua. Mexico is in the top five countries with the fastest-growing urbanization degree (cf. United Nations, 2018); additionally, Ciudad Juarez is the fifth largest city in Mexico, and its population is expected to increase its number of inhabitants to the point that it becomes a large city in the following decades. A town with a fast-increasing population must provide structures that rapidly broadcast knowledge among all the members of its community.

In Ciudad Juárez, the local newspaper El Diario publishes, on average, 40 news in RSS (Really Simple Syndication) format per day. Like most newspapers, the articles presented by El Diario are not organized with precise tags; instead, they classify them under general topics that they belong to. These topics are too broad, which makes the process of doing manual specific filtering of these reports not possible; this condition represents an evident problem when people are trying to find the news that talks about particular topics like traffic incidents. It is clear to determine that there is a need to develop an algorithm that analyzes El Diario's content so that it gets the news articles that involve a traffic incident.

The purpose of this chapter is to recognize the effectiveness level of different areas of Natural Language Processing when it comes to the classification of news articles that imply any kind of traffic incident. This information, which has already been classified, will then be used to extract the exact location of the event reported in these articles to be able to provide this data through a web application. The result of such a process is a service that notifies citizens about traffic incidents.

This chapter is structured as follows: In Section 2, we introduce some techniques and methods, concepts, and ideas that are related to the aiming of this project and a brief review of previous studies and approaches made to classify news that are not written in the English language. In Section 3, we describe the product of this project and the process of developing it through several phases; it presents the libraries and methods employed in each stage along with early results obtained during the testing. In Section 4, we present the results we got after finishing the project and discuss and explain these results. In Section 5, we describe the areas whose additional research could help to refine this proposal. Finally, in Section 6, we suggest some ideas that may slightly improve the performance of this classification and the opinion of the authors about the obtained results.

BACKGROUND

This section presents the main concepts regarding this chapter, as well as previous works that are related to the topic at hand.

Smart City

The concept of Smart City is not one that has a single established definition; in fact, looking into the literature related to such topic brings within multiple variations of the meaning of Smart City (cf. Ochoa Ortiz-Zezzati, Rivera, Gómez-Santillán, & Sánchez-Lara, 2019). For such reason, it is pertinent to present more than one definition of what a Smart City is; these definitions are shown in the next list:

- A Smart city is considered a city that has an intelligently competitive industry, taking in special consideration the areas of information and communication technologies. This term is used during the discussions regarding modern technology in everyday urban life (Giffinger et al., 2007; Mejía, Ochoa-Zezzati, Contreras-Masse & Rivera, 2020).
- The Smart Cities Council (n.d.) defines the concept of Smart City as a city that uses information and communication technologies to enhance life, work, and sustainability. Smart Cities are a manifestation of the Internet of Things: they make use of sensors to generate data that may be transferred, integrated and analyzed to let some aspects of the city function in a better way (cf. Holguin, Ochoa-Zezzati, Larios, Cossio, Maciel & Rivera, 2019).

It is also possible to find that some authors prefer the concept of Smart Communities over Smart Cities. One of these authors is Williams (2016) who suggests that utilizing the concept Smart Communities leads to a more neutral notion rather than cities; this is taken as such because the term city does not have an exact definition when it comes to factors such as population, size, geographic location, among other factors. For Williams (2016), a Smart Community can be one that has any size or significance, that utilizes the Internet of Things to:

- Enhance certain aspects of their operations or other factors inside or outside of its borders, that are valuable to its economic vitality, security, environmental footprint, quality of life, among other factors that are considered essential.
- Answer to the community's changing necessities quickly and efficiently.
- Make the community take part in it and allows the informed comprehension of, and where consent is appropriate for what it is doing.
- Allow the collaboration with other communities whenever it is required or desired.

In the work presented by Washburn et al. (2010), they identify several infrastructure components and services of a smart city in action:

- **City Administration:** The government services are informed about the city's condition and can reach its citizens effectively; it also provides a reliable infrastructure to give an efficient service of transportation. According to Gil-García (2012), the governance must use information technologies to interconnect and integrate information, processes, institutions, and physical infrastructure to better serve citizens and communities.
- **Education:** The intention in this component is that the citizens become able to use and even innovate their own sustainable solutions for the growth and development of a smart city; Wolf, Kortuem and Cavero (2015) suggest to solve how to teach data skills to 5-18 years olds as a way of achieving this. According to Washburn et al. (2010), the use of technology in the field of education will improve its quality and reduce costs.
- **Healthcare:** The purpose is to provide a quicker and more accurate diagnosis to patients. More than a decade ago, Istepanian, Laxminarayan and Pattichis (2006) predicted the potential impact of technologies like electronic health records and personal health records on healthcare services. The usage of Information and Communication Technologies offers a more global view of the health status of a community and allows them to design new ways to approach some health problems (Cook, Duncan, Sprint & Fritz, 2018).
- **Public Safety:** Real-time information is used to answer quickly to emergencies and threats. On this point, we could include the report of accidents that occur in the streets: vehicle crashes, traffic jams, obstructed ways, among many other things. On this aspect, authors focus on smart medical attention: intelligent management of medical materials, support for digital processing of data and supervision of public health; indeed, the health sector receives a lot of attention due to its importance and, particularly, the high potential of sensors and data links to monitor a patient's symptoms and needs, applicable even to the general population and not only in hospitals (Xue, 2010; Sourla, Paschou Sakkopoulos & Tsakalidis, 2013). However, there are other examples of public safety events: emerging crimes, traffic accidents, emergencies, hazards, among others (Roitman, Mamou, Mehta, Satt & Subramaniam, 2012).
- **Real Estate:** The implementation of smart systems in this field would be reflected in the amount of energy-saving and reduction in both operational and capital costs, according to Al-Hader and Rodzi (2009). These systems may also facilitate the maintenance and enhance the return of investment in a short period of time; additionally, this smart environment may attract the people because of the control it gives and the better management of resources.
- **Transportation:** Although Washburn et al. (2010) focus on encouraging the use of public transportation, it is also crucial on this aspect to reduce the traffic congestion and, in the cases where it

is not possible to control this kind of situations completely, to improve the situation by taking the less-likely time from drivers. In their study, Su, Li and Fu (2011) mention that a smart city may change the traditional transport system, establishing the smart traffic management system; this includes adaptive traffic signal, urban traffic control system, and so on.

- **Utilities:** Smart Cities should be able to optimize the use of energy distribution networks and natural resources, as well as human capital and some other assets. This goal may be achieved through different technologies applied for better management of production, energy distribution, transportation, logistics, waste management, and pollution control (Neirotti, De Marco, Cagliano, Mangano & Scorrano, 2014).

From these aspects, this proposal's focus is the *Transportation* point, since its purpose is to reduce traffic congestion by preventing people from driving through routes where accidents have happened recently and therefore having a less interrupted flow of traffic.

Data Scraping

It is significant to present that data scraping is not something new; the automated gathering of data from the Internet is nearly as old as the Internet itself. Commonly, this is done by a program that requests data to a website (generally in the form of HTML) that parses the data and extracts the needed information; web scraping involves a wide variety of programming techniques such as data analysis, natural language parsing and information security (Mitchell, 2018).

However, the scraped data is not too useful because it contains a high quantity of unnecessary information; this leads to an apparent necessity: we need to clean the data so we can have just what we will use. According to Rahm and Do (2000), *data cleaning* deals with detecting and removing errors and inconsistencies from data to improve its quality. Some common data problems are misspellings, missing information, or invalid data; another concern related to such a topic is redundant data, so the cleaning process must take this into consideration.

Text Classification

Classification is the activity of selecting the precise class label for a presented input. When it comes to basic classification means that each input is regarded as in isolation from the other data, and the group of labels is defined beforehand (Bird, Klein & Loper, 2009). A classifier can be called supervised because it is created based on a training corpus that has all the correct labels for each input given.

Due to the nature of the project at hand, the process of text classification is of great importance, so, for such reason, it is valuable to analyze multiple methods that can be used for the classification of text. The methods to classify text that are taken into consideration are the next ones:

- **Decision Tree:** It is a simple diagram that selects tags for the input values. It consists of decision nodes, that check every value, and leaf nodes, which assign the tags. In order to choose the tag for a given entry value, we must start at the root node, which selects the branch based on the value; this process continues until it reaches a leaf (Bird et al., 2009).
- **Naïve Bayes Classifier:** Every feature helps to determine to which category the input value belongs to. To select the tag, the Naïve Bayes Classifier calculates the prior probability of each tag

and determines it after checking the frequency of every tag in the training set. After that, the contribution of each feature is combined with its prior probability to get a possible value for each tag; the tag with the higher value is assigned to the input value (Bird et al., 2009).

- **Maximum Entropy:** It uses a model like the employed by the Naïve Bayes classifier, but instead of using probabilities to assign the characteristics, uses search techniques to find a set of features that maximize the performance of the classifier. Notably, it looks for a set of features that maximize the total probability of the training corpus. These classifiers choose the model parameters through iterative optimization methods that initialize the parameters with random values and then repeatedly improve them to get them the nearest to the optimal solution (Bird et al., 2009).
- **Support Vector Machine:** A Support Vector Machine (SVM) is a machine learning procedure that utilizes a linear classifier to be able to classify information into two different categories (Ranganathan, Nakai & Schonbach, 2018). The algorithm generates, from a training dataset, an optimal hyperplane to classify new inputs.

Taking into consideration the problem dealt with in this chapter, and along with the solution proposed, it is essential to point out that there are many other studies in the area of NLP whose purpose is to classify news according to their content. One of these studies is by Kroha and Baeza-Yates (2005), who processed a corpus of the news reports published from 1999 to 2002 to explore the impact of several factors on the actual news classification. In another study, Van and Thanh (2017) used a neural network with Bag of Words (BoW) to classify Vietnamese news, testing classifiers such as Random Forest and SVMs.

On the other hand, some authors have developed different applications that visually inform about events related to the news. An example of such is *Newspaper Map* (Franchi, 2005), which allows seeing some indexed newspapers from 238 countries; it is possible to filter the results by language, newspaper, or location. Another application is *Live Universal Awareness Map* (Rozhkovsky & Bil'chenko, 2014), which is an interactive map that reports news from all around the world by using smart web crawlers from different sources and sending the data to an analyst group to check them.

Furthermore, news articles are not the only way to gather information and detect traffic accidents occurring in a city; social media data is a popular source that can be used for the same purpose, which presents its own advantages and limitations. Kumar and Toshniwal (2016) applied k-means algorithm to group accident locations into three categories according to how often accidents occur in these places, and then used association rule mining to extract the characterization of these locations; this study intended to help identifying high-frequency accident locations to take preventive efforts. Zhang, He, Gao and Ni (2018) used deep learning to detect traffic accidents using 3 million tweets collected during a year based on two cities from the United States, obtaining an overall accuracy of 85%.

As we mentioned earlier, gathering the data is not a big deal, but filtering it to get only reports about traffic incidents is another issue; so, we must apply a text classification technique on this problem. Text classification is the process of assigning the items to a particular predefined category or class. Most of the research on text classification is done based on documents written in the English language, while other languages like Spanish are mostly ignored, and therefore, there is a very limited amount of research. Pérez-Rosas, Banea and Mihalcea (2012) presented in their work a framework to derive sentiment lexicons in Spanish from identifying private states, such as opinions, emotions, sentiments, evaluations, beliefs, and speculations in natural language. In their study, they mention there are few lexicons for sentiment and subjectivity analysis, while a considerable part exists for the English language. In the area of classification applied to Spanish texts, Gutiérrez Esparza et al. (2017) developed a classifier for reviews written by students about their teachers, distinguishing three categories: positive, negative, or neutral. They applied sentiment analysis methods and SVMs, presenting a model called SocialMining that obtained an accuracy of 80% using a linear kernel for the SVM.

Therefore, our proposal also represents a contribution to Natural Language Processing for text written in Spanish. The importance of our study relies on the many applications of Natural Language Processing that are currently almost exclusive to English texts. Nadkarni, Ohno-Machado and Chapman (2011) mention a few NLP tasks: on the low-level, sentence boundary detection, tokenization, part-of-speech assignment to individual words (POS tagging), morphological decomposition of compound works, shallow parsing (chunking), and problem-specific segmentation; on the higher-level, spelling/grammatical error identification and recovery, and named entity recognition.

MAIN FOCUS OF THE CHAPTER

In order to gather the information needed, we send requests to El Diario's RSS endpoint to get the information that is uploaded throughout the day. It is essential to point out that since the source is updated with new content regularly, we need to run a script that frequently checks if new information has been generated, and if so, this same script saves it in a database to classify it next. The structured format of RSS endpoints simplifies the process of extracting the information and makes it a fast procedure.

For this application, the data used is only obtained from the newspaper El Diario. However, it is possible to use any other platform or even combine multiple sources to get information regarding traffic incidents. Another thing to take into consideration is that an RSS endpoint is not a necessary thing, but it helps facilitate the process at hand, as mentioned before. The obtainment of the information is done every two hours, and the web application is intended to work on any modern web explorer (Chrome, Firefox, Internet Explorer 10+, Microsoft Edge, Opera, Safari).

In this particular case, we had to personally talk with the company's administrative personal to obtain permission to access their information and use it for research purposes. We requested two things:

- Access to the local news articles that were published in 2017. These were used to generate the training corpus.
- Continuous access to local news articles through the RSS service they offer to manipulate it later.

Generating the Training Corpus

The classifying technique that was applied in this project is a supervised learning algorithm, meaning that it is based on previously classified data. As a consequence, we had to generate our own corpus because there was not a specific one that would be useful for the necessities of this project. The corpus was created with the information provided by El Diario: a history of news published from January to September 2017, which consisted of a total of 11,218 articles. However, since it had only essential elements like title, content, and publishing date (no classification mark of any sort), we had to classify every article manually.

In order to make this process easier, we made a simple web application whose function was to show ten random news, each one with a menu that enabled us to select its corresponding category; the articles' data was updated in the database, and the application showed the next ten news articles. If the title of the news did not specify the category it belonged in, it was possible to click it to show the article's content to be able to determine its class; this is shown in **Figure 1** and **Figure 2**.

Figure 1. Web application to manually classify news

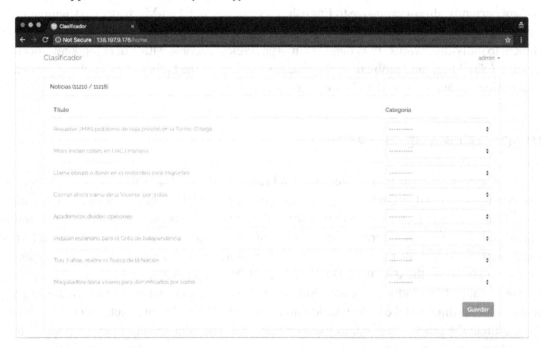

This process could have been done on a localhost application, but to make the classification process faster, we requested help to third parties. Therefore, since the website was exposed in a public IP server, we had to implement a login system to protect the application and prevent an outside user from accessing the site and modifying the information without permission.

For the category assignment, we defined the following criteria formed by two rules:

- Each article can have only one category.
- If the news article presents information related to a traffic incident, it must be classified as such.

The following list shows the technologies and tools used in the development of this web application:

- Server with Ubuntu Server on a public IP.
- MySQL 8.0 used as the database management system.
- NGINX as the webserver.
- Laravel 5.5 as the framework used in the application's backend.
- Bootstrap 3 and jQuery 3.2, used in the development of the application's frontend.

Figure 2. Display of the article's content

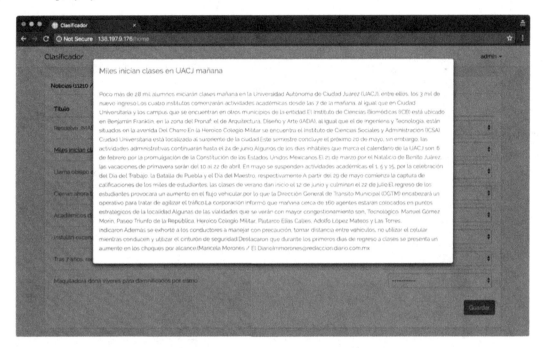

Once the manual classification of the news articles was finished, it was possible to determine that only about 10% of the news articles obtained were about traffic incidents. The distribution of the categories taken into consideration is shown in **Figure 3.**

Development Of Scripts To Manipulate The Information

In this second stage of the project, we worked on the process of automatically handling the information; this was divided into three parts, which are described briefly in the list below:

- **Automatic gathering of data:** Obtaining the new content generated and published on El Diario's RSS endpoint.
- **Classification of the information:** Assigning the category of *traffic incident* to each of the news collected with the previous script.
- **Extraction of the information:** Searching and extracting the location of the incidents from the articles classified as traffic incidents. This part is not covered in this chapter.

These scripts are executed sequentially in that order. The configuration performs the process every two hours daily through 'cron jobs' on the server where the scrips are hosted.

Automatic Gathering of the Information

The gathering of information is done through a straightforward procedure. El Diario gives an RSS endpoint where they publish their articles, and from there, we can manipulate the information in any

Figure 3. Category distribution

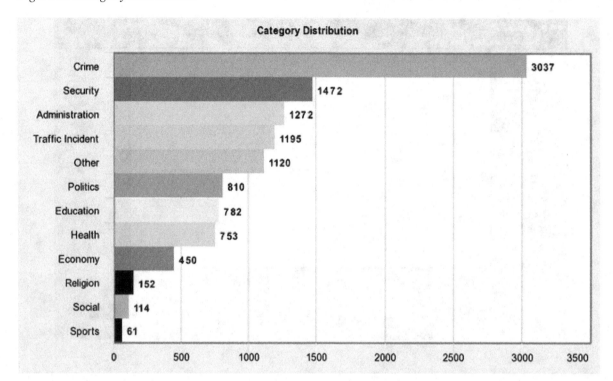

way we want, either using the unprocessed XML file, using some RSS reader, or with some library that facilitates this process.

The RSS feed serves thirty entries with the latest news published, ordered by the most recent publishing date. As we can see in Source Code 1, the title and description are not clean; they have embedded HTML tags that we need to remove and change some special characters.

Source Code 1. Example of an RSS entry of a news article

```
<item>
  <title>
    <![CDATA| Accidente en Juan Pablo II deja un herido ]]>
  </title>
  <link>
    https://diario.mx/Local/2018-02-13_68664d5b/accidente-en-juan-pablo-ii-
    deja-un-herido/
  </link>
  <pubDate> Tue, 13 Feb 2018 17:57:19 GMT-07:00 </pubDate>
  <category> Local </category>
  <description>
    <![CDATA|
```

```
<a href="https://diario.mx/Local/2018-02-13_68664d5b/accidente-en-juan-
pablo-ii-deja-un-herido/" target="_blank"><img src="
http://diario.mx/imagesnotas/2018/02/LOCI383116920b68b9_0.jpg"></a><br>
Un choque entre dos veh&iacute;culos en el bulevar Juan Pablo II
dej&oacute; una persona lesionada, informaron las autoridades.<br><br>
El accidente ocurri&oacute; a la altura del centro de convenciones Las
Fuentes, donde el conductor de un veh&iacute;culo Geo Metro azul
circulaba de poniente a oriente y se qued&oacute; dormido, invadiendo
el carril contrario, lo que ocasi&oacute;n&oacute; que impactara de frente a
una camioneta Oldsmobile Bravada.<br><br> El conductor responsable tuvo
que ser trasladado a un hospital, se inform&oacute;.<br><br>
    </description>
</item>
```

To obtain the RSS entries and clean the retrieved information, we wrote a Python script using the following libraries:

- **feedparser:** to process files in RSS format.
- **SQLAlchemy:** as Object Relational Mapper (ORM) to access the database from classes.
- **BeautifulSoup:** to process and clean texts.

The process is the following:

1. Send a request to the RSS endpoint and process the information.
2. Search in the database the entry with the most recent publishing date.
3. For each RSS entry, with a most recent publishing date than the stored news, process it and clean the fields to store it in table *news* on the database. Until this moment, all these entries have the field *is_traffic* as *null*, so with this, we know they have to be processed in the next script (the process of classifying).

Classification of the Information

The classification is the second step of the process in this stage. It binarily categorizes the collected news articles that have been stored in the database; it is either a traffic incident or not. For this process, we used a library named *scikit-learn* along with the training news articles corpus generated in the first stage of the project.

Before running the script, it is necessary to extract the descriptive words from the articles' classifications; this is done through a Bag of Words technique, which takes all the different words in a text with their respective occurrences. The Bag of Words intends to identify all the unique words that describe each news' category. Table 1 shows some of the words obtained from an article classified as a traffic incident in the training corpus; we can notice that the words with the highest occurrence are not descriptive of a specific category.

The script follows the process described next:

Table 1. Words obtained with BoW

Word (Spanish)	Translation	Occurrences
accidente	accident	1
de	from	6
bulevar	boulevard	1
calle	street	1
el	the	5
vehículo	vehicle	1

1. Retrieve all the entries from table *news* that have not been classified (those whose *is_traffic* column has a *null* value).
2. Load the training corpus that contains the 11218 news that already have an assigned category.
3. The learning process with the corpus information is started, processing the data through a Bag of Words.
4. After finishing the learning process, an SVM classifier takes all the non-categorized items previously retrieved from the database and emits a classification for each one.
5. After the classifier assigns a category to each element, the database is updated so that the field *is_traffic* now has a true or false value instead of a null.

RESULTS AND DISCUSSIONS

Like it was mentioned throughout the development of this section, the training corpus of the classifier was generated in the first part of this project with a set of news articles that contained articles from the year 2017, provided by the newspaper El Diario. During the making of this training corpus, only one classification was assigned to each news article, even though these articles could have been associated with multiples categories. This was decided as such to speed up the process of classification, but also due to the scope of this project.

The process of classification described in the second stage of this project starts off with the learning process, where everything from the corpus is loaded, and the bag of words is obtained from the news articles associated with their corresponding category. In Table 2, it is possible to observe the accuracy percentages that were obtained from the traffic incidents classification, plus the accuracy percentages regarding the 12 classes, named Global Accuracy in the table; these results were obtained through 10-fold cross-validation. By doing an average of the obtained results, it was possible to conclude that the correct classification of traffic incidents was 68%, while the global one was 63%. A reason as to why the obtained percentages were relatively low was because it was decided to associate each news article to only one category; this decision presents the next problem: when there is a news article in which the selected class is predominant only by a little bit regarding other classes, the bag of words of this article did not significantly represent unique traits of this category.

According to the objectives taken into consideration for the project, it was enough for the classifier to detect if a news article was a traffic incident or not. Due to this reason, the training corpus was treated differently than the way that was mention previously in the text.

Table 2. Simplified accuracy results from the classifier with two classes (is a traffic incident or is not)

Iteration	Traffic Incident Accuracy	Global Accuracy
1	0.68	0.63
2	0.66	0.62
3	0.68	0.64
4	0.61	0.64
5	0.64	0.62
6	0.65	0.63
7	0.74	0.64
8	0.68	0.61
9	0.76	0.64
10	0.75	0.64

An aggrupation was done with all the categories that aren't traffic incidents, considering in this way only two classifications: is or is not a traffic incident. With this simplification, the unique features of the news classified as a traffic incident became more significant; this allowed us to get better predictions from the classifier. To verify this last statement, we evaluated the effectiveness of the classifier through a cross-validation process with ten iterations. The detailed results are shown in Table 3; we noticed that the precision percentage was increased significantly, compared with those obtained with the previous method, getting an average of 96%. The following list explains the columns of Table 3 for a better understanding.

- **Iteration:** The number of iteration in the crossed validation process.
- **Is it TI (Traffic Incident)?:** This indicates if the news article is a traffic incident.
- **CM:** Confusion matrix where each quadrant C_{ij} (where i is the row, and j is the column, both indexes are binary) is denoted as follows:
  - $C_{0,0}$ – **True Positives (TP).** This is the number of news articles that have information about a traffic incident and in which the classifier predicted that they were part of the *traffic incident* category.
  - $C_{0,1}$ – **False Negatives (FN).** This is the number of news articles that have information about a traffic incident and in which the classifier predicted that they were not part of the traffic incident category.
  - $C_{1,0}$ – **False Positives (FP).** This is the number of news articles that do not have information about a traffic incident and in which the classifier predicted that they were part of the traffic incident category.
  - $C_{1,1}$ – **True Negatives (TN).** This is the number of news articles that do not have information about a traffic incident and in which the classifier predicted that they were not part of the traffic incident category.
- **Precision (P):** It is the proportion of the correctly predicted positive observations over the total number of predicted positive observations, defined by Equation 1.

$$P = \frac{TP}{TP + FP} \#$$

(1)

- **Recall (R):** It is the proportion of correctly predicted observations over the total number of observations predicted in the class, defined by Equation 2.

$$R = \frac{TP}{TP + FN} \#$$

(2)

- **F-Value:** It is the weighted average of precision and recall, defined by Equation 3.

$$F_{Value} = \frac{2P \cdot R}{P + R} \#$$

(3)

- **Support:** The number of observations in the sample.

The classifier was trained using all the news articles published in 2017 by El Diario. Afterward, it was tested on a compilation, including 3768 news articles published from January 20, 2018, to April 30, 2018, from which 207 were classified as a traffic incident.

CONCLUSION

Many works have studied the information classification field in Natural Language Processing; we can find in the literature various effective algorithms that have been proven to reach high precision levels with a low failure rate in some cases. Previous research tried with different classifiers like neural networks and random forest classifiers; this proposal applied Support Vector Machine with the Bag of Words technique.

Our aim in this project was to reach an acceptable level of precision like previous studies have, and at the conclusion, the results were favorable. Although the effectiveness level obtained from this news classifier is around 96%, it was directly affected by the quality of the training corpus, which was specifically designed for the necessities of the project, and the proper selection of a classifying algorithm. It is important to note that even though other works might show a better precision level, those results cannot be compared to the ones in this chapter since this work was done using a different language, which is Spanish.

FUTURE RESEARCH

This proposal did the classification process through a Support Vector Machine and a Bag-of-Words implementation. In their study, Van et al. (2017) got an average accuracy of 99.75% using a new neural network architecture; the employment of other classifying methods may help to get a better level for this proposal, although it is remarkable that Van et al. (2017) worked on texts written in Vietnamese while we use texts written in Spanish. Therefore, a direction for future research is to get a better performance

Table 3. Detailed results of the classifier with two classes (is a traffic incident or is not)

Iteration	Is it TI?	CM		Precision	Recall	F-Value	Support
1	Yes	73	60	0.95	0.55	0.70	133
	No	4	985	0.94	1.00	0.97	989
	average / total			0.94	0.94	0.94	1122
2	Yes	58	48	0.92	0.55	0.69	106
	No	5	1011	0.95	1.00	0.97	1016
	average / total			0.95	0.95	0.95	1122
3	Yes	66	52	1.00	0.56	0.72	118
	No	0	1004	0.95	1.00	0.97	1004
	average / total			0.96	0.95	0.95	1122
4	Yes	61	53	0.90	0.54	0.67	114
	No	7	1001	0.95	0.99	0.97	1008
	average / total			0.94	0.95	0.94	1122
5	Yes	62	63	0.98	0.50	0.66	125
	No	1	996	0.94	1.00	0.97	997
	average / total			0.95	0.94	0.93	1122
6	Yes	75	61	0.97	0.55	0.70	136
	No	2	984	0.94	1.00	0.97	986
	average / total			0.95	0.94	0.94	1122
7	Yes	68	45	0.91	0.60	0.72	113
	No	7	1002	0.96	0.99	0.97	1009
	average / total			0.95	0.95	0.95	1122
8	Yes	60	50	0.92	0.55	0.69	110
	No	5	1007	0.95	1.00	0.97	1012
	average / total			0.95	0.95	0.95	1122
9	Yes	74	51	0.97	0.59	0.74	125
	No	2	994	0.95	1.00	0.97	996
	average / total			0.95	0.95	0.95	1121
10	Yes	63	52	0.94	0.55	0.69	115
	No	4	1002	0.95	1.00	0.97	1006
	average / total			0.95	0.95	0.94	1121

through other classifiers for texts written in Spanish (or languages other than English, which has more studies), although the current results are satisfactory.

On the other hand, an improvement that could be made is to design a classifier that retrieves data from multiple sources. The main concern when it comes to this new version would be to remove effectively any duplicated news articles gathered from various sources; the usefulness of this suggested approach may differ depending on the coverage that each online newspaper (or the selected source of reports) gives. In a community where all sources offer almost the same information, the current approach employed in this proposal may be enough. However, in big cities, a single newspaper can't cover all the happening events; the use of multiple sources could highly improve the usefulness of this project in that case since the coverage would be noticeably increased.

For the development of the project, a classic Bag of Words technique was used to extract the descriptive words for each category. Table 1 showed that the descriptive terms for the *traffic incident* category were not too descriptive at all; one of the issues may be that synonyms and words with similar meanings are grouped separately. The use of a more advanced version of Bag-of-Words (e.g., Kim, Kim & Cho, 2017) would improve the results, leading to better descriptive words by grouping into the same point all the words that have a similar meaning (e.g., clustering all the words that refer to transit routes: *calle, avenida, carretera, bulevar*, among others). We are also going to deal with the severe class imbalance of the training data set to improve the classifier performance (cf. García, Sánchez, Marqués, Florencia & Rivera, 2019).

ACKNOWLEDGMENT

We thank El Diario for the support given and for granting us the permissions to use their information in the proposal presented throughout this chapter.

REFERENCES

Al-Hader, M., & Rodzi, A. (2009). The Smart Infrastructure Development & Monitoring. *Theoretical and Empirical Researches in Urban Management*, *4*(2), 87–94.

Bird, S., Klein, E., & Loper, E. (2009). *Natural Language Processing with Python*. O'Reilly Media, Inc.

Cook, D. J., Duncan, G., Sprint, G., & Fritz, R. (2018). Using Smart City Technology to Make Healthcare Smarter. *Proceedings of the IEEE*, *106*(4), 708–722. doi:10.1109/JPROC.2017.2787688 PMID:29628528

Franchi, F. (2005). *Newspaper Map*. Retrieved from https://newspapermap.com/

García, V., Sánchez, J. S., Marqués, A. I., Florencia, R., & Rivera, G. (2019). Understanding the apparent superiority of over-sampling through an analysis of local information for class-imbalanced data. *Expert Systems with Applications*, *113026*, 113026. Advance online publication. doi:10.1016/j.eswa.2019.113026

Giffinger, R., Fertner, C., Kramar, H., Kalasek, R., Pichler-Milanović, N., & Meijers, E. (2007). Smart cities – Ranking of European medium-sized cities. Vienna, Austria: Centre of Regional Science (SRF), Vienna University of Technology.

Gil-García, R. (2012). *Enacting Electronic Government Success: An Integrative Study of Government-wide Websites, Organizational Capabilities, and Institutions*. Springer. doi:10.1007/978-1-4614-2015-6

Gutiérrez Esparza, G., Ochoa Zezzatti, A., Hernández, A., Ponce, J., Álvarez, M., … Nava, J. (2017). A Sentiment Analysis Model to Analyze Students Reviews of Teacher Performance Using Support Vector Machines. In S. Omatu, S. Rodríguez, G. Villarubia, P. Faria, P. Sitek & J. Prieto (Eds.), *Distributed Computing and Artificial Intelligence, 14th International Conference. DCAI 2017. Advances in Intelligent Systems and Computing. 620.* Cham: Springer.

Holguin, L., Ochoa-Zezzatti, A., Larios, V. M., Cossio, E., Maciel, R., & Rivera, G. (2019). Small steps towards a smart city: Mobile application that provides options for the use of public transport in Juarez City. In *2019 IEEE International Smart Cities Conference* (ISC2) (pp. 100-105). IEEE. doi: 10.1109/ISC246665.2019.9071728

Istepanian, R., Laxminarayan, S., & Pattichis, C. S. (2006). *M-Health: Emerging Mobile Health Systems.* Springer. doi:10.1007/b137697

Kim, H. K., Kim, H., & Cho, S. (2017). Bag-of-concepts: Comprehending document representation through clustering words in distributed representation. *Neurocomputing, 266,* 336–352. doi:10.1016/j.neucom.2017.05.046

Kroha, P., & Baeza-Yates, R. (2005). A Case Study: News Classification Based on Term Frequency. In *16th International Workshop on Database and Expert Systems Applications (DEXA'05)* (pp. 428-432). Copenhagen, Denmark: IEEE. 10.1109/DEXA.2005.6

Kumar, S., & Toshniwal, D. (2016). A data mining approach to characterize road accident locations. *Journal of Modern Transportation, 24*(1), 62–72. doi:10.100740534-016-0095-5

Mejía, J., Ochoa-Zezzatti, A., Contreras-Masse, R., & Rivera, G. (2020). Intelligent System for the Visual Support of Caloric Intake of Food in Inhabitants of a Smart City Using a Deep Learning Model. In *Applications of Hybrid Metaheuristic Algorithms for Image Processing* (pp. 441–455). Springer. doi:10.1007/978-3-030-40977-7_19

Mitchell, R. (2018). *Web Scraping with Python.* O'Reilly Media, Inc.

Nadkarni, P. M., Ohno-Machado, L., & Chapman, W. W. (2011). Natural language processing: An introduction. *Journal of the American Medical Informatics Association, 18*(5), 544–551. doi:10.1136/amiajnl-2011-000464 PMID:21846786

Neirotti, P., De Marco, A., Cagliano, A. C., Mangano, G., & Scorrano, F. (2014). Current trends in Smart City initiatives: Some stylised facts. *Cities (London, England), 38,* 25–36. doi:10.1016/j.cities.2013.12.010

Ochoa Ortiz-Zezzatti, A., Rivera, G., Gómez-Santillán, C., & Sánchez Lara, B. (2019). *Handbook of Research on Metaheuristics for Order Picking Optimization in Warehouses to Smart Cities.* IGI Global. doi:10.4018/978-1-5225-8131-4

Pérez-Rosas, V., Banea, C., & Mihalcea, R. (2012). Learning Sentiment Lexicons in Spanish. In K. Jokinen, & S. Tenjes (eds.), *Proceedings of the Eighth International Conference on Language Resources and Evaluation (LREC'12)* (pp. 3077-3081). Istanbul, Turkey: European Language Resources Association (ELRA).

Rahm, E., & Do, H. H. (2000). Data cleaning: Problems and current approaches. *A Quarterly Bulletin of the Computer Society of the IEEE Technical Committee on Data Engineering*, *23*(4), 3–13.

Ranganathan, S., Nakai, K., Gribskov, M., & Schonbach, C. (2019). *Encyclopedia of Bioinformatics and Computational Biology: ABC of Bioinformatics*. Elsevier.

Roitman, H., Mamou, J., Mehta, S., Satt, A., & Subramaniam, L. V. (2012). Harnessing the Crowds for Smart City Sensing. In *Proceedings of the 1st international workshop on Multimodal crowd sensing (CrowdSens '12)*. New York: ACM. 10.1145/2390034.2390043

Rozhkovsky, R., & Bil'chenko, A. (2014). *Live Universal Awareness Map*. Retrieved from https://liveuamap.com/

Sourla, E., Paschou, M., Sakkopoulos, E., & Tsakalidis, A. (2013). Health Internet of Things: Metrics and methods for efficient data transfer. *Simulation Modelling Practice and Theory*, *34*, 186–199. doi:10.1016/j.simpat.2012.08.002

Su, K., Li, J., & Fu, H. (2011). Smart City and the Applications. *2011 International Conference on Electronics, Communications and Control (ICECC)*, 1028-1031. 10.1109/ICECC.2011.6066743

United Nations. (2018). *World Urbanization Prospects 2018*. Retrieved from https://population.un.org/wup/

Van, T. P., & Thanh, T. M. (2017). Vietnamese news classification based on BoW with keywords extraction and neural network. In *2017 21st Asia Pacific Symposium on Intelligent and Evolutionary Systems (IES)* (pp. 43-48). Hanoi, Vientnam: IEEE. 10.1109/IESYS.2017.8233559

Washburn, D., Sindhu, U., Balaouras, S., Dines, R., Hayes, N., & Nelson, L. (2010). *Helping CIOs Understand "Smart City" Initiatives: Defining the Smart City, Its Drivers, and the Role of the CIO*. Forrester Research Inc.

Williams, P. (2016). *What, Exactly, is a Smart City?* Retrieved from Meeting of the Minds: https://meetingoftheminds.org/exactly-smart-city-16098

Xue, Q. (2010). Smart Healthcare: Applications of the Internet of Things in Medical Treatment and Health. *Informes de la Construcción*, *5*, 56–58.

Zhang, Z., He, Q., Gao, J., & Ni, M. (2018). A deep learning approach for detecting traffic accidents from social media data. *Transportation Research Part C, Emerging Technologies*, *86*, 580–596. doi:10.1016/j.trc.2017.11.027

Chapter 11
Author Profiling Using Texts in Social Networks

Iqra Ameer
Instituto Politécnico Nacional, Mexico

Grigori Sidorov
Instituto Politécnico Nacional, Mexico

ABSTRACT

The automatic identification of an author's demographic traits (e.g., gender, age group) from their written text is termed as author profiling. This problem has become an essential problem in fields like linguistic forensics, marketing, and security. In recent years, online social setups (e.g., Twitter, Facebook, blogs, hotel reviews) have extended remarkably; however, it is easy to provide fake profiles. This research aims to predict the traits of the authors for a benchmark existing corpus, based on Twitter, hotel reviews, social media, and blogs' profiles. In this chapter, the authors have explored four sets of features, including syntactic n-grams of part-of-speech tags, traditional n-grams of part-of-speech tags, combinations of word n-grams, and combinations of character n-grams. They used word unigram and character three-gram as a baseline approach. After analyzing the results, they concluded that the performance improves when the combination of word n-grams is used.

INTRODUCTION

Author Profiling Task

Author profiling (AP) is the identification process of a person's gender, age, native language, personality traits, and other demographic information from his/her written text (Iqbal, Ashraf & Nawab, 2015). We are living in an era where technology is growing rapidly and arising many challenging problems for researchers related to the availability of much written textual data; one of such issues is author profiling. Nowadays, most of the text is available online. People sometimes write and share their opinions and ideas

DOI: 10.4018/978-1-7998-4730-4.ch011

Copyright © 2021, IGI Global. Copying or distributing in print or electronic forms without written permission of IGI Global is prohibited.

behind the curtain of anonymity. The problem of AP has become an essential problem in the fields like linguistic forensics, marketing, and security. Authorship analysis can be of two types:

- **Author verification tasks:** Where the style of individual authors is observed, to check whether a text belongs to a specific author or not.
- **Author profiling:** Discriminates between classes of authors examining their socialist aspects, that is, the way how people share the language. This benefits in classifying profiling characteristics such as gender, age, native language, education, profession, or personality type. Therefore, AP can be stated as follows: given the set of texts, it is necessary to identify age, gender, occupation, education, native language, and similar personality-related traits of the author.

Importance and Applications of Author Profiling

Recently, online social setups like Twitter, Facebook, Blogs, Hotels Review, etc. have extended remarkably and have allowed lots of clients of all age groups to grow and support personal and professional relationships. However, a shared characteristic of these digital bodies is that it is simple to keep a fake name, age, gender, and location to conceal one's actual identity providing criminals like pedophiles with new options to look for their victims. When trying to identify these internet predators, law enforcement agencies and social network moderators faced with two main difficulties: (i) the significant amount of profiles on social setups make manual evaluation unmanageable and (ii) internet predators frequently make a fake identification, posing as youths to make interaction with their victims. So, proficient automatic systems for identity uncovering and inspection are essential.

Chapter Focus

The main aim of this study is to discover what feature set is appropriate for author profiling. We conduct experiments on the same genre using word n-grams and character n-grams, as well as part-of-speech tag n-grams (traditional ad syntactic). We also try the cross genre, but only for part-of-speech n-grams. The concept of syntactic n-grams is introduced by Sidorov (2013a; 2013b; 2014; 2019). Sn-grams of POS tags are distinctive from traditional n-grams in the manner of what elements are considered neighbors. For syntactic n-grams, the neighbors are taken from the dependency parse tree, and not from the surface structure of the text. This technique builds an image of the style of an author by the information enclosed in dependency trees for sn-grams. This information is characterized as syntactic n-grams of POS tags and is applied to fit a vector space model. We also examine how traditional n-grams of POS tags can be helpful in the AP task. The supervised machine learning approach is used in this research. We explain the features that are utilized and the engaged supervised algorithms of Machine Learning.

Moreover, in this project, we also deal with different machine learning techniques and methods for training the model and compare the results to identify the best and most suitable techniques for this research work. Thus, we use those Machine Learning methods to distinguish the age group of an author and gender. Our focus is to analyze as much textual data as possible and classify methods to identify the writer's age group and gender.

As we have mentioned above, author profiling is a vast field covering different aspects related to the personality, behavior, and emotions of the author. Still, in this chapter, our primary focus is covering mainly two points, namely, age group and gender of author profiling using PAN 2014 and PAN 2016 corpora.

Scope of the Study

Author profiling task has a rising significance in research field belonging to the scientific community. It has immense applications in various areas like marketing, intelligence, forensics, security related to defense. This study aims to analyze and predict the different demographic traits, i.e., age and gender of the author from the Pan-14 and Pan-16 corpora, which consist of sub-corpora of blog posts, hotel reviews, social media, and tweets.

The general objective of the study is to develop a method for automatic classification of author traits related to the age group and gender, with the focus on feature selection and classification algorithm. We want to consider how the usage of words in routine communication in social networking reflects personality, opinions, and behavior. This study aims to achieve the following specific objectives:

- Exploration of the problem of the same genre and cross genre for author profiling.
- Collection of the benchmark corpora from different genres (social media, hotel reviews, twitter, and blogs) for cross genre prediction of authors' age and gender.
- Data pre-processing of the collected corpora to make the text more meaningful after removing tags, e.g., HTML tags, URLs.
- Features extraction for pre-processed corpora. We plan to extract syntactic and traditional n-grams of Part-of-Speech tags (POST), word and character n-grams, and their combinations.
- Design the experiments for the pre-processed corpora.
- Performance of the experiments on benchmark corpora to predict the authors' age group and gender.
- Evaluation of four benchmark corpora from different genres, such as social media, hotel reviews, Twitter, and blogs.

Chapter Outline

The remaining chapter is organized as follows. Section 2 is providing an overview of the current work in Author Profiling (AP) and explaining the existing benchmark AP corpora. It does not only provide background information, the possible methods to adopt in, but also the current study also highlights the research gap along with explaining available techniques for Author Profiling. This section also represents the table of results of the literature review study. Section 3 describes the state-of-the-art approaches for Author Profiling. The authors are following an overview of the used set of features and a summary of the achieved results. Section 4 presents the proposed method for AP as a multi-class classification problem. In addition, it explains the creation of syntactic n-grams of part-of-speech tags and traditional n-grams of part-of-speech tags. This section also aims to demonstrate the experimental setup of how this proposed technique can be used for the development and analysis of the author profile classification systems. Section 5 explains and analyzes the results of experiments to classify the age group and gender of the authors for the mentioned corpora. Section 6 concludes the chapter.

BACKGROUND

State-of-the-Art for Age and Gender Prediction

State-of-the-art methods aim to detect an unknown document author's trait from a set of considered authors. In this section, the authors described the state-of-the-art approaches of the Author Profiling problem for the same genre[1] and cross genre[2], respectively. Following, there is an overview of their feature engineering and a summary of the obtained results.

Age and Gender-Related Research for the Data of the Same Genre

The authors Kiprov, Hardalov, Nakov, and Koychev (2015) used Lexicon, Twitter-specie, orthographic, and Term Level Features. They analyzed that most of the orthographic features improving the age and gender accuracy and achieved 84% accuracy for authors' gender prediction and more than 70% for the age group on the same genre, by using Support Vector Machine (SVM). Kiprov et al. (2015) also investigated that sustainable performance among the best feature groups were POS-tag counts, word unigrams, and bigrams. The gender identification task also tackled by bringing together function words and parts-of-speech (POS) tags (Argamon, Koppel, Fine, & Shimoni, 2003). They used properly written texts taken out from the British National Corpus and attained approximately 80% accuracy.

Due to the popularity of electronic media nowadays, there is a lot of text on social media. For that reason, social media is the pivot of research; some researchers handled the task of automatically identify gender an author by considering the combinations of simple lexical and syntactic features and obtained an accuracy of about 80% (Koppel, Argamon, & Shimoni, 2002). Schler et al. (2006) examined the effects of age and gender over the blog's writing style; the writers collected more than 71,000 blogs. They established a set of stylistic features as the words are not in the dictionary (parts-of-speech, function words) and hyperlink merged with content-based features, such as word unigrams with the highest information gain. They obtained an accuracy of about 80% and 75% to identify gender and age, respectively.

The authors pointed out that the earlier time studies handled with at least 250 words of length. The size of the data set affects the results (Stamatatos, Potthast, Rangel, Rosso, & Stein, 2015). Some researchers carried out trials with short segments of a blog post, particularly 10,000 segments with 15 tokens per segment. They obtained 72.1% accuracy for gender classification, compared to more than 80% in the previous studies (Zhang & Zhang, 2010). Stamatatos et al. (2015) mentioned that most of the contributors used combinations of style-based features like frequency of punctuation marks, capital letters, quotations, together with part-of-speech tags. The content-based features like Latent Semantic Analysis, a bag of words, TF-IDF, dictionary-based words, topic-based words are also considered.

The researchers investigated the excellent performance of n-gram features (Houvardas & Stamatatos, 2006). The content-based method based on the bag of words with TF-IDF values is simple and efficient in classification problems (Ameer et al., 2019; Siddiqui et al., 2019). The authors worked on the task with 3 million features in a MapReduce configuration and achieved higher accuracies with fractions of processing time (Holmes & Meyerhoff, 2008). Poulston, Stevenson, and Bontcheva (2015) have shown that topic models produced good results when used separately and in conjunction with other features. They have pointed out that grams in conjunction with LDA topics are more stable than n-grams on their own, the scores obtained for the English corpora is in the range of 0.79 to 0.52.

It can be observed that n-grams and topic models are beneficial elements in the development of AP systems throughout several languages and providing consistent performance without any additional features. Usually, a 10-fold cross-validation methodology is used.

Pre-Processing Methodology

The primary pre-processing step used by Kiprov et al. (2015) and Poulston et al. (2015) was tokenization. Other authors (e.g., Grivas, 2015; Iqbal, 2015; Najib, 2015) first removed the HTML code from the tweets and handled hashtags, URLs and mentions (González-Gallardo, 2015; Najib, 2015; Nowson, 2015; Maharjan, 2015). Gonzalez et al. (2015) changed mentions, URLs, and hashtags for predefined tokens. Similarly, Maharjan et al. (2015) substituted the URLs with the URL token or the removed URLs entirely. However, the corpus was cleaned before publishing; in the pre-processed tweets were eliminated RTs and shares (Bartoli, Lorenzo, Laderchi, Medvet, & Tarlao, 2015). The author lowercased the text, removed numbers and stop words, and used stemming over training datasets (Weren, 2015). Nowson et al. (2015) terminated all character sequences depicting emojis in the original tweets; also, the authors eliminated tweets with fewer words (Posadas-Durán, Sidorov, Batyrshin & Mirasol-Meléndez, 2015).

Features

Stamatatos et al. (2015) reported that many participants approximate the problem with different combinations of style-based and content-based features. Kiprov et al. (2015) and Poulston et al. (2015) used n-gram models in the composition of style-based and content-based features. For instance, Maharja et al. (2015), González-Gallardo et al. (2015) and Sulea et al. (2015) used character n-grams; Najib et al. (2015), Palomino-Garibay, (2015), Giménez, (2015) and Nowson et al. (2015) worked with word n-grams, using TF-IDF values; whereas González-Gallardo et al. (2015) and Palomino-Garibay et al. (2015) took advantage of part-of-speech n-grams.

The content-based features were also used in topic modeling with Latent Semantic Analysis (LSA) (Maharja, 2015; McCollister, 2015; Werlen, 2015; Iqbal, 2015). Maharjan et al. (2015) played family tokens (my wife/husband, my girlfriend/boyfriend, my hubby, my bf, etc.). The best performing team at PAN-15 (Álvarez-Carmona et al., 2015) integrated the Latent Semantic Analysis (LSA) with second-order features based on relationships among terms, documents, proles, and sub-proles. Gonzalez-Gallardo et al. (2015) employed combinations of character and POS n-grams, while Grivas et al. (2015) combined style-based features with TF-IDF n-grams. Posadas-Durán et al. (2015) presented that syntactic n-grams can be used as features to model the author related aspects such as gender and age. They considered syntactic n-grams as dimensions in a vector space model and used a supervised machine learning approach. They observed that syntactic n-grams of words provided excellent results when predicting personality traits (RMSE); however, their application is not that positive when predicting the age group and gender.

Results

Table 1 shows a summary of state-of-the-art results for English language author profiling in the same genre.

Table 1. Summary of state-of-the-art results on the same genre

Team	Achieved accuracy	
	Age	Gender
Busger et al.	0.3046	0.5575
Dichiu & Rancea	0.2989	0.5345
Agrawal & Gonçalves	0.3103	0.5431
Bougiatiotis & Krithara	0.3046	0.5345
Modaresi	0.3218	0.5057
Bilan et al.	0.2902	0.5374
Gencheva et al.	0.2902	0.5287
Kocher & Savoy	0.2816	0.5144
Ashraf et al.	0.2902	0.4971
Bakkar et al.	0.2874	0.5029
Pimas et al.	0.0086	0.0201

Age and Gender-Related Research for the Data of the Cross Genre

To analysis the effect of the cross genre calculation on the performance of the various AP approaches, the researchers used corpora with varying genres for training and testing their systems.

Pre-Processing Methodology

The pre-processing methodology used in this task is practically the same as mentioned in the previous section, although Bougiatiotis and Krithara (2016) applied lemmatization. However, the authors observed no development in their results. Agrawal et al. (2016) and Bougiatiotis et al. (2016) considered the writers detached the punctuation signs and eliminated stop words. The authors lowercased the texts and eliminated the digits (Bougiatiotis et al., 2016; Markov et al., 2016). Still, the most common pre-processing is seen in Twitter-specific components such as hashtags, mentions, RTs, or URLs (Agrawal et al., 2016; Bougiatiotis et al., 2016).

Features

A large number of authors studied various types of stylistic-based features. Such as the frequency of function words, words that are not in a predefined dictionary, slang, capital letters, unique words (Bougiatiotis et al., 2016; Bilan et al., 2016; Gencheva et al., 2016; Pervaz et al., 2015; Pimas et al., 2016; Sittar et al., 2018). The adoption of correct sentences per gender (e.g., "my man", "my wife", "my girlfriend") and age ("I'm" followed by a number) used in and sentiment words are handled by Gencheva et al. (2016) and Pimas et al. (2016).

The researchers take into account the parts-of-speech, collocations, and LDA (Bilan et al., 2016; Gencheva et al., 2016; Ashraf et al., 2016; Vollenbroek et al., 2016).

Results

Table 2 presents a summary of state-of-the-art results for English language author profiling in the same genre. They trained their systems on tweets and tested by using Social Media texts (different corpora are used in different studies).

Table 2. Summary of state-of-the-art results on the cross genre

Team	Features	Accuracy Achieved	
		Age	Gender
Kiprov et al.	Lexicon, Twitter Specific, Orthographic, Term Level	0.7	0.8
Argamon et al.	Function words, POS	N/a	0.8
Shler et al.	Stylistic-based, Content-based	0.7	0.8
Koppel et al.	Simple Lexicon, Stylistic	N/A	0.8
Zhang et al.	Words, Sentence Length	N/A	0.7
Poulston et al.	N-Grams, LDA Topics	0.5	0.7
Peersman et al.	Token, Character Features	0.7	0.7
Posadas et al.	Syntactic n-grams of words	0.5	0.5

Proposed Approach

The proposed method is designed for the automatic classification of the author's age group and gender. The proposed approach is based on feature selection and application of supervised Machine Learning methods (traditional classification algorithms). We consider features and character n-grams of various sizes, syntactic n-grams, and traditional n-grams of part-of-speech tags. We consider that these features support us in taking a set of elements of writings. Since male and female are two opposite genders, this difference also reflects in their writings, the same is applied for different age groups. This fact leads us to predict an author's age group and gender-based on his/her written text. We tried both the same genre setting and cross genre setting when the training corpus is in one genre, and the test corpus is in another genre. Therefore, these features are anticipated to identify author attributes correctly, even if they are trained and tested on different datasets. **Figure 1** shows the detailed architecture diagram of the proposed method. The main input/output components of the proposed method are presented in **Figure 2.**

The output of each analysis is hand over to the Machine Learning classifiers, which defines the age group and gender of the author.

Pre-Processing

For the implementation, we used the training corpora of PAN-2014[3] and PAN-2016[4]. We considered only English language documents. The data set tagged with age group and gender. The corpora consist of different XML documents, which had to be tackled in an offline (social media, blogs, and hotel reviews) and online (tweets) mode.

Figure 1. Architecture diagram of the method

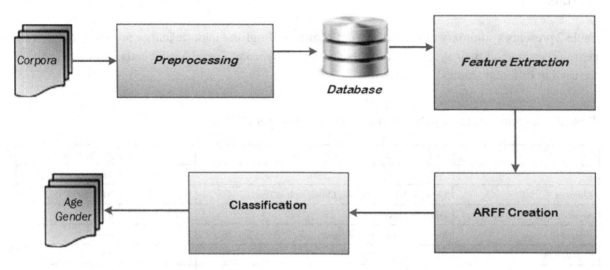

After crawling the data in both modes, corpus cleaned by removal of the XML contents, user mentions (twitter), URLs, etc., the original text, written by the author, is extracted from each XML file and saved in a

Figure 2. Main input/output components of the proposed method

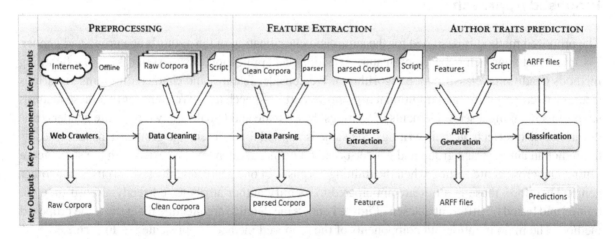

individual user file. The cleaned data is then stored in a database. The detailed procedure of preprocessing described in **Figure 3.**

- **Crawlers:** PAN-14 and PAN-16 provide the corpora, which contain the files in the XML form. However, for certain datasets like Twitter and Blogs, the data must be taken from the HTML URLs in the XML document. Thus, there are two methods of crawlers: one for offline datasets (Social Media and Hotel Review) and another for online datasets (Twitter and Blogs).

Figure 3. The main components of the pre-processing stage with their key inputs and outputs

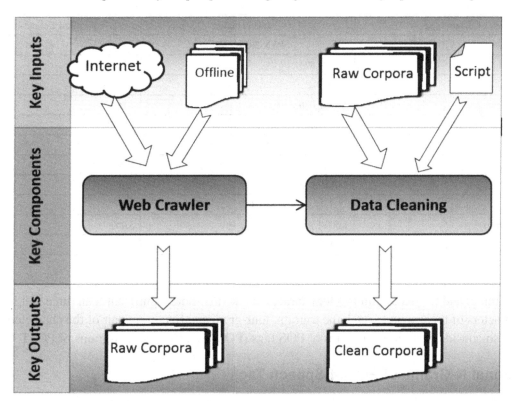

- **Data Cleaning:** The raw content got from the crawlers must be cleaned to eliminate noisy data like \ufff, XML labels, URLs, twitter client mentions, hashtags, and so forth. The presence of this noisy data could affect and decrease the accuracy of the study — the cleaned corpora at that point were saved in a database for experiments.

Statistics of the PAN Corpora

Dataset statistics are provided in Tables 3 to 5. Table 3 is stating the gender count of PAN-14, PAN-16, and PAN-17 corpora, whereas Table 4 is describing age group statistics of PAN-14 and PAN-16 corpora. The language group data set to count for the PAN-2017 corpus is presented in Table 5.

Combination of Word and Character-Based N-Grams

As a document consists of words, and words composed of characters, the form of word/character arrangements can provide valuable information about the text and style of a specific author. Therefore, to achieve better accuracy, we used a combination of word n-grams (1-3, minimum and maximum grams) and combination of character n-grams (3-5, minimum and maximum grams) as well. The term (1-3) means the minimum length is one, and the maximum is 3 for words: take the first three words of the text and search the unigram, bigram, and trigram pairs. The term (3-5) refers to the minimum length,

Table 3. Gender data set statistics for the PAN-2014, PAN-2016, and PAN-2017 corpora

Corpus Type	Male/Female	Total Count
PAN-2014		
Social Media	3,873/3,873	7,746
Blogs	73/74	147
Hotel Reviews	2,080/2,080	4,160
Total	**6,026/6,027**	**12,053**
PAN-2016		
Twitter (tweets)	2,018/2,018	436
Total	**2,018/2,018**	**436**
PAN-2017		
Twitter (tweets)	1,500/1,500	3,000
Total	**1,500/1,500**	**3,000**

which is three, and the maximum is 5 for characters: take the more significant than three and less than five characters of the text and search the trigram, four-gram and five-gram pair of the characters.

We also consider traditional n-grams of POS tags (POST) and syntactic n-grams of POST.

Traditional N-Grams of Part-of-Speech Tags

The term traditional n-grams of POS tags refers to a series of sequential POS tags in sentences. The series can be of length 1 (unigrams), length 2 (bigrams) and length 3 (trigrams), etc. towards the generalized term n-grams. They represent morphosyntactic information and are effectively expended in various computational linguistic problems. For example, the sentence in English is the following:

Example: *Iqra reads an interesting book.*
Traditional bigrams: *Iqra reads, reads an, an interesting, interesting book.*
Traditional trigrams: *Iqra reads an, reads an interesting, an interesting book.*
Traditional 4-grams: *Iqra reads an interesting, reads an interesting book.*

Table 4. Age group data set to count for the PAN-2014 and PAN-2016 corpora

Age Group	PAN-2014				PAN-2016	
	Blogs	Hotel Reviews	Social Media	Total Count	Twitter	Total Count
18-24	06	359	1550	1915	28	28
25-34	60	998	2098	3156	140	140
35-49	54	1000	2246	3300	182	182
50-64	23	999	1838	2826	80	80
65 or above	04	799	14	817	06	06
Total				**5071**	**Total**	**436**

Traditional 5-grams: *Iqra reads an interesting book.*

Then each word is replaced by its corresponding one of the part-of-speech tags in each sentence by using some correct and robust text analysis tools. For example, it can be Stanford Log-linear part-of-speech tagger as it gave a 97.2% accuracy on the Penn Treebank Wall Street Journal corpus. For example, after processing the text by using POS tagger, the following sentence obtained:

Processed sentence: *Iqra/NNP reads/VBZ an/DT interesting/JJ book/NN*
Traditional bigrams of POS Tags: *NNP VBZ, VBZ DT, DT JJ, JJ NN.*
Traditional trigrams of POS Tags: *NNP VBZ DT, VBZ DT JJ, DT JJ NN.*
Traditional 4-grams of POS Tags: *NNP VBZ DT JJ, VBZ DT JJ NN.*
Traditional 5-grams of POS Tags: *NNP VBZ DT JJ NN.*

The established relation is "follow another POS tag".

Syntactic N-Grams of Part-of-Speech Tags

Syntactic n-grams of POS tags are constructed by following the path in syntactic trees. Syntactic n-grams represent syntactic information (relations between words). As though, still dealing with n-grams but escape the noise led by the surface structure of the language due to the fact that syntactically "distant" POS tags may appear together. This anomaly can be geared if we consider the actual syntactic-relations that associate the POS tags even though those tags are not actual neighbors. Let us consider the same example sentence as above:

Example: Iqra reads an interesting book.

In the proposed methodology, we used Stanford Parser[5] for the English language example. **Code 1** presents the generated output of the parser. The direct output of Stanford parse consists of two parts:

- In the first part, the information is showed in terms of constituency grammars.
- In the second part, the information is showed in terms of dependency grammars.

The second part of the out is more concerned; in this part, it can be seen that the syntactic dependencies between the pair of words. The parser shows the type of syntactic relation between each pair of words and position in the sentence.

Code 1
```
nsubj (reads-2, Iqra-1)
root (ROOT-0, reads-2)
det (book-5, a-3)
amod (book-5, interesting-4)
dobj (reads-2, book-5)
```

Figure 4 is demonstrating the syntax tree. By using this tree, one directly generates the syntactic n-grams. Obtained syntactic n-grams are:

Syntactic Bigrams: *reads Iqra, reads book, book an, book interesting.*
Syntactic Trigrams: *reads book an, reads book interesting.*

In this case, there are no four and 5-grams. Then in the next step, each word is replaced by its corresponding part-of-speech tags (one of 36 existing tags). It is done in each sentence by using Stanford Log-linear Part-Of-Speech Tagger. Thus, the collected syntactic n-grams of Part-of-Speech Tags are the following:

Syntactic Bigrams of POS tags: *VBZ NNP, VBZ NN, NN DT, NN JJ.*
Syntactic Trigrams of POS tags: *VBZ NN DT, VBZ NN JJ.*

There are also other categories of syntactic n-grams depending on the information that is adopted for their construction (lemmas, tags of syntactic relations). All of them are linked through a dependency tree, but they represent different linguistic aspects of a sentence. We extracted these features from the mentioned data set and applied Naïve Bayes, SMO, Logistic, Random Forest, and J48 classifiers for training and testing purposes. We use WEKA software in our experimental phase.

RESULTS AND ANALYSIS

In this section, we report and analyze the results achieved in the experimental phase using various sizes of word and character n-grams, as well as traditional n-grams of part-of-speech tags and syntactic n-grams of part-of-speech tags.

Experimental Setup

Dataset

For evaluation of the proposed method, three data sets used. The specifications of these data sets have been shown in section proposed approach.

Evaluation Methodology

The identification problem of an authors' age group and gender from the text, handled as a supervised learning problem. Gender detection is a binary classification problem because the aim is to differentiate between two classes: (1) male and (2) female. The age group classification is a multiple class classification problem, i.e., the target is to discriminate between five age groups:

1) 18-24,
2) 25-34,
3) 35-49,

Figure 4. Example of a syntax tree

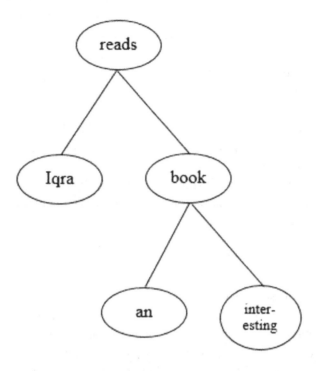

4) 50-64,
5) 65-xx.

We have utilized five Machine Learning classifiers, using the WEKA toolkit to find the best classifier for each trait. N-fold cross-validation is used to estimate the functioning of the considered approach better; in our case, we used n=10, i.e., 10-fold cross-validation applied on the dataset. The Machine Learning algorithms considered in this study include J48, Logistic, Random Forest (RF), Support Vector Machines (SMO) and Naive Bayes (NB). We calculated the percentage of correctly predicted authors' profiles for three traits (PAN-17 corpus for only native language identification task).

Classifiers (Machine Learning Algorithms)

We applied five machine learning classification algorithms as classifiers by using the WEKA toolkit to find out the best classifier for each trait. The classifiers that used are:

- **Naive Bayes:** Naive Bayes is the simplest statistical-based classifier. Naive Bayes classifier works using Bayesian rules and takes all the attributes available in the data sample and analyzes variables individually, independently of each other. The classifier with simple probabilistic properties with no complicated repetitious parameter evaluation mostly performs worse as compare to different complicated algorithms, but sometimes it can obtain better results.

- **Logistic regression:** Logistic regression is a statistical technique for examining a corpus in which one or more than one independent variable which controls a result. The result restrained with a dichotomous variable (in which there are only two possible outcomes).
- **SMO:** SMO is a supervised Machine Learning algorithm used for the classification task. The need behind the use of this classifier in the experimental setup is to perform a classification task for the identification of different demographic traits. SMO is a WEKA implementation of Support Vector Machines.
- **J48:** J48 classifier follows a decision tree model for the classification of a dataset. It develops a binary tree for the classification process. It decides the dependent variable by analyzing all independent variables available in the dataset.
- **Random Forest:** Random Forest classifier generates multiple numbers of decision trees. Each of the decision trees gives classification for a new object. The random forest then combines the results of all trees for final prediction.

Features Selection Methods

The raw machine learning data set consists of a mix of attributes, some of which are significant in generating predictions. Automatically dominating features can be selected, the features that are most useful or most suited for the problem. This procedure called feature selection. Every person has his/her writing style, which can differentiate the person from others. Two things that can vary in a person's written text can be his interests, and the usage of vocabulary in daily routine life as a study says that the female witting style enriched with adverbs and adjectives. As previously discussed, that feature selection is based on the approach proposed for this work: a content model based feature selection.

Feature selection algorithm: For selected content-based features, only one feature selection algorithm is used: Information Gain (IG). This feature selection method applies a statistical measurement to allocate a scoring to each feature. The score ranks the features, and features are either nominated to be saved or dropped from the corpus.

Information Gain: Information gain (IG) is a quantitative technique. It is utilized for evaluation of the efficiency of features. By using entropy, IG of a feature t can be stated as:

$$IG(t) = \mathrm{H}(S) - \sum \frac{|S_v|}{|S|} H(S)$$

IG is information gain to calculate for the feature t, H(S) is the entropy of dataset S, S_v is a subset of dataset S for which feature t hold value v.

- **Benefits of feature selection:** The feature selection methods are easy to use and give the following benefits when used in experiments:
- **Reduces overfitting:** If the duplication in data or irrelevant data is reduced, one can have a better chance of making predictions on data.
- **Improves accuracy:** On a less ambiguous data, one can greatly increase modeling accuracy.
- **Reduce training time:** On a minimal size of data, algorithms produce faster results.

Results for Gender Identification

For the tables presented in this section, the following expressions are used. The "Training/Testing dataset" is referring to the specific corpora used in training and testing phases. The corpora include PAN-2014, PAN-2016, and PAN-2017. The "features" are describing various features and number of selected n-grams chosen for experiments

In "Classifier" column, Machine Learning (ML) algorithms are listed, which produced the highest accuracy for a given corpus (note that five main ML algorithms including Logistic Regression (LR), Random Forest (RF), J48, Naive Bays (NB) and SMO are explored). The "Accuracy" describes the accuracy of a classifier for particular features.

Table 6 presents the best results for gender identification tasks on the same genre and cross genre using traditional and syntactic n-grams of POST. Note that only the best results are reported for each technique. Results were produced by using the content-based methods for the same genre (the same genre means training and testing of the models were on the same genre) using 10-fold cross-validation (CV). Overall, the highest accuracy for gender is obtained using 3-grams of n-grams of POST, i.e., information gain as feature selection (accuracy = 0.6326) with Logistic Regression, and using 3-grams of sn-grams of POST with J48 (accuracy = 0.5846) classifier on Blogs corpus on PAN-2014. Whereas in cross-genre model building, training was on one genre, and testing of the model was on another genre different from the training corpus. Notably, in the first column of the table, "Twitter/blogs" stated that training of the model was on Twitter data of PAN-2014, and the prediction of the trained model was on blogs of PAN-2014. For this setting, the model performed best on 4-grams of n-grams of POST with Naive Bayes (accuracy = 0.6054), while on SM/Blogs settings, the highest accuracy achieved by using 2-grams of sn-grams of POST with Logistic Regression classifier (accuracy = 0.5615).

Table 5. Gender identification, best results using n-grams of various features on the same genre, and cross genre.

Training/Testing Dataset	Features	Classifier	Accuracy
Same genre			
Blogs-14	3 (n-grams of POST)	Logistic	0.6326
Blogs-14	3 (sn-grams of POST)	J48	0.5846
Cross genre			
Twitter/Blogs-14	4 (n-grams of POST)	NB	0.6054
SM/Blogs-14	2 (sn-grams of POST)	Logistic	0.5615

Table 7 presents the best results for the age group identification problem on the same genre and cross genre using traditional n-grams of POST and syntactic n-grams of POST. For the same genre, accuracy for the age group is the same using unigrams of n-grams of POST and sn-grams of POST (accuracy = 0.4625) with Naïve Bayes on blogs corpus of PAN-2014. Whereas in cross-genre model building, the best scores achieved on Twitter/Blogs-14 settings (accuracy = 0.4081) using 2-grams of n-grams of POST and on SM/Blogs-14 using 2-grams of sn-grams of POST (accuracy = 0.3968). The accuracy

Table 6. Age identification, best results using n-grams of various sizes on the same genre and cross genres

Training/Testing Dataset	Features	Classifier	Accuracy
Same genre			
Blogs-14	1 (n-grams of POST)	NB	0.4625
Blogs-14	1 (sn-grams of POST)	NB	0.4625
Cross genre			
Twitter/Blogs-14	2 (n-grams of POST)	NB	0.4081
SM/Blogs-14	2 (sn-grams of POST)	Logistic	0.3968

is slightly lower than the same genre 's results because most probably, features that are used to test the model are different from features that captured in training the model.

In the final approach, we further tested the combination of two groups of textual features, word n-grams, and character n-grams, in the conjunction of SMO classifier to classify age group and gender of the producer of the text. The combination of 1-4 and 3-5 for both word n-grams and character n-grams obtained, respectively. To better estimate, 10-fold cross-validation performed on the dataset. Tables 8 and 9 are presenting the results on benchmark corpora of Pan-2014 (Blogs, Hotel Reviews, Social Media) and Pan-2016 (Twitter Tweets) and comparing the results with state-of-the-art and two baseline methods. In mentioned state-of-the-art results, López-Monroy et al. (2014) applied intra-profile information method which examines the existing information among documents which are the part of the same class. Team liau14 at PAN-2014 context use bag-of-words to identify the gender and age group of the author. Maharjan et al. (2014) used word n-grams with TF-IDF as features along with emoticons to predict age group and gender of the writer.

Table 7. Gender results comparison of various features with baseline and state-of-the-art (same genre)

Datasets	Features						State-of-the-art
	Sn-grams of POST	N-grams of POST	Combination of wn-grams (1-4)	Combination of char-grams (3-5)	Word uni-gram (baseline)	Char 3-gram (baseline)	
Blogs-14	0.5846	0.6326	**0.7074**	0.5918	0.6734	0.6612	0.6795 (López-Monroy et al., 2014)
HR	0.5341	0.6062	**0.6659**	0.6151	0.6612	0.5656	0.7259 (liau14)
SM	0.5107	0.5178	0.5559	0.5225	0.6743	**0.6932**	0.5382 Maharjan et al. (2014)
Twitter	0.5343	0.5874	**0.7062**	0.5850	0.6932	0.6363	NA

During the experimentation, it became apparent that the consolidation of word n-grams produced better results and outperformed the start-of-the-art accuracy on the same genre of blogs and social media. For Twitter, state-of-the-art results are not available (NA), because authors are using Tweets corpus of PAN-2016, and in that year, they were considering the cross genre task of AP. In Table 8, the

Table 8. Age results comparison of various features with baseline and state-of-the-art (same genre)

Datasets	Features						State-of-the-art
	Sn-grams of POST	N-grams of POST	Combination of wn-grams (1-4)	Combination of char-grams (3-5)	Word uni-gram (baseline)	Char 3-gram (baseline)	
Blogs-14	0.4625	0.4625	**0.4693**	0.4013	0.4064	0.4539	0.3974 (López-Monroy et al., 2014)
HR	0.2712	0.2712	**0.3217**	0.2618	0.2994	0.2956	**0.3502** (liau14)
SM	0.3329	0.3329	**0.3892**	0.2843	0.3675	0.2999	0.3652 Maharjan et al. (2014)
Twitter	0.4209	0.4209	**0.4731**	0.4289	0.3635	0.3363	NA

highest accuracy 0.7074 on gender attribute is achieved on Blogs-14 corpus with the combination of word n-grams (1, 2, 3, 4), and it is comparable to the best result obtained on blogs corpus (English) in PAN-2014 Author Profiling Competitions. Table 9 presented the results of age group identification. The highest accuracy of 0.473 is achieved on Twitter-16 corpus with a combination of word n-grams (1, 2, 3, 4). It can be appreciated that for gender, a combination of word-based n-gram technique surpassed the baseline techniques for all the datasets except social media corpus; for the age group, it outperformed the baseline in all cases. However, the performance of the combination of character n-grams is not suitable for gender trait but age group.

Inclusively, the word-based features outperformed other features for both tasks: age group and gender classification. The conceivable reasoning is, communication on blogs and twitter is usually formal, and word-based features are prospective to catch more discriminative content.

CONCLUSION

In this research work, we discussed the author's profiling problem. For this purpose, we used the benchmark corpora of PAN 2014 and 2016. We pre-processed the collected corpora and cleaned it by removing tags, e.g., HTML tags and URLs to get meaningful information out of the text. We explored various features such as syntactic n-grams of POS tags, traditional n-grams of POS tags, the combination of word-based n-grams, and a combination of character-based n-grams. The core contribution of the approach is that syntactic and traditional n-grams of part-of-speech tags can be used as features to predict the author's attributes, such as gender and age group, with comparable results. It is possible to tackle the author profiling problem by considering syntactic n-grams of POS tags and traditional n-grams of POS tags as dimensions in a vector space model and using a supervised Machine Learning approach. In this research, various machine learning algorithms were applied, including Naive Bayes, Logistic Regression, SMO, J48, and Random Forest. Best scores are achieved using the combination of word-based n-grams with SMO on blogs and twitter corpora. We considered word uni-grams and character 3-grams as baseline methods for comparison of the results. The results showed that a combination of word-grams

(1-4) technique outperforms the baseline technique, and some of the state-of-the-art scores on the same corpora, combinations of character-based n-grams (3-5) are not performing well.

REFERENCES

Agrawal, M., & Gonçalves, T. (2016). Age and Gender Identification using Stacking for Classification—Notebook for PAN at CLEF 2016. In K. Balog, L. Cappellato, N. Ferro, & C. Macdonald (Eds.), CLEF 2016 Evaluation Labs and Workshop – Working Notes Papers. Évora, Portugal: CEUR-WS.org.

Álvarez-Carmona, M., López-Monroy, A., Montes-y-Gómez, M., Villaseñor-Pineda, L., & Escalante, H. J. (2015). INAOE's participation at PAN'15: Author Profiling task—Notebook for PAN at CLEF 2015. In L. Cappellato, N. Ferro, G. Jones, & E. San Juan (Eds.), CLEF 2015 Evaluation Labs and Workshop – Working Notes Papers. Toulouse, France: CEUR-WS.org.

Ameer, I., Siddiqui, M. H. F., Sidorov, G., & Gelbukh, A. (2019). CIC at SemEval-2019 task 5: Simple yet very efficient approach to hate speech detection, aggressive behavior detection, and target classification in twitter. In *Proceedings of the 13th International Workshop on Semantic Evaluation*. Minneapolis, MN: Association for Computational Linguistics. 10.18653/v1/S19-2067

Ameer, I., Sidorov, G., & Nawab, R. M. A. (2019). Author profiling for age and gender using combinations of features of various types. *Journal of Intelligent & Fuzzy Systems, 36*(5), 4833–4843. doi:10.3233/JIFS-179031

Argamon, S., Koppel, M., Fine, J., & Shimoni, A. R. (2003). Gender, genre, and writing style in formal written texts. *Text, 23*(3), 321–346. doi:10.1515/text.2003.014

Ashraf, S., Iqbal, H. R., & Nawab, R. M. A. (2016). Cross genre Author Profile Prediction Using Stylometry-Based Approach— Notebook for PAN at CLEF 2016. In K. Balog, L. Cappellato, N. Ferro, & C. Macdonald (Eds.), CLEF 2016 Evaluation Labs and Workshop – Working Notes Papers. Évora, Portugal: CEUR-WS.org.

Bartoli, A., De Lorenzo, A., Laderchi, A., Medvet, E., & Tarlao, F. ((2015). An author profiling approach based on language-dependent content and stylometric features - notebook for PAN at CLEF 2015. In Working Notes for CLEF 2015 Conference, Toulouse, France.

Bilan, I., & Zhekova, D. (2016). CAPS: A Cross genre Author Profiling System—Notebook for PAN at CLEF 2016. In K. Balog, L. Cappellato, N. Ferro, & C. Macdonald (Eds.), CLEF 2016 Evaluation Labs and Workshop – Working Notes Papers. Évora, Portugal: CEUR-WS.org.

Bougiatiotis, K., & Krithara, A. (2016). Author Profiling using Complementary Second Order Attributes and Stylometric Features— Notebook for PAN at CLEF 2016. In K. Balog, L. Cappellato, N. Ferro, & C. Macdonald (Eds.), CLEF 2016 Evaluation Labs and Workshop – Working Notes Papers. Évora, Portugal: CEUR-WS.org.

Gencheva, P., Boyanov, M., Deneva, E., Nakov, P., Kiprov, Y., Koychev, I., & Georgiev, G. (2016). PANcakes Team: A Composite System of Genre-Agnostic Features For Author Profiling—Notebook for PAN at CLEF 2016. In CLEF 2016 Evaluation Labs and Workshop – Working Notes Papers. Évora, Portugal: CEUR-WS.org.

Giménez, M., Hernández, D. I., & Pla, F. (2015). Segmenting Target Audiences: Automatic Author Profiling Using Tweets—Notebook for PAN at CLEF 2015. In L. Cappellato, N. Ferro, G. Jones, & E. San Juan (Eds.), CLEF 2015 Evaluation Labs and Workshop – Working Notes Papers. Toulouse, France: CEUR-WS.org.

González-Gallardo, C. E., Montes, A., Sierra, G., Núñez-Juárez, J. A., Salinas-López, A. J., & Ek, J. (2015). *Tweets classification using corpus dependent tags, character and pos n-grams-Notebook for PAN at CLEF 2015*. In Working Notes for CLEF 2015 Conference, Toulouse, France.

Grivas, A., Krithara, A., & Giannakopoulos, G. (2015). *Author profiling using stylometric and structural feature groupings-Notebook for PAN at CLEF 2015*. In Working Notes of CLEF 2015 -Conference and Labs of the Evaluation forum, Toulouse, France.

Holmes, J., & Meyerhoff, M. (2008). *The handbook of language and gender, 25*. John Wiley & Sons.

Houvardas, J., & Stamatatos, E. (2006). N-gram feature selection for authorship identification. In *International Conference on Artificial Intelligence: Methodology, Systems, and Applications*, (pp. 77–86). Springer.

Iqbal, H. R., Ashraf, M. A., & Nawab, R. M. A. (2015). Predicting an author's demographics from text using topic modeling approach-Notebook for PAN at CLEF 2015. In *CLEF 2015 Evaluation Labs and Workshop – Working Notes Papers*. Toulouse, France: CEUR-WS.org.

Kiprov, Y., Hardalov, M., Nakov, P., & Koychev, I. (2015). Experiments in Author Profiling—Notebook for PAN at CLEF 2015. In L. Cappellato, N. Ferro, G. Jones, & E. San Juan (Eds.), CLEF 2015 Evaluation Labs and Workshop – Working Notes Papers. Toulouse, France: CEUR-WS.org.

Koppel, M., Argamon, S., & Shimoni, A. R. (2002). Automatically categorizing written texts by author gender. *Literary and Linguistic Computing, 17*(4), 401–412. doi:10.1093/llc/17.4.401

López-Monroy, A. P., Gómez, M. M., Escalante, H. J., & Pineda, L. V. (2014). Using Intra-Profile Information for Author Profiling—Notebook for PAN at CLEF 2014. CLEF.

Maharjan, S., Shrestha, P., & Solorio, T. (2014). A simple approach to author profiling in MapReduce. In *Proceedings of the Working Notes of CLEF 2014—Conference and Labs of the Evaluation Forum* (vol. 1180, pp. 1121–1128). CEUR.

Maharjan, S., & Solorio, T. (2015). Using wide range of features for author profiling. In *Working Notes Papers of the CLEF 2015 Evaluation Labs. Volume 1391 of CEUR Workshop Proceedings*. CEUR.

Markov, I., Gómez-Adorno, H., Sidorov, G., & Gelbukh, A. (2016). Adapting Cross genre Author Profiling to Language and Corpus— Notebook for PAN at CLEF 2016. In K. Balog, L. Cappellato, N. Ferro, & C. Macdonald (Eds.), CLEF 2016 Evaluation Labs and Workshop – Working Notes Papers. Évora, Portugal: CEUR-WS.org.

McCollister, C., Huang, S., & Luo, B. (2015). Building Topic Models to Predict Author Attributes from Twitter Messages—Notebook for PAN at CLEF 2015. In L. Cappellato, N. Ferro, G. Jones, & E. San Juan (Eds.), CLEF 2015 Evaluation Labs and Workshop – Working Notes Papers. Toulouse, France: CEUR-WS.org.

Najib, F., Cheema, W. A., & Nawab, R. M. A. (2015). Author's traits prediction on twitter data using content based approach. In *CLEF 2015 Evaluation Labs and Workshop – Working Notes Papers*. Toulouse, France: CEUR-WS.org.

Nowson, S., Perez, J., Brun, C., Mirkin, S., & Roux, C. (2015). Xrce personal language analytics engine for multilingual author profiling. *Working Notes Papers of the CLEF*.

Palomino-Garibay, A., Camacho-González, A., FierroVillaneda, R., Hernández-Farias, I., Buscaldi, D., & Meza-Ruiz, I. (2015). A Random Forest Approach for Authorship Profiling—Notebook for PAN at CLEF 2015. In L. Cappellato, N. Ferro, G. Jones, & E. San Juan (Eds.), CLEF 2015 Evaluation Labs and Workshop – Working Notes Papers. Toulouse, France: CEUR-WS.org.

Pervaz, I., Ameer, I., Sittar, A., & Nawab, R. M. A. (2015). Identification of Author Personality Traits using Stylistic Features, In *CLEF 2015 Evaluation Labs and Workshop – Working Notes Papers*. Toulouse, France: CEUR-WS.org.

Pimas, O., Rexha, A., Kröll, M., & Kern, R. (2016). Profiling Microblog Authors Using Concreteness and Sentiment—Notebook for PAN at CLEF 2016. In K. Balog, L. Cappellato, N. Ferro, & C. Macdonald (Eds.), CLEF 2016 Evaluation Labs and Workshop – Working Notes Papers. Évora, Portugal: CEUR-WS.org.

Posadas-Durán, J., Sidorov, G., Batyrshin, I., & Mirasol-Meléndez, E. (2015). Author Verification Using Syntactic N-grams—Notebook for PAN at CLEF 2015. In L. Cappellato, N. Ferro, G. Jones, & E. San Juan (Eds.), *CLEF 2015 Evaluation Labs and Workshop – Working Notes Papers*. Toulouse, France: CEUR-WS.org.

Poulston, A., Stevenson, M., & Bontcheva, K. (2015). Topic Models and n-gram Language Models for Author Profiling—Notebook for PAN at CLEF 2015. In L. Cappellato, N.Ferro,G. Jones, & E. San Juan (Eds.), CLEF 2015 Evaluation Labs and Workshop – Working Notes Papers. Toulouse, France: CEUR-WS.org.

Schler, J., Koppel, M., Argamon, S., & Pennebaker, J. (2006). Effects of age and gender on blogging. *AAAI Spring Symposium: Computational Approaches to Analyzing Weblogs, 6*, 199–205.

Siddiqui, M. H., Ameer, I., Gelbukh, A., & Sidorov, G. (2019). Bots and Gender Profiling on Twitter. In L. Cappellato, N. Ferro, D. Losada, & H. Müller (Eds.), *CLEF 2019 Labs and Workshops, Notebook Papers. CEUR-WS.org*.

Sidorov, G. (2013a). *Non-linear construction of n-grams in computational linguistics*. Sociedad Mexicana de Inteligencia Artificial.

Sidorov, G. (2013b). Syntactic dependency based n-grams in rule based automatic English as second language grammar correction. *International Journal of Computational Linguistics and Applications, 4*(2), 169–188.

Sidorov, G. (2019). *Syntactic n-grams in computational linguistics*. Springer. https://link.springer.com/book/10.1007%2F978-3-030-14771-6

Sidorov, G., Velasquez, F., Stamatatos, E., Gelbukh, A., & Chanona-Hernández, L. (2014). Syntactic n-grams as machine learning features for natural language processing. *Expert Systems with Applications*, *41*(3), 853–860. doi:10.1016/j.eswa.2013.08.015

Sittar, A., & Ameer, I. (2018). Multi-lingual Author Profiling Using Stylistic Features. In *Working Notes for MAPonSMS at FIRE'18 - Workshop Proceedings of the 10th International Forum for Information Retrieval Evaluation (FIRE'18)*. CEUR-WS.org.

Stamatatos, E., Potthast, M., Rangel, F., Rosso, P., & Stein, B. (2015). Overview of the PAN/CLEF 2015 Evaluation Lab. In J. Mothe, J. Savoy, J. Kamps, K. Pinel-Sauvagnat, G. Jones, E. SanJuan, L. Cappellato, & N. Ferro (Eds.), *Experimental IR Meets Multilinguality, Multimodality, and Interaction. 6th International Conference of the CLEF Initiative (CLEF 15)*, (pp. 518–538). Springer. 10.1007/978-3-319-24027-5_49

Sulea, O., & Dichiu, D. (2015). Automatic Profiling of Twitter Users Based on Their Tweets—Notebook for PAN at CLEF 2015. In L. Cappellato, N. Ferro, G. Jones, & E. San Juan (Eds.), CLEF 2015 Evaluation Labs and Workshop – Working Notes Papers. Toulouse, France: CEUR-WS.org.

Vollenbroek, M. B., Carlotto, T., Kreutz, T., Medvedeva, M., Pool, C., Bjerva, J., & Nissim, M. (2016). GronUP: Groningen User Profiling—Notebook for PAN at CLEF 2016. In CLEF 2016 Evaluation Labs and Workshop – Working Notes Papers. Évora, Portugal: CEUR-WS.org.

Weren, E. R. (2015). Information Retrieval Features for Personality Traits—Notebook for PAN at CLEF 2015. In L. Cappellato, N. Ferro, G. Jones, & E. San Juan (Eds.), CLEF 2015 Evaluation Labs and Workshop – Working Notes Papers. Toulouse, France: CEUR-WS.org.

Werlen, L. M. (2015). Statistical Learning Methods for Profiling Analysis—Notebook for PAN at CLEF 2015. In L. Cappellato, N. Ferro, G. Jones, & E. San Juan (Eds.), CLEF 2015 Evaluation Labs and Workshop – Working Notes Papers. Toulouse, France: CEUR-WS.org.

Zhang, C., & Zhang, P. (2010). Predicting gender from blog posts. Technical report. University of Massachusetts Amherst.

ENDNOTES

[1] Models are trained on one genre, for example, trained on Twitter, and evaluated on the same genre, but on unseen tweets.

[2] Models are trained on one genre, for example, trained on Twitter, and evaluated on another genre different from Twitter.

[3] https://pan.webis.de/clef14/pan14-web/author-profiling.html

[4] https://pan.webis.de/clef16/pan16-web/author-profiling.html

[5] Parser is a program that generates syntactic trees. The trees are usually based on formal grammars of various types.

Chapter 12
A Comparison of Personality Prediction Classifiers for Personnel Selection in Organizations Based on Industry 4.0

Roberto Contreras-Masse
Tecnológico Nacional de México, Mexico & Instituto Tecnológico de Ciudad Juárez, Mexico

Juan Carlos Bonilla
Universidad Autónoma del Estado de Morelos, Mexico

Jose Mejia
Universidad Autónoma de Ciudad Juárez, Mexico

Alberto Ochoa
ⓘ https://orcid.org/0000-0002-9183-6086
Universidad Autónoma de Ciudad Juárez, Mexico

ABSTRACT

Nowadays, the internet has an astonishing amount of useful material for personality mining; nevertheless, many companies fail to exploit the information and screen job candidates using personality tests that fail to grasp the very information they are trying to gather. This research aims to highlight and compare the different machine learning classifiers that can be used to predict the personality of a Spanish-speaking job applicant based on the written content posted on their social networks. The authors conduct experiments considering the most critical measures (such as accuracy, precision, and recall) to evaluate the classification performance. The results show that the random-forest classifier outperforms the other classifiers. It is of utmost importance to correctly assess the resumes to determine the most qualified people in a smart manufacturing position.

DOI: 10.4018/978-1-7998-4730-4.ch012

Copyright © 2021, IGI Global. Copying or distributing in print or electronic forms without written permission of IGI Global is prohibited.

INTRODUCTION

Personality defines many aspects of life, and it explains human behavior and how people interact with the outside world. To this date, there have been many attempts to define the different types of existent personalities, Myers-Briggs Indicator (Hulth, 2003) is one of the most notable we could find. This indicator is based in the Carl Jung studies and basically defines four main axes of personality: energy source, information collection, decision making, and relationship with the outside world. According to these four axes, a person may be a: introvert or extrovert, intuitive or sensing, thinker or feeler, and judger or perceiver. On a normal basis, you may determine your personality, taking the Myers-Briggs indicator. It generally involves answering about 30 simple questions on a scale from 1 to 5. Where 1 represents the complete disagreement with the statement, and 5 represents full agreement. Nevertheless, in Mexico, an average person spends 8 hours a day on social networks; therefore, there is more than enough useful information to predict the personality of Mexican users using their "online footprint", without the need to take the traditional test. This is possible because previous studies have found a strong relationship between the written content and the personality of individuals (Hulth, 2003). These studies generally use a combination of analysis techniques like "Linguistic Inquiry and Word Count" (LIWC) that allows researchers to determine the polarity of the words written by any user, related to the positive or negative self-concept, sex, or religion-related beliefs, to mention a few. Here, some classifiers are used with machine learning techniques to work on a dataset and train a model for classifying. The objective of this chapter is to compare three well-known machine learning classifiers (Support Vector Machine, Random Forest, and Naive Bayes) to automatically classify the personality of job candidates based on their social media content and find the most accurate classifier.

This article has the following structure: Section 2 introduces the theory behind the three algorithms, also a summary on the Myers-Briggs theory; in Section 3, we describe the preprocessing of the dataset and the case study; Section 4 presents results and discussion; and finally, Section 5 includes the conclusion.

RELATED RESEARCH

Machine Learning and e-recruitment systems are booming nowadays (De Meo, Quattrone, Terracina, & Ursino, 2007); however, many of them don't focus on user personality despite the huge amount of user data available. This appears as a good opportunity to broaden the existent recruiting systems' boundaries; also, such a tool could be of value to recruitment centers that can't afford to screen all the candidates' personalities through personal interviews. Faliagka et al. (2012) created an e-recruitment system that included automatic personality mining for job applicants, and they measured introversion/ extroversion through the polarity of the words that a candidate uses in their personal blog and then rank them according to the needs of the recruiter. The extroversion score was calculated using the LIWC model developed by Tausczik & Pennebaker (2010). On the other hand, Tandera et al. (2017) developed a personality classifier for Facebook users using deep learning techniques and the Big Five personality model, achieving 74.14% of accuracy. A study by Ortigosa et al. (2014) shows their success finding patterns in Facebook interactions of people with similar personalities based on the Big Five Alternative model. The before mentioned research studies personality prediction using social media and a personality model. This collection of previous work suggests that a machine learning classifier is a viable tool to find a user personality.

Analysis of Sentiment Related to Suicide

Even though there are no details in the studies about social media use, we can observe that it is one of the most important ways to maintain communication among individuals. This interaction makes it more attractive to gather insights from the huge quantities of information that are generated constantly. If this is treated in the correct way, it will be converted into an important source of data for analysis and knowledge acquisition for multiple applications, for example, marketing, politics, government, and any other discipline that need to extract knowledge from opinions and emotions (e.g., product and service reviews). In order to obtain this knowledge, there are computer-science disciplines that classify posts, short texts, or whole documents according to the sentiment, emotion, or opinion that is being expressed. These techniques are known by Sentiment Analysis or Opinion Mining (Hulth, 2003; Jiménez, García, Florencia-Juárez, Rivera, & López-Orozco, 2018).

Sentiment analysis can be used as an auxiliary tool in the detection of text with depressive or suicide content. Nowadays, there are alarming numbers around the topics of depression and suicide. Suicide is the second cause of death among the population in the15–29 years-old range. In general terms, more than 800,000 persons commit suicide each year, resulting in a death every forty seconds all over the world (De Meo, Quattrone, Terracina, & Ursino, 2007). There is a wide list of causes and risk factors related to suicidal behavior (Faliagka, Tsakalidis, & Tzimas, 2012; Tausczik & Pennebaker, 2010; De Meo, Quattrone, Terracina, & Ursino, 2007).

In the present research, we propose a dictionary of words with a depressive notion that could help us as a tool in sentiment analysis to detect potentially suicidal behavior. During the sentiment analysis in words or texts, there are some challenges to face: most words can potentially have affective content, although some seem to denote neutrality. Another case may occur with the word "cry" whose emotional meaning will depend in some cases on the context in which it is expressed, for example, "I want to cry of happiness" would imply a different emotion to the phrase "I want to cry of courage". The first would denote enjoyment, and the second statement denotes anger, when generally cry is caused by sadness (Tandera, Suhartono, Wongso, Prasetio, & others, 2017). For the identification of emotions in texts, there are several techniques that can be implemented. In Table 1, we show the ones that are proposed

Figure 1.

as the most important after a study by Ortigosa, Carro and Quiroga (2014), including the Circumplex Model (**Figure 1**):

Triad Cognitive Proposed

Table 1. Approaches to the detection of emotions, constructed from Hulth (2003) and Ortigosa, Carro and Quiroga (2014).

Concept	Emotions	Evaluation
Descriptions based on evaluations Scherer y Ekman, 1984	Positive or Negative	Result of event evaluation processes based on a set of evaluation criteria
Emotional Dimensions Wundt, 1896	Valence (Polarity) Activation Control	Positive / Negative Active /Pasive Domination / Submision
Emotional categories Smith, 1989	Anger, Repulsion, fear, joy, sadness, surprise, anger. Proposal by Ekman, Friese y Ellsworth.	

One of the fundamental and critical stages in the medical area is made at the time of diagnosis, which is also the basis for effective treatment; this is based on symptoms (medically relevant indications provided by the patient), signs (revealed in physical examinations made by medical personnel), in addition to findings of complementary explorations. In our case, which is to identify texts specifically with depressive content, we propose to focus beyond the emotional level; the proposal is to assign a depressive degree to the sentence without identifying the basic emotional category it denotes.

Considering the above, the Beck's cognitive model of depression is one that best we can adapt to our objective since, to diagnose the depression, it is based on three aspects that are fundamental in the way that an individual perceives life:

1. Negative perception of themself.
2. Negative perception of the environment.
3. Negative perception of the future.

In a cognitive triad, the person has a negative vision of the future and tends to interpret the experience of the day in a negative way.

These persons look themselves miserable, clumsy, with little worth, tend to underrate, and to criticize themselves based on those defects they have. They believe that the world interposes them insuperable obstacles, facing a frustrating environment continuously. From the future, they only expect sorrow, frustration, and endless deprivation. When a person faces a circumstance, the scheme (stable cognitive patterns) is the basis for transforming the data into cognitions. Schemes activated in a specific situation determine how a person responds. In depression, these schemes are inadequate. The subject loses a big part of the voluntary control over their thought processes and is unable to attend to other more appropriate schemes. In the cognitive triad, the person has a negative vision of the future, itself, and tend to interpret the experience of the day in negative ways.

As depression worsens, thinking is increasingly dominated by negative ideas. In the most serious depressive states, the subject's thinking can become totally absorbed in negative, repetitive, persevering thoughts, finding it extremely difficult to concentrate on external stimuli (e.g., reading) or undertaking voluntary mental activities (problem-solving, memories)

The systematic errors that occur in the thinking of the depressive mind maintain the subject's belief in the validity of their negative concepts, despite the existence of contrary evidence (Suykens & Vandewalle, 1999).

Construction of Dictionary

The main objective is to construct a dictionary that contains a label (weighting) with a depressive degree in each word. To carry it out, they took 3000 messages from the social network Tumblr; first, the messages were extracted from chat rooms tagged with the subjects of suicide, sadness, pain, depression in the social network Tumblr (**Figure 2**). For the extraction of these messages, we used the API offered by the social network in the section for developers, and this was implemented in a script in the PHP programming language. The following image shows the interface that was developed to extract messages from the social network. This screen shows the messages extracted from the chat rooms with the tags of our interest:

Figure 2. The crawler of messages from the chat rooms of the social networking Tumblr

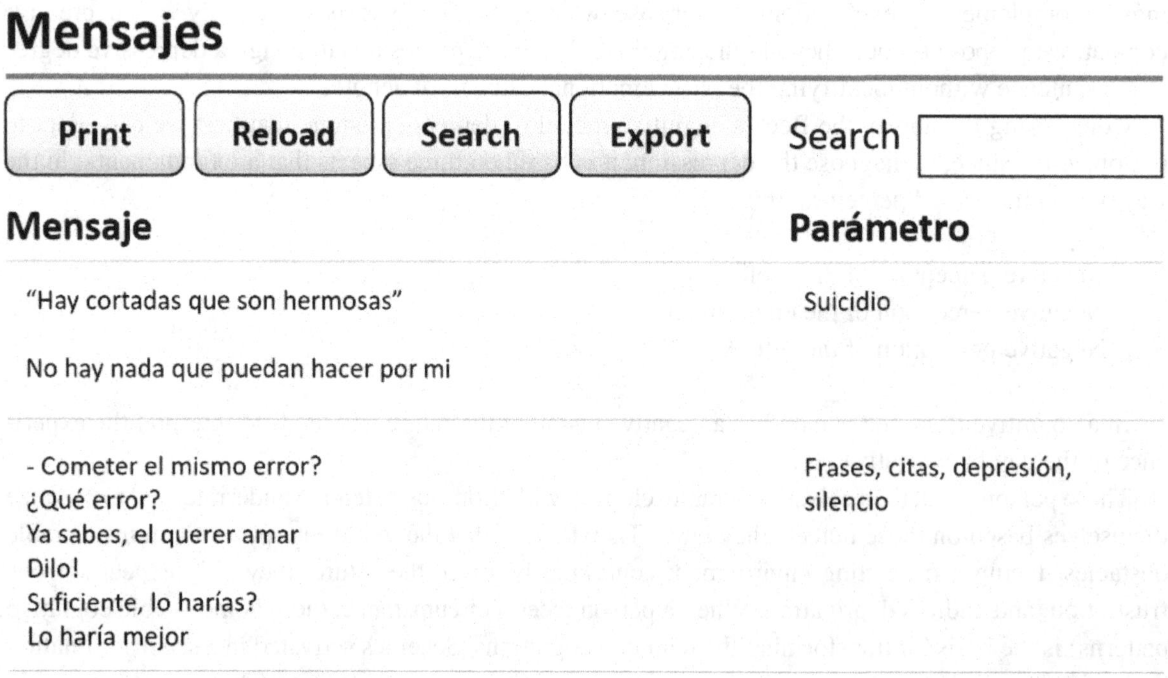

Mensajes

Print	Reload	Search	Export	Search

Mensaje	**Parámetro**
"Hay cortadas que son hermosas" No hay nada que puedan hacer por mi	Suicidio
- Cometer el mismo error? ¿Qué error? Ya sabes, el querer amar Dilo! Suficiente, lo harías? Lo haría mejor	Frases, citas, depresión, silencio

Once the messages were crawled, then the evaluators perform on each message, the assessment that corresponds to them (**Figure 3**). To each message, several evaluators assign a value based on their expe-

Figure 3. Graphical Interface to evaluators

rience about the depressive content that they observe within the message; based on this, we performed a concordance analysis with the weighted kappa method.

Evaluation of the Experts

The objective of the evaluators was to assign each message with the so-called depressive content through five characteristics, of which three were taken from Beck's cognitive triad. The fourth characteristic is the depressive content itself, and the fifth is to determine if the message has suicide information. We will calculate the depressive grade from the values assigned in the Likert scale used (null, low, medium, high). This scale is chosen for its popularity, simplicity, and its frequent use in survey applications. Unlike the dichotomous questions with yes / no answer, the Likert scale allows us to measure attitudes and know the degree of conformity of the respondent with any affirmation we propose.

It is especially useful in situations where we want the person to clarify their opinion. In this sense, the categories of response will serve to capture and see if the intensity of the feelings perceived by the evaluator was captured by the author of the message. The criteria for each scale value for our evaluators are described below. The variable "Depressive Degree" was used as an example to exemplify the characteristics to be evaluated.

Scale Values

• "Null": 0%

Depressive Degree: The message shows zero indications that the author tries to express depressive feelings or behaviors.

Beck's Triad (Negative Considerations): The message shows zero indications that the author has negative considerations (of themself, of their environment, and their future).

• "Low": 33.33%

Depressive Degree: The message shows slight indications that the author tries to express depressive feelings or behaviors.

Beck's Triad (Negative Considerations): The message shows slight indications that the author has negative considerations (of themself, of their environment, and their future)

- "Medium": 66.66%

Depressive Degree: The message shows moderately indications that the author tries to express depressive feelings or behaviors.

Beck's Triad (Negative Considerations): The message shows moderately indications that the author has negative considerations (of themself, of their environment, and their future).

- "High": 99.99%

Depressive Degree: The message shows clear indications that its author tries to express depressive feelings or behaviors.

Beck's Triad (Negative Considerations): The message shows clear indications that the author has negative considerations (of themself, their environment, and their future).

Table 2. Assignment of values by area experts (psychiatrists and psychologists)

	Characteristics of depressive content, according to Beck cognitive triad		
	Negative perception of self	**Negative perception of the environment**	**Negative perception of the future**
"Él no sabía amar, yo quizás… demasiado."	Null Low Medium High	Null Low Medium High	Null Low Medium High

As a result, we will have a message evaluated by several evaluators; then, to assign them a unique value, we used the technique of analysis of concordance with the Kappa index. The introduction of this kappa coefficient was proposed in a publication in the journal Educational and Psychological Measurement in the 1960s (Cohen, 1960). A similar measure called Scott's pi is also known, the difference being in the way they calculate the hypothetical probability of agreement by randomness. We must be clear that Cohen's kappa is only a measure for two observers. This Cohen kappa coefficient is a value used as a measure that adjusts the effect of randomness proportionally with the observed agreement applied to qualitative values (categorical variables). This index can be substituted for the calculation of the percentage of concordance since, in most cases, this measure gives a better representation of the values obtained from the observation than when calculating the percentage. Mitchell et al. (1997) and Alpaydin (2020) have a concern about the tendency to assure the frequencies of the observed categories, which could cause the agreement to be underestimated in a category of habitual use and is by That k is considered an excessively conservative measure. Also, Tausczik and Pennebaker (2010) make the observation and take the issue that kappa "considers" the fact that it is possible to reach an agreement. To deal with this possibility, the model must capture the effect of chance when the observer makes the decision. Therefore, if there is not full security, the evaluators give an answer that does not coincide with reality.

The agreement of two observers is what the Cohen kappa index or coefficient delivers as a result of measurement at the time of classifying n elements into C mutually exclusive categories expressed in equation

$$k = \frac{\left[\Pr(a) - \Pr(e)\right]}{\left[1 - \Pr(e)\right]} \tag{1}$$

Where $\Pr(a)$ is the calculated relative agreement between observers, and $\Pr(e)$ is the hypothetical probability of agreement by randomizing, using the observed data to calculate the probabilities that each observer will rank each category randomly. If the observers are completely in agreement k will take the value of 1, otherwise, since there is no agreement between the two evaluators that differs from that expected according to chance, this is $\Pr(e)$, then k takes the value of zero.

Table 3. Format of the data of a concordance study

Observer 1	Observer 2				Total
	1	2	...	C	Total
1	X_{11}	X_{12}	...	X_{1c}	X_1
2	X_{21}	X_{22}	...	X_{2c}	X_2
.					.
C					Xc
Total	X_{c1}	X_{c2}	...	X_{cc}	n

In our case, we have more than two evaluators so that we will use a proposed adaptation (Hulth, 2003). Where it is proposed to work in pairs of evaluators so that the latter is calculated the total average with all values obtained.

Once the agreement of the evaluators for each message is calculated, a single value will be obtained for each of the characteristics c_1 to c_5 evaluated, leaving as a vector of depressive characteristics of the message, as shown below:

$$fm_n = \{c_{1n} \cdots c_{5n}\} \tag{2}$$

Where each characteristic represents:

c_1	c_2	c_3	c_4	c_5
General Depressive Degree	Suicidal tendency shows?	Negative Vision of Self	Negative Consideration of Your Environment	Negative Consideration of the Future

Then we will have a corpus of n messages m_n of w_{kn} words where k is the number of words w of message n. Each message will be its characteristic vector fm_n. These characteristics will be assigned to each of the words w_{kn} of the message m_n. We know that words are repeated within the corpus of messages, then the characteristic vector of each word $fw\text{i}$ was obtained by calculating the average as follows:

Table 4. Some messages in the corpus of messages with high depressive load

Characteristics = >	C3	C4	C5	*FPDm*
Cada pensamiento es una batalla. Cada inspiración es una guerra y no creo que gane más.	1	1	1	1
Es triste como un día parezco tenerlo todo y al día siguiente lo pierdo todo tan rápido.	1	0.75	0.75	0.83
La depresión es como ahogarse, excepto que nadie te puede ver.	0.75	1	1	0.91
A veces me siento triste, cansado y desgraciado sin ninguna razón.	1	0.75	0.75	0.83
Cada pensamiento es una batalla. Cada inspiración es una guerra y no creo que gane más.	1	0.75	1	0.91
Necesito dormir unos meses, por favor.	0	0	0.75	0.25
Mamá tu hija ahora mismo está llorando en su habitación porque tiene unas ganas inmensas de morir.	0.75	0.33	1	0.69
¿Qué tiene de malo la muerte? Ella me promete esa felicidad que no logro conseguir en vida.	0.333	1	1	0.77
Solo quiero dormir y nunca más despertar	0.33	0.33	1	0.55
Mi madre me dice que necesito descansar ya. Quizá me está concediendo el permiso de suicidarme y descansar de este mundo enfermo.	0.75	1	1	0.91
Algunos duermen con el deseo de no despertar y dejar de pensar.	0.75	0.3	1	0.69

$$fw\text{i} = \sum_{i=0}^{n} \frac{\{c_1,\ldots,c_5\}}{n} \tag{3}$$

The following messages shown in the following table obtained a high depressive load score:

As we can see, each message has a depressive value perceived by the evaluator. The proposed value *FPDm* for the message results from computing the average of the value assigned by the evaluators in each of the characteristics $c_1 \ldots c_5$ of fm_n. Then we have that the Depressive Use Probability Factor of each word is:

$$FPDm = \sum_{x=1}^{5} \frac{c_x}{5} \tag{4}$$

Some of the messages that were rated with high depressive content are shown in the table above. Already with that value, each word will have its weighting that will be calculated from the average values that each word corresponds to each message that appears. Then we have that the Depressive Use Probability Factor of each word is given by the average of each of the characteristics in $fw\text{i}$

A Comparison of Personality Prediction Classifiers for Personnel Selection in Organizations

$$FPDw = \sum_{x=1}^{5} \frac{c_x}{5}$$ (5)

Table 5. Dictionary of weighted words with their depressive use factor FPDw their relative frequency fr.

	Word w	FPDw	fr_i
1	profundas	0.99851	0.10%
2	cuerpo	0.99851	0.10%
3	dolorosas	0.99851	0.10%
4	cualquiera	0.99851	0.10%
5	rompemos	0.859911	0.05%
6	valioso	0.859911	0.05%
7	haber	0.859911	0.05%
8	perdido	0.859911	0.05%
9	duro	0.839046	0.05%
10	mente	0.827124	0.20%
11	paciente	0.827124	0.10%
12	brillante	0.827124	0.10%
13	ningún	0.769001	0.10%
14	corte	0.769001	0.05%
15	comenzó	0.754098	0.05%
16	empezó	0.754098	0.05%
17	entonces	0.754098	0.05%
18	intentas	0.754098	0.05%
19	recordar	0.754098	0.05%
20	hablar	0.721311	0.15%
21	rodeado	0.721311	0.10%
22	mucha	0.721311	0.05%
23	confiar	0.721311	0.05%
24	solitario	0.721311	0.05%
25	sentirte	0.721311	0.05%
26	hace	0.716344	0.15%
27	muy	0.713115	0.10%
28	heridas	0.712866	0.15%
29	era	0.69225	0.10%
30	romper	0.684054	0.05%

Resulting Dictionary and Conclusions

In Table 5, we show the dictionary that resulted from processing messages, assigning finally depressive use Factor *FPDw* of each word and its frequency relative fr_i. This factor denotes the calculated depressive degree from messages in depressive contexts where the word was used.

Is interesting to see as shown an important difference between *FPDw* compared with fr_i; This can be an important factor in the calculation of depressive content in messages since we will not only rely on the frequency of words as calculation elements but also the *FPDw* to use it separately, in conjunction and compare results in the resulting depressive content. This factor can be used in automatic classification systems (neural networks, super vector machine, associative memories, etc.) As a value of depressive content and thus improve the classifiers that are developed. The concordance calculation method was used to improve the quality of the data obtained from the expert evaluations of the messages. Although we use the kappa method with adaptation to multiple evaluators, other techniques that serve the same purpose can be tried. The words that make up the dictionary are a result of the first 3000 messages valued. The number of words and the factor should improve as more text messages are evaluated. Although we do not know an optimum number of messages to obtain good classifiers, we intend to reach the necessary number of messages for optimum results. We must keep in mind that each Hispanic speaking region has different words to denote depression; although there will be coincidences, it is recommended to add the region to the dictionary for better performance.

MACHINE LEARNING TECHNIQUES

Support Vector Machine

A support vector machine is a discriminative classifier formally defined by a separating hyperplane developed by Cortes and Vapnik (Suykens & Vandewalle, 1999). In other words, given a labeled dataset, the algorithm returns the optimal division or hyperplane that classifies new data. In a bi-dimensional space, this hyperplane is a line that divides the space in two, and each class is on each side. To build this hyperplane, support vector machines use an iterative training algorithm that minimizes the error in the function. When data is not linearly separable, the algorithm allows us to apply a transformation and

Figure 4. Decision Tree

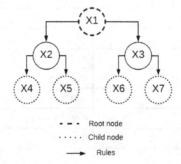

add another dimension, for instance, axis z, in such a way that you can split the data dividing it from the new axis perspective, and then just return to the original plane. These transformations are called kernels (Suykens & Vandewalle, 1999). In case that classes in the dataset are too close together or that some points of a class are mixed inside another we can use a parameter called tolerance, that indicates how many points of another class are allowed past the frontier, this is useful when we don't want to over train our classifier. Another important parameter is Gamma. This one allows us to define the influence of the points closer to the frontier; by this, we mean, when you have a low gamma value, the points further from the frontier are considered; otherwise, the influence corresponds to the points closer to the frontier. Adapting these parameters allows us to find a suitable frontier with more accuracy in less time.

Random Forest Algorithm

The random forest algorithm has a simple structure. To understand how it works, we first must know how a decision tree works (Xu, Guo, Ye, & Cheng, 2012).

- Given a dataset, a tree makes levels or partitions data according to if-else rules. These are determined based on the contribution of each variable to the purity of the child nodes.
- In **Figure 4**, the variable $X1$ gives out two child nodes with the highest purity; therefore, those variables are also root nodes. A root node is one of the most important in a dataset.
- Entropy is used to determine where the tree splits. Entropy is a measure of node's impurity (Alpaydin, 2020).

$$H(x) = -X(x)\log p(x) \tag{6}$$

So, a node splits if its impurity is higher than the established threshold. Once we know how decision trees work, we make a group of decision trees that turn into a forest, and then:

- A training subset is formed (S_2), with sample size n and random sampling replacement from the original set (S_1).

Figure 5. Random Forest Creation

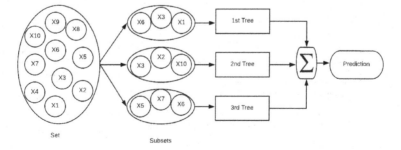

- If we have M input variables, a number $m < M$ must be specified, so m variables are selected from M. After this, the purity method is employed to divide the subsets and create child nodes with the highest purity level. The value of m is constant along with the forest's growth.
- Each tree grows without depth limit.
- Finally, several trees have grown, and a final prediction is made through voting or median **Figure 5.**

Naive Bayes Classifier

This classifier is very practical, and its performance has proven similar to that of more complex neural network classifiers. Also, this classifier was elected for this article because it has an amazing ability to work with text. This classifier uses classifying techniques where each element x in a set has an

$F(x)$ function that may take only one value from the finite set V.

First, the classifier is trained with a training data set; after this, a new set is introduced to the classifier. Then, it must classify new data or predict its class.

$$V_{MAP} = \arg\max_{v_j V} P(v_j \mid a_1, a_2, ..., a_n) \tag{7}$$

The technique used by this classifier to predict the new data's class is to assign the most probable value V_{MAP} (Equation 7) given the previous values $(a_1, a_2, ..., a_n)$ that describe that instance (Alpaydin, 2020; Mitchell et al., 1997).

If we add the Bayes theorem to the last equation, we get the following (Equation 8):

$$V_{MAP} = \arg\max_{v_j V} (a_1, a_2, ..., a_n \mid v_j) P(v_j) \tag{8}$$

With Equation 8, we would be able to calculate the probability of both terms. It is easy to estimate $P(vj)$ counting the frequency of each expected value in the training data, but to calculate the $P(a1, a2, ..., an|vj)$ terms, in the same way, would be very expensive. Therefore, the Naive Bayes Classifier is based on the simple theory that the values of the attributes are independent among them. Given an ex-

Table 6. Myers-Briggs Indicator

Preference	Dichotomies
Favorite world: Inside or Outside?	Extroversion(E) / Introversion(I)
Information: Do you prefer to focus on the basic information you are receiving, or do you prefer to add meaning?	Sensing(S)/Intuition(N)
Decision making: When you make decisions do you first see the logic and then the circumstances	Thinking(T)/Feeling(F)
Structure: Do you prefer to take sides immediately or stay open to new information	Judging(J)/Perceiving(P)

Figure 6. The 16 personality types according to the Myers-Briggs Indicator

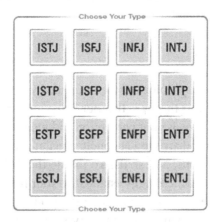

pected value, for instance, the probability to observe the union of *a1,a2,…,an* is just the product of the individual probabilities of the attributes:

P(a1, a2, …, an|vj) = Qi(ai|vj).

If we substitute this into Equation 3, we get the formula for the Bayes classifier:

$$V_{NB} = \max_{v_j V} P\left(v_j\right)_i^Y P(a_i \mid v_j) \tag{9}$$

Where v_{NB} is the expected value returned by the classifier.

To summarize, the Naive Bayes classifier is the one that assumes the independence among elements in a set; for instance, it says that the probability of finding the word 'machine' followed by the word 'learning' it's the same as the probability of finding the word 'duck'. Even if this is not real, it is neces-

Figure 7. Sample of questions and answer scale of the MBTI

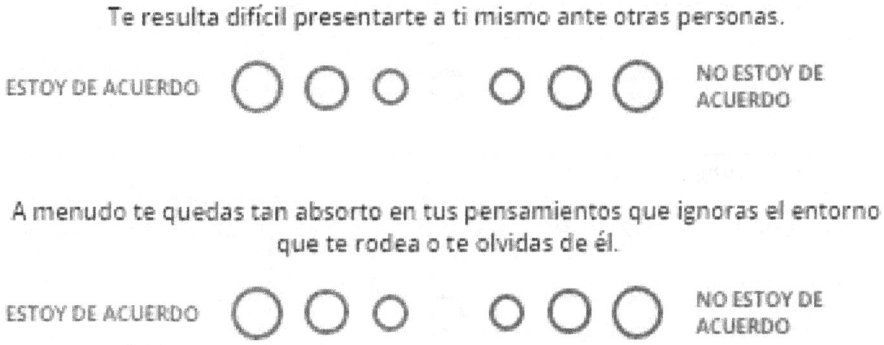

Te resulta difícil presentarte a ti mismo ante otras personas.

ESTOY DE ACUERDO   ◯ ◯ ◯   ◯ ◯ ◯   NO ESTOY DE ACUERDO

A menudo te quedas tan absorto en tus pensamientos que ignoras el entorno que te rodea o te olvidas de él.

ESTOY DE ACUERDO   ◯ ◯ ◯   ◯ ◯ ◯   NO ESTOY DE ACUERDO

sary to make this assumption because if not, the number of probabilities for each term would be too big (Alpaydin, 2020; Mitchell & others, 1997).

Myers-Briggs Indicator

This indicator was born to make the psychological theory made by C.G Jung accessible and useful to the general population. The essence of this theory is that our behavior is more consistent than we think; we all have basic differences in the way we use our perception and judgment. Suppose people have different ways of receiving new information and arriving at conclusions; it is only logical that they have different interests, reactions, values, motivations, and skills. To divide the different types of personality Isabel Briggs Myers, and her mother, Katharine Briggs established four main axes (Barrick & Mount, 1991):

Once each of the four categories is settled for a certain candidate, the test shows their personality results with a 4-letter code. The 16 possible personality types are showed in the next **Figure 6**.

Figure 8. Machine Learning Approach

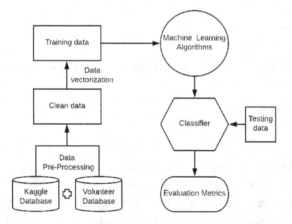

Figure 9. Sample of training data set

4	ENTP	"Creí en Dios toda mi vida hasta hace un año. Mi madre creía mucho en Dios y nos alentó a mí y a mis hermanos a ser de la misma manera. Ella no nos forzó en nuestras gargantas o ...			Me acecho en todas partes para ser honesto.			Tuve un cone...
5	INTP	"Estoy rebotando dentro y fuera de este hilo como lo permite mi temperamento, lo admitiré. Estoy usando mis reservas de temperamento para responder esto. La letra cursiva no es razonable. Eso no va a argumentar en contra. En ...			Solo diré que ...
6	ISFJ	"Vencí eso buscando a un compañero de casa que trabajaba meses a la vez, y cuando estaba en casa, visitó a sus compañeros después de que terminaron el trabajo, así que estaba solo el 80% del tiempo. D oh, yo no ...			No hay pegajoso para que s...

Figure 10. Sample of training data set

32	ENTP	Cada vez que tomo decisiones, trato de reducir los riesgos y problemas que puedan existir ????????? Si una persona no tiene sueños no tiene razón de vivir, soñar es necesario aun cuando el sueño va más allá de la re... https://t.co/Q8dO2IU68X
33	ENTP	RT @_Cinthhya: Exactamente un mes para mi cumple ! ???? #PaPendiente ???? Pensando en ti! ???????????? https://t.co/6M8Y7nX9F @lapizito123 Carnal yo solo veía acábatelo por ti! Haaa eres quien hacía reir!!! #Uvimeza @_Cinthhya vamos!
34	INTP	RT @MegBucher: Heading to bed, hopefully we hit 700 RTs and I can give you guys this #ArcadeMF code in the morning! https://t.co/PdMgTYVbUG RT @cdollarsc: Need 40 more followers! RT @cdollarsc: 34 more followers! RT @freddyomana94: Follo...

Traditionally one can take this personality test answering questions like the ones shown in **Figure 7**

Personality and Job Performance

Organizational researchers are now focusing more than ever on the relationship between an employee and their personality. A previous study done by Barrick and Mount (1991) using the Big Five model suggests that certain personality traits are strongly related to the employees' performance. For instance, a sales position is perfect for someone with a high level of judgment and extroversion (Hurtz & Donovan, 2000). This automatic personality predictor is intended to work as a tool for human resources recruiters that need to find a certain characteristic in a candidate. This tool reduces the probability of biased answers from job applicants since the content used to evaluate their personality is from their own social media profiles.

METHODOLOGY

Figure 8 shows the method used to prepare and test each one of the three classifiers. First, data was collected, and after data cleaning, it was vectorized and finally separated to train the classifiers.

Table 7. Distributions of different datasets

Feature	Distributions of Datasets		
	Training	**Data Collected**	**Whole Dataset**
Introversion (I) / Extroversion (E)	191/661	33/11	224/672
Intuitive (N) Sensing (S)	165/687	6/38	171/725
Think (T) Feel (F):	426/426	17/27	443/453
Judging (J) Perceiving (P):	523/3	27/17	550/346

Figure 11. Sample of the vocabulary vector of size 432 with the selected words from the dataset

{'moment': 259, 'mejor': 244, 'jug': 214, 'brom': 40, 'cual': 84, 'sid': 350, 'vid': 420, 'mayor': 241, 'part': 296, 'dia': 10
3, 'perc': 303, 'ultim': 400, 'amig': 19, 'public': 326, 'escuch': 138, 'relacion': 341, 'perfect': 305, 'tiemp': 386, 'cad': 4
4, 'intent': 206, 'dificil': 108, 'bienv': 39, 'jueg': 213, 'men': 245, 'minut': 254, 'mientr': 252, 'sent': 357, 'mism': 256,
'mod': 257, 'tal': 377, 'ver': 417, 'prueb': 325, 'salud': 349, 'tres': 398, 'probabl': 322, 'tip': 388, 'des': 99, 'usar': 40
2, 'cuent': 87, 'funcion': 164, 'dem': 95, 'dej': 94, 'tod': 390, 'cos': 81, 'hech': 183, 'buen': 41, 'not': 276, 'muert': 263,
'ningun': 271, 'dad': 90, 'quer': 330, 'crec': 83, 'favorit': 153, 'parec': 295, 'demasi': 96, 'tard': 381, 'trist': 399, 'algu
i': 15, 'esper': 140, 'pens': 300, 'mund': 265, 'voy': 427, 'trabaj': 395, 'disfrut': 114, 'preocup': 319, 'gent': 170, 'siemp
r': 360, 'cerc': 54, 'medi': 243, 'social': 369, 'inclus': 203, 'entonc': 134, 'realment': 337, 'gust': 176, 'hil': 187, 'com':
61, 'segu': 352, 'pud': 327, 'piens': 310, 'ver': 415, 'pelicul': 299, 'tont': 393, 'clas': 59, 'clar': 58, 'grup': 175, 'gra
n': 173, 'cant': 50, 'razon': 335, 'dos': 119, 'beb': 37, 'propi': 324, 'hombr': 191, 'escrib': 137, 'hoy': 193, 'par': 294, 'v
eo': 414, 'vuelv': 428, 'ide': 196, 'form': 161, 'orgull': 290, 'tom': 392, 'habit': 178, 'cam': 46, 'aprend': 23, 'compart': 6
4, 'viej': 421, 'music': 266, 'secundari': 351, 'años': 33, 'algun': 14, 'man': 238, 'pod': 313, 'volv': 426, 'mental': 248, 'c
iert': 56, 'comienz': 63, 'nuev': 278, 'pas': 297, 'mes': 250, 'junt': 215, 'plan': 311, 'podr': 314, 'imagin': 200, 'tant': 38

Figure 12. Sample of the normalized vector between 0 and 1 for the first user

```
[0.          0.          0.          0.          0.          0.
 0.          0.          0.          0.          0.          0.
 0.          0.04366567  0.04916774  0.          0.          0.
 0.          0.04438111  0.          0.          0.          0.13246047
 0.          0.          0.          0.          0.          0.
 0.          0.          0.          0.10104016  0.          0.
 0.          0.07860859  0.          0.13126557  0.08156512  0.14652168
 0.          0.          0.171365    0.          0.08680048  0.
 0.          0.          0.08156512  0.          0.          0.
 0.06671746  0.          0.06177086  0.          0.08014684  0.15989984
 0.          0.07577311  0.          0.08860757  0.08486753  0.
 0.          0.          0.          0.          0.          0.
 0.          0.          0.          0.          0.          0.
 0.          0.          0.          0.03860427  0.          0.09291923
 0.13777469  0.          0.          0.10780087  0.          0.
 0.09111488  0.          0.          0.          0.05405699  0.07167368
 0.15516824  0.          0.          0.0664728   0.          0.
 0.          0.11354773  0.          0.          0.          0.
```

Data Set

The training dataset was downloaded through Kaggle, where a database with more than 8,000 records of users' posts, and the results of the Myers-Briggs indicator is found. We were able to translate 852 to Spanish; these were used as training data for our three classifiers. The testing data were obtained with the support of 44 volunteers of the Faculty of Information Technology from the Universidad Autónoma de Queretaro. These 44 volunteers agreed to take the Myers-Briggs indicator and let us save their tweets from their profile. **Figure 9** and **Figure10** show a sample of the training and testing dataset:

The distribution of the personality types across our sample is presented in Table 7.

Table 8. Accuracy results for each of four preferences with different algorithms

Algorithm	Accuracy (in percentage)				
	I-E	S-I	T-F	J-P	Average
SVM	25.00	84.09	47.73	61.36	54.55
Random Forest	25.00	86.36	45.45	63.64	55.11
Naïve Bayes	25.00	86.36	45.45	61.36	55.04

Preprocessing

After preprocessing the data, which includes eliminating punctuation signs, HTML, emojis, numbers, URLs, extra characters, change everything to lower case, and leave only the root of the words in both datasets, we proceeded to train and test the classifiers. Nevertheless, first, we must vectorize the data; this was done through a process known as feature extraction.

Feature Extraction

This process is often used in machine learning settings where it's necessary to transform images or words, like in this study, into vectors. There are many techniques and algorithms that can be used to model the data and turn it into something easier to process for a machine. These techniques are then a way of simplifying the data, and then feed this newly transformed data to the classifier and obtain more accurate results. In this case, we used a very simple technique that includes tokenization or word splitting, followed by the frequency of each word, and finally, a normalization that ensures that no word weighs more than another when defining a class. The vectorizer, in this case, was set to use only 80% of the whole vocabulary found in the posts, **Figure 11** shows a sample of the selected vocabulary that has 432 words in total.

The next step is to obtain the vocabulary vector for each user, that is, to map the vocabulary of each user to the main vocabulary vector obtained in the previous step. For this task, the Term Frequency-Inverse Document Frequency algorithm was used. The first part of the algorithm is the Term-Frequency

Table 9. SVM Precision, recall and F1 results (in percentages)

	I-E	S-N	T-F	J-P	Average
Precision	6.00	74.00	51.00	58.00	47.25
Recall	0.00	84.00	48.00	61.00	48.25
F1	10.00	79.00	48.00	55.00	48.00

Table 10. Naive Bayes Precision, recall and F1 results (in percentages)

	I-E	S-N	T-F	J-P	Average
Precision	6.00	75.00	51.00	38.00	42.50
Recall	25.00	86.00	45.00	61.00	54.25
F1	10.00	80.00	45.00	47.00	45.50

Table 11. Random Forest Precision, recall and F1 results (in percentages)

	I-E	S-N	T-F	J-P	Average
Precision	6.00	75.00	77.00	58.00	58.75
Recall	25.00	86.00	45.00	64.00	55.00
F1	10.00	80.00	35.00	52.00	44.25

(Luhn, 1957) and, as it is stated in its name, it counts the occurrence of the word in the user's posts, nevertheless, in this case, we normalize the frequency to avoid long posts from having a higher count. To do this, the frequency is divided by the maximum frequency count of the same word in all the posts.

Inverse Document Frequency (Robertson & Jones, 1988) is a measure to reduce the weight of words that repeat across several posts and, therefore, they aren't as important as words that are less common throughout the whole database. This is calculated by dividing the total number of documents by the number of documents that include that term, and then you calculate the logarithm of that division:

Applying this transformation to the data, we get a matrix with the document-term components. In **Figure 12** the vector for the first user is shown

Table 12. Accuracy results for each of four preferences with different algorithms with 80% training data

Algorithm	Accuracy (in percentage)				
	I-E	S-I	T-F	J-P	Average
SVM	70.00	77.23	62.05	57.59	66.74
Random Forest	77.23	77.23	64.73	57.14	69.08
Naïve Bayes	76.34	77.23	64.29	57.14	68.75

Table 13. SVM Precision, recall and F1 results (in percentages)

	I-E	S-N	T-F	J-P	Average
Precision	70.00	60.00	62.00	56.00	62.00
Recall	0.00	84.00	48.00	61.00	48.25
F1	10.00	79.00	48.00	55.00	48.00

Table 14. Naive Bayes Precision, recall and F1 results (in percentages)

	I-E	S-N	T-F	J-P	Average
Precision	6.00	75.00	51.00	38.00	42.50
Recall	25.00	86.00	45.00	61.00	54.25
F1	10.00	86.00	45.00	47.00	45.50

Table 15. Random Forest Precision, recall and F1 results (in percentages)

	I-E	S-N	T-F	J-P	Average
Precision	6.00	75.00	77.00	58.00	58.75
Recall	25.00	86.00	45.00	64.00	55.00
F1	10.00	86.00	35.00	52.00	44.25

RESULTS

Test A: Accuracy

For this first test, the dataset was set up so that the 852 translated records from the original Kaggle database were used as training data, and the remaining 44 records obtained from students of the faculty used as the test data. In Table 8, the accuracy results are presented by the classifier, and for each one of the four preferences.

Test A: Precision, Recall, and F1

Besides accuracy, another three metrics where obtained because our data is not equally balanced. The precision, the recall, and the F1 metrics are found in the tables below for each classifier.

For test A, the best result of right classification or accuracy was 25% for Introversion-Extroversion in Table 10, 86.36% for Sensing-Intuition, 47.73% for Think-Feel (Table 8), and 63.64% for Judge-Perceive. The classifier with the best performance was the one created with the Random Forest Algorithm that had an average accuracy of 55.11%; this classifier also had the best precision, recall, and F1 metrics.

Test B: Accuracy

For this first test, the dataset was randomly separated, data obtained from the volunteers and the translated records from the Kaggle database were mixed, and then 80% of the data was used as training data and the rest as testing data. The results appear in the Tables below.

Test B: Precision, Recall, and F1

Precision, Recall and F1 metrics are found in the tables below for each classifier.

The best results for test B were 77.23% of accuracy for Introversion/Extroversion, 77.23% for Sensing/Intuitive, 64.73% for Think/Feel, and 57.59% for Judge/Perceive (Tables 12-15). Two out of the four best accuracy scores were obtained with the random forest algorithm, that on average, had 69.08%. Also, it had the highest precision and recall metrics. Better results were obtained with test B. Nevertheless, in both experiments, the classifier with the greatest accuracy and metrics turned out to be the Random Forest Classifier with an average accuracy of 55.11% in test A and 69.08% in test B. These results may be since the algorithm of random forest breaks data into sets and subsets that reduce the effect of outliers; still, as stated in the study by Wolpert and Macready (1997), there are always going to be datasets where a certain classifier is better than others.

CONCLUSION

This research reviewed the performance of three well-used algorithms due to their high accuracy levels and low complexity to classify a Spanish speaking job applicant's personality automatically. The results of two separate tests showed the results of classification using Support Vector Machine, Random Forest, and Naive Bayes. The best results were obtained using the Random Forest Algorithm. With the treatment,

Figure 13. Implementation of an intelligent chatbot that can determine the size of a group of applicants and can dedicate quality time to online interviews and their distribution with respect to the totality of jobs in the Industry 4.0 paradigm.

the dataset received by classifier was able to classify correctly 69.08% of all data. This indicates that the general results of the experiment were positive and with the use of certain improvements like increasing the amount of data, and a more detailed preprocessing, this classifier could improve and obtain higher accuracy to process job applicants' tweets in order to become a solid tool for human resources recruiters.

FUTURE RESEARCH

In our future research, we determined to implement a chatbot that uses an avatar appropriate to the type of interview to be conducted so that they can determine the maximum extent of each applicant skills and their best skills (Zhou, Wang, Mark, Yang, & Xu, 2019; Følstad, Nordheim, & Bjørkli, 2018; Gulenko, 2014; Vladova, Haase, Rüdian, & Pinkwart, 2019), with the intention of determining if they can survive in the long term in the position of the organization that is under the paradigm of Industry 4.0, considering the minimum model level of continuous employment within organizations, as due to the industrialization of the metropolitan area of Queretaro at least a thousand applications are received with curriculums for a single position considering Smart manufacturing within Industry 4.0.

ACKNOWLEDGMENT

This research received no specific grant from any funding agency in the public, commercial, or not-for-profit sectors.

REFERENCES

Alpaydin, E. (2020). *Introduction to machine learning*. MIT Press.

Barrick, M. R., & Mount, M. K. (1991). The big five personality dimensions and job performance: A meta-analysis. *Personnel Psychology*, *44*(1), 1–26. doi:10.1111/j.1744-6570.1991.tb00688.x

De Meo, P., Quattrone, G., Terracina, G., & Ursino, D. (2007). An XML-based multiagent system for supporting online recruitment services. *IEEE Transactions on Systems, Man, and Cybernetics. Part A, Systems and Humans*, *37*(4), 464–480. doi:10.1109/TSMCA.2007.897696

Faliagka, E., Tsakalidis, A., & Tzimas, G. (2012). An integrated e-recruitment system for automated personality mining and applicant ranking. *Internet Research*, *22*(5), 551–568. doi:10.1108/10662241211271545

Følstad, A., Nordheim, C. B., & Bjørkli, C. A. (2018). What makes users trust a chatbot for customer service? An exploratory interview study. *International Conference on Internet Science*, 194-208. 10.1007/978-3-030-01437-7_16

Gulenko, I. (2014). Chatbot for IT Security Training: Using Motivational Interviewing to Improve Security Behaviour. *AIST*, (Supplement), 7–16.

Hulth, A. (2003). Improved automatic keyword extraction given more linguistic knowledge. *Proceedings of the 2003 conference on Empirical methods in natural language processing*, 216-223. 10.3115/1119355.1119383

Hurtz, G. M., & Donovan, J. J. (2000). Personality and job performance: The Big Five revisited. *The Journal of Applied Psychology*, *85*(6), 869–879. doi:10.1037/0021-9010.85.6.869 PMID:11125652

Jiménez, R., García, V., Florencia-Juárez, R., Rivera, G., & López-Orozco, F. (2018). Minería de opiniones aplicada a la evaluación docente de la Universidad Autónoma de Ciudad Juárez. *Research in Computing Science*, *147*(6), 167–177. doi:10.13053/rcs-147-6-13

Luhn, H. P. (1957). A statistical approach to mechanized encoding and searching of literary information. *IBM Journal of Research and Development*, *1*(4), 309–317. doi:10.1147/rd.14.0309

Mitchell, T. M., & ... (1997). *Machine learning*. McGraw-Hill.

Ortigosa, A., Carro, R. M., & Quiroga, J. I. (2014). Predicting user personality by mining social interactions in Facebook. *Journal of Computer and System Sciences*, *80*(1), 57–71. doi:10.1016/j.jcss.2013.03.008

Robertson, S. E., & Jones, K. S. (1988). *Document retrieval systems. chapter Relevance weighting of search terms*. Taylor Graham Publishing.

Suykens, J. A., & Vandewalle, J. (1999). Least squares support vector machine classifiers. *Neural Processing Letters, 9*(3), 293–300. doi:10.1023/A:1018628609742

Tandera, T., Suhartono, D., Wongso, R., Prasetio, Y. L., & ... (2017). Personality prediction system from facebook users. *Procedia Computer Science, 116*, 604–611. doi:10.1016/j.procs.2017.10.016

Tausczik, Y. R., & Pennebaker, J. W. (2010). The psychological meaning of words: LIWC and computerized text analysis methods. *Journal of Language and Social Psychology, 29*(1), 24–54. doi:10.1177/0261927X09351676

Vladova, G., Haase, J., Rüdian, L. S., & Pinkwart, N. (2019). *Educational Chatbot with Learning Avatar for Personalization*. Association for Information Systems.

Wolpert, D. H., & Macready, W. G. (1997). No free lunch theorems for optimization. *IEEE Transactions on Evolutionary Computation, 1*(1), 67–82. doi:10.1109/4235.585893

Xu, B., Guo, X., Ye, Y., & Cheng, J. (2012). An Improved Random Forest Classifier for Text Categorization. *JCP, 7*(12), 2913–2920. doi:10.4304/jcp.7.12.2913-2920

Zhou, M. X., Wang, C., Mark, G., Yang, H., & Xu, K. (2019). *Building Real-World Chatbot Interviewers: Lessons from a Wizard-of-Oz Field Study*. IUI Workshops.

Chapter 13
Improving the K–Means Clustering Algorithm Oriented to Big Data Environments

Joaquín Pérez Ortega
Tecnológico Nacional de México, Mexico & CENIDET, Mexico

Nelva Nely Almanza Ortega
Tecnológico Nacional de México, Mexico & Instituto Tecnológico de Tlalnepantla, Mexico

Andrea Vega Villalobos
Tecnológico Nacional de México, Mexico & CENIDET, Mexico

Marco A. Aguirre L.
(iD) https://orcid.org/0000-0002-2551-1881
Tecnológico Nacional de México, Mexico & Instituto Tecnológico de Ciudad Madero, Mexico

Crispín Zavala Díaz
Universidad Autónoma del Estado de Morelos, Mexico

Javier Ortiz Hernandez
(iD) https://orcid.org/0000-0002-6481-1537
Tecnológico Nacional de México, Mexico & CENIDET, Mexico

Antonio Hernández Gómez
Tecnológico Nacional de México, Mexico & CENIDET, Mexico

ABSTRACT

In recent years, the amount of texts in natural language, in digital format, has had an impressive increase. To obtain useful information from a large volume of data, new specialized techniques and efficient algorithms are required. Text mining consists of extracting meaningful patterns from texts; one of the basic approaches is clustering. The most used clustering algorithm is k-means. This chapter

DOI: 10.4018/978-1-7998-4730-4.ch013

Copyright © 2021, IGI Global. Copying or distributing in print or electronic forms without written permission of IGI Global is prohibited.

proposes an improvement of the k-means algorithm in the convergence step; the process stops whenever the number of objects that change their assigned cluster in the current iteration is bigger than the ones that changed in the previous iteration. Experimental results showed a reduction in execution time up to 93%. It is remarkable that, in general, better results are obtained when the volume of the text increase, particularly in those texts within big data environments.

INTRODUCTION

In recent years the amount of data has increased dramatically, contributing to this increase, for example, the Internet, social media, patient data, and book repositories in digital format, among others. To give an idea of the accelerated growth of the volume of data, we will mention that according to the International Data Corporation (Gantz, & Reinsel, 2011), the world generated 1.8 zettabytes of digital information in 2011 and it is expected that in 2020 it will be the product of multiplying for 50 such amount (Ingersoll, Morton, & Farris, 2012). Much of the information generated is textual because it is the most natural way to store it. This amount of text is an invaluable source of information and knowledge, which allows us to make better decisions or improve our understanding of parts of reality for study. However, the handling and processing of large and complex volumes of data with standard tools is generally limited by computer resources. In this sense, our contribution here is to provide a strategy to deal with the problem of grouping objects (documents, paragraphs, and terms) according to their attributes (dimensions, characteristics, properties) in the context of Big Data.

The problem being addressed is complex and requires the integration of knowledge from several disciplines, including natural language processing, text mining, combinatorial optimization, and Lloyd's K-Means algorithm, among others.

The rest of the chapter proceeds as follows. In the Background section, the clustering problem is formulated as an optimization problem. The K-Means algorithm is described, and its behavior is analyzed. The subsection Literature Review on K-Means briefly reviews the most relevant research to improve K-Means. Highlights of work related to Text Mining applications are shown in the Literature review of K-Means in Text Mining subsection. In the Proposed Algorithm section, the behavior of K-Means is analyzed, and it was observed:

a) a strong correlation between the decreasing value of the objective function and the number of objects that change group by iteration and

b) that the value of the number of objects that change group starts to oscillate when the value of the objective function changed very little between one iteration and another.

These observations inspired our proposal for a new convergence criterion. In the Experimental validation section, we discuss the validation of our proposal by testing with real and synthetic datasets. Possible extensions of our research are shown in the Future Research Directions section. Finally, our conclusions are presented in the Conclusions section.

BACKGROUND

The K-Means Algorithm

The clustering problem has long been studied and consists in partitioning a set of n objects in $k \geq 2$ non-empty subsets (called clusters) in such a way that the objects in any cluster have similar attributes and, at the same time, are different from the objects in any other cluster.

In this paper we assume that the objects' attributes are measurable. Let $N = \{x_1, \ldots, x_n\}$ denote the set of n objects to be grouped by a closeness criterion, where $x_i \in \mathfrak{R}^d$ for $i = 1, \ldots, n$, and $d \geq 1$ is the number of dimensions (the objects' attributes). Further, let $k \geq 2$ be an integer and $K = \{1, \ldots, k\}$. For a k-partition $\mathrm{P} = \{G(1), \ldots, G(k)\}$ of N, denote μ_j the centroid of group (cluster) $G(j)$, for $j = 1, \ldots, k$, let $M = \{\mu_1, \ldots, \mu_k\}$, and $W = \{w_{11}, \ldots, w_{ij}\}$.

Thus, the clustering problem can be posed as a constrained optimization one (cf. Selim and Ismail, 1984):

$$\boldsymbol{P} : \text{minimize } z\left(W, M\right) = \sum_{i=1}^{n}\sum_{j=1}^{k} w_{ij} d(x_i, \mu_j)$$

Subject to:

$$\sum_{j=1}^{k} w_{ij} = 1, \text{ for } i = 1, \ldots, n,$$

$w_{ij} = 0$ or 1, for $i = 1, \ldots, n$, and $j = 1, \ldots, k$

where $w_{ij} = 1 \Leftrightarrow$ object x_i belongs to cluster $G(j)$, and $d(x_i, \mu_j)$ denotes the Euclidean distance between x_i and μ_j, for $i = 1, \ldots, n$, and $j = 1, \ldots, k$.

Since the pioneering studies by Steinhaus (1956), Lloyd (1982), and Jancey (1966), many investigations have been devoted to finding a k-partition of N that solves $\boldsymbol{P}$ above. It has been proved that this problem belongs to the so-called *NP*-hard class for $k \geq 2$ or $d \geq 2$ (Aloise, Deshpande, Hansen, & Popat, 2009; Mahajan, Nimbhorkar & Varadarajan, 2012); thus, obtaining an optimal solution of a moderate size instance or dataset is in general intractable.

Therefore, a variety of heuristic algorithms have been proposed to approach the optimal solution of $\boldsymbol{P}$, the most conspicuous being those generally designed as *K-Means* (MacQueen, 1967) with straightforward implementation (Wu et al., 2008). It must be said that the establishment of useful gaps between the optimal solution of the problem $\boldsymbol{P}$ and the solution obtained by *K-Means* remains an open problem. The computational complexity of *K-Means* is $O(nkdr)$, where r stands for the number of iterations (Jain, 2010; Bock, 2008), limiting their use in large instances since, in general, at every iteration, all distances from objects to cluster centroids must be considered. Thus, numerous strategies to stop iterating have been investigated where, usually, increasing the computational effort entails the reduction of the objective function. Algorithm 1 shows the Lloyd version of the *K-Means* algorithm.

Algorithm 1. Lloyd *K*-means algorithm

```
 1:              # Initialization:
 2:                  N:= {x₁, ..., xₙ};
 3:                  M:= {μ₁, ..., μₖ};
 4:              # Classification:
 5:                  For xᵢ ∈ N and μₖ ∈ M
 6:                      Calculate the Euclidean distance from each xᵢ to the μₖ
          centroids;
 7:                      Assign object xᵢ to the closest centroid μₖ;
 8:              # Centroid calculation:
 9:                  Calculate centroid μₖ;
10:          # Convergence:
11:              If M:= {μ₁, ..., μₖ} remains unchanged in two consecutive
          iterations
      then:
12:                  Stop the algorithm;
13:              else:
14:                  Go to Classification
15:          End
```

In the Lloyd version of K-Means, the following four steps have been identified (Pérez et al., 2007):

Step 1: Initialization. In this step, the initial centroids are defined for each of the *k* clusters (lines 1-3).

Step 2: Classification. For each data point, its distance to each of the centroids is calculated, and it is assigned to the cluster whose centroid is the closest (lines 4-7).

Step 3: Centroid calculation. For each cluster generated in the classification step, its centroid is recalculated (lines 8 and 9).

Step 4: Convergence. If the set of centroids remains unchanged in two consecutive iterations, the algorithm stops; otherwise, it continues in step 2 (lines 10-15).

Literature Review on K-Means

In the more than 60 years since the K-Means algorithm was proposed, many improvements to the K-Means algorithm have been published. Below are some of the most outstanding works organized according to the phases or stages of the algorithm, except for the Centroid calculation phase, of which no improvements have been reported.

In the initialization phase, the improvements have been oriented to select sets of initial centroids that make it possible to reduce the number of iterations of the algorithm and/or improve the quality of the solution.

In one of the most recent articles (Fränti & Sieranoja, 2019), two heuristics are proposed to improve the initialization phase of the K-Means algorithm. It is remarkable the study made by the authors about the most important factors that affect the performance of the algorithm in this phase. One of the most prominent articles (Arthur & Vassilvitskii, 2006) proposes a random method to generate the initial centroids of the algorithm. The first centroid ($i=1$) is generated using a uniform distribution rule over the set of objects. The centroids ($i=2,3,...,k$) are generated by a probability function proportional to the square of the minimum distances of the set of centroids already obtained ($1,...,i-1$).

Katsavounidis, Kuo and Zhang (1994) made an improvement to the algorithm presented by Lloyd (1982). It focuses on the idea that the more distant two objects are, the more likely it belongs to different groups, so it is proposed that the first centroid will be the object with the greatest Euclidean distance to the rest of the objects. Subsequently, the centroids ($i=2,...,k$) are selected in a decreasing way, with respect to the greater distance towards the centroid c_1.

The algorithm presented by Khan and Ahmad (2004) establishes that the closer or similar two objects are, the greater the possibility that both belong to the same group; therefore, they are eliminated from the initial centroid selection method. This method is based on density-based multiscale data condensation (DBMSDC) and allows identifying regions of higher density data with which it forms a descending order list. Subsequently, one of the first objects in the list is selected as the first initial centroid and, all objects that have a radius inversely proportional to the first centroid are discarded. The second centroid will be the next item on the list, which has not been deleted, and the objects around it are discarded. This process is repeated until all initial centroids are obtained.

Saini, Minocha, Ubriani and Sharma (2016) propose an efficient method for the selection of initial centroids with a parallel approach, solving some of the limitations of the K-Means++ algorithm.

In the classification phase, the improvements seek to reduce the number of object-centroids distance calculations. Pérez et al. (2013) propose a heuristic to reduce the number of objects in object-centroid distance calculations. This heuristic is based on the fact that the objects closest to a centroid are less likely to change cluster membership; therefore, identifies and excludes them from future distance calculations. The lower probability of changes cluster membership is determined if the difference in distances between an object x_i to its two closest centroids (c_1, c_2) is greater than the sum of the two largest displacements of centroids (c_x, c_y) in the current iteration. The results show that, in real instances, this heuristic reduces the execution time up to 50.16%, while the quality is reduced only by 6.94%. Pérez et al. (2018) presented an improvement is to this work for instances of Big Data environment, which reduces up to 98% the processing time, and the average quality reduction is 3%.

Poteraş, Mihăescu and Mocanu (2014) observed that after a certain number of iterations, only a small number of objects change cluster membership and propose an exchange boundary between objects that cannot change cluster membership in the next iteration and those who can change. To produce the exchange boundary, the displacement of the centroids is considered, as the number of iterations increases, the number of objects located within the exchange boundary is reduced.

Fahim, Salem, Torkey and Ramadan (2006) presented an improvement to reduce the number of object-centroid distance calculations. To achieve this, an exclusion criterion is established based on the object-centroid distance information, in two successive iterations. This criterion allows us to exclude an object x from the calculations of distance to the rest of the centroids if the distance to the centroid in the iteration $i+1$ is less than the distance in the iteration i. An improvement in the efficiency of this work is presented by Lee and Lin (2012), which allows one or more centroids to be excluded from the calculations by means of a maximum distance criterion.

Pérez et al. (2012) proposed a heuristic that reduces the number of object-centroids calculation of the algorithm. It was observed, by experimental visualization, that an object can only change its membership to a neighboring cluster. Based on this observation, a heuristic is proposed that reduces the number of object-centroids calculations to eight per object in each iteration. They assume that the number of clusters is greater than eight.

In the convergence phase, it is decided when to stop the algorithm. Pérez et al. (2007) proposed a new convergence criterion, which is composed of two conditions, the first is to stop the algorithm when in two successive iterations the squared error of the last iteration exceeds the value the squared error from the previous iteration, the second is to stop the execution when exchanges of objects between clusters are no longer made.

Mexicano et al. (2016) proposed an early convergence criterion, which allows reducing the number of iterations. For this, the centroid with the greatest displacement (denoted by ψ) is calculated in the second iteration, and they stop the algorithm if, in two successive iterations, the greatest displacement in the position of a centroid is less than 0.05ψ.

Pérez, Almanza, and Romero (2018) proposed to stop the algorithm when a balance is reached between the processing time and the quality of the solution; that is when the number of objects that change cluster membership is less than a certain threshold. This heuristic is aimed at solving instances of Big Data type.

In addition to the proposals for improvement in the phases of the K-Means algorithm, there are other works that use other paradigms to improve the performance and quality of the solution. In this sense, there are two studies that use parallelism (Cui, Zhu, Yang, Li & Ji, 2014; Sreedhar, Kasiviswanath & Reddy, 2017).

Literature Review of K-Means in Text Mining

One of the most recent publications on the use of K-Means in document clustering is presented by Sabbagh and Ameri (2020). This article proposes a hybrid unsupervised learning methodology using the K-Means algorithm and the topic modeling technique. The methodology allows building clusters of suppliers based on their capabilities, from data extracted from the websites of manufacturing companies.

Fukuoka, Lindgren, Mintz, Hooper and Aswani (2018) identified motivational profiles (physical activity) in a sample of women who completed a defined time of various physical activities. The process is as follows:

1. The participants answer a survey,
2. The answers are processed using *Word2vec*,
3. Apply the K-Means clustering algorithm, 4) apply the *PCA* technique to reduce the dimensions of the clusters formed by the K-Means algorithm, from 100 to 2 dimensions, to facilitate its visualization.

Kim, Yin, Soto, Blaby and Yoo (2018) presented a project to gather biological data from various sources and evaluate them through computational analysis techniques. The process is as follows

1) Normalize the dataset.
2) Apply PCA to reduce the dimensions and be able to select the most relevant characteristics.
3) Apply the K-Means algorithm contained in the *scikit-learn* package, to group the data by its similarity, through a set of labels (number of groups) and inertia, finally.
4) Find and graph the maximum entropy of the data set.

Alhawarat and Hegazi (2018) grouped, through Text Mining techniques, a set of Arabic documents. It makes use of the Latent Diricklet Allocation and K-Means algorithms. In addition, it evaluates various data sets, cited in other articles, through the use of K-Means. The results emphasize an increase in quality by combining the K-Means and VSM algorithm with respect to K-Means with Euclidean distance.

El Abdouli, Hassouni and Anoun (2017) analyzed the tweets of Moroccan users in order to discover the topics that most interest Moroccan society and then locate the areas where the tweets come from on a map. The tweets were stored in a *Hadoop Distributed File System* (HDSFS), then analyzed using *MapReduce* and *Phyton*. To group the tweets into general topics, they were converted to numerical values, and subsequently, the K-Means algorithm was applied, and through their geographical coordinates, it was possible to plot them on a map. Other authors have performed text analysis of social networks, especially Twitter, through K-Means to extract information, geolocate users, analyze opinions on topics or services, among others (Chen, Shipper & Khan, 2010; Godfrey, Johns, Meyer, Race & Sadek, 2014; Kim, Jeon, Kim, Park & Yu, 2012; Yee Liau & Pei Tan, 2014).

Yao, Pi and Cong (2012) presented a variant K-Means algorithm for grouping texts in Chinese. The main idea is to select the most similar documents from each other. First,

1) Pre-processing of the text,
2) Transformation of the text is done, using the Frequency of the Terms (TF) and Inverse Document Frequency (IDF),
3) To obtain the weighted text, the algorithm K-Means is applied.

When compared to the original K-Means algorithm, the temporal complexity was not affected, while the results of the final grouping were improved.

Habibpour and Khallilpour (2014) proposed a hybrid algorithm between K-Means and K-Nearest-Neighbor (KNN), called NB-K-Means, for the classification of text documents. The proposed algorithm is mainly composed of two phases:

1) Text processing and
2) Document clustering.

In the first phase, a reduction in the number of features of each text document is made, and then, K-Means is applied. In the second phase, KNN is applied to assign each document to one of the clusters, in order to increase the accuracy. The results indicate that the NB-K-Means hybrid algorithm is more accurate than the standard K-Means algorithm. Other authors have proposed hybrid algorithms, due to the favorable results presented, for example, K-Means and Naive Bayes (Allahverdipour & Soleimanian, 2017), K-Means and SOM (Isa, Kallimani & Lee, 2009; Chen, Qin, Liu, Liu & Li, 2010), K-Means and PSO (Cui & Potok, 2005; Sethi & Mishra, 2013; Daoud, Sallam & Wheed, 2017).

Akter, Asa, Uddin, Hossain, Roy and Afjal (2017) presented a summary approach based on the K-means and inverse document frequency term (TF-IDF) algorithms. Its aim is to select and extract important sentences from one or several Bengali documents. First, the incoming documents are pre-processed by tokenization, bypass operation, among others. Then, TF-IDF is applied to score the words, and the sentence score is obtained by adding the score of each word that forms it. Finally, K-Means is applied to select the best-punctuated sentences and produce the final summary. Similar works have been presented (e.g., Shetty & Kallimani, 2017; Prathima & Divakar, 2018; Khan, Qian & Naeem, 2019), in which the K-Means algorithm is combined with various text processing techniques, among which stand out PCA and TF-IDF.

Al-Azzawy and Al-Rufay (2017) applied the K-Means algorithm and a similarity function to a group similar words through their morphology and their syntactic and semantic characteristics. Through stemming, the root words were obtained, which were given to the K-Means algorithm as initial centroids to form groups with a similar or related lexicon.

Proposed Algorithm

To date, several improvements have been made to the K-Means clustering algorithm; however, its complexity is still high, which limits the solution of large instances such as those presented in the paradigm of Big Data. In this sense, this research proposes a new criterion for stop or convergence of the K-Means algorithm, which reduces its temporal complexity.

The improvement of the algorithm proposed in this work arises as a result of the observation of the behavior of the K-Means algorithm, in particular, the values of the objective function and the number of objects changing cluster membership in each iteration. As an example, **Table 1** shows the results of solving an instance of 2500 objects, two dimensions, and eight groups with K-Means. The first column shows the iteration number, the second column the values objective function (SSE) with a precision of 6 decimal places to facilitate the contrast of the values in each iteration, and the third column the objects changing cluster membership.

A large number of executions of the algorithm were analyzed, mostly with large instances, and the following was observed:

a) There is a correlation between the value of the objective function and the number of objects changing cluster membership in each iteration. See **Table 1** (Iterations 2-14).
b) In the firsts iterations, there are large values of the objective function and the number of objects changing cluster membership. See **Table 1** (Iterations 2-14).
c) In general, it was observed that in more than 50% of the last iterations of the algorithm, the value of the objective function was reduced by less than 1%. See the iterations 14-34 in **Figure 1**, **Figure 2**, and **Table 1**.
d) In general, it was observed in iteration sequences that when the number of objects changing clusters no longer has a decreasing monotonic value, the value of the objective function is very close to its optimal value. See iteration 13 and 14 in **Figure 1**, **Figure 2,** and **Table 1**.

Based on these observations, the research question arose: When should the algorithm be stopped so that the execution time is reduced without significantly affecting the quality of the solution?

To answer this question, a new heuristic was developed to accelerate the convergence of the algorithm. We call the *Quick Convergence* heuristic (QC). The QC heuristic establishes a new convergence criterion, which consists of stopping the algorithm when there are no changes in the centroids or when the number of objects changing cluster membership in a previous iteration is less than the number of objects changing cluster membership in the current iteration. That is, the observation d is being used, stopping the algorithm in the first oscillation of the number of objects changing cluster membership.

In the following, we will refer to our improvement and its implementation as QC and the standard or Lloyd algorithm simply as K-Means.

Table 1. Objects changing cluster membership

Iteration	Values of the objective function (SSE)	Objects changing cluster membership
1	5715.397920	NA
2	5260.005051	419
3	5135.289153	194
4	5064.809004	124
5	5021.062415	98
6	4988.064563	77
7	4963.676304	65
8	4947.006291	54
9	4933.333273	46
10	4920.063748	43
11	4909.721229	36
12	4901.495332	24
13	4896.738022	16
14	4891.781032	17
15	4888.977437	13
16	4885.184028	14
17	4882.706662	10
18	4880.974982	9
19	4878.413241	10
20	4875.551467	11
21	4873.604618	11
22	4872.308891	8
23	4870.747080	7
24	4869.136272	8
25	4865.495953	12
26	4865.260470	2
27	4864.948440	2
28	4864.723055	2
29	4863.180195	5
30	4861.970753	4
31	4861.293881	3
32	4860.914155	2
33	4860.774784	1
34	4860.774784	0
35	4860.774784	0

Figure 1. Number of objects changing cluster membership in each iteration

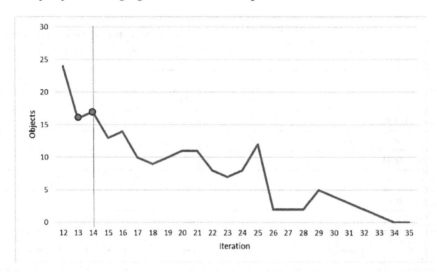

Algorithm 2 describes the proposed improvement of QC. Next, the steps of the algorithm will be described. Lines 2 and 3 show the initialization of the algorithm, in particular the iteration counter t and the variable v^0, which expresses the number of objects changing cluster membership in each iteration, to comply with the logic of the algorithm, a value of $n + 1$ is set. From lines 5 to 8, the object is assigned to the group whose distance to the centroid is closest, note in lines 9 and 10 if the object changes cluster membership, the value of v^t is increased by 1. Line 12 contains the instructions to calculate the new centroids. Line 14 expresses the stop condition of the proposed heuristic, which consists in stopping the algorithm when the number of objects changing cluster membership in the current iteration is greater than the number of objects changing cluster membership in the previous iteration or when there is no change of centroids in two successive iterations. Lines 19 and 20 have instructions for the algorithm to continue iterating when the stop condition is not met.

It is noteworthy to mention that the QC algorithm and its implementation require a minimum of changes to the K-Means algorithm, and the use of additional data structures is minimal since it is reduced to stor-

Figure 2. Value of the objective function in the iterations 12 to 35

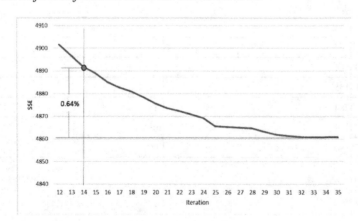

ing the number of objects changing cluster membership in each iteration. These aspects are extremely important in the solution of instances with large volumes of data, such as those presented in Big Data.

Algorithm 2. *Quick Convergence* (QC)

```
1:           # Initialization:
2:               N:= {x₁, ..., xₙ},      M:= {μ₁, ..., μₖ},      t:= 0, v:= 0;
3:               v⁰:= n + 1;
4:           # Classification:
5:               For xᵢ ∈ N and μₖ ∈ M
6:                   Calculate the Euclidean distance from each xᵢ to the μₖ
         centroids;
7:
8:                   Assign object xᵢ to the closest centroid μₖ;
             If xᵢ change of cluster
             then vᵗ is increased by 1
9:
10:
11:          # Centroid calculation:
12:              Calculate centroid μₖ;
13:          # Convergence:
14:              If vᵗ⁻¹ < vᵗ or M:= {μ₁, ..., μₖ} remains unchanged in two con-
    secutive
             iterations
         then:
15:
16:
17:                  Stop the algorithm;
18:              else:
19:                  t = t +1;
20:                  Go to Classification;
21:          End
```

Experimental Validation

This section describes the experimentation to evaluate the performance of QC. The QC enhancement and the K-Means algorithm were implemented in the C programming language. The experiments were carried out on a computer with Intel (Core) i3-2330 processor at 2.20 GHz, 6 GB of RAM, and CentOs 7 operating system.

To validate QC, real and synthetic datasets were used. We used three real datasets or instances, *Letters*, *Skin* taken from the repository of the University of California at Irving, UCI (Blake, & Merz, 2015), and

Table 2. Datasets description

Dataset	N	D	Type
D1	2,250,000	2	
D2	2,248,091	3	Synthetic
D3	2,085,136	4	
Letters	20,000	16	
Skin	245,057	3	Real
Paris	414,528	2	

the Paris dataset taken from the *KEEL*-dataset repository (Alcalá-Fdez et al., 2011). Synthetic datasets D1, D2, and D3 were generated with a uniform distribution.

Table 2 describes the test datasets, in the first column the name of the instance, in the second the number of objects, in the third the number of dimensions and in the fourth, the type of instance. Each instance was resolved 30 times with QC and with K-Means. In each of the 30 executions, different initial centroids randomly generate, were used. In each run, the two algorithms used the same initial centroids.

Table 3. Synthetic dataset results

Dataset	k	K-Means		Quick Convergence		% Reductions	
		Quality (SSE)	Time	Quality (SSE)	Time	Quality	Time
D1	2	500540544	5919	502187323	4108	**-0.33**	**31**
	3	397756095	29036	401238215	13038	-0.88	55
	6	272305798	63102	272613295	35175	-0.11	44
	12	188980538	239963	189213438	88494	-0.12	63
	25	129306907	903698	130227863	152648	-0.71	83
	50	91178737	2622223	91644594	343074	-0.51	87
	100	64247646	7233221	64511427	787373	-0.41	89
D2	2	60697860	9883	60907967	6148	-0.35	38
	3	53891915	24286	53983382	13013	-0.17	46
	6	40346548	202380	40603848	32517	-0.64	84
	12	31636184	345460	31714346	77066	-0.25	78
	25	24251690	1114414	24383167	179858	-0.54	84
	50	19207845	3806789	19277860	436698	-0.36	89
	100	15164566	13332233	15217470	929394	**-0.35**	**93**
D3	2	19933028	8390	20007529	4330	-0.37	48
	3	18413861	24668	18453100	11485	-0.21	53
	6	15353302	552208	15370694	54102	-0.11	90
	12	12174491	464988	12286689	76247	-0.92	84
	25	10061861	1356848	10131358	207058	-0.69	85
	50	8391218	3744178	8431616	420726	-0.48	89

Table 3 shows the results in the solution of synthetic instances. They answer the questions "How much is the quality of the final grouping affected with respect to K-Means?" and "What percentage of K-Means time is reduced with QC?". The first column shows the name of the instance, the second the number of k groups, the third and fourth show the results of K-Means. Time and quality reduction of QC are shown in the fifth and sixth columns. In the seventh and eighth columns are the percentages of reduction of time and quality of QC with respect to K-Means.

The results in **Table 3** are encouraging because they show, in the best case, a reduction of up to 93% of the QC execution time compared to K-Means and a quality reduction of just 0.35%. The worst case had a reduction of 31% of the time and a quality reduction of 0.33%. In general, it was noted that the difference between the best and the worst case is related to the number of groups. Experimentally it was observed that as the number of groups in the instances increases, the number of objects that change groups tend to oscillate more than in those instances with a reduced number of groups.

Figure 3. Reduction time

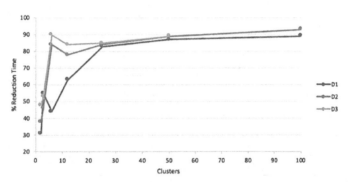

The results of time reduction and quality reduction of QC with respect to K-Means are shown graphically in **Figure 3** and **Figure 4**. It is noteworthy to mention that as the number of groups increases, the reduction in time is greater. On the other hand, **Figure 4** shows that in no case the reduction in quality was greater than 1% and for values of k between 50 and 100, the loss of quality was in the range of approximately 0.3% to 0.5%.

Figure 4. Reduction quality

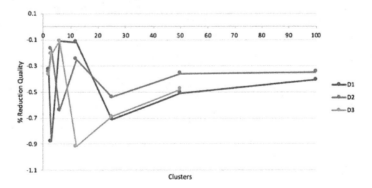

Table 4. Real dataset results

Dataset	k	K-Means		Quick Convergence (QC)		% Reductions	
		Quality (SSE)	Time	Quality (SSE)	Time	Quality	Time
Letters	40	99771	26035	100448	5103	-0.67	80
	50	94613	45502	95572	6171	-1.01	86
	60	91263	41009	92115	9502	-0.93	77
	70	88549	42470	88785	13861	-0.26	67
	80	86347	48416	86953	11123	-0.7	77
	90	83953	56225	84343	12868	-0.46	77
	100	82630	66254	83260	13638	-0.76	79
Skin	3	11812247	1805	12650321	521	-7.09	71
	6	8163138	2777	8436028	1294	**-3.34**	**53**
	12	5557820	9130	5801603	2260	-4.38	75
	25	3909001	27702	4119158	5355	-5.37	81
	50	2678633	76735	2794209	10187	-4.31	87
	100	1899908	231356	2020253	20116	**-6.33**	**91**
Paris	2	9794	1446	10038	410	-2.48	72
	3	8130	2244	8338	1018	-2.56	55
	6	6094	5989	6239	2027	-2.38	66
	12	4233	16776	4382	3499	-3.53	79
	25	2683	29387	2811	6529	-4.77	78
	50	1791	74954	1835	15517	-2.45	79
	100	1216	135626	1236	34159	-1.7	75

Table 4 shows the results of solving real instances. The first column shows the name of the instance, the second the number of *k* groups, the third and fourth show the results of K-Means. Time and quality

Figure 6. Reduction quality

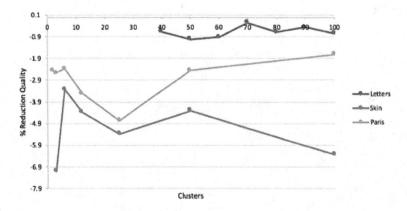

Figure 5. Reduction time

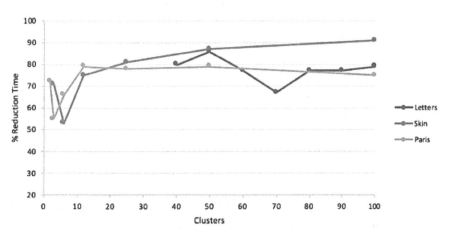

reduction of QC are shown in the fifth and sixth columns. In the seventh and eighth columns are the percentages of reduction of time and quality of QC with respect to K-Means.

The results shown in **Table 4** show that the greatest reduction in QC execution time compared to K-Means was 91%, with a quality reduction of 6.33%. The worst case has a 53% time reduction with a quality reduction of 3.34%.

The results of time reduction and quality reduction of QC with respect to K-Means are shown graphically in **Figure 5** and **Figure 6**. It is noteworthy to mention that as the number of groups increases, the reduction in time is greater. On the other hand, in **Figure 6,** it is observed that with the *Letters* instance, the quality reduction in no case exceeds 1%. In the case of the *Skin* instance, the quality reduction is in the range between approximately 3% and 7%.

FUTURE RESEARCH DIRECTIONS

We believe that the principles of this work can be useful in the generation of new hybrid algorithms, which integrate relevant aspects of other heuristics reported in the literature in order to include other factors that intervene in the performance of the clustering algorithms, for example, heuristics to obtain better initial centroids.

In recent years, parallel processing technology has been significantly improved, and its use is increasingly increasing. It is reasonable to think that if some improvements of K-Means are parallelized, the solution time can be reduced, contributing to the solution of Big Data instances.

CONCLUSION

This work presents an improvement to the K-Means algorithm, which we call *Quick Convergence*. In this improvement, a new stop condition or convergence criterion is proposed, which consists of stopping the algorithm when the number of objects that change group membership in the current iteration is greater than in the previous iteration.

From intensive computer experimentation on real and synthetic data sets, we have found that, in general, our heuristics significantly reduce the number of iterations with a relatively small decrease in the quality of the solutions produced. To compare the results quantitatively, the QC time was expressed as a percentage of the time used by the standard K-Means algorithm. Similarly, the quality was expressed as a percentage of the quality of the standard K-Means algorithm. The results are encouraging because they show a reduction of up to 93% in QC execution time compared to K-Means and a reduction in quality of only 0.35% in synthetic data sets. In real data sets, time is reduced by 91% and quality by less than 6.33%.

An important feature of QC is that its implementation requires minimal change to the standard K-Means algorithm code and negligible additional memory resources, which may have advantages over other proposed heuristics. Furthermore, our proposed convergence criterion is not inconsistent with any improvement related to the other K-Means steps.

Finally, it is noteworthy that in the experiments, the best results tend to correspond to the largest data sets considered, namely those in which the *nkd* product is high, which is encouraging for use in solving large instances like Big Data.

REFERENCES

Akter, S., Asa, A. S., Uddin, M. P., Hossain, M. D., Roy, S. K., & Afjal, M. I. (2017). An extractive text summarization technique for Bengali document (s) using K-means clustering algorithm. In *2017 IEEE International Conference on Imaging, Vision & Pattern Recognition (icIVPR)* (pp. 1-6). IEEE. 10.1109/ICIVPR.2017.7890883

Al-Azzawy, D. S., & Al-Rufaye, F. M. L. (2017). Arabic words clustering by using K-means algorithm. In *2017 Annual Conference on New Trends in Information & Communications Technology Applications (NTICT)* (pp. 263-267). IEEE.

Alcalá-Fdez, J., Fernández, A., Luengo, J., Derrac, J., García, S., Sánchez, L., & Herrera, F. (2011). Keel data-mining software tool: data set repository, integration of algorithms and experimental analysis framework. *Journal of Multiple-Valued Logic & Soft Computing*, 17.

Alhawarat, M., & Hegazi, M. (2018). Revisiting K-Means and Topic Modeling, a Comparison Study to Cluster Arabic Documents. *IEEE Access: Practical Innovations, Open Solutions*, 6, 42740–42749. doi:10.1109/ACCESS.2018.2852648

Allahverdipour, A., & Gharehchopogh, F. (2017). A New Hybrid Model of K-Means and Naïve Bayes Algorithms for Feature Selection in Text Documents Categorization. *Journal of Advances in Computer Research*, 8(4), 73–86.

Aloise, D., Deshpande, A., Hansen, P., & Popat, P. (2009). NP-hardness of Euclidean sum-of-squares clustering. *Machine Learning*, 75(2), 245–248. doi:10.100710994-009-5103-0

Arthur, D., & Vassilvitskii, S. (2006). k-means++: The advantages of careful seeding. Stanford.

Blake, C., & Merz, C. J. (2015). *UCI repository of machine learning databases*. Department of Information and Computer Science, University of California, Irvine, CA. Retrieved from https://www.ics.uci.edu/mlearn/MLRepository

Bock, H. H. (2008). Origins and extensions of the k-means algorithm in cluster analysis. *Journal Electronique d'Histoire des Probabilités et de la Statistique Electronic Journal for History of Probability and Statistics*, *4*(2).

Chen, Q., Shipper, T., & Khan, L. (2010). Tweets mining using WIKIPEDIA and impurity cluster measurement. In *2010 IEEE International Conference on Intelligence and Security Informatics* (pp. 141-143). IEEE. 10.1109/ISI.2010.5484758

Chen, Y., Qin, B., Liu, T., Liu, Y., & Li, S. (2010). The Comparison of SOM and K-means for Text Clustering. *Computer and Information Science*, *3*(2), 268–274. doi:10.5539/cis.v3n2p268

Cui, X., Potok, T. E., & Palathingal, P. (2005, June). Document clustering using particle swarm optimization. In *Proceedings 2005 IEEE Swarm Intelligence Symposium, 2005. SIS 2005.* (pp. 185-191). IEEE. 10.1109/SIS.2005.1501621

Cui, X., Zhu, P., Yang, X., Li, K., & Ji, C. (2014). Optimized big data K-Means clustering using MapReduce. *The Journal of Supercomputing*, *70*(3), 1249–1259. doi:10.100711227-014-1225-7

Daoud, A. S., Sallam, A., & Wheed, M. E. (2017, September). Improving Arabic document clustering using K-means algorithm and Particle Swarm Optimization. In *2017 Intelligent Systems Conference (IntelliSys)* (pp. 879-885). IEEE. doi:10.1109/IntelliSys.2017.8324233

El Abdouli, A., Hassouni, L., & Anoun, H. (2017, April). Mining tweets of Moroccan users using the framework Hadoop, NLP, K-means and basemap. In *2017 Intelligent Systems and Computer Vision (ISCV)* (pp. 1-7). IEEE.

Fahim, A. M., Salem, A. M., Torkey, F. A., & Ramadan, M. A. (2006). An efficient enhanced K-Means clustering algorithm. *Journal of Zhejiang University. Science A*, *7*(10), 1626–1633. doi:10.1631/jzus.2006.A1626

Fränti, P., & Sieranoja, S. (2019). How much can k-means be improved by using better initialization and repeats? *Pattern Recognition*, *93*, 95–112. doi:10.1016/j.patcog.2019.04.014

Fukuoka, Y., Lindgren, T. G., Mintz, Y. D., Hooper, J., & Aswani, A. (2018). Applying natural language processing to understand motivational profiles for maintaining physical activity after a mobile app and accelerometer-based intervention: The mPED randomized controlled trial. *JMIR mHealth and uHealth*, *6*(6), e10042. doi:10.2196/10042 PMID:29925491

Gantz, J., & Reinsel, D. (2011). Extracting value from chaos. *IDC iview*, *1142*(2011), 1-12.

Godfrey, D., Johns, C., Meyer, C., Race, S., & Sadek, C. (2014). *A case study in text mining: Interpreting twitter data from world cup tweets.* arXiv preprint arXiv:1408.5427

Habibpour, R., & Khalilpour, K. (2014). A new hybrid k-means and k-nearest-neighbor algorithms for text document clustering. *International Journal of Academic Research*, *6*(3), 79–84. doi:10.7813/2075-4124.2014/6-3/A.12

Ingersoll, G. S., Morton, T. S., & Farris, A. L. (2012). Taming text: How to find, organize and manipulate it. Shelter Island.

Isa, D., Kallimani, V. P., & Lee, L. H. (2009). Using the self organizing map for clustering of text documents. *Expert Systems with Applications*, *36*(5), 9584–9591. doi:10.1016/j.eswa.2008.07.082

Jain, A. K. (2010). Data clustering: 50 years beyond K-means. *Pattern Recognition Letters*, *31*(8), 651–666. doi:10.1016/j.patrec.2009.09.011

Jancey, R. C. (1966). Multidimensional group analysis. *Australian Journal of Botany*, *14*(1), 127–130. doi:10.1071/BT9660127

Katsavounidis, I., Kuo, C. C. J., & Zhang, Z. (1994). A new initialization technique for generalized Lloyd iteration. *IEEE Signal Processing Letters*, *1*(10), 144–146. doi:10.1109/97.329844

Khan, R., Qian, Y., & Naeem, S. (2019). Extractive based Text Summarization Using K-Means and TF-IDF. *International Journal of Information Engineering and Electronic Business*, *3*(3), 33–44. doi:10.5815/ijieeb.2019.03.05

Khan, S. S., & Ahmad, A. (2004). Cluster center initialization algorithm for K-means clustering. *Pattern Recognition Letters*, *25*(11), 1293–1302. doi:10.1016/j.patrec.2004.04.007

Kim, C., Yin, P., Soto, C. X., Blaby, I. K., & Yoo, S. (2018). Multimodal biological analysis using NLP and expression profile. In 2018 New York Scientific Data Summit (NYSDS) (pp. 1-4). IEEE. doi:10.1109/NYSDS.2018.8538944

Kim, S., Jeon, S., Kim, J., Park, Y. H., & Yu, H. (2012). Finding core topics: Topic extraction with clustering on tweet. In *2012 Second International Conference on Cloud and Green Computing* (pp. 777-782). IEEE. 10.1109/CGC.2012.120

Lee, S. S., & Lin, J. C. (2012). An accelerated K-Means clustering algorithm using selection and erasure rules. *Journal of Zhejiang University SCIENCE C*, *13*(10), 761–768. doi:10.1631/jzus.C1200078

Lloyd, S. (1982). Least squares quantization in PCM. *IEEE Transactions on Information Theory*, *28*(2), 129–137. doi:10.1109/TIT.1982.1056489

MacQueen, J. (1967). Some methods for classification and analysis of multivariate observations. In *Proceedings of the fifth Berkeley symposium on mathematical statistics and probability* (*Vol. 1*, No. 14, pp. 281-297). Academic Press.

Mahajan, M., Nimbhorkar, P., & Varadarajan, K. (2012). The planar k-means problem is NP-hard. *Theoretical Computer Science*, *442*, 13–21. doi:10.1016/j.tcs.2010.05.034

Mexicano, A., Cervantes, S., Rodríguez, R., Pérez, J., Almanza, N., Jiménez, M. A., & Azuara, A. (2016). Identifying stable objects for accelerating the classification phase of k-means. In *International Conference on P2P, Parallel, Grid, Cloud and Internet Computing* (pp. 903-912). Springer.

Pérez, J., Almanza, N., Ruiz-Vanoye, J., Pazos, R., Sáenz, S., Rodríguez, J., & Martínez, A. (2018). A-means: Improving the cluster assignment phase of k-means for Big Data. *International Journal of Combinatorial Optimization Problems and Informatics*, *9*(2), 3–10.

Pérez, J., Almanza, N. N., & Romero, D. (2018). Balancing effort and benefit of K-means clustering algorithms in Big Data realms. *PLoS One*, *13*(9). PMID:30183705

Pérez, J., Mexicano, A., Santaolaya, R., Hidalgo, M., Moreno, A., & Pazos, R. (2012). Improvement to the K-Means algorithm through a heuristics based on a bee honeycomb structure. In *2012 Fourth World Congress on Nature and Biologically Inspired Computing (NaBIC)* (pp. 175-180). IEEE. 10.1109/NaBIC.2012.6402258

Pérez, J., Pazos, R., Cruz, L., Reyes, G., Basave, R., & Fraire, H. (2007). Improving the efficiency and efficacy of the K-Means clustering algorithm through a new convergence condition. In *International Conference on Computational Science and Its Applications* (pp. 674-682). Springer. 10.1007/978-3-540-74484-9_58

Pérez, J., Pires, C. E., Balby, L., Mexicano, A., & Hidalgo, M. Á. (2013). Early classification: A new heuristic to improve the classification step of K-Means. *Journal of Information and Data Management*, *4*(2), 94–103.

Poteraş, C. M., Mihăescu, M. C., & Mocanu, M. (2014). An optimized version of the K-Means clustering algorithm. In *2014 Federated Conference on Computer Science and Information Systems* (pp. 695-699). IEEE. 10.15439/2014F258

Prathima, M. R., & Divakar, H. R. (2018). Automatic Extractive Text Summarization Using K-Means Clustering. *International Journal on Computer Science and Engineering*, *6*(6), 782–787.

Sabbagh, R., & Ameri, F. (2020). A Framework Based on K-Means Clustering and Topic Modeling for Analyzing Unstructured Manufacturing Capability Data. *Journal of Computing and Information Science in Engineering*, *20*(1), 1–13. doi:10.1115/1.4044506

Saini, A., Minocha, J., Ubriani, J., & Sharma, D. (2016). New approach for clustering of big data: DisK-Means. In *2016 International Conference on Computing, Communication and Automation (ICCCA)* (pp. 122-126). IEEE. 10.1109/CCAA.2016.7813702

Selim, S. Z., & Ismail, M. A. (1984). K-means-type algorithms: A generalized convergence theorem and characterization of local optimality. *IEEE Transactions on Pattern Analysis and Machine Intelligence*, *PAMI-6*(1), 81–87. doi:10.1109/TPAMI.1984.4767478 PMID:21869168

Sethi, C., & Mishra, G. (2013). A Linear PCA based hybrid K-Means PSO algorithm for clustering large dataset. *International Journal of Scientific and Engineering Research*, *4*(6), 1559–1566.

Shetty, K., & Kallimani, J. S. (2017). Automatic extractive text summarization using K-Means clustering. In *2017 International Conference on Electrical, Electronics, Communication, Computer, and Optimization Techniques (ICEECCOT)* (pp. 1-9). IEEE. 10.1109/ICEECCOT.2017.8284627

Sreedhar, C., Kasiviswanath, N., & Reddy, P. C. (2017). Clustering large datasets using K-means modified inter and intra clustering (KM-I2C) in Hadoop. *Journal of Big Data*, *4*(1), 27. doi:10.118640537-017-0087-2

Steinhaus, H. (1956). Sur la division des corp materiels en parties. *Bull. Acad. Polon. Sci*, *1*(804), 801–804.

Wu, X., Kumar, V., Quinlan, J. R., Ghosh, J., Yang, Q., Motoda, H., ... Steinberg, D. (2008). Top 10 algorithms in data mining. *Knowledge and Information Systems*, *14*(1), 1–37. doi:10.100710115-007-0114-2

Yao, M., Pi, D., & Cong, X. (2012). Chinese text clustering algorithm based k-means. *Physics Procedia*, *33*, 301–307. doi:10.1016/j.phpro.2012.05.066

Yee Liau, B., & Pei Tan, P. (2014). Gaining customer knowledge in low cost airlines through text mining. *Industrial Management & Data Systems*, *114*(9), 1344–1359. doi:10.1108/IMDS-07-2014-0225

KEY TERMS AND DEFINITIONS

Big Data: Although there is no consensus on how much should be considered Big Data, it is possible to define it as the point at which the computing capabilities of a given piece of equipment are exceeded.

Clustering: The clustering consists in partitioning a set of n objects in $k \geq 2$ non-empty subsets (called clusters) in such a way that the objects in any cluster have similar attributes and, at the same time, are different from the objects in any other cluster.

Data Mining: Process of discovering relevant patterns in a dataset.

Filtering: Set of techniques for removing words from a text.

Lemmatization: Relates a derived word to its canonical form.

NLP: Part of Artificial Intelligence that allows machines to understand and interpret human language.

Normalization: Tasks aimed at putting all text on an equal footing, i.e. removing punctuation, converting numbers into words, among others.

Stemming: Methods aimed to convert the derived words into the word origin or root.

Text Mining: Process of analyzing textual sources, with the aim of identifying relevant patterns.

Tokenization: Task of dividing a sentence, paragraph or a whole text into smaller units such as words or terms (tokens).

Chapter 14
Pronominal Anaphora Resolution on Spanish Text

Alonso García
Universidad Autónoma de Ciudad Juárez, Mexico

Martha Victoria González
https://orcid.org/0000-0002-9366-9998
Universidad Autónoma de Ciudad Juárez, Mexico

Francisco López-Orozco
Universidad Autónoma de Ciudad Juárez, Mexico

Lucero Zamora
Universidad Autónoma de Ciudad Juárez, Mexico

ABSTRACT

Recent technological advances have allowed the development of numerous natural language processing applications with which users frequently interact. When interacting with this type of application, users often search for the economy of words, which promotes the use of pronouns, thereby highlighting the well-known anaphora problem. This chapter describes a proposal to approach the pronominal anaphora for the Spanish language. A set of rules (based on the Eagle standard) was designed to identify the referents of personal pronouns through the structure of the grammatical tags of the words. The proposed algorithm uses the online Freeling service to perform tokenization and tagging tasks. The performance of the algorithm was compared with an online version of Freeling, and the proposed algorithm shows better performance.

DOI: 10.4018/978-1-7998-4730-4.ch014

Copyright © 2021, IGI Global. Copying or distributing in print or electronic forms without written permission of IGI Global is prohibited.

1 INTRODUCTION

Natural Language Processing (NLP) is a branch of Artificial Intelligence (AI) that helps computers understand, interpret, and manipulate human language. This branch has a lot of problems where each one has a specific treatment. Anaphora resolution is one of these problems, where the main objective is to understand references to earlier items in a text fragment or a sentence (Karthikeyan & Karthikeyani,2013). On the other hand, cataphora is another problem where the main objective is to understand references to later items in the discourse or a sentence. This chapter deals with the anaphora resolution, specifically with the pronominal anaphora in the Spanish language.

Pronoun anaphora has relevant importance because it is used in different application areas such as the case of computerized translators, which process text and even voice in order to rewrite it in some other language. This process requires the application of the pronominal anaphora in order to identify all the cases in which there is an anaphora, and by solving it, it is possible to transcribe the text as best as possible and preserve the same meaning or idea that it was originally intended to express. Another area where anaphora is applied is in the area of automatic text summarization, which seeks to summarize texts through various NLP techniques, but as in the previous case, it is important to maintain the original idea of the text, for which it is important to treat anaphora cases with the aim of preserving the meaning of the idea or the original text. Even in areas such as voice recognition, in which users interact with software applications through their voice by entering commands or instructions, pronouns are generally used to avoid repeating names of devices or tasks previously mentioned by users, so the anaphora resolution is of great relevance.

Exist different kinds of pronouns like *personal pronouns, demonstrative pronouns, possessive pronouns, interrogative pronouns* (Palomar et al., 2001). This chapter describes a proposal to approach the pronominal anaphora in texts in the Spanish language. For this purpose, it is important to identify the grammatical information of the words that make up a sentence. For this task, a Freeling endpoint was used. Freeling endpoint assigns a tag to words according to their grammatical function within the sentence. A tag contains the grammatical information of a word, encoded based on the Eagle standard. This grammatical information was used in this proposal to generate a set of rules that allowed addressing the anaphora problem.

The remaining chapter is organized as follows. Section 2 is providing a general description of the types of anaphora that have been addressed in the literature. In addition, some of the considerations to be taken into account during the process of co-referencing the anaphora and its possible references are shown. Finally, the Eagle standard tag and its importance for the word tagging process are mentioned. Section 3 describes the problem of the resolution of the pronominal anaphora and describes the types of pronouns most addressed in the literature, as well as some examples of them and the morphological analysis carried out on each example. Finally, the importance of anaphora resolution in different areas of NLP is mentioned. Section 4 presents the state of the art of anaphora resolution in the Spanish language in which some of the works carried out addressing this problem using different techniques are described. In addition, some of the tools mostly used in the literature for the resolution of the anaphora, and some of its applications and restrictions are shown since not all of them have support for the resolution of the anaphora for the Spanish language. Section 5 describes the proposed solution for the resolution of the pronominal anaphora in texts in the Spanish language for personal pronouns. This section shows the architecture of the proposed algorithm, the main phases, and what each of these phases consists of are described. Section 6 describes the tests performed on the algorithm. In addition, a comparison was made with the online Freeling service. Finally, the results obtained from both tools are shown. Section 7 presents some of the future work that may be developed from the proposal made in this chapter. Finally, Section 8 describes the conclusions obtained from the development of this proposal, as well as from the tests carried out on the algorithm.

2 TYPES OF ANAPHORA

This section describes the types of anaphora and some considerations that could help treat the anaphora resolution. Some examples of them are described below.

In computational linguistics, anaphora resolution is concerned with determining the relation between two entities in the text. The main task of this process is to find the antecedent of an anaphora (Seddik & Farghaly, 2014). There are various types of anaphora:

- **Pronominal anaphora:** This is the anaphora addressed in this chapter, which has the characteristic what do not have an independent meaning, necessarily needs to have an antecedent before the pronoun has a concrete meaning.
- **Lexical anaphora:** This anaphora occurs when the expression reference is defined by a description or proper nouns. Generally, synonyms or superordinates are used.
- **Comparative anaphora:** This type of anaphora occurs when exists a lexical modifier in the sentence or when exists comparative adjectives. An example of a lexical modifier could be the word *other* or *another,* and an example of a comparative adjective could be the word *better* or *greater.*
- **One-anaphora:** One-anaphors are anaphoric noun phrases headed by one. Determining the sense of a one-anaphora requires using at least one other noun phrase in the text (Gardiner, 2003). Below is an example of this type of anaphora:
  a. *John has a red jumper.*
  b. *He wears it on Sundays.*
- **Definite noun phrase anaphora:** The processing of NP anaphors in discourse is argued to be grounded in cognitive representation and communicative principles. Derived from the Griceian maxim of quantity, the proposed theory views NP anaphora processing as an optimization process based on the principle that processing cost, defined in terms of conceptual representation, should serve some discourse function identifying the antecedent and/or adding new information (Almor,1970). Below is an example of this type of anaphora:
  a. *A robin ate the fruit. The robin seemed very satisfied.*

Considerations for the Anaphora Resolution Process

Exist some characteristics that help to find the antecedent of an anaphor. These characteristics provide information about the analyzed word, such as Khadiga (2014) mentions in his work.

- **Distance between the anaphoric expression and its antecedent:** In some languages such as English and in some cases Spanish, the referent of a pronoun is usually very close in terms of words, that is, when there is a pronoun, the proximity with its referent is a short length of words.

- **Lexical restrictions:** This feature is very important because it provides information about each word that is analyzed. Among the information provided is: the gender, and if the word is plural or singular, in other words, a pronoun must agree in gender and number with the noun. These data are important because they help in the process of identifying referents since, in the case of a male gender pronoun, it must have a referent of the same gender. In the same sense, if the pronoun is singular, it means that its referent must also be singular. It is worth mentioning that there are exceptions due to the grammatical complexity that derives from each language; this chapter describes some of the exceptions that were addressed in order to develop the proposed algorithm.
- **Syntactic roles (Grammatical relationship):** They are functional relationships between constituents in a clause. The standard examples of syntactic roles from traditional grammar are the subject, a direct object, and an indirect object. In recent times, the syntactic roles typified by the traditional categories of subject and object, have assumed an important role in linguistic theorizing, within a variety of approaches ranging from generative grammar to functional and cognitive theories.

For the Spanish language, the distance between the anaphoric expression and its antecedent seems to be a good key-point, but there are tokens used in the texts which prevent correctly identifying the disagreement between both expressions, that is, the anaphora and its antecedent. In the other hand, lexical restrictions provide important information like the gender and the number of a word as already mentioned above. This helps to treat the Spanish language with a subset of pronouns and backgrounds, but there are special cases of pronouns such as "*ellos, quienes, nosotros*" which apply to both male and female gender.

Eagle Standard

Computer Science Department (2020) provides a series of word tagging rules which are widely used in the literature generally in NLP areas. The importance of these rules or norms is that through them, there are various tag methods which are based on this standard. The proposal presented in this chapter is based on the identification of pronouns and nouns, for which the specifications defined by the Eagle standard were used. For the identification of pronouns, the specification shown in Table 1 was used, and for the identification of nouns, the specification shown in Table 2 was used. Table 1 describes the composition of tags in the case of pronouns, and Table 2 describes the composition of the tags in the case of nouns. These tags have important relevance in the development of the proposed algorithm since, by means of these tags, it is possible to identify pronouns and referents.

Tables 1 and 2 are composed of four columns. The first column refers to the position of the first component of the tag. The second column refers to the attribute that this component represents. The third column refers to the value or characteristic to which it refers. The fourth column refers to the letter to be placed on the tag. An example of the meaning of a tag is described below:

Tag: *NPMS000*

The tag shown above can be interpreted with the information provided in Table 1 because it is a noun. Based on the order of each letter on the tag from left to right, the meaning is the following "*singular masculine proper name*".

Table 1. Subjects tag composition

Subjects			
Pos.	**Attribute**	**Value**	**Code**
1	Category	Name	N
2	Type	Common	C
		Own	P
3	Genre	Male	M
		Female	F
		Common	C
4	Number	Single	S
		Plural	P
		Invariable	N
5	Case	-	0
6	Semantic Gender	-	0
7	Grade	Appreciative	A

3 PRONOMINAL ANAPHORA RESOLUTION

Pronominal anaphora can occur before any type of pronoun such as interrogative, personal, possessive, relative, among others. For each type of pronoun, a different treatment corresponds to how the anaphora is approached to find its referent in a text. In this chapter, the proposal is focused on the resolution of the anaphora of personal pronouns.

Personal Pronouns

As already mentioned above, pronominal anaphora resolution solves the references to earlier items in the discourse or sentence. An example of this in the Spanish language could be the following sentence:

"Antonio considera que es una barbaridad que sigan subiendo los precios. Él sería partidario de no aumentar el coste de la vida."

The previous sentence is an example that has a third person personal pronoun whose earlier referent appears at the start of the sentence. Below is an example of how the morphological analyzer assigns a tag to each word in the previous sentence.

sigan ... subiendo ... los precios.... Él sería
NPMS000 VMIP3S0 CS VSIP3S0 DI0FS0 NCFS000 PR0CN00
Antonio ... considera ... que ... es una ... barbaridad ... que
VMSP3P0 VMG0000 DA0MP0 NCMP000 Fp PP3MS00 VSIC1S0
partidario ... de no ... aumentar ... el coste ... de la
AQ0MS00 SP RN VMN0000 DA0MS0 NCMS000 SP DA0FS0

Table 2. Pronouns tag composition

Pronouns			
Pos.	**Attribute**	**Value**	**Code**
1	Category	Pronoun	P
2	Type	Personal	P
		Demonstrative	D
		Possessive	X
		Undefined	I
		Interrogative	T
		Relative	R
3	Person	First	1
		Second	2
		Third	3
4	Genre	Male	M
		Female	F
		Common	C
5	Number	Single	S
		Plural	P
		Invariable	N
6	Case	Nominative	N
		Accusative	A
		Dative	D
		Oblique	O
7	Holder	1st person-sg	1
		2nd person-sg	2
		3rd person	0
		1st person-pl	4
		2nd person-pl	5
8	Politeness	Polite	P

vida .
NCFS000 Fp

In the sentence shown above, the anaphora is between the pronoun "*Él*" and the noun "Antonio", whose tags can be interpreted with the specifications shown in Table 1 and Table 2. The tag of the word "*Antonio*" (*NPMS000*) is interpreted as a singular masculine proper name. On the other hand, the tag of the pronoun "*Él*" (*PP3MS00*) is interpreted as a singular masculine third person personal pronoun.

Based on the literature, it has been found that the components of a tag help identify this type of co-reference. This is because, in the literature, it refers to the fact that in the pronominal anaphor, a pronoun refers to a noun as was done in the previous example.

The pronominal anaphora for the case of personal pronouns, as shown above, is the issue addressed in this chapter as well as the documentation of some features that may help during the solution of the anaphora.

Possessive Pronouns

Possessive pronouns have possession as their main value, but they also have a relational value, since they link the possessed with one or more possessors. An example of this type of pronoun is presented below:

"Antonio no está convencido de que pueda recuperar su coche. Su amigo le ha recomendado comprarse otro. El problema es que a Antonio le gustaba mucho el suyo."

The output obtained from the morphological analyzer applied to the previous sentence is presented below:

Antonio … no está … convencido … de que … pueda … recuperar
NPMS000 RN VMIP3S0 VMP00SM SP CS VMSP3S0 VMN0000
su … coche. … Su … amigo … le ha
DP3CSN NCMS000 FP DP3CSN NCMS000 PP3CSD0 VAIP3S0
recomendado … comprarse … otro. … El problema … es
VMP00SM VMN0000 PI0MS00 FP DA0MS0 NCMS000 VSIP3S0
que … a Antonio … le gustaba … mucho … el suyo
CS SP NPMS000 PP3CSD0 VMII3S0 RG DA0MS0 PX0MS3N

As can be seen in the morphological analysis presented above, the pronoun "*suyo*" is an indicator of possession, which refers to *Antonio's car*, which is finally the referent of this type of anaphora in this example.

Relative Pronouns

A relative pronoun is used to refer to nouns mentioned previously, whether they are people, places, things, animals, or ideas. Relative pronouns can be used to join two sentences. There are only a few relative pronouns in the English language. The most common are *which, that, whose, whoever, whomever, who*, and *whom*. In some situations, the grammatical function of the words *what, when*, and *where* is that of a relative pronoun. Because there are only a few of them, there are also just a few rules for using relative pronouns. In the case of the Spanish language, some examples of this are "*el que*", "*quienes*", "*cuyo*", "*donde*". An example of this type of pronouns are shown below:

"El ciclista que ganó la carrera entrenó duro."

The output obtained from the morphological analyzer applied to the previous sentence is presented below:

El ciclista … que … ganó … la Carrera … entrenó

DA0MS0 NCCS000 PR0CN00 VMIS3S0 DA0FS0 NCFS000 VMIS3S0
duro .
AQ0MS00 FP

As can be seen in the previous analysis, the pronoun *"que"* is a relative pronoun that refers to the cyclist, who is a noun and who also won the race.

As can be seen in the previous examples, there exist different types of pronouns, and although the resolution of the anaphora is similar for all types, each pronoun type needs specific rules to be treated by a pronominal anaphora resolution algorithm. Even with the new AI techniques, it is too difficult to deal with anaphora resolution, especially for the Spanish language, because understanding natural language is a daunting task for computers. The main difficulty arises from the fact that natural languages are inherently ambiguous (Mitkov, 2014). Generally, humans can select the appropriate meaning from a set of possible interpretations of a sentence, which is a complex task for a computer due, among other reasons, to its limited "knowledge" and lack of ability to deal with complex contextual situations (Lappin & Leass, 1994).

Among the different types of anaphora, pronominal anaphora resolution is applied to all new smart technologies from voice or written text to other AI technologies that address some NLP issues. The treatment for the resolution of the anaphora has evolved conforming to the implementation of new tools provided by IA, such as ontologies. Such is the case of Toledo, Valtierra, Guzmán, Cuevas, and Méndez (2014), who wrote a document in which he describes how to build a tool for the solution of anaphora in the Spanish language. In this work, the authors developed a tool that addresses anaphora resolution by using a morphological analyzer, which is used to write rules for each type of pronominal anaphora case. For special cases where it is difficult to write a rule, the authors implemented ontologies that allow them to deal with special cases of pronouns when the rules do not allow it. Another similar case is the work of Ruiz (2012), which treat with pronominal anaphora through a software tool called *FungramKB*. FungramKB is another language processing suite tool that offers some functions and techniques to deal with natural language. The author uses morphological, semantic, and syntax analysis to solve the anaphora problems presented in texts. However, there are special cases of pronouns in which the aforementioned analysis fails, and the author uses AI techniques to solve these special cases.

At this point, it is important to mention the large number of tools, articles, and documents that treat the anaphora resolution for the English language. On the other hand, for the Spanish language, there is not a great variety of tools, articles, or any document that treat with the anaphora resolution. Exist a lot of commercial tools that people can use to solve pronominal anaphora resolution. Additionally, there are also public and open source tools. However, in both cases, the existing tools are designed to process text in English and Chinese languages, but not for the Spanish language. Anaphora researches agree with the mean of using semantic analysis to solve complete and suitable anaphora problems. The problem with this approach is that semantic analyzers are not dependable, and a few exist just for the English language.

4 STATE OF THE ART FOR PRONOMINAL ANAPHORA RESOLUTION

In this section, some of the works related to anaphora resolution are presented. Additionally, some tools that address some type of anaphora are also described.

Research Work

The anaphora problem has been addressed in the literature through different approaches and tools. Such is the case of the work of Toledo and Valtierra (2011), which describes the construction of a tool for the detection of pronominal anaphora in the Spanish language through the implementation of a morphological analyzer and the adaptation of a set of rules to define the correlation between pronouns and references.

Another work that addresses the anaphora problem for the Spanish language is that of Toledo, Valtierra, Guzman, Cuevas and Mendez (2014). In this work, a tool called *AnaPro* was developed. This tool solves problems of direct anaphora. They approached the anaphora problem through ontologies that belong to the area of AI and through the use of a grammar tagger. Through a series of tests, they have fed the knowledge bases so that through the processing of each tagged word and the use of ontologies, the co-reference between the pronoun and the noun can be established. That is, when a word is processed, it is analyzed through ontologies to find relationships that have already been defined within the ontology database and thus be able to identify the referent of that word. The use of ontologies was very useful because it allows for disambiguating the text to be processed, which facilitates the process of identification of referents.

The work of Palomar et al. (2001) addresses the pronominal anaphora for personal, demonstrative, and reflexive pronouns. In their proposal, they have developed a list of restrictions and preferences for the different types of pronouns mentioned above. In addition to this, they have documented the importance of knowledge factors such as lexical, morphological, syntactic, and statistical factors to address the anaphora problem.

In the work of Peral and Fernandez (2003) in which the anaphora problem is addressed by translating texts between Spanish and English. They are based on the manipulation of the text by translating it to English since this language has even greater support in this type of problem in which, in addition, they have developed a dictionary of preferences for each type of pronoun and thus identify its possible referent. The motivation of this work arises from an analysis of the importance of anaphora in automated translation systems.

Techniques have recently been developed to address the problem of anaphora through different branches of Artificial Intelligence. An example of this is the work proposed by Mahato, Thomas and Sahu (2020), in which the development of an anaphora resolution algorithm for the Hindi language is described, which works with the help of a heuristic algorithm. They also mention that the technique they propose can be improved and adapted even to be able to work with other languages as well. Another example of this is the work of Guo, Li and Ma (2020), in which an a priori algorithm is implemented with which, through association rules and information mining regarding anaphora and pronouns, both first, second, and third person and their characteristics. With this, the link of the analyzed speech or text between a pronoun and its referent begins to be built through the association rules.

One of the areas within NLP is speech recognition, which involves solving the anaphora as a subtask. The importance that speech recognition has also gained today has been so great that within speeches, it is increasingly difficult to identify co-reference between mentions and referents. In the work of Agarwal (2020), this importance is discussed and, furthermore, they propose a work in which hierarchically stacked neural networks are implemented to solve more complex anaphoric relationships within speech recognition.

The importance of pronominal anaphora is so great that it increasingly attracts the attention of researchers due to its potential as a subtask in a variety of complex NLP problems. In the study by Ferreira, Rocha and Lopes (2020), in which they describe the research they carried out regarding trends in anaphora resolution techniques and the integration of a point-to-point service model in order to offer a wide range of techniques for Anaphora resolution in order to gradually break down barriers such as language limitation and excessive consumption of resources.

Anaphora Resolution Tools

There are various tools that address issues related to the area of NLP, including anaphora resolution. Most of these tools have a different way of addressing this problem, and even though they are constantly developing, some of their applications do not cover most languages. Table 3 describes some NLP tools and some functions that offer. It is important to mention that not all the modules that these tools offer are developed for the Spanish language, as well as that their functionality may be limited.

Table 3. NLP Tools

Tool	Modules	Languages
Spacy (Spacy, 2020)	Text summarization, sentence splitter, and tokenizer, **co-reference resolution**, named entity recognition, parts of speech tagging, relationship extraction.	English, German, French, **Spanish**, Portuguese, Italian, Dutch, Greek, Norwegian and Lithuanian.
Standford NLP (NLP, 2020)	**Co-reference resolution**, neural network dependency parser, speech tagger, named entity recognizer.	English, Arabic, Chinese, French, German, and **Spanish**.
NLTK (NLTK, 2020)	Parsing and chunker, relationship extraction, sentence splitter and tokenizer, text summarization, **co-reference resolution.**	Danish, Dutch, English, Finnish, French, German, Hungarian, Italian, Norwegian, Porter, Portuguese, Romanian, Russian, **Spanish,** and Swedish.
Freeling (Freeling, 2020)	Tokenization and sentence splitting, morphological analysis, multiword recognition, proper noun detection, date-time expression recognition, currency expression recognition, numerical expression recognition, part of speech tagging, **co-reference resolution.**	English, **Spanish**, Portuguese, French, Italian, German, Russian, Norwegian, Catalan, Galician, Croatian, Slovene, and Asturian, Welsh.

Table 3 shows some of the tools developed for NLP tasks, as well as the languages they support. It should be mentioned that even though the majority support the Spanish language, it does not mean that they address the anaphora resolution for the Spanish language, in fact, only Freeling offers support for the anaphora resolution for the Spanish language. The tools that are shown in Table 3 address the pronominal anaphora problem for cases of *personal*, *relative*, and *possessive* pronouns, although, as mentioned earlier, the efficiency of the results of these tools varies depending on the language in which they are applied.

5 PROPOSED APPROACH

This section presents the algorithm developed for the resolution of the pronominal anaphora for personal pronouns cases.

The algorithm proposed in this chapter focuses on words that are grammatically tagged as personal pronouns (*PP*). It is important to emphasize that the chapter addresses the pronominal anaphora in the case of personal pronouns. It is for this reason that emphasis is placed on words whose tag begins with (*PP*). The corresponding tag for each word is provided by a tool known as a morphological analyzer. This tool plays an important role during data processing. On the other hand, it is necessary to identify the type of words that could be a possible candidate as a referent of a pronoun. The grammatical category of this type of word is a *noun*. According to the Eagle standard, the grammatical category of the tag assigned by the morphological analyzer to nouns is *N* (shown in Table 1). When the first component of a tag begins with the letter *N*, it indicates that the word refers to a name. The next component of a tag could be a C or a P, denoting that it is a common name or a proper name, respectively. Finally, the next five components just give additional information to the analyzed word. It is worth mentioning that in subject words, the genre and the number are important elements that could solve the pronominal anaphora. The morphological analyzer is a complex algorithm that returns the information mentioned above, among some other features, which depend on the language being processed (Proószéky, 1996). The morphological text analyzer implemented in this chapter is a Freeling API hosted by the Universidad Nacional Autónoma de México (UNAM) (2020). Freeling is an open-source language analysis tool suite that offers a lot of functions to analyze words in some languages. Each of the phases of the proposed algorithm is shown in **Figure 1.**

Figure 1. Phases of the proposed algorithm

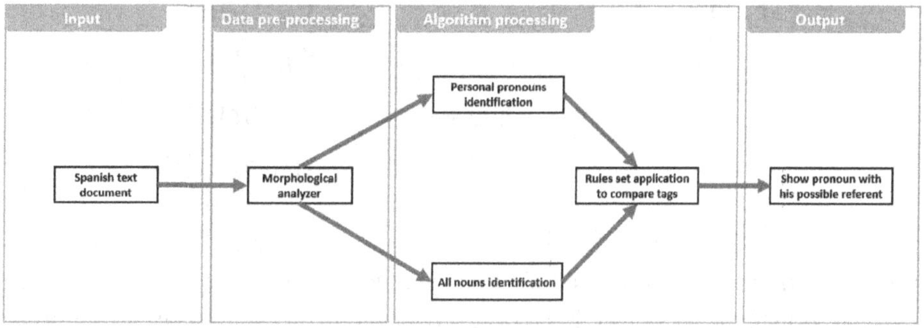

Input

The entry consists of a Spanish text file that has the paragraph or sentences to process. It should be mentioned that the text to be processed must be correctly written without spelling mistakes. This has great importance to pre-processing because the Spanish language has a lot of grammatical rules, and these rules can give another sense instead of the real meaning word.

Data Pre-Processing

The text to be processed is tokenized to obtain individual *tokens*. These tokens are often referred to as words, numbers, or symbols. Subsequently, the morphological analyzer parses each of the tokens to obtain their grammatical information. As a result of this process, the morphological analyzer returns the *lemma* and the *tag* of each one of the analyzed tokens. The lemma is the natural base form of a word, for example, the lemma of the word "*fue*" is "*ser*". The tag is a character string in which each character that composes it has a specific meaning. As mentioned previously, the grammatical tags considered in this proposal can be interpreted based on the Eagle standard (Table 1 and Table 2).

Here is an example of a token returned by the morphological analyzer:

Lemma: él
Token: Ella
Tag: PP3FS00

In this case, the tag "*PP3FS00*" could be interpreted with the information provided in Table 2. The tag can be interpreted, as shown in **Figure 2:**

Figure 2. Example of the interpretation of a tag

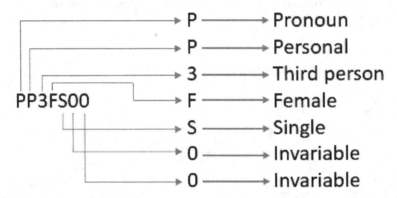

The grammatical information described above, generated by the morphological analyzer for each token, is stored individually in an object. Each object is stored in an array to be further processed by the algorithm. This array allows the algorithm to know the words that are before a pronoun, which is used to identify the referent.

Algorithm Processing

After the morphological analyzer finishes processing all the words in the text file, the algorithm starts with the array that contains all the words with all lemmas, tokens, and tags. The algorithm has some key points which are described below:

Step 1: Personal pronoun identification.
Step 2: Nouns identification.
Step 3: Coreference association.

In the first step, each identified pronoun is stored in an array, which is used exclusively to store the grammatical information of the pronouns.

The second step corresponds to the part of identifying possible candidates through the same object that contains all the tokens analyzed and grammatically tagged by the morphological analyzer. Each element of the array is analyzed in order to detect those tokens that are nouns. When a token is identified as a noun, it is added to an exclusive array of possible referents.

In the third step, once the algorithm has identified all the pronouns and all the nouns, in other words, the possible referents, it takes the first possible referent and submits it to a set of association rules by means of which it is sought to determine its correlation with some pronoun of those that were identified. There are specific rules to establish the correlation between a noun and a pronoun. These rules were developed from the contents of Table 1 and Table 2.

As mentioned above, the first two components of the tag must start with (PP), which indicates that it is a personal pronoun. Once a case of this type has been identified, then the algorithm takes the third component of the label to begin identifying it through the grammatical rules that have been defined in order to associate it with some possible noun or referent. This identification process is carried out by means of each component of the label since, as mentioned before, each component provides specific information about that word, and this finally helps the algorithm to select the indicated referent of that pronoun.

Output

After having identified the referents of each of the pronouns, the proposed algorithm stores the pronoun-referent pair in an array. Finally, each pair of solutions are displayed on the screen to the user.

6 RESULTS

The evaluation of the proposed algorithm was carried out using two corpora from which texts were taken to be able to test the algorithm. It was determined to use these two corpora for testing due to the difficulty of finding a corpus for tests of anaphora resolution in Spanish. On the one hand, one of the corpora consists of a website (Jiménez, 2020), of which a total of sixteen sentences have been implemented, each of which consists of sixteen anaphoric references derived from personal pronouns. On the other hand, a corpus found in the work of Torner, López and Martín (2011) was used, whose work is related to the one proposed in this chapter, however, it approaches a different perspective regarding the common problems that arise in the solution of anaphora in Spanish. From this work, eight paragraphs of text were taken, which had a total of 18 anaphoric references that were derived from personal and demonstrative pronouns. This is because some paragraphs had more than one pronoun, including personal and demonstrative. It should be mentioned that the proposed algorithm covers the case only for personal pronouns.

The algorithm correctly identified all the anaphoric references within each of the texts to which it was submitted. There were cases where the reference identified by the algorithm was not entirely correct. This is because the referent mapping for each pronoun is mapped out of a queue where all the pronouns are stored. In addition, there were cases of pronouns in which, based on the grammatical rules defined in the algorithm, they could be a candidate for one or more nouns. The following pronoun is an example of this particular case, "they" is a pronoun that can refer to a masculine plural, but it is a pronoun that can be correctly used to speak of a group of people of a different gender.

Finally, a comparison of the results obtained using the same test cases has been made. This comparison was made with the tool offered by Freeling (2020). This tool allows solving pronominal anaphora for texts in Spanish, as already mentioned before. The metrics used to evaluate the algorithm are shown below.

The metrics used to evaluate the performance of both algorithms were *precision* and *recall*, which are metrics widely used in the literature to evaluate the resolution of the anaphora, which refers to *accuracy* and *completeness*, respectively. The formulas for these metrics are presented below:

$$Precision = \frac{TP}{TP + FP}$$

$$Recall = \frac{TP}{TP + FN}$$

Where: TP means *True Positive*, TN means *True Negative*, FP means *False Positive,* and FN means *False Negative*. Table 4 describes these formulas.

Table 4. Formulas description

Correct Identification		Obtained Identification
TP (True Positive)	FP (False Positive)	
FN (False Negative)	TN (True Negative)	

Table 5 shows the results obtained from the evaluation performed on the proposed algorithm and the Freeling online service, using the metrics described above.

Table 5. Performance comparison of algorithms for the first test corpus

Parameter	Recall	Precision
Freeling Online Service	62.25%	56.25%
Proposed algorithm	70%	68.75%

As can be seen in Table 5 and Table 6, in both cases, the algorithm proposed in this chapter maintains a margin of good results, except in cases where there are other pronouns that are not personal within the same text. The opportunity areas of the proposed algorithm focus on solving the way in which the candidates of each pronoun are assigned because, as mentioned before, all personal pronouns are correctly identified by the algorithm, however, the assignation of candidates tends to fail when texts with various anaphoric references are used.

Table 6. Performance comparison of algorithms for the second test corpus

Parameter	Recall	Precision
Freeling Online Service	25%	15%
Proposed algorithm	38.75%	54.25%

In conclusion, the objective of the evaluation is to measure the ability of both algorithms to identify the referents of each pronoun. Among the metrics presented above, the one of greatest interest is recall. This is because this metric indicates the ability of both algorithms to identify the referent of each pronoun correctly. As can be seen in Table 5, the recovery percentage obtained by the proposed algorithm is 70%, and that obtained by Freeling's online service is 62.25%, and finally, in Table 6, it is shown that the percentage of Recovery obtained is 38.75% for the proposed algorithm and a total of 25% for the case of the online Freeling tool. As you can see, the proposed algorithm improves the performance of Freeling's online service. However, there is a wide area of improvement for future works in which the grammatical rules of the algorithm can be extended to cover more types of pronouns and to improve the results obtained.

7 FUTURE RESEARCH DIRECTIONS

Anaphora resolution is a complex task due to the ambiguity that exists at all levels of NLP. During the evaluation of the proposed algorithm, it was identified that the algorithm was not able to identify the referent of some types of pronouns, for example, in the sentences: "*Carlos y Lupita se acaban de casar. Ellos van a formar una familia pronto*", the pronoun "*Ellos*" apparently it is a third-person male personal pronoun, but in the context of these sentences, this pronoun refers to both, "*Carlos*" and "*Lupita*". This implies to write extra rules for special cases like this and for the other pronoun types that exist, which are fewer addresses in the literature.

Considering the previous examples, it is necessary to conduct new research with the aim of integrating into the applications focused on the anaphora problem a deeper natural language analysis, as well as developing linguistic resources such as ontologies to model common sense knowledge that allows addressing this type of problem, especially for the Spanish language.

8 CONCLUSION

In this chapter, the anaphora problem was described, which remains an open research problem in the scientific community. The architecture of the proposed algorithm to address the type of pronominal anaphora for the Spanish language was presented. To identify the referents of personal pronouns, basic rules were designed based on the grammatical tag of each of the words of the processed text. These grammatical tags are based on the Eagle standard. The algorithm uses the online Freeling service to perform tokenization and grammatical tagging tasks.

To evaluate the performance of the proposed algorithm, texts, and sentences downloaded from a website were used, which were used in a study related to the topic of anaphora. The evaluation consisted of determining the ability of the algorithm to identify the referents of the personal pronouns. The results obtained by the proposed algorithm were compared with an online version of Freeling.

The metrics used to evaluate the performance of both algorithms were Precision and Recall metrics, widely used in the literature. The results obtained show that the proposed algorithm obtained better performance.

The resolution of the anaphora is a complex task due to the ambiguity existing at all levels of processing of any natural language. In the Spanish language, people can say the same sentence in different ways due to the richness of this language. For this reason, the anaphora problem represents a great area of opportunity for the development of research work, as could be seen in this chapter. Currently, most research works only deals with anaphora resolution from the perspective of exclusively personal pronominal pronouns, but there are other types of pronouns, such as demonstrative, possessive, relative, interrogative, as well as other types of anaphora which are less addressed. Unfortunately, common sense knowledge is often required to address more complex types of anaphora. Likewise, there is a large amount of research work and software tools focused on the English language, but not on the Spanish language, so research works for this language is necessary.

REFERENCES

Almor, A. (2020, March 9). *ResearchGate*. Retrieved from ResearchGate: https://www.researchgate.net/publication/2659482_Noun-Phrase_Anaphora_and_Focus_The_Informational_Load_Hypothesis

André Ferreira Cruz, G. R. (2020, January 30). *MDPI Open Access Journals*. Retrieved from MDPI Open Access Journals: https://www.mdpi.com/2078-2489/11/2/74

Computer Science Department. (2020, February 18). *Introducción a las etiquetas Eagle*. Retrieved from Introducción a las etiquetas Eagle: https://www.cs.upc.edu/~nlp/tools/parole-sp.html#pronombres

Freeling. (2020a, March 8). *Freeling*. Retrieved from Freeling: http://nlp.lsi.upc.edu/freeling/demo/demo.php

Freeling. (2020b, February 19). *Freeling*. Retrieved from Freeling: http://nlp.lsi.upc.edu/freeling/node/1

Gardiner, M. (2020, March 09). *Identifying and resolving one-anaphora*. Retrieved from Puzzling: https://files.puzzling.org/academic/gardiner03honours%20%28Identifying%20and%20resolving%20one-anaphora%29.pdf

Grupo de Ingeniería Lingüística. (2020, February 18). *Corpus lingüísticos desde la UNAM*. Retrieved from Corpus lingüísticos desde la UNAM: http://www.corpus.unam.mx/servicio-freeling/

Guo, S. X. L. (2020, January 1). *ACM Digital Library*. Retrieved from ACM Digital Library: https://dl.acm.org/doi/abs/10.1145/3379247.3379277

Jesús Peral, A. F. (2003). Translation of Pronominal Anaphora between English and Spanish. *Journal of Artificial Intelligence Research*, *18*, 117–147. doi:10.1613/jair.1115

Jiménez, L. M. (2020, March 8). *Scielo*. Retrieved from Scielo: https://scielo.conicyt.cl/scielo.php?script=sci_arttext&pid=S0718-09342001004900009

Karthikeyan, K. V. K. (2013). Understanding text using Anaphora Resolution. *2013 International Conference on Pattern Recognition, Informatics and Mobile Engineering*, 346-350. 10.1109/ICPRIME.2013.6496498

Kumar, U. (2018). *Review on the techniques of Anaphora Resolution.* Review on the Techniques of Anaphora Resolution.

Manuel Palomar, L. M. (2001). An Algorithm for Anaphora Resolution in. *Computational Linguistics, 27*(4), 545–567. doi:10.1162/089120101753342662

Mitkov, R. (2014). *Anaphora Resolution.* Routledge. doi:10.4324/9781315840086

NLP. S. (2020, February 19). *Stanford NLP.* Retrieved from Stanford NLP: https://nlp.stanford.edu/

NLTK. (2020, February 19). *NLTK.* Retrieved from NLTK: https://www.nltk.org/

Palomar, M. (2001, December 1). *Universidad De Alicante.* Retrieved from Universidad De Alicante: https://www.dlsi.ua.es/~mpalomar/p545_s.pdf

Peral, J. (2003). Translation of Pronominal Anaphora between English andSpanish: Discrepancies and Evaluation. *Journal of Artiðcial Intelligence Research*, 117-147.

Prószéky, G. (1996). Morphological Analyzer as Syntactic Parser. In *Proceedings of the 16th conference on Computational linguistics* (pp. 1123-1226). Budapest: DBLP. 10.3115/993268.993381

Puneet Agarwal, P. K. (2020, January 16). *Google Patents.* Retrieved from Google Patents: https://patentimages.storage.googleapis.com/8c/5a/d9/8c6d5faeff865b/US20200019610A1.pdf

Ruiz Frutos, M. J. (2012, October 23). *Resolución de la anáfora correferencial con FunGramKB.* Retrieved from Resolución de la anáfora correferencial con FunGramKB: http://e-spacio.uned.es/fez/eserv/bibliuned:master-Filologia-TICETL-Mjfrutos/Frutos_mariajose_TFM.pdf

Seddik, K. M. (2014). Anaphora resolution. In I. Zitouni (Eds.), Natural language processing of semitic languages (pp. 247-277). doi:10.1007/978-3-642-45358-8_8

Seddik, K. M. (2014). *Natural Language Processing Applications.* Academic Press.

Seddik, K. M. (2014, March 1). *ResearchGate.* Retrieved from ResearchGate: https://www.researchgate.net/publication/300822578_Anaphora_Resolution

Seema Mahato, A. T. (2020). Heuristic Algorithm for Resolving Pronominal Anaphora in Hindi Dialects. In A. T. Seema Mahato (Eds.), Advanced Computing and Intelligent Engineering (pp. 41-51). Springer Link.

Sergi Torner Castells, C. L. (2011). Problemas en el uso de las anáforas en producciones escritas de español como lengua extranjera. *Revista Española de Lingüística*, 147-174.

Shalom Lappin, H. J. (1994). *An Algorithm for Pronominal Anaphora Resolution.* Academic Press.

Spacy. (2020, February 19). Retrieved from Spacy: https://spacy.io/

Stanford N. L. P. Group. (2020, February 18). *Stanford NLP Group.* Retrieved from Stanford NLP Group: https://nlp.stanford.edu/

Toledo Gómez Israel, V. R. (2011). *Academia.* Retrieved from Academia: https://www.academia.edu/1588476/Construcci%C3%B3n_de_una_herramienta_para_la_identificaci%C3%B3n_y_resoluci%C3%B3n_de_pronombres_an%C3%A1foras_en_una_oraci%C3%B3n

Universidad Politécnica de Cataluña. (2020, March 9). *Computer science deparment.* Retrieved from https://www.cs.upc.edu/~nlp/tools/parole-sp.html#pronombres

Valtierra Romero, E. (2014, February 1). *AnaPro, Tool for Identification and Resolution of Direct Anaphora inSpanish.* Retrieved from AnaPro, Tool for Identification and Resolution of Direct Anaphora inSpanish: https://www.academia.edu/10482656/201._AnaPro_Tool_for_Identification_and_Resolution_of_Direct_Anaphora_in_Spanish

Chapter 15
Geospatial Situation Analysis for the Prediction of Possible Cases of Suicide Using EBK:
A Case Study in the Mexican State of Aguascalientes

Carlos Manuel Ramirez López
Universidad Politécnica de Aguascalientes, Mexico

Martín Montes Rivera
https://orcid.org/0000-0003-3897-6212
Universidad Politécnica de Aguascalientes, Mexico

Alberto Ochoa
https://orcid.org/0000-0002-9183-6086
Universidad Autónoma de Ciudad Juárez, Mexico

Julio César Ponce Gallegos
Universidad Autónoma de Aguascalientes, Mexico

José Eder Guzmán Mendoza
Universidad Politécnica de Aguascalientes, Mexico

ABSTRACT

This research presents the application of Empirical Bayesian Kriging, a geostatistical interpolation method. The case study is about suicide prevention. The dataset is composed of more than one million records, obtained from the report database of the Emergency Service 911 of the Mexican State of Aguascalientes. The purpose is to get prediction surfaces, probability, and standard error prediction for completed suicide cases. Here, the variations in the environment of suicide cases are relative to and dependent on economic, social, and cultural phenomena.

DOI: 10.4018/978-1-7998-4730-4.ch015

Copyright © 2021, IGI Global. Copying or distributing in print or electronic forms without written permission of IGI Global is prohibited.

INTRODUCTION

The Mexican State of Aguascalientes is currently experiencing a social problem that undermines the tranquility of its citizens: the phenomenon of suicide, which has been on the rise in the last decade, with repercussions in multiple sectors, such as public health and economy. To effectively prevent the issue of suicide, we should use a multi-sectoral approach that addresses the phenomenon in a comprehensive manner (World Health Organization, 2014).

The National Institute of Statistics and Geography (INEGI), responsible for regulating and coordinating the National System of Statistical and Geographical Information, shows alarming data where the Mexican State of Aguascalientes ranks as the second-highest rate of suicides (10.1%), only below the State of Chihuahua with a rate of 10.7% per 100,000 inhabitants (INEGI, 2019).

From January 2016 to October 2019, according to statistics from the 911 Emergency Service, there has been an upward trend in this indicator, as shown in **Figure 1**.

Figure 1. The trend in the phenomenon of suicide for the period 2016-2019

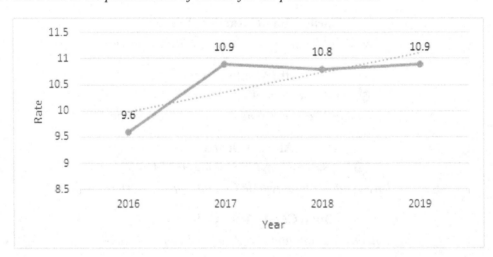

The same statistic shows that, in 2019, the suicidal tendency was more pronounced in men in the age range of 19–40 years; from a total of 120, seventy committed suicides were reported until October. In the case of women, 24 completed suicides were reported by the same date, being more pronounced in 19–40 years-old.

The member states of the WHO (*World Health Organization*) presented an action plan on mental health for the period 2013-2020, which set a global goal of reducing the suicide rate by 10% by the end of it (World Health Organization, 2014).

The database used for the application of the method contains records from the period 2010-2018, with more than one million reports stored, where a total of 537 cases of suicides are in Aguascalientes. Table 1 presents the features of the database of reports.

In general, these social problems are of interest for the whole population, but the databases and analysis results related to the behavior are commonly expressed using numerical tables, equations, or other types

Table 1. Characteristics of the database of reports of the Emergency Service 911 of the Aguascalientes State.

Features	Case_1	Case_2	Case_3
Id_Mode	1	1	1
Id_Rol_Person	2	2	2
Full Name	OMITTED	OMITTED	OMITTED
Date	06/12/2014	06/11/2014	06/10/2014
Hour	05:58:07 p. m.	10:31:23 p. m.	01:37:17 p. m.
Age	0	0	0
Inc_No_Int			
Id_Community	1	1	1
Telephone	OMITTED	OMITTED	OMITTED
Id_street	1967	636	2215
Domestic_Violence	0	0	0
Alcoholic	1	0	1
Age1	0	0	0
Drug Consumption	0	0	0
Id_Colony	54	328	61
Inc_No_Ext		105	
Domestic_Violence2	0	0	0
Municipality_Code	8	3	3
Psychological Support	0	0	0
Dating Violence	0	0	0
Diagnostic			
Suicide Threat	0	1	0
Id_Sex	1	1	0
Suicide	0	0	0

of specialized information, nevertheless, not all people can understand these representations; therefore, more understandable information, like visual data, must be generated (MacEachren et al., 2005).

Geospatial information is a visualization tool extendedly used when geographical data is involved, this kind of information allows to detect new patterns and infer conclusions that could not be easily identified in the original database (MacEachren et al., 2005; Omre,1987).

Furthermore, geospatial information is commonly expressed using maps that are understandable for the majority of the population, which is desired, since in several social problems there are several knowledge areas that must deal with the information before taking any action oriented to solve or improve the situation associated with that social problem (MacEachren et al., 2005).

Since geospatial information allows us to analyze and infer conclusions with different perspectives, it would be useful for making the prediction of the next possible suicide cases of Aguascalientes, and even to compare the collected data with other maps to identify possible causes for this phenomena.

The geospatial information for predicting suicides in Aguascalientes must be based on all the information obtained from the previous cases, with that in mind all variables must be taken into account instead of only consider geographical information, the area related with this kind of analysis is spatial statistics (Cressie, 1990).

Kriging has become synonymous of spatial optimal predicting in spatial statistics because it considers observations in nearby locations to perform predictions, so that database information available in other locations supports its prediction (Cressie, 1990).

Despite its utility and capabilities, Kriging is based on the idea that data are a Gaussian distribution with covariance function exactly known, but this is not a valid basis in practice, because of the possible variability of the data in real analysis. Moreover, if these suppositions are made, then the predictions may not be correct for the observed phenomena(Pilz & Spöck, 2008).

An alternative for dealing with the variability and possible uncertainties in the data is the Bayesian approach because it is based on the prior distribution of the database, making that the calculation of the model for prediction and its parameters be based on that distribution, and therefore to obtain more accurate predictions (Pilz & Spöck, 2008).

In this sense, the technique capable of obtaining the Kriging analysis using the Bayesian approach is the method *Empirical Bayesian Kriging*.

The EBK variant of the Kriging method has demonstrated its effectiveness when applied to the analysis of irregular data with uncertainties and variabilities like it is shown in Krivoruchko (2009) and Strand et al. (2014). Moreover, it has been previously used for analyzing databases related with the suicide problem with pleasant results in Barros et al. (2017), Dantas et al. (2018), Fontanella et al. (2018), Froberg et al. (2019), Helbich et al. (2012), Kanamori and Kondo (2020), Kim et al. (2011), Larsen et al. (2019), MacEachren et al. (2005), Min and Min (2018), Mahaki et al. (2015), Oka et al. (2015) and Omre (1987).

The main objective of this study is, with the use of the analysis variables, to obtain a graphic representation using the EBK method, to identify the areas with a high probability of this phenomenon in Aguascalientes, México, so that be possible to obtain a map that can be compared with other data in the city or analyzed by other knowledge areas.

BACKGROUND

There is a great variety of works related to the application of the EBK method, oriented to medical research, soil study, agriculture, but fundamentally it is used in those fields of research where it is necessary to carry out an analysis where the conditions of geographical distribution are not the same, either by levels of contamination, socio-economic level or exploitation of the soil, the variability of these indicators does not allow them to be evaluated in the same way, so the EBK method, provides this characteristic of the variability of the geographical conditions.

The EBK method, as mentioned above, is a variant of the Kriging method, applied in "*Intelligent system for prediction motorcycle accident by reaching into a Smart city using a Kriging model to achieve its reduction and the reduction of deaths in the medium term*", which focuses on the predictive model used to describe the places and situations that cause accidents, in order to design a solution for this specific problem (Ochoa et al., 2019).

The application of this method is of great versatility, can be used in any branch of research, in "*Epidemiologic Mapping using the "Kriging" Method: Application to an Influenza-like Illness Epidemic in France*", the analysis is applied in the field of geographical epidemiology, where a spatial prediction is made (Carrat & Valleron, 1992).

The research work *"Empirical Bayesian Kriging, Implemented in ArcGIS Geostatistical Analyst"*, shows the predictions of 6 subsets of soil contamination by radiocaesium, for the study of soil contamination near the Fukushima Daiichi Nuclear Power Plant in Japan, followed by the well-known accident at that facility in 2011 (Krivoruchko, 2009).

Studies related to soil quality employ this method for improving efficiency, in this case, the *"Use of Empirical Bayesian Kriging for Revealing Heterogeneities in the Distribution of organic Carbon on Agricultural Lands"*, focuses on the comparison of cartograms obtained by the Kriging method with the EBK method, for the organic carbon content in an isolated field with agro-gray soils. Within the conclusions obtained, it is found that the EBK errors reveal the spatial variability structure of the property, which cannot be revealed by other methods (Samsonova et al., 2017).

The special analysis of the information is applied in the study *"Analysis of suicide mortality in Brazil: spatial distribution and socio-economic context"*, where the phenomenon of suicide is analyzed, the variables as the spatial distribution, intensity and meaning of the groups are analyzed with the Global Moral Index, Moran Map and Local Indicators of Spatial Association (LISA), with the purpose of identifying patterns through the geostatistical analysis, where one was found a weak correlation very close to zero between all the dependent and independent variables (Dantas et al., 2018).

Also, the ecological study, *"Mapping suicide mortality in Ohio: A spatial epidemiological analysis of suicide clusters and area level correlates"*, which aims to identify groups at high risk of suicide in Ohio as well as assess the level of correlation in the area of those groups. It estimates the standardized mortality rate using the Bayesian Conditional Autoregressive Model, so this model is used to determine the association between area level correlates and suicide clusters (Fontanella et al., 2018).

The analysis of the suicide phenomenon has been carried out on different fronts, as is the case with the publication *"Suicide detection in Chile: proposing a predictive model for suicide risk in a clinical sample of patients with mood disorders"*, which aims to analyze behavior and build a predictive model of suicide risk, using Data Mining and Machine Learning tools with the Support Vector Machine technique (Barros et al., 2017).

In the current technological era, this phenomenon manifests itself in different ways, the paper *"Information extraction from text messages using data mining techniques"* approaches the analysis from electronic messaging, where its objective is to estimate the suicidal tendencies of a person by applying Data Mining techniques to the text messages sent by this person to other people, analyzing components of the text such as keywords, emoticons (Ahmad & Varma, 2018).

These papers describe the phenomenon of suicide among university students, as well as some of its effects on the educational environment and the need for the application of public policies for its attention and follow-up. Features that have the greatest impact on suicidal behavior were identified via deep neural networks. The neural network used is a dense deep model built with three hidden layers, and its precision is greater than 90% (Torres et al., 2019).

An analysis of these publications was carried out, identifying the methods used and the type of results they sought with the analysis done; this is shown in the following table (see Table 2).

Table 2. Analysis of the related work

Title	Year	Method		Results
"Intelligent system for predicting motorcycle accident by reaching into a smart city using a kriging model to achieve its reduction and the reduction of deaths in the medium term"	2019	Kriging		Areas with possible risk routes
"Epidemiologic Mapping using the "Kriging" Method: Application to an Influenza-like Illness Epidemic in France"	1992	Kriging		Z* (x0, y0) = 3-39 WNCP of influenza-like illness (WNCP) Weekly Number of Cases per Practitioner
Empirical Bayesian Kriging, Implemented in ArcGIS Geostatistical Analyst	2009	EBK		Prediction 14.72 and 3.52 Standard Error 2.19 and 0.52
Use of Empirical Bayesian Kriging for Revealing Heterogeneities in the Distribution of organic Carbon on Agricultural Lands	2017	Ordinary Kriging	EBK	Standard Error
		0.00005 0.38291	0.00594 0.36979	
Analysis of suicide mortality in Brazil: spatial distribution and socio-economic context	2018	GMI MM LISA		Weak Spatial Correlation Moran's I=0.2608
Mapping suicide mortality in Ohio: A spatial epidemiological analysis of suicide clusters and area level correlates	2018	Bayesian conditional autoregressive models		Nine statistically significant (p < 0.05)
Suicide detection in Chile: proposing a predictive model for suicide risk in a clinical sample of patients qith mood disorders	2017	DM SVM		Accuracy = 0.78, Sensitivity = 0.77, and Specificity = 0.79
Information extraction from text messages using data mining techniques	2018	DM SVM		"Normal" "Critical"
Suicidal Tendency Neural Identifier in University Students from Aguascalientes, Mexico	2019	DNN		critical factors

Theoretical Framework

Kriging's method is a probabilistic predictor, and as such establishes a statistical model of the data, this method has the standard error parameter, which quantifies the associated uncertainty of the predicted values, it uses a semivariogram that consists of a distance and direction function separating two places to quantify the spatial dependence of the data (Krivoruchko, 2009), the following is the semivariogram of a classic Kriging (see **Figure 2**).

Suppose that the dataset to be processed could be modeled according to a stochastic process in a two-dimensional Euclidean space $\mathbb{R}^2$. Such a stochastic process is a collection of random variables $\{Z(x, y); (x, y) \in D\}$, where D is a subset of $\mathbb{R}^2$ and (x, y) is the spatial index of the process (in our case, the geographic coordinates). We will now assume that the spatial data $\{Z_{obs}(x_1, x_1); i = 1, ..., N\}$ observed at the locations $\{(x_1, y_1); i = 1, ..., N\} \subset D$ are in fact a realization of a multivariate random variable $\{Z(x_1, x_1); i = 1, ..., N\}$ generated by the stochastic process $\{Z(x,y); (x,y) \in D\}$.

The application of statistical methods to this process generally requires an assumption of its stationarity, at least "second-order stationarity". The latter assumption is satisfied if the mean is constant and if the covariance function depends only on the distance (h) between the locations of the random variables, expressed as:

$$E\left[Z\left(x,y\right)\right]=\mu$$

$$cov\left[Z\left(x+h_{x},y+h_{y}\right),Z\left(x,y\right)\right]=C\left(h\right)$$

$$\forall\left(x,y\right),\left(x+h_{x},y+h_{y}\right)\in D,\text{where }h=\sqrt{h_{x}^{2}+h_{y}^{2}}$$

In the case of "ordinary kriging", the underlying hypothesis is less restrictive: it is assumed that, up to the first two moments, the difference in the value of the variables between two positions depends only on the distance between them. This assumption is known as the "intrinsic hypothesis" and is expressed as follows:

$$E\left[Z\left(x+h_{x},y+h_{y}\right)-Z\left(x,y\right)\right]=0$$

$$var\left[Z\left(x+h_{x},y+h_{y}\right)-Z\left(x,y\right)\right]=2^{3}\left(h\right)$$

Figure 2. Representation of the semivariogram of the classical Kriging method (Krivoruchko, 2009).

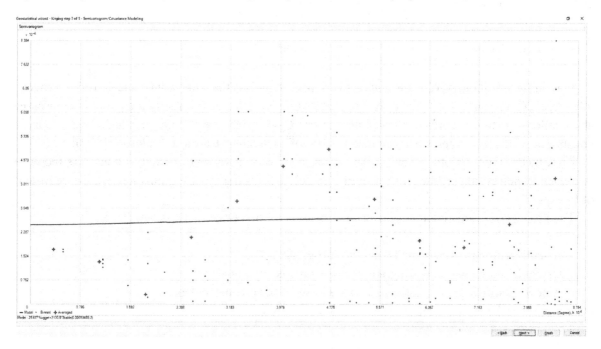

$$\forall (x,y),(x+h_x,y+h_y) \in D$$

The quantity $\gamma(h)$, which depends only on the distance h, is defined as the "semivariogram function". The intrinsic hypothesis is more general than second-order seasonality. Any stationary second-order process satisfies the intrinsic hypothesis, while the opposite is not true (Carrat & Valleron, 1992).

The following is a step-by-step process for developing the Kriging method:

Estimation of the semivariogram. The first step of Kriging is to perform a "structural analysis" of the geographical data. This involves the estimation $\hat{\gamma}(h)$ of the function of the distance semivariogram $\gamma(h)$. The usual estimator of the semivariogram for a given distance h is:

$$\hat{\gamma}(h) = \frac{1}{2N(h)} \Sigma_{i=1}^{N(h)} (Z_{obs}(x_1 + h_x, y_1 + h_y) - Z_{obs}(x_1, y_1))^2$$

where the subscript "obs" indicates the observed sample values, and $N(h)$ is the number of pairs of sample points at distance h from each other. The calculations of $\hat{\gamma}(h)$ are repeated for $2h, 3h, 4h,...,kh$. When spatial sampling is irregular, estimates are calculated for the offset h using points at a distance less than $h \pm h/2$ from each other.

In the second step, the observed semivariogram is used to estimate the parameters of the theoretical models using a weighted least-squares technique.

The expression of $\gamma(h)$ in this model is given by:

$$\gamma(h) = \begin{cases} 0 & \text{if } h = 0, \\ C_0 + C_1 \left[\frac{3}{2} \frac{h}{C_2} - \frac{1}{2} \left(\frac{h}{C_2} \right)^3 \right] & \text{if } 0 < h < C_2, \\ C_0 + C_1 & \text{otherwise.} \end{cases}$$

In Kriging terminology, C_0 is the "nugget variance", $C_0 + C_1$ is the "threshold," and C_2 is the "range of influence". C_0 measures the variance due to a measurement error or variability that would be observed at a smaller scale than the smallest sampling interval. $C_0 + C_1$ gives the maximum value of $\gamma(h)$. C2 is the distance at which the samples become independent of each other (Carrat & Valleron, 1992).

EBK method, on the other hand, differs from the classical Kriging method, it considers the error introduced when estimating the semivariogram model, so several semivariogram models are used instead of just one.

The process of estimating the semivariograms is as follows (ArcGis Desktop, 2016):

1. A semivariogram is estimated from the subset data.
2. Using the previous semivariogram, the new data is simulated.
3. A new semivariogram is estimated on the basis of the estimated data.
4. Steps 2 and 3 are repeated a specified number of times.

The following are the semivariograms generated by the EBK method (see **Figure 3**).

Figure 3. Representation of the semivariograms generated by the EBK method

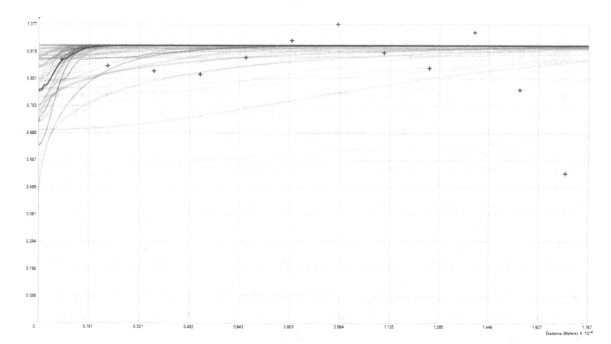

The procedure of EBK method differs from other versions of Kriging by the use of variograms, the principle of operation is that for interpolation of any point within the mapping, which is independent of mapped data, a restricted neighborhood is formed, a variogram is estimated and the predicted value of the point is calculated only from the data of this neighborhood, in other words, the interpolation at any point of the mapping is performed using only its subpopulation of available observations, making the method independent of trends (Samsonova et al., 2017).

The importance of highlighting this methodology focuses on some of the advantages it represents, such as (ArcGis Desktop, 2016):

- Standard errors of prediction are more accurate than in other Kriging methods.
- It enables accurate prediction of moderately non-stationary data.
- It is more accurate than other Kriging methods for small datasets.

In the same way, it is important to highlight the disadvantages of using the method, here are some of the most important (ArcGis Desktop, 2016):

- Processing time increases rapidly as the number of input points, subset size, or overlap factor increases.
- Empirical Logarithmic transformation is particularly sensitive to outliers.

This process for the application of the EBK method involves the following steps:

1. From the data, a semivariogram model is estimated.
2. Using this semivariogram, a new value is simulated at each of the input data locations.
3. A new semivariogram model is estimated from the simulated data. A weight is then calculated for this semivariogram using Bayes' rule, which shows the probability that the observed data can be deleted from the semivariogram.

Steps 2 and 3 are repeated. With each repetition, the semivariogram estimated in step 1 is used to simulate a new set of values at the entry points. The simulated data is used to estimate a new semivariogram model and its weight. Predictions and standard errors of prediction then occur at the unsampled locations using these weights.

Each semivariogram is an estimate of the true semivariogram from which the observed process could be generated.

The default kriging model in EBK is called the intrinsic random function of order 0, and the spatial correlation model is the power model, where b, c, and α (the allowed value of the power value α is between 0 and 2) are the parameters of the model. This correlation model corresponds to the fractional Brownian motion, also known as the random walk process. It consists of steps in a random direction and filters out a moderate trend in the data.

Although the default EBK model makes the distribution of the residue data closer to a Gaussian distribution by eliminating the local trend, the residue distribution can still be non-Gaussian. In this case, a model with the data transformation option may produce better predictions.

Therefore, the variation of the local distribution of the data is clearly an essential feature of the optimal interpolation model. The EBK offers an option to transform the observed process into a Gaussian process, using a data transformation function.

EBK with the data transformation option estimates the distribution of the data many times using the following algorithm:

1. The data are transformed into a Gaussian distribution, and a semivariogram model is simultaneously estimated from the data.
2. Using this semivariogram, the new data is unconditionally simulated and then transformed again at each of the input data locations.
3. The new data is transformed, and a new semivariogram model is simultaneously estimated from the simulated data.
4. Steps 2 and 3 are repeated a specific number of times. Each repetition produces a new transformation and a semivariogram.
5. The weights for the semivariograms are calculated using Bayes' rule.
6. Predictions and standard errors of prediction are made using weights and then transformed again with bias correction.

These associated predictive uncertainties must be taken into account when using these results for decision making (Krivoruchko, 2009)

Methodology

For the application of the EBK method, the database of reports from the Emergency Service 911 of the state of Aguascalientes is used, which, as mentioned above, contains reports corresponding to the period 2010 - 2018 and where the first step was to filter the information and thus obtain a total of 537 cases of completed suicides in the state.

The database has 25 characteristics which are mentioned below:

1.- Date-Format-Date
2.- Hour-Format-Hora
3.- Alcoholic-Format-Numeric
4.- Suicide Threat-Format-Numeric
5.- Psychological Support-Format-Numeric
6.- Drug Consumption-Format-Numeric
7.- Violence against Women-Format-Numeric
8.- Dating Violence-Format-Numeric
9.- Domestic Violence-Format-Numeric
10.- Domestic violence_2-Format-Numeric
11.- Id_Street-Format-Numeric
12.- Inc_No_Int-Format-String
13.- Id_Colony-Format-Numeric
14.- Id_Community-Format-Numeric
15.- Municipality_Code-Format-Numeric
16.- Full Name-Format-String
17.- Id_Sex-Format-Numeric
18.- Age-Format-Numeric
19.- Age1-Format-Numeric
20.- Id_Rol_Person-Format-Numeric
21.- Diagnostic-Format-String
22.- Id_Mode-Format-Numeric
23.- Telephone-Format-Numeric
24.- Inc_No_Ext-Format-String
25.- Suicide-Format-Numeric

As can be seen in the case study, only some characteristics are of interest, and they are also necessary to carry out the geolocation of points representing the places where cases of suicide occurred since the dataset does not have a field corresponding to the coordinates of the incident.

The selected attributes or characteristics are presented below:

Id_Street
Inc_No_Int
Inc_No_Ext
Id_Colony
Id_Community

Municipality_Code

As mentioned above these features allow to generate the geolocation of each of the 537 cases of suicide previously filtered, for this pre-processing is used the web tool Google Maps ®, then lists the steps to perform this stage:

1. Create a new map.
2. Assign a name to it, preferably referring to the topic of study.
3. Click on the Import button. In this step, the filtered file is selected, which generates a data table with the selected attributes and records.
4. In the generated table, a column is added for the capture of the " Latitude, Longitude".
5. Once the column is added, it is filled with the coordinates thrown in each of the points.

As shown in **Figure 4** (a), you have the coordinates of the points in Google Maps®, the next step is to import them into the ArcMap® tool, for which the following procedure is performed:

1. The data table generated in Google Maps® is copied to a .xlsx file.
2. Within the ArcMap® software, in the "File" tab, "Add Data" is selected and then "Add XY Data", where the origin of the data is selected (.xlsx file of coordinates), and the column that contains them is specified.
3. The previous step generates a data table that will be converted into .dbf format, for which it is necessary to right-click on the table, select "Data" and then "Export". This step generates a table in .dbf format with its respective column "OID".
4. The coordinates are not yet shown in the base map, so it is necessary to convert them, with the tool "Convert Coordinate Notation" to the format DD_1 (Both Longitude and Latitude values are in the single field).

The last step shows the georeferenced points in the ArcMap® software, as shown in **Figure 4** (b).

The application of the EBK method within the ArcMap® software requires that the .dbf table be open. To do this, select the "Geostatistical Analist" button on the toolbar, then "Geostatistical Wizard", which displays a window with two boxes:

- Deterministic methods
- Geostatistical methods
- Interpolation with barriers

The Empirical Bayesian Kriging method —that we are dealing with— is within the Geostatistical methods group, therefore, when selecting it, the second box shows the options for the selection of the dataset origin that will be processed, in the "Source Dataset" field, the coordinates converted in the previous stage are selected and in "Data Field" the "ID" column is selected (see **Figure 5**).

When making this selection, the next step is to configure the properties of the method that will allow us to tune it to obtain the greatest efficiency (see **Figure 6**).

The configuration was done in this way in order to obtain the most accurate results:

Figure 4. Geolocation of suicides - Google Maps® (a); Geolocation of suicides - ArcMap® (b)

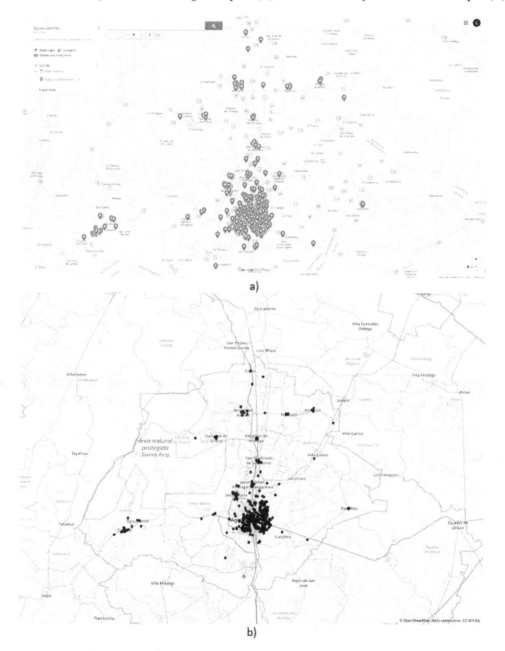

a)

b)

The default setting of 100 points for the size of the subset is maintained since the semivariogram is estimated from this data, obtaining slower processing as its size increases.

The overlap factor is placed at number 2 so that each entry point can enter into two different subsets in addition to obtaining a smoother exit surface.

Regarding the number of simulations, the default setting is kept, which shows the number of semi-variograms to be simulated per subset, taking into account that increasing this number will increase the processing time proportionally.

Figure 5. Selection of the EBK method and the data source to be processed

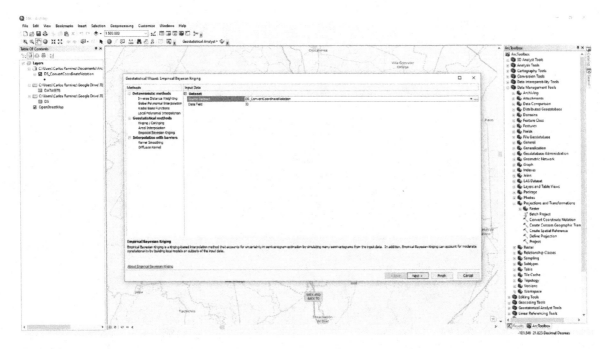

An Empirical transformation is used since it applies a non-parametric core mixture to the dependent variable. This option is recommended when the dependent variable is not normally distributed

Figure 6. Tuned method properties

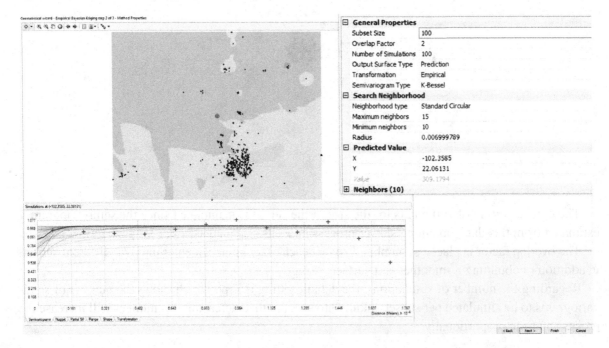

The selection of the semivariogram supposes the existence of a special autocorrelation and defines how its similarity with distance decreases, where the key to obtaining more optimal results is to select the semivariogram that is closest to the behavior of the phenomenon, so it was decided to select a K-Bessel type semivariogram, which turns out to be more flexible and precise, allowing the spatial autocorrelation of the error term to decrease slowly, quickly or anywhere in between, its application requires an additional parameter so it takes longer to calculate, being that its main disadvantage, which can generate slow calculations, unlike those semivariograms that turn out to be faster in terms of processing speed but with low precision as in the case of the Linear or Spline.

RESULTS

The results stage obtained with the above-mentioned configuration of characteristics is presented below.

Figure 7. Prediction surface and semivariograms generated by the EBK method

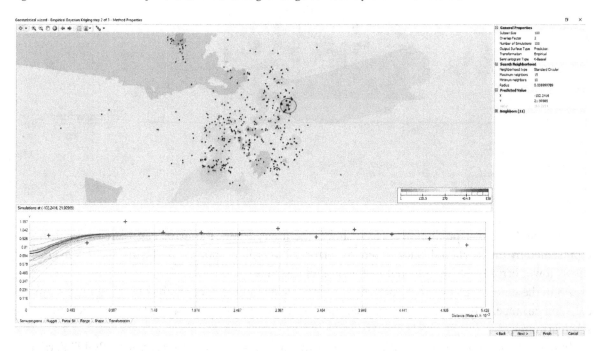

In the previous figure the geolocation of the points can be seen, as well as the prediction surface focused on the area with the most cases, where based on the legend it is possible to identify the zones in blue color where the prediction distance is less and on the contrary in orange color where the prediction distance is greater.

Likewise, a correct visual adjustment can be observed for the empirical semivariances (blue crosses), where it can be seen that they are located in the central part of the spectrum of the semivariogram.

The following is the probability surface, in the same way as the previous surface, based on the legend, it is possible to identify the areas in red, with a higher probability of occurrence of suicide and on the other hand in blue with a lower probability of occurrence.

Likewise, a correct visual adjustment can be observed for the empirical semivariances, where it can be seen that they are located in the central part of the spectrum of the semivariogram.

Figure 8. Probability area and semivariograms generated by the EBK method

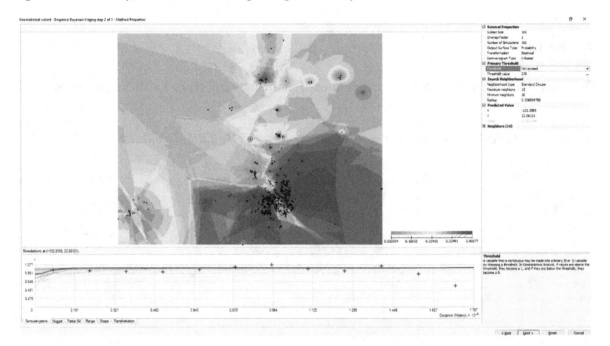

The standard error prediction surface shows the areas where the error can increase or decrease, represented by the bright red color, where the error is larger in proportion to the distance; conversely, it shows lower error levels in light yellow for smaller distances.

As in the case of the previous surfaces, a correct visual adjustment can be observed for the empirical semivariance, where it can be seen that they are located in the central part of the spectrum of the semivariogram.

In the case of the probability surface, an adjustment is made to the "Primary Threshold" parameter in order to establish the threshold value that allows the probability to be interpreted more clearly and effectively.

FUTURE RESEARCH DIRECTIONS

We are going to extend the analysis using additional data related to other social problems that affect the east of Aguascalientes for identifying other potential causes so that the local government could be informed, allowing them to apply politics and actions to decrease the number of suicidal cases in the city.

Figure 9. Standard error prediction surface and semivariograms generated by the EBK method

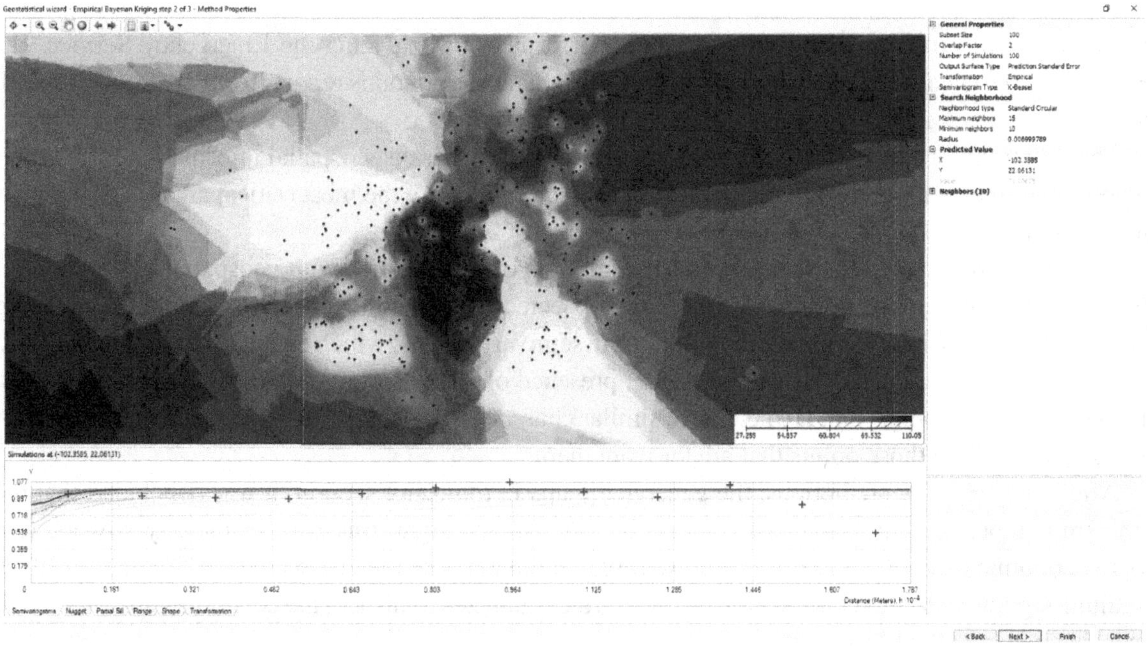

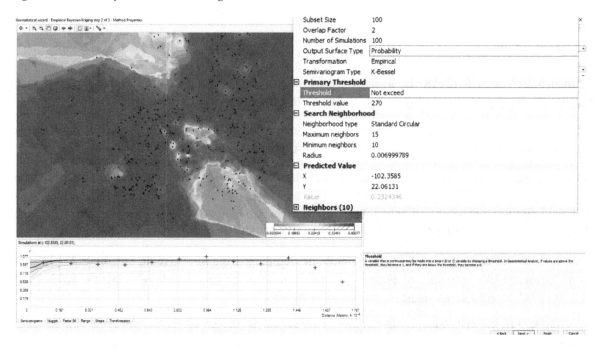

Figure 10. Primary Threshold Setting in Not Exceeded Mode

CONCLUSION

In this research, Empirical Bayesian Kriging is performed for analyzing the Emergency Service 911 database of the Mexican State of Aguascalientes. This database contains reports from 2010 to 2018 with information related to 537 cases that completed suicide.

The examination of this database with EBK allows us to generate geospatial information for predicting possible suicide cases in Aguascalientes, and therefore identify the most critical areas in the city for this phenomenon.

The application of the EBK method for the analysis of case studies with geospatial orientation allows to have a more exact approximation to the expected values, unlike other variants of the Kriging method, this one makes the calculation of multiple semivariograms, which evaluate different zones in a different way: through the subsets allowing the presence of spatial autocorrelation between the points. In other words, the points that are near have similar characteristics and, at the same time, have different characteristics from those points that are far from them.

After analyzing the predictions, the generated maps in the result section, it was concluded that the problem is more present in the east zone of the city. At first sight, this zone of the city is where the socio-economic level of life is medium-low, unlike in the north of the city where the standard of life is medium-high, which could take to consider for further analyzes to inspect the economic situation of the ones that generate the 911 report.

However, these observations must be extended comparing the locations identified with other possible conflicts in the critical area detected, like schooling or access to psychological attention.

REFERENCES

Ahmad, S., & Varma, R. (2018). Information extraction from text messages using data mining techniques. *Malaya Journal of Matematik*, *S*(1), 26–29. doi:10.26637/MJM0S01/05

ArcGis Desktop. (2016). *¿Qué es un Kriging bayesiano empírico?* Retrieved from https://desktop.arcgis.com/es/arcmap/10.4/extensions/geostatistical-analyst/what-is-empirical-bayesian-kriging-.htm

Barros, J., Morales, S., Echávarri, O., García, A., Ortega, J., Asahi, T., Moya, C., Fischman, R., Maino, M. P., & Núñez, C. (2017). Suicide detection in Chile: Proposing a predictive model for suicide risk in a clinical sample of patients with mood disorders. *Revista Brasileira de Psiquiatria (Sao Paulo, Brazil)*, *39*(1), 1–11. doi:10.1590/1516-4446-2015-1877 PMID:27783715

Carrat, F., & Valleron, A. J. (1992). Epidemiologic mapping using the "kriging" method: Application to an influenza-like epidemic in France. *American Journal of Epidemiology*, *135*(11), 1293–1300. doi:10.1093/oxfordjournals.aje.a116236 PMID:1626546

Cressie, N. (1990). The origins of Kriging. *Mathematical Geology*, *22*(3), 239–252. doi:10.1007/BF00889887

Dantas, A., De Azevedo, U., Nunes, A., Amador, A., Marques, M., & Barbosa, I. (2018). Analysis of suicide mortality in brazil: Spatial distribution and socio-economic context. *Revista Brasileira de Psiquiatria (Sao Paulo, Brazil)*, *40*(1), 12–18. doi:10.1590/1516-4446-2017-2241 PMID:28832751

Fontanella, C., Saman, D., Campo, J., Hiance-Steelesmith, D., Bridge, J., Sweeney, H., & Root, E. (2018). Mapping suicide mortality in Ohio: A spatial epidemiological analysis of suicide clusters and area level correlates. *Preventive Medicine*, *106*, 177–184. doi:10.1016/j.ypmed.2017.10.033 PMID:29133266

Froberg, B., Morton, S., Mowry, J., & Rusyniak, D. (2019). Temporal and geospatial trends of adolescent intentional overdoses with suspected suicidal intent reported to a state poison control center. *Clinical Toxicology*, *57*(9), 798–805. doi:10.1080/15563650.2018.1554186 PMID:30696297

Helbich, M., Leitner, M., & Kapusta, N. (2012). Geospatial examination of lithium in drinking water and suicide mortality. *International Journal of Health Geographics*, *11*(1), 1–8. doi:10.1186/1476-072X-11-19 PMID:22695110

INEGI. (2019). Estadísticas a propósito del día mundial para la prevención del suicidio. In *Estadísticas a Propósito Del Día Mundial Para La Prevención Del Suicidio (10 De Septiembre)*. Retrieved from https://www.google.com.mx/ url?sa=t&rct=j&q=&esrc=s &source=web&cd=3&cad=rja &uact=8&ved= 2ahUKEwjFlOuJpbDlAhULL a0KHRpTDrMQFjA CegQIBBAC&url=https %3A%2F%2Fwww.inegi.org. mx%2Fcontenidos%2 Fsaladeprensa%2Faproposito %2F2019%2Fsuicidios 2019_Nal.docx&usg=AOvVaw2IN9e

Kanamori, M., & Kondo, N. (2020). Suicide and Types of Agriculture: A Time-Series Analysis in Japan. *Suicide & Life-Threatening Behavior*, *50*(1), 122–137. doi:10.1111ltb.12559 PMID:31215073

Kim, N., Mickelson, J., Brenner, B., Haws, C., Yurgelun-Todd, D., & Renshaw, P. (2011). Altitude, Gun Ownership, Rural Areas, and Suicide. *The American Journal of Psychiatry*, *168*(1), 49–54. doi:10.1176/appi.ajp.2010.10020289 PMID:20843869

Krivoruchko, K. (2009). Empirical Bayesian Kriging Implemented in ArcGIS Geostatistical Analyst. *Shanghai Jiaotong Daxue Xuebao. Journal of Shanghai Jiaotong University*, *43*(11), 1813–1817.

Larsen, M., Torok, M., Huckvale, K., Reda, B., Berrouiguet, S., & Christensen, H. (2019). Geospatial suicide clusters and emergency responses: An analysis of text messages to a crisis service. In *2019 41st Annual International Conference of the IEEE Engineering in Medicine and Biology Society (EMBS)* (pp.6109–6112). doi:10.1109/EMBC.2019.8856909

MacEachren, A., Robinson, A., Hopper, S., Gardner, S., Murray, R., Gahegan, M., & Hetzler, E. (2005). Visualizing geospatial information uncertainty: What we know and what we need to know. *Cartography and Geographic Information Science, 32*(3), 139–160. doi:10.1559/1523040054738936

Mahaki, B., Mehrabi, Y., Kavousi, A., Mohammadian, Y., & Kargar, M. (2015). Applying and comparing empirical and full Bayesian models in study of evaluating relative risk of suicide among counties of Ilam province. *Journal of Education and Health Promotion*, *4*(1), 50. doi:10.4103/2277-9531.162331 PMID:26430677

Min, J., & Min, K. (2018). Night noise exposure and risk of death by suicide in adults living in metropolitan areas. *Depression and Anxiety*, *35*(9), 876–883. doi:10.1002/da.22789 PMID:29953702

Ochoa, A., Urrea, B., Mejía, J., & Avelar, L. (2019). Intelligent system for predicting motorcycle accident by reaching into a smart city using a kriging model to achieve its reduction and the reduction of deaths in the medium term. Smart technologies for smart cities.

Oka, M., Kubota, T., Tsubaki, H., & Yamauchi, K. (2015). Analysis of impact of geographic characteristics on suicide rate and visualization of result with Geographic Information System. *Psychiatry and Clinical Neurosciences*, *69*(6), 375–382. doi:10.1111/pcn.12254 PMID:25384900

Omre, H. (1987). Bayesian kriging-Merging observations and qualified guesses in Kriging. *Mathematical Geology*, *19*(1), 25–39. doi:10.1007/BF01275432

Pilz, J., & Spöck, G. (2008). Why do we need and how should we implement Bayesian kriging methods. *Stochastic Environmental Research and Risk Assessment*, *22*(5), 621–632. doi:10.100700477-007-0165-7

Samsonova, V. P., Blagoveshchenskii, Y. N., & Meshalkina, Y. L. (2017). Use of empirical Bayesian Kriging for revealing heterogeneities in the distribution of organic carbon on agricultural lands. *Eurasian Soil Science*, *50*(3), 305–311. doi:10.1134/S1064229317030103

Strand, P., Aono, T., Brown, J. E., Garnier-Laplace, J., Hosseini, A., Sazykina, T., ... Batlle, J. (2014). Assessment of Fukushima-Derived Radiation Doses and Effects on Wildlife in Japan. *Environmental Science & Technology Letters*, *1*(3), 198–203. doi:10.1021/ez500019j

Torres, M. D., Torres, A., Barajas, D., Campos, N., Ponce De León, E. E., & Velázquez, C. (2019). Suicidal tendency neural identifier in university students from aguascalientes, Mexico. In *2019- 14th Latin American Conference on Learning Technologies (LACLO)* (pp.387–392). doi:10.1109/LACLO49268.2019.00071

World Health Organization. (2014). *Prevención del suicidio un imperativo global*. Retrieved from https://apps.who.int/iris/bitstream/handle/10665/136083/9789275318508_spa.pdf;jsessionid=3449688B7BB864F3D4D35DCB65E13970?sequence=1

Chapter 16
Location Extraction to Inform a Spanish–Speaking Community About Traffic Incidents

Alejandro Requejo Flores
Universidad Autónoma de Ciudad Juárez, Mexico

Alejandro Ruiz
iD https://orcid.org/0000-0002-7913-5682
Universidad Autónoma de Ciudad Juárez, Mexico

Ricardo Mar
Universidad Autónoma de Ciudad Juárez, Mexico

Raúl Porras
iD https://orcid.org/0000-0002-6772-5351
Universidad Autónoma de Ciudad Juárez, Mexico

ABSTRACT

Around the world, cities suffer from a large variety of problems. One of them is urban mobility, and the most common cause is related to traffic incidents, which unexpectedly provoke delays to people and produce losses to businesses. Through natural-language-processing methods, this chapter proposes a way to inform people about events that could have happened on the road. The proposed application takes information from news reports (published by a local newspaper) that have been previously classified as 'traffic incidents'; the app tries to extract the location where these events occurred. These data are then served on a web application, which shows a map that marks all the recent incidents. In this way, the authors offer an alternative to allow citizens to be informed about this kind of event so they can take preventive actions.

DOI: 10.4018/978-1-7998-4730-4.ch016

Copyright © 2021, IGI Global. Copying or distributing in print or electronic forms without written permission of IGI Global is prohibited.

INTRODUCTION

One of the leading causes of delays, when a person must arrive at a particular place, is because an accident has occurred on the road (generally, a car crash obstructing some street or slowing down the traffic). Since most times people get informed of this incident after they observe it personally, they do not have many options besides waiting for the traffic to move at a slow rhythm, which represents itself a problem because of many reasons such as arriving late to their job or ruining their planned schedule (some parents leave their children at the school right before going to their work, and a traffic jam could make the children be late to class, or the parents arrive late to their workplace), practically causing people to lose time. Although some authors have researched about the clustering of traffic incidents in a spatiotemporal manner (Eckley & Curtin, 2013), we are not able to predict this type of events. Therefore, the only way to know of such events is after they have already happened, and someone has reported it through a means of communication.

There are two ways to deal with this problem: getting informed through social media networks in advance, or by checking the online newspaper from a community to find reports about these incidents. The first one is the most inefficient because we can get all kinds of news and information from social media, and it is hard to filter the publications we are really interested in. On the other hand, in order to get informed through newspaper articles, we need to read lots of them, determine which ones imply traffic incidents and then find in the entire text the exact point of where the incident happened. Doing so would mean a significant loss of time and would not be very useful to do it every time before we drive since events do not occur every day in our daily route, but in order for such technology to work, we would need to be checking the newspaper daily in search of news reports that are related to traffic incidents.

It is possible to visualize that a solution to such a problem is through the use of a local online newspaper since its information is a little more organized than random posts from social media. However, this is only viable through the application of technology by delegating the activity to a machine. This is done through an algorithm, which enables faster analysis and extraction of the location from the events the news articles mention, meaning that this algorithm goes through a higher number of reports than that a person could in the same amount of time. This chapter uses this approach to offer to the society an application the allows them to be informed about traffic incidents in the city.

The information used for application development is obtained from a local newspaper via a classification algorithm. Once the reports are classified, they are put through a process of information extraction that finds the location of the incident, so they are displayed on a map of the city. The application works in real-time and serves its results to all the community. However, it should be emphasized that the extractor proposed in this chapter does not depend on the mentioned classifier; the extraction process can be used to obtain a location in a Spanish-written text, and this text is only required to include an address. A classifier is only mentioned for the developed application that informs about places where accidents have occurred based on news articles that it classified as traffic incidents; feeding the app with manually filtered reports would not be efficient. This chapter focuses merely on the extraction of the location from Spanish-written texts.

The structure of the chapter is as follows. Section 2 provides a review of the previous works and more recent advances in the area of information extraction, as well as some brief introductions to some useful concepts used for the project. Section 3 presents the development that was followed to accomplish the objectives of the project. There, the three phases in which the proposal was divided are explained: generation of the training corpus, manipulation of the information scripts, and the web application. Section

4 presents the results obtained in the classification and extraction of information process and; finally, Section 5 discusses some conclusions derived from the project.

BACKGROUND

The automatic extraction of structured information is commonly known as information extraction; structured information can be an entity, a relationship between entities, or an attribute describing a not structured source. The popularization of the internet expanded the use of applications that depended on the extraction of data; nowadays with roots in the Natural Language Processing (NLP), the extraction of structured information was extended to topics like machine learning, information retrieval, databases, and document analysis (Sarawagi, 2008).

There were firstly simple rule-based with manually coded rule systems to cope with the demand of automatic extraction; afterward, algorithms for automatically learning rules were developed; after that, the age of statistical methods bloomed, in which there were two main approaches: generative models based on Hidden Markov Models and conditional models based on maximum entropy. These were re-placed with a new model called Conditional Random Fields, and, finally, the techniques for the grammar construction were created since most systems required a more holistic analysis of document structure (Sarawagi, 2008).

Many applications generate massive amounts of data: email, texts, web pages, social media postings, news articles, business reports, research papers, and so on. Doan, Ramakrishnan and Vaithyanathan (2006) made a tutorial for the development of a unified framework for the management of information extraction, which involves a process including extraction, storage, indexing, querying and maintenance of both the original raw data and the extracted information. Doan et al. (2006) also discuss three real-world applications that can use in information extraction management:

- **Business Intelligence:** Information stored in structured attributes with semantic information extracted from textual attributes. This approach can solve questions related to businesses and commercial strategies.
- **Community Information Management:** information extraction can help a researcher who wants to track all the citations or all the connections of a paper.
- **Semantic Search:** Information extraction can help to solve more advanced queries in a precise way.

Engels and Bremdal (2000) mention that most applications of information extraction fall into one of the following classes:

- **Abstracting and Summarizing:** Delivering of short informative representations of larger texts. An automatic summarization system is designed to take a single article or a cluster of multiple articles and produce a concise and fluent summary of essential information (Nenkova & McKeown, 2011). These systems could play a significant role in helping to find relevant and useful information on the Internet (Jizba, 1997).

- **Visualization:** Recognizing the involved concepts and relationships in a text, seen in a thoughtful manner or on some model. It intends to detect and characterize the semantic relations between entities in a text (Jiang, 2012).

- **Indexing and Classification:** Identifying representative information that helps to either classify it or to search specific contents on it. Its development aims to help in handling unstructured documents; it needs to compare different texts, rank the importance and relevance, or find patterns and trends across multiple documents (Sagayam, Srinivasan & Roshni, 2012).

- **Translation:** Context-driven translation of texts from one language into another; this task requires a semantic representation of meaning to translate correctly. It is also known as Cross-Language Information Retrieval (CLIR). The most widely used approach is a dictionary-based query translation; however, this method needs to address three major issues: phrase identification and translation, translation ambiguity, and out of vocabulary terms (Zhang & Vines, 2004).

- **Question formulation and Query answering:** Recognizing what item is searched or guiding a user to discover its needs in human-computer interaction systems. It makes it possible to ask a fact-based question in natural language and receive a specific answer rather than an entire document where the users must further search for the particular answer themselves (Kosseim, Plamondon & Guillemette, 2003).

- **Extraction of Information:** Generating additional knowledge that is not explicit in the original text. It must infer information or relations not explicitly stated in the text but known from the discourse itself or the domain; this is also known as *discourse inferencing* (Kosseim, Beauregard & Lapalme, 2001).

In their study, Marzinotto, Damnati and Béchet (2019) proposed a new semantic frame parsing model adapted to process spoken documents to perform information extraction from broadcast contents. Their experiments were done over two corpora: a specialized lot of encyclopedic materials about three subjects and a more general corpus of podcast transcriptions with questions and answers from a broader set of general knowledge topics. The result was a semantic frame parser with improved generalization capacities, suggesting that their approach could be successfully applied on Spoken Language Understanding tasks. Loos and Biemann (2008) used unsupervised learning to extract addresses from webpages that involved locations that could be interesting or useful tourist information. The data was processed by an unsupervised part-of-speech tagger and applied a Conditional Random Field on a labeled training set of addresses to extract the locations from the retrieved data.

Among the previously mentioned studies, different applications have been developed to inform about events related to the news. To give an example, *Newspaper Map* (at https://newspapermap.com) shows some newspapers indexed from 238 countries around the world; it lets to filter the results by language, newspaper's name, or location. Each marker in the map represents a newspaper and, by clicking in one of them, it is possible to select a language to translate the original newspaper's page through the support of Google Translate services.

Another application is *US News Map* (at https://usnewsmap.com), which allows its users to search through more than 11 million newspaper pages between 1789 and 1922 from *Chronicling America: Historic American Newspapers* and visualize the results in a map. It is possible to filter the results by a date range.

On the other hand, social media presents a way to implement a crowdsourcing technique to detect incidents reported by the users. Some platforms provide a way to fetch free content created by their users through APIs that most times are open (although they could have a limit of requests that can be done per day). In their study, Chen, Chen and Qian (2014) presented a social-media based approach to monitoring traffic congestion using human sensors (pedestrians, drivers, and passengers) and their posted tweets on Twitter to observe traffic status. After analyzing traffic congestion patterns in Twitter, they proposed a novel statistical framework that integrated topic models and hinge-loss Markov random field (HLMRF): Language enhanced Hinge Loss Markov Random Fields (L-HLMRF). Their language model and HLMRFs helps to identify traffic congestion points.

In another study, Gu, Qian and Chen (2016) present a methodology to crawl, process, and filter public tweets to detect those that report traffic incidents, using Twitter again as a data source. Their data crawling was performed through the Twitter API with an initial list of keywords, which was expanded with the words of the queried tweets that were not part of this list and were considered relevant to incidents; then a new iteration was performed to obtain more tweets with this updated keyword list. Then, the tweets were classified in their corresponding category of incident reports (accident, road work, hazards and weather, events, and obstacle vehicles) using a Semi-Naïve-Bayes model, and finally, they tried to identify the location from the tweet's text (although Twitter allows to geo-tag the tweets, less than 0.1% of the users use this feature). Moreover, Rajwani, Somvanshi, Upadhye, Vaidya and Dange (2015) developed an application that extracts tweets from Twitter and, after applying NLP techniques (tokenization, stop word filtering, stemming, stem filtering, and feature representation), categorizes those tweets related to traffic and notifies the users about it.

Furthermore, Waze (https://www.waze.com) is a navigation application that, through crowdsourced user reports, notifies about traffic crashes, congestion, hazards, and other issues that slow down the traffic. According to Amin-Naseri, Chakraborty, Sharma, Gilbert and Hong (2018), Waze is the fourth most contributing source of incident detection in Iowa, recognizing it as a reliable crowdsourced traffic incident report service with a competent coverage.

Smart Cities

This concept refers to cities that have the infrastructure of digital and telecommunications technologies to send and receive information and uses data to makes more efficient all the operations that occur in the city with the purpose of improving the life quality of its inhabitants. Smart Cities take advantage of technologies like the Internet of Things (IoT) and Big Data, which helps to make cities more efficient and responsive (Ochoa Ortiz-Zezzatti, Rivera, Gómez-Santillán & Sánchez Lara, 2019).

Smart Cities need to have intelligence, interconnection, and instrumentation; this is something that IoT can provide. IoT embraces smartphones, smart sensors, networks, and Radio Frequency Identification (RFID) devices, but it also has software and firmware components that, when combined, help to connect and communicate different systems and applications to provide smart, reliable and secure systems (Holguin, Ochoa-Zezzatti, Larios, Cossio, Maciel & Rivera, 2019).

Big Data is interrelated with IoT, and both need each other. Big Data solves the problem of processing the information generated by a Smart City through all the sensors, databases, emails, websites, and social media it uses; hence, new approaches are necessary to process data that enable enhanced decision making, insight discovering and process optimization. These kinds of tools are essential for Smart Cities because it allows to search and extract knowledge from Big Data and IoT (Mohanty, Choppali & Kougianos, 2016).

Chourabi et al. (2012) proposed a framework with the success factors of a Smart City that allows to envision and design initiatives for its development, and ultimately helps with the implementation, and improves the sustainability and livability of a smart city. These factors are briefly described below:

- **Management and Organization:** There are needed some strategies for the administration and organization in a Smart City: project team skills and expertise, end-user involvement, planning, clear and realistic goals, clear milestones and measurable deliverables, good communication, adequate training, and best practices reviews.
- **Technology:** These are the smart computing technologies that support Smart Cities; these technologies include all the hardware and software and network technologies that provide the infrastructure and essential services that communicate the information about the city in real-time.
- **Governance:** It is vital in the implementation of Smart Cities because it allows them to exist. Smart Cities are commonly the base for smart governance because they are based on Information and Communication Technologies (ICT); this field involves a collection of technologies, people, policies, practices, resources, social norms, and information that support city governing activities. The main characteristics that should have a government are accountability, collaboration, leadership, participation, communication, data exchange, service and application integration, and transparency.
- **Policy context:** Transforming a city into a Smart City requires changes in how politics and institutions interact with technology, so it is essential to change the policies to ensure a successful transition.
- **People and Communities:** The most benefited from Smart Cities are their citizens because their quality of life rises; they also are more informed, which allows them to become active users by participating in the governance and management.
- **Economy:** This is a significant driver for Smart Cities, and it is based on six main components: smart economy, smart people, smart governance, smart mobility, smart environment, and smart living. The smart economy is also supported by economic competitiveness factors such as innovation, entrepreneurship, trademarks, productivity, and flexibility.
- **Built Infrastructure:** It is crucial for a Smart City to have an infrastructure for ICT with the quality and reliability needed for all the operations that a Smart City performs.
- **Natural Environment:** One of the main objectives of a smart city is to increment sustainability and to manage natural resources better.

Text Segmentation

The process of extracting coherent blocks of text is known as *text segmentation*; this technique is useful for text analysis because it splits the text into smaller parts and more coherent than the whole document. Text segmentation is used in a lot of areas like emotion extraction, sentiment mining, opinion mining, language detection, and information retrieval (Pak & Teh, 2018).

The text segmentation is the precursor for other techniques such as text retrievals, automatic summarization, information retrievals like language modeling and NLP. Text segmentation helps to identify the boundaries between words, phrases and sentences or topics in a text (Huang & Zhanng, 2009).

Beeferman, Berger and Lafferty (1999) expose in their research the application of a statistical approach to divide the text into coherent segments, based on a technique that incrementally builds a correlational model to extract features that are correlated with the presence of boundaries in a labeled training text. These techniques are applied in two different domains, like the Wall Street Journal news articles and television broadcast transcription news stories.

One example of the implementation of text segmentation is presented by Cabeza Ruiz (2016), where he shows two methods to perform a text segmentation by language: in the first one he applies the text segmentation and analyze every sentence trying to identify the language of these; on the second one, he adapts the hidden Markov models to the task of Text Segmentation by language.

The text segmentation can also be considered a supervised learning problem according to the study from Koshore, Cohen, Mor, Rotman and Berant (2018). To create segmentation models based on a dataset, in this case, their dataset was extracted and labeled from Wikipedia to validate if the model acceptably generalizes (using unseen natural text).

Tokenization

In NLP studies, it is essential to identify tokens; Webster and Chunyu (1992) defined tokens as the basic units that cannot be discomposed in a subsequent process. They also discuss two approaches to recognize tokens:

- **Lexical Information Retrieval as a Basis for Token Recognition:** Propose to train a neural network to recognize tokens based on their companion relations. This way, the neural network would be able to tokenize and solve ambiguity issues by matching the input with the learned patterns of companion relations.
- **Table-Look-Up Matching:** This is the simplest way to identify tokens. This approach tokenizes each word, then continues matching to find if there are any compound tokens among these words.

In their study, Pak and Teh (2018) said that the tokenization process is like text segmentation because both split the text into words, symbols, phrases, and meaningful linguistic units.

Part of Speech Tagging

Part of Speech tagging (abbreviated as *POS tagging*) enables robust and accurate tagging using the context of other words; this is useful when words are ambiguous, and we cannot detect if it is a noun or a verb. The importance of the POS tagging is that it helps to discover the linguistic structure of a large text and facilities a high-level analysis (Cutting, Kupiec, Pedersen & Sibun, 1992).

According to Kupiec, Pedersen and Sibun (1992), a tagger must include the following characteristics:

- **Robust:** It is necessary that the tagger handles all the elements of that text that could be a problem, such as titles, tables, or words that are unknown by the tagger itself.
- **Efficient:** It must be skilled to analyze all the text even if it is large; also, the training that it requires must be fast, enabling a rapid turnaround of the text and the genre.
- **Accurate:** It must attempt so assign the correct part-of-speech tag to every word in the text.
- **Tunable:** It must be able to take advance of linguistic insights and must be able to take into consideration hints to be able to correct systematic errors.
- **Reusable:** It must be usable with different text with minimal changes in the tagger itself.

POS tagging has different types of approach, like the rule-based approach that was used in the TAG-GIT program employed to tag the Brown corpus; there are also statistical approaches that provide the ability to resolve the ambiguity of most likely interpretation (one example is a form of Markov model that assumes a word depends probabilistically on the text-of-speech category); this kind of methods has two types of training: the first one makes use of tagged training corpus, and the second one does not require a corpus already trained (Cutting, Kupiec, Pedersen & Sibun, 1992).

Named Entity Recognition

Named Entity Recognition is a task of the information extraction processes; its objective is to find names of entities like people, locations, organizations, and products. The named entity can be divided into two main phases: entity detection and entity typing. Named entity recognition is also a prerequisite for many other tasks of information extraction.

Derczynski et al. (2015) analyzed entity disambiguation using an entity recognition and link analysis on a Twitter dataset to research how robust a number of state-of-the-art systems are on noisy texts, among with the main issues that could cause an error to occur and the problems that need to be investigated.

INFORMATION EXTRACTION

The script for information extraction is the last process that is held in the development of the project. A news classifier was previously developed, although the application could work with manually filtered content or, as it was already mentioned, any Spanish-written text that includes a location. Here, a technique of information extraction is applied to all the news that we have marked as road accidents; this conformed the input set and is done to extract the location of the road accidents in the news content to serve it later in the application.

For the extraction process, a library of NLP called spaCy (Honnibal & Montani, 2017) was used. This module employs a *Rule-based matching*. The way this module works is by defining a group of rules composed by different elements like grammatical tags, the length of a token, punctuation marks, tokens in uppercase or lowercase, among others. Once the set of rules are defined, they are applied to a previously loaded text; in case there are one or more matches, the location is obtained from the text. The creation of the set of rules for the extraction of the location was elaborated, analyzing the structure with which you can describe the location of a road incident. The rules that form the description of a road are the following.

- An optional prefix to mention the type of road either in singular or plural, followed by an optional grammatical article and preposition. Examples: *"calle", "avenida de la", "Bulevar", "carreteras de"*.
- The name of the road integrated with an optional number continued by as far as four words in lowercase format with an optional grammatical article and preposition between each one of them. Examples: *"calle Sur", "Avenida de la Raza", "avenida López Mateos", "bulevar Independencia", "calle 16 de Septiembre"*.

These sets of rules that are used to describe a road are optionally repeated one time with a conjunction between themselves; this forms the complete pattern used in this process. Some examples are: *"calles Sur del Emir y Bolivia"*, *"avenida Vicente Guerrero y calle Morín"*, *"Bulevar Independencia y carretera Casas Grandes"*, *"calle 16 de Septiembre y bulevar Óscar Flores"*.

The process that the script follows during its execution is as follows:

1. The rows that were classified as traffic incidents and have not been processed from the table *news* are taken; in other words, the rows that have *true* as their value in the column *is_vialidad* and *false* as their value in the column *is_processed*.
2. The Rule-based matching module is loaded with the set of keys previously defined.
3. The content of each one of the previously obtained news is processed by *spaCy* to get all the tokens of the text with their respective grammar tags.
4. Once all the tokens are obtained, the *matcher* is applied to find all the *matches*.
5. Save all the matches obtained in the previous step in the table locations from the database associated with the respective news article. Update all the news records (in the *news* table) that were processed. Specifically, it is assigned to the *is_processed* column the value of *true*.

Figure 1 shows an example of how the process works over a report (all the mentioned classes are part of spaCy). In **Figure 1(a)**, we have the original article, which is only plain text in Spanish; in **Figure 1(b)**, it is divided into its composing sentences using the *Sentencizer* class; this set of sentences is then processed by the *Tokenizer* class to break down the text into the most basic units of the text (tokens), as shown in **Figure 1(c)**; the tokenization step is useful for the following POS tagging, where each token gets assigned the function of the word in the text, shown in **Figure 1(d)** and performed by the *Tagger* class; finally, for the required preprocessing, **Figure 1(e)** shows the Named Entity Recognition part done using the *EntityRecognizer* class, which identifies the entities in the text that we are interested in as they may be useful to find the location. For the *EntityRecognizer*, the only entities we were interested in were those that refer to a transit line (in Spanish, this list includes *calle, avenida, bulevar, carretera*, among others). In the example shown in **Figure 1(e)**, *"bulevar"* is the only meaningful word.

When all these steps are done, the *Matcher* class tries to find a sequence of tokens that coincide with the pattern rules we defined before. In this case, the extraction is exact, and it is only able to perform a single match: *bulevar Juan Pablo II*. Since no additional steps are needed, this is stored in the database as the extracted location; if there were recognized multiple locations, it would require a human to select the correct answer among these results.

WEB APPLICATION

The web application has different functions depending on the perspective from which it is used:

*   **End-user:** The functionality for this type of user is to show all the news detected as a road accident and its respective point on a city map.
*   **Administrator user:** The functionality for this user is to show an interface where the information handling process can be completed to show the news on the map. Here, the administrator can see

Figure 1. Preprocessing for the Information Extraction process: (a) Original Text; (b) Text Segmentation; (c) Tokenization; (d) POS Tagging; (e) Named Entity Recognition

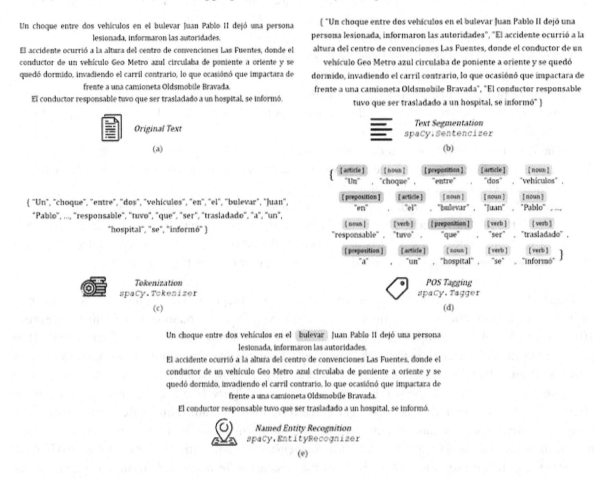

a list of all the news classified like a road accident, and the *matches* obtained for each one of them and select what location is the correct and insert the corresponding coordinates.

The technologies and tools used for the development of this web application are presented in the following list:

- Server with Ubuntu Server with a public IP. A domain and an SSL certificate were acquired for the application.
- PHP 7.1 as the server-side programming language.
- Laravel 5.6 was used as the development framework for the backend of the application.
- Bulma 0.7.0 as a CSS library.
- Vue 2.5 as a JS framework.
- Axios 0.18 as a JS library for the asynchronous HTTP petitions.
- Google Maps API for the visualization of the city map.
- Google Geocoding API for the obtention of the coordinates of a point.

The backend development of the application was done by applying Test-Driven Development (TDD). TDD implements a test per system functionality before the implementation of such functionality. At first, the execution of the test will show that the code fails because the functionality has not been implemented yet. The next step is to implement the functionality and verify its behavior through the test. Once the test is successful, the code can be refactored as many times as necessary as long as the test is still successful. TDD helps to reduce the number of errors generated during the development stage and strengthens the refactoring process by offering security when it comes to checking the functionality of the code whenever a change is made to the program.

Figure 2. The relational model of the database

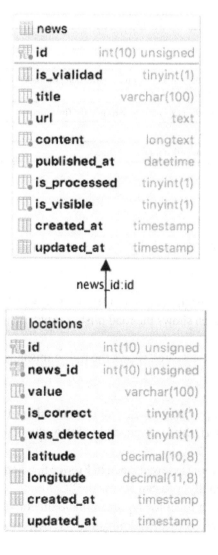

Preparation of the Database

Before developing the scripts that would manipulate the information, the implementation of a database was necessary to allow the correct storage of all the data from the news articles. After analyzing the entities that would be used and their possible attributes, the final relational model ended, as shown in **Figure 2**.
Tables 1-3 briefly describe the structure of each one of the tables in the database.

Table 1. Structure of table "news" where all the news records collected from the RSS are saved. It is periodically modified in the second and third phases of the project.

Column	Description
id	Unique identifier of the row
is_vialidad	Boolean type column in which it is specified if the row is either an accident road or not. If it has been collected from the RSS source, this column will have a 'null' value as it has not been classified yet.
title	Title of the news
url	Link to the news in El Diario's website
content	Content of the news
published_at	Date of the publication of the news
is_processed	Boolean type column where it is specified if the extraction of the information process has already been applied. It has a 'false' value by default.
is_visible	Boolean type column where it is specified if the news must be shown to the final user.
created_at	Date where it is specified when the row was created.
updated_at	Date where it is specified when the row was modified for the last time.

Application Views

Figure 3 shows the main view. Here is where the final users can see all the news on a map, based on all the applicated filters that are described below:

- If any filter is present, the search shows all the road mishaps registered from January 2018 to date.
- If nothing more than "De" (From) is present, the search shows the road mishaps that are registered on that same day in specific.
- If both filters "De" (From) and "A" (To) are present, the search shows the traffic mishaps between the date range.

When one of the pins shown is clicked, a small popup window with information about the traffic incident appears, which contains the title of the news report, the location, and a link to the news article. This window is shown in **Figure 4**.
From the main view, you can access the "*Acerca de*" (About) view, as seen in **Figure 5**, where a popup window shows a small description of the project. Additionally, you can access the "*Contacto*" (Contact) view, as seen in **Figure 6**, where a popup window shows a form for reporting incidents or submitting comments about the application; such information is received by the administrator via electronic mail.

Table 2. Structure of table "locations" where all the extracted points from the news classified as road accidents are saved

Column	Description
id	Unique identifier of the row
news_id	Foreign key that references to the news table.
value	Text of the detected location.
is_correct	Boolean type column where it is specified if the row is the correct location of the news. Only one row per news entry can be marked as true.
was_detected	Boolean type column where it is specified if the row either was automatically generated during the information extraction processing or was manually done.
latitude	Latitude of the point of the row.
longitude	Longitude of the point of the row.
created_at	Date when the row was created
updated_at	Date when the row was modified for the last time.

The first step to access the application as an administrator user is through a login, which is shown in **Figure 7**. The user (i.e., the administrator) must type in a valid email and password that grants him the authorization to access with the mentioned role, with the possibility to mark the "Remember me" checkbox to keep the session open and avoid to log in again from the same browser in the future.

The user (being logged in) is redirected to the list of collected news classified as a road accident, as seen in **Figure 8** in the News List View. Here is presented a list of the processed news, sorted by the date of the most recent publication, including its visibility (that denotes if it is shown in the main view or not), the number of matches, and the date of the publication. The list can be filtered by four different modes: all, only the public, only the private, and all that cannot be located. The visibility of a news report can be changed in this view by clicking on the visibility of the register. Shaded records denote that they are private and non-shaded that they are public.

From the News Listing is possible to move to a view for manual register (see **Figure 9**), where the manipulation of the information process gets to a point in which it must be done manually. This view includes multiple elements:

Table 3. Structure of table "users" where are stored all the users that have the credentials to access the backend of the application

Column	Description
id	Unique identifier of the row
name	Name of the user.
email	Email of the user
password	Password hash of the user.
remember_token	User hash for the automatic login.
created_at	Date when the row was created.
updated_at	Date when the row was modified form the last time.

Figure 3. The main view of the application. Each pin in the map represents a point where a traffic incident has occurred; depending on the filters, it may only show accidents that have occurred recently.

- General information about the news article can be visualized in the upper left part, such as the title, the date it was published on, and the content.
- We can find a list that has the locations of the news article in the lower left part of this view. This list includes all the points that were automatically detected through the information extraction script and created manually. Because we have the information of the news available, it is possible to verify where the traffic incident happened (in case of its existence) and check if any of the locations given by the list is the exact match of the actual location of the news article. If none of the locations found in the list is the correct one, it is possible to register the right position manually. When a point is manually registered, the *was_detected* column in the *locations* table (from the database) gets assigned a *false* value. To select a point as correct, it is necessary to fill in the latitude and longitude fields of the location and update the register (this step is required to display a pin in the map correctly). Once we have a correct point (with its latitude and longitude), we can select it as the correct one and the visibility of that particular entry changes to 'public'.
- In the upper-right part of the view is a search field, where it is possible to enter any location. When searching for a location, a petition is sent to the Google Geocoding API, and it tries to find a match to such search. The search results are shown through the usage of pins on the map. If the point is not found or pinned correctly, it is possible to move the map to search for the correct location and create a pin through a double click or drag an existing pin.
- All the pins of the map are listed with their respective latitude and longitude coordinates in the lower right part of the screen.

Figure 4. View with information about a road mishap that occurred in one of the points marked by a pin

Figure 5. "About" view

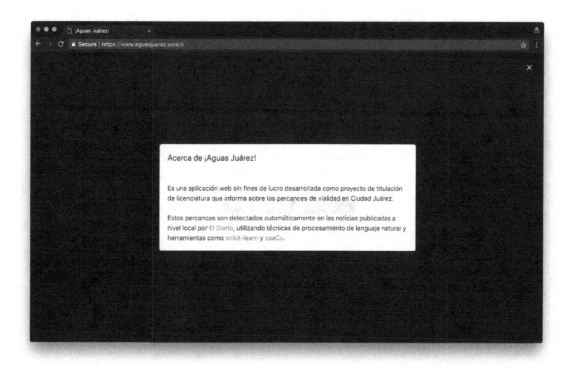

Figure 6. Contact view

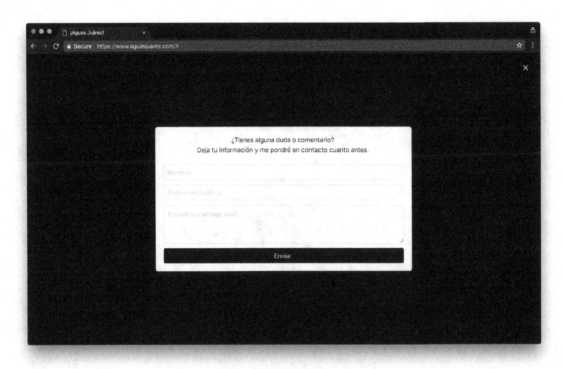

Figure 7. Login view

Figure 8: News Listing view

Figure 9. Individual register view

When a location, with its respective latitude and longitude, is marked as correct, the news article is considered wholly processed, and from that moment on, it is available to be shown in the main view of the web application.

RESULTS

From the 207 new reports that included a road accident and were using to test the effectiveness of the extractor, we carried a filtering process before analyzing the results. Those items that included at least one of the following characteristics were not considered in the analysis:

- There are mentioned multiple road mishaps (usually grouping past news).
- It is about a road, but not a road accident.
- The event occurred outside the city.
- It is not related to a road accident.
- Other news reports about the same road accident and does not significantly change the redaction (repeated news).
- It is a road accident but does not specify the location.

These filters allowed to remove 69 elements, and then the evaluation of the information extraction process was performed over the 138 news reports that were relevant to the project. From this group of 138 items, using the extraction rules previously defined the extractor found matches in all of the news, and therefore had a 100% rate of success in finding locations in a Spanish-written text; however, the extractor presented issues in 47% of the cases as shows data in Table 4, mainly because the report included multiple street names (usually referring to an intersection), or it mentioned an address in a way that was not expected when the extraction rules were created. In these cases, it was necessary to manually select the correct result among the multiple matches that were found. A characteristic that stands out is that the extractor was always able to extract a location from a Spanish report if it contained one.

Table 4. Results of the extraction of location in the news classified as a road accident

Detection	Total news
Partial. The location was detected in parts, incompletely, or with words to spare.	64
Exactly. The location was exactly detected, as described in the news.	74

CONCLUSION

The presented proposal intends to mitigate the consequences (time losses) caused by accidents that happened in the roads of an individual's route. In most cities, there are everyday situations that vary from blocked roads or traffic jams to car crashes and some other incidents that require a street to be blocked; these situations may cause people to arrive late to their destination. The proposed solution allows drivers in a Mexican city to know where has happened an accident recently, where a roadblock is, or get informed about any kind of road incident that could slow down the traffic. This project is done using NLP to extract locations from texts written in Spanish language and displaying those points pinned in a map; this allows people to take preventive actions (taking other routes or preparing earlier).

The news articles that the extractor used for this project were obtained from a local newspaper of a Mexican city (specifically Ciudad Juárez); those were previously classified in order to avoid reports that did not include any location or did not refer to a traffic incident since there is no reason to try to find something where it is not.

After that processing, the location was extracted by applying the extraction rules specified in this chapter, which were always found successful when there was a location (although it could identify not a single correct result when multiple extraction rules found matching sentences in the text).

FUTURE RESEARCH

As we mentioned in the conclusions, the extraction process encountered many issues that made it difficult to get the location of the incidents. The leading cause is the lack of a regular structure in the news reports; in some cases, there were articles that did not mention any location at all, but some others vaguely mentioned an address and therefore was difficult for the algorithm to detect it. Since newspaper articles do not present a strict structure in their writing style, it would be useful to develop an algorithm that is capable of identifying whether a document may or not include a location (without the need of explicitly identifying it); it would allow to discard those that do not present this information and reduce the time wasted in a search that will not yield anything at all. Additionally, the extractor used in this chapter did not detect all the locations exactly (as shown in Table 4) and required human intervention to decide which one of all the matchings was the correct result. Future research could focus on improving the extraction rules, so it does not produce multiple matches because of the lack of a more specific extraction rule.

On the other hand, since this application was designed as a web application, the improvement must be made to develop a mobile app that does not require the user to type a web address but to simply click an icon in their smartphone to get informed about incidents that have occurred in the city. Therefore, the development of an Application Program Interface (API) could be useful to communicate the information with a smartphone application and then adequately inform the community about these events. This approach could then be widely extended through the implementation of a crowdsourcing interface so that the information gathering does not only depend on news articles, but also on reports that citizens post and share. Also, the usage of different sources (other newspapers, social media content, or some crowdsourcing methods) could increase the coverage for a city about traffic incidents.

REFERENCES

Amin-Naseri, M., Chakraborty, P., Sharma, A., Gilbert, S. B., & Hong, M. (2018). Evaluating the Reliability, Coverage, and Added Value of Crowdsourced Traffic Incident Reports from Waze. *Transportation Research Record: Journal of the Transportation Research Board*, *2672*(43), 1–10. doi:10.1177/0361198118790619

Beeferman, D., Berger, A., & Lafferty, J. (1999). Statistical Models for Text Segmentation. *Machine Learning*, *34*(1-3), 177–210. doi:10.1023/A:1007506220214

Cabeza Ruiz, R. (2016). *Text segmentation by language*. Academic Press.

Chen, P., Chen, F., & Qian, Z. (2014). Road Traffic Congestion Monitoring in Social Media with Hinge-Loss Markov Random Fields. In R. Kumar, H. Tolvonen, J. Pel, J. Zhexue Huang, & X. Wu (Eds.), *14th IEEE International Conference on Data Mining* (pp.80-89). 10.1109/ICDM.2014.139

Chourabi, H., Nam, T., Walker, S., Gil-García, J. R., Mellouli, S., Nahon, K., ... Scholl, H. J. (2012, January). Understanding Smart Cities: An Integrative Framework. In *2012 45th Hawaii International Conference on System Sciences* (pp. 2289-2297). IEEE.

Cutting, D., Kupiec, J., Pedersen, J., & Sibun, P. (1992). A Practical Part-of-Speech Tagger. In M. Bates, & O. Stock (Eds.), *Proceedings of the third Conference on Applied Natural Language Processing* (pp.133-140). Stroudsburg, PA: Association for Computational Linguistics. 10.3115/974499.974523

Derczynski, L., Maynard, D., Rizzo, G., van Erp, M., Gorrell, G., Troncy, R., Petrak, J., & Bontcheva, K. (2015). Analysis of named entity recognition and linking for tweets. *Information Processing & Management*, *51*(2), 32–49. doi:10.1016/j.ipm.2014.10.006

Doan, A., Ramakrishnan, R., & Vaithyanathan, S. (2006). Managing information extraction: state of the art and research directions. In *Proceedings of the 2006 ACM SIGMOD international conference on Management of data* (pp. 799-800). ACM. 10.1145/1142473.1142595

Eckley, D. C., & Curtin, K. M. (2013). Evaluating the spatiotemporal clustering of traffic incidents. *Computers, Environment and Urban Systems*, *37*, 70–81. doi:10.1016/j.compenvurbsys.2012.06.004

Engels, R., & Bremdal, B. (2000). *Information Extraction: State-of-the-Art Report*. On-To-Knowledge Consortium.

Gu, Y., Qian, Z., & Chen, F. (2016). From Twitter to detector: Real-time traffic incident detection using social media data. *Transportation Research Part C, Emerging Technologies*, *67*, 321–342. doi:10.1016/j.trc.2016.02.011

Holguin, L., Ochoa-Zezzatti, A., Larios, V. M., Cossio, E., Maciel, R., & Rivera, G. (2019). Small steps towards a smart city: Mobile application that provides options for the use of public transport in Juarez City. In *2019 IEEE International Smart Cities Conference* (pp. 100-105). IEEE. 10.1109/ISC246665.2019.9071728

Honnibal, M., & Montani, I. (2017). *spaCy 2: Natural language understanding with Bloom embeddings, convolutional neural networks and incremental parsing*. Academic Press.

Huang, H., & Zhang, B. (2009). Text Segmentation. In L. Liu & M. T. Özsu (Eds.), *Encyclopedia of Database Systems*. Springer. doi:10.1007/978-0-387-39940-9_421

Jiang, J. (2012). Information extraction from text. In C. Aggarwal & C. Zhai (Eds.), *Mining text data* (pp. 11–41). Springer. doi:10.1007/978-1-4614-3223-4_2

Jizba, L. (1997). Reflections on Summarizing and Abstracting. *Journal of Internet Cataloging*, *1*(2), 15–39. doi:10.1300/J141v01n02_03

Koshorek, O., Cohen, A., Mor, N., Rotman, M., & Berant, J. (2018). Text Segmentation as a Supervised Learning Task. In *Proceedings of NAACL-HLT* (pp. 469-473). 10.18653/v1/N18-2075

Kosseim, L., Beauregard, S., & Lapalme, G. (2001). Using information extraction and natural language generation to answer email. *Data & Knowledge Engineering*, *38*(1), 85–100. doi:10.1016/S0169-023X(01)00018-0

Kosseim, L., Plamondon, L., & Guillemette, L. J. (2003, June). Answer formulation for question answering. In *Conference of the Canadian Society for Computational Studies of Intelligence* (pp. 24–34). Springer.

Loos, B., & Biemann, C. (2008). Supporting Web-based Address Extraction with Unsupervised Tagging. In C. Preisach, H. Burkhardt, L. Schmidt-Thieme, & R. Decker (Eds.), *Data Analysis, Machine Learning and Applications. Studies in Classification, Data Analysis, and Knowledge Organization* (pp. 577–584). Springer. doi:10.1007/978-3-540-78246-9_68

Marzinotto, G., Damnati, G., & Béchet, F. (2019). Adapting a FrameNet Semantic Parser for Spoken Language Understanding using Adversarial Learning. *Proc. Interspeech*, *799-803*, 799–803. Advance online publication. doi:10.21437/Interspeech.2019-2732

Mohanty, S. P., Choppali, U., & Kougianos, E. (2016). Everything you wanted to know about smart cities: The Internet of things is the backbone. *IEEE Consumer Electronics Magazine*, *5*(3), 60–70. doi:10.1109/MCE.2016.2556879

Nenkova, A., & McKeown, K. (2011). Automatic summarization. *Foundations and Trends in Information Retrieval*, *5*(2-3), 103–233. doi:10.1561/1500000015

Ochoa Ortiz-Zezzatti, A., Rivera, G., Gómez-Santillán, C., & Sánchez Lara, B. (2019). *Handbook of Research on Metaheuristics for Order Picking Optimization in Warehouses to Smart Cities*. IGI Global. doi:10.4018/978-1-5225-8131-4

Pak, I., & Teh, P. L. (2018). Text Segmentation Techniques: A Critical Review. In I. Zelinka, P. Vasant, V. Duy, & T. Dao (Eds.), *Innovative Computing, Optimization and its Applications* (pp. 167–181). doi:10.1007/978-3-319-66984-7_10

Rajwani, H., Somvanshi, S., Upadhye, A., Vaidya, R., & Dange, T. (2015). Dynamic Traffic Analyzer Using Twitter. *International Journal of Scientific Research (Ahmedabad, India)*, *4*(10), 984–987.

Sagayam, R., Srinivasan, S., & Roshni, S. (2012). A survey of text mining: Retrieval, extraction and indexing techniques. *International Journal of Computational Engineering Research*, *2*(5), 1443–1446.

Sarawagi, S. (2008). Information Extraction. *Foundations and Trends in Databases*, *1*(3), 261–377. doi:10.1561/1900000003

Webster, J. J., & Kit, C. (1992). Tokenization as the initial phase in NLP. In *COLING1992: The 15th International Conference on Computing Linguistics*. 10.3115/992424.992434

Zhang, Y., & Vines, P. (2004, July). Using the web for automated translation extraction in cross-language information retrieval. In M. Sanderson, K. Järvelin, J. Allan, & P. Bruza (Eds.), *Proceedings of the 27th annual international ACM SIGIR conference on Research and development in information retrieval* (pp. 162-169). New York, NY: ACM. 10.1145/1008992.1009022

Chapter 17

Text Summarization and Its Types:
A Literature Review

Namrata Kumari
(iD) https://orcid.org/0000-0001-6880-4206
National Institute of Technology, Hamirpur, India

Pardeep Singh
(iD) https://orcid.org/0000-0002-4019-604X
National Institute of Technology, Hamirpur, India

ABSTRACT

Text summarization is a compressing technique of the original text to form a summary which will provide the same meaning and information as provided by the original version. Summarizer helps in saving time and increasing efficiency. This chapter gives the full insight of text summarizers, which can be categorized based on methodology, function and target reader, dimension, and language. Various researches have been conducted in the field of text summarization using different approaches. Consequently, the chapter aims to provide an overview of how text summarizers work with different methods and state their domain-oriented applications. Additionally, the authors discuss multi-lingual text summarization in detail. This chapter focuses on showing the effectiveness and shortcomings of text summarization approaches by comparing them.

INTRODUCTION

In the present era, nobody has enough time to go through the full documentation to get the full meaning. So, there is an immense need for automatic text summarization to save time and to make it easy for humans. Text summarization helps in creating bulletin, headings, summary, brief description, finding out the essential words, and so on. Text summarization helps in creating a summary of the data set without altering the actual meaning of data, which includes essential information as well. The need for text

DOI: 10.4018/978-1-7998-4730-4.ch017

Copyright © 2021, IGI Global. Copying or distributing in print or electronic forms without written permission of IGI Global is prohibited.

summarization can also be understood by an example suppose someone wants to read documents which are related to text mining from a vast miscellaneous database, and he starts reading all documents one by one and hence consumes much time, but if there is a list of all headings, then the person can directly read materials related to text mining. Other examples are – news headlines in the newspaper, the title of a book, and many more. Text summarization is essential because a massive growth in the information requires high maintenance.

Abstractive text summarization and extractive text summarization are the two major categories in text summarization. Abstractive summarization refers to recreate the whole document in a few words or lines, which may include new words as well. Extractive summarization refers to extract the critical words or lines from the original document. To clear the difference between abstractive and extractive to consider an example – a man is reading a document, and while reading, he is highlighting the main sentences to remember the vital part; after that, he writes the whole document using a pen to make notes. The highlighted sentences and pen-written notes both describes the original document in brief but are placed in different categorization. A highlighted summary is an example of extractive summarization, and a pen-written summary is an abstractive summarization. Machines or tools used to create a summary are known as summarizers. These tools are language-dependent.

Summarizers take text data as input to produce a summary. If the tool produces a summary in one or more languages other than the original language, then it is referred to as multilingual text summarization. The main idea of multilingual text summarization is to save time and complexity. Earlier summarizers worked for the single document, but now many documents can be feed to the machine as input and referred as multiple document summarizer. Tools are mainly designed by keeping the target reader in mind. It can be indicative, informative of query focused. Without giving much content, indicative summaries help in providing an idea about the text, while informative summaries provide a shortened version of the content. Necessary steps in creating a summary are:

a)   feed text input to the machine in one or more languages;
b)   pre-processing and feature extraction;
c)   sentence selection and assembly;
d)   summary generation in the desired language.

Figure 1 shows a generic architecture of text summarization. Text data is taken as input; important terms are extracted, and on their basis sentence ranking is done; high ranked sentences are selected, and low-rank sentences are rejected and then combined to form a summary; output can be in one (monolingual) language or different (multilingual) language.

The proposed chapter will be helpful to all the readers in understanding the basics of text summarization. To make this chapter enjoyable and to make concepts more precise, a proper flow will be maintained. Real-life examples will be given to clear the picture of text summarization. Pictorial explanations will support this chapter to make the chapter more interesting for the students, notably. Different Multilingual text summarization approaches will be discussed in detail, explaining the importance of each and difference among all. Comparison of different Multilingual text summarization tools will be made based on their accuracy (in percentage), shortcomings, and effectiveness. Queries like how to calculate accuracy and what are the parameters to calculate the accuracy will be covered in this chapter. While reviewing the tools, the dataset used will also be the significant concerned area for comparisons as efficiency and accuracy can be depicted based on the dataset used. The trend of text summarization will help the reader to know about the past, present, and future of text summarization.

The chapter will begin with describing text summarization and its architecture to get the basic knowledge of summarization techniques. After this, various types of text summarizers will be described in detail, including their architecture and working. The chapter will focus on the various approaches used in Multilingual summarization and tools used for it. Once Multilingual summarization is explained in detail, then the chapter will move towards challenges in Multilingual summarization. Trends in text summarization will be discussed by mentioning it past, present, and future. A comparison of various text summarization techniques will be covered in two tables. One table will be showing a comparison of text summarization techniques based on abstractive text summarization, and another table will show comparison based on extractive text summarization techniques.

In this chapter architecture of multilingual summarization will be discussed in detail. Multilingual text summarization can also be used to depict the day to day trend analysis on Twitter and other social sites data, which leads to telling about a trending topic and most wanted product in the market. Summarization can be done either line by line or word by word. There are specific approaches for doing Multilingual summarization, such as the statistical approach, syntactical approach, rule-based approach, neural network approach, deep learning approach, machine-learning approach, and many more.

Figure 1. The generic architecture of text summarization

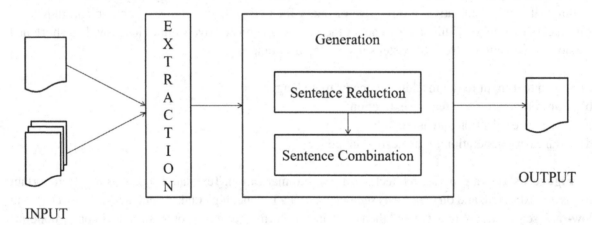

BACKGROUND

Day by day data is increasing, and similarly, a technique to handle the data is also increasing and enhancing. In-text summarization, previously human used to summarize manually, which was efficient but much time taken. As technology grows, text summarization techniques discovered. Two main techniques (abstractive summarization and extractive summarization) were introduced. Both are having different capabilities and features. Like abstractive is challenging to do but always produces a precise and grammatically correct summary.

On the other hand, extractive produce summary in no time, but it lacks semantic structure. A detailed description of each text summarization approach is provided in the tables mentioning technique they use to summarize along with their advantage, disadvantage, and performance of the summaries produces using the particular approach. Some performance is written about the precision measure, some about accuracy level, and some rouge values. Based on text summarization classification, tables are constructed. In total, there are three tables in this section. One for various extractive text summarization techniques, second for structured based abstractive text summarization and third for semantic-based abstractive text summarization.

TYPES OF TEXT SUMMARIZATION

Text summarization can be classified based on input, language, and an approach used (as shown in **Figure 2**). As an input, document feed to the system can be a single document or multiple documents. As per the requirement, text summarization can be needed in different (multilingual) language or one (monolingual) language only. Broadly, text summarization can be categorized as Extracting Summarization and Abstract Summarization. An extractive summary collects essential information and consolidate all together to form a meaningful summary. In the case of abstractive text summarization, knowledge of source text is essential to interpret the data.

Figure 2. Categorization of text summarization

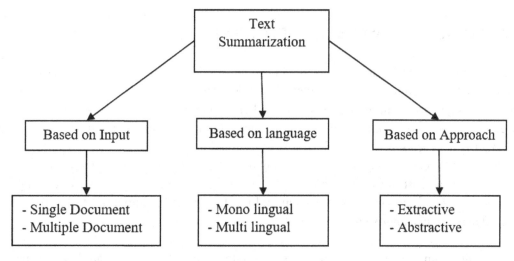

1. Extractive Text Summarization

The informative sentences are selected from the document as they appeared in the source based on specific criteria to create summaries. For extractive text summarization, one must know which sentences are meaningful and are supposed to be covered in summary. For this purpose, a sentence is referred to as features. After assigning the score, rank is calculated for every sentence.

a)   TF-IDF Method
b)   Cluster-Based Method
c)   Text Summarization with Neural Network
d)   Graph-based Method
e)   Query-based summarization

2. Abstractive Text Summarization

Abstractive summarization refers to recreate the whole document in a few words or lines, which may include new words as well.

a)   Structured Based Approach
    i.   Tree-Based Method.
    ii.   Template Based Method
    iii.   Ontology-Based Method
    iv.   Lead and Body Phrase Method
    v.   Rule-Based Method
b)   Semantic-Based Approach
    i.   Multimodal semantic model
    ii.   Information item-based method
    iii.   Semantic Graph-Based Method

MULTILINGUALGUAL TEXT SUMMARIZATION

These multilingual summaries are language-independent summaries. In different languages, a summary is generated by the system based on the relevant corpora. An example of a news channel can also understand multilingual text summarization. Suppose there is a channel 'A' broadcast news in the English language, and viewers do not know the English language but know the Hindi language; therefore, that news channel is hard work becomes null. If a news channel uses multilingual systems, then news can be broadcast in different languages without writing them again. For multilingual text summarizer, the system must work at least in two different languages. The generated summary must be compiled in a single document. The summary must be fluent and must cover every important topic from the input document. There are two approaches:

a)   Documents from source language are translated into the target language and then summarized on target language;
b)   Language-specific tools are used for condensation in the source language, and then machine translation is applied to the summarized text.

Review of Various Multilingual Text Summarizers

The table shown below tells about the various multilingual text summarizers by mentioning their features and availability. The software is freely available, few have a trial period, and rest is paid. An important topic covered in the table is that it tells about the size of the summary produced by different tools. Some produce a summary with the constraint of several lines and some with the compression percentage. Some summarizers are available in the form of API, software, and online web pages.

Table 1. Comparison study of various text summarization tools

S.No.	Tools/Software	Features	Availability
1.	Ultimate Research analyst	It is an online search engine. It can be used for text summarization, clustering of hierarchical concepts. It produces a summary in 10 lines.	It is an online multiple document Summarizer Tool that is available freely, but for a limited trial, later services will be charged.
2.	SMMRY	It is an online summarizer, and it also has an API. It produces a summary in 7 lines.	It is free API, but for only the first 100 trials, later on, works on payment mode. It is a single document summarizer.
3.	Esummarizer	Esummarizer is an online text summarization system. It produces a summary in 10 lines.	It is a paid single document text summarizer.
4.	iResearch Reporter	It is an online summarizer, and they provide API as well. It is not restricted to produce a summary in a fixed number of sentences.	It is a multiple document text summarizer. It is a fully paid summarizer and limited to produce 45 summaries per day.
5.	Columbia Newsblaster	It is restricted to produces news summary. As a result, it produces a web page that includes important news of the day.	It is a multiple document text summarizer. It is paid.
6.	JistWb	It is a query-based text summarizer. It is available as JistWeb and Jistdesktop.	Majorly it is used for single-document summarization.
7.	Tools4noobs	It is an online text summarizer. Summary size can be customized as per user requirement. The summary must have a sentence of at least 50 characters.	It is a single document text summarizer. It is a free text summarizer.
8.	Wiki-Summarizer	It is a web-based text summarizer	Open source Freely available.
9.	MEAD	It is an extractive text summarizer. It is a publicly available toolkit. The summary size can be customized.	It is a multilingual text summarizer. It is available for free but for limited trials.
10.	RESOOMER	An API based text summarization. It is a multilingual text summarizer.	It is freely available.
11.	SplitBrain	It is a web-based multilingual text summarizer. Summary size can be fixed in percentage (5% to 80%).	It is a single document based text summarizer. Freely available.
12.	Intellexer Summarizer	It is for professionals and is available as API and SDK.	It is a paid multiple document text summary generator.
13.	SummarizeBot	It is a professional multilingual text summarizer. It is an API based text summarizer. It is not limited to text summarization; it also does auto summarization.	It is a paid service.
14.	NLP V.4	It is a professional tool for text summarization and extraction.	It is a paid software, but there is a free trial.
15.	Mirplacid Text	It is available as SDK and server edition.	It is the license based text summarizer.

Challenges

Evaluation of summary is the biggest challenge for any text summarizer. Summarizers must be efficient enough to produce a relevant summary. The produced summary must include all the essential terms discussed in the input document. The flow of the document should be preserved in the produced summary. Otherwise, the summary is of no use. The summary should not include any irrelevant information and hence should be removed efficiently. The summary should be readable and precise. The summary generated must be grammatically correct.

Applications of Multilingual Text Summarization

Text summarization is not limited to one field. Instead, it is applied in various fields such as medical, multimedia, news, and many more. Text summarization is helpful in various scenarios such as headlines helps in knowing world's activity; last-minute notes of any book for the students in exam time; in making last-minute notes from the meeting; a synopsis of daily soaps; share market bullet-in reports; chronologically arranged titles help in history; review of any product, book, movie.

Evaluation Metrics

Evaluating a summary is not an easy and direct task. The evaluation must tell about be the accuracy of the summary of whether a summary is complete and precise or not. A comparison of the summary generated is made to find its accuracy. One can compare the summary in two ways. One way is to compare generated summary with a manually generated summary, and another way is to compare some evaluation metrics of generated summary and summary generated by other systems. Therefore, evaluation can be of two types:

a) intrinsic
b) extrinsic

To check the quality of the summary, it should be grammatically correct, non-redundant, and good structure. A summary is judged based on the compression ratio, i.e., how much generated summary is shorter than the original text and retention ratio, i.e., ration of information in summary to the information in full data. There are some gold standards to measure intrinsic evaluation. Intrinsic focuses on text coherence and information coverage in summary. There are some metrics in intrinsic evaluation, such as precision, recall, and sentence rank. The ratio of sentences that are common in both (in generated an ideal summary) to the sentences in the source. Extrinsic evaluation judge or measure the summary based on efficiency and acceptability.

All the comparative measures such as advantages, disadvantages, techniques, performance measure evaluation are covered for each of the text summarization in the above tables. **Table 2** shows the details of all the extractive text summarization techniques and, based on that, Text summarization With Neural Networks outperforms. **Table 3** shows the comparison of all the structured based abstractive text summarization and **Table 4** shows the comparison of semantic-based abstractive text summarization. Using the data provided in the above tables, **Table 5** is constructed in which all the performance metrics values are used to calculate the average performance.

Table 2. Comparison of various extractive text summarization techniques

S. No.	Technique/ Method	Content Selection	Summary Generation	Advantage	Disadvantage	Performance
1.	Term Frequency-Inverse Document Frequency Method	Terms that are occurring mostly are ranked as TF. Terms that are not occurring frequently as ranked as IDF.	Words having a high TF-IDF score are selected to form a summary.	Respondents can understand a summary with an average of 83.8%.	In advance, the user cannot know about terms.	67% accuracy, evaluated by Christian H. in 2016
2.	Cluster-Based Method	Word frequency and sentence location features are used to calculate the sentence score.	From each cluster, high ranked sentences are selected to form a summary.	Clustering makes it less redundant.	It only performs for a single document.	Rouge1=0.431, Rouge2=0.10142, calculated by Zhang et al. (2009)
3.	Graph-Theoretic Approach	It uses a ranking algorithm to rank sentences.	High ranked sentences were selected and combined to form a summary.	Removes redundant information; improves coherency.	It cannot summarize multiple documents.	Rouge1 = 0.5312, Rouge L = 0.4978, calculated by Kuppan(2009).
4.	Text summarization With Neural Networks	The network is pruned and generalize to classify data as a summary and non-summary.	Detailed data as 'summary' is selected.	As per the user's requirements, the set of features can be altered.	Training is slow, and it is complex to understand its processing.	0.778 precision, calculated by Sinha et al. (2018).
5.	Query Based Extractive Text Summarization	The ranking is done based on the frequency of the query term.	Sentences with high rank were selected.	Language independent.	Lacks in sentence simplification techniques	Rouge1=0.4025, Rouge2=0.09324, calculated by Zhao (2009).

CONCLUSION

Text summarization is an emerging field in natural language processing. The purpose of this chapter is to provide a detailed description of various text summarization techniques. The review helps in understanding the current trend in text summarization. Multilingual text summarization is the need in the market now. Most of the work has been done in extractive text summarization, and it is the time to explore abstractive text summarization. From the observations made in **Table 5**, it is concluded that abstractive text summarization is more accurate and grammatically correct than extractive text summarization. From the extractive techniques categorization, query-based methodology outperforms and in case of abstractive Lead and Body phrase technique produce a more precise summary. A literature survey comes up with the idea of combining various techniques to provide a complete, informative, and precise summary.

Table 3. Comparison of various structure-based abstractive text summarization techniques

S. No.	Technique/ Method	Content Selection	Summary Generation	Advantage	Disadvantage	Performance
1.	Tree-based	Theme Intersection algorithm	Sentence fusion	The language generator helps in improving summary quality.	While capturing the content selection, the main context of the sentences gets rejected	0.98 precision, calculated by Barzilay R. (2005).
2.	Template-based	Linguistic pattern or extraction rule	IE-based summarization algorithm	It generates a highly coherent summary.	It is challenging as designing and generalizing phase.	78.7% accuracy, calculated by Geng et al. (2006).
3.	Ontology-based	Classifier	New Agent	The handling of uncertain data is possible while it is not possible in the simple domain ontology.	It is time-consuming because it can be defined by domain experts only.	Rouge1=0.4636, Rouge2=0.2040, calculated by Henning et al. (2008).
4.	Lead & Body Phrase	Revision candidates	Insertion & substitution operation on phrases	It is good for semantically appropriate summary	A grammatical error will occur.	Precision=0.97, calculated by Hideki (2009).
5.	Rule-based	Information extraction rules	Generate patterns	Generate a meaningful summary.	Time-consuming and complex task because the rules are manually constructed.	Precision=0.98, calculated by John (2013).

Table 4. Comparison of various semantic-based abstractive text summarization techniques

S. No.	Technique/ Method	Content Selection	Summary Generation	Advantage	Disadvantage	Performance
1.	Multimodal Semantic-based	Simple NLG	Generation technique synchronous tree	A semantic model captures concepts and relations among concepts.	The evaluation is to be done manually.	Rouge1 = 0.333, Rouge2 = 0.200, calculated by Shumming et al. (2017).
2.	Information item based	Generated sentences can be ranked based on document frequency	NLG realize simple NLG	The summary is a small, coherent, and information-rich summary.	Sometimes useful information item is complicated in constructing grammatically correct sentences. It reduces the linguistic quality of the summary.	Rouge1=0.418, Rouge2=0.102, calculated by Genest et al. (2011).
3.	Semantic graph-based	Calculation of each concept and their sentences	Reduced semantic graph	Grammatically correct and less redundant summary.	It is limited to a single document.	54% accuracy, calculated by Dalal (2017).

Table 5. Comparison of performance on average between extractive and abstractive technique

S. No.	Technique	Average Performance
1.	Extractive Text Summarization	59% 0.778 precision
2.	Abstractive Text Summarization	75.35% 0.796 precision

REFERENCES

Barzilay, R., & McKeown, K. R. (2005). Sentence fusion for multidocument news summarization. *Computational Linguistics*, *31*(3), 297–328. doi:10.1162/089120105774321091

Christian, H., Agus, M. P., & Suhartono, D. (2016). Single Document Automatic Text Summarization using Term Frequency-Inverse Document Frequency (TF-IDF). ComTech: *Computer. Mathematics and Engineering Applications*, *7*(4), 285–294.

Dalal, V., & Malik, L. (2017, March). Semantic Graph Based Automatic Text Summarization for Hindi Documents Using Particle Swarm Optimization. In *International Conference on Information and Communication Technology for Intelligent Systems* (pp. 284-289). Springer.

Genest, P. E., & Lapalme, G. (2011, June). Framework for abstractive summarization using text-to-text generation. In *Proceedings of the workshop on monolingual text-to-text generation* (pp. 64-73). Academic Press.

Geng, H., Zhao, P., Chen, E., & Cai, Q. (2006, July). A novel automatic text summarization study based on term co-occurrence. In *2006 5th IEEE International Conference on Cognitive Informatics* (Vol. 1, pp. 601-606). IEEE. 10.1109/COGINF.2006.365553

Hennig, L., Umbrath, W., & Wetzker, R. (2008, December). An ontology-based approach to text summarization. In *2008 IEEE/WIC/ACM International Conference on Web Intelligence and Intelligent Agent Technology* (Vol. 3, pp. 291-294). IEEE. 10.1109/WIIAT.2008.175

John, A., & Wilscy, M. (2013, December). Random forest classifier based multi-document summarization system. In 2013 IEEE Recent Advances in Intelligent Computational Systems (RAICS) (pp. 31-36). IEEE. doi:10.1109/RAICS.2013.6745442

Kuppan, S., & Sobha, L. (2009, June). An Approach to Text Summarization. In *Proceedings of the Third International Workshop on Cross Lingual Information Access: Addressing the Information Need of Multilingual Societies (CLIAWS3)* (pp. 53-60). Academic Press.

Ma, S., Sun, X., Xu, J., Wang, H., Li, W., & Su, Q. (2017). *Improving semantic relevance for sequence-to-sequence learning of Chinese social media text summarization*. arXiv preprint arXiv:1706.02459

Sinha, A., Yadav, A., & Gahlot, A. (2018). *Extractive text summarization using neural networks*. arXiv preprint arXiv:1802.10137

Tanaka, H., Kinoshita, A., Kobayakawa, T., Kumano, T., & Kato, N. (2009, August). Syntax-driven sentence revision for broadcast news summarization. In *Proceedings of the 2009 Workshop on Language Generation and Summarisation* (pp. 39-47). Association for Computational Linguistics. 10.3115/1708155.1708163

Zhang, P. Y., & Li, C. H. (2009, August). Automatic text summarization based on sentences clustering and extraction. In *2009 2nd IEEE international conference on computer science and information technology* (pp. 167-170). IEEE. 10.1109/ICCSIT.2009.5234971

Zhao, L., Wu, L., & Huang, X. (2009). Using query expansion in graph-based approach for query-focused multi-document summarization. *Information Processing & Management, 45*(1), 35–41. doi:10.1016/j.ipm.2008.07.001

KEY TERMS AND DEFINITIONS

Abstractive: Paraphrasing of the data.

Coherent: Summary should be in flow as same as in input data.

Completeness: Summary comprising of all-important information covered in input data.

Extractive: Selection of relevant sentences.

Extrinsic: It measures the summary on the basis of efficiency and acceptability.

Intrinsic: Used for evaluation by calculating evaluating metrics.

Multi-Document: More than one document file.

Precision: It indicates the true-positive predictive value.

Recall: It indicates the true-positive value.

Redundant: Summary should not include any unwanted information.

Semantic: Branch of linguistics and logic, concerned with meaning.

Summary: Brief description of the full document while preserving the full meaning.

Chapter 18
Extractive Text Summarization Methods in the Spanish Language

Irvin Raul Lopez Contreras
Universidad Autónoma de Ciudad Juárez, Mexico

Alejandra Mendoza Carreón
Universidad Autónoma de Ciudad Juárez, Mexico

Jorge Rodas-Osollo
iD https://orcid.org/0000-0001-6588-8336
Universidad Autónoma de Ciudad Juárez, Mexico

Martiza Concepción Varela
Universidad Autónoma de Ciudad Juárez, Mexico

ABSTRACT

The quantity of information in the world is increasing every day on a fast level. This fact will be an obstacle in some situations; text summarization is involved in this kind of problem. It is used to minimize the time that people spend searching for information on the web and in a lot of digital documents. In this chapter, three algorithms were compared; all of them are an extractive text summarization algorithm. Popular libraries that influence the performance of these kinds of algorithms were used. It was necessary to configure and modify these methods so that they work for the Spanish language instead of their original one. The authors use some metrics found in the literature to evaluate the quality and performance of these algorithms.

DOI: 10.4018/978-1-7998-4730-4.ch018

Copyright © 2021, IGI Global. Copying or distributing in print or electronic forms without written permission of IGI Global is prohibited.

INTRODUCTION

Today, the information is growing fast every day; for that reason, it is important to have tools that can deal with some issues like the problem of search quality information in a fast way. This information can be used to solve a problem, to understand how something works, among other things. This information is often found in web pages, articles, books, among others, which may contain an extensive amount of text that makes what is important be lost in the content.

There are algorithms that seek to summarize the text based on certain summarization techniques; many of these techniques use Python libraries to perform this function. The two basic strategies used in the literature are extractive and abstractive. In this chapter, a review of some algorithms that focus on extractive techniques is presented. There are several areas that can take advantage of these tools, such as journals, magazines, newspapers, social networks, etc.

The present work has as main objective to analyze, according to metrics found in the literature, the operation of algorithms used in the text summarization field on text from the computer science field in the Spanish language. The algorithms that were implemented were previously used in studies found for texts in the English language. For these algorithms to work for the Spanish language, the obstacles that appear in this language should be satisfactorily faced. This chapter contains a report of the results of three algorithms based on extractive text summarization working with Spanish texts.

The proposed study consists of the following main steps:

1. Find some algorithms of text summarization that work on the English language (or another language).
2. Configure the algorithms to run in the Spanish language.
3. Evaluate the performance of the algorithms.

Currently, there are several algorithms in the literature that allows users to summarize texts in the English language, but unfortunately, there are a few for the Spanish language. It is for this reason that we consider that the present work could help to explore the area of text summarization in the Spanish language.

The Spanish language can present grammar problems that have to be considered in the text summarization algorithms, which can affect their performance. The work to be done compares the results obtained from the algorithms according to the language, so it is intended to contrast the operation of one algorithm with another and, in this way, identify which of those approaches can work best in the Spanish language.

The importance of this lies in the considerations that must be considered so that the algorithm performs the task correctly and subsequently; also, a comparison of their performance can be made. For the evaluation, parameters found in the literature were used. The result of the application of the algorithm must make sense and not lose the direction of what is in the content of the text.

This research could contribute to the development of algorithms for extracting information from texts in the Spanish language. This contribution will allow a better algorithm selection when using any of those utilized in the research to obtain better results according to the text to be summarized.

BACKGROUND

This section will present the background of text summarization, as well as related studies that have dealt with these algorithms with the Spanish language or other than the English language.

Text Summarization Approaches

On some occasions in our lives, there has been a need to read and understand the content of long text documents, whether for academic issues, work, or personal reasons. To more easily understand that large amount of text, people generally make a summary.

A summary is a reduced representation of the content of a text, which is made by extracting the sentences that a reader considers to be the central ideas of the original text. In other words, it is about building a condensed text that is concise and accurate from the original text. In this sense, automatic text summarization systems have become increasingly interesting within Natural Language Processing area.

To date, many automatic text summarization systems have been developed using different approaches. In the study by Hovy and Lin (1998), three main characteristics are defined to classify the different approaches based on:

a)   characteristics of the text to be processed (input);
b)   characteristics of the generated summary (output);
c)   characteristics of the use of the summary to be generated (purpose).

These characteristics are defined by Hovy and Lin (1998) as follows:

Input: It is subdivided into the following three characteristics:
- **Single or multiple documents:** This characteristic is given by the number of input documents that will be processed. If it is a single input text, it is defined as a *Single-Document* system, and, in the case of more than one text, it is defined as a *Multiple-Document* system.
- **Specificity:** This feature refers to the text domain for which the summarization system was designed. If it is only designed to process texts from a single domain, it is defined as a *Domain-specific* system. If the system is capable of processing texts from different domains, it is defined as a *General* system.
- **Genre and scale:** The *genre* refers to the nature of the document to be processed, that is, whether it is a newspaper article, novel, short story, book, etc. *Scale* refers to the size of the text to be processed, which can vary depending on whether it is a book or a paragraph.

Purpose: It is subdivided into the following three characteristics:
- **Audience:** When it comes to preserving the main ideas of the input text in the summary to be generated, and it is oriented to all types of users, it is defined as a *Generic* summary. If the system is oriented to the preferences of the user; that is, it considers specific ideas or aspects of the text, the summary that is generated is defined as a *Query-oriented* summary.
- **Usage:** If the summary to be generated contains the main ideas of the input text; that is, it is possible to describe the content of the input text, it is defined as an *Informative* summary. If the summary only contains a general description of the input text, that is, it does not contain informative content, it is defined as an *Indicative* summary.

- ◦ **Expansiveness:** If the summary to be generated includes an explanation as prior information of the topics because it is considered that the knowledge of the user is not adequate, it is defined as *Background* summary. If it only contains the main news or topics, assuming that the user has the necessary prior knowledge to interpret the news or topics, it is defined as a *Just-the-news* summary.

Output: As mentioned above, this characteristic focuses on the structure of the summary that will be generated.

- ◦ **Coherence:** Refers to the writing of the summary to be generated. If the grammatical rules are respected in all the sentences and a coherent structure is generated, that is, there is a relationship between the sentences, it is defined as a *Fluent* summary. On the other hand, if the sentences are fragmented, the grammatical rules are not respected, or there is no coherence between the sentences, it is defined as a *Disfluent* summary.
- ◦ **Partiality:** It refers to whether in the summary there is a bias towards an idea, concept, theme, etc. When the summary is generated without bias; that is, it reflects the idea of the input document, it is defined as a *Neutral* summary. If the summary is generated, highlighting a particular idea, that is, if there is a bias, the summary is defined as an *Evaluative* summary.
- ◦ **Conventionality:** This feature refers to the format of the summary. If the summary has a fixed format or is aimed at a specific type of user, that is, it is designed for a specific purpose, it is defined as a *Fixed* summary. If the summary is created in a variety of configurations, it can be aimed at different user types or different purposes, it is defined as a *Floating-situation* summary.
- ◦ **Derivation:** It refers to the way the summary is generated. If, when generating the summary, it is contemplated to extract units from the text, generally sentences, it is defined as an *Extractive* summary. If it is intended to generate new text from the input text, it is defined as an *Abstractive* summary.

Some of the characteristics described above are of interest to this research chapter: *Single Document* and *Derivation*. Addressing the processing of multiple documents involves dealing with multiple sources of information, which could mean that it is possible to have contradictory ideas specified in different documents. This implies that the generation of a consistent and complete summary becomes a highly complex task. In relation to Derivation, the functioning of abstractive methods is heavily based on linguistic techniques and advanced techniques of natural language generation, making them difficult to implement. This type of summary is very similar to how humans summarize texts. On the other hand, extractive methods are based on features such as keywords, word frequency, position in the text, etc., to determine the relevance of a sentence. The interest of this exploration work focuses on the extractive text summarization methods applied to single-document input.

As mentioned above, extractive text summarization methods generate summaries by selecting the most important statements in the input document. Because some sentences are more important than others, the challenge of extractive methods is to identify the most important sentences (Basiron, 2016; Das, 2007). According to Halizah Basiron (2016), the three most addressed approaches to sentence extraction are *Frequency-based* approach (Word Probability, Term Frequency – Inverse Document Frequency), *Feature-based* approach (Title / Headline Word, Sentence Position, Sentence Length, Term Weight, Proper Noun), and *Machine Learning*-based approach (Naive Bayes, Neural Network).

Abstractive Methods

This method is based on learning a representation of the internal language to generate summaries as a person would, paraphrasing the original text. In order to obtain a good result, it is necessary to create a model that allows creating effective summaries, for this, it is necessary to train said model with training values, the more they are used to train the model, the better the results will be.

The Google algorithm, named *Texsum,* uses a database of 4 million records for training, so it can yield good results if used properly. Otherwise, if little data is used to train the model, a poor-quality summary can be obtained, so it is an important factor in the abstract methods of text summarization that it uses as much training data as possible.

Extractive Methods

This method of text summarization is based on the extraction of words and phrases that are then used to create summaries. In this chapter, we will cover three algorithms that use this method of text summarization. These algorithms consider the *repetition of words*, *keywords*, *stopwords*, text length, and some other factors that the algorithm author has added.

There are Python libraries that contain functions that perform text summarization; these libraries are included in the Text summarization tools section. These libraries allow the text summarization process to be carried out if the preprocessing is carried out correctly, thus saving time in the coding of algorithms of this type.

Cases have been documented that are based on bioinspired algorithms for the elaboration of text summarization models by the extractive method. These summaries managed to obtain up to 43% similarity with the original text (Dalal & Malik,2013).

Steps for Text Summarization

Text summarization algorithms can be divided into two steps. The first step is the preprocessing phase, and the second step is the processing phase. The first phase searches for keywords that can be used to obtain a quality result, based on the repetition of the words and saving the sentences to analyze later how difficult they are for the text. In the second phase, the text is composed by considering what was preprocessed.

The result of the algorithm can vary according to the rules that have been taken in the preprocessing phase since the keywords and the keywords can vary according to the language and the criteria of the author.

There is a Python library named *Gensim* that performs text summarization using the extractive method; it performs the following series of steps to make a summary:

1.   Remove *stopwords* from text input along with words that are not relevant.
2.   Create a graph where the vertices are sentences.
3.   Connect each sentence with each of the other sentences; the weight of each edge indicates how similar they are to each other.
4.   Run the Google PageRank algorithm on the graph generated.
5.   Take the sentences with the best result.

With this practical example, we can see how a text summarization algorithm works, in this case, the *Gensim* algorithm does it by the extractive method, however, if the abstract method is used to perform an algorithm, the preprocessing phase and processing may be different from this example.

THE STATE-OF-THE-ART STUDIES

This section presents the related work of text summarization in other languages. Algorithms on the English language are found in the literature, but for a different language, their application is difficult. In many of the following researches, text summarization algorithms are used for various areas such as medicine, news, research, among others, but the purpose of such research is to treat these algorithms with a language other than English.

Research Work

In the paper "An Approach for Bengali Text Summarization using Word2Vector", a similar study is conducted in which the following is mentioned: Several studies have already been discussed for English language summarizers, but a few have already done for the Bengali language (Abujar, Kaisar, Masum, Mohibullah, Ohidujjaman & Hossain, 2019). In the Spanish language, we can find a similar case.

In the study "Arabic Text Keywords Extraction using Word2vec", the semantics of the Arabic language is worked for the extraction of the most relevant summary of a text (Suleiman, 2019).

In the paper "Text Summarization of Spanish Documents", the authors try to extract summaries of documents in Spanish, this without leaving relevant information outside the output text. In the paper, they document the steps that are carried out for the management of this information (Umadevi et al., 2018).

In the paper "Information Retrieval by Text Summarization for an Indian Regional Language", the authors try to extract summaries from large volumes of data. They work on Indian regional language (Kannada), so the text summarization algorithm they use must take this into account. For this, they develop an incorporate a Kannada dictionary to the algorithm (Kallimani,2010).

In the paper "Extractive Summarization for Myanmar Language" text summarization is worked in the Myanmar language, for this objective, it is also considered that an extractive text summarization method will be used, and it will be processed by single document using latent semantic analysis (Nwet, 2018).

In the paper "An Approach for Bengali Text Summarization using Word2Vector", a word2vector approach has been discussed for the Bengali language with algorithms for text summarization. It is mentioned how text summarization methods exist in the English language, but there is no documentation for the Bengali language. In addition, he mentions that the application of neural networks for these types of problems usually has better results (Abujar et al., 2019).

In the paper "A Survey of Extractive and Abstractive Text Summarization Techniques", the authors talk about how a text summarization algorithm is based on a bioinspired one and obtains better results than the summaries made by Microsoft Word. Also, they carry out text summarization by means of the abstractive method (Dalal & Malik 2013).

In the paper "Graph-Based Suggestion for Text Summarization", it is mentioned how the summary may be based on the graphs obtained through the sentences of the text. The authors explore the possibility of their model working for different languages. Furthermore, in the proposed model, they are based on an extractive model, since in-depth knowledge on the subject is not required to carry out the process (Cengiz et al.,2018).

Text Summarization Tools

Some tools used in natural language processing are described below.

Spacy has functions for text summarization, sentence splitter, and tokenizer, coreference resolution, named entity recognition, parts of speech tagging, relationship extraction, and others. Spacy has support for the following languages: English, German, French, Spanish, Greek, Norwegian, Swedish, Indonesian, and Persian.

Gensim has functions for modeling unsupervised topics and natural language processing, which uses modern automatic machine learning statistics.

NLTK has functions for parsing and chunker, relationship extraction, sentence splitter and tokenizer, text summarization, coreference resolution, and others. The following languages are supported by this library: Czech, Danish, Dutch, English, Estonian, Finnish, French, German, Greek, Italian, Norwegian, Polish, Portuguese, Slovene, Spanish, Swedish, Turkish. It is a leading library platform for industrial-powered natural language processing algorithms.

The *Heapq* library is used for implementing the heap sort algorithm, suitable for lists in Python. In text summarization algorithms, this library is usually used to find the best sentences of the input text.

COMPARISON OF EXTRACTIVE ALGORITHMS FOR THE SPANISH LANGUAGE

In the literature, three algorithms were found that fulfill the function of summarizing large texts in the English language. These algorithms implement different techniques that allow taking the most important part of the English text. In this way, according to the technique implemented, the most relevant of said literature is obtained. To perform an analysis of these algorithms in Spanish texts, it is necessary to configure these algorithms since they are not found in the literature in this way. The intention of this work is to compare the results using metrics found in the literature, in which the quality of the result is evaluated, as well as the performance of the algorithms.

It is necessary to make the adjustment to these algorithms so that they can operate correctly with the text that is going to summarize, which in this case will be in the Spanish language, so that in this way a correct summary of the processed text is obtained, since if the algorithm if the corresponding adjustments the summary or result of the text processing could give a summary with lack of meaning or poor quality.

The algorithms were taken from Internet sites in which the article reviews were positive by the users. These were selected from among several algorithms that were compiled. These three being the ones that best adapt to the problem that we want to cover since they work on the English language. They are relatively easy to adapt to the Spanish language, and they are duly documented in the place where they were taken.

Issues, Controversies, Problems

Currently, there are no algorithms in the literature that have been developed for the Spanish language; this presents a conflict with the algorithm because if the original algorithm is used to perform the analysis of Spanish texts, the result will be unconvincing or meaningless. Since the Spanish language presents many rules that differentiate the English language, it makes it difficult to perform the algorithm well.

The algorithms selected to perform the tests work for the English language, so it is necessary to adjust them so that they can work correctly with the Spanish texts. These modifications will be made only with the intention that the algorithm can process text in Spanish, leaving the rest of the code unchanged, so even though the algorithm is maintained in the same way, it can perform differently.

It is not easy to find a tool that can evaluate the result of these algorithms, especially when the result is in Spanish, a person has to evaluate the meaning of the text, as well as the purpose of the text to obtain an effective result.

There are some difficulties when validating the information because the best way to evaluate the result of the algorithms is for an expert to make a summary of the evaluated text and then compare it with the outputs of the algorithms; thus a comparison of both summaries can be made by identifying the summary more similar to the one by the expert.

Due to the little documentation found in the literature, it is difficult to find libraries that work with this type of problem in the Spanish language. This complicates the ease of being able to apply libraries already preloaded with functions that help to accomplish this task, since most of the libraries and frameworks that exist are oriented to the English language, so it is necessary to work with this type of problem to contribute to the construction of knowledge in this field for the Spanish language.

Although there are several studies related to text summarization for a language other than English, there are differences in the language structures that complicate the adaptation easily for any other language, this is because each language has grammatical rules that can affect algorithm performance, whether in the preprocessing phase rather than in the processing part, may still affect both phases.

General Operation

Text summarization works under the processing of natural language, so the algorithms that are used in this branch should result in a summary of a text, and that result should make sense, this is an important point for the quality assessment of the algorithm.

The text summarization algorithms follow a process as we see it below:

Step 1: Capturing key aspects of the text and storing it as an intermediate representation.
Step 2: Scoring sentences in the text based on that representation.
Step 3: Composing a summary by selecting several sentences.

The first and second steps are part of the preprocessing of the process since these are aimed at preparing the characteristics that the algorithm intends to address, to cover later the processing, which is the part where text summarization focuses, which is the composition of the summary or result.

In the first step, the paragraphs become sentences, and the most common delimiter is when a point is found, in this way, we have divided the paragraphs into small segments. Then, in the second step, a list of the words that are used in the sentences is made to be able to analyze the most used words in the text and identify the times that each word is repeated. Each sentence is then replaced with the sum of the times each word is used in the sentence. Finally, in the last step, by identifying the concurrence of the sentences in the text, an algorithm for extracting the most relevant information from the text is carried out.

The algorithms were taken to work with Python 2, but they were adapted to work with Python 3 since Python 2 support was terminated, and some libraries presented warnings; however, the performance of the algorithms is the same.

The First Algorithm

The first algorithm found was developed in Python in version 2. This algorithm is an extraction method. It was developed by Usman Malik, and it can be found on the "Stackabuse" site.

For this algorithm to work in the Spanish language, it was only necessary to modify the line in which the *stopwords* are called through the NTLK library, changing the language of the libraries to the Spanish language since the library already contains these *stopwords* in this language.

With this implementation, the algorithm worked correctly for the Spanish language, so it can perform the corresponding tests to compare it with the other algorithms.

In the algorithm, we can know how it is that the *stopwords* of the NTLK library are stored in a variable, and subsequently, the counting of the words in the text is carried out. Subsequently, the percentage of importance in the text is obtained (according to the maximum number of repetitions, in a word).

The Second Algorithm

The second algorithm was developed by Shivangi Sareen. It was developed in Python version 2. It is an extraction method, and it can be found on the medium site.

For the algorithm to work in the Spanish language, it was necessary to modify the function that takes the text of an Internet site since the function that was not working with "utf-8" characters, in addition to changing the *stopwords* with the NTLK library to the Spanish language.

In this way, the algorithm worked correctly with the Spanish text, and the tests could be performed correctly.

This algorithm, once the text of the site is obtained online, cleans the text of spaces, line breaks, special characters, and numbers.

Subsequently, the text summarization process is carried out using a function of the *Gensim* library.

According to the *Gensim* documentation, this function will yield a summary text based on the *TextRank* algorithm (NLP APIs, 2016).

The Third Algorithm

The third algorithm was developed by Anannya Uberoi and was developed in Python version 2. It is an extraction method, and it is located on the "Geeks for geeks" site.

This algorithm works with the *Spacy* Natural Language Processing library to preprocess the text before translating it with *Gensim*.

Subsequently, the code is processed with Gensim to perform the text summarization process, and then in the code, it can be seen how two text processes are carried out. In the first one, it is specified that only 5% of the text is wanted original as a summary, while the other specifies that a 200 words summary is wanted. Although the algorithm can be customized, it was left as the author of the specific algorithm.

In general, the three algorithms fulfilled the task of making a summary in the Spanish language; in the next section, we present the results and their comparison.

COMPARATIVE RESULTS

To put the algorithms into practice, a chapter of the book "Fundamentals of Databases" (Abraham Silberschatz, 2006) was used to evaluate these algorithms. The text of the selected chapter was transferred to a text file keeping the original format without images. This so that it could be read by the algorithm.

The selected chapter of the book was Chapter 1, which deals with a general introduction to the subject of databases. For this purpose, a summary was carried out by a person skilled in the subject, in this way we can compare the results of the algorithms using the *Precision*, *Recall* and *F-Measure* measures to evaluate the effectiveness of each algorithm. It is worth mentioning that the expert made the summary without considering keywords, so the performance of the algorithms can decrease a bit because they consider the repetition of words, not including empty words.

To obtain these measures, it is necessary to recognize the *True-Positive* (TP, successes that the algorithm obtained), the *False-Positive* (FP, errors obtained by the algorithm), the *False-Negative* (FN, the errors that the algorithm did not generate) and *True-Negative* (TN, these are the rest of the results, rated as wrong and has not considered).

Due to the size of the summaries, the obtaining of the data was complicated manually, so it was necessary to code a program that would automate the number of sentences that coincide with the summary of the expert.

The algorithm separates the results by points and saves them in a space in an array, and it does the same with the summary of the expert to subsequently find out if each value of the array is contained in the values of the summary of the expert array. In this way, the *True-Positive* are counted, then all the values contained in the full text are counted to obtain the total values, and the values that are also part of the summary of the expert are counted.

With this program, it was obtained that the summary was composed of 608 sentences, of which the expert used 149 to make his summary. The summary of the first algorithm gives only eight sentences as output, the second algorithm gives 121 sentences, and the third algorithm gives as output only six sentences.

As a result, the first algorithm only had one similarity to the expert summary, the second algorithm had 15 similarities to the expert summary, and the third algorithm had zero similarities to the expert summary. In this way, the values of each of the algorithms were obtained. The results are shown in Table 1.

Table 1. Values obtained by the three algorithms

Algorithm	FN	TP	FP	TN
1	148	1	7	452
2	134	15	106	353
3	149	0	6	459

With these results, the *Precision*, *Recall,* and *F-Measure* metrics were calculated, also get the percentage amount compared to the original text. The results are shown in Table 2.

As seen in Table 1, the best is the second algorithm, since it obtains a better measurement in the *F-Measure*. This measure indicates that the relationship between successes and the values obtained incor-

Table 2. Precision, Recall and F-Measure metrics calculated for each of the algorithms

Algorithm	Precision	Recall	F-Measure	Percentage
1	0.12500	0.00671	0.01273	1.31%
2	0.12396	0.10067	0.11110	19.90%
3	0	0	0	0.98684%

rectly is good, so compared to the other results, it is the highest. One factor that helped the algorithm is that the result that is obtained from itself is much broader than the others, so it had a greater advantage.

The first algorithm, despite obtaining a very short summary, 1.31% of the summary of the original text, obtained an *F-measure* value of 0.01273, which is low if the methodology of the expert to carry out the summary is not considered. Regarding the last algorithm, no sentence was match based on the summary made by the expert, so the result for all its metrics was 0.

FUTURE RESEARCH DIRECTIONS

Nowadays, text summarization is very useful in terms of research; this can save a lot of time when searching for information by extracting the most important fragments of large texts. In the future, we are going to work on the improvement and accuracy of the algorithms; in this way, the performance of the algorithms could be increased.

In this research, text summarization algorithms were modified for allowing to process texts in the Spanish language. This opens the research area so that this language can be entered to expand the researches of these algorithms in Spanish.

Something to consider is that on some occasions that for the person seeking information in large texts, some aspects that the algorithm does not consider may be relevant, so it would be convenient if the algorithm could be configured in some way before carrying out the process.

A better result can be obtained if a methodology is followed according to how the algorithms work to obtain a higher acceptance percentage. Therefore, this research can be used to improve the characteristics of the algorithms. An opportunity area is to find an appropriate technique to evaluate Spanish text summarization algorithms.

CONCLUSION

The process of text summarization is very useful when performing a search; it is a process that involves the processing of natural language to obtain an acceptable result.

Although the text summarization process is structured by a series of steps, it varies according to the functions that are implemented in the programming of the algorithm, so the result varies according to the method with which it was coded. This does not mean that one algorithm is better than another, but according to the text to analyze, some algorithms can obtain a better result than another.

As can be seen, the results are low because the expert made the summary without considering keywords to perform the exercise, so if we follow a methodology according to it, a more approximate result could be obtained.

The use of the *Spicy* library of Natural Language Processing helps make the result meaningful, obtaining better quality in the generated text.

REFERENCES

Abraham Silberschatz, H. F. (2006). Fundamentals of Databases. Aravaca: McGraw-Hill.

Abujar, S., A. K. (2019). An Approach for Bengali Text Summarization using Word2Vector. *10th International Conference on Computing, Communication and Networking Technologies (ICCCNT)*, 1-5. 10.1109/ICCCNT45670.2019.8944536

Abujar, S., Kaisar, A., Masum, M., Mohibullah, M. O., & Hossain, S. (2019). An Approach for Bengali Text Summarization using Word2Vector. In *2019 10th International Conference on Computing, Communication and Networking Technologies (ICCCNT)* (pp.1-5). Academic Press.

Dalal, V. L. M. (2013). A Survey of Extractive and Abstractive Text Summarization Techniques. *6th International Conference on Emerging Trends in Engineering and Technology*, 109-110. 10.1109/ICE-TET.2013.31

Eduard Hovy, C.-Y. L. (1998). Automated text summarization and the summarist system. *Proceedings of a workshop on held at Baltimore.*

Fenstermacher, K. D. (2005). The Tyranny of Tacit Knowledge: What Artificial Intelligence Tells us About Knowledge Representation. IEEE.

Gudivada, N. V. (2018). Handbook of Statistics. Greenville: Elsevier.

Gupta, V., & Lehal, G. S. (2010). A Survey of Text Summarization Extractive Techniques. *Journal of Emerging Technologies in Web Intelligence*, 2(3), 258–268. doi:10.4304/jetwi.2.3.258-268

Hark, T. U. (2018). Graph-Based Suggestion For Text Summarization. *International Conference on Artificial Intelligence and Data Processing (IDAP)*, 1-6.

Indu, M., K. V. (2016). Review on text summarization evaluation methods. *International Conference on Research Advances in Integrated Navigation Systems (RAINS)*, 1-4.

Kallimani, J. S., K. G. (2010). Information retrieval by text summarization for an Indian regional language. *Proceedings of the 6th International Conference on Natural Language Processing and Knowledge Engineering*, 1-4. 10.1109/NLPKE.2010.5587764

Kallimani, J. S., K. G. (2011). Information extraction by an abstractive text summarization for an Indian regional language. *7th International Conference on Natural Language Processing and Knowledge Engineering*, 319-322. 10.1109/NLPKE.2011.6138217

Kumar, J. N. (2019). Extractive Text Summarization Using Sentence Ranking. *International Conference on Data Science and Communication (IconDSC)*, 1-3.

Malik, U. (2018, September 4). *Text Summarization with NLTK in Python*. Retrieved from Stack Abuse: https://stackabuse.com/text-summarization-with-nltk-in-python/

NLP APIs. (2016). Retrieved November 18, 2019, from https://tedboy.github.io/nlps/generated/generated/gensim.summarization.summarize.html

Nwet, S. S. (2018). Extractive Summarization for Myanmar Language. *International Joint Symposium on Artificial Intelligence and Natural Language Processing (iSAI-NLP)*, 1-6.

Parida, S. M. (2019). Abstract Text Summarization: A Low Resource Challenge. *Proceedings of the 2019 Conference on Empirical Methods in Natural Language Processing and the 9th International Joint Conference on Natural Language Processing*, 5996-6000. 10.18653/v1/D19-1616

Pranay Mathur, A. G. (2017, April 5). *Text Summarization in Python: Extractive vs. Abstractive techniques revisited*. Retrieved from Rare Technologies: https://rare-technologies.com/text-summarization-in-python-extractive-vs-abstractive-techniques-revisited/

Sareen, S. (2018, July 4). *Medium*. Retrieved November 18, 2019, from https://medium.com/@shivangisareen/text-summariser-in-python-da5557d31aa0

Sareen, S. (2018, Jul 4). *Text Summariser in Python*. Retrieved from Medium: https://medium.com/@shivangisareen/text-summariser-in-python-da5557d31aa0

Sarkar, K. (2013). Automatic Single Document Text Summarization Using Key Concepts in Documents. *Journal of Information Processing Systems*.

ScienceDirect. (2020). *Text Summarization - an overview*. Retrieved from ScienceDirect: https://www.sciencedirect.com/topics/computer-science/text-summarization

Sharma, M. (2018, September 15). *Text Summarization*. Retrieved from Medium: https://medium.com/incedge/text-summarization-96079bf23e83

Spacy. (2020). Retrieved from Spacy: https://spacy.io/usage/adding-languages#_title

Suleiman, D., A. A. (2019). Arabic Text Keywords Extraction using Word2vec. *2nd International Conference on new Trends in Computing Sciences (ICTCS)*, 1-7.

tedboy. (2016). *gensim*. Retrieved from NLP APIs: https://tedboy.github.io/nlps/generated/generated/gensim.summarization.summarize.html

Umadevi, K. S., R. C. (2018). Text Summarization of Spanish Documents. *International Conference on Advances in Computing, Communications and Informatics (ICACCI)*, 1793-1797.

Vijay, S., V. R. (2017). Extractive text summarisation in hindi. *International Conference on Asian Language Processing (IALP)*, 318-321. 10.1109/IALP.2017.8300607

Section 3
Text Mining Systems

Chapter 19
NLP and the Representation of Data on the Semantic Web

Jose L. Martinez-Rodriguez
Universidad Autónoma de Tamaulipas, Mexico

Ivan Lopez-Arevalo
(iD) https://orcid.org/0000-0002-7464-8438
CINVESTAV Tamaulipas, Mexico

Jaime I. Lopez-Veyna
Tecnológico Nacional de México, Mexico & Instituto Tecnológico de Zacatecas, Mexico

Ana B. Rios-Alvarado
Universidad Autónoma de Tamaulipas, Mexico

Edwin Aldana-Bobadilla
(iD) https://orcid.org/0000-0001-8315-1813
Conacyt, Mexico & Cinvestav Tamaulipas, Mexico

ABSTRACT

One of the goals of data scientists and curators is to get information (contained in text) organized and integrated in a way that can be easily consumed by people and machines. A starting point for such a goal is to get a model to represent the information. This model should ease to obtain knowledge semantically (e.g., using reasoners and inferencing rules). In this sense, the Semantic Web is focused on representing the information through the Resource Description Framework (RDF) model, in which the triple (subject, predicate, object) is the basic unit of information. In this context, the natural language processing (NLP) field has been a cornerstone in the identification of elements that can be represented by triples of the Semantic Web. However, existing approaches for the representation of RDF triples from texts use diverse techniques and tasks for such purpose, which complicate the understanding of the process by non-expert users. This chapter aims to discuss the main concepts involved in the representation of the information through the Semantic Web and the NLP fields.

DOI: 10.4018/978-1-7998-4730-4.ch019

Copyright © 2021, IGI Global. Copying or distributing in print or electronic forms without written permission of IGI Global is prohibited.

INTRODUCTION

The Web provides a wealth data source that can be consumed by humans and applications in diverse areas such as Data Analytics, Information Retrieval, Information Extraction, Machine Learning, and so forth, which can benefit Smart Environments, Smart Business, Educational and Learning, and, also, the Internet of Things (IoT) as a whole (Liu, Fang, & Ansari, 2016). Diverse elements of information can be obtained from the Web (e.g., product descriptions, relevant information from organizations, profiles of persons, contextual information, etc.), which can be connected in a way to provide new insights, later represented as knowledge that can be useful for organizations for decision making. Several actors from diverse domains (education, healthcare, logistics, tourism, energy, etc.) can be benefited from gathering such kind of information for providing digital services and products with added value for consumers. Typically, the data published in the Web is mainly represented as plain text for human consumption, which has no structure or descriptions that facilitate its comprehension (even in a human visual understanding format as HTML). Thus, computers cannot easily process the text to obtain its underlying information (and meaning). In this way, to get information organized and represented for further consumption by humans or applications, the following aspects should be taken into account:

a) A representation model. This model should be useful for representing and querying facts about real-world objects and their connections. Moreover, it should allow computers to infer new information according to rules and already represented facts, which is a step for obtaining knowledge.

b) Feed representation model. Once a model is defined, the next task is to represent data following the specifications and rules of such a model. However, this task is often unfeasible for humans when the data source is huge and constantly increasing (as the Web).

According to the previous subjects, there exist two fields directly involved in the modeling and representation of data: the *Semantic Web* (Berners-Lee, Hendler, & Ora, 2001) and the *Natural Language Processing (NLP)* (Hirschberg & Manning, 2015). The first refers to an extension of the Web aimed at the representation, integration, sharing, reuse, and connection of information through a format readable by humans and applications. The Semantic Web relies on the Resource Description Framework (RDF), which provides a model for the formal representation of information based on a basic unit of information, the RDF triple. A set of RDF triples can represent information in the form of a graph (*Knowledge Graph –KG–* (Ehrlinger & Wöß, 2016)), where nodes represent real-world elements (resources) and the edges define the relationship or description between the nodes. On the other hand, NLP is aimed at preparing and processing text, so that computers can handle it. Thus, by the nature of its tasks, NLP has become a cornerstone for the representation of data on the Semantic Web, providing methods and techniques (e.g., segmenting text into sentences and words, grammatical analysis and parsing) for the identification and extraction of two main elements from text: named entities and semantic relations. Named entities refer to real-world objects that can be classified in a specific class (e.g., person, location, place), while semantic relations refer to the existing relationship between the identified named entities. In this way, named entities and semantic relations can be represented in the RDF model as nodes and edges (properties), respectively. For example, a KG from the sentence *"LeBron James plays basketball for Los Angeles Lakers. He was born in Ohio"* contains named entities (LeBron James, Los Angeles Lakers, Ohio), which are linked by predicates (isA, play, birthplace). From such relations, additional information (not explicitly stated in the sentence) can be inferred (basketball team, country, marital status, age, hobbies, etc.). Explicit and implicit types of information are useful to feed and enrich, respectively, the KG.

A generic process to represent data on the Semantic Web is shown in **Figure 1**. The process starts by obtaining a statement that might be provided as text by diverse data sources. Next, a first (and optional) data enrichment step might be to create a relation of those data sources mentioning the same statement. The next step involves the identification of the real-world elements (i.e., named entities) and their relationships. Thereafter, relationships and implicit connections between elements are formalized through vocabularies (and ontologies) that provide semantics. Finally, the represented and enriched information can be consumed by applications such as *Question Answering*, *Web Search Engines*, *Inferencing Engines*, and so forth.

Figure 1. The generic process to represent data on the Semantic Web

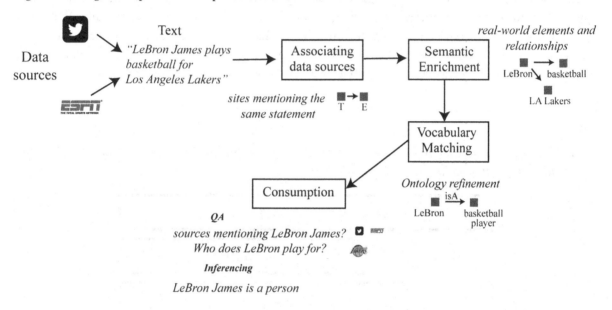

Diverse organizations have supported the incorporation of the Semantic Web for representing their data (by generating and exploiting their own KGs). For example, BBC (Kobilarov, et al., 2009), Oracle (Wu, et al., 2008), Facebook (Facebook, 2017), Google (Bollacker, et al., 2008), Amazon (Amazon, 2019), to mention a few. They use such representation in diverse applications such as Information Retrieval, to facilitate the presentation of relevant results; Smart Services, for defining preferences according to contextual information; Advertising, according to topics and textual contents; Question Answering, and so forth. Although the construction of KGs following the Semantic Web principles has been mostly addressed for (semi)-structured data sources such as Wikipedia (Lehmann, et al., 2015), a huge challenge is to extract relevant structured information from an unstructured text (plain text). This is due to diverse linguistic and technical issues such as inconsistency, ambiguity, synonymy, and large-scale data sources.

The purpose of this chapter is to provide scholars and researchers the theoretical foundations (definitions and techniques) of NLP involved in the task of representing data extracted from a text on the Semantic Web. The chapter starts by describing basic concepts of the Semantic Web to explain later

NLP classical Information Extraction tasks and their evolution for its integration within the Semantic Web. The aim is to describe and explain the traditional flow of procedures and activities involved in the construction of KGs; in consequence, some metrics and strategies will also be described to evaluate them. Additionally, a revision of some existing approaches from the literature addressing such a representation task is presented to give a general overview of the work done and possible tendencies according to open challenges and opportunities for applying NLP on the Semantic Web.

THE SEMANTIC WEB

The Semantic Web (Berners-Lee, Hendler, & Ora, 2001) provides an extension of the traditional Web with the purpose of representing, sharing and reusing large textual sources (such as the Web) through a semantic representation that keeps human readability but at the same time allows being exploited by applications to obtain the underlying meaning of a text. The components of the Semantic Web were first proposed by Berners-Lee in an architecture covering layers for the representation and querying of information, as shown in **Figure 2**. From bottom to top of the architecture, semantics is added to the representation of text — particularly, incorporating ontologies and schemes for describing the data. Ac-

Figure 2. The Semantic Web architecture provides the components for the representation, consumption, and validation of information on the Semantic Web.

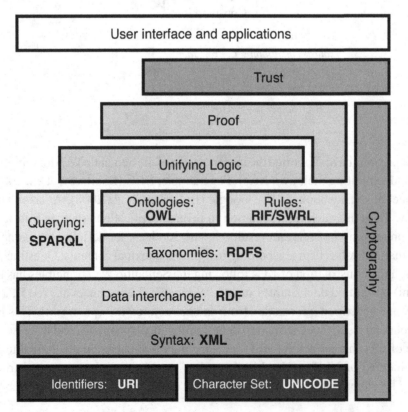

cording to Breitman, Casanova and Truszkowski (2007) and Hogan (2014), the main concepts regarding representation aspects involved in such an architecture are presented in the following subsections.

Representation Components

The representation on the Semantic Web is mainly provided by three components: RDF, RDFS, and OWL. Thus, this section presents a brief description of these components together with some examples to help clarify their usability.

Resource Description Framework (RDF)

RDF represents the central model for data interchange on the Semantic Web (Manola, Miller, & McBride, 2014). RDF allows descriptions of resources (i.e., electronically identifiable things) to be modeled through *RDF triples*. Every triple is composed of three elements with the form (*Subject*, *Predicate*, *Object*). While the *Subject* and *Object* represent members of a class (e.g., person, organization, place, among others), the *Predicate* defines the description or relationship between them. Each element of the triple can be identified by an IRI (Internationalized Resource Identifiers) or URI (Uniform Resource Identifier), and additionally, the object may also take Literal values (instead of an identifier), for example, strings and data types provided by the XMLSchema specification (Klyne, Carroll, & McBride, 2014). Note that, for space reasons, an IRI is often abbreviated using the CURIE notation (Birbeck & McCarron, 2010) with prefixes denoting namespaces in documents. For example, the prefix **ex:** is used to denote a contraction of the IRI "http://example.com/ns/". A list of popular RDF namespace prefixes was published by Cyganiak (2011).

RDF triples are represented by means of serialization formats such as RDF/XML (McBride, 2004), Turtle (Beckett & Berners-Lee, 2011), N-Triples (Beckett, 2011), N-Quad (Carothers, 2014), and additionally, NIF (Hellmann, Lehmann, Auer, & Brümmer, 2013), to mention the most common formats. These formats are capable of being stored or transmitted via HTTP and are intended to be parsed (analyzed) by humans and machines.

RDF Schema (RDFS)

RDF does not provide the meaning of elements in a triple by itself. In this sense, RDFS provides an extension to the RDF model that incorporates semantic features for the definition of relations between classes and properties (McBride, 2004). In consequence, RDFS provides the definition of vocabularies used to make descriptions about resources and their relationships. Some common keywords supplied by RDFS are depicted in Table 1.

Web Ontology Language (OWL)

Another way to declare vocabularies is by means of OWL, which is a language for the definition of ontologies in the Semantic Web. However, OWL provides more expressiveness than RDFS to represent terms and interrelations in the creation of ontologies. Ontologies are important because they define concepts and terms used by machine-readable metadata (Fensel, et al., 2007). In addition to the features

Table 1. Common keywords provided by RDFS for the definition of classes and properties

Predicate	Definition
Resource	Represents the superclass of everything (all things in RDF)
Class	It represents a collection of resources with similar features
subClassOf	Instances of one class are transitively part of another class
Property	It refers to a relation between subject and object resources
subPropertyOf	Resources related to one property also have a relation with another
domain	It specifies the class of the admitted resources to use a property (valid subject)
range	It specifies the class of the admitted values of a property (valid objects)

provided by RDFS, popular features of OWL are depicted in ***Table 2***, where a commonly used OWL feature is **owl:sameAs,** employed to declare that two resources are equivalent.

Table 2. Popular features defined in OWL

Predicate	Definition
sameAs	Used to represent that two resources are the same thing
differentFrom	It is the opposite of sameAs
equivalentClass	This property is used to define equivalent classes and thus, the same instances membership
disjointWith	Used to define disjoint classes (e.g., Man and Woman)
ObjectProperty	Indicates that a property can only accept IRI resources as values (i.e., as object)
DatatypeProperty	Indicates that a property can only accept *Literal* values

Figure 3 presents an RDF example of the equivalence between resources from the DBpedia and Wikidata KBs. The upper part of the figure denotes the RDF triple in Turtle format, and the lower part denotes the graph representation of such a triple.

Figure 3. Example of RDF triple using an OWL property

```
dbr:Batman  owl:sameAs  wikidata:Q2695156 .
```

dbr:Batman

owl:sameAs

wikidata:Q2695156

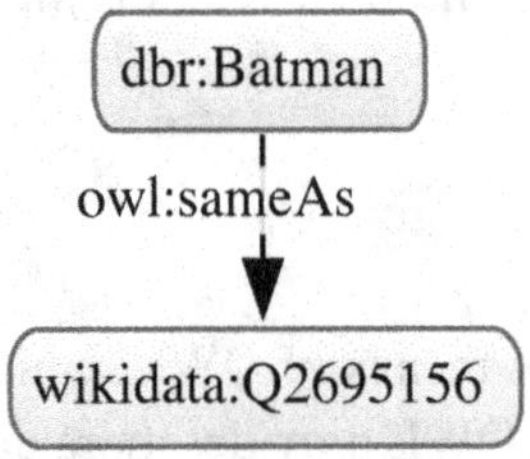

Vocabularies

Vocabularies define concepts and relations used to describe and represent a domain (W3C community, 2014). Ontologies provide the same functionality as vocabulary but provide more expressiveness for defining concepts. As stated by Vandenbussche, Atemezing, Poveda-Villalón and Vatant (2017), there are many standardized ontologies and vocabularies in the Semantic Web community, some popular ones are FOAF (Friend of a Friend), the Friend of a Friend project aimed at linking information from people using the Web (http://www.foaf-project.org); SKOS, the Simple Knowledge Organization System provides a representation model for defining schemes, taxonomies, thesaurus, and vocabularies (http://www.w3.org/2004/02/skos/); Dublin Core, provides features to describe any resource at a basic level (http://www.dublincore.org); among others. Finding the resources and a suitable vocabulary for describing a particular dataset is not a trivial task. However, sites like LOV (Linked Open Vocabularies) (http://lov.okfn.org/dataset/lov/) provide an extensive database with information about ontologies and vocabularies that can be accessed through literal queries for finding a useful property that describes the correct relationship between resources.

While RDF, RDFS, and OWL provide the representation model and vocabularies, other layers of the architecture such as the XML, URI, and UNICODE give support for the underlying representation of the information. After defining a set of RDF triples (following vocabulary descriptions), a Knowledge Base (KB) can then be generated. Moreover, once the information is represented, it can be queried through the SPARQL query language and processed by reasoners to create an inference model comprised of deductions (new knowledge). Several approaches about reasoners have been published so far d'Amato, Fanizzi, Fazzinga, Gottlob and Lukzsiewicz (2013); Zhong (2012); Mileo, Abdelrahman, Policarpio and Hauswirth (2013); and regarding reasoning tools: KAON2 (KAON, 2006) and FaCT++ (Tsarkov & Horrocks, 2007). However, reasoning and querying are not within the focus of this chapter.

With the support of vocabularies, a resource of a triple may also participate in several other triples, and thus create an *RDF Graph*. This fact can be observed in **Figure 4**, where, according to the running sentence "*LeBron James plays basketball for Los Angeles Lakers. He was born in Ohio*", every element is identified by a resource (even properties) from the DBpedia KB. For example, the entity 'LeBron James' is represented by the resource **dbr:LeBron_James**, which is associated with the resource **dbr:Akron,_Ohio** through the property **dbo:birthPlace**. The object property **rdf:type** (often indicated only by the letter "**a**") denotes the membership of a resource to a class, in this case describing '*LeBron James*' as a '*Basketball Player*'. Note that blurred nodes and edges refer to implicit facts obtained from the stated information.

The components described in this subsection allow the information to be represented through RDF triples and vocabularies. However, to get such information connected with other resources on a global scale, an initiative of the Semantic Web for publishing and disseminating structured information is described in the following subsection.

Linked Data

Linked Data defines a set of principles for publishing and interlinking structured data on the Web. As a way to increase the Semantic Web dissemination and to provide browsing capabilities (as presented by the traditional Web), Berners-Lee (2006) stated four Linked Data principles as follows:

Figure 4. Example of RDF graph

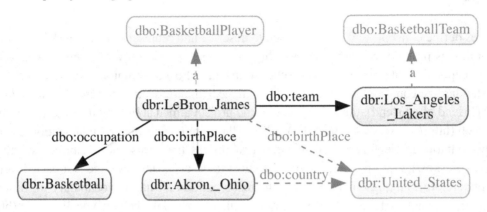

- Use URIs as names for things (Identifiers)
- Use HTTP URIs so that people can look up those names (Dereferencing).
- When someone looks up a URI, provide useful information using standards (RDF, SPARQL)
- Include links to other URIs so that they can discover more things.

Indeed, these principles could be adapted to modifications in the standards. For example, RDF switched to IRIs (instead of URIs) to identify resources. Several organizations such as BBC, Thomson Reuters, The Library of Congress, The New York Times, among others, support the Linked Data principles through the Linked Open Data (LOD) project. Since 2007, LOD has grown rapidly; this fact has been analyzed by Fensel, Facca, Bontas and Toma (2011); Auer, Ermilov, Lehmann and Martin (2018) and McCrae (2018) that present the LOD growth concerning the number of RDF triples and the links between central datasets during the interval of years from 2007 to 2019 as depicted in *Table 3*. Central datasets refer to those that contain more than ten thousand triples, where the most popular datasets of KB are DBpedia (http://wiki.dbpedia.org), YAGO (http://www.yago-knowledge.org), FreeBase (http://www.freebase.com), Wikidata (https://www.wikidata.org), and so forth. Datasets published under the Linked Data principles form a huge knowledge graph known as the *LOD cloud*.

Table 3. LOD cloud growth since 2007, (-) means no information available

Date	RDF Triples (billions)	RDF Links (millions)	Central Datasets
Oct. 2007	2	2	-
May 2009	4.2	142	203
Sep. 2010	25	400	295
Sep. 2011	31.6	503	295
Jan. 2014	61.9	-	928
Nov. 2015	85.5	-	1,014
Sep. 2018	149.4	-	1,163
Mar. 2019	-	16,147	1,239

The representation of information on the LOD cloud often requires a model that combines RDF triples to convey descriptions of the same fact or idea. However, there is a lack of expressivity using only one RDF triple for representing information regarding a particular situation (an event involving diverse roles such as participants, places, time, and so forth) and thus, making such a process complicated. Thus, the following section provides a description of diverse models for representing information using more than one RDF triple.

Reification

RDF provides a model based on binary relations (two elements joined by a predicate). However, a relation often needs to be modeled using several resources and descriptions. This is the case of *n*-ary relations (Hayes & Welty, 2006), where two or more resources are involved in describing an RDF statement. As such, RDF statements with several descriptions follow a model called *reification* (Fossati, Dorigatti, & Giuliano, 2018), in which every argument in a relationship should be individually specified, producing several triples from a single one. The idea of reification is to provide descriptions about a triple or additional features and participants on it. In this sense, and following ontology design patterns and standards, four RDF reification options according to Hernández, Hogan and Krötzsch (2015) are described as follows:

- **Standard Reification**. This is the basic idea to create complex descriptions with the built-in vocabulary provided by the RDF reification specification (Manola, Miller, & McBride, 2014). Where every element of the triple must be described with properties (*rdf:subject*, *rdf:predicate*, *rdf:object*) for an individual of type *Statement*. Note that this representation provides four triples for describing a single binary relation.
- **Singleton properties/subproperties**. Proposed by Nguyen, Bodenreider and Sheth (2014), this model works by declaring a *subproperty* as a single statement to include additional information using it as the subject of new triples.
- ***n*-ary relations.** This model relies on modeling a relationship as a resource rather than a property. This model is used for the Neo-Davidsonian representation (Rouces, de Melo, & Hose, 2015), in which an event or situation is described by its participants, actions, and the thematic roles they represent.
- **Named Graphs**. This option consists of an RDF graph allocated with an IRI (or a blank node) that appends the context or domain of a group of triples.

The standard reification option is criticized because of its nature to represent an RDF statement using four triples and due to the difficulty of query data. Thus, typically the used option is the *n*-ary relation because it requires fewer triples to indicate an assertion or event (Hernández, Hogan & Krötzsch, 2015; Fossati, Dorigatti & Giuliano, 2018).

The NLP field has supported the representation of RDF triples through diverse preprocessing and parsing techniques, which are useful for obtaining features and elements from text. Thus, NLP and its Information Extraction subfield are presented in the next section.

NLP AND INFORMATION EXTRACTION

According to the RDF model, the information that can be represented through RDF triples is about real-world things and their relationships. In this sense, the NLP and its derived Information Extraction (IE) tasks have demonstrated their usefulness in extracting representable elements from a text. In this sense, this section provides a description of the NLP and IE tasks aimed at the representation of data on the Semantic Web. The idea is to describe tasks from a classical perspective to explain a connection to the Semantic Web standards. The general process where both fields are involved is illustrated in **Figure 5**.

Figure 5. Overview of general NLP and IE processes

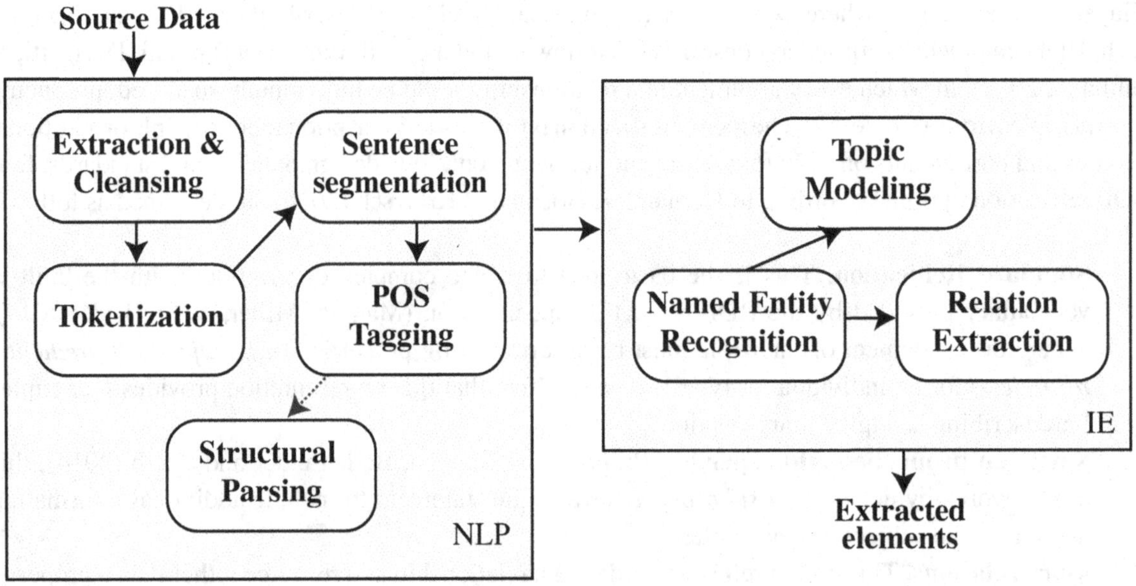

Although all the tasks presented in the previous Figure are part of the NLP field, the following subsection describes them according to NLP tasks for the treatment of text features and IE tasks for extracting elements of information.

NLP Tasks

NLP covers a wide range of phases that span diverse text cleansing, preprocessing, and parsing tasks. In this sense, some common tasks oriented for the representation of text in the Semantic Web are as follows:

- **Extraction & Cleansing**. One of the original goals of the Semantic Web is to represent the information published in the Web formally. However, information on it may come from diverse formats and structures such as plain text, documents (e.g., Word, PDF), or with some markup (e.g., HTML). Therefore, this task covers the extraction of text from such formats. Note that it may also involve the extraction of text from diverse media files (e.g., images, video) and the removal of punctuation marks, tags, blank spaces, etc.

- **Sentence Segmentation**. Once the tokens were delimited, the next step is to organize the text into sentences (aka sentence breaking). The idea is to analyze the text and identify the beginning and end of sentences with the purpose of extract independent and grammatically self-contained clauses or ideas. This is useful in the RDF representation because the triples are aimed at the description of single ideas. An example of sentence segmentation from the running example may be: ['*LeBron James plays basketball for Los Angeles Lakers.*','*He was born in Ohio*']. There are two sentences obtained from such a text fragment. The first sentence will be used in following examples.

- **Tokenization**. This task refers to the identification of linguistic units as atomic tokens such as words, punctuations, numbers, and so forth. Tokenization using the running example may be: ['LeBron','James','plays','basketball','for','Los','Angeles,'Lakers','.']. Note that the sentence dot is also counted as a token.

- **Part-Of-Speech Tagging**. This is a process of assigning the grammatical category to each word in a sentence (or text). There are many categories that can be assigned, for example, verbs, nouns, adjectives, and so forth. To do so, the context of the text is fundamental to select the corresponding tag for each word. This is a relevant task for subsequent extraction processes that seek units of information guided by, for example, nouns or verbs. A POS tagging using the running example sentence as input may be: "*LeBron_NNP James_NNP plays_VBZ basketball_NN for_IN Los_ NNP Angeles_NNP Lakers_NNP ._.*".

- **Structural Parsing.** The structure of the words in a sentence is also described by grouping tokens into phrases with a particular role. There are two popular structural parsing strategies:
  - Constituency parsing. Represent the syntactic structure of a text. It groups words into phrases such as noun phrases (NP), Prepositional phrases (PP), and Verb phrases (VP). The output of a constituency parsing is a syntactic tree representing a structure of non-terminal nodes (phrases) and terminal nodes (words).
  - Dependency parsing. This is a complementary representation to the constituency parsing where the out is also an ordered tree composed of relations between words (dependencies). In this case, verbs are the dominant words in a sentence (governors), and other terms are dependents (subordinates). Particularly, the verb may have a subject and object as dependents.

An example of structural parsing from the running sentence is illustrated in **Figure 6**, where a) represents the constituency tree, and b) represents the dependency tree.

It is worth mentioning that the tasks mentioned here are focused on plain text as input. Thus, other approaches leveraging structured and/or semi-structured data sources may involve distinct processing techniques such as direct (manual) mappings and pattern-based associations to extract the intended elements and features.

IE Tasks

Once the NLP tasks were applied over a text, diverse elements of information can be extracted. In this sense, the IE field has the goal of extracting structured information from an unstructured/semi-structured text source. In particular, three components are often obtained through the IE: topics, named entities, and semantic relations. Such components are represented by the following tasks:

Figure 6. Example of structural parsing trees

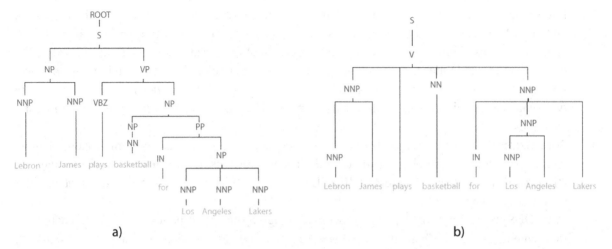

a)   b)

- **Topic Modeling**. This task is aimed at extracting topics or themes discussed in a set of documents. In this context, a topic refers to a group of keywords that represent a latent semantic theme present in a document. Topics are obtained according to mixed probability distributions over terms in a text. Topic Modeling requires several documents to get such distributions. Two hypothetical examples of topics detected from the running sentence are: 'basketball', 'Los Angeles Lakers'.

- **Named Entity Recognition (NER)**. This task refers to the identification of (a set of) words that point to named entities and their type in a text. For example, named entity types such as persons, organizations, and locations, to mention a few. NER can be addressed from diverse aspects: as a classification problem, and pattern-based matching. Features as a classification involve orthography (punctuation), grammar (POS, chunks), contextual information, and so on, and algorithms such as Naive Bayes, Conditional Random Fields, and Hidden Markov Models, to mention a few. On the other hand, a pattern-based approach requires handcrafted rules (often based on regular expressions) to detect entities, which are time consuming and incomplete.

  - Coreference resolution. The NER task finds mentions of named entities in text. However, named entities are sometimes referred by pronouns (e.g., he, she, it). In this case, the coreference resolution aims at finding named entities by such fragments with the support of the contextual information and already identified named entities. For instance, the entities found in the running example are *LeBron James, basketball, Los Angeles Lakers, He (LeBron James), Ohio*.

- **Relation Extraction (RE)**. This task is aimed at recognizing the semantic relation between entities found in the text. A semantic relation is a tuple composed of two arguments (entities or concepts) and a fragment/predicate joining them (verb, preposition). RE applies several steps going from preprocessing steps (POS, dependency parse tree), NER, and classification tasks. A popular RE approach is called OpenIE (Banko, Cafarella, Soderland, Broadhead, & Etzioni, 2007), whose purpose is to obtain semantic relations with no restriction of a specific information domain.

Two important tasks in the representation of information are NER and RE. Considering the running sentence, an example of such tasks is presented in **Figure 7**, where boxes indicate named entities,

Figure 7. Example of elements extracted for the NER and RE tasks

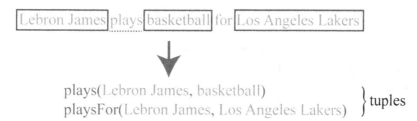

and the dotted line indicates the verb used in the relationship later organized on tuples of the form *predicate(subject, object)*.

It can be noted that RE is a step towards the creation of RDF triples. The next Section presents the continuation of NER and RE for the construction of triples on the Semantic Web, the association with resources of a KB.

NLP AND THE SEMANTIC WEB

This section provides the description of two important tasks for the representation of information on the Semantic Web, the extraction of named entities and semantic relations and their linking to resources and properties from a KB. Their obtainment is crucial for the generation of RDF triples from unstructured text.

Entity Extraction and Linking

An RDF triple is composed of named entities (for Subject and Object elements) of a diverse type such as persons, organizations, places, and so forth. As previously mentioned, the NER task is responsible for identifying mentions of named entities and their type from a text. However, according to the Linked Data principles of the Semantic Web, the elements of an RDF triple must be identified by IRIs. That is, every named entity is associated with a resource from a KB. Hence, the *Entity Extraction and Linking* (EEL) refers to the task of identifying named entity mentions from text and their association with their respective resources from a KB.

Going into details, the EEL task is commonly composed of two stages: *Recognition* and *Disambiguation* (Martinez-Rodriguez, Hogan, & Lopez-Arevalo, 2018). Such stages are briefly described as follows:

- **Recognition**. This stage refers to finding mentions of named entities in the text. There are three common ways to obtain them: applying traditional NER techniques, grammatical tagging, and dictionary matching. First, NER techniques are useful for determining typical mentions such as persons, organizations, places, among others. Second, since entities are considered as nouns (see **Figures 5** and **6**), another way to detect entity mentions is through a POS tagging, which helps to identify the *nouns* in the text. Finally, a dictionary-based strategy consists of creating an index with resource labels extracted from a KB and then performing string matching of text keywords (i.e., words, tokens, n-grams) against the created index.

- **Disambiguation**. Given a mention of named entity, this stage is in charge of retrieving a set of entity candidates (resources) from a KB and then selects the most appropriate one to assign it to such mention. Nevertheless, more than one entity candidate can be retrieved for a given mention, and thus, the disambiguation stage must choose the most likely match. The disambiguation relies on diverse techniques such as linguistic-based and graph-based. First, linguistic-based strategies are based on string similarity techniques and comparison of features (POS or NER). Second, graph-based approaches take into consideration the structure of the KB containing the retrieved candidate resources (and contextual information) to create a subgraph that is processed by measures (e.g., centrality, relatedness) to select or associate a weight indicating confidence in the matches to choose which links to trust.

The EEL task has been addressed by diverse systems and approaches such as TagMe (Ferragina & Scaiella, 2010), DBpedia SpotLight (Mendes, Jakob, García-Silva, & Bizer, 2008), Babelfy (Moro, Raganato, & Navigli, 2014), ADEL (Plu, Rizzo, & Troncy, 2016), Sieve (D'Souza & Ng, 2015) and (Zheng, et al., 2015), to mention a few, where DBpedia and YAGO are the main sources to be linked with.

EEL systems can also be combined in an ensemble approach (as seen in Machine Learning algorithms). The purpose is to integrate two or more EEL systems to get better performance than using a single one. This is because the EEL systems may be configured to particular text features, KBs, information domains, and/or focused on trade-offs between precision and recall. An example of the EEL process is shown in **Figure 8**, where the two EEL stages are carried out, *Recognition* (1), and *Disambiguation* divided into two steps (2 and 3). First, three mentions of named entities are obtained (**LeBron James, basketball, Los Angeles Lakers**). Second, according to the obtained mentions, a list of resource candidates are obtained from the DBpedia KB for linking (e.g., **dbr:LeBron_James, dbr:Gram_LeBron**). For the last step of the disambiguation, the resource is assigned for each mention.

Figure 8. Example of the EEL process

From **Figure 8**, it can be noted that the resource candidates might have no relation with the mention, and thus, the contextual information (neighboring words, types, resources) is used to disambiguate the corresponding resource. Moreover, even if only one resource is retrieved as a candidate, it may or not be selected for the mention; it depends on the confidence score assigned by the disambiguation strategy and a threshold value selected by the user.

Relation Extraction and Linking

The relations between entities are primordial elements for the creation of any KB of the Semantic Web (Sheth, Arpinar, & Kashyap, 2004). Thus an important IE task in the context of the Semantic Web is the *Relation Extraction* (RE), which is the process of finding relationships between entities (e.g., born-in, plays-for, is-a, etc.). Relations extracted may be binary relations or even higher arity *n*-ary relations. Similar to the EEL, elements in a semantic relation (particularly the predicate) must be linked to a KB to produce RDF triples. Moreover, while binary relations can be represented directly as triples, *n*-ary relations require some form of reification model. Hence, the *Relation Extraction and Linking* (REL) process aims at extracting and representing semantic relations from unstructured text, subsequently linking their elements to the named entities and properties of a KB.

Although the steps for the REL task are varied from one approach to another, the general steps can be stated as follows:

1. Entity Extraction and Linking. Named entities are first extracted from the text. This step is performed through traditional NER tools or by EEL systems, where approaches described previously are typically used.
2. Relation Extraction. The relations between the entities found in the text are recognized. This process is often coupled to the entity extraction when traditional NER tools are used, otherwise first, the relations are extracted, and then entities are recognized and linked to a KB. As previously mentioned, there are commonly three types of approaches for obtaining semantic relations (relationship structures): Discourse-based (frames), Pattern-based, and Distant supervised-based (features). While the first and second approaches are mainly based on the semantic and syntactic analysis of the text, the third approach is based on training machine learning algorithms.
3. Representation. The aim is to link elements of the relation (i.e., entities and their relation) with resources from a KB to represent them through RDF triples later. In this sense, strategies for linking entities and predicates with resources and properties from a KB are required.

According to the RDF graph example presented in **Figure 4**, a hypothetical REL process of the three followed steps performed for such example is depicted in **Figure 9**, where the entity tuples and semantic relation extracted in the EEL (Step 1) and RE (Step 2) tasks, respectively, are reused for this example regarding the running sentence. The entity resources are directly associated with the named entities in the semantic relations (Step 2). Finally, Step 3 retrieves property candidates and selects the corresponding one to be used for the final RDF triple. Note that although a property candidate is **dbo:plays**, it is not used for the predicate '**play**' because it is a *Datatype property* (used for specifying a literal value to the object), and what we need is an *Object property* for linking resources.

For clarity, **Figure 9** exemplifies only direct binary relations using the graph representation. Thus, in the case of *n*-ary relations, the complete set of resources could be part of descriptions regarding a single event (using a reification model).

The selection of a property also takes into consideration the contextual information such as the entities, the type of predicate (verb sense), the structure, descriptions, and number of property candidates.

Figure 9. Relation Extraction and Linking example

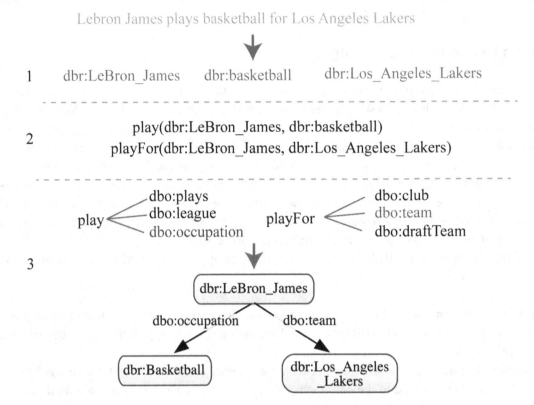

Rather than syntactically comparing the information of the predicate against the property candidates, it is common to apply a comparison that considers semantic features in text. Therefore, the next section describes the *Sentence Similarity* task, which is used in the property selection.

SENTENCE SIMILARITY

Sentence similarity refers to the process of judging the similarity between natural language sentences. This process is used in many tasks such as question answering, text mining, text summarization, among others. Although there are some measures used to determine the similarity between sentences (e.g., the Jaccard index or the Levenstein distance, based on the comparison of terms/characters) (Cheatham & Hitzler, 2013), this section is focused on two particular types of measures: corpus-based and knowledge-based. In general, these measures determine whether the sentences are semantically equivalents or not by considering the variability of natural language expressions. Hence, this section presents details of these two sentence similarity measures, which are aimed at providing a module for the representation of RDF statements in the selection and disambiguation of properties.

Corpus-Based Measures

The measures of this type rely on information derived from large corpora for obtaining a degree of similarity between words. Popular measures in this group are the Pointwise Mutual Information (PMI) and Latent Semantic Analysis (LSA). While PMI measures the word co-occurrence using word counts derived from very large corpora, LSA captures term co-occurrences expressed in a matrix vectorization (constructed from large corpora) that are compared using the cosine similarity between the vectorial representation of two words.

Related to the idea of LSA, word embeddings (Mikolov, Sutskever, Chen, Corrado, & Dean, 2013) provides a feature extraction method for representing words in a vectorial space, where words with similar meaning have a similar vectorial representation. In this sense, each word is mapped to a vector in which the vector values are learned through a strategy based on neural networks. The key to word embeddings is the idea of using a densely distributed representation for each word. That is, each word is represented by a vector composed of (commonly) hundreds of dimensions, which differs from traditional vector space models where every distinct word adds a dimension to the model, producing thousands or millions of dimensions. A popular algorithm for learning word-embedding representations is Word2Vec (Mikolov, Chen, Corrado, & Dean, 2013), which uses a neural network to model words vectors with a defined context window. More information about word embeddings and Word2Vec is available through the machine learning libraries Gensim (https://radimrehurek.com/gensim/index.html) and TensorFlow (https://www.tensorflow.org/tutorials/representation/word2vec).

Based on the representation provided by word embeddings, the Word Movers Distance (WMD) (Kusner, Sun, Kolkin, & Weinberger, 2015) is a typical measure that has been used in recent years to obtain the dissimilarity between two text documents --Dissimilarity or distance measures (Goshtasby, 2012) determine the dependency of two values/words. Unlike similarity measures, a higher value in dissimilarity measures means that the two values are less dependent (similar)--. The general idea of WMD is presented in **Figure 10**, which calculates the distance between two documents through the weighted cumulative cost required to move the words from one document to another (Kusner, Sun, Kolkin, & Weinberger, 2015). Note that the words are represented by their embeddings (vectorial representations).

It is worth mentioning that although this Section is mainly based on the WMD measure, there are other traditional measures such as Mahalanobis, Cosine, and Euclidean distances (Srivastava & Sahami, 2009). However, the description of such measures is omitted for brevity.

Knowledge-Based Measures

Measures in this category employ information represented on a semantic network or KB. The most common measures in this category are based on the taxonomy of WordNet (http://wordnet.princeton.edu). In this sense, the measures take as input two concepts to later compute their semantic relatedness. As presented by Meng, Huang and Gu (2013), a brief description of some of these measures is as follows:

- Short path (PATH). This measure takes into consideration the length between two concepts in the taxonomy.
- Leacock & Chodorow (LCH). This measure is a variation of the PATH measure, which additionally takes into account the maximum depth of the taxonomy and the length between the concepts.

Figure 10. WMD principle. This figure is based on the work of Kusner, Sun, Kolkin and Weinberger (2015).

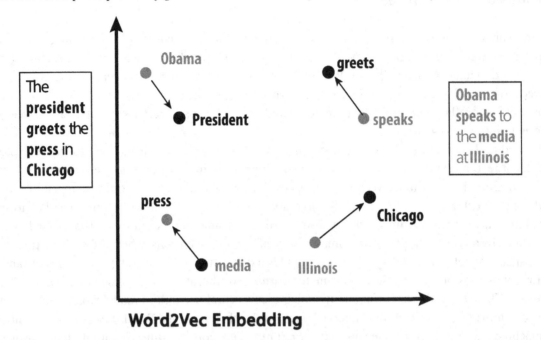

- Wu and Palmer (WUP). This measure takes into account the depth of two concepts in the taxonomy and the depth of the least common subsumer (LCS) --The LCS between two concepts refers to the most specific concept (in the taxonomy) that is an ancestor of the two concepts.-- to later combine them into a similarity score.
- LIN. This measure uses the LCS between concepts and the specificity provided by Information Content (IC), which provides the association of concepts according to frequency counts of words as found in a corpus of text.

Note that the above measures are aimed at obtaining the similarity between pairs of concepts rather than words. However, it is possible to compare words by retrieving their most common concept or by selecting the concept that leads to the highest concept-to-concept similarity (McCarthy, Koeling, Weeds, & Carroll, 2004). Additional details of the measures have been provided by Meng et al. (2013).

Information represented with binary or *n*-ary statements on the LOD cloud has been possible due to publishing strategies to convert text extracted from a variety of formats and organization levels. Thus, a primordial task in the Semantic Web is the conversion of information into a machine-understandable representation. Some approaches for the representation and publication of information on the Semantic Web are described in the next section.

Representation and Publication Schemes

Information representation and publication schemes must follow the technologies and standards of the Semantic Web (e.g., formats, protocols, LD principles) to guarantee the minimum conditions to reuse and consume information from a data source. However, the information may come from documents under distinct structuring levels, such as structured, semi-structured, and unstructured text. In this regard, the difficulty of parsing and processing text increases according to the lack of textual structures (Chang, Kayed, Girgis, & Shaalan, 2006). Several approaches have been proposed to represent information on the Semantic Web. For example, approaches that convert (semi) structured data (databases, tables, spreadsheets, and others) into RDF triples using rules, wrappers, or templates (Bizer, Cyganiak, & Gauss, 2007; Erling & Mikhailov, 2009; Arenas, Bertails, Prud'hommeaux & Sequeda, 2012; Gualán, Freire, Tello & Saquicela, 2017). Nevertheless, a lot of work is required for transforming unstructured text into a structured format. In this regard, some general strategies and recommendations for the information representation on the Semantic Web are presented in the following paragraphs.

Regarding representation architectures, Heath and Bizer (2011) described the Linked Data Operation sequence for publishing semantic information. Their architecture is organized into three stages that consider distinct kinds of input source. First, a preparation stage is carried out, where the applied technique depends on the kind of input data to be processed, be it structured data to be converted/parsed into a similar format or unstructured data to be processed by NLP tools. The second stage is intended to store entities and parsed elements obtained from the text. Finally, the information is published using a web server.

In a similar way, Criado-Fernandez (2009) determined three steps to make semantic annotations over websites. First, he identified the appropriate vocabulary employing word occurrence measurements; in other words, the vocabulary with more word co-occurrences is selected. Second, a morphosyntactic analysis task ensures the extraction of features from unstructured text through a textual parser. And third, he produced a mapping function in which the parsed data are matched against some manually selected vocabularies.

Another representation strategy is provided by the FOX (*Federated knOwledge eXtraction*) framework (http://aksw.org/Projects/FOX.html), which is a project whose purpose is the RDF data generation by using NER, KE and RE algorithms within an architecture composed of three layers: Automatic Learning layer, for training a module with the best-performing tools and categories; Controller layer, to coordinate information and parsing tools; and Tools layer, containing a repository of tools such as NLP services and data mining algorithms.

Similarly, Auer, Lehmann, Ngomo, & Zaveri (2013) identified three branches for extracting features used for representing RDF triples from unstructured text: Named Entity Recognition (NER) to extract entity labels from the text, Keyword Extraction (KE) to recognize central topics, and Relation Extraction (RE) to extract properties that link entities. Moreover, authors also assert that a disambiguation task is necessary to obtain adequate URIs for every resource within the extracted RDF triples. This task is conducted employing entity matching over KBs like DBpedia or FreeBase. Along these lines, based on the previous steps, approaches provided by Rusu, Fortuna and Mladenic (2011); Augenstein, Padó, and Rudolph (2012); and Nuzzolese, Gangemi, Presutti, Draicchio, Musetti, and Ciancarini (2013)obtain entities through NLP tools, apply morphosyntactic analysis and lexical databases like WordNet to extract and disambiguate individuals from text using preset vocabularies.

The above approaches are consistent in the step of obtaining features from the text as a core part for extracting the elements to be represented. Moreover, such approaches provide a brief overview of basic architectures to publish information on the Semantic Web. In consequence, the general steps for publishing RDF data on the Semantic Web are presented in **Figure 11**. Note that the input source is considered as unstructured or structured, where additional processing is needed for the former input.

Figure 11. General steps for extracting and representing RDF triples from structured or unstructured data sources.

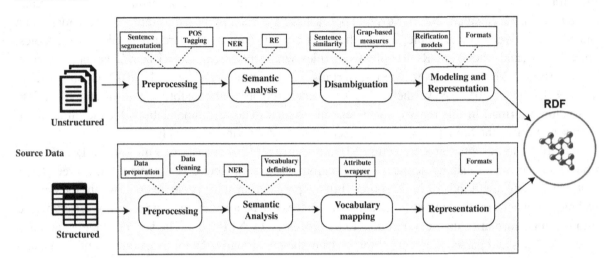

The representation approaches typically rely on techniques defined in multiple areas such as Ontology Learning & Population (OL&P) and Information Extraction (IE). OL&P is mainly focused on the knowledge representation and the construction of ontologies from text. This is commonly based on IE and machine learning tasks and sometimes requires a manually annotated and domain-specific large corpus (Nuzzolese, Gangemi, Presutti, Draicchio, Musetti, & Ciancarini, 2013). Hence, an alternative solution is given by IE tasks to obtain knowledge from a text; for example, Named Entity Recognition (NER), relation extraction (RE), and their linking with resources from a KB. Although the focus of this chapter is not regarding processing structured data, the steps presented in **Figure 11** demonstrate some of the required tasks for processing such data, where the relationship is commonly obtained by the schema describing the data (e.g., database schema) and according to (manually) selected vocabularies to create RDF triples.

EVALUATION OF INFORMATION EXTRACTION TASKS

EEL and REL tasks involve two high-level steps; recognition (of entity mentions or semantic relations) and linking/disambiguation (with identifiers from a KB). Thus, the evaluation could consider the recognition phase separately or the entire process as a whole. This section presents common ways to evaluate the two most important tasks of this chapter for the representation of information on the Semantic Web. Additionally, the evaluation of sentence similarity techniques is presented, which represents a crucial step for the disambiguation of properties.

Evaluation of EEL

As previously mentioned, the EEL task is composed of two steps; recognition and disambiguation. The evaluation of the recognition step (identification of named entities) has been widely covered by traditional

NER literature; this section considers the evaluation of the complete EEL process in terms of whether or not the recognized mentions are correct and whether or not the assigned KB identifier is correct. Although there are several EEL approaches proposed in the literature for diverse domains, languages, text structures, and evaluation strategies, this section presents some of the common datasets, metrics, and strategies used for the EEL evaluation.

Datasets

Several datasets have been proposed to evaluate the EEL process in different domains and features (e.g., languages, formats, text length). A dataset commonly contains the text (i.e., sentence, document) and the entity tuples on it, each one consisting of the named entity mention, offsets (beginning and ending index), and URI. As presented by Usbeck et al. (2015), some common datasets used to evaluate EEL systems are:

- AQUAINT. The AQUAINT dataset contains 50 English documents collected from news services such as the Xinhua News, New York Times, and the Associated Press. The documents contain 250-300 words (on average), where the mentions are manually linked to Wikipedia.
- IITB. The IITB dataset contains 103 English webpages taken from a handful of domains relating to sports, entertainment, science, and technology; the text of the webpages was scraped and semi-automatically linked with Wikipedia.
- Meij. This dataset contains 562 manually annotated tweets sampled from 20 "verified users" on Twitter and linked with Wikipedia.
- KORE-50. The KORE-50 dataset contains 50 English sentences designed to offer a challenging set of examples for Entity Linking tools; the sentences relate to various domains, including celebrities, music, business, sports, and politics. The dataset emphasizes short sentences, entity mentions with a high number of occurrences, highly ambiguous mentions, and entities with low prior probability.
- MSNBC. The MSNBC dataset contains 20 English news articles from 10 different categories, which were semi-automatically annotated.
- VoxEL. The VoxEL dataset contains 15 news articles (on politics) in 5 different languages sourced from the VoxEurop website.

Metrics

EEL approaches are evaluated by applying traditional metrics such as Precision, Recall, and F-measure, as presented in the Information Extraction field. Moreover, *micro* and *macro* variants are also applied in diverse EEL systems such as AIDA (Yosef, Hoffart, Bordino, Spaniol, & Weikum, 2011), DoSeR (Zwicklbauer, Seifert, & Granitzer, 2016), and frameworks such as BAT (Cornolti, Ferragina, & Ciaramita, 2013) and GERBIL (Usbeck, et al., 2015). For example, with respect to the Precision measure, macro-Precision considers the average Precision over individual documents or sentences, while micro-Precision considers the entire gold standard as one test without distinguishing the individual documents or sentences. Other systems and frameworks may use measures that distinguish the type of entity or the type of mention; for example, GERBIL is a general Linked Data benchmarking framework that provides the option of evaluating diverse EEL systems over several datasets through different measures. It distinguishes results for KB entities from emerging entities. The measures Precision (P), Recall (R), and their micro and macro versions are presented in Eqs. (1) and (2), respectively.

$$P = \frac{tp}{tp + fp}, MicroP = \frac{\sum_i^n tp_i}{\sum_i^n (tp_i + fp_i)}, MacroP = \frac{\sum_i^n P_i}{n} \tag{1}$$

$$R = \frac{tp}{tp + fn}, MicroR = \frac{\sum_i^n tp_i}{\sum_i^n (tp_i + fn_i)}, MacroR = \frac{\sum_i^n R_i}{n} \tag{2}$$

where tp refers to true-positive cases, fn to false-negative cases, and n to the number of documents/sentences.

Finally, the F1-measure is used to combine the values of precision and recall in one metric, as presented in Eq. (3), where micro and macro variants can also be used (instead of P and R).

$$F1 = \frac{2PR}{P + R} \tag{3}$$

Matching Configuration

There are two types of configuration for comparing the extracted entity tuples from a text with the gold standard datasets: *strong* and *weak* matching. In other words, for *strong* matching configuration, an entity is deemed correct if the extracted entity tuple (the named entity mention and its IRI) exactly matches the entity tuple annotated in the dataset. In contrast, for *weak* matching configuration, the extracted entity tuple is considered as correct if the IRI exactly matches the IRI of the entity tuple in the dataset, but the extracted named entity mention exactly or partially matches the named entity mention in the dataset.

EEL Evaluation Frameworks

There are frameworks such as BAT (Cornolti, Ferragina, & Ciaramita, 2013) and GERBIL (Usbeck, et al., 2015), which provide the option of evaluating diverse EEL systems over several datasets through different measures under the two matching strategies (strong and weak). In particular, the GERBIL framework allows systems to be compared throughout diverse subtasks of the EEL process (i.e., recognition and disambiguation). Hence, such a framework is commonly used in the evaluation of such systems.

Evaluation of REL

The evaluation of the REL process is not a straightforward task, where a number of fundamental factors are involved (e.g., RE, NER, element linking, semantic and pragmatic representation). In general, human judgment is often required to assess the quality of the output of REL systems performing such a task, but such assessments can sometimes be subjective. Thus, creating a gold-standard dataset can be complicated, particularly for those systems producing *n*-ary relations, where there is a need of human experts on the particular information domain by which the entities and relations are extracted. However, manually labeling data may be a tedious task, where the annotations may not be widely accepted by all the experts. Thus, rather than creating a gold-standard dataset, another approach is to apply *a posteriori* assessment of the output by human judges, i.e., obtain RDF triples from plain text, and have the output validated by human judges; while this would appear more reasonable for systems based on Discourse or Pattern-based relations, there are still problems in assessing, for example, recall.

In other words, approaches for evaluating REL are diverse, and in many cases, there are no standard criteria for assessing the adequacy of a particular evaluation method. Therefore, this section presents some of the main points for evaluation, broken down by used datasets, how evaluators are employed to judge the output, and what are the typical metrics considered.

Datasets

Although there are a few available datasets for evaluating the REL process, most approaches consider applying the process to general-domain corpora extracted, for example, from Wikipedia articles, newspaper articles, or webpages. In general, three common data sources and techniques are preferred for the evaluation of REL approaches:

- Data sample. Many approaches may restrict REL to consider a domain-specific subset of a corpus, a fixed subset of KB properties or classes, a sample of documents, and so forth. For example, Fossati, Dorigatti and Giuliano (2018) extract relation from Wikipedia articles about Italian soccer players using a selection of relevant frames; Augenstein, Maynard and Ciravegna (2016) apply evaluation for relations pertaining to entities in seven Freebase classes for which relatively complete information is available, using the Google Search API to find relevant documents for each such entity, and so forth.
- Machine Learning oriented. A number of standard evaluation datasets have emerged, particularly for approaches based on Machine Learning. A widely reused gold-standard dataset was proposed by Riedel, Yao and McCallum (2010) for evaluating their system, where they select Freebase relations pertaining to people, businesses, and locations (corresponding also to NER types) and then link them with New York Times articles.
- Labeled data. Other such evaluation resources have since emerged. For example, Google Research (https://code.google.com/archive/p/relation-extraction-corpus/downloads) provides five REL corpora, with relation mentions from Wikipedia linked with manual annotation to five Freebase properties indicating institutions, date of birth, place of birth, place of death, and education degree.

It is worth mentioning that all previously mentioned datasets and strategies are focused on binary relations of the form *Subject-Predicate-Object* but limited to particular types of relations. However, contents provided as plain text are not commonly restricted to a set of relations. On the other hand, creating gold standard datasets for *n*-ary relations is complicated by the heterogeneity of representations that can be employed in terms of frames, or other theories used. In this sense, Gangemi, Recupero, Mongiovì, Nuzzolese and Presutti (2016) proposed the construction of RDF graphs by means of logical patterns known as *motifs* that are extracted by the FRED tool and thereafter manually corrected and curated by evaluators to follow best Semantic Web practices; the result is a corpus annotated by instances of such motifs that can be reused for evaluation of REL tools producing similar such relations.

Metrics

REL is a process often involving Machine Learning, IE, and mapping strategies. In this sense, varied evaluation measures are typically applied, including Precision, Recall, F-measure, accuracy, Area-Under-Curve (AUC-ROC), and so forth. However, given that relations may be extracted for multiple properties, sometimes macro-measures such as Mean Average Precision (MAP) are applied to summarize precision across all such properties rather than taking a micro precision measure (Dutta, Meilicke, & Stuckenschmidt, 2014). Given the subjectivity inherent in evaluating REL, Fossati, Dorigatti and Giuliano (2018) use a *strict* and *lenient* version of typical measures such as precision/recall/F-measure, where the former requires the relation to be exact and complete, while the latter also considers relations that are partially correct; relating to the same theme.

Given that REL is composed of several steps, some approaches evaluate distinct parts of the task. For example, according to the triples extracted from text, Dutta, Meilicke and Stuckenschmidt (2015) considers the evaluation of the property precision (i.e., evaluate if the mapped property is correct), instance precision (i.e., evaluate if the mapped subjects/objects are correct), triple precision (i.e., if the complete triple is correct), among other measures.

As presented by the evaluation of REL approaches, the Precision and Recall measures are obtained a bit different than described in the EEL experiments. Such measures are described in the following way:

- Precision (P). It specifies the correct amount of information retrieved. In other words, it refers to the proportion of correct members assigned to the class that they are really members of. The precision can be obtained by the Eq. (4).

$$P = \frac{Correct\ Elements\ Obtained}{Total\ Elements\ Obtained} \tag{4}$$

- Recall (R). It represents the degree of correct information retrieved. In other words, it is the proportion of class members that the system assigns to the class. The recall can be obtained by the Eq. (5)

$$R = \frac{Correct\ Elements\ Obtained}{Total\ Elements\ Correct} \tag{5}$$

Sampling

In cases where *a posteriori* evaluation is applied, it is recommended to select a sample from the represented data that will be assessed by human judges. Although some approaches select a random sample between 100-200 elements, a popular way to determine the sample size is through the Eq. (6), which was proposed by Krejcie and Morgan (1970).

$$s = \frac{X^2 NP(1-P)}{d^2(N-1) + X^2 P(1-P)} \tag{6}$$

where s is the sample size, X^2 is the desired confidence level (expressed by a constant obtained from the table value of chi-square for 1 degree of freedom (https://people.richland.edu/james/lecture/m170/tbl-chi.html), N is the size of the population, P is the population proportion with the feature of the study (it is unknown in advance, and it is assumed to be 0.5 since it represents the maximum sample size), d is the margin of error (expressed in percentage)

Evaluators

Generating a gold standard dataset is not a straightforward task, and thus, when a dataset is not available, the output triples returned by a REL process are often manually evaluated by human experts in the domain. Although the details of the evaluation for each proposed approach are often incomplete, the process commonly involves the selection of a determined number of triples to be evaluated by the experts, and then a rater agreement is obtained (the overall agreement refers to the relative amount of samples in which the human evaluators agree for a particular feature (Van den Berge, Schouten, Boomstra, van Drunen Littel, & Braakman, 1979) expressed as Cohen's or Fleiss' k-measure for a fixed number of evaluators. Typically, the Kappa (Randolph, 2005) value is used to determine the inter-rater agreement between observed data and prior data, which is described in the Eq. (7).

$$K_{free} = \frac{\left[\frac{1}{Nn(n-1)} \left(\sum_{i=1}^{N} \sum_{j=1}^{k} n_{ij^2} - Nn \right) \right] - \left[\frac{1}{k} \right]}{1 - \left[\frac{1}{k} \right]} \tag{7}$$

where N is the number of cases, n is the number of human judges, k is the number of categories, and n_{ij} is the number of judges who assigned the case to the same category; see Randolph (2005) for a complete example.

In addition to the evaluation guided by experts in a domain, some approaches leverage crowdsourcing platforms for labeling training and test datasets, where several users check the information (according to guides) for a relatively low price. For example, some works relying on crowdsourcing evaluation are (Mintz, Bills, Snow, & Jurafsky, 2009) using Amazon's Mechanical Turk (https://www.mturk.com/mturk/welcome) for evaluating relations, while Presutti, Nuzzolese, Consoli, Gangemi and Recupero (2016) and Fossati, Dorigatti and Giuliano (2018) use the Crowdflower (https://www.figure-eight.com/) platform (now called Figure Eight).

Evaluation of Sentence Similarity

The sentence similarity measures can be evaluated in two distinct ways according to the used dataset. Firstly, by comparing the level of similarity obtained by the measure against a gold standard dataset. Secondly, according to the application dataset, for example, using a dataset for either paraphrasing detection or question answering. Hence, some existing datasets and metrics to perform such tasks are described.

Datasets

There are diverse datasets proposed for the sentence similarity task, mainly proposed as a part of challenge events. Some relevant datasets are:

- TREC9 (Achananuparp, Hu, Zhou, & Zhang, 2008). It is composed of 193 paraphrased pairs used in the TREC9 Question Answering task. This dataset was constructed by human assessors supported with information from a query log.
- Microsoft Research paraphrase corpus (MSRP) (Dolan, Quirk, & Brockett, 2004). It is composed of 1725 sentence pairs constructed by two human assessors about new web sources.
- Recognizing textual entailment challenge (RTE3) (Dagan, Glickman, & Magnini, 2005). It contains 800 sentence pairs comprised of topics regarding information retrieval, multi-document summarization, question answering, and information extraction.
- Semantic Textual Similarity (STS) (Cer, Diab, Agirre, Lopez-Gazpio, & Specia, 2017). STS dataset contains documents about News, Caption, and Forum. This dataset was derived from the SevEval-2017 Task1. The dataset contains 8628 sentence pairs divided into three categories: *train*, *dev*, and *test*. This is useful for training a machine learning technique because the two first parts of the dataset can be used for training and configuration steps and the latter for testing.

Metrics

The Pearson correlation (Goshtasby, 2012) is a commonly used measure to compare the similarity result against a gold standard dataset. This is because it provides a correlation coefficient that measures the linear relationship between corresponding values in X and Y (two sets with n number of individuals). The Pearson correlation can be obtained, as shown in Eq. (8).

$$r = \frac{\sum_{i=1}^{n}(x_i - \bar{x})(y_i - \bar{y})}{\sqrt{\sum_{i=1}^{n}(x_i - \bar{x})^2}\sqrt{\sum_{i=1}^{n}(y_i - \bar{y})^2}} \tag{8}$$

where n is the sample size, x_i, y_i are the individual sample points indexed with i. Finally, $\bar{x} = \frac{1}{n}\sum_{i=1}^{n}x_i$; and similarly for $\bar{y}$.

TRENDS AND CHALLENGES

The representation of text on the Semantic Web covers a process consisting of several concepts, techniques, tools, formats, and specifications from several areas such as Information Retrieval, Natural Language Processing, Information Extraction, Machine Learning, and so on. Although such areas and tasks suppose progress in the representation of new information for the Semantic Web, their learning curve makes people reuse the incorporation of RDF standards for the representation. However, recent solutions based on systems and information published in knowledge bases encourage the production and dissemination of RDF data. For example, the Semantic Web has been applied in the areas of Education (Dietze, Yu, Giordano, Kaldoudi, Dovrolis, & Taibi, 2012), Tourism (Sabou, Arsal, & Brasoveanu, 2013), Biomedicine (Friedman & Elhadad, 2013), Search engines (Sánchez-Cervantes, et al., 2019), to mention a few. Likewise, knowledge graphs have been recently incorporated in many services and companies such as Facebook, Microsoft, Google, Amazon, among others. The idea is to use such representations to exploit data sources to gain information and, thus, knowledge of users, preferences, connections, and so on.

Although many efforts have been performed for the representation and consumption of RDF triples from text, there are still several challenges to overcome, some of them are:

- Although there are solutions such as Protégé (Tudorache, Nyulas, Noy, & Musen, 2013) and Jena (Zhong, 2012) that allow the edition and development of ontologies and RDF data, more applications and editors are still needed to facilitate and assist the representation of information statements as RDF triples. Such an application would alleviate the breach of learning standards and rules of the Semantic Web.

- New vocabularies/ontologies and ways to link predicates from semantic relations to properties are also required. In this sense, it is required a thorough characterization of the type of relations that can be associated to such properties, where different solutions cover relations used for the ontology learning, and representation of logical facts (Gangemi, Recupero, Mongiovì, Nuzzolese, & Presutti, 2016), and general domain relations (Banko, Cafarella, Soderland, Broadhead, & Etzioni, 2007).

- Diverse data sources such as social networks suppose a process that involves cleansing and pre-processing operations and due to their reduced context and text characteristics (noisy, short), difficult the extraction of entities and relations.

- There is no one solution to cover all domains of information and languages. Thus, specialized models and techniques are required to exploit information from different domains such as finance, construction, biology, and languages (Gracia et al., 2012; Gómez-Pérez, Villa-Suero, Montiel-Ponsoda, Gracia & Aguado-de-Cea, 2013).

- According to the data source, the data may contain quality issues such as consistency, truth, completeness, and timeliness (data updated) (Zaveri, Rula, Maurino, Pietrobon, Lehmann, & Auer, 2016). Thus, such information must be verified by strategies that cover either represented data and those tools that extract new facts.

- Finally, in recent years, the Deep Learning has been demonstrated an impact in the area of NLP and Information Extraction (Sengupta, et al., 2020), encouraging the improvement of the precision in the tagging and extraction of elements of information and grammatical descriptions from text. However, the integration of different Deep Learning techniques supposes the obtainment of representative data models and algorithms, which are costly to obtain due to the large scale of documents to train and the configuration of required parameters by the algorithms.

CONCLUSION

An appropriate representation of text is mandatory in the Semantic Web for achieving the required organization of the Web. Starting from the basic syntactic representation at the lower layer to the top layer of the Semantic Web model, the text is transformed for adding semantics. At each layer, the representation of text is enhanced for such aim. The goal of this chapter is to give the reader the underlying concepts, methods, and tools that give support to the representation of text through several steps for the generation of RDF triples on the Semantic Web. Thus, it presented some of the main concepts regarding the Semantic Web and its standards and the relation with diverse tasks from NLP. The idea is to give an overview of benefits from NLP tasks, and how these can be exploited for the representation of data in the Semantic Web. Moreover, some common representation and publication schemes from text to RDF data were also presented. These schemes introduced the need for the two main tasks involved in the representation of information on the Semantic Web, Entity Extraction and Linking and Relation Extraction and Linking. Likewise, the ways used to evaluate such tasks were also provided, where EEL is commonly evaluated through existing gold standard datasets and REL through a posteriori evaluation performed by human judges over a sample of extractions.

REFERENCES

W3C Community. (2014). *Vocabularies*. Retrieved from W3C: http://www.w3.org/standards/semanticweb/ontology

Achananuparp, P., Hu, X., Zhou, X., & Zhang, X. (2008). Utilizing Sentence Similarity and Question Type Similarity to Response to Similar Questions in Knowledge-Sharing Community. In *Workshop on Question Answering on the Web*. IEEE.

Amazon. (2019). *Amazon Neptune: Fast, reliable graph database built for the cloud*. Retrieved from Amazon: https://aws.amazon.com/es/neptune/

Arenas, M., Bertails, A., Prud'hommeaux, E., & Sequeda, J. (2012). *A Direct Mapping of Relational Data to RDF*. Retrieved from W3C: https://www.w3.org/TR/rdb-direct-mapping/

Auer, S., Ermilov, I., Lehmann, J., & Martin, M. (2018). *LODstats*. Retrieved from aksw: http://lodstats.aksw.org

Auer, S., Lehmann, J., Ngomo, A.-C. N., & Zaveri, A. (2013). *Introduction to Linked Data and Its Lifecycle on the Web. In Reasoning Web, Semantic Technologies for Intelligent Data Access*. Springer.

Augenstein, I., Maynard, D., & Ciravegna, F. (2016). Distantly supervised Web relation extraction for knowledge base population. *Semantic Web, 7*(4), 335–349.

Augenstein, I., Padó, S., & Rudolph, S. (2012). LODifier: Generating Linked Data from Unstructured Text. In *The Semantic Web: Research and Applications - 9th Extended Semantic Web Conference, ESWC 2012* (pp. 210-224). Springer.

Banko, M., Cafarella, M. J., Soderland, S., Broadhead, M., & Etzioni, O. (2007). Open Information Extraction from the Web. *International Joint Conference on Artificial Intelligence*.

Beckett, D. (2011). *N-Triples - A line-based syntax for an RDF graph*. Retrieved from W3C: http://www.w3.org/TR/n-triples/

Beckett, D., & Berners-Lee, T. (2011). *Turtle - Terse RDF Triple Language*. Retrieved from W3C: http://www.w3.org/TeamSubmission/turtle/

Berners-Lee, T. (2006). *Linked Data*. Retrieved from W3C: http://www.w3.org/DesignIssues/Linked-Data.html

Berners-Lee, T., Hendler, J., & Ora, L. (2001). The semantic web. *Scientific American, 284*(5), 34–43. PMID:11681174

Birbeck, M., & McCarron, S. (2010). *CURIE Syntax 1.0*. Retrieved from W3C: https://www.w3.org/TR/curie/

Bizer, C., Cyganiak, R., & Gauss, T. (2007). The RDF Book Mashup: From Web APIs to a Web of Data. *Workshop on Scripting for the Semantic Web*.

Bollacker, K., Evans, C., Paritosh, P., Sturge, T., & Taylor, J. (2008). Freebase: a collaboratively created graph database for structuring human knowledge. In *Proceedings of the ACM SIGMOD International Conference on Management of Data, SIGMOD 2008* (pp. 1247-1250). Vancouver: ACM.

Breitman, K. K., Casanova, M. A., & Truszkowski, W. (2007). *Semantic Web: Concepts, Technologies and Applications*. Springer.

Carothers, G. (2014). *RDF 1.1 N-Quads*. Retrieved from W3C: http://www.w3.org/TR/n-quads/

Cer, D. M., Diab, M. T., Agirre, E., Lopez-Gazpio, I., & Specia, L. (2017). SemEval-2017 Task 1: Semantic Textual Similarity - Multilingual and Cross-lingual Focused Evaluation. *Proceedings of the 11th International Workshop on Semantic Evaluation*.

Chang, C.-H., Kayed, M., Girgis, M. R., & Shaalan, K. F. (2006). A survey of web information extraction systems. *IEEE Transactions on Knowledge and Data Engineering, 18*(10), 1411–1428.

Cheatham, M., & Hitzler, P. (2013). String Similarity Metrics for Ontology Alignment. *International Semantic Web Conference* (pp. 294-309). Springer.

Cornolti, M., Ferragina, P., & Ciaramita, M. (2013). A Framework for Benchmarking Entity-Annotation Systems. *World Wide Web Conference*.

Criado-Fernandez, L. (2009). Procedimiento semi-automático para transformar la web en web semántica. Universidad Nacional de Educación a Distancia (España).

Cyganiak, R. (2011). *Top 100 most popular RDF namespace prefixes*. Retrieved from cyganiak: http://richard.cyganiak.de/blog/2011/02/top-100-most-popular-rdf-namespace-prefixes/

d'Amato, C., Fanizzi, N., Fazzinga, B., Gottlob, G., & Lukasiewicz, T. (2013). *Semantic Web Search and Inductive Reasoning. In Uncertainty Reasoning for the Semantic Web II, International Workshops URSW*. Springer.

D'Souza, J., & Ng, V. (2015). Sieve-Based Entity Linking for the Biomedical Domain. In *Proceeding of the 53rd annual Meeting of the Association for Computational Linguistics: Short Papers* (pp. 297-302). ACL.

Dagan, I., Glickman, O., & Magnini, B. (2005). The PASCAL Recognising Textual Entailment Challenge. In *First PASCAL Machine Learning Challenges Workshop* (pp. 177-90). Springer.

Dietze, S., Yu, H. Q., Giordano, D., Kaldoudi, E., Dovrolis, N., & Taibi, D. (2012). Linked education: interlinking educational resources and the Web of data. In *Proceedings of the ACM Symposium on Applied Computing* (pp. 366-371). Trento: ACM.

Dolan, B., Quirk, C., & Brockett, C. (2004). *Unsupervised Construction of Large Paraphrase Corpora: Exploiting Massively Parallel News Sources. In COLING*. ACL.

Dutta, A., Meilicke, C., & Stuckenschmidt, H. (2014). Semantifying Triples from Open Information Extraction Systems. *European Starting AI Researcher Symposium (STAIRS)*, 111-120.

Dutta, A., Meilicke, C., & Stuckenschmidt, H. (2015). Enriching Structured Knowledge with Open Information. In *Proceedings of the 24th International Conference on World Wide Web* (pp. 267-277). ACM.

Ehrlinger, L., & Wöß, W. (2016). Towards a Definition of Knowledge Graphs. In *Joint Proceedings of the Posters and Demos Track of the 12th International Conference on Semantic Systems - SEMANTiCS2016 and the 1st International Workshop on Semantic Change & Evolving Semantics (SuCCESS'16)* (pp. 1-4). Leipzig: CEUR-WS.org.

Erling, O., & Mikhailov, I. (2009). RDF Support in the Virtuoso DBMS. In Networked Knowledge - Networked Media - Integrating Knowledge Management, New Media Technologies and Semantic Systems (pp. 7-24). Springer.

Facebook. (2017). *Introduction to The Open Graph Protocol*. Retrieved from The Open Graph Protocol: https://ogp.me/

Fensel, D., Facca, F. M., Simperl, E., & Toma, I. (2011). *Semantic Web Services*. Springer.

Fensel, D., Lausen, H., Bruijn, J. d., Stollberg, M., Roman, D., Polleres, A., & Domingue, J. (2007). *Enabling Semantic Web Services*. Springer.

Ferragina, P., & Scaiella, U. (2010). TAGME: On-the-fly Annotation of Short Text Fragments (by Wikipedia Entities). In *Conference on Information and Knowledge Management (CIKM)* (pp. 1625-1628). ACM.

Fossati, M., Dorigatti, E., & Giuliano, C. (2018). N-ary Relation Extraction for Simultaneous T-Box and A-Box Knowledge Base Augmentation. *Semantic Web*, *9*(4), 413–439.

Friedman, C., & Elhadad, N. (2013). Natural Language Processing in Health Care and Biomedicine. In *Biomedical informatics*. Springer.

Gangemi, A., Recupero, D. R., Mongiovì, M., Nuzzolese, A. G., & Presutti, V. (2016). Identifying motifs for evaluating open knowledge extraction on the Web. *Knowledge-Based Systems*, *108*, 33–41.

Gómez-Pérez, A., Vila-Suero, D., Montiel-Ponsoda, E., Gracia, J., & Aguado-de-Cea, G. (2013). Guidelines for multilingual linked data. In *Proceedings of the 3rd International Conference on Web Intelligence, Mining and Semantics* (p. 3). Madrid: ACM.

Goshtasby, A. A. (2012). Similarity and dissimilarity measures. In *Image registration* (pp. 7–66). Springer.

Gracia, J., Montiel-Ponsoda, E., Cimiano, P., Gómez-Pérez, A., Buitelaar, P., & McCrae, J. P. (2012). Challenges for the multilingual Web of Data. *Journal of Web Semantics*, *11*, 63–71.

Gualán, R., Freire, R., Tello, A. E., Espinoza, M., & Saquicela, V. (2017). *Automatic RDF-ization of big data semi-structured datasets*. Maskana.

Hayes, P., & Welty, C. (2006). *Defining N-ary Relations on the Semantic Web*. Retrieved from W3C: https://www.w3.org/TR/swbp-n-aryRelations/

Heath, T., & Bizer, C. (2011). *Linked Data: Evolving the Web into a Global Data Space*. Morgan & Claypool Publishers.

Hellmann, S., Lehmann, J., Auer, S., & Brümmer, M. (2013). Integrating NLP Using Linked Data. In *International Semantic Web Conference* (pp. 98-113). Springer.

Hernández, D., Hogan, A., & Krötzsch, M. (2015). Reifying RDF: What Works Well With Wikidata? *International Workshop on Scalable Semantic Web Knowledge Base Systems co-located with ISWC* (pp. 32-47). CEUR.org.

Hirschberg, J., & Manning, C. (2015). Advances in natural language processing. *Science*, *349*(6245), 261–266. doi:10.1126cience.aaa8685 PMID:26185244

Hogan, A. (2014). *Linked Data & the Semantic Web Standards. In Linked Data Management*. Chapman and Hall/CRC.

KAON. (2006). *KAON2*. Retrieved from SemanticWeb: http://kaon2.semanticweb.org

Klyne, G., Carroll, J. J., & McBride, B. (2014). *RDF 1.1 Concepts and Abstract Syntax*. Retrieved from W3C: https://www.w3.org/TR/2014/REC-rdf11-concepts-20140225/#section-Datatypes

Kobilarov, G., Scott, T., Raimond, Y., Oliver, S., Sizemore, C., Smethurst, M., . . . Lee, R. (2009). Media Meets Semantic Web - How the BBC Uses DBpedia and Linked Data to Make Connections. In *The Semantic Web: Research and Applications, 6th European Semantic Web Conference* (pp. 723-737). Springer.

Krejcie, R. V., & Morgan, D. W. (1970). Determining sample size for research activities. *Educational and Psychological Measurement*, *30*(3), 607–610. doi:10.1177/001316447003000308

Kusner, M. J., Sun, Y., Kolkin, N. I., & Weinberger, K. Q. (2015). From Word Embeddings To Document Distances. In *International Conference on Machine Learning* (pp. 957-966). JMLR.

Lehmann, J., Isele, R., Jakob, M., Jentzsch, A., Kontokostas, D., Mendes, P. N., ... Bizer, C. (2015). DBpedia - A large-scale, multilingual knowledge base extracted from Wikipedia. *Semantic Web, 6*(2), 167–195. doi:10.3233/SW-140134

Liu, J., Fang, C., & Ansari, N. (2016). Request Dependency Graph: A Model for Web Usage Mining in Large-Scale Web of Things. *IEEE Internet of Things Journal, 3*(4), 598–608.

Manola, F., Miller, E., & McBride, B. (2014). *RDF 1.1 Primer*. Retrieved from W3C: https://www.w3.org/TR/2014/NOTE-rdf11-primer-20140624/

Martinez-Rodriguez, J. L., Hogan, A., & Lopez-Arevalo, I. (2018). Information Extraction meets the Semantic Web: A Survey. *Semantic Web, 11*(2), 1–81. doi:10.3233/SW-180333

McBride, B. (2004). *RDF/XML Syntax Specification*. Retrieved from W3C: http://www.w3.org/TR/REC-rdf-syntax/

McBride, B. (2004). *The Resource Description Framework (RDF) and its Vocabulary Description Language RDFS. In Handbook on Ontologies*. Springer.

McCarthy, D., Koeling, R., Weeds, J., & Carroll, J. A. (2004). Finding Predominant Word Senses in Untagged Text. In *Proceedings of the 42nd Annual Meeting of the Association for Computational Linguistics*. (pp. 279-286). ACL.

McCrae, J. P. (2018). *The Linked Open Data Cloud*. Retrieved from lod-cloud: https://lod-cloud.net

Mendes, P. N., Jakob, M., García-Silva, A., & Bizer, C. (2011). DBpedia spotlight: shedding light on the web of documents. In *Proceedings of the 7th International Conference on Semantic Systems, I-SEMANTICS* (pp. 1-8). ACM.

Meng, L., Huang, R., & Gu, J. (2013). A review of semantic similarity measures in Wordnet. *International Journal of Hybrid Information Technology, 6*(1), 1–12.

Mikolov, T., Chen, K., Corrado, G., & Dean, J. (2013). Efficient Estimation of Word Representations in Vector Space. *Proceedings of the International Conference on Learning Representations* (pp. 1-12). Academic Press.

Mikolov, T., Sutskever, I., Chen, K., Corrado, G. S., & Dean, J. (2013). Distributed Representations of Words and Phrases and their Compositionality. In Advances in Neural Information Processing Systems (pp. 3111-3119). NIPS.

Mileo, A., Abdelrahman, A., Policarpio, S., & Hauswirth, M. (2013). StreamRule: A Nonmonotonic Stream Reasoning System for the Semantic Web. In Web Reasoning and Rule Systems (pp. 247-252). Springer.

Mintz, M., Bills, S., Snow, R., & Jurafsky, D. (2009). Distant Supervision for Relation Extraction Without Labeled Data. In *Proceedings of the Joint Conference of the 47 Annual meeting of the Association for Computational Linguistics* (pp. 1003-1011). ACL.

Moro, A., Raganato, A., & Navigli, R. (2014). Entity Linking meets Word Sense Disambiguation: A Unified Approach. *Transactions of the Association for Computational Linguistics, 2*, 231–244. doi:10.1162/tacl_a_00179

Nguyen, V., Bodenreider, O., & Sheth, A. (2014). Don't Like RDF Reification?: Making Statements About Statements Using Singleton Property. In *Proceedings of the 23 rd International conference on World Wide Web* (pp. 759-770). ACM.

Nuzzolese, A. G., Gangemi, A., Presutti, V., Draicchio, F., Musetti, A., & Ciancarini, P. (2013). *Tipalo: A Tool for Automatic Typing of DBpedia Entities. In The Semantic Web: ESWC*. Springer.

Plu, J., Rizzo, G., & Troncy, R. (2016). Enhancing Entity Linking by Combining NER Models. In *Extended Semantic Web Conference (ESWC)*. Springer.

Presutti, V., Nuzzolese, A. G., Consoli, S., Gangemi, A., & Reforgiato Recupero, D. (2016). From hyperlinks to Semantic Web properties using Open Knowledge Extraction. *Semantic Web, 7*(4), 351–378.

Randolph, J. J. (2005). Free-Marginal Multirater Kappa (multirater K [free]): An Alternative to Fleiss' Fixed-Marginal Multirater Kappa. *Joensuu Learning and Instruction Symposium*.

Riedel, S., Yao, L., & McCallum, A. (2010). *Modeling Relations and Their Mentions without Labeled Text. In Machine Learning and Knowledge Discovery in Databases*. Springer.

Rouces, J., de Melo, G., & Hose, K. (2015). Framebase: Representing n-ary relations using semantic frames. In *Extended Semantic Web Conference* (pp. 505-521). Springer.

Rusu, D., Fortuna, B., & Mladenic, D. (2011). Automatically Annotating Text with Linked Open Data. In *Workshop on Linked Data on the Web*. CEUR.

Sabou, M., Arsal, I., & Braşoveanu, A. M. (2013). TourMISLOD: A tourism linked data set. *Semantic Web, 4*(3), 271–276.

Sánchez-Cervantes, J. L., Colombo-Mendoza, L. O., Alor-Hernández, G., García-Alcaráz, J. L., Álvarez-Rodríguez, J. M., & Rodríguez-González, A. (2019). LINDASearch: A faceted search system for linked open datasets. *Wireless Networks*, 1–19.

Sengupta, S., Basak, S., Saikia, P., Paul, S., Tsalavoutis, V., Atiah, F., ... Peters, A. (2020). A review of deep learning with special emphasis on architectures, applications and recent trends. *Knowledge-Based Systems*, 1–100.

Sheth, A., Arpinar, I. B., & Kashyap, V. (2004). *Relationships at the heart of Semantic Web: Modeling, discovering, and exploiting complex semantic relationships. In Enhancing the Power of the Internet*. Springer.

Srivastava, A. N., & Sahami, M. (2009). *Text mining: Classification, clustering, and applications*. Chapman and Hall/CRC.

Tsarkov, D., & Horrocks, I. (2007). *FaCT++ resoner*. Retrieved from FaCT: http://owl.man.ac.uk/factplusplus/

Tudorache, T., Nyulas, C., Noy, N. F., & Musen, M. A. (2013). WebProtégé: A collaborative ontology editor and knowledge acquisition tool for the Web. *Semantic Web*, *4*(1), 89–99. PMID:23807872

Usbeck, R., Röder, M., Ngomo, A.-C. N., Baron, C., Both, A., Brümmer, M., ... Wesemann, L. (2015). GERBIL: General Entity Annotator Benchmarking Framework. In *Proceedings of the 24th International Conference on World Wide Web* (pp. 1133-1143). ACM.

Van den Berge, J., Schouten, H., Boomstra, S., van Drunen Littel, S., & Braakman, R. (1979). Interobserver agreement in assessment of ocular signs in coma. *Journal of Neurology, Neurosurgery, and Psychiatry*, *42*(12), 1163–1168. PMID:533856

Vandenbussche, P.-Y., Atemezing, G., Poveda-Villalón, M., & Vatant, B. (2017). Linked Open Vocabularies (LOV): A gateway to reusable semantic vocabularies on the Web. *Semantic Web*, *8*(3), 437–452. doi:10.3233/SW-160213

Wu, Z., Eadon, G., Das, S., Inseok, E., Kolovski, V., Annamalai, M., & Srinivasan, J. (2008). Implementing an Inference Engine for RDFS/OWL Constructs and User-Defined Rules in Oracle. In *Proceedings of the 24th International Conference on Data Engineering* (pp. 1239-1248). Cancún, México: IEEE.

Yosef, M. A., Hoffart, J., Bordino, I., Spaniol, M., & Weikum, G. (2011). AIDA: An online tool for accurate disambiguation of named entities in text and tables. *PVLDB, 4*(12).

Zaveri, A., Rula, A., Maurino, A., Pietrobon, R., Lehmann, J., & Auer, S. (2016). Quality assessment for Linked Data: A Survey. *Semantic Web*, *7*(1), 63–93.

Zheng, J., Howsmon, D., Zhang, B., Hahn, J., McGuinness, D. L., Hendler, J. A., & Ji, H. (2015). *Entity Linking for biomedical literature. In BMC Med. Inf. & Decision Making*. BMC Springer.

Zhong, L. (2012). The Jena-Based Ontology Model Inference and Retrieval Application. *Intelligent Information Management*, *4*(4), 157–160.

Zwicklbauer, S., Seifert, C., & Granitzer, M. (2016). DoSeR - A Knowledge-Base-Agnostic Framework for Entity Disambiguation Using Semantic Embeddings. *Extended Semantic Web Conference*, 182-198.

Chapter 20
Opinion Mining for Instructor Evaluations at the Autonomous University of Ciudad Juarez

Rafael Jiménez
https://orcid.org/0000-0001-9904-3059
Universidad Autónoma de Ciudad Juárez, Mexico

Vicente García
https://orcid.org/0000-0003-2820-2918
Universidad Autónoma de Ciudad Juárez, Mexico

Abraham López
Universidad Autónoma de Ciudad Juárez, Mexico

Alejandra Mendoza Carreón
Universidad Autónoma de Ciudad Juárez, Mexico

Alan Ponce
Universidad Autónoma de Ciudad Juárez, Mexico

ABSTRACT

The Autonomous University of Ciudad Juárez performs an instructor evaluation each semester to find strengths, weaknesses, and areas of opportunity during the teaching process. In this chapter, the authors show how opinion mining can be useful for labeling student comments as positives and negatives. For this purpose, a database was created using real opinions obtained from five professors of the UACJ over the last four years, covering a total of 20 subjects. Natural language processing techniques were used on the database to normalize its data. Experimental results using 1-NN and Bagging classifiers shows that it is possible to automatically label positive and negative comments with an accuracy of 80.13%.

DOI: 10.4018/978-1-7998-4730-4.ch020

Copyright © 2021, IGI Global. Copying or distributing in print or electronic forms without written permission of IGI Global is prohibited.

INTRODUCTION

Opinions are central activities for almost all human beings. When we need to make important decisions, it is essential to know the view of others; therefore, opinions are a valuable source of information. The sentiments analysis or opinion mining is an area that automatically classifies sentiments expressed by a person about a given object, as positive, negative, or neutral (Cortizo, 2019). Opinion mining is used by companies to understand the perceptions that customers have about their products or services and identify areas of opportunity or improve the marketing strategies used (Huddy, 2017).

Teacher evaluations are carried out by the Autonomous University of Ciudad Juárez (UACJ) each semester as a method by which the written opinion of students is recorded to identify strengths, weaknesses, and areas of opportunity in the performance of teachers (Universidad Autonoma de Ciudad Juarez, 2019).

During the period of evaluation, the teaching evaluation office makes available to students a platform in which, in addition to other metrics, two boxes appear where they can freely write positive and negative comments about their teachers during the semester in progress. In this process, a student might mistakenly write negative comments in the positive box and vice versa, as well as a combination of both. It causes the teacher evaluation to not provide easy feedback to teachers as the positive and negative comments are mixed.

During the evaluation process, the student is presented with a series of specific questions about how the teacher leads their class. These questions are answered from bad to excellent, represented with values ranging from 1 to 5. Before finishing the evaluation, the student is allowed to write textual comments about the teacher's performance.

Once the teachers assign a final grade to students, the university's portal allows teacher access to the results of the teacher through the teacher's portal. The results are an average of the grades obtained in each of the specific questions, and positive and negative comments are received. These results help them identify strengths and weaknesses within their teaching model by receiving immediate feedback, which allows them to make relevant changes to their practices to promote better teaching and better learning.

This chapter is an extension of a previous study (Jiménez, García, Florencia-Juárez, Rivera & López-Orozco, 2018). Here, we use sentiment analysis techniques on opinions issued by the students to categorize the comments into positive and negative in their native Spanish language. For this, a comment repository was built with student opinions issued over four years, manually categorized as positive and negative, to build later feature vectors, which were used to train a 1-NN and the Bagging algorithm. Work in the same line was presented by Gutiérrez, Ponce, Ochoa, and Álvarez (2018), in which the performance of teachers was analyzed using reviews written by students of the Polytechnic University of Aguascalientes.

It is important to mine text in Spanish because there is not much work being done in the fields of natural language processing and opinion mining using Spanish language tools and libraries, despite the fact that opinion mining methodologies in English might not fit other languages without making major modifications.

The chapter is organized in the following manner. Section 2 briefly describes related works in opinion mining. In Section 3, the methodology undertaken in the development of research. Section 4 shows the experimental configuration adopted. Subsequently, in Section 5, the results are described and discussed. Finally, Section 6 concludes and proposes future lines of research.

RELATED WORKS

Sentiment analysis, or opinion mining, is the process of automatically extracting opinions using artificial intelligence and natural language processing to understand expressed emotions better, primarily online. Microsoft (2019) states that natural language processing is a tool that aims to design and build software that can analyze, understand, and generate languages that humans can naturally use so that they can eventually communicate with a computer as if it did with another.

An opinion is a "view, judgment, or appraisal formed in mind about a particular matter" (Merriam-Webster, 2019). Liu (2004) classifies opinions into two types:

1. **Direct Opinions:** The opinion is expressed directly at the object or entity. This type of opinion is the one we are interested in mining.
2. **Comparative Opinions:** In which the opinion is expressed by comparing two or more objects or entities in a hierarchical way. This type of opinion aims at giving a reference to which an 'object 1' is better or worse in comparison to 'object 2'.

The role that natural language processing plays in opinion mining is to provide the linguistic information necessary for the extraction of information. This linguistic information is used through the grammatical labeling of words of a sentence to remove stop words and during stemming that allows to reduce a word to its morphological root, discussed in Section 3.

As such, opinion mining has a great field of application. There are large and small companies that only engage in opinion mining to sell analytics to their customers like Revuze (2018), Aspectiva (2019), Brandwatch (2019) and Google (2018); while others use it as an essential tool of their daily operations like Amazon (Amazon Web Services, 2018).

Web Reviews

Opinion mining on the web (Jadhavar & Komarraji, 2018) is used to automate the maintenance of reviews and opinions since social networks are a rich source of large-scale information. Users use them to express their feelings on various topics, many of them, about products. These comments can be classified as positive, negative, or neutral, and from them, valuable information can be extracted for the company's market reports. Some examples of applications in the market are:

- **Meaning cloud:** It is an online application that offers text classification, topic extraction, language identification, thematization, morphosyntactic analysis, corporate reputation, and text clustering (Meaning Cloud, 2019). The application has support for several languages, including English, Spanish, French, Italian, Portuguese, and Catalan. How Meaning Cloud works is through an Excel plugin or through an online service API that contains all the libraries in a single package to perform the extraction of opinions.
- **Vivek Sentiment:** This web application was created using a Naïve Bayes model and utilizes reviews from IMDB.com, a movie database (Narayanan, Arora, & Bhatia, 2016). The system evaluates the comments as positive, negative, or neutral left by registered users in movies and tv shows, in addition to providing the classifier's level of confidence in the result. The application has an

API to use the classifier externally, but only if there is an Internet connection. Another limitation of this application is that its domain only covers the English language.

In Businesses

Companies interested in knowing customers' perceptions of their products or services use opinion mining. The information collected from surveys is classified, making it possible to improve a product, identify areas of opportunity, or improve the marketing strategies used (Smeureanu, 2012). An example of this is Meltwater (2019), which is a consultancy that offers services and packages that help create an analysis of the presence of the brand before consumers and competitors. Among the analyzes that are performed is the sentiment analysis, which monitors how well-received was a message from the company in social networks.

The ability to automatically extract meaningful information from users is of great use for businesses who have or aim to have a great online presence, as they can monitor social networks by analyzing real-time user activity and detecting negative feedback just minutes after the brand issues a new marketing campaign, product or service. Many customer metrics and data analytics are tailor-made for each company by marketing companies using sentiment analysis. An example of this is Brandwatch (2019), who offers brand name analytics for customers looking to track how well they are perceived by users by positive and negative comments and how well users perceive their competitors. One key aspect of Brandwatch is that they offer their customers a way to redefine comment's sentiment if they think it was misclassified. This is because sentiment analysis is an automatic process, which is not completely free of mistakes and primarily because sentiments are subjective, and as such, their perception is influenced by personal feelings.

Government Agencies

Government opinion mining extracts public behavior and opinions on political issues. The use of sentiment analysis helps identify the opinions of voters regarding a candidate before the elections in order to improve campaign strategies (Smeureanu, 2012). An example of this is the National Institute of Statistics, Geography, and Informatics (INEGI), which developed a tool that classified 63 million georeferenced tweets written between 2014 and 2015, with the purpose of generating mobility and tourism statistics, as well as knowing the mood of the population by the state of the country (National Institute of Statistics and Geography, 2017).

METHODOLOGY

The steps that were carried out for the classification of comments of the teacher evaluation were the following:

1) Collection of comments of the teacher evaluation.
2) Preprocessing of the comments.
3) Creation of a feature vector.
4) Validation of our classification model.

These steps are briefly described in the following sections.

Comment Collection

The collection of comments was carried out during the month of January 2017 with the help of the professors of the Multidisciplinary Division of the UACJ in Ciudad Universitaria (CU). The comments collected correspond to four years, 20 subjects, and five professors. Since neither the university nor other teachers have access to other teacher's evaluation results and comments, we had to ask each teacher who was willing to participate in this project to extract their own comments by performing the following steps:

Step 1: Access their teacher evaluation results page, which shows all the courses they have ever imparted. This results page is only available to each teacher and can only be accessed using the credentials issued to them by the university's Information technology (IT) department.

Step 2: Select a subject already evaluated, as current semester courses might be in the process of evaluation.

Step 3: Locate the comments area as featured in Figure 1, where we can find two comment boxes, one for positive comments and one for negative comments.

Step 4: Copy all comments in either the positive comments and paste them into the positive comment's repository, copy all negative comments, and paste them into their corresponding repository.

Figure 1. Positive comments area and negative comments area

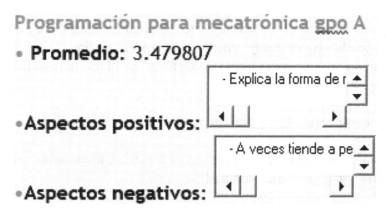

Having all positive and negative comments stored in separate simple text files (.txt) makes it easy to preprocess, as Java can easily read the utf-8 encoding.

Comment Preprocessing

During the preprocessing stage of the project, the sentiment analysis techniques described by Quratulain, Sajjad, and Sayeed (2016) were followed. Below are the steps carried out.

- Validation of comments by reading all comments to find those which had no relevance to teacher evaluation. All comments found to be outside the domain of the teacher evaluation had to be eliminated. It is important since only those comments in which students provide feedback on their experience when taking classes with a professor should be taken into account since comments outside this domain could cause noise to the classifier. For example, the comment shown below was marked as invalid because it does not provide feedback on teacher knowledge, teaching style, or teaching competence, but rather is just a student complaint about something that did.

"Profesor en serio, yo nunca le explique a Yair el método mini, Max el asumió que sí, pero está tonto. Se lo juro."

Translation: "Professor seriously, I never explained Yair the mini max method, assumed that I did, but he is stupid. I swear."

- Identification of comments that were erroneously assigned by the student in the negative comments area, being that the comment is positive and vice versa. Once these comments were identified, they were reassigned to their corresponding repository. This step is necessary to establish what comments represent a positive comment or a negative comment. It is important to consider that tagging comments as positive or negative is a reflection of the personal subjective interpretation of those comments, and therefore, will likely be a difficult endeavor to tag them as a consensus.
- Writing validation was also done manually since all comments had to be read to validate them. All misspelled words were manually edited to correct their spelling. This was done manually as automatically fixing spelling errors lands outside the scope of this project. Example of a spelling correction: "inpuntual" → "impuntual".

Automatic preprocessing with the normalization function was also used, which consisted of:

- Case conversion of characters from uppercase to lowercase to eliminate possible errors when comparing words using Java's toLowerCase() method.

Example:

```
String str = "Hello";
str = str.toLowerCase();
```

- Elimination of accents in some letters since the students do not accentuate the words correctly or simply avoid accents altogether. This caused that the words were being compared correctly. To do this, the replaceAll() method was used. This method takes two parameters x and y. Where parameter *x* is the character to be replaced by the *y* character in a string. Example of the method to replace the character 'á' with 'a'.

```
str = str.replaceAll("á", "a");
```

- Elimination of characters, quotes, and underscores. These types of characters contribute nothing. To eliminate these characters, we also used the replaceAll() method explicitly imputing each character to be replaced and its replacement. Example of the elimination of the underscore character, which is then replaced by a no character, shortening the string by one character:

```
str = str.replaceAll("_", "");
```

- Elimination of emojis and other symbols such as ideograms were also removed. An example of this is:

"es una muy buena maestra ♥" → *"es una muy buena maestra"*

- Since FreeLing requires all comments to end with a full stop, a period was added at the end of all comments, while also deleting other characters in the comment added automatically by the teacher evaluation system such as the hyphen character ("-") found at the beginning of all comments recollected. Since we know how to remove characters using the replaceAll() method, we use the concatenation operator to add the period character, ".", at the end of the string. Below is an example of the method used:

```
str = str.replaceAll("_", "");
str += ".";
```

The following is an example of the processed comment:

"- Tiene dominio sobre su tema" → *"Tiene dominio sobre su tema."*

- Word tokenization of comments into a list of single words. This process makes it easier to do word matching during the creation of feature vectors in Section 3.3. Word tokenization should be done after the removal of characters and just before stop word removal as it can add punctuations such as ".", "-", "?", "!" to the end of word tokens. Tokenization can be achieved either by utilizing Freeling's tokenizer or Java's StringTokenizer.

Example of Java's StringTokenizer to split a string using its default space delimiter:

```
String message = "Hello Word";
StringTokenizer st = new StringTokenizer(message);
while (st.hasMoreTokens())
{
    System.out.println(st.nextToken());
}
Program output:
Hello
World
```

- Removal of stop words. Stop words are commonly used words like prepositions or articles and do not provide useful information, the stop words list used as a reference to identify words to be removed was printed to a text file from Python's NLTK corpus list of Spanish stop words. This can be done by using the following code in python:

```
import nltk
from nltk.corpus import stopwords
stop_words = set(stopwords.words('spanish'))
with open('Stop Word List.txt', 'w', encoding='utf-8') as f:
    for item in stop_words:
        f.write("\n" + item)
```

Creating a Feature Vector

A feature vector is a vector of n-elements or attributes that describe an object. In order to convert a comment to a vector, the attributes that formed it were previously defined. From a list of opinion-indicating words in Spanish independent of the domain, which contain positive and negative words, the feature vector was constructed. The list of words to be used as a dictionary was provided by the Thematic Network on Multilingual and Multimodal Information Treatment (Molina-González, 2013), which consists of 2509 positive words and 5626 negative words. This dictionary is based on Bing Liu's Opinion Lexicon.

To reduce the dimensionality of the vector, we used a package library called FreeLing (2019), which is a morphosyntactic tagger. This library allows to automatically extract the stem of each of the word in the dictionary. By stemming each word, we can reduce the inflected words to their base form, which allows us to remove duplicate stems. By stemming the dictionary words, we saw a decrease of words in the dictionary to 1313 positive and 2949 negative words, or a 47.60% reduction of attributes while still retaining the same value of the dictionary.

To further reduce the dimensionality, an analysis of the stem of the words was performed. During this analysis, a word w was taken and compared to all the words in the same file (positive or negative) were searched to find if the word w was contained within at the start of another word v. That is that a word w can be considered a base for word v, *or* its morphological root. This decreased the number of features to only 584 positive words and 1270 negative words.

Table 1. Example of positive and negative words as characteristics of a vector

List of words	Positive	bueno	proactivo	decisivo	mejor
	Negative	impuntual	fastidio	aburrir	inexperto

The creation of a feature vector was carried out from the stem words of positive and negative type as shown in Table 1, where the words "bueno" (good), "proactivo" (proactive), "decisivo" (decisive) and "mejor" (better) are examples of positive word, and "impuntual" (unpunctual), "fastidio" (nuisance), "aburrido" (bored) and "inexperto" (inexperienced) are examples of negative words.

To create a feature vector, the complete 1852 attributes from our dictionary were used to create a list of words vector or attributes vector. This vector is created specifically for the task of word matching the attributes with the words in each instance, and the quantity of words in the dictionary dictates the dimensionality of our vector. After adding all our dictionary words to our attributes vector, a class attribute, called "class", is added at the end of the attribute vector to determine the class value of our vectors.

Table 2. Resulting vector from a comment and the characteristics vector

List of words	bueno	proactivo	decisivo	mejor	impuntual	fastidio	aburrir	inexperto
Vector	1	0	0	1	1	0	0	0

Given a comment "Es un buen professor pero podria ser mejor si no fuera tan imputual", this is preprocessed with the normalization function before being converted to tokens with the help of FreeLing, which would look like {"es", "un", "buen", "profesor", "pero", "podría", "ser", "mejor", "si", "no", "fuera", "tan", "impuntual"}, later the lemma is extracted from the words {"ser", "uno, "bueno", "profesor", "pero", "podria", "ser", "mejor", "si", "no", "ser", "tan", "impuntual"}. Subsequently, the value of 1 is assigned to each attribute if the word exists and 0 in the opposite case. An example of this can be seen in Table 2. At the end of each vector, we added 1 if the comment used to create the vector is positive or cero if the comment used is negative, which corresponds to the class attribute.

After the feature vectors are created, we need to save our vectors and we can either save them to a comma-separated values (CSV) file and use WEKA's built-in ARFF-Viewer to transform our CSV to a relation attribute format file (ARFF) or to write our vectors directly to ARFF.

An ARFF is a text file with an. arff extension and consists of three parts:

1. The relation area is the @Relation header followed by the relation name. The relation name can be given by the user and the name given does not affect the classification product.
    Example: @Relation TeacherEvaluation

2. The attributes area follows after the heading and describes all the characteristics in the attributes vector by listing them with the word: @Attribute followed by the characteristic and the type of values that this attribute can have inside square brackets or NUMERIC if the value it is numerical. To end the attribute area, the Class attribute is included with the possible class values in the relation.
    Attribute example: @ATTRIBUTE triumphant {1,0}
    Example of class attribute: @ATTRIBUTE Class {positive, negative}

3. The data area begins after the word @Data and contains all the vectors created with the values separated by a comma and, at the end, the class to which it belongs or the sign "?" if the feature vector must be evaluated. By using the data shown in Table 2, the following instances must be created:
    For training: 1,0,0,1,1,0,0,0, 1
    For classification: 1,0,0,1,1,0,0, 0,?

The last step we need to do is to determine if any attributes that do not vary at all or that vary too much, and therefore, we can safely remove with the help of the "RemoveUseless" filter in Weka. After applying this filter, our attributes went down from 1852 to only 111, as shown in Table 3.

Table 3. Brief description of the database during the experiments

Number of instances			Number of attributes		
Positive	Negative	Total	Positive	Negative	Total
187	110	297	48	63	111

Validation

Cross-validation is a technique to estimate the performance of a classification model. The main idea of cross-validation is to divide the collected data to estimate the classifier error. One part of the data,

Table 4. K-folds example of 5 iterations

Iteration	1	2	3	4	5
Dataset	**Testing**	Training	Training	Training	Training
	Training	**Testing**	Training	Training	Training
	Training	Training	**Testing**	Training	Training
	Training	Training	Training	**Testing**	Training
	Training	Training	Training	Training	**Testing**

the largest, is used to train the classifier, and the remaining part is used for testing the trained classifier with unseen data.

To validate our model, cross-validation using K-folds was performed, where K is the number of iterations used. To carry out the tests, the total set of elements used is divided into K number of equal parts, and during each iteration, one of the K parts is rotated as testing while the remaining parts are used as training until completing K iterations. Table 4 exemplifies the cross-validation algorithm using K = 5 iterations and how test pieces are rotated during each iteration.

EXPERIMENT CONFIGURATION

All tests were performed with the WEKA software, which is an open-source data mining software that includes machine language algorithms for classification and data preparation (WEKA, 2020). The classification algorithms offered by the WEKA library were analyzed to have a reasonable idea of which of them we should use to classify. The following considerations were taken into account:

- The number of comments used for training.
- The dimensionality of feature vectors.
- The attribute type in the vector, in this case, only a binary value of 0 and 1.

Since we have less than 100,000 comments and the feature vector only contains binary values composed of 0 and 1, it was decided to try the following classifiers:

- Bagging is an ensemble method that feeds base classifiers a random subset of the training set since Bagging resamples the training set with replacement, some instances can be represented multiple times while others might not be. Then it evaluates each classifier's prediction, either by voting or by average, to form a final prediction for a new test instance (Opitz, 1999).
- 1-NN is an algorithm that measures the Euclidean distance from one instance to another (already-classified instance or neighbor) and classifies the new instance as the same class as its nearest neighbor (See, 2016).

WEKA allows users to apply classification algorithms, and to validate using cross-validation of K partitions and the database that is briefly detailed in Table 3. The comments contained in the database went through a preprocessing that was described in Section 3.2., where finally 187 and 110 positive and negative comments could be constructed, respectively.

Table 5. Confusion matrix of two classes

		Predicted Tag	
		Positive	Negative
Real Label	Positive	d	c
	Negative	b	a

The dimensionality of the vectors is 111, of which 63 attributes describe positive words and 48 negative words.

For the Bagging and 1-NN classifiers, the default configurations in WEKA were used where the Bagging classifier uses a REPTree for fast decision tree learning, and the 1-NN classifier uses a Euclidean distance kernel and a K = 1.

As evaluation metrics to measure the performance of the Bagging and 1- NN classifiers, a two-class confusion matrix was used, as shown in Table 5. With this matrix, we can determine the performance of a classifier with the following formulas.

The accuracy of the classification model is a statistical measure of how well the model correctly identifies positive and negative comments, and it is determined by the formula:

$$accuracy = \frac{a+d}{a+b+c+d} \tag{1}$$

The precision is the proportion of correctly classified instances based on the total number of instances classified as belonging to the positive class, and it is determined by the formula:

$$precision = \frac{d}{d+b} \tag{2}$$

The true positive rate (TP) is the proportion of positive instances that were correctly classified, and it is determined by the formula:

$$TP = \frac{d}{c+d} \tag{3}$$

The true negative rate (TN) is the proportion of negative instances that were correctly classified, and it is determined by the formula:

$$TN = \frac{a}{a+b} \tag{4}$$

The false-positive rate (FP) is the proportion of negative instances classified as positive, determined by the formula:

$$FP = \frac{b}{a+b} \tag{5}$$

The false-negative rate (FN) is the proportion of negative instances classified as positive, determined by the formula:

$$FN = \frac{c}{c+d} \tag{6}$$

RESULTS

The overall accuracy results are shown in Table 6. We can observe that the Bagging algorithm obtained the best results of the two classifiers by scoring 3.37% points higher than 1-NN. It indicates a good score for the Bagging algorithm.

Table 6. The global accuracy results table

	Bagging	1-NN
Global Accuracy	80.13%	76.76%

Table 7 shows the accuracy by class for each of the classifiers. As can be seen, the negative comments obtain a low classification rate of 59.1% and 62.7% on both algorithms. In contrast, positive comments get results greater than 90%. The low negative results affect the overall classification rate.

Table 7. Precision table by class

	Bagging	**1-NN**
Positive	90.4%	90.4%
Negative	62.7%	59.1%

To analyze the behavior by the class of the classifiers, Tables 8 and 9 show the confusion matrix for the Bagging and 1-NN classifiers, respectively.

Table 8. Confusion matrix for the Bagging classifier

	Bagging	
	Positive	**Negative**
Positive	169	18
Negative	41	69

Table 9. Confusion matrix for the 1-NN classifier

	1-NN	
	Positive	Negative
Positive	169	18
Negative	45	65

The confusion matrix M shows that the model correctly classified the elements of the upper left M [1,1] and the lower right M [2,2]. In the lower-left M [2,1] and upper right M [1,2], false positives and negatives are shown, respectively.

From the confusion matrix for the Bagging classifier in Table 8, a TP of 0.9037, TN of 0.6272, the FP of 0.3727, and the FN of 0.0962 is obtained. Given the rates of FP and FN, we can observe that this classification algorithm has a lower rate of FP than FN, which indicates that there was a lower percentage of negative comments classified as positive than positive comments classified as negative. For the 1- NN classifier in Table 9, a TP of 0.9037, a TN of 0.5909, the FP of 0.4090, and the FN of 0.0962 are obtained.

The Bagging algorithm, unlike the 1-NN algorithm, has a higher TN rate than FP, so fewer negative comments were classified as positive than using 1-NN.

Given the FP and FN of the two classifiers, the Bagging algorithm has the lowest rate of false positives and false negatives. This indicates that with this algorithm had fewer positive comments classified as negative and less negative comments classified as positive.

To give a better idea of how the instances are located in a two-dimensional space and why we get those results, Multidimensional Scaling (MDS) was used to graph the vector database by mapping the instances by their similarities and dissimilarities. It is usually used to visualize data with high dimensionality, in a low dimensions space. In Figure 2, we can see how the positive (red) and negative (cyan) instances are plotted in a cartesian plane. In the figure, it is possible to see how the data gets grouped into three groups marked with the letters A, B, and C. In group A, it is possible to see a convergence of positive instances and does not have the presence in or around that group another class of instances. So, it could be said that the instances that belong to this space will be correctly classified.

The opposite occurs in group C, where there is a slight overlap between positive and negative instances, as some positive instances make their way into a group of negative instances. These positive instances have a minimum effect on the ability classification model.

Group B is precisely the area where the classifier usually makes mistakes. Looking at group C in detail, one could say that positive comments in that area will be classified as negative. In contrast, in group B, negative comments will be classified as positive, given that the nearest instances are all mostly positive.

This overlap that occurs in group B happens since some comments may contain the same particular words in both positive and negative comments. For example, the word "bien" (good). This word is repeated both in negative comments such as:

"realmente la puedo considero como una maestra que enseña del todo bien aunque cumpla con todos los puntos previos, considero que no es su culpa, el salón que nos tocó este semestre se batalla mucho para escuchar (d4-210)." Translation "I can really consider her as a teacher who teaches everything

Figure 2. The two-dimensional layout of the instances used for training

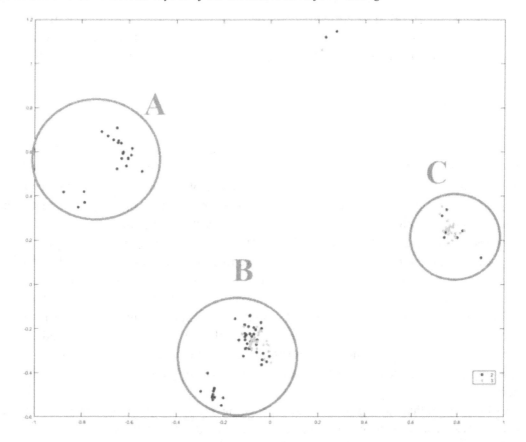

well even though she meets all the previous points, I consider that it is not her fault, the classroom that we had this semester made it hard to listen (d4-210)."

It also occurs in positive comments such as:

"sus grupos casi siempre están vacíos, eso habla bien de él, ya que da la clase bien y les da a los alumnos la calificación que se merecen, no deberían abrir esta materia en veranos, los que no hacen nada buscan como pasar y si se gradúan eso da mala imagen a la UACJ en la industria, a veces se vuelve difícil conseguir un buen trabajo cuando tienen catalogado a los alumnos de la UACJ como inútiles y flojos." Translation: "his groups are almost always empty, that speaks well of him, since he imparts the class well and gives the students the grade they deserve, they should not open this course in summer classes, those who do nothing look for how to pass and if they graduate, that gives the UACJ a bad image in the industry, sometimes it becomes difficult to get a good job when they have classified the UACJ students as useless and lazy"

Having such comments that contain the same amount of positive and negative words and are subjectively ambiguous; therefore, this comment, along with the comments from group B, could be considered neutral. We did not consider making a neutral class as it was not part of the original teacher evaluation, which only has two types of comments. Creating a new class might allow what we call neutral comments from Figure 2 group B to be correctly classified, but it can also lead to misclassifying positive and negative comments as we might introduce noise to those classes by subtraction of Groups A and B's sample size and possibly removing key instances that help correctly classify all instances in Group A.

CONCLUSION

In this work, it was understood that document classification covers many other areas of knowledge, including natural language processing. These methods are not recent since they have been used for many years but still have a long work to be done, especially in terms of semantics and detecting context.

During this study, opinion mining techniques were applied to a database of student comments emitted during the university's teacher evaluation period. These comments correspond to four years, 20 subjects, and five professors. So, a series of steps were taken that went from collecting comments, applying natural language processing techniques to those comments, we took those comments and built a database of vectors to represent them, and we utilized those vectors for training and testing two classifiers.

The use of opinion mining is the science of analyzing text to understand users' feelings about a teacher. By exploring student sentiments about a teacher, a strategy can be made to uncover weaknesses and strengths areas in the way a teacher carries out their class. Even though we can find all positive comments about a teacher, we cannot guarantee those comments will contain relevant information to suggest an improvement to be made by the teacher and will require further human analysis to find improvement ideas.

The results showed that, among the classifiers Bagging and 1-NN, the most accurate was Bagging with which a classification accuracy of 80.13 could be achieved. Also, it was observed that errors were produced by a series of comments that were labeled as positive or negative, but are characterized as comments that could be considered neutral; therefore we could try adding a third class for neutral comments, barring we end up with a class disbalance. We can also continue working on adding more real comments to our dataset of comments and seeing if the global accuracy increases.

Future work will try to integrate the Stanford University CoreNLP library to help with word dependencies and identify entities such as people, places, and organizations. Also, a new comment class label, called neutral, might be added to allow comments shown in their own group to be correctly classified.

REFERENCES

Amazon Web Services. (2018). *Big Data on AWS*. Retrieved from https://aws.amazon.com/big-data/

Aspectiva. (2019). *Aspectiva About Us*. Retrieved from Aspectiva: https://www.aspectiva.com/company/

Brandwatch. (2019). Retrieved from https://www.brandwatch.com/about/

Cortizo, J. C. (2019). *Mineria de Opiniones*. Retrieved from BrainSINS: https://www.brainsins.com/es/blog/mineria-opiniones/3555

Freeling. (2019). *Freeling: FreeLing Home Page*. Retrieved from http://nlp.lsi.upc.edu/freeling/node/1

Google. (2018). *Sentiment Analysis Tutorial*. Retrieved from https://cloud.google.com/natural-language/docs/sentiment-tutorial

Gutiérrez, G., Ponce, J., Ochoa, A., & Álvarez, M. (2018). Analyzing Students Reviews of Teacher Performance Using Support Vector Machines by a Proposed Model. In C. Brito-Loeza & A. Espinosa-Romero (Eds.), *Intelligent Computing Systems. 820* (pp. 113–122). Springer International Publishing AG. doi:10.1007/978-3-319-76261-6_9

Huddy, G. (2017). *What Is Sentiment Analysis? The importance of understanding how your audience feels about your brand*. Retrieved from https://www.crimsonhexagon.com/blog/what-is-sentiment-analysis/

Jadhavar, R., & Komarraju, A. K. (2018). Sentiment Analysis of Netflix and Competitor Tweets to Classify Customer Opinions. *SAS Global Forum*. Retrieved from https://www.sas.com/content/dam/SAS/support/en/sas-global-forum-proceedings/2018/2708-2018.pdf

Jiménez, R., García, V., Florencia-Juárez, R., Rivera, G., & López-Orozco, F. (2018). Minería de opiniones aplicada a la evaluación docente de la Universidad Autónoma de Ciudad Juárez. *Research in Computing Science*, *147*(6), 167–177. doi:10.13053/rcs-147-6-13

Liu, B., & Hu, M. (2004). *Opinion Mining, Sentiment Analysis, and Opinion Spam Detection*. Retrieved from https://www.cs.uic.edu/~liub/FBS/sentiment-analysis.html

Meaning Cloud. (2019). *General questions*. Retrieved from Meaning Cloud: https://www.meaningcloud.com/

Meltwater. (2019). *About Meltwater*. Retrieved from Meltwater: https://www.meltwater.com/about/

Merriam-Webster. (2019). *Opinion*. Retrieved from Merriam-Webster Dictionary: https://www.merriam-webster.com/dictionary/opinion

Microsoft. (2019). *Natural Language Processing*. Retrieved from https://www.microsoft.com/en-us/research/group/natural-language-processing/

Molina-GonzálezD.Martínez-CámaraE.Martín-ValdiviaM.Perea-OrtegaJ. (2013). *iSOL*. Retrieved from http://timm.ujaen.es/recursos/isol/

Narayanan, V., Arora, I., & Bhatia, A. (2016). *Fast and accurate sentiment classification using an enhanced Naive Bayes model*. Retrieved from http://sentiment.vivekn.com/about/

National Institute of Statistics and Geography. (2017). *State of mind of the tweeters in the United Mexican States*. Retrieved from http://internet.contenidos.inegi.org.mx/contenidos/Productos

Opitz, D. (1999). *Bagging Classifiers*. Retrieved from Popular Ensemble Methods: An Empirical Study: https://www.cs.cmu.edu/afs/cs/project/jair/pub/volume11/opitz99a-html/node3.html

Revuze. (2018). *Revuze Products*. Retrieved from http://revuze.it/product/

See, A. (2016). *Nearest Neighbors*. Retrieved from Stanford Computer Science: https://cs.stanford.edu/people/abisee/nn.pdf

Smeureanu, I., & Bucur, C. (2012). Applying Supervised Opinion Mining Techniques on Online User Reviews. *Informações Econômicas*, *16*(2), 81–91.

Universidad Autonoma de Ciudad Juarez. (2019). *Universidad Autonoma de Ciudad Juarez*. Retrieved from https://www.uacj.mx/sa/ed/Paginas/default.aspx

WEKA. (2020). *What is Weka*. Retrieved from University of Auckland School of Computer Science: https://www.cs.auckland.ac.nz/courses/compsci367s1c/tutorials/IntroductionToWeka.pdf

Chapter 21
An Opinion Mining Approach for Drug Reviews in Spanish

Karina Castro-Pérez
iD https://orcid.org/0000-0002-1709-0087
Tecnológico Nacional de México, Mexico & IT Orizaba, Mexico

José Luis Sánchez-Cervantes
iD https://orcid.org/0000-0001-5194-1263
CONACYT, Mexico & Instituto Tecnológico de Orizaba, Mexico

María del Pilar Salas-Zárate
Tecnológico Nacional de México, Mexico & ITS Teziutlán, Mexico

Maritza Bustos-López
Tecnológico Nacional de México, Mexico & Instituto Tecnológico de Orizaba, Mexico

Lisbeth Rodríguez-Mazahua
Tecnológico Nacional de México, Mexico & Instituto Tecnológico de Orizaba, Mexico

ABSTRACT

In recent years, the application of opinion mining has increased as a boom and growth of social media and blogs on the web, and these sources generate a large volume of unstructured data; therefore, a manual review is not feasible. For this reason, it has become necessary to apply web scraping and opinion mining techniques, two primary processes that help to obtain and summarize the data. Opinion mining, among its various areas of application, stands out for its essential contribution in the context of healthcare, especially for pharmacovigilance, because it allows finding adverse drug events omitted by the pharmaceutical companies. This chapter proposes a hybrid approach that uses semantics and machine learning for an opinion mining-analysis system by applying natural-language-processing techniques for the detection of drug polarity for chronic-degenerative diseases, available in blogs and specialized websites in the Spanish language.

DOI: 10.4018/978-1-7998-4730-4.ch021

Copyright © 2021, IGI Global. Copying or distributing in print or electronic forms without written permission of IGI Global is prohibited.

INTRODUCTION

Opinion mining is an area of great importance for the coarse application that has, focuses on analyzing opinions, sentiments, evaluations, assessments, attitudes, and emotions of people towards entities such as products, services, organizations, individuals, problems, and events (Liu, 2012; Jiménez et al., 2018). This technique, emerged thanks to the accelerated growth of resources available on the web, a representative work of the application, in its beginnings, of opinion mining is the study of Das and Chen (2004) in which they found that, in the case of Amazon Inc., there were cumulatively 70,000 messages by the end of 1998 on Yahoo's message board, and this had grown to about 750,000 messages by early 2004. The authors found that many of the messages from Amazon's board offered favorable, pessimistic, confusing, and even spamming opinions, so in their study, they demonstrated the possibility of capturing sentiment by applying statistical language and natural language processing techniques. Thus, sentiment analysis, also known as opinion mining, began to take on relevance. Also, the availability of potential resources for analysis continued to grow exponentially, now through online review sites, shopping sites, and blogs, which increased the challenge of understanding people's opinions, those opinions important to the decision-making process. Pang and Lee (2008) analyzed surveys of American adults, where they found that consumers reported being willing to pay 20% to 99% more for a 5-star item than a 4-star item in an online store, clearly identifying the importance of knowing other people's opinions and feelings about a product.

It is noteworthy that opinion mining is not only applied for analysis in the consumption of goods and services; it has also been applied in the field of politics; generally, it recognized by the full range of applications it has at present. On the other hand, to implement opinion mining, it is necessary to use lexical resources that help to carry out sentiment classification. A widely known resource is SENTIWORDNET 3.0 (Baccianella et al., 2014) created for research purposes, which provides automatic annotation of all WORDNET synsets according to their degrees of positivity, negativity, and neutrality. The process presented by the authors consists of two steps,

1) weak-supervision, semi-supervised learning step;
2) a random-walk step, used to support sentiment classification in opinion mining.

Thus, the industry surrounding sentiment has grown due to the proliferation of analytics for commercial applications, as well as the exponential increase, in recent years, of social networks and video blogs accessed by millions of users, which generate large amounts of unstructured data. Given this fact, manual revision of data is not very feasible, as a consequence of the number of data continuously generated; therefore, it highlights the use and implementation of opinion mining in current systems (Liu, 2012).

Notwithstanding, opinion mining in the area of health care has increased because of the benefits provided for decision-making, one of the analyses that can be performed using this technique is pharmacovigilance, defined as the science and activities related to the detection, assessment, understanding, and prevention of adverse effects or any other drug-related problem (*World Health Organization*, 2015).

In this context, according to the World Health Organization in 2016, diabetes mellitus, hypertension, cardiovascular diseases, cancer, among other diseases, classified as chronic-degenerative, are positioned among the top ten causes of death in Mexico and the world (World Health Organization, 2020). This means that health systems and experts need to analyze important aspects such as eating habits, exercise, and treatments. Therefore, the application of opinion mining is useful because it allows the analysis of patient and health professionals' comments published on the web to identify symptoms and medicines related to the condition. Hence, the main contribution of this work is an approach for an opinion analysis system for drugs in Spanish by applying Web Scraping techniques and Natural Language Processing (NLP) for detection of drugs for chronic-degenerative diseases published in blogs, specialized websites and video blogs in the Spanish language, using a hybrid approach, with the use of supervised machine learning and a Snomed-based medical domain ontology.

The application of Web Scraping techniques and opinion mining is important in our approach because it allows summarizing the information and obtaining accurate knowledge, providing a useful result for health experts. Our system aims, firstly, to provide specialists with the information that helps to speed up the process of identifying and selecting the medicines they prescribe, and also to know the adverse effects that other patients have with the medicines prescribed for their condition, to identify the adverse effects of their patients more quickly, allowing them to spend more time on the physical examination and thus avoid additional complications to the disease, leading to a higher quality of care for patients. The application of Web Scraping and opinion mining techniques are important in our approach because it allows information to be summarized and accurate knowledge to be obtained, providing a useful outcome for health experts. Secondly, to provide patients with information to find out what others think about the medicines they use, and with expert validation, patients can identify comments that do not represent a danger to their health and those that encourage self-medication. The present document is structured as follows: in the background section, a set of recent works related to our proposal is presented, as well as a comparison of the proposals of each revised work. The focus section describes the main proposal and the final architecture and describes the modules that make up the architecture. The Web Scraping section is a fundamental part of our approach, so the use of it is presented. It continues with the Ontology section, which shows and describes the medical domain ontology used in this work. The section on opinion mining describes the tasks performed and shows a brief example. Finally, we present a case study to complement our proposal, showing the proposed approach applied in a functional system. Finally, the conclusions and future work presented.

BACKGROUND

Lee et al. (2017) developed an analysis that describes the difficulty of finding adverse effects in clinical trials conducted by pharmaceutical organizations and the lack of monitoring required in the market to identify side effects of drugs not previously discovered. For this reason, the authors examined a semi-supervised approach because it is a potential resource for detecting ADE in real-time in Twitter publications. In this context, they built models based on Convolutional Neural Network (CNN) using a semi-supervised architecture for the classification of ADE in tweets, making selective use of a variety of untagged data. Experiments conducted from random tweets with:

1) Medical names;
2) Health conditions;
3) Sentences from scientific articles in the medical literature and Wikipedia and,
4) Simulated health-related sentences created from lexicons, and combinations of these data types;

The experiments demonstrate that the ADE classification exceeds the supervised classification models, a +9.9% F1 measurement, and the state-of-the-art supervised models with an accuracy of +14.58%.

An analysis of opinion mining for drug review in which patients express their experiences and opinions about treatments or medications was focused by Cavalcanti and Prudêncio (2017). Besides, they identified that pharmacovigilance benefits drug manufacturers because particular adverse reactions to a drug quickly tracked from publications in social networks or public forums. Therefore, the authors proposed the adoption of a linguistic method and the inclusion of a supervised learning algorithm for the classification of opinion pairs (an aspect term and an opinion term) into one of the four types of aspects: Condition, Adverse Drug Reactions (ADR), Dosage or Effectiveness. Finally, the experiments involved three diseases, Attention Deficit Hyperactivity Disorder (ADHD), AIDS, and anxiety. The results revealed an improvement in performance to extract relevant aspects compared to the reference methods, where the highest F-Measure values appear for all data sets.

A simple and effective method for extracting ADE from Twitter was proposed by (Peng et al., 2016). The authors used a five-step pipeline:

1) Capturing tweets;
2) Data preprocessing;
3) Drug-related classification;
4) Tweet sentiment analysis and,
5) ADE extraction.

The analysis realized by the authors identified that pharmaceutical companies often do not find in the time the secondary effects caused by the drugs, due to the limited size of the clinical trials, which favors withdrawing drugs from the market, resulting in a significant financial loss for pharmaceutical companies. For this reason, it argues the great importance of monitoring and predicting ADEs. However, social media websites, such as Twitter, Facebook, and Google Circle, provides consumers with a way to share experiences with drugs that they do not report to health care providers or the Food and Drug Administration (FDA). The tests performed provided positive information, because the proposed method successfully extracted 1,239 ADEs via the Twitter social network, including 22% new ADE, for five drugs in four months, which is five times more compared to the results of the reference method.

Pharmacovigilance is an area of great importance because it is related to the detection, evaluation, understanding, and prevention of ADE or any other drug-related problem; also, it evaluates the safety of each medication to enhance the safety profile of the marketed drug. In this context, a system called CSIRO Adverse Drug Event Miner (CADEminer) was presented by Karimi et al. (2015). CADEminer which extracts comments from consumers in drug forums, using search and NLP techniques to extract mentions of side effects and other relevant concepts such as drug names and diseases, to compensate for the shortcomings of passive surveillance, that relies on individual reports of potential adverse drug events from different sources, such as health professionals and manufacturers. On the other hand, using a machine learning-based approach that implements conditional random fields for concept extraction, as well as the rules of association mining method that relies on the support and trust of a potential rule. Similarly, the work incorporated an information retrieval approach to filter out the known information extracted from a drug and thus emphasize the potentially unknown side effects, through the use of ontologies that helped map out the concepts, such as SNOMED CT, AMT, and MedDRA. Finally,

CADEminer is useful for regulatory agencies, pharmaceutical companies, and anyone else interested in exploring information about ADE.

A framework for Semantic Extraction and Sentiment Assessment of Risk Factors (SESARF), which combines and maps relevant concepts, finds adjectives and adverbs that reflect the level of severity was proposed by Sabra et al. (2018). It also incorporates a method for semantic enrichment of Venous Thromboembolism (VTE) risk factors to analyze the clinical narratives of Electronic Health Records (EHR) and predict a VTE diagnosis using the SVM (Support Vector Machine) classifier. Studies show that the death rate associated with Pulmonary Embolism (PE) and the rate of VTE is unacceptably high but is consistent with being listed as the third most common cardiovascular disorder; however preventive efforts begin with lifestyle measures to reduce the risk of VTE. On the other hand, the authors evaluated the framework using an NLP approach to assess accuracy and completeness with the use of Semantic Web technologies and machine learning to identify risk factors that are essential to diagnosis and to distinguish levels of severity using Unified Medical Language System (UMLS) of MetaMap and LOD (Linked Open Data). Besides, three analyses performed on the data:

1) General;
2) Gender-based;
3) Age-based, these analyses showed that the age groups did not contribute to any specific observations.

The work presented demonstrates a strong association between the emergence of VTE and the combination of the following three risk factors: diabetes, obesity, and smoking. Finally, it demonstrates that the prediction is feasible and with accuracy without presenting symptoms of 54.5% and completeness of 85.7%.

An analysis describing facets and potentials of sentiment analysis in the context of medicine and health was developed by Denecke and Deng (2015). The authors also developed an extraction method to quantify parts of speech, determine the frequency of occurrence, and calculate term matches with sentiment lexicons from a dataset obtained from clinical narratives and medical social networks from six different sources. In the analysis conducted by the authors, they found that physicians describe their personal views and observations, what may be a judgment or an evaluation, an affective state that ends up influencing clinical decision making. For this reason, the analysis of medical records is crucial for obtaining a complete vision of the patient's health status to provide automated support for decision making and, with the help of opinion mining, determine the impact of written documents. In conclusion, in work found that clinical analyses written by nurses are more subjective than those of radiology reports, but even more objective than social media data; also, the work identified that the lexicons used have different coverage, but many more sentiment terms exist in the SentiWordNet tool.

A neuronal approach as a hierarchical representation of tweets was proposed by Wu et al. (2019). The initiative of the authors arises because detecting the drug name and detecting adverse reactions mentioned in tweets is very difficult, since tweets are usually very noisy and informal, and there are huge spelling errors and user-created abbreviations for these mentions. Besides, these mentions are usually context-dependent. The approach is to learn from the representations of people's words and then to learn the representations of tweets. The authors used an additive attention mechanism to select informative words in tweets to build more informative representations of tweets. Also, they identified that Twitter's social network provides tweets that can be easily collected in real-time and the number of tweets is enormous. Therefore, detecting tweets that mention drug names and ADEs helps uncover serious or unknown consequences of drug use that are not covered by medical records. To address word representation, the authors made three sub-modules, the first being a character embedding layer, the second a CNN, and the third a word embedding that incorporates rich semantic information from tweets. The representation of the tweet consists of three modules:

1)   A Bi-directional Long Short Term Memory (Bi-LSTM);
2)   Multi-head self-care network, and
3)   An additive care network.

Experimental results in two reference data sets validate the effectively the proposed approach in detecting tweets mentioning drug names and ADRs.

A study on the impact of implementing opinion mining for Online Support Groups (OSGs) on breast cancer related to the drug tamoxifen, as it is of great importance in understanding the emotions and opinions of users, was conducted by Cabling et al. (2018). The analysis included the application for 498 users, with the most active users accounting for 80% and the rest being less active users. The aim of comparing the two groups is to explore the possible reasons why users decided to post a comment and how their feeling plays a role in finding or providing online support compared to those who did not post a comment. The authors identified that the higher the stage of cancer a user had, the less likely that she would have posted, and if she were to post, the post would have focused on her side effects and the anxiety/sadness that tailgates those side effects. The lower the stage of cancer a user had, the more likely that she would have posted, additionally remained active on the forum and encouraged more social support. Finally, analysis of user feelings provides an understanding of how specific interactions that promote support lead to the development of intra-group and out-of-group dynamics, as well as hyper-personal communication within OSGs. However, through the Big Data, sentiment analysis and research exploring the development of group cohesion within Computer Mediated Communication (CMC) revealed a richer narrative of what occurs in OSGs and reflected for facilitators to be aware of the dynamics of sentiment.

A method based on opinion mining to detect the emotional reaction of patients with an asthmatic disease on risk factors, physical activities, among other concepts, were proposed by Luna-Aveiga et al. (2018). The disease of asthma is a serious health problem that affects all age groups. Asthma-related hospitalizations and deaths have decreased in some countries; however, the authors argue that the number of patients with symptoms has increased in recent years. On the other hand, the growth of information on health and disease management in forums, blogs, microblogs, and social networks, specifically Twitter, was identified as a powerful tool to disseminate experiences and encourage conversations on disease self-management. The authors present a method that takes advantage of Semantic Web technologies, specifically ontologies, to represent the asthma domain, as well as the SentiWordNet tool to determine the polarity of asthma concepts contained in Twitter messages. In addition, they designed an ontology called OASM that describes concepts such as risk factors, drugs, symptoms, and other concepts related to asthma care. The proposed method is composed of four elements:

1)   Normalization module;
2)   Semantic annotation module;
3)   The ontology for asthma self-management;
4)   A polarity identification of feeling module.

Evaluations of approach through the collected tweets gave encouraging results with 82.95% accuracy, 82.27% recall 82.36% F measure. Furthermore, it proved to help raise asthma awareness, thereby motivating additional help-seeking behavior.

Currently, Web 2.0 allows individuals to share valuable data and opinions about products or services purchased online. Shared data and unstructured opinions include emotions, feelings, characteristics, numbers, dates, and facts, so it represents the focus of most researchers trying to collect and capture popular sentiments. In this context, a review of NLP techniques for opinion extraction was conducted by Solangi et al. (2019). Their study identified the preprocessing stages required to structure texts, which are: feature extraction, segmentation, tokenization, grammatical tagging, and analysis in opinion extraction, where tokenization is an essential strategy for most NLP-related tasks. However, for Chinese and Japanese dialects, among others, words are composed differently. The authors added in the review the tools that address Chinese word segmentation and tokenization, such as

1) Fudan NLP in JAVA language
2) The Language Technology Platform (LTP) in the open-source C++ system for lexical analysis
3) Niu Parser in C++ language which is a semantic analyzer and syntactic toolkit in Chinese
4) Gensim Python
5) Stanford CoreNLP

Further, it is exposed that opinion mining aims to extract sentimental orientation from writings, through opinion mining, divided into three levels: document level, sentence level, and fine grain level. Finally, for the preprocessing of texts the techniques designed to consist of checks to track or classify the data, however, detection is not always adequate, so the authors suggest to make modifications to the techniques of the NLP or other relevant techniques since the user or beneficiary provides and receives adequate information data.

Alayba et al. (2017) presented an Arabic language dataset that discusses health services topics collected from the social network Twitter. While there has been a lot of research on sentiment analysis in English, the number of researches and datasets in the Arabic language is limited, so the authors detail the four main steps taken to obtain the Arabic dataset for opinion mining purposes, such as:

1) Data collection;
2) Data filtering;
3) Preprocessing of Arabic text by removing unwanted data, deleting some words and unrelated text, and standardizing the text; and
4) Applying machine learning to the dataset collected.

For the experiments, implemented algorithms such as Machine Learning (Naïve Bayes, SVM, and Logistic Regression) alongside Deep and Convolutional Neural Networks. The results show accuracy results were roughly between 85% and 91%, and the best classifiers were SVM using Linear Support Vector Classification and Stochastic Gradient Descent. The SVM classifier accuracy is similar to the first annotator's accuracy.

An analysis that discusses in detail opinion mining, how the value of polarity relates to something positive or negative, and how to address blog reviews written in the Roman language was conducted by Rathi et al. (2016). In this context, the analysis of the authors shows the existence of different tasks applied in opinion mining, such as opinion mining, sentiment mining and emotional analysis, however, the vital aspect of the action is to collect the information from the comments found in the blogs or other sites and then discover the behavior of that information. There are many opinions on the web, and some opinions contain context-dependent words which present a polarity classification, therefore, to catalog the feelings correctly, it is necessary to eliminate the ambiguity with the help of the tool called word polarity disambiguation, which refers to the computer identification of the polarity of a word in a given context. Likewise identified that existing works focus on the English language and not the Roman language, for this reason, the authors present the possibility of creating a database to provide the opinion value of Roman words for comparison with the English language, which leads to increasing the performance rating of websites related to any product that includes Roman language reviews.

A method for sentiment analysis that effectively detects aspects of diabetes in tweets, using ontologies to semantically describe relationships between concepts in the specific domain, in the English language was developed by Salas-Zárate et al. (2017). The feeling that determines the aspects gets calculated considering the words around the aspect obtained through the methods of "N-gram". On the other hand, the analysis identified that diabetes is a chronic condition that occurs when the body does not produce or use enough insulin; for that reason, it is one of the most significant health emergencies worldwide. It estimated that more than half a million children under age 14 are living with diabetes, 415 million adults have diabetes, and an additional 318 million adults are estimated to have impaired glucose tolerance, putting them at high risk for developing the disease in the future. Thus, social networks such as Twitter are an excellent resource for patients as they connect with people who have similar conditions and similar experiences. However, opinion seeking is a difficult task, because a simple search on Twitter using "Diabetes" returns thousands of tweets; therefore, opinion summary systems using sentiment analysis or opinion mining technologies are needed. Hence, the proposed approach to the classification of feelings consists of three main components: the preprocessing module for cleaning and correcting text, the semantic annotation module for detecting aspects, and the sentiment rating module that calculates the polarity of each aspect found in the SentiWordNet lexicon. Finally, the set of experiments gave results that showed that the "N-gram around" method obtained the best results with an accuracy of 81.93%, a recovery of 81.13%, and an F measure of 81.24%. Also, the experiments showed that the lexicon of general feeling is not sufficient to capture the meanings in health texts. Furthermore, the proposed method requires an ontology that models the domain to identify aspects of the diabetes domain.

On the other hand, a comparison that reviews the different techniques of opinion mining and emphasizes the need to address the specific challenges of the NLP in collecting and examining words related to opinion mining was developed by Khan et al., (2016). They also stressed the need for standard data sets and assessment methodologies to improve models that capture context and proximity. Also, they identified that machine learning techniques are beneficial for opinion mining; such techniques apply in two ways; 1) Supervised, which require tagged data, and 2) Semi-supervised, which require manual adjustment by domain experts. On the other hand, opinion mining is a diversified field of research that includes machine learning, NLP, language identification, and text summarization, in which review texts come from different languages, and for each one, the evaluative and subjective phrases get recognized. Therefore, it has close relevance to NLP, so opinion mining faces problems such as co-reference resolution, negation management, and disambiguation of word meaning.

Usually, the patients who use drugs often search the Internet for stories of patients like themselves, which they usually find among their friends and family. However, exist a few studies investigating the impact of social networks on patients show that, for some health problems, online community support results in a positive effect. A method of opinion extraction that focuses on predicting the level of satisfaction among other patients who have already experienced the effect of a drug, addressing Neural Networks to understand how the general population perceives the safety, reactions, and efficiency of a drug was proposed by Gopalakrishnan and Ramaswamy (2017). In the particular domain of pharmacies, positive, negative, and neutral reactions are equally important in deciding on drug use. On the other hand, from the results, it was demonstrated that the Neural Network-based approach to opinion creation surpasses the SVM method in terms of accuracy, recovery, and F-score. Also, it found that prediction models based on the Radial Base Function of the Neuronal Network (RBFN) performed well in all aspects, better than the Probabilistic Neuronal Network (PNN), because of the deficiencies that tend to get trapped in unwanted local minima to reach the global minimum of a very complex search space. Thus, the approach shows a better result in terms of various performance measures compared to other drug reviews of existing works collected, as well as being a viable and optimal solution for increasing ranking performance.

A study on existing lexicons was conducted by Ding et al. (2008). One of them, WordNet, in which the authors found that it has important deficiencies since it does not have an effective mechanism to deal with the words of opinion depending on the context, therefore, it probably is not possible to know the semantic orientation of the words. The authors propose a lexically based, holistic approach, which focuses on the opinions expressed by customers about products in reviews. The approach, instead of examining only the actual sentence, exploits the information by a method of aggregating the orientations of such words by considering the distance between each word of the opinion and the characteristic of the product. The proposed approach was implemented in the system called Opinion Observer; the experiments carried out by the authors focused on eight products, two digital cameras, a DVD player, an MP3 player, two cell phones, a router, and antivirus software; however, they found that deciding if a sentence offers an opinion for some confusing cases is difficult, so, for the difficult sentences, they made a consensus between the primary human note-takers (the first author of the paper and two students) and the secondary note-taker (the second author of the paper). On the other hand, the proposed method turned out to be useful and effective because it considers explicit and implicit opinions; this makes the proposed technique more complete.

Similarly, Pak and Paroubek (2010) presented an analysis describing how Microblogging has become a popular communication tool, which is why websites are a rich source of data because of the rapidly growing number of users who post messages about their lives, about various topics, examine current issues or about the products and services they use. This data can be used effectively to perform opinion mining analysis and with the results obtained help in decision making in marketing or social studies, to mention a few. The authors presented a method that extracts opinions from the social network Twitter, the content of which varies from personal thoughts to public statements. With the data obtained, they made a corpus that determines the positive, negative, and neutral feeling. Using the corpus, they constructed a sentiment classifier and performed experiments on a set of microblogging posts to prove that the technique presented is effective and performs better than the methods analyzed. In the study, the authors used the classifier is based on the multinomial Naïve Bayes classifier that uses N-gram and POS-tags as features.

As shown in Table 1, the analyzed works use one of several approaches, such as the application of algorithms for the classification of sentiment and the use of semantic methods, which involve the hybrid approach presented in this chapter. Unlike (Lee et al., 2017; Wu et al., 2019; Cabling et al., 2018; Luna-Aveiga et al., 2018; Salas-Zárate et al., 2017; Gopalakrishnan & Ramaswamy, 2017) our approach

Table 1. Related work comparative

Author	Domain	Approach	Polarity detection	NLP	Data Source
Lee et al. (2017)	Medical	Semi-supervised Convolutional Neural Network.	✓	X	Twitter
Cavalcanti (2017)	Medical	Linguistic method based on Dependency Paths in the Syntactic Tree.	✓	✓	Drugs.com
Peng et al. (2016)	Medical	Supervised Machine learning.	✓	✓	Twitter
Karimi et al. (2015)	Medical	Semantic and Machine learning.	X	✓	Drugs.com RxList.com MedlinePlus.
Sabra et al. (2018)	Medical	Semantic and Supervised Machine Learning.	✓	✓	Biomedical Documents and Clinical Narratives from PubMed.
Denecke and Deng (2015)	Medical	Review of Sentiment Lexicons and Machine Learning.	✓	X	Clinical Narratives, Social Networks, and Specialized Websites.
Wu et al. (2019)	Medical	Neural approach using Multi-Head Self-Attention.	X	X	Twitter
Cabling et al. (2018)	Medical	------	✓	X	Specialized Website
Luna-Aveiga et al. (2018)	Medical	Semantic	✓	X	Twitter
Solangi et al. (2019)	------	Opinion mining for various levels are analyzed and reviewed	✓	✓	-----
Alayba et al. (2017)	Medical	Machine Learning	✓	X	Twitter
Rathi et al. (2016)	------	Semantic	✓	X	Blogs
Salas-Zárate et al. (2017)	Medical	Semantic	✓	✓	Twitter
Khan et al. (2016)	------	Reviews sentiment analysis techniques and NLP.	✓	✓	------
Gopalakrishnan and Ramaswamy (2017)	Medical	Neural Network.	✓	✓	askapatient.com
Ding et al. (2008)	e-commerce	Opinion mining, NLP	✓	✓	amazon.com.
Pak and Paroubek (2010)	General	Opinion mining, NLP and Machine Learning	✓	✓	Twitter

gets comments from a variety of sources such as forums, blogs, and video blogs, where there is relevant information to analyze in detail, so the scarcity of comments does not prove to be an obstacle as it is with getting tweets about medication from the social network Twitter.

Our approach makes a review on chronic-degenerative diseases, so a vast amount of comments is obtained through Web Scraping and contain information about sentiments regarding a drug, the dosage of the drug, the price, and even the adverse effects that it has on patients. On the other hand, in Cavalcanti and Prudencio (2017), Peng et al. (2016), Karimi et al. (2015) and Sabra et al. (2018) they propose hybrid approaches using semantic web technologies and sentiment classification algorithms such as supervised machine learning and Syntactic dependency paths as well as linguistic methods through external tools. As mentioned by the authors Pak and Paroubek (2010), the use of a corpus for classification in opinion mining is important because it allows training the algorithm to obtain better results; nevertheless, it makes use of a corpus with general opinions of any topic to classify opinions on Twitter, in contrast, as mentioned by Ding et al. (2008) a corpus must contain opinions according to the context to be analyzed to obtain a better classification, therefore, in our approach, we propose a semantic method through the integration of a corpus with opinions focused on the health area, in the Spanish language, which was labeled with the use of supervised machine learning the resulting corpus was reviewed by a specialist in the health area. Besides, it should be noted that our approach, we propose a semantic method through the integration of a corpus that we label automatically, the use of supervised machine learning. Furthermore, our approach gets first-hand comments from patients, unlike the clinical narratives discussed by Denecke and Deng (2015), which are subject to interpretation by third parties by doctors and nurses, so they are less accurate.

Finally, as mentioned in Solangi et al. (2019), Alayba et al. (2017), Rathi et al. (2016) and Khan et al. (2016), very scarce work has been done in the implementation of opinion mining and NLP for data sets in languages other than English, such as Chinese and Japanese, among others, because it requires a great effort for implementation and analysis, while our approach addresses opinion mining and NLP for comments in the Spanish language, recognized as the second most spoken language in the world.

APPROACH

Our work uses a hybrid approach, through supervised machine learning because we use tags in the opinions with the desired solution to generate a model for training the algorithm that allows the classification of new opinions and the linguistic semantics can refer either to the study of meaning in o far as this is expressed in language or to the study of meaning within linguistics, through the use of a medical domain ontology and the bag of words (Lyons, 1995).

With the following approach implemented in a system, it will allow to summarize the information obtained from forums, blogs and video blog, to obtain accurate knowledge and provide health specialists and patients with information about the opinions that speak about medicines, as well as the adverse effects. The following describes the parts that make up our approach, through an architecture.

Architecture

Figure 1 depicts the Spanish opinion analysis system for chronic-degenerative disease drugs, based on Web Scraping techniques that it is integrated by six main modules and a corpus:

1) Data collection module;
2) Pre-processing module;
3) Domain identification module;
4) Processing module;
5) Opinions repository;

6) Expert Validation Module,
7) Data presentation.

Data Collection Module

Figure 1. Architecture of system

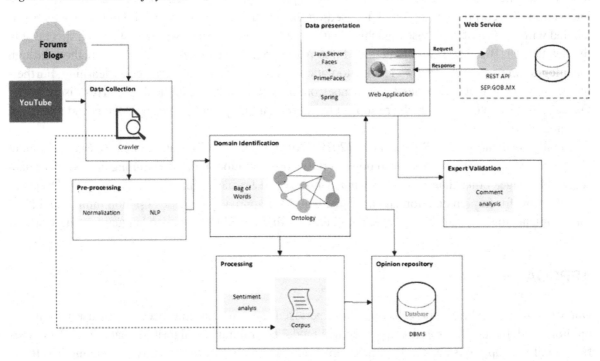

In this module, we collected the comments that mention drugs and symptoms of chronic-degenerative diseases published in forums, blogs, specialized websites, and video blogs through a crawler with a series of URLs that it accesses to obtain the comments. This work considers only three types of chronic degenerative diseases: diabetes, hypertension, and hepatitis.

Pre-Processing Module

The preprocessing of data is an important step for the normalization of the text; therefore, we chose to use three phases for the treatment of our data.

1. **Delete unusual characters:** Unique characters that do not provide information removed from the comments.
2. **Delete duplicate comments:** This step is essential because duplicate comments affect the final result of the analysis; therefore, it is crucial to ensure that no duplicate comments exist.

3. **Delete comments that only have URLs**: Comments that only link to other sites do not contribute information to be considered as comments so that no analysis can be applied, for this reason, eliminated.

The application of these tasks on the comments ensures a better analysis of sentiments, but the incorrect use of language is a common scenario, created by the use of abbreviations or spelling errors on behalf of the users, requiring a more considerable effort to carry out opinion mining activities, for that reason, this module also makes use of a spell checker.

Domain Identification Module

The identification of the words is highly relevant within architecture because it allows verifying that the comments collected include the mention of a drug prescribed for diabetes, hypertension, and hepatitis diseases. The result of this module provides a more specific data set with valuable information for the analysis in the next module. In this context, a bag of words was created through a medical domain ontology, based on Snomed an organization nonprofit, which determines standards for a codified language that represents groups of clinical terms, this enables healthcare information to be exchanged globally for the benefit of patients and other stakeholders (NCBO BioPortal, 2019).

The Bag of Words (BoW) is a key element for the approach because it allows corroborating that the comments are of the medical domain, BoW is known to be a model widely used in the domain of NLP because it based on the idea that the frequency of appearance of a word in a text serves as a measure of the meaning that the word (Thanaki, 2017).

Processing Module

Once the data collected are clean of unusual characters and corroborated that they belong to the medical domain, is adopts the supervised machine learning approach which makes use of a semi-automatic labeled corpus, necessary to train the algorithm that performs the sentiment analysis, this permits it to recognize new opinions in the Spanish language and to classify them correctly according to polarity.

Opinions Repository Module

The opinions and polarity of the drugs resulting from the analysis are stored in a database to keep the data available for consultation, as well as the expert's data when validating the comments. The repository adds speed to our system for information retrieval.

Expert Validation Module

The module examines the validation obtained by the expert to verify whether it is a valid comment or a comment that should be attended to by a specialist. This module makes it clear that our system does not encourage self-medication.

Figure 2 depicts in a conceptual way what the expert's validation consists of, i.e., the specialist in the domain can validate the comments shown obtained from Web Scraping. To validate the comments, the expert registers his name, professional license, and comment; these data as validated through a public domain web service provided by the SEP (Secretary of Public Education).

Data Presentation Module

Figure 2. Representation of the expert validation module process

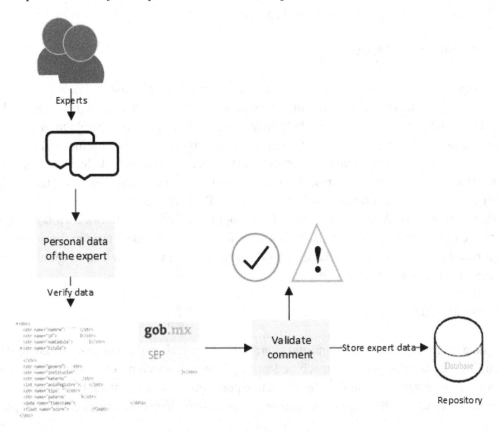

This module refers to the presentation of a web interface that supports the interaction of users with the application to know the comments and the polarity of the drugs prescribed for chronic-degenerative diseases, specifically diabetes mellitus, hepatitis, and hypertension.

3.2 Web Scraping

For carrying out our approach, we use two web scraping techniques, the first, Web Crawling or also known as spider or robots, is characterized by being computer programs to collect web pages automatically has a behavior similar to the navigation performed by users and, first, specifies the set of URLs to which you have to access and then enter each page and download the content, making a repetitive process to complete all the assigned URLs. The second technique used is web information extraction, which allows the identification of structured and semi-structured information that interests users. The main objective is to obtain the text from web pages, images, audios, videos, and other media (Liu,2011; Cho & Garcia-Molina, 2002; Mo et al. 2012).

Figure 3 shows the process that this module performs for the collection of comments. The first step is the sending of a computer agent with a list of URLs from which it extracts the comments, giving, as a result, a set of comments necessary for the analysis of opinions.

Figure 3. Web scraping workflow

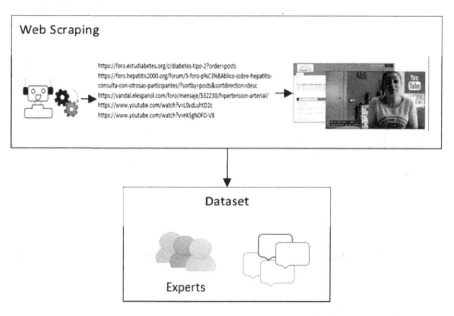

3.3 Ontology

An ontology is an explicit description of a domain that specifies a concept by describing its properties, attributes, and constraints in an organized way to limit complexity (Porras et al., 2018). It is necessary to extract information to populate and improve the ontology, allowing identification and classification using a system with a deeper level of analysis (Abirami et al., 2018).

In this context, the ontology used is important for the creation of the bag of words used for the identification of the medical domain. The ontology is designed in Spanish, and it is populated with drug names, to ensure that the collected comments contain a mention of some drug. The bag of words is widely used in the NLP domain because based on the idea that the frequency of appearance of each word in a text serves as a measure of the word's meaning (Thanaki, 2017). **Figure 4** shows the composition of the ontology used in this work, which contains four main instances called:

1) Medicamento - Drug
2) Efectos adversos - Adverse effects
3) Farmaco - Pharmaco
4) Farmacéutica - Pharmaceutical.

Figure 4. The general structure of the ontology

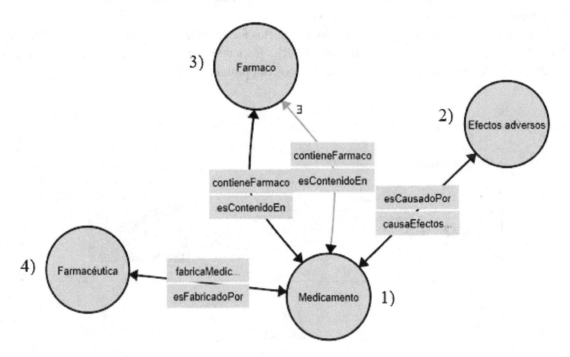

The ontology used in this work contains many instances of the class Drug, as shown in **Figure 5**, some of them are:

1) Antihipertensivos - Anti-hypertensives;
2) Bloqueadores - Blockers;
3) Antidiabéticos - Anti-diabetics;
4) Inhibidores - Inhibitors;
5) Antivirales - Antivirals;
6) Diuréticos - Diuretics;
7) Beta bloqueadores - Beta-blockers;
8) Inmunosupresores - Immunosuppressant.

The Ontology populated with names of drugs used for the treatment of chronic degenerative diseases in the Spanish language, which is listed below:

1) Valsartán - Valsartan
2) Metildopa - Methyldopa
3) Nateglinida - Nateglinide
4) Repaglinida - Repaglinide
5) Telmisartán - Telmisartan
6) Prazosina - Prazosin
7) Metformina - Metformin

Figure 5. Attributes of the Drug instance

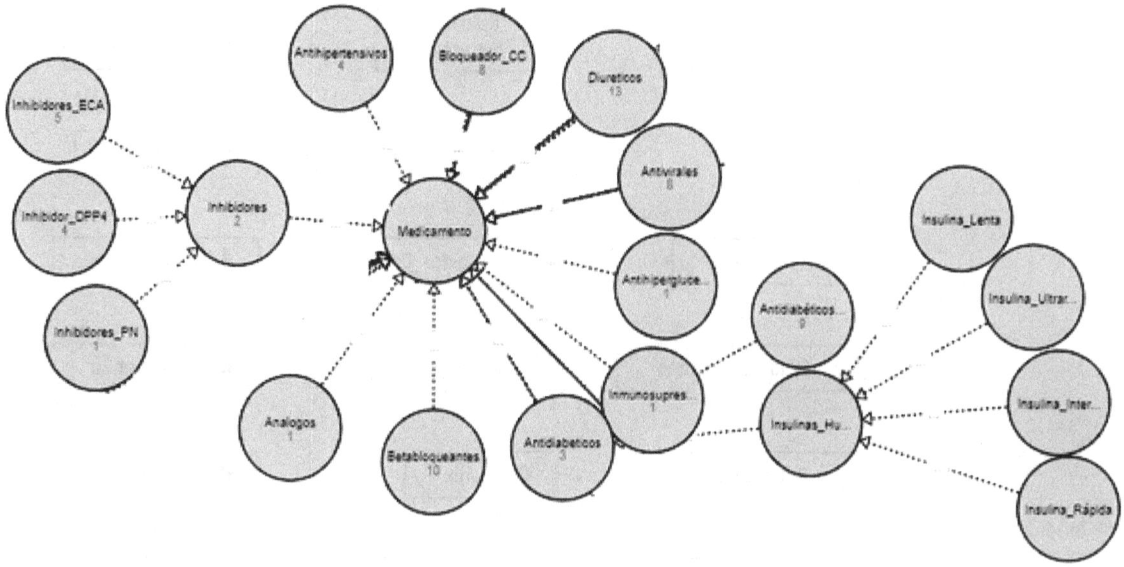

8) Sitagliptina - Sitagliptin
9) Gliclazide - Gliclazide
10) Vildagliptina - Vildagliptin
11) Saxagliptina - Saxagliptin
12) Tolbutamida - Tolbutamide
13) Linagliptina - Linagliptin
14) Glimepirida - Glimepiride
15) Clorpropamida - Chlorpropamide
16) Glibenclamida – Glibenclamide
    to name a few.

Opinion Mining

Opinion mining, or also called sentiment analysis, is the process of extracting subjective information from user-generated content, also, using NLP and computational intelligence. This field of study analyzes user's opinions, feelings, assessments, emotions, and attitudes towards entities such as products, services, organizations, individuals, events, topics, and their attributes. Some names and tasks are differentiated as sentiment analysis, opinion extraction, sentiment extraction, subjectivity analysis, damages analysis, emotion analysis, mining analysis, among others. Sentiment analysis is a highly restricted NLP problem because the system does not need to understand the semantics of each sentence or document fully but only needs to understand some aspects of it, i.e., positive or negative sentiments and their target entities or topics. In this context, the application of opinion mining involved three key tasks, which are described below:

Figure 6. Populated Ontology

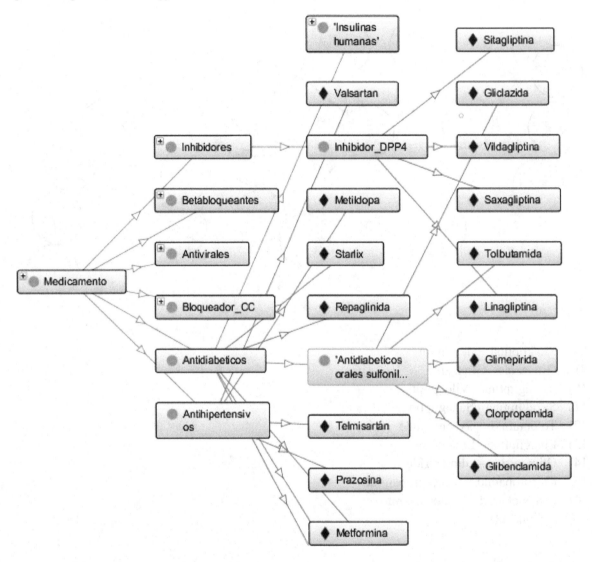

Task 1 (entity extraction and categorization): Extract all entity expressions and categorize or group entity.

Task 2 (opinion holder extraction and categorization): Extract opinion holders for opinions from text or structured data and categorize them.

Task 3 (aspect sentiment classification): Determine whether an opinion on an aspect is positive, negative or neutral, or assign a numeric sentiment rating to the aspect (Kishore & Kumar, 2016; Liu, 2012).

It is important to note that neutral comments are discarded in our work because they do not contain relevant information, i.e., it means that the user does not have an opinion on the subject matter.

Figure 7 shows two of the comments collected, which read as follows:

1) Curing me of hepatitis c is over!! halfway through my treatment, I've been on 360 of these magic antivirals! Only 312 remains. Although the adverse effects keep me away and I have difficulty concentrating and counting as it is to kill the hepatitis c bug. I have been feeling the amazing sensation of being cured ever since the treatment began. And now that I have conquered this half of the alienation, I will be able to resist it and finish it. I take a day 1 sofosbuvir 1 daclatasvir and 6 ribavirins divided into two takes of 3, and I continue to receive it! With a lot of will to live!!! Thank you for joining me.

2) Hi, everybody, my news is not good. I can't continue the treatment. It turns out that when I was admitted I didn't know how serious I was, the doctor explained to me that my situation was very critical and that this is the first case he sees like mine. The leukocytes went down in about 2 hours to 2.44 and the platelets to 3o.ooo (when I arrived I had 45,100); the most serious thing of all is that it was the neutrophils he says that below 700 there is a danger for the person and I suddenly went down to 270, so I was really in danger...they injected me with neupogen and this increased my leukocytes with 2 doses, but my platelets are a big problem for me. The only solution they see is the medicine I said tombopag and when they arrange to try it again.

In these two comments was identified the entities (drugs), the words that distinguish a comment positive a negative one, and with it, the classification according to polarity.

Corpus

The computerized corpus has proven to be a practical resource for the solution of problems arising from computational linguistics, its importance and relevance because these are considered pieces of the language selected and ordered according to a linguistics criterion to use as a language sample that facilitates an analysis of large amounts of data.

The linguistic criteria are

1) external, when they refer to author data, the means of transmission used, the social level of the participants, the communicative function of the texts, among others; or
2) criteria internal when they refer to linguistic patterns present in the texts (Sinclair, 1996).

For our approach, we use computerized corpus with external linguistic criteria, since we require linguistic patterns of a specific language, the Spanish language.

The polarity detection is limited in the Spanish language due to the lack of data sets; therefore, a corpus was made that includes 280 comments obtained from forums and video blogs on diseases such as type 2 diabetes mellitus, hepatitis, and hypertension. The corpus was tagged semi-automatically with the use of a dictionary that was manually built, from the analysis of comments found in specialized forums, blogs, and video blogs to identify the words that tell a positive comment from a negative one. To ensure the effectiveness of the labeling, two health specialists reviewed the corpus; they manually reviewed each comment to corroborate that both the positive and negative comments presented the corresponding tag. An example of comments included within-corpus is depicted in **Figure 8**, highlighting the words that are of interest to this work, the comments read as follows:

Figure 7. Comment analysis

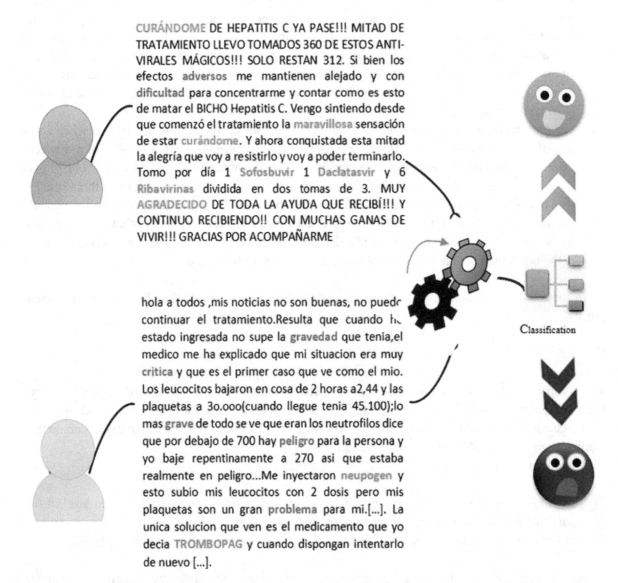

CURÁNDOME DE HEPATITIS C YA PASE!!! MITAD DE TRATAMIENTO LLEVO TOMADOS 360 DE ESTOS ANTIVIRALES MÁGICOS!!! SOLO RESTAN 312. Si bien los efectos adversos me mantienen alejado y con dificultad para concentrarme y contar como es esto de matar el BICHO Hepatitis C. Vengo sintiendo desde que comenzó el tratamiento la maravillosa sensación de estar curándome. Y ahora conquistada esta mitad la alegría que voy a resistirlo y voy a poder terminarlo. Tomo por día 1 Sofosbuvir 1 Daclatasvir y 6 Ribavirinas dividida en dos tomas de 3. MUY AGRADECIDO DE TODA LA AYUDA QUE RECIBÍ!!! Y CONTINUO RECIBIENDO!! CON MUCHAS GANAS DE VIVIR!!! GRACIAS POR ACOMPAÑARME

Classification

hola a todos ,mis noticias no son buenas, no puedo continuar el tratamiento.Resulta que cuando he estado ingresada no supe la gravedad que tenia,el medico me ha explicado que mi situacion era muy critica y que es el primer caso que ve como el mio. Los leucocitos bajaron en cosa de 2 horas a2,44 y las plaquetas a 3o.ooo(cuando llegue tenia 45.100);lo mas grave de todo se ve que eran los neutrofilos dice que por debajo de 700 hay peligro para la persona y yo baje repentinamente a 270 asi que estaba realmente en peligro...Me inyectaron neupogen y esto subio mis leucocitos con 2 dosis pero mis plaquetas son un gran problema para mi.[...]. La unica solucion que ven es el medicamento que yo decia TROMBOPAG y cuando dispongan intentarlo de nuevo [...].

1) POSITIVE: Hello, everyone, and I'm starting off with a lot of courage and strength. I'm 37 years old and I found out about hepatitis C B1 when I had the special tests because I got pregnant, this is already 3.5 years ago. Well, my little girl was born phenomenal (3,500 kg) without infection, at first if it had, but it was negative, I was told that was normal because it was very difficult to transmit to the fetus, especially in hepatitis c [...]; treatment has been phenomenal, no symptoms (no hair loss, no fever, no weight loss, nothing at all) the doctor told me it was a weirdo, I broke statistics, according to them. I took 5 pills a day and the injection (150mcg) once a week. Some days I was more tired, but I took eferalgan 1g or espidifen and it went away, in the end, you get used to that kind of tiredness [...] Now I can't start the treatment again, not because I want to, I'm very excited

but because I have to rest. I'm very happy because my hepatitis is supposed to be the worst, well it's the most difficult to cure, and so far it's effective [...];

2)   NEGATIVE: Greetings again, on December 15 I have the exam again to see my state, the truth because of the work I have felt stressed and every time I pass it hurts my right side, the liver, I doubt because I felt a little itch in my body again, could I again present the picture that I present at the beginning of jaundice, and fall back to those levels? How difficult this is.

Figure 8. Sample of the tagged corpus

Tagged comments

1)   POSITIVO   Hola a todos y empiezo también con mucho ánimo y fuerza. Tengo 37 años y me enteré de que la hepatitis C B1 cuando me hicieron los análisis especiales porque me quedé embarazada, de esto ya hace 3.5 años. Bueno, mi nenita nació fenomenal (3.500 kg) sin contagio, al principio si lo tenía, pero se negativizo, me dijeron que era lo normal porque era muy difícil el contagio al feto, sobretodo en la hepatitis c [...]; el tratamiento me ha ido fenomenal, ningún síntoma (ni caída de pelo, ni fiebre, ni perdida de peso, nada de nada) el médico me decía que era un bicho raro, he roto estadísticas, según ellos. Tomaba 5 pastillas diarias y la inyección (150mcg) una vez a la semana. Algunos días estaba más cansada, pero tomaba eferalgan 1g o espidifen y se me pasaba, al final te acostumbras a esa especie de cansancio [...] Ahora no puedo empezar otra vez el tratamiento, no por ganas porque estoy muy animada sino porque tengo que descansar. Estoy muy contenta porque se supone que mi hepatitis es la peor, bueno es la más difícil de curar y hasta ahora me va funcionando [...]

2)   NEGATIVO Saludos de nuevo, en diciembre 15 me toca de nuevo el examen para ver mi estado, la verdad a raíz del trabajo me he sentido estresado y cada vez que me pasa me duele la parte derecha, el hígado, tengo una duda porque volvi a sentí un poco la comezón en mi cuerpo, podría de nuevo volver a presentar el cuadro que presente al inicio de ictericia, y caer de nuevo a esos niveles? Que difícil esto.

Case Study

Polarity analysis in comments published in blogs, forums and video blogs in the Spanish language about prescription drugs for chronic - degenerative diseases

The medical community has detected a lack of records of patients describing symptoms ADE's, even those not previously identified by the pharmaceutical companies. This fact represents misinformation by the health specialists, as well as the patients themselves, for not letting the doctor know in consultations about symptoms added to their condition.

On the other hand, chronic-degenerative diseases are among the top 10 causes of death in Mexico, which represents a large number of people who go to their doctor for routine consultations and examinations. However, because of this requirement, health specialists have little time to check on patients in consultations, and consequently, physical examinations are not very useful as they require additional time. Given this fact, health specialists omit new symptoms independent of the initial condition, that derive from drugs or some other disease, ending up by not being adequately treated as a consequence of the absence of detection.

Similarly, it was found that it is important for patients to investigate, read, ask questions and give feedback to others who publish on the web about the drugs prescribed to their condition, the reasons are:

1) Know the adverse effects,
2) Learn about other treatments,
3) Ask about the adverse effects they suffer and
4) Comment on the percentage of progress they have with treatment, to mention but a few.

Therefore, we present the system called, SentiScrap, it allows the user to analyze the forums that are on the Web and video blogs about medicines for chronic diseases, specifically for diseases: Diabetes, Hypertension, and Hepatitis. The system is capable of performing the necessary extraction of these sources to obtain the opinions of patients and health specialists, resulting in a very valuable set of information to be analyzed through domain recognition and polarity detection.

For this case study, suppose a health specialist needs to know the opinions of patients receiving treatment for diabetes:

- How will the specialist be able to identify the medications that patients talk about for the treatment of diabetes?
- How will the specialist know the comments of patients who publish in forums and video blogs in the Spanish language?
- How will the specialist know the positive and negative impact on the comments?
- How will the specialist be able to validate under his/her medical experience the comments that patients share?
- How will it impact the specialist to know the comments made by patients?
- How will the health specialist be able to contribute to increasing the knowledge of our system?

The healthcare specialist has access to the information provided by patients through a web system, which we call SentiScrap. The system offers a menu of five options which are listed in order of appearance:

1) Diabetes
2) Hepatitis
3) Hypertension
4) Add Sources
5) Statistics

Figure 9 depicts the content of the main screen.

Figure 9. SentiScrap home page

Suppose a healthcare specialist wants to know about medications that are prescribed for the treatment of diabetes, specifically those medications that patients discuss on forums, blogs, and video blogs. In this case, the specialist selects the disease diabetes a menu; consequently, the system generates a query to a repository to show the medicines, as well as the positive and negative polarity (through an iconography that represents the polarity) of medicines, as shown in **Figure 10**.

The specialist may need to read the collected feedback to identify, evaluate, and prevent adverse effects caused by the medications their patients take to reduce health and quality of life risks. In other words, the specialist obtains concise feedback for a specific disease, which helps to improve the care of their patients. To consult the feedback repository, click on the "+" button.

The SentiScrap system displays all comments with their corresponding classification, positive or negative, as shown in **Figure 11**. Also, each comment contains a button called Expert Validations to find out the data of the specialists who have validated the comment. Likewise, at the bottom, the Validate button to validate the comment according to the health professional's experience.

When the health specialist reads the collected comments, he may find malicious comments encouraging self-medication, which can have serious consequences such as adverse effects, which are harmful to health. Due to the situation previously explained, expert validation considered in this work.

Figure 10. Diabetes options of the SentiScrap system

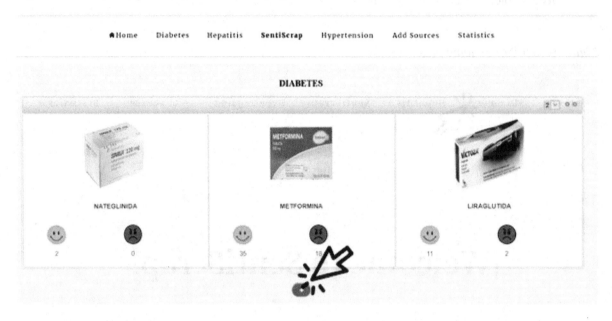

Figure 11. Comments collected about diabetes

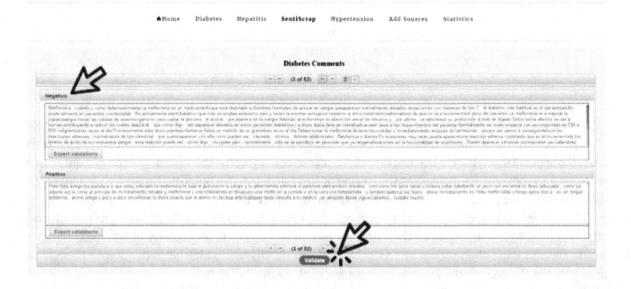

The specialist has the possibility of validating the comments shown in SentiScrap, under his medical experience, as shown in **Figure 12**.

When selecting a comment and clicking on the Validate button, the system displays the following interface, which corresponds to a personal data form with the following information: professional license, name, and surname, to verify his identity. To perform the expert validation, surgeon Rogelio Romero Vázquez made use of our system and validated some of the comments collected.

Figure 12. Expert validation form, professional card fields, name and surname

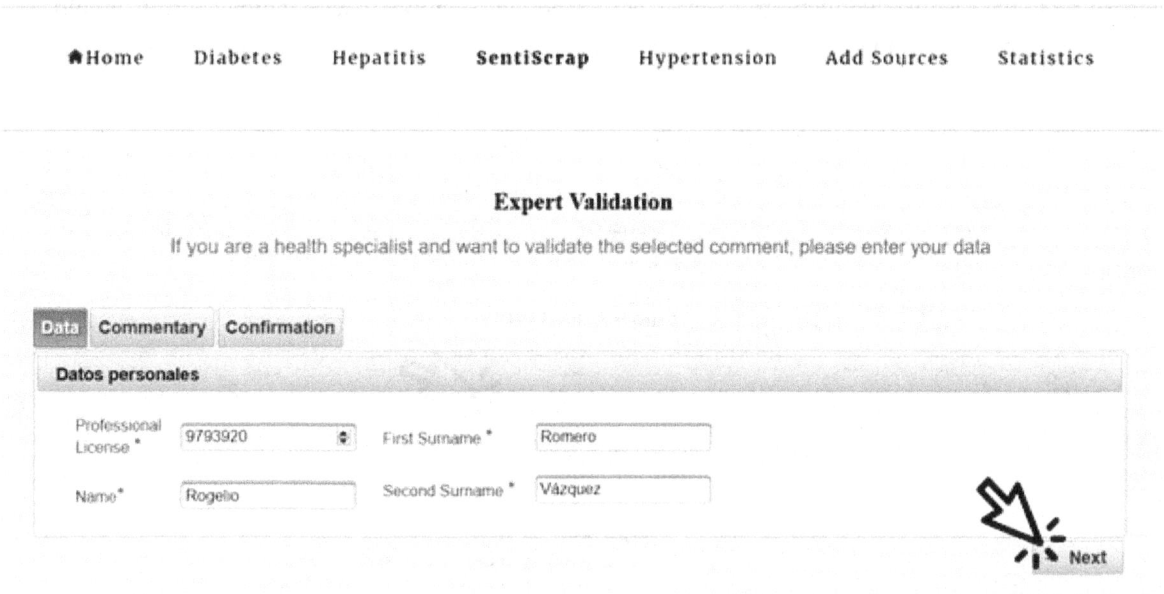

The system driver receives the full name of the expert and calls the Restful service to find out if it exists; if so, then it temporarily saves the response of the invocation and then iterates until it finds the record that matches the professional card and the name of the expert. Once the response of the method is true, it allows to continue with the form, shown in **Figure 13**, in which you select an option regarding your opinion on the comment you want to validate; also, the expert must enter an email. Finally, the system shows the data entered so that the specialist can review them one last time and confirm the sending of the data to the repository.

Figure 13. Continuation of the expert validation form

When the experts validate the collected comments, the system adds a representation iconography according to the received validations, to show at a glance the comments with which caution should take and the comments that do not represent health risks for the reader, as shown in **Figure 14**.

Figure 14. Data of the expert who validated the commentary

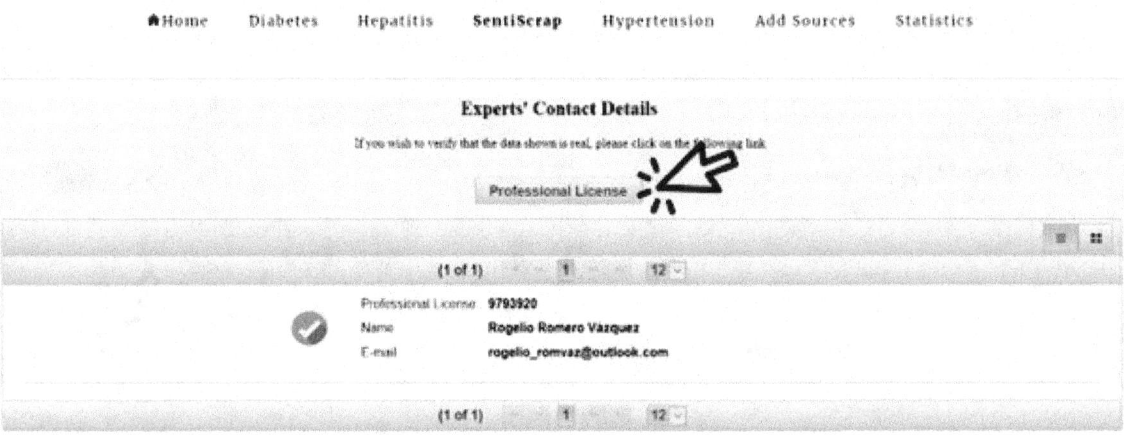

Also, in the case of non-expert users who need to verify the veracity of the data, we added a button called professional license to go to the official website of the Secretary of Public Education (SEP), in which the user can enter the full name of the health specialist in the record search form, as shown in **Figure 15**.

Besides, SentiScrap provides a form for the healthcare specialist and even patients to add feeds from a file or a single URL for forums and video blogs.

Once the file or URL is sent to the system, the driver takes the URLs and sends them to the class with the method that extracts the information, and then the resulting set goes through the preprocessing method to remove the unusual characters and emoticons. The preprocessed data is then temporarily stored in a file.

Then, the data goes through the class in charge of classifying the data, in this class, the instance is made to the Bang of Word class to invoke the method that makes the bag of words with the names of the medicines contained in the corpus, the system continues the process with the domain identification method that is in charge of checking that the data resulting from the extraction is of medical domain since it has a mention of at least one medicine, if it is so, then it goes to the resulting set that is analyzed later with the classification method, and that is when it is determined if the comment has a positive or negative polarity. When the process is successful, a message is displayed, as shown in **Figure 16**.

Finally, when the specialist needs to compare the polarity between the comments of the diseases, he can visualize able it in Statistics, as shown in **Figure 17**. In this view, we present charts on the number of the polarity of the comments, positive and negative ones, besides, the polarity corresponding to each disease, and the chart with the mentions of the drugs referred to for each disease. Also, a pie chart is shown with the ten most mentioned drugs.

Figure 15. Official website of professional licenses
Source: SEP,2020

Our work aims to show that the information contained in the forums and blogs is of high relevance to health specialists. Because by accessing the comments of patients, the doctor can know the experience and symptoms of each patient, for consulting first-hand data, which are useful for decision making and for improving medical care in clinics and hospitals.

FUTURE RESEARCH DIRECTIONS

As future work, we have contemplated including more aspects to be analyzed, such as the analysis of adverse effects, identifying the treatment time taken by patients who comment on chronic-degenerative diseases, and identifying prices. Likewise, we would like to incorporate this information into the web

Figure 16. Interface to add new URLs for forums, specialized websites and video blogs

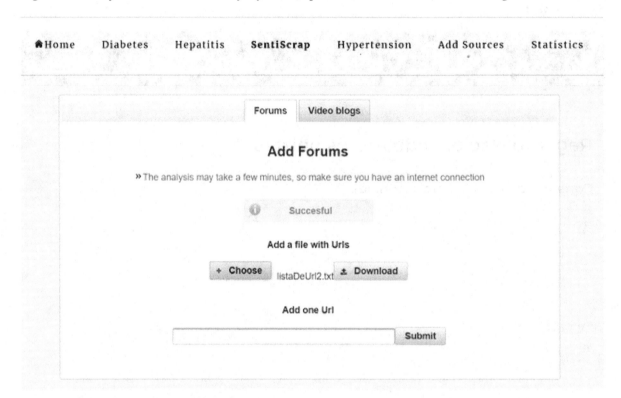

application through different types of graphs that allow better visualization and understanding of the information, to provide a concise and summarized analysis for health specialists, which helps to improve the decision making in the hospitals and clinics.

CONCLUSION

The analysis of the related work shows a lack of application of studies that implement opinion mining in the Spanish language. Besides, a large part of the current studies focusses on extracting data from social networks, which, while it is true that it is a rich source of resources, we should not forget that there are other resources with multiple data, such as those addressed in this work. Our approach obtains comments from blogs, specialized websites and video blogs, which focus on the health care context, specifically for hypertension, diabetes and hepatitis diseases, to classify them according to polarity, positive or negative, making use of a tagged corpus to train the model and a medical domain ontology to contrast and obtain those comments that talk about the drugs prescribed for the mentioned diseases. The proposed approach was implemented in a system called SentiScrap, which aims to help health specialists with pharmaco-vigilance since it allows to know first-hand the comments of patients, which mention the symptoms of the conditions, and ADE that are unknown to the patients themselves, and that attribute these symptoms to other conditions and with expert validation help to prevent and reduce the risks to the patient's health. On the other hand, there are a lot of people who self-medicate which is a mistake that affects the qual-

Figure 17. Chart board with statistics of the analyzed information

ity of life and compromises health; therefore, SentiScrap, provides information to patients or about the medications prescribed for their condition, and also the comments collected identify what other people think, including expert validations that they can contact if they have any questions.

In conclusion, with the presented case study, a result of the interaction that the health specialist had with SentiScrap, we verified the functionality of each module presented in the architecture; also, the correct functioning of the proposed hybrid approach, with which we classified the opinions of the blogs and video blogs entered through a URL to be analyzed, also, we obtained the polarity of the drugs for chronic-degenerative diseases, specifically for diabetes, hypertension, and hepatitis.

ACKNOWLEDGMENT

This research work was sponsored by the National Council for Science and Technology (CONACYT) and the Secretary of Public Education (SEP). The authors are grateful to Tecnológico Nacional de México (TNM) for supporting this work.

REFERENCES

Abirami, A. M., Askarunisa, A., Shiva, R. A., & Revathy, R. (2018). Ontology Based Feature Extraction from Text Documents. In M. Thangavel & P. Karthikeyan (Eds.), Applications of Security, Mobile, Analytic, and Cloud (SMAC) Technologies for Effective Information Processing and Management (p. 175). IGI Global. doi:10.4018/978-1-5225-4044-1.ch009

Alayba, A. M., Palade, V., England, M., & Iqbal, R. (2017). Arabic Language Sentiment Analysis on Health Services. In *2017 1st International Workshop on Arabic Script Analysis and Recognition (ASAR)* (pp.114–118). 10.1109/ASAR.2017.8067771

Baccianella, S., Esuli, A., & Sebastiani, F. (2014). *SentiWordNet 3 . 0 : An Enhanced Lexical Resource for Sentiment Analysis and Opinion Mining*. Academic Press.

Cabling, M. L., Turner, J. W., Hurtado-de-Mendoza, A., Zhang, Y., Jiang, X., Drago, F., & Sheppard, V. B. (2018). Sentiment Analysis of an Online Breast Cancer Support Group: Communicating about Tamoxifen. *Health Communication, 33*(9), 1158–1165. doi:10.1080/10410236.2017.1339370 PMID:28678549

Cavalcanti, D. & Prudêncio. (2017). Aspect-Based opinion mining in drug reviews. In *Progress in Artificial Intelligence* (Vol 10423, pp.815–827). doi:10.1007/978-3-319-65340-2

Cho, J., & Garcia-Molina, H. (2002). Parallel Crawlers. In *Proceedings of the 11th International Conference on World Wide Web* (pp.124–135). doi:10.1145/511446.511464

Das, S. R., & Chen, M. Y. (2004). Yahoo! for Amazon : Sentiment Extraction from Small Talk on the Web. *Management Science, 53*(9), 1–16.

Denecke, K., & Deng, Y. (2015). Sentiment analysis in medical settings: New opportunities and challenges. *Artificial Intelligence in Medicine, 64*(1), 17–27. doi:10.1016/j.artmed.2015.03.006 PMID:25982909

Ding, X., Liu, B., & Yu, P. (2008). A holistic lexicon-based approach to opinion mining. *WSDM'08 - Proceedings of the 2008 International Conference on Web Search and Data Mining*. 10.1145/1341531.1341561

Gopalakrishnan, V., & Ramaswamy, C. (2017). Patient opinion mining to analyze drugs satisfaction using supervised learning. *Journal of Applied Research and Technology, 15*(4), 311–319. doi:10.1016/j.jart.2017.02.005

Jiménez, R., García, V., Florencia-Juárez, R., Rivera, G., & López-Orozco, F. (2018). Minería de opiniones aplicada a la evaluación docente de la Universidad Autónoma de Ciudad Juárez. *Research in Computing Science, 147*(6), 167–177. doi:10.13053/rcs-147-6-13

Karimi, S., Metke-Jimenez, A., & Nguyen, A. (2015). CADEminer: A System for Mining Consumer Reports on Adverse Drug Side Effects. *Proceedings of the Eighth Workshop on Exploiting Semantic Annotations in Information Retrieval - ESAIR '15*, 47–50. 10.1145/2810133.2810143

Khan, M. T., Durrani, M., Ali, A., Inayat, I., Khalid, S., & Khan, K. H. (2016). Sentiment analysis and the complex natural language. *Complex Adaptive Systems Modeling, 4*(1), 2. Advance online publication. doi:10.118640294-016-0016-9

Kishore, B., & Kumar, A. (2016). Evaluation of Faculty Performance in Education System Using Classification Technique in Opinion Mining Based on GPU. In H. S. Behera & D. P. Mohapatra (Eds.), *Computational Intelligence in Data Mining—Volume 2* (pp. 109–111). Springer India. doi:10.1007/978-81-322-2731-1

Lee, K., Qadir, A., Hasan, S. A., Datla, V., Prakash, A., Liu, J., & Farri, O. (2017). Adverse drug event detection in tweets with semi-supervised convolutional neural networks. In *Proceedings of the 26th International World Wide Web Conference, WWW 2017*, (pp.705–714). 10.1145/3038912.3052671

Liu, B. (2011). *Web Data Mining: Exploring Hyperlinks, Contents, and Usage Data*. Springer Berlin Heidelberg. doi:10.1007/978-3-642-19460-3

Liu, B. (2012). Sentiment Analysis: A Fascinating Problem. In Sentiment Analysis and Opinion Mining (p. 7). Morgan & Claypool Publishers.

Luna-Aveiga, H., Medina-Moreira, J., Lagos-Ortiz, K., Apolinario, O., Paredes-Valverde, M. A., Salas-Zárate, M., & Valencia-García, R. (2018). Sentiment Polarity Detection in Social Networks: An Approach for Asthma Disease Management. In N.-T. Le, T. van Do, N. T. Nguyen, & H. A. Le Thi (Eds.), *Advanced Computational Methods for Knowledge Engineering* (pp. 141–152). Springer International Publishing. doi:10.1007/978-3-319-61911-8_13

Lyons, J. (1995). Metalinguistic preliminaries. In *Linguistic Semantics: An Introduction* (p. 2). Cambridge University. Retrieved from https://books.google.com.mx/ books?id=Na2g1ltaKuAC&printsec= frontco ver&dq=semantics+linguistic&hl= es-419&sa=X&ved=0ahUKEwiohJ_27NLmAhUQ2qwKHWyZD ocQ6AEIKTAA#v=onepage &q=semanticslinguistic&f=false

Mo, Q., & Chen, Y. (2012). Ontology-Based Web Information Extraction. In M. Zhao & J. Sha (Eds.), *Communications and Information Processing* (Vol. 288, pp. 118–119). Springer Berlin Heidelberg. doi:10.1007/978-3-642-31965-5_14

NCBO BioPortal. (2019). *BioPortal*. Retreived from https://bioportal.bioontology.org/ontologies

Pak, A., & Paroubek, P. (2010). Twitter as a Corpus for Sentiment Analysis and Opinion Mining. In LREc (pp.1320–1326). Academic Press.

Pang, B., & Lee, L. (2008). Opinion mining and sentiment analysis. *Foundations and Trends in Information Retrieval, 2*(1), 94.

Peng, Y., Moh, M., & Moh, T. S. (2016). Efficient adverse drug event extraction using Twitter sentiment analysis. In *Proceedings of the 2016 IEEE/ACM International Conference on Advances in Social Networks Analysis and Mining, ASONAM 2016*, (pp. 1011–1018). 10.1109/ASONAM.2016.7752365

Porras, J., Florencia-Juárez, R., Rivera, G., & García, V. (2018). Interfaz de lenguaje natural para consultar cubos multidimensionales utilizando procesamiento analítico en línea. *Research in Computing Science, 147*(6), 153–165. doi:10.13053/rcs-147-6-12

Rathi, S., Shekhar, S., & Sharma, D. K. (2016). Opinion Mining Classification Based on Extension of Opinion Mining Phrases. In S. C. Satapathy, A. Joshi, N. Modi, & N. Pathak (Eds.), *Proceedings of international conference on ICT for sustainable development* (pp. 717–724). Springer Singapore. 10.1007/978-981-10-0129-1_74

Sabra, S., Mahmood Malik, K., & Alobaidi, M. (2018). Prediction of venous thromboembolism using semantic and sentiment analyses of clinical narratives. *Computers in Biology and Medicine*, *94*, 1–10. doi:10.1016/j.compbiomed.2017.12.026 PMID:29353160

Salas-Zárate, M. D. P., Medina-Moreira, J., Lagos-Ortiz, K., Luna-Aveiga, H., Rodríguez-García, M. Á., & Valencia-García, R. (2017). Sentiment Analysis on Tweets about Diabetes: An Aspect-Level Approach. *Computational and Mathematical Methods in Medicine*, *2017*, 1–9. Advance online publication. doi:10.1155/2017/5140631 PMID:28316638

Sinclair, J. (1996). Preliminary Recommendations on Corpus Typology. *EAGLES (Expert Advisory Group on Language Engineering Standards) EAG-TCWG- CTYP/P*, 4–27. Retrieved from http://www.ilc.cnr.it/EAGLES96/corpustyp/node4.html

Solangi, Y. A., Solangi, Z. A., Aarain, S., Abro, A., Mallah, G. A., & Shah, A. (2019). Review on Natural Language Processing (NLP) and Its Toolkits for Opinion Mining and Sentiment Analysis. In *2018 IEEE 5th International Conference on Engineering Technologies and Applied Sciences, ICETAS 2018* (pp. 1–4). doi:10.1109/ICETAS.2018.8629198

Thanaki, J. (2017). Feature Engineering and NLP Algorithms. In Python Natural Language Processing (p. 102). Academic Press.

World Health Organization. (2015). *Pharmacovigilance*. Retrieved from https://www.who.int/medicines/areas/quality_safety/safety_efficacy/pharmvigi/en/

World Health Organization. (2020). *The top 10 causes of death*. Retrieved from www.who.int/newsroom/fact-sheets/detail/the-top-10-causes-of-death

Wu, C., Liu, J., Wu, F., Huang, Y., Yuan, Z., & Xie, X. (2019). MSA: Jointly detecting drug name and adverse drug reaction mentioning tweets with multi-head self-attention.I n *WSDM 2019 - Proceedings of the 12th ACM International Conference on Web Search and Data Mining*, (pp.33–41). doi:10.1145/3289600.3290980

APPENDIX

Listing 1 corresponds to the dataPreprocessing() method receives each collected opinion to remove unusual characters, then with the help of the API used for rating the opinions, we perform the tokenization to remove the commonly used emoticons.

Listing 1. The method dataPreprocessing()

```
1. private String dataPreprocessing(String cadena) {
2.     String cadCaracteres, aux1, aux2, aux3, aux4, frase = "";
3.     cadCaracteres = cadena.replaceAll("[||'|/|<|>|+||_|@|•|♥|]", "");
4.     Properties props = new Properties();
5.     props.setProperty("annotators", "tokenize,ssplit");
6.     StanfordCoreNLP pipeline = new StanfordCoreNLP(props);
7.     CoreDocument exampleDocument = new CoreDocument(cadCaracteres);
8.     pipeline.annotate(exampleDocument);
9.     //access tokens from a CoreDocument, a token is represented by a CoreLabel
10.    List<CoreLabel> firstSentenceTokens = exampleDocument.tokens();
11.        for (CoreLabel token: firstSentenceTokens) {
12.            if (!token.word().contains("http")) {
13.                if (!token.word().contains(":-RRB-")) {
14.                    if (!token.word().contains(":D")) {
15.                        if (!token.word().contains(":-LRB-")) {
15.                            if (!token.word().contains(";D")) {
17.                                frase += token.word() + " ";
18.        } else
19.            frase += "";
20.        }
21.        aux1 = frase.replace("-LRB- ", "(");
22.        aux2 = aux1.replace(" -RRB-", ")");
23.        aux3 = aux2.replace("-LSB- ", "[");
24.        aux4 = aux3.replace(" -RSB-", "]");
25.        return aux4;
26.    }
```

The next code (Listing 2) corresponds to the method for the creation of the bag of words, which obtains from the ontology the list of the Individuals to obtain the names of the drugs, these drugs can be recognized by another name, in those cases, each individual is gone through, and the sameAsLista is obtained; finally, the drugs are added to the bag of words that is used later.

Listing 2. The method for the creation of the bag of words

```
1. public Bag createBoW() {
2.     //load the ontology model
3.     this.model = ModelFactory.createOntologyModel();
4.     this.model.read(new File(this.file).toURI().toString());
5.     ExtendedIterator<Individual> listaInd = this.model.listIndividuals();
6.     Individual ind = null;
7.     ArrayList medicines = new ArrayList();
8.     Bag drugsBag = model.createBag();
9.     String aux="";
10.        //list of Individuals and each individual their own list SameAs
11.        while (listaInd.hasNext()) {
12.            ind = listaInd.next();
13.            medicines.add(ind.getLocalName());
14             ExtendedIterator sameAsLista = ind.listSameAs();
15.           while (sameAsLista.hasNext()) {
16.               Object ind2 = sameAsLista.next();
17.               int numPosFar = ind2.toString().indexOf("#");
18.               aux = ind2.toString().substring(numPosFar + 1);
19.               medicines.add(aux);
20.           }
21.        }
22.
23.        for (int j = 0; j < farmacos.size(); j++) {
24.            drugsBag.add(farmacos.get(j));
25.        }
26.        return drugsBag;
27     }
```

The domainIdentification() method (Listing 3) invokes the BoW class to obtain the bag of words and compare it with each comment to identify the comments that if they talk about any medication, those comments that do not mention medications are discarded. The resulting comments are stored temporarily in a .txt file.

Listing 3. The Method DomainIdentification()

```
1. public void domainIdentification()
2.             throws FileNotFoundException, IOException {
3.    String cadCom;
4.    int intIndex = 0;
5.    //BoW class instance to load the ontology and create the bag of words
6.    BoW l = new BoW(rutOnt);
7.    l.load();
8.    Bag BagOfW = l.crearBoW();
9.    FileReader f = new FileReader(arcOpiScr);
10.    BufferedReader buffer = new BufferedReader(f);
11.    /*compare each comment with the bag of words for those commentsthat
mention  12.    *a BoW drug */
13.    while ((cadCom = buffer.readLine()) != null) {
14.        StringTokenizer st = new StringTokenizer(cadCom);
15.        while (st.hasMoreTokens()) {
16.            cadCom = st.nextToken("\n");
17.            NodeIterator iter2 = BagOfW.iterator();
18.            while (iter2.hasNext()) {
19.                String mdicamto = iter2.next().toString().toLowerCase();
20.                intIndex = cadCom.toLowerCase().indexOf(mdicamto);
21.                if (intIndex != -1) {
22.                    opinion.add(cadCom);
23.                    break;
24.                }
25.            }
26.        }
27.    }
28.    buffer.close();
29.        //saves the opinions in a Opiniones.TEST file
30.        BufferedWriter bw = new BufferedWriter(new FileWriter(rutOpiTest));
31.        bw.write("");
32.        for (int i = 0; i < opinion.size(); i++) {
33.            bw.write("\t" + opinion.get(i).toString());
34.            bw.newLine();
35.        }
36.        bw.write("");
37.        bw.close();
38.    }
```

The opinionSorting method (Listing 4) loads three files, the file to be sorted, the corpus tagged and a property file, necessary to perform the sorting, the Stanford CoreNLP API allows the sorting making use of ObjectBank that takes the comment and compares it with the corpus to determine the polarity, the result of this process are the commentaries with their final tag which are stored in a temporary .txt file

Listing 4. The Method opinionSorting()

```
1. public void opinionSorting() throws IOException {
2.    BufferedWriter bw = new BufferedWriter(new OutputStreamWriter(new
3.            FileOutputStream(rutaOpiClasif), "ISO-8859-1"));
4.    String cadena;
5.    //ColumnDataClassifier to make a context-free (independent)
7.    ColumnDataClassifier cdc = new ColumnDataClassifier(rutArcProp);
8.    //Creation of the classifier from the training data.
10.    Classifier<String, String> cl =
9.            cdc.makeClassifier(cdc.readTrainingExamples(rutArcTrain));
10. // ObjectBanks are taken from the source
11.        for (String line:
12.        ObjectBank.getLineIterator(rutOpiTest, "ISO-8859-1")) {
13.            Datum<String, String> d = cdc.makeDatumFromLine(line);
14.        cadena = cl.classOf(d) + "\t" + line;
15.            bw.write(cadena);
16.            bw.newLine();
17.    }
18.        bw.close();
19. }
```

Chapter 22
Identifying Suggestions in Airline–User Tweets Using Natural Language Processing and Machine Learning

Rafael Jiménez
Universidad Autónoma de Ciudad Juárez, Mexico

Vicente García
https://orcid.org/0000-0003-2820-2918
Universidad Autónoma de Ciudad Juárez, Mexico

Karla Olmos-Sánchez
https://orcid.org/0000-0002-9145-6761
Universidad Autónoma de Ciudad Juárez, Mexico

Alan Ponce
Universidad Autónoma de Ciudad Juárez, Mexico

Jorge Rodas-Osollo
https://orcid.org/0000-0001-6588-8336
Universidad Autónoma de Ciudad Juárez, Mexico

ABSTRACT

Social networks have moved from online sites to interact with your friends to a platform where people, artists, brands, and even presidents interact with crowds of people daily. Airlines are some of the companies that use social networks such as Twitter to communicate with their clients through messages with offers, travel recommendations, videos of collaborations with YouTubers, and surveys. Among the many responses to airline tweets, there are users' suggestions on how to improve their services or processes. These recommendations are essential since the success of many companies is based on offering what

DOI: 10.4018/978-1-7998-4730-4.ch022

Copyright © 2021, IGI Global. Copying or distributing in print or electronic forms without written permission of IGI Global is prohibited.

the client wants or needs. A database of tweets was created using user tweets sent to airline accounts on Twitter between July 30 (2019) and August 8 (2019). Natural language processing techniques were used on the database to preprocess its data. The latest classification results using Naive Bayes show an accuracy of 72.44%.

INTRODUCTION

Nowadays, the influence that social networks have on people's lives has caused marketing companies to change their business model (Saravanakumar & SuganthaLakshmi, 2012), going from advertisements in print media, radio and television to modern digital media, seeking to increase the reach of potential customers to whom transmit their advertising messages.

New digital platforms promote customer interaction and reward them with greater exposure as it becomes viral. Greater exposure to other potential customers by way of followers sharing their content creates value for the brands who use social media and their products (Ahmed, 2017). Social networks have moved from online sites primarily created to interact with our friends to a platform where people, artists, brands, and even presidents interact daily with crowds of people.

Through social networks, companies like DeWalt are making available the ability to co-create new products based on suggestions from their consumers (DeWalt, 2010). It has helped them stay on top of the construction tool manufacturing companies and win several awards with their products (DeWalt, 2019). This kind of innovation is called customer-driven innovation (Penisi & Kim, 2003) and requires an organization focused on delivering products with quality and attributes that consumers can assess positively.

According to a study published by the company Hootsuite (Kemp, 2019), Twitter is the seventh most accessed website in the world. It is a site where 500 million tweets are sent daily (Stricker, 2017). In Mexico, Twitter has 7.22 million users (Kemp, 2019), a figure that is on the rise and has shown a 3.7% increase in the last quarter of 2018.

Airlines are some of the companies that use social networks, such as Twitter, to interact with their customers through tweets, seeking to promote their services, offers, travel recommendations for a specific time of year, videos of collaborations with YouTubers or other companies, and publishing surveys to know the opinion of their customers on a particular topic, such as where in the world they would like to spend a weekend. Twitter users have three options to interact with each other through tweets:

1.   Sharing a tweet to the user's followers through a retweet.
2.   Tagging a tweet as "Like" when users like an airline tweet, and
3.   Responding to a tweet issued by the airline through a comment in which users express their opinion or suggestion about the services provided.

In some comments that users respond to tweets issued by airlines, they express suggestions on how to improve their services or processes. The suggestions are important since the success of many of the companies is based on giving the customer what they want or need (Brun & Hagege, 2013; García, Florencia-Juárez, Sánchez-Solís, Rivera, & Contreras-Masse, 2019) and these needs may change over time.

Currently, Mexican airlines are going through a stage of growth in the international market in which their participation in international flights has increased. This, added to the increase in domestic flights, has created a large number of suggestions that could be used by companies to offer a product focused on the user, seeking to increase the number of satisfied customers, reduce the loss of customers and even make an effective evaluation of the advertising campaigns that are being carried out. Twitter users tend to make suggestions naturally without the need to be asked for one. These suggestions are aimed at various areas and stages centered around the services given and expected from an airline when traveling using such airlines. Thus, having a cognitive system capable of automatically identifying suggestions among all tweets can be of great help to companies. It is worth mentioning that systems of this type are few and only exist for the use of the English language.

This chapter aims to serve this niche of opportunity by developing a prototype based on machine learning and natural language processing to classify tweets issued by airline customers in the Spanish language into suggestions and non-suggestions. The technological challenge of implementing a cognitive system to identify suggestions in the Spanish language lies in formulating a keyword dictionary that, using natural language processing techniques, allows a data mining classification algorithm to identify the suggestions.

The chapter is organized as follows. Section 2 briefly describes work found in the scientific literature related to suggestion mining. Section 3 describes the methodology used in the development of this research. Section 4 shows the configuration of the experiments carried out. Section 5 presents the results obtained in this research work and, finally, Section 6 presents the conclusions and proposes future lines of research.

RELATED WORKS

At this time, few works have been published for opinion mining trying to find suggestions in reviews and social media as opposed to the vast number of opinion mining projects aimed at sentiment analysis. Compared to sentiment analysis —which seeks to classify comments as positive, negative, or neutral— suggestion mining attempts to identify such comments that contain an opinion towards a target. These opinions are of information given by the writer as advice, warnings, and recommendations. This kind of information is important for stakeholders in a product being reviewed and is usually overlooked by sentiment mining because some suggestions might not have a sentiment polarity.

To easily identify the frontier of knowledge regarding the subject of research, these related works describe the extent of research in suggestion mining. Suggestion mining has been applied to open domain reviews by Negi (2016), in social networks by Negi, Asooja, Mehrotra, and Buitelaar (2016), and in consumer reviews by Brun and Hagage (2013).

A suggestion, according to the Royal Spanish Academy (Real Academia Española, 2019), is a hint, inspiration, idea that is given. In general, this definition of suggestion makes it possible to distinguish suggestions from other types of comments. Suggestions implicitly or explicitly convey ideas to brand owners that lead to improvements in their product. An example of an explicit suggestion comment made to an airline is "if you'd answered the phone, everything would be easier" this could suggest that the user has been calling for support and has not received one yet, or it took too long to get an agent on the phone.

The first works related to the detection of customer needs were more focused on the wishes made by the customers (Goldberg, et al., 2009) and in (Ramanand, Bhavsar, & Pedanekar, 2010), where they tried to detect what the customer wanted, in the form of characteristics they wanted from a product or suggestions for the decision to buy a product. These systems were free context and used a dictionary to detect the desires of both products and the new year.

Suggestion mining is a recent area; the first related case dates to 2013. Brun and Hagege (2013), noticed the growing sources of online information such as review sites and personal blogs. They developed an automatic feelings extraction system to understand the opinions and subjectivity of people better. While developing this system, they realized that there was interesting information from customers within the opinions and feelings that were being expressed. The collection of this type of information is not contemplated in a standardized way in sentiment analysis applications. They used it to know the degree of satisfaction of the customers, as well as to devise improvements either to include characteristics or components that the customer wishes or to indicate when a customer regrets the absence of a feature or component.

The system used four main components to detect suggestions, which are also detailed in the patent acquired by Brun and Hagege (2014). These components are:

- **A structured terminology**: This component consists of a vocabulary of products that want to know information, such as printer, copier, scanner, etc.
- **A dictionary of words**: This dictionary of expressions contains the words frequently used in comments that denote suggestions, such as "I would like, suggest, missing, strange".
- **A linguistic analyzer**: This component is the one that contains the morphological features of the words and uses the components of structured terminology and the dictionary of words to detect the suggestion and determine to which product it is applied.
- **A suggestion extractor**: This component is in charge of extracting suggestions from comments using a set of semantic and syntactic patterns, which then tries to match with previously analyzed reviews.

The corpus used in this project was built from 3500 printer reviews found on Epinions.com. 3440 training reviews were used to test the system created, and sixty random reviews were used as test cases. The described results are 77% accurate.

The following suggestion mining work was presented by Negi and Buitelar (2015). They began to identify that in specific reviews they used in their exploration of sentiment mining, they could also detect a "subjective mood" within those reviews. This subjective mood is a desire by the reviewer that is described as the description of an action that has not occurred yet. Just by trying to identify wishes and suggestions, they formed a corpus of phrases obtained from grammar pages and forums.

Negi and Buitelar (2015) also presented a project to detect customer suggestions. This project focused on extracting suggestions from comments made to hotels on TripAdvisor and comments reviewing electrical appliances on the website Yelp. This project was aimed at detecting at what part of the product or department was the suggestion meant, and if the suggestion is implicit or explicit in the comment.

During the development of this system, 8050 hotel reviews, and 3782 comments on electrical appliances were collected. These comments were manually tagged according to their positive, negative, or neutral sentiment. This labeling was done using crowdsourcing using a platform called Crowdflower, which scores a confidence score according to the percentage of labeling given to it. To be able to use a comment, the comment must have a minimum confidence level of 0.6.

The detection of suggestions was based on identifying keywords in a dictionary obtained from Word-Net and the grammatical labeling of words in a comment. The classification was made using a Support Vector Machine in Weka, and cross-validation with ten iterations was used to test the accuracy of the classification model. The authors concluded their investigation, indicating that the suggestions could not be classified correctly since the syntactic and lexical features were ineffective in most cases.

The suggestion mining also entered into social networks. The first one was presented by Pitchay-aviwat (2016) when implementing a system that collected information from insurance service clients on Facebook and Twitter. User complaints were being detected and given a priority by the insurance company to maintain a quality standard set by such an insurance company.

To train this system, 800 comments were used. To use a grouping model, a feature vector was created using the words that repeated themselves more than five times in the comments stored on a corpus. A *k*-means clustering method was used as the grouping model with the help of which three groups were created. Group one contained questions made by the user about insurance policies, group two was feedback claims about services offered by an insurance company, and group three covered general inquiry of information questions.

Similarly, suggestions have been used to find areas of opportunity in student comments to their teachers in the project developed by Gottipati (2018). This project dealt with student surveys made each semester by several institutions. These surveys consist of two parts, a quantitative one where a teacher is evaluated on a numerical scale and a qualitative one, where the student can express in a comment their personal opinion in relation to the teaching method of a teacher, the content in relation to the class syllabus and their academic performance.

In Gottipati's project, a database was built to store the collected surveys. These surveys were processed in two ways: 1) the calculation of an average grade for the scores obtained in the quantitative portion of the survey, and 2) the identification of suggestions using the Negi and Buitelar (2015) text processing methods and a decision tree classifier.

Since the project dealt with surveys with two types of characteristics, the project applied the quantitative average load to each comment in a survey, this to denote the priority in which suggestions should be addressed.

The database used to carry out this project included 5342 instances from a school in Singapore, and they were all manually labeled as positive, negative, with suggestions or without suggestions. The author mentioned that the removal of stop words, which is a technique commonly used to improve performance, reduced the accuracy of the classifier from 0.78 to 0.18. Hence they ended not removing any stop words to maintain the highest level of accuracy.

METHODOLOGY

During this project, the steps that were carried out follow the same steps stated before in projects dealing with sentiment analysis, mainly following the Negi and Buitelar (2015) project. These steps are as follows:

1. Collection of comments
2. Preprocessing of the comments

3. Creation of a feature vector
4. Classification of the comments

These steps are briefly described in the following sections.

Collection of Comments

Using the Twitter Archiver tool, we were able to collect 5026 comments issued by Twitter users to Mexican airline accounts: *Aeromexico, Volaris, Interjet, VivaAerobus,* and *Tar.* These comments correspond to tweets and responses made during July 30 (2019) and August 8 (2019).

Since comments made on Twitter lack a label that could help identify them as suggestions, a tagging process had to be done using a method called *crowd tagging* or *mass tagging,* which has been utilized by Chai, Fan, Li, Wang, & Zheng (2018). Sophomore and junior students of Software Engineering and Computer Systems Engineering at the *Multidisciplinary Division in University City* of the *Autonomous University of Ciudad Juárez* were asked for help to apply a crowd tagging method on the collected comments. This method of tagging aims to attach a tag to comments contained in a dataset using the collective knowledge of crowds to substitute an expert in the evaluation of comments containing suggestions. These annotators tag a comment as a suggestion. Then these comments were verified to be really a suggestion.

The first stage in the preparation of the collected data for tagging was to remove all useless comments. A useless comment is that comment that does not include enough meaningful information to determine if it is a suggestion or referencing a topic. This is because most of its content consists of tagged accounts and/or hashtags, and the remaining content is not textually significant enough to mark it as a suggestion or even a comment. An example of these types of useless comment is:

"@Aeromexico @Aeromexico #vamos diablos"

As we can see in the previous example, the comment includes two tags to the same airline (@Aeromexico), a hashtag (#vamos), and a word (diablos), which by itself has no explicit or implicit value to the airline or to other customers reading the tweet. Therefore, we can assume that this comment would only add noise to the classification model.

The dataset was split into 74 subsets, of which 73 were made up of 50 comments and the last one subset of 5 comments. Each subset was then given to a sophomore student, and the same subset was then given to a junior student to be tagged with a '1', meaning true, if there exists a suggestion within the comment or '0' if there is not a suggestion within the comment. After all, subsets were tagged by the students, comments in which there were discrepancies in the tags assigned by the students were identified. This indicates that there was no consensus on the tag that the comment should have. In these cases, the comments were again analyzed, and a tag was assigned.

Lastly, we merged all correctly tagged subsets into a single dataset, which was then divided into two subsets, one subset of comments containing suggestions and one subset of comments that do not contain suggestions to proceed with preprocessing techniques.

Comment Preprocessing

Given the use of informal language by Twitter users, text preprocessing is an important step when working with machine learning algorithms, because it helps to reduce noise, variation between words in the dataset and it facilitates text analysis. Avoiding some of the steps could lead to missing important information included in the raw text.

Before creating the feature vector from the comment text, manual preprocessing was performed. The preprocessing consisted of validating the text of the comments and their respective tags, as well as text normalization using the NLTK library of tools available in Python 3.6, which consisted of:

- Tokenization of the text of a comment into a list of words. Tokenization is a useful way to prepare a comment for processing as each word in the token list can be easily iterated, and normalization functions applied. Example of tokenization in Python 3 using NLTK tokenize:

```
from nltk.tokenize import word_tokenize
str = "hello world!"
stylist = word_tokenize(str)
print(strList)

Output: ['hello', 'world!']
```

- Case-folding of all comments by changing all letters in a comment from uppercase to lowercase. It allows for possible errors to be minimized when matching words. Although capitalization is a way of distinguishing proper nouns from common nouns, the fast and improper way of typing by Twitter users cannot justify keeping words apart by leaving in the capitalization of words. Example of case-folding a comment to lower case using Python 3:

```
str = "Hello WORLD"
str = str.lower()
print(str)

Output: hello world
```

- Elimination of accents because users do not tend to accentuate words on their tweets correctly. It caused mismatches of words even though the users intended the same meaning of the word. Example of the elimination of accents via the replacement of letters in Python 3:

```
def normalize(str):
    replacements = (
```

```
              ("á", "a"),
              ("é", "e"),
              ("í", "i"),
              ("ó", "o"),
              ("ú", "u"),
    )
        for a, b in replacements:
            str = str.replace(a, b)
return str
Example of the elimination of accents using Unicode library:
import unidecode
str = "Acción"
strUni = unicode(str, "utf-8")  // converts raw text into UTF-8 format
str = unidecode.unidecode(strUni)

print(str)

Output: Accion
```

- Elimination of emoticons quotes and underscore. This type of character does not contribute to meaningful information. Example of how to remove special characters in Python 3:

```
str = "Hello World 1"
str = str.encode('ascii', 'ignore').decode('ascii')
print(str)
inputString.encode('ascii', 'ignore').decode('ascii')s
Output: Hello World
```

- Elimination of stop words in the Spanish language using the Python NLTK library. Stop words are common terms that do not contain meaningful information, or their semantic content is negligible, such as determiners, prepositions, among others. Additionally, words that begin with '@' or '#' were removed since they are meant to tag other users into tweets or create a hashtag, and do not add information relevant to the project.

```
from nltk.corpus import stopwords

stop_words = set(stopwords.words('spanish'))
str = "Michael likes to play inside, not outside"
word_list = str.split() //splits the string into a list of strings
clean_list = [] //a list to store the list without stop words
```

```
for x in word_list:
if x not in stop_words:
                clean_list.append(x)

str = ' '.join(clean_list)
print(str)

Output: Michael likes play inside outside
```

- Elimination of digits. Because the digits themselves do not denote the existence of a suggestion in a comment, they were removed.

```
str = "abc123def"
str = ''.join([x for x in str if not x.isdigit()])
print(str)

Output = abcdef
```

- Word validation. The words in the comments were compared against a list of existing words in the Current Spanish Reference Corpus of the Real Academia Española (2019), which is a list of words approved by the Spanish Royal Academy as being relevant to day-to-day conversations in person and online conversations and postings. This step is meant to verify that each word in a comment exists in the Spanish language. This operation is necessary because all the comments in the repository come from a social network, where tweets are written in an informal manner, and it is commonly used to elongate words to give those words emphasis by typing a letter in that word multiple times (i.e., "pleeeease") or substituting entire words for single letters (i.e., "okay → "k"). For simplicity and to avoid stepping into another area of NLP, a word marked as invalid, cannot be considered a real word and it is eliminated from the comment.
- Word stemming. It was used to extract the root of each of the words in the comments to get to their basic form using SnowballStemmer from the Python NLTK library.

```
from nltk import SnowballStemmer
spanishstemmer = SnowballStemmer('english') //Switch english to available
    //language
nlp = spacy.load('es_core_news_sm')

str = "Compute computer computed computing"
strList = word_tokenize(str) //stemmer only works on single words so you
 //need to tokenize the string beforehand
```

```
stemList = [] //you need a list to save the stemmed words
for x in strList:
    stemList.append(spanishstemmer.stem(x))

str = ' '.join(stemList])
print(str)

Output: compute compute compute compute
```

Creating a Suggestion Dictionary

A dictionary for text analysis is like a map that guides the conversion of unstructured text into structured data (vectors). When working on sentiment analysis, a dictionary would likely be available on the web or using nltk.download('opinion_lexicon')if the project is being developed in Python. Since suggestion mining is relatively new and there are not dictionaries available for a domain dealing with suggestions for airline tweets, a niche dictionary had to be built.

The feature dictionary was built after performing preprocessing on a text corpus. This preprocessing was performed on both the suggestion subset and the non-suggestion subset, and it can be done with the help of a word frequency distribution in each of the subsets.

By using Gutenberg Corpus, part of NLTK, we can easily load our repositories with comments containing suggestions to apply a frequency distribution. To create an NLTK corpus, we use the following command, where *"Comments with suggestions.txt"* is the repository containing comments with suggestions. Another corpus was created for the repository containing comments without suggestions.

corpus = nltk.corpus.gutenberg.words("Comments with suggestions.txt")

After we load our repository as a corpus, we then need to apply a frequency distribution function and tabulate.

freqdist = nltk.FreqDist(corpus)
freqdist.tabulate()

This frequency distribution is used to create a list of tuples consisting of the number of times a word appeared in the corpus and the corresponding word. It considers distinct words in each subset and their occurrence within that subset to reveal how often a word appears. A high amount of appearance in a subset can describe the subset by showing its most relevant content. Since this frequency distribution does not contain stop words, we can say the most frequent words are the most important to describe their subset. Afterward, a frequency distribution of the subset is built. Words that appear less than five times are removed since these are defined as rare and are less likely to reappear in a new tweet to classify in the future. Example of a dictionary with words appearing more than five times in all the corpus:

SuggestionDictionary = list (filter(lambda x:x[1]>4 and (len(x[0])>1), freqdist.items()))

The last thing needed to create a dictionary is to create a list of words from the *SuggestionDictionary* tuple list. This can be done by copying all the words in the tuple list using the following code line:

SuggestionDictionaryList = [word for (word, _) in SuggestionDictionary]

With a list of words used in comments with suggestions stored in *SuggestionDictionaryList*, we need to append this list to the list of words used in comments without suggestions to create the dictionary. When adding both lists to create the dictionary, duplicate words were removed. After eliminating rare words, the number of words used to create the suggestion dictionary was a combined 556 words from both subsets.

Creating a Feature Vector

A feature vector is a vector composed of *n*-elements or attributes that describe numerically or symbolically the properties of an object. In this case, that object is a comment made on Twitter and a feature vector that describes a text comment. Feature vectors are widely used in machine language due to their ability to represent objects in a numerical way that helps the analysis of the object by a classifier.

To create a feature vector from a comment, we need to take the attributes previously defined in a suggestion dictionary as a list or array and create a dictionary-size vector, i.e., if the dictionary is composed of 400 words, the feature vector will have 400 features to describe a comment according to the dictionary accurately, subsequently, a feature vector is generated for each comment in the dataset. To populate a feature vector, it is needed to be initialized to 0, and in each attribute of the feature vector set 1 if the word in comment exists in correspondence with the position of that word attribute in the dictionary list. The following code is an example of creating, initializing, and generating a feature vector from a given comment, based on the dictionary structure.

```
featureVector = [0] * (len(dictionary)) //creates a vector

  for w in tweetComment: //iterates all words in a given comment
w = spanishstemmer.stem(w) //extracts the stem for the current word
featureIndex = find_element_in_list(w, dictionary) //finds the position of the
word in the dictionary list
if featureIndex > -1: //checks if the word returned index is valid
featureVector [featureIndex] = 1 //populates according to index

stringVector = ", ".join(map(str, featureVector)) //concatenates
fileWrite.write(stringVector + "\n") //writes vector to file
```

After creating all vectors, duplicate vectors were removed from the dataset. It resulted in only 3,330 unique vectors in the dataset for both comments containing suggestions and non-suggestions comments.

EXPERIMENT CONFIGURATION

All tests were performed using WEKA software and 5-fold cross-validation. The dataset used consisted of 556 attributes and 3330 comments. Of these comments, only 88 contained a suggestion, and the remainder were non-suggestions. The comments contained in the dataset were preprocessed, as described in Section 3.2. The classifiers used were Bagging and Naïve Bayes. For both classifiers, the default configurations in WEKA were used. Bagging utilizes a REPTree classifier.

To evaluate the performance of each classifier, a two-class confusion matrix is automatically generated by WEKA during the testing process. An example of a confusion matrix is presented in Table 1, where we can see the four basic combinations of actual data category and predicted category: *TP*, *FP*, *FN*, and *TN*. These four outcomes can be explained as:

Table 1. Confusion matrix for the classification of two classes

	Actual: Suggestion	Actual: Non-suggestion
Predicted: Suggestion	TP	FP
Predicted: Non-suggestion	FN	TN

- TP (True Positives): Comments labeled as suggestions that are actually suggestions.
- FP (False Positives): Comments labeled as suggestions that are actually non-suggestions.
- FN (False Negatives): Comments labeled as non-suggestions that are actually suggestions
- TN (Ture Negatives): Comments labeled as non-suggestions that are actually non-suggestions.

To understand the performance of the classifiers, accuracy, precision, and recall metrics were used. Accuracy is the number of correctly predicted instances. Precision is the proportion of correctly classified instances among the ones classified as positive. Recall, also called Sensitivity, is the fraction of positive instances that were correctly classified. Below is the definition of each of these metrics:

$$accuracy = \frac{TP + TN}{TP + FP + FN + TN}$$

$$precision = \frac{TP}{TP + FP}$$

$$recall = \frac{TP}{TP + FN}$$

Table 2. Cross-validation using a 5-fold variation

Iteration	1	2	3	4	5
Dataset	**Testing**	Training	Training	Training	Training
	Training	**Testing**	Training	Training	Training
	Training	Training	**Testing**	Training	Training
	Training	Training	Training	**Testing**	Training
	Training	Training	Training	Training	**Testing**

Table 3. Global accuracy results table

	Bagging	**Naïve Bayes**
Global Accuracy	97.35%	93.90%

Table 4. Precision table by class

	Bagging	**Naïve Bayes**
Suggestions	0%	19.3%
No Suggestions	1.0%	95.9%

Validation

To get a statistical estimation of the performance of the selected classifiers, the cross-validation method is applied to both Bagging and Naïve Bayes. Validation is a method used to estimate the prediction skill of a classifier on new data. The idea of cross-validation using five-folds is to divide the dataset into five equal parts using four of them as training data and one of them as new data for *testing*. Table 2 shows

Table 5. Confusion matrix for the Bagging classifier

	Suggestion	**No Suggestion**
Suggestions	0	88
No Suggestions	0	3242

Table 6. Confusion matrix for the Naïve Bayes classifier

	Suggestion	**No Suggestion**
Suggestions	17	71
No Suggestions	132	3110

the change of testing and training data parts during each of the five iterations of cross-validation. During these iterations, it is important that the instances in the dataset be assigned to a group 1 thru 5 and stay on that group for all five iterations, with this we ensure that instance will be used one time for testing and four times for training.

RESULTS

To compare the performance of the Bagging and Naïve Bayes classifiers, Table 3 shows each of the overall accuracy results obtained by each of the classifiers. Based on these results, the Bagging algorithm obtained the best performance, but as can be seen in Table 4, all suggestions were incorrectly classified using this classifier.

The high accuracy scores and the low precision scores in the classification of suggestions indicate a high degree of imbalance between classes, as shown in Tables 5 and 6. It can also be seen in the low recall scores, shown in Table 7.

Table 7. Recall values by the classifier

	Bagging	Naïve Bayes
Recall	0%	11.4%

To achieve a better true positive rate of classification for suggestions, a subsampling of the majority class by using Weka's SpreadSubsample filter with a distributionSpread of 5.0 was performed. It gives subsample of the majority class of 5 times the size of the minority class; in this case, 440 no suggestion instances as the minority class is composed of only 88 instances. A classification using subsampling and Naïve Bayes reduces accuracy but increases the recall score from 11.4% to 44.7% by increasing the number of correctly classified suggestions, as shown in 8.

Table 8. Confusion matrix of the Naïve Bayes classifier and a subsample of the majority class.

	Suggestion	No Suggestion
Suggestions	38	50
No Suggestions	47	217

Given the low precision for both classifiers, it is needed to see how the dataset is visualized in a 2D space. First, tSNE was used to see how the instances in the dataset are arranged in a high-dimensional space. The tSNE method reduces dimensionality by using local relationships between points to create a low dimension map of the dataset. When tSNE was used to represent the original database of 3330 instances in two dimensions, the map in Figure 1 was obtained, where we can see instances marked as suggestions in blue and non-suggestions in red. This visualization can give the idea of how the classes are grouped, and as we can see, suggestions are overlapping non-suggestions. Additionally, it is also possible to see the formation of small disjuncts that characterize the high error rate, as well as the low precision.

Figure 1. The two-dimensional layout of the dataset using tSNE

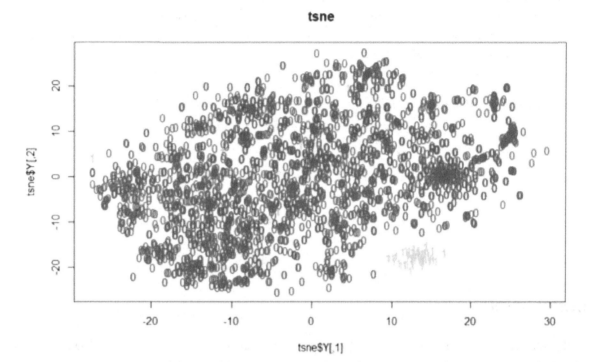

Since we see the formation of small disjuncts in our tSNE map, we created a heatmap in MATLAB to view a 2D data matrix, shown in Figure 2, to view how the features in the dictionary are being utilized

Figure 2. Heatmap of data contained in the dataset

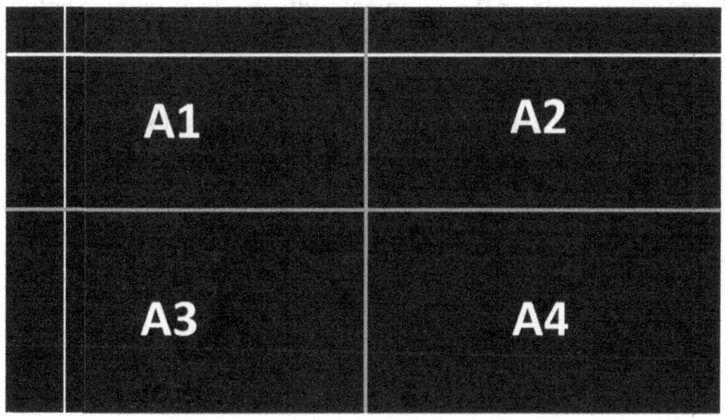

by all instances for both classes. With this, it is possible to identify if there are features that cause our instances to form small clusters in the map generated with tSNE.

To better illustrate the features shown by the heatmap in Figure 2, the second quadrant in this figure is shown in Figure 3, where the regions displayed in B1 and B2 contain the suggestion instances, and B3 and B4 contain the non-suggestion instances. As can be seen, there are small dots in all four regions. These small dots represent the presence of a feature in an instance. In a best-case scenario, we could only see the presence of features in regions B1 and B4. Since the dataset used shows the presence of features in B2 and B3, we can deduce that the features used to describe a suggestion are also present in non-suggestion comments, and vice versa.

Figure 3. Heatmap of the second quadrant

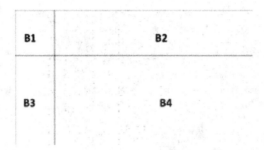

CONCLUSION

In this chapter, the development of a prototype based on machine learning and natural language processing to classify tweets issued by airline customers in the Spanish language into suggestions and non-suggestions was presented.

For the development of this research project, a dataset of comments extracted from Twitter was created. The dataset consists of 5026 comments which were issued by Twitter users to Mexican airline accounts: Aeromexico, Volaris, Interjet, VivaAerobus, and Tar, corresponding to tweets and responses made during July 30 (2019) and August 8 (2019).

The classifiers used were Bagging and Naïve Bayes. For both classifiers, the default configurations in WEKA were used. Bagging uses a REPTree classifier.

Because some features extracted from the comments with suggestions also belong to non-suggestions, small disjunctions were created, representing common features, and taking precedence for the classifier as it makes its prediction on new data. To address this situation, only comments expressing a direct suggestion were used, so comments expressing an indirect or implicit suggestion were reassigned to the non-suggestion class. In this way, the precision improved, but almost a sixth of the suggestions in the dataset were lost.

The problem we need to address is a small disjunct problem, which could improve accuracy without losing suggestions.

REFERENCES

Ahmed, R. I. (2017). The influence of perceived social media marketing activities on brand loyalty: The mediation effect of brand and value consciousness. *Asia Pacific Journal of Marketing and Logistics, 29*(1), 129–144. doi:10.1108/APJML-10-2015-0154

Brun, C., & Hagege, C. (2013). Suggestion Mining: Detecting Suggestions for Improvement in Users' Comments. *Research in Computing Science,* (70), 199-209.

Brun, C., & Hagege, C. (2014, Mayo 27). *United States of America Patent No. US 8,738,363 B2.* US Patent Office.

DeWalt. (2010). *Facebook.* Retrieved 03 19, 2019, from Idea Submission Brochure: https://www.facebook.com/DEWALT/posts/356194591449

DeWalt. (2019). *Best of 2019.* Retrieved 03 12, 2019, from Awards: https://www.dewalt.com/company-info/dewalt-awards

García, V., Florencia-Juárez, R., Sánchez-Solís, P., Rivera, G., & Contreras-Masse, R. (2019). Predicting Airline Customer Satisfaction using k-nn Ensemble Regression Models. *Research in Computing Science, 148*(6), 205–215. doi:10.13053/rcs-148-6-15

Goldberg, A. B., Fillmore, N., Andrzejewski, D., Xu, Z., Gibson, B., & Zhu, X. (2009). May All Your Wishes Come True: A Study of Wishes and How to Recognize Them. *The Annual Conference of the North American Chapter of the ACL.* 10.3115/1620754.1620793

Gottipati, S., Shankararaman, V., & Lin, J. (2018). Text analytics approach to extract course improvement suggestions from students' feedback. *Research and Practice in Technology Enhanced Learning,* 6.

Kemp, S. (2019). *Digital 2019: essential insights into how people around the world use the internet, mobile devices, social media, and e-commerce.* Hootsuite.

Negi, S. (2016). Suggestion Mining from Opinionated Text. Association for Computational Linguistics, 119–125.

Negi, S. (2019). *Suggestion mining from text.* Retrieved from Access to Research at NUI Galway: https://aran.library.nuigalway.ie/bitstream/handle/10379/14987/2019SapnaNegiPhD.pdf

Negi, S., Asooja, K., Mehrotra, S., & Buitelaar, P. (2016). A Study of Suggestions in Opinionated Texts and their Automatic Detection. *Conference on Lexical and Computational Semantics.* 10.18653/v1/S16-2022

Negi, S., & Buitelaar, P. (2015). Curse or Boon? Presence of Subjunctive Mood in Opinionated Text. *International Conference on Computational Semantics,* 101-106.

Negi, S., & Buitelaar, P. (2015). Towards the Extraction of Customer-to-Customer Suggestions from Reviews. In *Conference on Empirical Methods in Natural Language Processing,* (pp. 2159-2167). 10.18653/v1/D15-1258

Penisi, R., & Kim, G. (2003). Customer Driven Innovation Process. *IEEE/CPMT/SEMI International Electronics Manufacturing Technology (IEMT) Symposium.*

Pitchayaviwat, T. (2016). A Study on Clustering Customer Suggestion on Online Social Media about Insurance Services by Using Text Mining Techniques. *Management and Innovation Technology International Conference, 1*, 148-151. 10.1109/MITICON.2016.8025228

Ramanand, J., Bhavsar, K., & Pedanekar, N. (2010). Wishful Thinking: Finding suggestions and 'buy' wishes from product reviews. *Workshop on Computational Approaches to Analysis and Generation of Emotion in Text.*

Real Academia Española. (2019). *Banco de datos (CORDE).* Retrieved from Corpus diacrónico del español: http://www.rae.es

Real Academia Española. (2019). *Diccionario de la lengua española.* Retrieved 03 18, 2019, from Sugerencia: https://dle.rae.es/?id=YfTKl7q

Saravanakumar, M., & SuganthaLakshmi, T. (2012). Social Media Marketing. *Life Science Journal, 9*(4), 4444–4451.

Stricker, G. (2017, Diciembre 10). *The 2014 #YearOnTwitter.* Retrieved Julio 02, 2019, from https://blog.twitter.com/official/en_us/a/2014/the-2014-yearontwitter.html

Compilation of References

Abdul-Kader, S., & Woods, J. (2015). Survey on Chatbot Design Techniques in Speech Conversation Systems. *International Journal of Advanced Computer Science and Applications*, 6(7), 72–80. doi:10.14569/ijacsa.2015.060712

Abirami, A. M., Askarunisa, A., Shiva, R. A., & Revathy, R. (2018). Ontology Based Feature Extraction from Text Documents. In M. Thangavel & P. Karthikeyan (Eds.), Applications of Security, Mobile, Analytic, and Cloud (SMAC) Technologies for Effective Information Processing and Management (p. 175). IGI Global. doi:10.4018/978-1-5225-4044-1.ch009

Abraham Silberschatz, H. F. (2006). Fundamentals of Databases. Aravaca: McGraw-Hill.

Abujar, S., Kaisar, A., Masum, M., Mohibullah, M. O., & Hossain, S. (2019). An Approach for Bengali Text Summarization using Word2Vector. In *2019 10th International Conference on Computing, Communication and Networking Technologies (ICCCNT)* (pp.1-5). Academic Press.

Abujar, S., A. K. (2019). An Approach for Bengali Text Summarization using Word2Vector. *10th International Conference on Computing, Communication and Networking Technologies (ICCCNT)*, 1-5. 10.1109/ICCCNT45670.2019.8944536

Achananuparp, P., Hu, X., Zhou, X., & Zhang, X. (2008). Utilizing Sentence Similarity and Question Type Similarity to Response to Similar Questions in Knowledge-Sharing Community. In *Workshop on Question Answering on the Web*. IEEE.

Agrawal, M., & Gonçalves, T. (2016). Age and Gender Identification using Stacking for Classification—Notebook for PAN at CLEF 2016. In K. Balog, L. Cappellato, N. Ferro, & C. Macdonald (Eds.), CLEF 2016 Evaluation Labs and Workshop – Working Notes Papers. Évora, Portugal: CEUR-WS.org.

Ahmad, S., & Varma, R. (2018). Information extraction from text messages using data mining techniques. *Malaya Journal of Matematik*, S(1), 26–29. doi:10.26637/MJM0S01/05

Ahmed, R. I. (2017). The influence of perceived social media marketing activities on brand loyalty: The mediation effect of brand and value consciousness. *Asia Pacific Journal of Marketing and Logistics*, 29(1), 129–144. doi:10.1108/APJML-10-2015-0154

Akter, S., Asa, A. S., Uddin, M. P., Hossain, M. D., Roy, S. K., & Afjal, M. I. (2017). An extractive text summarization technique for Bengali document (s) using K-means clustering algorithm. In *2017 IEEE International Conference on Imaging, Vision & Pattern Recognition (icIVPR)* (pp. 1-6). IEEE. 10.1109/ICIVPR.2017.7890883

Alayba, A. M., Palade, V., England, M., & Iqbal, R. (2017). Arabic Language Sentiment Analysis on Health Services. In *2017 1st International Workshop on Arabic Script Analysis and Recognition (ASAR)* (pp.114–118). 10.1109/ASAR.2017.8067771

Al-Azzawy, D. S., & Al-Rufaye, F. M. L. (2017). Arabic words clustering by using K-means algorithm. In *2017 Annual Conference on New Trends in Information & Communications Technology Applications (NTICT)* (pp. 263-267). IEEE.

Alcalá-Fdez, J., Fernández, A., Luengo, J., Derrac, J., García, S., Sánchez, L., & Herrera, F. (2011). Keel data-mining software tool: data set repository, integration of algorithms and experimental analysis framework. *Journal of Multiple-Valued Logic & Soft Computing*, 17.

Al-Hader, M., & Rodzi, A. (2009). The Smart Infrastructure Development & Monitoring. *Theoretical and Empirical Researches in Urban Management*, 4(2), 87–94.

Alhawarat, M., & Hegazi, M. (2018). Revisiting K-Means and Topic Modeling, a Comparison Study to Cluster Arabic Documents. *IEEE Access: Practical Innovations, Open Solutions*, 6, 42740–42749. doi:10.1109/ACCESS.2018.2852648

Allahverdipour, A., & Gharehchopogh, F. (2017). A New Hybrid Model of K-Means and Naïve Bayes Algorithms for Feature Selection in Text Documents Categorization. *Journal of Advances in Computer Research*, 8(4), 73–86.

Almor, A. (2020, March 9). *ResearchGate*. Retrieved from ResearchGate: https://www.researchgate.net/publication/2659482_Noun-Phrase_Anaphora_and_Focus_The_Informational_Load_Hypothesis

Aloise, D., Deshpande, A., Hansen, P., & Popat, P. (2009). NP-hardness of Euclidean sum-of-squares clustering. *Machine Learning*, 75(2), 245–248. doi:10.100710994-009-5103-0

Alpaydin, E. (2020). *Introduction to machine learning*. MIT Press.

Álvarez-Carmona, M., López-Monroy, A., Montes-y-Gómez, M., Villaseñor-Pineda, L., & Escalante, H. J. (2015). IN-AOE's participation at PAN'15: Author Profiling task—Notebook for PAN at CLEF 2015. In L. Cappellato, N. Ferro, G. Jones, & E. San Juan (Eds.), CLEF 2015 Evaluation Labs and Workshop – Working Notes Papers. Toulouse, France: CEUR-WS.org.

Amazon Web Services. (2018). *Big Data on AWS*. Retrieved from https://aws.amazon.com/big-data/

Amazon. (2019). *Amazon Neptune: Fast, reliable graph database built for the cloud*. Retrieved from Amazon: https://aws.amazon.com/es/neptune/

Ameer, I., Siddiqui, M. H. F., Sidorov, G., & Gelbukh, A. (2019). CIC at SemEval-2019 task 5: Simple yet very efficient approach to hate speech detection, aggressive behavior detection, and target classification in twitter. In *Proceedings of the 13th International Workshop on Semantic Evaluation*. Minneapolis, MN: Association for Computational Linguistics. 10.18653/v1/S19-2067

Ameer, I., Sidorov, G., & Nawab, R. M. A. (2019). Author profiling for age and gender using combinations of features of various types. *Journal of Intelligent & Fuzzy Systems*, 36(5), 4833–4843. doi:10.3233/JIFS-179031

Amin-Naseri, M., Chakraborty, P., Sharma, A., Gilbert, S. B., & Hong, M. (2018). Evaluating the Reliability, Coverage, and Added Value of Crowdsourced Traffic Incident Reports from Waze. *Transportation Research Record: Journal of the Transportation Research Board*, 2672(43), 1–10. doi:10.1177/0361198118790619

André Ferreira Cruz, G. R. (2020, January 30). *MDPI Open Access Journals*. Retrieved from MDPI Open Access Journals: https://www.mdpi.com/2078-2489/11/2/74

Androutsopoulos, I., Ritchie, G. D., & Thanisch, P. (1995). Natural language interfaces to databases – An introduction. *Journal of Natural Language Engineering*, 1(1), 29–81. doi:10.1017/S135132490000005X

Angga, A., Fachri, E., & Angga, E., Suryadi, & Agushinta, D. (2015). Design of Chatbot with 3D Avatar, Voice Interface, and Facial Expression. In *International Conference on Science in Information Technology* (pp. 326-330). Yogyakarta, Indonesia. IEEE. 10.1109/ICSITech.2015.7407826

ArcGis Desktop. (2016). *¿Qué es un Kriging bayesiano empírico?* Retrieved from https://desktop.arcgis.com/es/arc-map/10.4/extensions/geostatistical-analyst/what-is-empirical-bayesian-kriging-.htm

Arenas, M., Bertails, A., Prud'hommeaux, E., & Sequeda, J. (2012). *A Direct Mapping of Relational Data to RDF.* Retrieved from W3C: https://www.w3.org/TR/rdb-direct-mapping/

Argamon, S., Koppel, M., Fine, J., & Shimoni, A. R. (2003). Gender, genre, and writing style in formal written texts. *Text*, *23*(3), 321–346. doi:10.1515/text.2003.014

Arthur, D., & Vassilvitskii, S. (2006). k-means++: The advantages of careful seeding. Stanford.

Asa, A. S., Akter, S., Uddin, M. P., Hossain, M. D., Roy, S. K., & Afjal, M. I. (2017). A Comprehensive Survey on Extractive Text Summarization Techniques. *American Journal of Engineering Research*, *6*(1), 226–239.

Ashraf, S., Iqbal, H. R., & Nawab, R. M. A. (2016). Cross genre Author Profile Prediction Using Stylometry-Based Approach— Notebook for PAN at CLEF 2016. In K. Balog, L. Cappellato, N. Ferro, & C. Macdonald (Eds.), CLEF 2016 Evaluation Labs and Workshop – Working Notes Papers. Évora, Portugal: CEUR-WS.org.

Aspectiva. (2019). *Aspectiva About Us*. Retrieved from Aspectiva: https://www.aspectiva.com/company/

Atserias, J., Casas, B., Comelles, E., González, M., Padró, L., & Padró, M. (2006). FreeLing 1.3: Syntactic and semantic services in an open-source NLP library. In *Proceedings of the Fifth International Conference on Language Resources and Evaluation (LREC'06)* (pp. 48-55). Genoa, Italy: Academic Press.

Auer, S., Ermilov, I., Lehmann, J., & Martin, M. (2018). *LODstats*. Retrieved from aksw: http://lodstats.aksw.org

Auer, S., Lehmann, J., Ngomo, A.-C. N., & Zaveri, A. (2013). *Introduction to Linked Data and Its Lifecycle on the Web. In Reasoning Web, Semantic Technologies for Intelligent Data Access*. Springer.

Augello, A., Gentile, M., Weideveld, L., & Dignum, F. (2016). A Model of a Social Chatbot. In G. De Pietro, L. Gallo, R. Howlett, & L. Jain (Eds.), *Smart Innovation, Systems and Technologies, 55* (pp. 5–7). doi:10.1007/978-3-319-39345-2

Augenstein, I., Padó, S., & Rudolph, S. (2012). LODifier: Generating Linked Data from Unstructured Text. In *The Semantic Web: Research and Applications - 9th Extended Semantic Web Conference, ESWC 2012* (pp. 210-224). Springer.

Augenstein, I., Maynard, D., & Ciravegna, F. (2016). Distantly supervised Web relation extraction for knowledge base population. *Semantic Web*, *7*(4), 335–349.

Babar, S. A., & Patil, P. D. (2015). Improving performance of text summarization. *Procedia Computer Science*, *46*, 354–363. doi:10.1016/j.procs.2015.02.031

Baccianella, S., Esuli, A., & Sebastiani, F. (2014). *SentiWordNet 3 . 0 : An Enhanced Lexical Resource for Sentiment Analysis and Opinion Mining*. Academic Press.

Baeza-Yates, R., & Ribeiro-Neto, B. (1999). *Modern Information Retrieval*. Addison-Wesley.

Bais, H., Machkour, M., & Koutti, L. (2016). A Model of a Generic Natural Language Interface for Querying Database. *International Journal of Intelligent Systems and Applications*, *8*(2), 35–44. doi:10.5815/ijisa.2016.02.05

Bais, H., Machkour, M., & Koutti, L. (2016). An independent-domain natural language interface for relational database: Case Arabic language. In *Proceedings of 2016 IEEE/ACS 13th International Conference of Computer Systems and Applications* (pp. 1-7). Agadir. Morocco: IEEE. 10.1109/AICCSA.2016.7945786

Banbury, A., Nancarrow, S., Dart, J., Gray, L., Dodson, S., Osborne, R., & Parkinson, L. (2019). Adding value to remote monitoring: Co-design of a health literacy intervention for older people with chronic disease delivered by telehealth - The Telehealth Literacy Project. *Patient Education and Counseling, 103*(3), 597–606. doi:10.1016/j.pec.2019.10.005 PMID:31744701

Banerjee, A., Dubey, A., Menon, A., Nanda, S., & Chand Nandi, G. (2018). *Speaker Recognition using Deep Belief Networks.* Retrieved from https://arxiv.org/ftp/arxiv/papers/1805/1805.08865.pdf

Banko, M., Cafarella, M. J., Soderland, S., Broadhead, M., & Etzioni, O. (2007). Open Information Extraction from the Web. *International Joint Conference on Artificial Intelligence.*

Barrick, M. R., & Mount, M. K. (1991). The big five personality dimensions and job performance: A meta-analysis. *Personnel Psychology, 44*(1), 1–26. doi:10.1111/j.1744-6570.1991.tb00688.x

Barros, J., Morales, S., Echávarri, O., García, A., Ortega, J., Asahi, T., Moya, C., Fischman, R., Maino, M. P., & Núñez, C. (2017). Suicide detection in Chile: Proposing a predictive model for suicide risk in a clinical sample of patients with mood disorders. *Revista Brasileira de Psiquiatria (Sao Paulo, Brazil), 39*(1), 1–11. doi:10.1590/1516-4446-2015-1877 PMID:27783715

Bartoli, A., De Lorenzo, A., Laderchi, A., Medvet, E., & Tarlao, F. ((2015). An author profiling approach based on language-dependent content and stylometric features - notebook for PAN at CLEF 2015. In Working Notes for CLEF 2015 Conference, Toulouse, France.

Barzilay, R., & McKeown, K. R. (2005). Sentence fusion for multidocument news summarization. *Computational Linguistics, 31*(3), 297–328. doi:10.1162/089120105774321091

Barzilay, R., McKeown, K., & Elhadad, M. (1999). Information fusion in the context of multi-document summarization. In *Proceedings of the 37th annual meeting of the Association for Computational Linguistics* (pp. 550-557). 10.3115/1034678.1034760

Basiron, H., Kumar, Y., Goh, S., Ngo, H. C., & Suppiah, C. (2016). A review on automatic text summarization approaches. *Journal of Computational Science, 12*(4), 178–190. doi:10.3844/jcssp.2016.178.190

Bates, M. (1989). Rapid porting of the parlance natural language interface. *Proceedings of the workshop on Speech and Natural Language*, 83-88. 10.3115/100964.100966

BBC. (2014). *Languages of the world - Interesting facts about languages.* Retrieved from http://www.bbc.co.uk

Beckett, D. (2011). *N-Triples - A line-based syntax for an RDF graph.* Retrieved from W3C: http://www.w3.org/TR/n-triples/

Beckett, D., & Berners-Lee, T. (2011). *Turtle - Terse RDF Triple Language.* Retrieved from W3C: http://www.w3.org/TeamSubmission/turtle/

Beeferman, D., Berger, A., & Lafferty, J. (1999). Statistical Models for Text Segmentation. *Machine Learning, 34*(1-3), 177–210. doi:10.1023/A:1007506220214

Berners-Lee, T. (2006). *Linked Data.* Retrieved from W3C: http://www.w3.org/DesignIssues/LinkedData.html

Berners-Lee, T., Hendler, J., & Ora, L. (2001). The semantic web. *Scientific American, 284*(5), 34–43. PMID:11681174

Bernstein, A., Kaufmann, E., & Kaiser, C. (2005). Querying the semantic web with ginseng: A guided input natural language search engine. *15th Workshop on Information Technologies and Systems*, 112-126.

Bhatia, N., & Jaiswal, A. (2016,). Automatic text summarization and it's methods-a review. In 2016 6th International Conference-Cloud System and Big Data Engineering (Confluence) (pp. 65-72). IEEE. doi:10.1109/CONFLUENCE.2016.7508049

Bhootra, R. A., & Parker, L. (2004). *Natural language interfaces: comparing english language front end and english query* (Doctoral dissertation). Virginia Commonwealth University.

Bilan, I., & Zhekova, D. (2016). CAPS: A Cross genre Author Profiling System—Notebook for PAN at CLEF 2016. In K. Balog, L. Cappellato, N. Ferro, & C. Macdonald (Eds.), CLEF 2016 Evaluation Labs and Workshop – Working Notes Papers. Évora, Portugal: CEUR-WS.org.

Birbeck, M., & McCarron, S. (2010). *CURIE Syntax 1.0*. Retrieved from W3C: https://www.w3.org/TR/curie/

Bird, S., Klein, E., & Loper, E. (2009). *Natural Language Processing with Python*. O'Reilly Media, Inc.

Bizer, C., Cyganiak, R., & Gauss, T. (2007). The RDF Book Mashup: From Web APIs to a Web of Data. *Workshop on Scripting for the Semantic Web*.

Blake, C., & Merz, C. J. (2015). *UCI repository of machine learning databases*. Department of Information and Computer Science, University of California, Irvine, CA. Retrieved from https://www.ics.uci.edu/mlearn/MLRepository

Bobrow, R. J., Resnik, P., & Weischedel, R. M. (1990). Multiple underlying systems: Translating user requests into programs to produce answers. *Proceedings of the 28th annual meeting on Association for Computational Linguistics*, 227-234. 10.3115/981823.981852

Bock, H. H. (2008). Origins and extensions of the k-means algorithm in cluster analysis. *Journal Electronique d'Histoire des Probabilités et de la Statistique Electronic Journal for History of Probability and Statistics, 4*(2).

Bollacker, K., Evans, C., Paritosh, P., Sturge, T., & Taylor, J. (2008). Freebase: a collaboratively created graph database for structuring human knowledge. In *Proceedings of the ACM SIGMOD International Conference on Management of Data, SIGMOD 2008* (pp. 1247-1250). Vancouver: ACM.

Booker, C. (2004). *The seven basic plots: Why we tell stories*. Continuum International Publishing Group.

Borker, S. (2006). Business intelligence data warehousing an open source approach (Report). Kansas State University, Manhattan, KS.

Borland International. (1988). *Turbo Prolog 2.0 reference guide*. Scotts Valley, Borland International.

Borland International. (1988). *Turbo Prolog 2.0 Reference Guide*. Scotts Valley.

Bougiatiotis, K., & Krithara, A. (2016). Author Profiling using Complementary Second Order Attributes and Stylometric Features— Notebook for PAN at CLEF 2016. In K. Balog, L. Cappellato, N. Ferro, & C. Macdonald (Eds.), CLEF 2016 Evaluation Labs and Workshop – Working Notes Papers. Évora, Portugal: CEUR-WS.org.

Bouras, A., Usop, K., & Popescu, M. (2018). Empowering diabetes self-management by gamifying intelligent system: MyTrybeCare concept. In *2018 IEEE 4*[th] *Middle East Conference on Biomedical Engineering, MECBME* (pp.137–140). doi:10.1109/MECBME.2018.8402421

Brandwatch. (2019). Retrieved from https://www.brandwatch.com/about/

Breitman, K. K., Casanova, M. A., & Truszkowski, W. (2007). *Semantic Web: Concepts, Technologies and Applications*. Springer.

Brixey, J., Hoegen, R., Lan, W., Rusow, J., Singla, K., Yin, X., Artstein, R., & Leuski, A. (2018). SHIHbot: A Facebook chatbot for Sexual Health Information on HIV/AIDS. In *Proceedings of the 18th annual SIGdial meeting on discourse and dialogue* (pp. 370–373).doi: 10.18653/v1/w17-5544

Brun, C., & Hagege, C. (2013). Suggestion Mining: Detecting Suggestions for Improvement in Users' Comments. *Research in Computing Science, (70)*, 199-209.

Brun, C., & Hagege, C. (2014, Mayo 27). *United States of America Patent No. US 8,738,363 B2.* US Patent Office.

Buschmeier, H., & Wlodarczak, M. (2013). TextGridTools: A TextGrid Processing and Analysis Toolkit for Python. In Tagungsband Der 24. Konferenz Zur Elektronischen Sprachsignalverarbeitung (ESSV 2013) (pp.152–157). Academic Press.

Cabeza Ruiz, R. (2016). *Text segmentation by language.* Academic Press.

Cabling, M. L., Turner, J. W., Hurtado-de-Mendoza, A., Zhang, Y., Jiang, X., Drago, F., & Sheppard, V. B. (2018). Sentiment Analysis of an Online Breast Cancer Support Group: Communicating about Tamoxifen. *Health Communication, 33*(9), 1158–1165. doi:10.1080/10410236.2017.1339370 PMID:28678549

Carothers, G. (2014). *RDF 1.1 N-Quads.* Retrieved from W3C: http://www.w3.org/TR/n-quads/

Carrat, F., & Valleron, A. J. (1992). Epidemiologic mapping using the "kriging" method: Application to an influenza-like epidemic in France. *American Journal of Epidemiology, 135*(11), 1293–1300. doi:10.1093/oxfordjournals.aje.a116236 PMID:1626546

Cavalcanti, D. & Prudêncio. (2017). Aspect-Based opinion mining in drug reviews. In *Progress in Artificial Intelligence* (Vol 10423, pp.815–827). doi:10.1007/978-3-319-65340-2

Cer, D. M., Diab, M. T., Agirre, E., Lopez-Gazpio, I., & Specia, L. (2017). SemEval-2017 Task 1: Semantic Textual Similarity - Multilingual and Cross-lingual Focused Evaluation. *Proceedings of the 11th International Workshop on Semantic Evaluation.*

Cerezo, J., Kubelka, J., Robbes, R., & Bergel, A. (2019). Building an expert recommender chatbot. In *Proceedings - 2019 IEEE/ACM 1st International Workshop on Bots in Software Engineering (BotSE)* (pp. 59–63). 10.1109/BotSE.2019.00022

Chander, S., Soundarya, J., Priyadharsini, R., & Bharathi, B. (2018). Data analysis of natural language querying using NLP interface. *International Journal of Applied Engineering Research, 13*(8), 5792–5795.

Chandra, Y., & Mihalcea, R. (2006). Natural language interfaces to databases. Masters Abstracts International, 45(4).

Chang, C.-H., Kayed, M., Girgis, M. R., & Shaalan, K. F. (2006). A survey of web information extraction systems. *IEEE Transactions on Knowledge and Data Engineering, 18*(10), 1411–1428.

Chatfuel. (n.d.). Retrieved from: https://chatfuel.com/

Cheatham, M., & Hitzler, P. (2013). String Similarity Metrics for Ontology Alignment. *International Semantic Web Conference* (pp. 294-309). Springer.

Chen, N. F., & Li, H. (2017). Computer-assisted pronunciation training: From pronunciation scoring towards spoken language learning. In *2016 Asia-Pacific Signal and Information Processing Association Annual Summit and Conference, APSIPA 2016* (pp. 1–7). doi:10.1109/APSIPA.2016.7820782

Chen, S. Z., Cafarella, M. J., & Adar, E. (2011). Searching for statistical diagrams. Frontiers of Engineering, National Academy of Engineering, 69-78.

Chen, P., Chen, F., & Qian, Z. (2014). Road Traffic Congestion Monitoring in Social Media with Hinge-Loss Markov Random Fields. In R. Kumar, H. Tolvonen, J. Pel, J. Zhexue Huang, & X. Wu (Eds.), *14th IEEE International Conference on Data Mining* (pp.80-89). 10.1109/ICDM.2014.139

Chen, Q., Shipper, T., & Khan, L. (2010). Tweets mining using WIKIPEDIA and impurity cluster measurement. In *2010 IEEE International Conference on Intelligence and Security Informatics* (pp. 141-143). IEEE. 10.1109/ISI.2010.5484758

Chen, Y., Qin, B., Liu, T., Liu, Y., & Li, S. (2010). The Comparison of SOM and K-means for Text Clustering. *Computer and Information Science*, *3*(2), 268–274. doi:10.5539/cis.v3n2p268

Cho, J., & Garcia-Molina, H. (2002). Parallel Crawlers. In *Proceedings of the 11th International Conference on World Wide Web* (pp.124–135). doi:10.1145/511446.511464

Chomsky, N. (1957). Syntactic Structures (463-480). The Hage: Mouton & Co.

Chourabi, H., Nam, T., Walker, S., Gil-García, J. R., Mellouli, S., Nahon, K., … Scholl, H. J. (2012, January). Understanding Smart Cities: An Integrative Framework. In *2012 45th Hawaii International Conference on System Sciences* (pp. 2289-2297). IEEE.

Christian, H., Agus, M. P., & Suhartono, D. (2016). Single Document Automatic Text Summarization using Term Frequency-Inverse Document Frequency (TF-IDF). ComTech: *Computer. Mathematics and Engineering Applications*, *7*(4), 285–294.

Chung, M., Ko, E., Joung, H., & Kim, S. J. (2018). Chatbot e-service and customer satisfaction regarding luxury brands. *Journal of Business Research*, 1–9. doi:10.1016/j.jbusres.2018.10.004

Ciechanowski, L., Przegalinska, A., Magnuski, M., & Gloor, P. (2019). In the shades of the uncanny valley: An experimental study of human-chatbot interaction. *Future Generation Computer Systems*, *92*, 539–548. doi:10.1016/j.future.2018.01.055

Cimiano, P., Haase, P., & Heizmann, J. (2007). Porting natural language interfaces between domains: an experimental user study with the orakel system. *Proceedings of the 12th international conference on Intelligent user interfaces*, 180-189. 10.1145/1216295.1216330

Cobos, J. (2013). *Integración de un chatbot como habilidad de un robot social con gestor de diálogos* (Master's thesis). Madrid: Universidad Carlos III de Madrid.

Codd, E. F. (1972). Further normalization of the data base relational model. *Data Base Systems*, 33-64.

Cohen, A. & Hosenfeld, C. (1981). *Some Uses of Mentalistic Data in Second Language Acquisition*. Academic Press.

Collobert, R., Weston, J., Buttou, L., Karlen, M., Kavukcuoglu, K., & Kuksa, P. (2011). Natural Language Processing (Almost) from Scratch. *Journal of Machine Learning Research*, *12*, 2493–2537.

Computer Science Department. (2020, February 18). *Introducción a las etiquetas Eagle*. Retrieved from Introducción a las etiquetas Eagle: https://www.cs.upc.edu/~nlp/tools/parole-sp.html#pronombres

Conlon, S. J., Conlon, J. R., & James, T. L. (2004). The economics of natural language interfaces: Natural language processing technology as a scarce resource. *Decision Support Systems*, *38*(1), 141–159. doi:10.1016/S0167-9236(03)00096-4

Consortium, L. D. (2019). *Linguistic Data Consortium*. Retrieved from https://catalog.ldc.upenn.edu/

Contreras-Masse, R., Ochoa-Zezzatti, A., García, V., Elizondo-Cortés, M., & Pérez-Dominguez, L. (2020). Implementing a Novel Use of Multicriteria Decision Analysis to Select IIoT Platforms for Smart Manufacturing. *Symmetry*, *12*(3), 368. doi:10.3390ym12030368

Cook, D. J., Duncan, G., Sprint, G., & Fritz, R. (2018). Using Smart City Technology to Make Healthcare Smarter. *Proceedings of the IEEE, 106*(4), 708–722. doi:10.1109/JPROC.2017.2787688 PMID:29628528

Cornolti, M., Ferragina, P., & Ciaramita, M. (2013). A Framework for Benchmarking Entity-Annotation Systems. *World Wide Web Conference.*

Corrales, K. (2009). Construyendo un segundo idioma. *Zona Próxima, 10*, 156–167.

Cortez, A., Vega, H., Pariona, J., & Huayna, A. (n.d.). Procesamiento de lenguaje natural. *Revista de Investigación de Sistemas e Informática, 6*, 45–54.

Cortizo, J. C. (2019). *Mineria de Opiniones.* Retrieved from BrainSINS: https://www.brainsins.com/es/blog/mineria-opiniones/3555

CourseFinders. (2017). *¿Cuál es el idioma más rápido del mundo?* (CourseFinders) Retrieved from https://coursefinders.com/blog/es/5637/espanol-cual-es-el-idioma-mas-rapido-del-mundo

Cressie, N. (1990). The origins of Kriging. *Mathematical Geology, 22*(3), 239–252. doi:10.1007/BF00889887

Criado-Fernandez, L. (2009). Procedimiento semi-automático para transformar la web en web semántica. Universidad Nacional de Educación a Distancia (España).

Cui, L., Huang, S., Wei, F., Tan, C., Duan, C., & Zhou, M. (2017). Superagent: A customer service chatbot for E-commerce websites. In *ACL 2017 - 55th Annual Meeting of the Association for Computational Linguistics, Proceedings of System Demonstrations*, (pp.97–102). 10.18653/v1/P17-4017

Cui, X., Potok, T. E., & Palathingal, P. (2005, June). Document clustering using particle swarm optimization. In *Proceedings 2005 IEEE Swarm Intelligence Symposium, 2005. SIS 2005.* (pp. 185-191). IEEE. 10.1109/SIS.2005.1501621

Cui, X., Zhu, P., Yang, X., Li, K., & Ji, C. (2014). Optimized big data K-Means clustering using MapReduce. *The Journal of Supercomputing, 70*(3), 1249–1259. doi:10.100711227-014-1225-7

Cutting, D., Kupiec, J., Pedersen, J., & Sibun, P. (1992). A Practical Part-of-Speech Tagger. In M. Bates, & O. Stock (Eds.), *Proceedings of the third Conference on Applied Natural Language Processing* (pp.133-140). Stroudsburg, PA: Association for Computational Linguistics. 10.3115/974499.974523

Cyganiak, R. (2011). *Top 100 most popular RDF namespace prefixes.* Retrieved from cyganiak: http://richard.cyganiak.de/blog/2011/02/top-100-most-popular-rdf-namespace-prefixes/

d'Amato, C., Fanizzi, N., Fazzinga, B., Gottlob, G., & Lukasiewicz, T. (2013). *Semantic Web Search and Inductive Reasoning. In Uncertainty Reasoning for the Semantic Web II, International Workshops URSW.* Springer.

D'Souza, J., & Ng, V. (2015). Sieve-Based Entity Linking for the Biomedical Domain. In *Proceeding of the 53rd annual Meeting of the Association for Computational Linguistics: Short Papers* (pp. 297-302). ACL.

Dagan, I., Glickman, O., & Magnini, B. (2005). The PASCAL Recognising Textual Entailment Challenge. In *First PASCAL Machine Learning Challenges Workshop* (pp. 177-90). Springer.

Dalal, V. L. M. (2013). A Survey of Extractive and Abstractive Text Summarization Techniques. *6th International Conference on Emerging Trends in Engineering and Technology*, 109-110. 10.1109/ICETET.2013.31

Dalal, V., & Malik, L. (2017, March). Semantic Graph Based Automatic Text Summarization for Hindi Documents Using Particle Swarm Optimization. In *International Conference on Information and Communication Technology for Intelligent Systems* (pp. 284-289). Springer.

Damljanovic, D., Agatonovic, M., & Cunningham, H. (2010). Natural language interfaces to ontologies: Combining syntactic analysis and ontology-based lookup through the user interaction. *Extended Semantic Web Conference*, 106-120.

Dantas, A., De Azevedo, U., Nunes, A., Amador, A., Marques, M., & Barbosa, I. (2018). Analysis of suicide mortality in brazil: Spatial distribution and socio-economic context. *Revista Brasileira de Psiquiatria (Sao Paulo, Brazil), 40*(1), 12–18. doi:10.1590/1516-4446-2017-2241 PMID:28832751

Daoud, A. S., Sallam, A., & Wheed, M. E. (2017, September). Improving Arabic document clustering using K-means algorithm and Particle Swarm Optimization. In *2017 Intelligent Systems Conference (IntelliSys)* (pp. 879-885). IEEE. doi:10.1109/IntelliSys.2017.8324233

Das, D., & Martins, A. F. (2007). *A Survey on Automatic Text Summarization.* Academic Press.

Das, R., & Sharma, U. (2016). Extracting acoustic feature vectors of South Kamrupi dialect through MFCC. In *2016 3rd International Conference on Computing for Sustainable Global Development, INDIACom 2016* (pp.2808–2811). Academic Press.

Das, S. R., & Chen, M. Y. (2004). Yahoo! for Amazon : Sentiment Extraction from Small Talk on the Web. *Management Science, 53*(9), 1–16.

De Meo, P., Quattrone, G., Terracina, G., & Ursino, D. (2007). An XML-based multiagent system for supporting online recruitment services. *IEEE Transactions on Systems, Man, and Cybernetics. Part A, Systems and Humans, 37*(4), 464–480. doi:10.1109/TSMCA.2007.897696

Debon, R., Coleone, J. D., Bellei, E. A., & De Marchi, A. C. B. (2019). Mobile health applications for chronic diseases: A systematic review of features for lifestyle improvement. *Diabetes & Metabolic Syndrome, 13*(4), 2507–2512. doi:10.1016/j.dsx.2019.07.016 PMID:31405669

Denecke, K., & Deng, Y. (2015). Sentiment analysis in medical settings: New opportunities and challenges. *Artificial Intelligence in Medicine, 64*(1), 17–27. doi:10.1016/j.artmed.2015.03.006 PMID:25982909

Derczynski, L., Maynard, D., Rizzo, G., van Erp, M., Gorrell, G., Troncy, R., Petrak, J., & Bontcheva, K. (2015). Analysis of named entity recognition and linking for tweets. *Information Processing & Management, 51*(2), 32–49. doi:10.1016/j.ipm.2014.10.006

Deshpande, A., Shahane, A., Gadre, D., Deshpande, M., & Joshi, P. M. (2017). A Survey of Various Chatbot Implementation Techniques. *International Journal of Computer Engineering and Applications, 11*, 7. Retrieved from www.ijcea.com

Deshpande, A. R., & Lobo, L. M. R. J. (2013). Text summarization using Clustering technique. *International Journal of Engineering Trends and Technology, 4*(8), 3348–3351.

DeWalt. (2010). *Facebook.* Retrieved 03 19, 2019, from Idea Submission Brochure: https://www.facebook.com/DEWALT/posts/356194591449

DeWalt. (2019). *Best of 2019.* Retrieved 03 12, 2019, from Awards: https://www.dewalt.com/company-info/dewalt-awards

Dietze, S., Yu, H. Q., Giordano, D., Kaldoudi, E., Dovrolis, N., & Taibi, D. (2012). Linked education: interlinking educational resources and the Web of data. In *Proceedings of the ACM Symposium on Applied Computing* (pp. 366-371). Trento: ACM.

Ding, X., Liu, B., & Yu, P. (2008). A holistic lexicon-based approach to opinion mining. *WSDM'08 - Proceedings of the 2008 International Conference on Web Search and Data Mining.* 10.1145/1341531.1341561

Doan, A., Ramakrishnan, R., & Vaithyanathan, S. (2006). Managing information extraction: state of the art and research directions. In *Proceedings of the 2006 ACM SIGMOD international conference on Management of data* (pp. 799-800). ACM. 10.1145/1142473.1142595

Dolan, B., Quirk, C., & Brockett, C. (2004). *Unsupervised Construction of Large Paraphrase Corpora: Exploiting Massively Parallel News Sources. In COLING.* ACL.

Dublin Core Metdata Initiative (DCMI). (2005). *DCMI.* Retrieved from Dublin Core Metdata Initiative: https://www.dublincore.org/

Dutta, A., Meilicke, C., & Stuckenschmidt, H. (2014). Semantifying Triples from Open Information Extraction Systems. *European Starting AI Researcher Symposium (STAIRS),* 111-120.

Dutta, A., Meilicke, C., & Stuckenschmidt, H. (2015). Enriching Structured Knowledge with Open Information. In *Proceedings of the 24th International Conference on World Wide Web* (pp. 267-277). ACM.

Eckley, D. C., & Curtin, K. M. (2013). Evaluating the spatiotemporal clustering of traffic incidents. *Computers, Environment and Urban Systems, 37,* 70–81. doi:10.1016/j.compenvurbsys.2012.06.004

Eduard Hovy, C.-Y. L. (1998). Automated text summarization and the summarist system. *Proceedings of a workshop on held at Baltimore.*

Ehrlinger, L., & Wöß, W. (2016). Towards a Definition of Knowledge Graphs. In *Joint Proceedings of the Posters and Demos Track of the 12th International Conference on Semantic Systems - SEMANTiCS2016 and the 1st International Workshop on Semantic Change & Evolving Semantics (SuCCESS'16)* (pp. 1-4). Leipzig: CEUR-WS.org.

El Abdouli, A., Hassouni, L., & Anoun, H. (2017, April). Mining tweets of Moroccan users using the framework Hadoop, NLP, K-means and basemap. In 2017 Intelligent Systems and Computer Vision (ISCV) (pp. 1-7). IEEE.

Ellis, R., Allen, T., & Tuson, A. (2007). *Applications and Innovations in Intelligent Systems XIV.* Springer-Verlag. doi:10.1007/978-1-84628-666-7

Engels, R., & Bremdal, B. (2000). *Information Extraction: State-of-the-Art Report.* On-To-Knowledge Consortium.

Erling, O., & Mikhailov, I. (2009). RDF Support in the Virtuoso DBMS. In Networked Knowledge - Networked Media - Integrating Knowledge Management, New Media Technologies and Semantic Systems (pp. 7-24). Springer.

Facebook. (2017). *Introduction to The Open Graph Protocol.* Retrieved from The Open Graph Protocol: https://ogp.me/

Fahad, S. K. A., & Yahya, A. E. (2018). Inflectional Review of Deep Learning on Natural Language Processing. In *2018 International Conference on Smart Computing and Electronic Enterprise, ICSCEE 2018,* (pp. 1–4). 10.1109/ICSCEE.2018.8538416

Fahim, A. M., Salem, A. M., Torkey, F. A., & Ramadan, M. A. (2006). An efficient enhanced K-Means clustering algorithm. *Journal of Zhejiang University. Science A, 7*(10), 1626–1633. doi:10.1631/jzus.2006.A1626

Faili, H. (2009). From partial toward full parsing. In *Proceedings of the International Conference RANLP-2009* (pp. 71-75). Borovets, Bulgaria: Academic Press.

Faliagka, E., Tsakalidis, A., & Tzimas, G. (2012). An integrated e-recruitment system for automated personality mining and applicant ranking. *Internet Research, 22*(5), 551–568. doi:10.1108/10662241211271545

Fariño, G. (2011). *Modelo en Espiral de un proyecto de desarrollo de software.* Universidad Estatal de Milagro. Retrieved https://es.ryte.com

Farzandipour, M., Nabovati, E., Sharif, R., Arani, M. H., & Anvari, S. (2017). Patient self-management of asthma using mobile health applications: A systematic review of the functionalities and effects. *Applied Clinical Informatics*, *8*(4), 1068–1081. doi:10.4338/ACI-2017-07-R-0116 PMID:29241254

Fei-Fei, L. (2017). *Querying RDBMS using natural language* (Doctoral dissertation). University of Michigan, Ann Arbor, MI.

Fensel, D., Facca, F. M., Simperl, E., & Toma, I. (2011). *Semantic Web Services*. Springer.

Fensel, D., Lausen, H., Bruijn, J. d., Stollberg, M., Roman, D., Polleres, A., & Domingue, J. (2007). *Enabling Semantic Web Services*. Springer.

Fenstermacher, K. D. (2005). The Tyranny of Tacit Knowledge: What Artificial Intelligence Tells us About Knowledge Representation. IEEE.

Ferguson, C. A. (1975). Toward a Characterization of English Foreigner Talk. *Anthropological Linguistics*, *17*, 1–14.

Ferragina, P., & Scaiella, U. (2010). TAGME: On-the-fly Annotation of Short Text Fragments (by Wikipedia Entities). In *Conference on Information and Knowledge Management (CIKM)* (pp. 1625-1628). ACM.

FinancesOnline. (2019). *EasyAsk review*. Retrieved on December 16, 2019, from https://reviews.financesonline.com/p/easyask/

Følstad, A., Nordheim, C. B., & Bjørkli, C. A. (2018). What makes users trust a chatbot for customer service? An exploratory interview study. *International Conference on Internet Science*, 194-208. 10.1007/978-3-030-01437-7_16

Fontanella, C., Saman, D., Campo, J., Hiance-Steelesmith, D., Bridge, J., Sweeney, H., & Root, E. (2018). Mapping suicide mortality in Ohio: A spatial epidemiological analysis of suicide clusters and area level correlates. *Preventive Medicine*, *106*, 177–184. doi:10.1016/j.ypmed.2017.10.033 PMID:29133266

Fossati, M., Dorigatti, E., & Giuliano, C. (2018). N-ary Relation Extraction for Simultaneous T-Box and A-Box Knowledge Base Augmentation. *Semantic Web*, *9*(4), 413–439.

Franchi, F. (2005). *Newspaper Map*. Retrieved from https://newspapermap.com/

Fränti, P., & Sieranoja, S. (2019). How much can k-means be improved by using better initialization and repeats? *Pattern Recognition*, *93*, 95–112. doi:10.1016/j.patcog.2019.04.014

Freeling. (2019). *Freeling: FreeLing Home Page*. Retrieved from http://nlp.lsi.upc.edu/freeling/node/1

Freeling. (2020a, March 8). *Freeling*. Retrieved from Freeling: http://nlp.lsi.upc.edu/freeling/demo/demo.php

Freeling. (2020b, February 19). *Freeling*. Retrieved from Freeling: http://nlp.lsi.upc.edu/freeling/node/1

Friedman, C., & Elhadad, N. (2013). Natural Language Processing in Health Care and Biomedicine. In *Biomedical informatics*. Springer.

Froberg, B., Morton, S., Mowry, J., & Rusyniak, D. (2019). Temporal and geospatial trends of adolescent intentional overdoses with suspected suicidal intent reported to a state poison control center. *Clinical Toxicology*, *57*(9), 798–805. doi:10.1080/15563650.2018.1554186 PMID:30696297

Fryer, L., & Carpenter, R. (2006). Bots as Language Learning Tools. *Language Learning & Technology*, *20*, 8–14.

Fukuoka, Y., Lindgren, T. G., Mintz, Y. D., Hooper, J., & Aswani, A. (2018). Applying natural language processing to understand motivational profiles for maintaining physical activity after a mobile app and accelerometer-based intervention: The mPED randomized controlled trial. *JMIR mHealth and uHealth*, *6*(6), e10042. doi:10.2196/10042 PMID:29925491

Gabrielli, S., Marie, K., & Corte, C. (2018). SLOWBot (chatbot) lifestyle assistant. In *Proceedings of the 12th EAI International Conference on Pervasive Computing Technologies for healthcare* (pp. 367–370). 10.1145/3240925.3240953

Gales, M., & Young, S. (2007). The application of hidden Markov Models in speech recognition. *Foundations and Trends in Signal Processing*, *1*(3), 195–304. doi:10.1561/2000000004

Galicia, S. (2002). Análisis sintáctico conducido por un diccionario de patrones de manejo sintáctico para lenguaje español. *Computación y Sistemas*, *6*(2), 143–152.

Galitsky, B. (2019). A Social Promotion Chatbot. Developing Enterprise Chatbots. doi:10.1007/978-3-030-04299-8_12

Galitsky, B. (2019). Chatbot Components and Architectures. In Developing Enterprise Chatbots (pp. 13–47). doi:10.1007/978-3-030-04299-8_2

Gangemi, A., Recupero, D. R., Mongiovì, M., Nuzzolese, A. G., & Presutti, V. (2016). Identifying motifs for evaluating open knowledge extraction on the Web. *Knowledge-Based Systems*, *108*, 33–41.

Gantz, J., & Reinsel, D. (2011). Extracting value from chaos. *IDC iview, 1142*(2011), 1-12.

Garcia Brustenga, G., Fuertes Alpiste, M., & Molas Castells, N. (2018). *Briefing paper: chatbots in education.* doi:10.7238/elc.chatbots.2018

García, O. (2008). Gramática contrastiva computacional: MTT vs. HPSG. *Proceedings of VIII congreso de Lingüística General*. Retrieved from http://www.lllf.uam.es/ clg8/actas/index.html

García, V., Florencia-Juárez, R., Sánchez-Solís, P., Rivera, G., & Contreras-Masse, R. (2019). Predicting Airline Customer Satisfaction using k-nn Ensemble Regression Models. *Research in Computing Science*, *148*(6), 205–215. doi:10.13053/rcs-148-6-15

García, V., Sánchez, J. S., Marqués, A. I., Florencia, R., & Rivera, G. (2019). Understanding the apparent superiority of over-sampling through an analysis of local information for class-imbalanced data. *Expert Systems with Applications*, *113026*, 113026. Advance online publication. doi:10.1016/j.eswa.2019.113026

Gardiner, M. (2020, March 09). *Identifying and resolving one-anaphora.* Retrieved from Puzzling: https://files.puzzling.org/academic/gardiner03honours%20%28Identifying%20and%20resolving%20one-anaphora%29.pdf

Gencheva, P., Boyanov, M., Deneva, E., Nakov, P., Kiprov, Y., Koychev, I., & Georgiev, G. (2016). PANcakes Team: A Composite System of Genre-Agnostic Features For Author Profiling—Notebook for PAN at CLEF 2016. In CLEF 2016 Evaluation Labs and Workshop – Working Notes Papers. Évora, Portugal: CEUR-WS.org.

Genest, P. E., & Lapalme, G. (2011). Framework for abstractive summarization using text-to-text generation. In *Proceedings of the 49 th Annual Meeting of the Association for Computational Linguistics* (pp. 64-73). Academic Press.

Genest, P. E., & Lapalme, G. (2011, June). Framework for abstractive summarization using text-to-text generation. In *Proceedings of the workshop on monolingual text-to-text generation* (pp. 64-73). Academic Press.

Genest, P. E., & Lapalme, G. (2012, July). Fully abstractive approach to guided summarization. In *Proceedings of the 50th Annual Meeting of the Association for Computational Linguistics* (pp. 354-358). Academic Press.

Geng, H., Zhao, P., Chen, E., & Cai, Q. (2006, July). A novel automatic text summarization study based on term co-occurrence. In *2006 5th IEEE International Conference on Cognitive Informatics* (Vol. 1, pp. 601-606). IEEE. 10.1109/COGINF.2006.365553

Ge, R., & Mooney, R. J. (2005). A statistical semantic parser that integrates syntax and semantics. *Proceedings of the ninth conference on computational natural language learning*, 9-16. 10.3115/1706543.1706546

Giffinger, R., Fertner, C., Kramar, H., Kalasek, R., Pichler-Milanović, N., & Meijers, E. (2007). Smart cities – Ranking of European medium-sized cities. Vienna, Austria: Centre of Regional Science (SRF), Vienna University of Technology.

Gil-García, R. (2012). *Enacting Electronic Government Success: An Integrative Study of Government-wide Websites, Organizational Capabilities, and Institutions.* Springer. doi:10.1007/978-1-4614-2015-6

Giménez, M., Hernández, D. I., & Pla, F. (2015). Segmenting Target Audiences: Automatic Author Profiling Using Tweets—Notebook for PAN at CLEF 2015. In L. Cappellato, N. Ferro, G. Jones, & E. San Juan (Eds.), CLEF 2015 Evaluation Labs and Workshop – Working Notes Papers. Toulouse, France: CEUR-WS.org.

Giordani, A., & Moschitti, A. (2012). Translating questions to SQL queries with generative parsers discriminatively reranked. In *Proceedings of the International Conference on Computational Linguistics (COLING)* (pp. 401-410). Mumbai, India: Academic Press.

Giordani, A., & Moschitti, A. (2009). Semantic mapping between natural language questions and SQL queries via syntactic pairing. In *International Conference on Application of Natural Language to Information Systems*, (pp. 207-221). Springer.

Githiari, L. M. (2014). *Natural Language Access to Relational Databases: An Ontology Concept Mapping (OCM) Approach.* PhD dissertation.

Godfrey, D., Johns, C., Meyer, C., Race, S., & Sadek, C. (2014). *A case study in text mining: Interpreting twitter data from world cup tweets.* arXiv preprint arXiv:1408.5427

Goldberg. (2017). Neural network methods for natural language processing. *Synthesis Lectures on Human Language Technologies, 10*(1).

Goldberg, A. B., Fillmore, N., Andrzejewski, D., Xu, Z., Gibson, B., & Zhu, X. (2009). May All Your Wishes Come True: A Study of Wishes and How to Recognize Them. *The Annual Conference of the North American Chapter of the ACL.* 10.3115/1620754.1620793

Gómez-Pérez, A., Vila-Suero, D., Montiel-Ponsoda, E., Gracia, J., & Aguado-de-Cea, G. (2013). Guidelines for multilingual linked data. In *Proceedings of the 3rd International Conference on Web Intelligence, Mining and Semantics* (p. 3). Madrid: ACM.

González, J. (2015). Trends and Directions in Computer-Assisted Pronunciation Training. In Investigating English Pronunciation (pp. 314–342). doi:10.1057/978113750943

González-Gallardo, C. E., Montes, A., Sierra, G., Núñez-Juárez, J. A., Salinas-López, A. J., & Ek, J. (2015). *Tweets classification using corpus dependent tags, character and pos n-grams-Notebook for PAN at CLEF 2015.* In Working Notes for CLEF 2015 Conference, Toulouse, France.

González, J. J., Florencia-Juarez, R., Fraire, H. J., Pazos, R. A., Cruz-Reyes, L., & Gómez, C. (2015). Semantic representations for knowledge modelling of a natural language interface to databases using ontologies. *International Journal of Combinatorial Optimization Problems and Informatics, 6*(2), 28–42.

Google Cloud. (n.d.). *Dialogflow.* Retrieved from https://cloud.google.com/dialogflow/?hl=en

Google. (2018). *Sentiment Analysis Tutorial.* Retrieved from https://cloud.google.com/natural-language/docs/sentiment-tutorial

Google. (2019). *Actions on Google.* Retrieved from https://developers.google.com

Google. (2019). *Productos de IA y aprendizaje automático.* Retrieved from https://cloud.google.com/dialogflow/docs/

Google. (n.d.). *Android Studio - Conoce Android Studio.* Retrieved from https://developer.android.com

Google. (n.d.). *Dialogflow - Agents Overview*. Retrieved from https://dialogflow.com

Gopalakrishnan, V., & Ramaswamy, C. (2017). Patient opinion mining to analyze drugs satisfaction using supervised learning. *Journal of Applied Research and Technology, 15*(4), 311–319. doi:10.1016/j.jart.2017.02.005

Goshtasby, A. A. (2012). Similarity and dissimilarity measures. In *Image registration* (pp. 7–66). Springer.

Gottipati, S., Shankararaman, V., & Lin, J. (2018). Text analytics approach to extract course improvement suggestions from students' feedback. *Research and Practice in Technology Enhanced Learning*, 6.

Gottlieb, N. (2009). The Rōmaji Movement in Japan. *The Royal Asiatic Society, 20*, 75–88.

Gracia, J., Montiel-Ponsoda, E., Cimiano, P., Gómez-Pérez, A., Buitelaar, P., & McCrae, J. P. (2012). Challenges for the multilingual Web of Data. *Journal of Web Semantics, 11*, 63–71.

Green, B. F., Jr., Wolf, A. K., Chomsky, C., & Laugh, K. (1961). Baseball: an automatic question-answerer. *Papers presented at the May 9-11, western joint IRE-AIEE-ACM computer conference*, 219-224. 10.1145/1460690.1460714

Green, B. F., Wolf, A. K., Chomsky, C., & Laughery, K. (1961). BASEBALL: An automatic question answerer. In *Proceedings of the Western Joint Computer Conference* (pp. 207-216). Los Angeles, CA: Academic Press.

Green, B. F., Wolf, A. K., Chomsky, C., & Laughery, K. (1961). BASEBALL: An automatic question answerer. In *Proceedings of the Western Joint Computer Conference* (pp. 207-216). Los Angeles, CA: Academic Press.

Greenbacker, C. F. (2011, June). Towards a framework for abstractive summarization of multimodal documents. In *Proceedings of the ACL 2011 Student Session* (pp. 75-80). Portland, OR: Association for Computational Linguistics.

Grivas, A., Krithara, A., & Giannakopoulos, G. (2015). *Author profiling using stylometric and structural feature groupings-Notebook for PAN at CLEF 2015*. In Working Notes of CLEF 2015 -Conference and Labs of the Evaluation forum, Toulouse, France.

Grosz, B. J., Appelt, D. E., Martin, P. A., & Pereira, F. C. (1987). TEAM: an experiment in the design of transportable natural-language interfaces. *Artificial Intelligence, 32*(2), 173–243. doi.org/10.1016/0004-3702(87)90011-7

Grupo de Ingeniería Lingüística. (2020, February 18). *Corpus lingüísticos desde la UNAM*. Retrieved from Corpus lingüísticos desde la UNAM: http://www.corpus.unam.mx/servicio-freeling/

Gualán, R., Freire, R., Tello, A. E., Espinoza, M., & Saquicela, V. (2017). *Automatic RDF-ization of big data semi-structured datasets*. Maskana.

Gudivada, N. V. (2018). Handbook of Statistics. Greenville: Elsevier.

Gulenko, I. (2014). Chatbot for IT Security Training: Using Motivational Interviewing to Improve Security Behaviour. *AIST*, (Supplement), 7–16.

Gunjal, U. P., Rathod, V., & Pise, N. N. (2017). An intelligent system for relational databases. *International Journal of Scientific Research (Ahmedabad, India), 6*(3), 1546–1550.

Guo, S. X. L. (2020, January 1). *ACM Digital Library*. Retrieved from ACM Digital Library: https://dl.acm.org/doi/abs/10.1145/3379247.3379277

Gupta, V., & Lehal, G. S. (2010). A Survey of Text Summarization Extractive Techniques. *Journal of Emerging Technologies in Web Intelligence, 2*(3), 258–268. doi:10.4304/jetwi.2.3.258-268

Gutiérrez Esparza, G., Ochoa Zezzatti, A., Hernández, A., Ponce, J., Álvarez, M., ... Nava, J. (2017). A Sentiment Analysis Model to Analyze Students Reviews of Teacher Performance Using Support Vector Machines. In S. Omatu, S. Rodríguez, G. Villarubia, P. Faria, P. Sitek & J. Prieto (Eds.), *Distributed Computing and Artificial Intelligence, 14th International Conference. DCAI 2017. Advances in Intelligent Systems and Computing. 620.* Cham: Springer.

Gutiérrez, G., Ponce, J., Ochoa, A., & Álvarez, M. (2018). Analyzing Students Reviews of Teacher Performance Using Support Vector Machines by a Proposed Model. In C. Brito-Loeza & A. Espinosa-Romero (Eds.), *Intelligent Computing Systems. 820* (pp. 113–122). Springer International Publishing AG. doi:10.1007/978-3-319-76261-6_9

Gu, Y., Qian, Z., & Chen, F. (2016). From Twitter to detector: Real-time traffic incident detection using social media data. *Transportation Research Part C, Emerging Technologies, 67,* 321–342. doi:10.1016/j.trc.2016.02.011

Habibpour, R., & Khalilpour, K. (2014). A new hybrid k-means and k-nearest-neighbor algorithms for text document clustering. *International Journal of Academic Research, 6*(3), 79–84. doi:10.7813/2075-4124.2014/6-3/A.12

Han, Y. J., Park, S. B., & Park, S. Y. (2016). A natural language interface concordant with a knowledge base. *Computational Intelligence and Neuroscience, 2016,* 1–15. doi:10.1155/2016/9174683 PMID:26904105

Harabagiu, S. M., & Lacatusu, F. (2002). Generating single and multi-document summaries with gistexter. In *Document Understanding Conferences* (pp. 11-12). Academic Press.

Haristiani, N. (2019). Artificial Intelligence (AI) Chatbot as Language Learning Medium: An inquiry. *Journal of Physics: Conference Series, 1387*(1), 012020. Advance online publication. doi:10.1088/1742-6596/1387/1/012020

Hark, T. U. (2018). Graph-Based Suggestion For Text Summarization. *International Conference on Artificial Intelligence and Data Processing (IDAP),* 1-6.

Harlowe, H. (2019). *40 Small Talk Questions Your Chatbot Needs To Know (And Why It Matters).* Retrieved from https://medium.com

Hayes, P., & Welty, C. (2006). *Defining N-ary Relations on the Semantic Web.* Retrieved from W3C: https://www.w3.org/TR/swbp-n-aryRelations/

Heath, T., & Bizer, C. (2011). *Linked Data: Evolving the Web into a Global Data Space.* Morgan & Claypool Publishers.

Heil, C. R., Wu, J. S., Lee, J. J., & Schmidt, T. (2016). A review of mobile language learning applications: Trends, challenges and opportunities. *The EUROCALL Review, 24*(2), 32. Advance online publication. doi:10.4995/eurocall.2016.6402

Helbich, M., Leitner, M., & Kapusta, N. (2012). Geospatial examination of lithium in drinking water and suicide mortality. *International Journal of Health Geographics, 11*(1), 1–8. doi:10.1186/1476-072X-11-19 PMID:22695110

Hellmann, S., Lehmann, J., Auer, S., & Brümmer, M. (2013). Integrating NLP Using Linked Data. In *International Semantic Web Conference* (pp. 98-113). Springer.

Hemphill, C., Godfrey, J., & Doddington, G. (n.d.). *The ATIS Spoken Language Systems Pilot Corpus.* Retrieved from: https://catalog.ldc.upenn.edu/docs/LDC93S4B/corpus.htmlhttps

Hendrix, G. G., Sacerdoti, E. D., Sagalowicz, D., & Slocum, J. (1978). Natural language interfaces to databases – An introduction. *ACM Transactions on Database Systems, 3*(2), 105–147. doi:10.1145/320251.320253

Hennig, L., Umbrath, W., & Wetzker, R. (2008, December). An ontology-based approach to text summarization. In *2008 IEEE/WIC/ACM International Conference on Web Intelligence and Intelligent Agent Technology* (Vol. 3, pp. 291-294). IEEE. 10.1109/WIIAT.2008.175

Hernández, D., Hogan, A., & Krötzsch, M. (2015). Reifying RDF: What Works Well With Wikidata? *International Workshop on Scalable Semantic Web Knowledge Base Systems co-located with ISWC* (pp. 32-47). CEUR.org.

Hill, J., Ford, W. R., & Ferreras, I. G. (2015). Real conversations with artificial intelligence: A comparison between human–human online conversations and human–chatbot conversations. *Computers in Human Behavior, 49*, 245–250. doi:10.1016/j.chb.2015.02.026

Hirschberg, J., & Manning, C. (2015). Advances in natural language processing. *Science, 349*(6245), 261–266. doi:10.1126cience.aaa8685 PMID:26185244

Hogan, A. (2014). *Linked Data & the Semantic Web Standards. In Linked Data Management.* Chapman and Hall/CRC.

Holguin, L., Ochoa-Zezzatti, A., Larios, V. M., Cossio, E., Maciel, R., & Rivera, G. (2019). Small steps towards a smart city: Mobile application that provides options for the use of public transport in Juarez City. In *2019 IEEE International Smart Cities Conference* (ISC2) (pp. 100-105). IEEE. doi: 10.1109/ISC246665.2019.9071728

Holmes, J., & Meyerhoff, M. (2008). *The handbook of language and gender, 25.* John Wiley & Sons.

Holmquist, L. E., Redström, J., & Ljungstrand, P. (1999). Token-Based Access to Digital Information. In *International Symposium on Handheld and Ubiquitous Computer.* Springer. 10.1007/3-540-48157-5_22

Honnibal, M., & Montani, I. (2017). *spaCy 2: Natural language understanding with Bloom embeddings, convolutional neural networks and incremental parsing.* Academic Press.

Houvardas, J., & Stamatatos, E. (2006). N-gram feature selection for authorship identification. In *International Conference on Artificial Intelligence: Methodology, Systems, and Applications,* (pp. 77–86). Springer.

Hoya. (n.d.). *NeoSpeech.* Retrieved from https://neospeech.com

Huang, Z., Chung, W., Ong, T., & Chen, H. (2002). A Graph-based Recommender System for Digital Library. JCDL'02. doi:10.1145/544220.544231

Huang, C. Y., Yang, M. C., Huang, C. Y., Chen, Y. J., Wu, M. L., & Chen, K. W. (2019). A Chatbot-supported Smart Wireless Interactive Healthcare System for Weight Control and Health Promotion. In *IEEE International Conference on Industrial Engineering and Engineering Management* (pp. 1791–1795). doi: 10.1109/IEEM.2018.8607399

Huang, H., & Zhang, B. (2009). Text Segmentation. In L. Liu & M. T. Özsu (Eds.), *Encyclopedia of Database Systems.* Springer. doi:10.1007/978-0-387-39940-9_421

Huang, J., Zhou, M., & Yang, D. (2006). Extracting Chatbot Knowledge from Online Discussion Forums. *IJCAI (United States), 7*, 423–428.

Huddy, G. (2017). *What Is Sentiment Analysis? The importance of understanding how your audience feels about your brand.* Retrieved from https://www.crimsonhexagon.com/blog/what-is-sentiment-analysis/

Hulth, A. (2003). Improved automatic keyword extraction given more linguistic knowledge. *Proceedings of the 2003 conference on Empirical methods in natural language processing,* 216-223. 10.3115/1119355.1119383

Hurtz, G. M., & Donovan, J. J. (2000). Personality and job performance: The Big Five revisited. *The Journal of Applied Psychology, 85*(6), 869–879. doi:10.1037/0021-9010.85.6.869 PMID:11125652

IBM. (1990). *IBM SAA LanguageAccess: A straighter way to your information.* Retrieved December 16, 2019, from https://archive.org/details/TNM_IBM_SAA_Language_Access_-_IBM_20171017_0041

IBM. (n.d.). *Watson - Speech To Text.* Retrieved from https://www.ibm.com/watson

Indu, M., K. V. (2016). Review on text summarization evaluation methods. *International Conference on Research Advances in Integrated Navigation Systems (RAINS)*, 1-4.

INEGI. (2019). Estadísticas a propósito del día mundial para la prevención del suicidio. In *Estadísticas a Propósito Del Día Mundial Para La Prevención Del Suicidio (10 De Septiembre)*. Retrieved from https://www.google.com.mx/url?sa=t&rct=j&q=&esrc=s&source=web&cd=3&cad=rja&uact=8&ved=2ahUKEwjFlOuJpbDlAhULLa0KHRpT-DrMQFjA CegQIBBAC&url=https %3A%2F%2Fwww.inegi.org. mx%2Fcontenidos%2 Fsaladeprensa%2Faproposito %2F2019%2Fsuicidios 2019_Nal.docx&usg=AOvVaw2IN9e

Ingersoll, G. S., Morton, T. S., & Farris, A. L. (2012). Taming text: How to find, organize and manipulate it. Shelter Island.

International Press en Español. (2018). *Abe: Japón quiere comenzar a recibir más trabajadores extranjeros desde abril.* Retrieved from https://internationalpress.jp

International, S. R. I. (2019). *Air Travel Information Service (ATIS)*. Retrieved December 2, 2019, from http://www.ai.sri.com/natural-language/projects/arpa-sls/atis.html

Iqbal, H. R., Ashraf, M. A., & Nawab, R. M. A. (2015). Predicting an author's demographics from text using topic modeling approach-Notebook for PAN at CLEF 2015. In *CLEF 2015 Evaluation Labs and Workshop – Working Notes Papers*. Toulouse, France: CEUR-WS.org.

Isa, D., Kallimani, V. P., & Lee, L. H. (2009). Using the self organizing map for clustering of text documents. *Expert Systems with Applications*, *36*(5), 9584–9591. doi:10.1016/j.eswa.2008.07.082

ISO. (1989). *ISO/IEC 9075:1989 International standard. Information processing systems – Database language SQL with integrity enhancement* (2nd ed.). ISO/IEC.

Istepanian, R., Laxminarayan, S., & Pattichis, C. S. (2006). *M-Health: Emerging Mobile Health Systems*. Springer. doi:10.1007/b137697

Jacques, F. (1999). *Multi-Agent System: An Introduction to Distributed Artificial*. Academic Press.

Jadhavar, R., & Komarraju, A. K. (2018). Sentiment Analysis of Netflix and Competitor Tweets to Classify Customer Opinions. *SAS Global Forum*. Retrieved from https://www.sas.com/content/dam/SAS/support/en/sas-global-forum-proceedings/2018/2708-2018.pdf

Jahangiri, N., Kahani, M., Ahamdi, R., & Sazvar, M. (2011). A study on part of speech tagging. *5th Symposium on Advance and Science and Technology*.

Jain, A. K. (2010). Data clustering: 50 years beyond K-means. *Pattern Recognition Letters*, *31*(8), 651–666. doi:10.1016/j.patrec.2009.09.011

Jancey, R. C. (1966). Multidimensional group analysis. *Australian Journal of Botany*, *14*(1), 127–130. doi:10.1071/BT9660127

Jelinek, F. (1997). *Statistical Methods for Speech Recognition*. Massachusetts Institute of Technology.

Jesús Peral, A. F. (2003). Translation of Pronominal Anaphora between English and Spanish. *Journal of Artificial Intelligence Research*, *18*, 117–147. doi:10.1613/jair.1115

Jettakul, A., Thamjarat, C., Liaowongphuthorn, K., Udomcharoenchaikit, C., Vateekul, P., & Boonkwan, P. (2018). A Comparative Study on Various Deep Learning Techniques for Thai NLP Lexical and Syntactic Tasks on Noisy Data. In *2018 15th International Joint Conference on Computer Science and Software Engineering* (pp.1–6). 10.1109/JCSSE.2018.8457368

Jia, J. (2009). CSIEC: A computer assisted English learning chatbot based on textual knowledge and reasoning. *Knowledge-Based Systems*, *22*(4), 249–255. doi:10.1016/j.knosys.2008.09.001

Jiang, J. (2012). Information extraction from text. In C. Aggarwal & C. Zhai (Eds.), *Mining text data* (pp. 11–41). Springer. doi:10.1007/978-1-4614-3223-4_2

Jiménez, L. M. (2020, March 8). *Scielo*. Retrieved from Scielo: https://scielo.conicyt.cl/scielo.php?script=sci_arttext&pid=S0718-09342001004900009

Jiménez, R., García, V., Florencia-Juárez, R., Rivera, G., & López-Orozco, F. (2018). Minería de opiniones aplicada a la evaluación docente de la Universidad Autónoma de Ciudad Juárez. *Research in Computing Science*, *147*(6), 167–177. doi:10.13053/rcs-147-6-13

Jizba, L. (1997). Reflections on Summarizing and Abstracting. *Journal of Internet Cataloging*, *1*(2), 15–39. doi:10.1300/J141v01n02_03

John, A., & Wilscy, M. (2013, December). Random forest classifier based multi-document summarization system. In 2013 IEEE Recent Advances in Intelligent Computational Systems (RAICS) (pp. 31-36). IEEE. doi:10.1109/RAICS.2013.6745442

Juang, B. H., & Rabiner, L. R. (2004). Automatic Speech Recognition – A Brief History of the Technology Development. Elsevier Encyclopedia of Language and Linguistics, 50(2), 637–655.

Jutte, B. (2012). *Project Risk Management Handbook*. Academic Press.

Kadariya, D., Venkataramanan, R., Yip, H. Y., Kalra, M., Thirunarayanan, K., & Sheth, A. (2019). KBot: Knowledge-enabled personalized chatbot for asthma self-management. In *Proceedings - 2019 IEEE International Conference on Smart Computing (SMARTCOMP)* (pp. 138–143). doi: 10.1109/SMARTCOMP.2019.00043

Kallimani, J. S., K. G. (2010). Information retrieval by text summarization for an Indian regional language. *Proceedings of the 6th International Conference on Natural Language Processing and Knowledge Engineering*, 1-4. 10.1109/NLPKE.2010.5587764

Kallimani, J. S., K. G. (2011). Information extraction by an abstractive text summarization for an Indian regional language. *7th International Conference on Natural Language Processing and Knowledge Engineering*, 319-322. 10.1109/NLPKE.2011.6138217

Kamath, U., Liu, J., & Whitaker, J. (2019). *Deep Learning for NLP and Speech Recognition*. doi:10.1007/978-3-030-14596-5

Kamath, S., & Wagh, R. (2017). Named entity recognition approaches and challenges. *International Journal of Advanced Research in Computer and Communication Engineering*, *6*(2), 259–262.

Kanamori, M., & Kondo, N. (2020). Suicide and Types of Agriculture: A Time-Series Analysis in Japan. *Suicide & Life-Threatening Behavior*, *50*(1), 122–137. doi:10.1111ltb.12559 PMID:31215073

Kanters, S., Cucchiarini, C., & Strik, H. (2009). The goodness of pronunciation algorithm: a detailed performance study. *Speech & Language Technology in Education -SLaTE*, (2), 2–5. Retrieved from http://www.eee.bham.ac.uk/SLaTE2009/papers%5CSLaTE2009-33.pdf

KAON. (2006). *KAON2*. Retrieved from SemanticWeb: http://kaon2.semanticweb.org

Karimi, S., Metke-Jimenez, A., & Nguyen, A. (2015). CADEminer: A System for Mining Consumer Reports on Adverse Drug Side Effects. *Proceedings of the Eighth Workshop on Exploiting Semantic Annotations in Information Retrieval - ESAIR '15*, 47–50. 10.1145/2810133.2810143

Karthikeyan, K. V. K. (2013). Understanding text using Anaphora Resolution. *2013 International Conference on Pattern Recognition, Informatics and Mobile Engineering*, 346-350. 10.1109/ICPRIME.2013.6496498

Kate, R. J., & Mooney, R. J. (2006). Using string-kernels for learning semantic parsers. *Proceedings of the 21st International Conference on Computational Linguistics and the 44th annual meeting of the Association for Computational Linguistics*, 913-920.

Katsavounidis, I., Kuo, C. C. J., & Zhang, Z. (1994). A new initialization technique for generalized Lloyd iteration. *IEEE Signal Processing Letters*, *1*(10), 144–146. doi:10.1109/97.329844

Kaufmann, E., Bernstein, A., & Fischer, L. (2007). NLP-Reduce: A naive but domain independent natural language interface for querying ontologies. *4th European Semantic Web Conference (ESWC)*.

Kaufmann, E., Bernstein, A., & Zumstein, R. (2006). Querix: A natural language interface to query ontologies based on clarification dialogs. *5th International Semantic Web Conference (ISWC 2006)*, 980-981. 10.1007/11926078_78

Kawabata, K. J., Twomey, T., Parker, O., Seghier, M. L., Haji, T., Sakai, K., & Devlin, J. T. (2013). *Inter- and Intra-hemispheric Connectivity Differences When Reading Japanese Kanji and Hiragana* (Vol. 24). Cerebral Cortex. Oxford University Press.

Kemp, S. (2019). *Digital 2019: essential insights into how people around the world use the internet, mobile devices, social media, and e-commerce*. Hootsuite.

Khan, A., & Salim, N. (2014). A Review on Abstractive Summarization Methods. *Journal of Theoretical and Applied Information Technology*, *59*(1), 64–72.

Khan, M. T., Durrani, M., Ali, A., Inayat, I., Khalid, S., & Khan, K. H. (2016). Sentiment analysis and the complex natural language. *Complex Adaptive Systems Modeling*, *4*(1), 2. Advance online publication. doi:10.118640294-016-0016-9

Khan, R., Qian, Y., & Naeem, S. (2019). Extractive based Text Summarization Using K-Means and TF-IDF. *International Journal of Information Engineering and Electronic Business*, *3*(3), 33–44. doi:10.5815/ijieeb.2019.03.05

Khan, S. S., & Ahmad, A. (2004). Cluster center initialization algorithm for K-means clustering. *Pattern Recognition Letters*, *25*(11), 1293–1302. doi:10.1016/j.patrec.2004.04.007

Khan, W., Daud, A., Nasir, J. A., & Amjad, T. (2016). A survey on the state-of-the-art machine learning models in the context of NLP. *Kuwait Journal of Science*, *43*(4), 95–113.

Khurana, D., Koli, A., Khatter, K., & Singh, S. (2017). *Natural Language Processing: State of The Art, Current Trends and Challenges*. Retrieved from https://arxiv.org/abs/1708.05148

Kim, C., Yin, P., Soto, C. X., Blaby, I. K., & Yoo, S. (2018). Multimodal biological analysis using NLP and expression profile. In 2018 New York Scientific Data Summit (NYSDS) (pp. 1-4). IEEE. doi:10.1109/NYSDS.2018.8538944

Kim, H. K., Kim, H., & Cho, S. (2017). Bag-of-concepts: Comprehending document representation through clustering words in distributed representation. *Neurocomputing*, *266*, 336–352. doi:10.1016/j.neucom.2017.05.046

Kim, N., Mickelson, J., Brenner, B., Haws, C., Yurgelun-Todd, D., & Renshaw, P. (2011). Altitude, Gun Ownership, Rural Areas, and Suicide. *The American Journal of Psychiatry*, *168*(1), 49–54. doi:10.1176/appi.ajp.2010.10020289 PMID:20843869

Kim, S., Jeon, S., Kim, J., Park, Y. H., & Yu, H. (2012). Finding core topics: Topic extraction with clustering on tweet. In *2012 Second International Conference on Cloud and Green Computing* (pp. 777-782). IEEE. 10.1109/CGC.2012.120

Kiprov, Y., Hardalov, M., Nakov, P., & Koychev, I. (2015). Experiments in Author Profiling—Notebook for PAN at CLEF 2015. In L. Cappellato, N. Ferro, G. Jones, & E. San Juan (Eds.), CLEF 2015 Evaluation Labs and Workshop – Working Notes Papers. Toulouse, France: CEUR-WS.org.

Kishore, B., & Kumar, A. (2016). Evaluation of Faculty Performance in Education System Using Classification Technique in Opinion Mining Based on GPU. In H. S. Behera & D. P. Mohapatra (Eds.), *Computational Intelligence in Data Mining—Volume 2* (pp. 109–111). Springer India. doi:10.1007/978-81-322-2731-1

Klyne, G., Carroll, J. J., & McBride, B. (2014). *RDF 1.1 Concepts and Abstract Syntax*. Retrieved from W3C: https://www.w3.org/TR/2014/REC-rdf11-concepts-20140225/#section-Datatypes

Kobilarov, G., Scott, T., Raimond, Y., Oliver, S., Sizemore, C., Smethurst, M., . . . Lee, R. (2009). Media Meets Semantic Web - How the BBC Uses DBpedia and Linked Data to Make Connections. In *The Semantic Web: Research and Applications, 6th European Semantic Web Conference* (pp. 723-737). Springer.

Kokare, R., & Wanjale, K. (2015). A natural language query builder interface for structured databases using dependency parsing. *International Journal of Mathematical Sciences and Computing*, *1*(4), 11–20. doi:10.5815/ijmsc.2015.04.02

Koller, A., & Striegnitz, K. (2002). Generation as dependency parsing. In *Proceedings of the 40th Annual Meeting of the Association for Computational Linguistics* (pp. 17-24). Philadelphia, PA: Academic Press.

Konsynski, B. R., Kottemann, J. E., Nunamaker, J. F. Jr, & Stott, J. W. (1984). plexsys-84: An Integrated Development Environment for Information Systems. *Journal of Management Information Systems*, *1*(3), 64–104. doi:10.1080/0742 1222.1984.11517710

Koppel, M., Argamon, S., & Shimoni, A. R. (2002). Automatically categorizing written texts by author gender. *Literary and Linguistic Computing*, *17*(4), 401–412. doi:10.1093/llc/17.4.401

Koshorek, O., Cohen, A., Mor, N., Rotman, M., & Berant, J. (2018). Text Segmentation as a Supervised Learning Task. In *Proceedings of NAACL-HLT* (pp. 469-473). 10.18653/v1/N18-2075

Kosseim, L., Beauregard, S., & Lapalme, G. (2001). Using information extraction and natural language generation to answer email. *Data & Knowledge Engineering*, *38*(1), 85–100. doi:10.1016/S0169-023X(01)00018-0

Kosseim, L., Plamondon, L., & Guillemette, L. J. (2003, June). Answer formulation for question answering. In *Conference of the Canadian Society for Computational Studies of Intelligence* (pp. 24–34). Springer.

Kostagiolas, P. A., Lavranos, C., Korfiatis, N., Papadatos, J., & Papavlasopoulos, S. (2015). Music, musicians and information seeking behaviour: A case study on a community concert band. *The Journal of Documentation*, *71*(1), 3–24. doi:10.1108/JD-07-2013-0083

Krashen, S. D. (1982). Principles and Practice in Second Language Acquisition. Academic Press.

Krejcie, R. V., & Morgan, D. W. (1970). Determining sample size for research activities. *Educational and Psychological Measurement*, *30*(3), 607–610. doi:10.1177/001316447003000308

Krivoruchko, K. (2009). Empirical Bayesian Kriging Implemented in ArcGIS Geostatistical Analyst. *Shanghai Jiaotong Daxue Xuebao. Journal of Shanghai Jiaotong University*, *43*(11), 1813–1817.

Kroenke, D. M., & Auer, D. (2012). *Database processing: Fundamentals, design and implementation*. Pearson Education, Inc.

Kroha, P., & Baeza-Yates, R. (2005). A Case Study: News Classification Based on Term Frequency. In *16th International Workshop on Database and Expert Systems Applications (DEXA'05)* (pp. 428-432). Copenhagen, Denmark: IEEE. 10.1109/DEXA.2005.6

Kubala, F., Barry, C., Bates, M., Bobrow, R., Fung, P., Ingria, R., ... Stallard, D. (1992). BBN Byblos and HARC February 1992 ATIS benchmark results. *Proceedings of the workshop on Speech and Natural Language*, 72-77. 10.3115/1075527.1075544

Kumar, J. N. (2019). Extractive Text Summarization Using Sentence Ranking. *International Conference on Data Science and Communication (IconDSC)*, 1-3.

Kumar, S., & Toshniwal, D. (2016). A data mining approach to characterize road accident locations. *Journal of Modern Transportation, 24*(1), 62–72. doi:10.100740534-016-0095-5

Kumar, U. (2018). *Review on the techniques of Anaphora Resolution.* Review on the Techniques of Anaphora Resolution.

Kuppan, S., & Sobha, L. (2009, June). An Approach to Text Summarization. In *Proceedings of the Third International Workshop on Cross Lingual Information Access: Addressing the Information Need of Multilingual Societies (CLIAWS3)* (pp. 53-60). Academic Press.

Kusner, M. J., Sun, Y., Kolkin, N. I., & Weinberger, K. Q. (2015). From Word Embeddings To Document Distances. In *International Conference on Machine Learning* (pp. 957-966). JMLR.

Larsen, M., Torok, M., Huckvale, K., Reda, B., Berrouiguet, S., & Christensen, H. (2019). Geospatial suicide clusters and emergency responses: An analysis of text messages to a crisis service. In *2019 41st Annual International Conference of the IEEE Engineering in Medicine and Biology Society (EMBS)* (pp.6109–6112). doi:10.1109/EMBC.2019.8856909

Latendresse, M., & Karp, P. D. (2010) An Advanced Web Query Interface for Biological Databases. *Database - The Journal of Biological Databases and Curation.*

Laustanou, K.(2007). *MySpace Music.* Academic Press.

Lavranos, C., Kostagiolas, P., Korfiatis, N., & Papadatos, J. (2015). Information seeking for musical creativity: A systematic literature review. *Journal of the Association for Information Science and Technology, 67*(9), 2105–2117. doi:10.1002/asi.23534

Lee, C. S., Jian, Z. W., & Huang, L. K. (2005). A fuzzy ontology and its application to news *summarization. IEEE Transactions on Systems, Man, and Cybernetics. Part B, Cybernetics, 35*(5), 859–880. doi:10.1109/TSMCB.2005.845032 PMID:16240764

Lee, D. L., Chuang, H., & Seamons, K. (1997). Document ranking and the vector-space model. *IEEE Software, 14*(2), 67–75. doi:10.1109/52.582976

Lee, K., Qadir, A., Hasan, S. A., Datla, V., Prakash, A., Liu, J., & Farri, O. (2017). Adverse drug event detection in tweets with semi-supervised convolutional neural networks. In *Proceedings of the 26th International World Wide Web Conference, WWW 2017*, (pp.705–714). 10.1145/3038912.3052671

Lee, S. S., & Lin, J. C. (2012). An accelerated K-Means clustering algorithm using selection and erasure rules. *Journal of Zhejiang University SCIENCE C, 13*(10), 761–768. doi:10.1631/jzus.C1200078

Lee, Y. J., Ghosh, J., & Grauman, K. (2012, June). *Discovering important people and objects for egocentric video summarization. In 2012 IEEE conference on computer vision and pattern recognition.* IEEE.

Lehmann, J., Isele, R., Jakob, M., Jentzsch, A., Kontokostas, D., Mendes, P. N., ... Bizer, C. (2015). DBpedia - A large-scale, multilingual knowledge base extracted from Wikipedia. *Semantic Web*, *6*(2), 167–195. doi:10.3233/SW-140134

Leung, W. K., Liu, X., & Meng, H. (2019). CNN-RNN-CTC Based End-to-end Mispronunciation Detection and Diagnosis. In *ICASSP 2019-IEEE International Conference on Acoustics, Speech and Signal Processing* (pp. 8132–8136). 10.1109/ICASSP.2019.8682654

Lewis, D. D. (1991). Evaluating text categorization. In *Proceedings of Speech and Natural Language Workshop*. Defense Advanced Research Projects Agency, Morgan Kaufmann. 10.3115/112405.112471

Lexico. (1920). *Formal language*. Retrieved from https://www.lexico.com/en/ definition/formal_language

Lexico. (n.d.). *Natural language*. Retrieved from https://www.lexico.com/en/ definition/natural_language

Li, F. (2017). *Querying RDBMS using natural language* (Doctoral dissertation). University of Michigan, Ann Arbor, MI.

Li, K., Li, J., Ye, G., Zhao, R., & Gong, Y. (2019). Towards Code-switching ASR for End-to-end CTC Models.In *ICASSP 2019-IEEE International Conference on Acoustics, Speech and Signal Processing* (pp.6076–6080). 10.1109/ICASSP.2019.8683223

Li, W., He, L., & Zhuge, H. (2016, December). Abstractive News Summarization based on Event Semantic Link Network. In *Proceedings of COLING 2016, the 26th International Conference on Computational Linguistics: Technical Papers* (pp. 236-246). Academic Press.

Liddy, E. D. (2001). Natural Language Processing. In *Encyclopedia of Library and Information Science* (2nd ed., pp. 1–15). Marcel Decker, Inc.

Li, K., Qian, X., & Meng, H. (2017). Mispronunciation Detection and Diagnosis in L2 English Speech Using Multidistribution Deep Neural Networks. *IEEE/ACM Transactions on Audio, Speech, and Language Processing*, *25*(1), 193–207. doi:10.1109/TASLP.2016.2621675

Linguistic Data Consortium. (1990). *The 2884 ATIS0 speaker-dependent training prompts*. Retrieved from https://catalog.ldc.upenn.edu/docs/LDC93S4B/trn_prmp.html

Little, J., de Ga, M., Özyer, T., & Alhajj, R. (2004). Query builder: A natural language interface for structured databases. In *International Symposium on Computer and Information Sciences* (pp. 470-479). Springer. 10.1007/978-3-540-30182-0_48

Litwin, E. (1995). *Tecnología educativa: Política, historias, propuestas*. Paidós SA.

Litwin, E. (2005). *Tecnologías educativas en tiempos de Internet*. Amorrotu.

Liu, B. (2012). Sentiment Analysis: A Fascinating Problem. In Sentiment Analysis and Opinion Mining (p. 7). Morgan & Claypool Publishers.

Liu, B., & Hu, M. (2004). *Opinion Mining, Sentiment Analysis, and Opinion Spam Detection*. Retrieved from https://www.cs.uic.edu/~liub/FBS/sentiment-analysis.html

Liu, B. (2011). *Web Data Mining: Exploring Hyperlinks, Contents, and Usage Data*. Springer Berlin Heidelberg. doi:10.1007/978-3-642-19460-3

Liu, J., Fang, C., & Ansari, N. (2016). Request Dependency Graph: A Model for Web Usage Mining in Large-Scale Web of Things. *IEEE Internet of Things Journal*, *3*(4), 598–608.

Li, Y., & Yang, T. (2017). Word Embedding for Understanding Natural Language : A Survey. In S. Srinivasan (Ed.), *Guide to Big Data Applications* (pp. 83–104)., doi:10.1007/978-3-319-53817-4

Lloberes, M., Castellón, I., & Padró, L. (2016). Enhancing FreeLing rule-based dependency grammars with subcategorization frames. In *Proceedings of the Third International Conference on Dependency Linguistic*s (pp. 201-210). Uppsala, Sweden: Academic Press.

Llopis, M., & Ferrández, A. (2013). How to make a natural language interface to query databases accessible to everyone: An example. *Computer Standards & Interfaces*, *35*(5), 470–481. doi:10.1016/j.csi.2012.09.005

Lloyd, S. (1982). Least squares quantization in PCM. *IEEE Transactions on Information Theory*, *28*(2), 129–137. doi:10.1109/TIT.1982.1056489

Long, M. H. (1981). Input, Interaction and Second Language Acquisition. [Pennsylvania.]. *Annals of the New York Academy of Sciences*, *379*(1), 259–278. doi:10.1111/j.1749-6632.1981.tb42014.x

Loos, B., & Biemann, C. (2008). Supporting Web-based Address Extraction with Unsupervised Tagging. In C. Preisach, H. Burkhardt, L. Schmidt-Thieme, & R. Decker (Eds.), *Data Analysis, Machine Learning and Applications. Studies in Classification, Data Analysis, and Knowledge Organization* (pp. 577–584). Springer. doi:10.1007/978-3-540-78246-9_68

López-Monroy, A. P., Gómez, M. M., Escalante, H. J., & Pineda, L. V. (2014). Using Intra-Profile Information for Author Profiling—Notebook for PAN at CLEF 2014. CLEF.

Löwgren, M. (2013). Chatbot como recurso didáctico en la enseñanza de español como lengua extranjera. Academic Press.

Luhn, H. P. (1957). A statistical approach to mechanized encoding and searching of literary information. *IBM Journal of Research and Development*, *1*(4), 309–317. doi:10.1147/rd.14.0309

Luna-Aveiga, H., Medina-Moreira, J., Lagos-Ortiz, K., Apolinario, O., Paredes-Valverde, M. A., Salas-Zárate, M., & Valencia-García, R. (2018). Sentiment Polarity Detection in Social Networks: An Approach for Asthma Disease Management. In N.-T. Le, T. van Do, N. T. Nguyen, & H. A. Le Thi (Eds.), *Advanced Computational Methods for Knowledge Engineering* (pp. 141–152). Springer International Publishing. doi:10.1007/978-3-319-61911-8_13

Luo, D., Xia, L., Zhang, C., & Wang, L. (2019). Automatic Pronunciation Evaluation in High-states English Speaking Tests Based on Deep Neural Network Models. In *2019 2nd International Conference on Artificial Intelligence and Big Data, ICAIBD* (pp.124–128). 10.1109/ICAIBD.2019.8836976

Lyons, J. (1995). Metalinguistic preliminaries. In *Linguistic Semantics: An Introduction* (p. 2). Cambridge University. Retrieved from https://books.google.com.mx/ books?id=Na2g1ltaKuAC&printsec= frontcover&dq=semantic s+linguistic&hl= es-419&sa=X&ved=0ahUKEwioh J_27NLmAhUQ2qwKHWyZD ocQ6AEIKTAA#v=onepage &q=semanticslinguistic&f=false

Ma, S., Sun, X., Xu, J., Wang, H., Li, W., & Su, Q. (2017). *Improving semantic relevance for sequence-to-sequence learning of Chinese social media text summarization.* arXiv preprint arXiv:1706.02459

MacEachren, A., Robinson, A., Hopper, S., Gardner, S., Murray, R., Gahegan, M., & Hetzler, E. (2005). Visualizing geospatial information uncertainty: What we know and what we need to know. *Cartography and Geographic Information Science*, *32*(3), 139–160. doi:10.1559/1523040054738936

Machine Learning Research Group. (2001). *Geoquery Data.* Retrieved from http://www.cs.utexas.edu/users/ml/nldata/ geoquery.html

MacQueen, J. (1967). Some methods for classification and analysis of multivariate observations. In *Proceedings of the fifth Berkeley symposium on mathematical statistics and probability* (*Vol. 1*, No. 14, pp. 281-297). Academic Press.

Mahajan, M., Nimbhorkar, P., & Varadarajan, K. (2012). The planar k-means problem is NP-hard. *Theoretical Computer Science*, *442*, 13–21. doi:10.1016/j.tcs.2010.05.034

Mahaki, B., Mehrabi, Y., Kavousi, A., Mohammadian, Y., & Kargar, M. (2015). Applying and comparing empirical and full Bayesian models in study of evaluating relative risk of suicide among counties of Ilam province. *Journal of Education and Health Promotion*, *4*(1), 50. doi:10.4103/2277-9531.162331 PMID:26430677

Maharjan, S., & Solorio, T. (2015). Using wide range of features for author profiling. In *Working Notes Papers of the CLEF 2015 Evaluation Labs. Volume 1391 of CEUR Workshop Proceedings*. CEUR.

Maharjan, S., Shrestha, P., & Solorio, T. (2014). A simple approach to author profiling in MapReduce. In *Proceedings of the Working Notes of CLEF 2014—Conference and Labs of the Evaluation Forum* (vol. 1180, pp. 1121–1128). CEUR.

Malik, U. (2018, September 4). *Text Summarization with NLTK in Python*. Retrieved from Stack Abuse: https://stackabuse.com/text-summarization-with-nltk-in-python/

Mamani, R. (2018). *Internet: ¿Cuántos megas consumen las redes sociales?* Retrieved from https://larepublica.pe

Manola, F., Miller, E., & McBride, B. (2014). *RDF 1.1 Primer*. Retrieved from W3C: https://www.w3.org/TR/2014/NOTE-rdf11-primer-20140624/

Manuel Palomar, L. M. (2001). An Algorithm for Anaphora Resolution in. *Computational Linguistics*, *27*(4), 545–567. doi:10.1162/089120101753342662

Mao, G., Su, J., Yu, S., & Luo, D. (2019). Multi-Turn Response Selection for Chatbots With Hierarchical Aggregation Network of Multi-Representation. *IEEE Access: Practical Innovations, Open Solutions*, *7*, 111736–111745. doi:10.1109/ACCESS.2019.2934149

Markov, I., Gómez-Adorno, H., Sidorov, G., & Gelbukh, A. (2016). Adapting Cross genre Author Profiling to Language and Corpus— Notebook for PAN at CLEF 2016. In K. Balog, L. Cappellato, N. Ferro, & C. Macdonald (Eds.), CLEF 2016 Evaluation Labs and Workshop – Working Notes Papers. Évora, Portugal: CEUR-WS.org.

Martinez-Rodriguez, J. L., Hogan, A., & Lopez-Arevalo, I. (2018). Information Extraction meets the Semantic Web: A Survey. *Semantic Web*, *11*(2), 1–81. doi:10.3233/SW-180333

Marukawa, K., Koga, M., Shima, Y., & Fujisawa, H. (1993). A Post-Processing Method for Handwritten Kanji Name Recognition Using Furigana Information. In *Proceedings of 2nd International Conference on Document Analysis and Recognition* (pp. 218-221). IEEE. 10.1109/ICDAR.1993.395745

Marzinotto, G., Damnati, G., & Béchet, F. (2019). Adapting a FrameNet Semantic Parser for Spoken Language Understanding using Adversarial Learning. *Proc. Interspeech*, *799-803*, 799–803. Advance online publication. doi:10.21437/Interspeech.2019-2732

McBride, B. (2004). *RDF/XML Syntax Specification*. Retrieved from W3C: http://www.w3.org/TR/REC-rdf-syntax/

McBride, B. (2004). *The Resource Description Framework (RDF) and its Vocabulary Description Language RDFS. In Handbook on Ontologies*. Springer.

McCarthy, D., Koeling, R., Weeds, J., & Carroll, J. A. (2004). Finding Predominant Word Senses in Untagged Text. In *Proceedings of the 42nd Annual Meeting of the Association for Computational Linguistics.* (pp. 279-286). ACL.

McCollister, C., Huang, S., & Luo, B. (2015). Building Topic Models to Predict Author Attributes from Twitter Messages—Notebook for PAN at CLEF 2015. In L. Cappellato, N. Ferro, G. Jones, & E. San Juan (Eds.), CLEF 2015 Evaluation Labs and Workshop – Working Notes Papers. Toulouse, France: CEUR-WS.org.

McCrae, J. P. (2018). *The Linked Open Data Cloud*. Retrieved from lod-cloud: https://lod-cloud.net

McKeown, K., Hirschberg, J., Galley, M., & Maskey, S. (2005, March). From text to speech summarization. In *Proceedings (ICASSP'05) IEEE International Conference on Acoustics, Speech, and Signal Processing, 2005 (Vol. 5*, pp. v-997). IEEE.

McKirdy, A. (2015). *Microsoft says Line's popular Rinna character is new way to engage customers.* Retrieved from https://www.japantimes.co.jp

Meaning Cloud. (2019). *General questions.* Retrieved from Meaning Cloud: https://www.meaningcloud.com/

Mejía, J., Ochoa-Zezzatti, A., Contreras-Masse, R., & Rivera, G. (2020). Intelligent System for the Visual Support of Caloric Intake of Food in Inhabitants of a Smart City Using a Deep Learning Model. In *Applications of Hybrid Metaheuristic Algorithms for Image Processing* (pp. 441–455). Springer. doi:10.1007/978-3-030-40977-7_19

Meltwater. (2019). *About Meltwater.* Retrieved from Meltwater: https://www.meltwater.com/about/

Mendes, P. N., Jakob, M., García-Silva, A., & Bizer, C. (2011). DBpedia spotlight: shedding light on the web of documents. In *Proceedings of the 7th International Conference on Semantic Systems, I-SEMANTICS* (pp. 1-8). ACM.

Méndez, E. M., & Moreiro, J. A. (1999). Lenguaje natural e Indización automatizada. *Ciencias de la Información, 30*, 11–24.

Meng, L., Huang, R., & Gu, J. (2013). A review of semantic similarity measures in Wordnet. *International Journal of Hybrid Information Technology, 6*(1), 1–12.

Merriam-Webster. (2019). *Opinion.* Retrieved from Merriam-Webster Dictionary: https://www.merriam-webster.com/dictionary/opinion

Mexicano, A., Cervantes, S., Rodríguez, R., Pérez, J., Almanza, N., Jiménez, M. A., & Azuara, A. (2016). Identifying stable objects for accelerating the classification phase of k-means. In *International Conference on P2P, Parallel, Grid, Cloud and Internet Computing* (pp. 903-912). Springer.

Microsoft. (2010). *Chapter 32 - English Query Best Practices.* Retrieved December 16, 2019, from http://technet.microsoft.com/es-mx/library/cc917659(en-us,printer).aspx

Microsoft. (2010). *How to Navigate & use the Query by Example (QBE) interface in Microsoft Access 2007.* Retrieved from https://ms-office.wonderhowto.com/how-to/navigate-use-query-by-example-qbe-interface-microsoft-access-2007-398173/

Microsoft. (2017). *Visual Studio - Edición del código.* Retrieved from https://visualstudio.microsoft.com

Microsoft. (2019). *Natural Language Processing.* Retrieved from https://www.microsoft.com/en-us/research/group/natural-language-processing/

Mikolov, T., Chen, K., Corrado, G., & Dean, J. (2013). Efficient estimation of word representations in vector space. In *1st International Conference on Learning Representations, ICLR 2013 - Workshop Track Proceedings* (pp.1–12). Academic Press.

Mikolov, T., Chen, K., Corrado, G., & Dean, J. (2013). Efficient Estimation of Word Representations in Vector Space. *Proceedings of the International Conference on Learning Representations* (pp. 1-12). Academic Press.

Mikolov, T., Sutskever, I., Chen, K., Corrado, G. S., & Dean, J. (2013). Distributed Representations of Words and Phrases and their Compositionality. In Advances in Neural Information Processing Systems (pp. 3111-3119). NIPS.

Mileo, A., Abdelrahman, A., Policarpio, S., & Hauswirth, M. (2013). StreamRule: A Nonmonotonic Stream Reasoning System for the Semantic Web. In Web Reasoning and Rule Systems (pp. 247-252). Springer.

Min, J., & Min, K. (2018). Night noise exposure and risk of death by suicide in adults living in metropolitan areas. *Depression and Anxiety*, *35*(9), 876–883. doi:10.1002/da.22789 PMID:29953702

Minock, M., Olofsson, P., & Näslund, A. (2008). Towards building robust natural language interfaces to databases. In *International Conference on Application of Natural Language to Information Systems*, (pp. 187-198). Springer. 10.1007/978-3-540-69858-6_19

Mintz, M., Bills, S., Snow, R., & Jurafsky, D. (2009). Distant Supervision for Relation Extraction Without Labeled Data. In *Proceedings of the Joint Conference of the 47 Annual meeting of the Association for Computational Linguistics* (pp. 1003-1011). ACL.

Mitchell, R. (2018). *Web Scraping with Python*. O'Reilly Media, Inc.

Mitchell, T. M., & ... (1997). *Machine learning*. McGraw-Hill.

Mitkov, R. (2014). *Anaphora Resolution*. Routledge. doi:10.4324/9781315840086

Moawad, I. F., & Aref, M. (2012, November). Semantic graph reduction approach for abstractive Text Summarization. In *2012 Seventh International Conference on Computer Engineering & Systems (ICCES)* (pp. 132-138). IEEE. 10.1109/ICCES.2012.6408498

Mohanty, S. P., Choppali, U., & Kougianos, E. (2016). Everything you wanted to know about smart cities: The Internet of things is the backbone. *IEEE Consumer Electronics Magazine*, *5*(3), 60–70. doi:10.1109/MCE.2016.2556879

Molina-GonzálezD.Martínez-CámaraE.Martín-ValdiviaM.Perea-OrtegaJ. (2013). *iSOL*. Retrieved from http://timm. ujaen.es/recursos/isol/

Mo, Q., & Chen, Y. (2012). Ontology-Based Web Information Extraction. In M. Zhao & J. Sha (Eds.), *Communications and Information Processing* (Vol. 288, pp. 118–119). Springer Berlin Heidelberg. doi:10.1007/978-3-642-31965-5_14

Morales, D., Nguyen, H., & Chin, T. (2017). *A Neural Chatbot with Personality*. Stanford University.

Moratanch, N., & Chitrakala, S. (2017, January). A survey on extractive text summarization. In *2017 International Conference on Computer, Communication and Signal Processing (ICCCSP)* (pp. 1-6). IEEE.

Moro, A., Raganato, A., & Navigli, R. (2014). Entity Linking meets Word Sense Disambiguation: A Unified Approach. *Transactions of the Association for Computational Linguistics*, *2*, 231–244. doi:10.1162/tacl_a_00179

Muangkammuen, P., Intiruk, N., & Saikaew, K. R. (2018). Automated Thai-FAQ chatbot using RNN-LSTM. In *2018 22nd International Computer Science and Engineering Conference* (pp. 1–4). 10.1109/ICSEC.2018.8712781

Muhammad, H. Z., Nasrun, M., Setianingsih, C., & Murti, M. A. (2018). Speech recognition for English to Indonesian translator using hidden Markov model. In *2018 International Conference on Signals and Systems, ICSigSys* (pp.255–260). 10.1109/ICSIGSYS.2018.8372768

Munroe, K. D., & Papakonstantiou, Y. (2000). BBQ: A visual interface for integrated browsing and querying of XML. In *Working Conference on Visual Database Systems* (pp. 277-296). Springer. 10.1007/978-0-387-35504-7_18

Murveit, H., Butzberger, J., & Weintraub, M. (1991). Speech Recognition in SRI's Resource Management and ATIS Systems. *Proceedings of the workshop on Speech and Natural Language (HTL'91)*, 94-100. Retrieved from: https://www.aclweb.org/anthology/H91-1015.pdf

Mvumbi, T. (2016). *Natural language interface to relational database: A simplified customization approach* (Master thesis). University of Cape Town. Cape Town, South Africa.

Nadkarni, P. M., Ohno-Machado, L., & Chapman, W. W. (2011). Natural language processing: An introduction. *Journal of the American Medical Informatics Association, 18*(5), 544–551. doi:10.1136/amiajnl-2011-000464 PMID:21846786

Naiman, N., Frohlich, M., & Todesco, A. (1975). The Good Second Language Learner. *TESL Talk, 6,* 58–76.

Najib, F., Cheema, W. A., & Nawab, R. M. A. (2015). Author's traits prediction on twitter data using content based approach. In *CLEF 2015 Evaluation Labs and Workshop – Working Notes Papers.* Toulouse, France: CEUR-WS.org.

Nakayama, T., Patterson, K. E., & Humphreys, G. W. (1993). Phonologically Mediated Access to Meaning for Kanji. *Journal of Experimental Psychology, 3,* 491–514.

Narayanan, V., Arora, I., & Bhatia, A. (2016). *Fast and accurate sentiment classification using an enhanced Naive Bayes model.* Retrieved from http://sentiment.vivekn.com/about/

National Institute of Statistics and Geography. (2017). *State of mind of the tweeters in the United Mexican States.* Retrieved from http://internet.contenidos.inegi.org.mx/contenidos/Productos

NCBO BioPortal. (2019). *BioPortal.* Retreived from https://bioportal.bioontology.org/ontologies

Negi, S. (2016). Suggestion Mining from Opinionated Text. Association for Computational Linguistics, 119–125.

Negi, S. (2019). *Suggestion mining from text.* Retrieved from Access to Research at NUI Galway: https://aran.library.nuigalway.ie/bitstream/handle/10379/14987/2019SapnaNegiPhD.pdf

Negi, S., & Buitelaar, P. (2015). Curse or Boon? Presence of Subjunctive Mood in Opinionated Text. *International Conference on Computational Semantics,* 101-106.

Negi, S., Asooja, K., Mehrotra, S., & Buitelaar, P. (2016). A Study of Suggestions in Opinionated Texts and their Automatic Detection. *Conference on Lexical and Computational Semantics.* 10.18653/v1/S16-2022

Negi, S., & Buitelaar, P. (2015). Towards the Extraction of Customer-to-Customer Suggestions from Reviews. In *Conference on Empirical Methods in Natural Language Processing,* (pp. 2159-2167). 10.18653/v1/D15-1258

Neirotti, P., De Marco, A., Cagliano, A. C., Mangano, G., & Scorrano, F. (2014). Current trends in Smart City initiatives: Some stylised facts. *Cities (London, England), 38,* 25–36. doi:10.1016/j.cities.2013.12.010

Nenkova, A., & McKeown, K. (2011). Automatic summarization. *Foundations and Trends in Information Retrieval, 5*(2-3), 103–233. doi:10.1561/1500000015

Nguyen, V., Bodenreider, O., & Sheth, A. (2014). Don't Like RDF Reification?: Making Statements About Statements Using Singleton Property. In *Proceedings of the 23 rd International conference on World Wide Web* (pp. 759-770). ACM.

Nguyen, D. T., Hoang, T. D., & Pham, S. B. (2012). A Vietnamese natural language interface to database. In *Proceedings of 2012 IEEE Sixth International Conference on Semantic Computing* (pp. 130-133). Palermo, Italy: IEEE. 10.1109/ICSC.2012.33

Nichante, R., Giripunje, S., Nikam, A., Arsod, S., & Sonwane, N. (2017). Hindi language as a graphical user interface to relational database for transport system. *International Research Journal of Engineering and Technology, 4*(3), 349–353.

Nihalani, N., Motwani, M., & Silaka, S. (2011). Natural language interface to database using semantic matching. *International Journal of Computers and Applications, 31*(11), 29–34.

Nihalani, N., Silakari, S., & Motwani, M. (2011). Natural language interface for database: A brief review. *International Journal of Computer Science Issues, 8*(2), 600–608.

Nimavat, K., & Champaneria, T. (2017). Chatbots: An Overview Types, Architecture, Tools and Future Possibilities. *International Journal of Scientific Research and Development, 5*(7), 1019–1026.

Niu, C., Zhang, J., Yang, X., & Xie, Y. (2018). A study on landmark detection based on CTC and its application to pronunciation error detection. In *2017 Asia-Pacific Signal and Information Processing Association Annual Summit and Conference (APSIPA ASC)* (pp. 636–640). doi:10.1109/APSIPA.2017.8282103

NLP APIs. (2016). Retrieved November 18, 2019, from https://tedboy.github.io/nlps/generated/generated/gensim.summarization.summarize.html

NLP. S. (2020, February 19). *Stanford NLP*. Retrieved from Stanford NLP: https://nlp.stanford.edu/

NLTK. (2020, February 19). *NLTK*. Retrieved from NLTK: https://www.nltk.org/

Noda, I., & Stone, P. (2003). The RoboCup Soccer Server and CMUnited Clients: Implemented Infrastructure for MAS Research. *Autonomous Agents and Multi-Agent Systems, 7*(1/2), 101–120. doi:10.1023/A:1024128904944

Nowson, S., Perez, J., Brun, C., Mirkin, S., & Roux, C. (2015). Xrce personal language analytics engine for multilingual author profiling. *Working Notes Papers of the CLEF.*

Nuruzzaman, M., & Hussain, O. K. (2018). A Survey on Chatbot Implementation in Customer Service Industry through Deep Neural Networks. In *2018 IEEE 15th International Conference on e-Business Engineering (ICEBE)* (pp. 54–61). 10.1109/ICEBE.2018.00019

Nuzzolese, A. G., Gangemi, A., Presutti, V., Draicchio, F., Musetti, A., & Ciancarini, P. (2013). *Tìpalo: A Tool for Automatic Typing of DBpedia Entities. In The Semantic Web: ESWC.* Springer.

Nwet, S. S. (2018). Extractive Summarization for Myanmar Language. *International Joint Symposium on Artificial Intelligence and Natural Language Processing (iSAI-NLP)*, 1-6.

Ochoa Ortiz-Zezzatti, A., Rivera, G., Gómez-Santillán, C., & Sánchez Lara, B. (2019). *Handbook of Research on Metaheuristics for Order Picking Optimization in Warehouses to Smart Cities.* IGI Global. doi:10.4018/978-1-5225-8131-4

Ochoa, A., Hernádez, A., Sánchez, J., Muñoz-Zavala, A., & Ponce, J. (2008). Determining the ranking of a new participant in eurovision using cultural algorithms and data mining. In *18th International Conference on Electronics, Communications and Computers. (CONIELECOMP).* IEEE. 10.1109/CONIELECOMP.2008.27

Ochoa, A., Tcherassi, A., Shingareva, I., Padméterakiris, A., Gyllenhaale, J., & Hernández, J.(2007). Italianitá: Discovering a Pygmalion effect on Italian communities using data mining. *Advances in Computer Science and Engineering, 57.*

Ochoa, A., Urrea, B., Mejía, J., & Avelar, L. (2019). Intelligent system for predicting motorcycle accident by reaching into a smart city using a kriging model to achieve its reduction and the reduction of deaths in the medium term. Smart technologies for smart cities.

Ochoa, A., González, S., Esquivel, C., Matozzi, G., & Maffucci, A. (2009). Musical Recommendation on Thematic Web Radio. *Journal of Computers, 4*(8), 742–746. doi:10.4304/jcp.4.8.742-746

Oka, M., Kubota, T., Tsubaki, H., & Yamauchi, K. (2015). Analysis of impact of geographic characteristics on suicide rate and visualization of result with Geographic Information System. *Psychiatry and Clinical Neurosciences, 69*(6), 375–382. doi:10.1111/pcn.12254 PMID:25384900

Okumura, M., Fukushima, T., & Nanba, H. (2001). Text Summarization Challenge 2/Text Summarization Evaluation at NTCIR Workshop3. In *Proceedings of the third NTCIR Workshop Meeting* (pp. 1-7). Academic Press.

Omre, H. (1987). Bayesian kriging-Merging observations and qualified guesses in Kriging. *Mathematical Geology, 19*(1), 25–39. doi:10.1007/BF01275432

Open Archives Initiative. (2019). *Open Archives Initiative (OAI).* Retrieved from Open Archives Initiative: http://openarchives.org/

Opitz, D. (1999). *Bagging Classifiers.* Retrieved from Popular Ensemble Methods: An Empirical Study: https://www.cs.cmu.edu/afs/cs/project/jair/pub/volume11/opitz99a-html/node3.html

Ortigosa, A., Carro, R. M., & Quiroga, J. I. (2014). Predicting user personality by mining social interactions in Facebook. *Journal of Computer and System Sciences, 80*(1), 57–71. doi:10.1016/j.jcss.2013.03.008

Oxford, R., & Crookall, D. (2014). Research on language learning strategies: Methods, Findings, and Instructional issues. *The Modern Language, 73*(4), 404–419. doi:10.1111/j.1540-4781.1989.tb05321.x

Pak, A., & Paroubek, P. (2010). Twitter as a Corpus for Sentiment Analysis and Opinion Mining. In LREc (pp.1320–1326). Academic Press.

Pak, I., & Teh, P. L. (2018). Text Segmentation Techniques: A Critical Review. In I. Zelinka, P. Vasant, V. Duy, & T. Dao (Eds.), *Innovative Computing, Optimization and its Applications* (pp. 167–181). doi:10.1007/978-3-319-66984-7_10

Palomar, M. (2001, December 1). *Universidad De Alicante.* Retrieved from Universidad De Alicante: https://www.dlsi.ua.es/~mpalomar/p545_s.pdf

Palomino-Garibay, A., Camacho-González, A., FierroVillaneda, R., Hernández-Farias, I., Buscaldi, D., & Meza-Ruiz, I. (2015). A Random Forest Approach for Authorship Profiling—Notebook for PAN at CLEF 2015. In L. Cappellato, N. Ferro, G. Jones, & E. San Juan (Eds.), CLEF 2015 Evaluation Labs and Workshop – Working Notes Papers. Toulouse, France: CEUR-WS.org.

Panayotov, V., Chen, G., Povey, D., & Khudanpur, S. (2015). Librispeech: An ASR corpus based on public domain audio books. In *2015 IEEE International Conference on Acoustics, Speech and Signal Processing (ICASSP)* (pp. 5206–5210). 10.1109/ICASSP.2015.7178964

Pang, B., & Lee, L. (2008). Opinion mining and sentiment analysis. *Foundations and Trends in Information Retrieval, 2*(1), 94.

Parida, S. M. (2019). Abstract Text Summarization: A Low Resource Challenge. *Proceedings of the 2019 Conference on Empirical Methods in Natural Language Processing and the 9th International Joint Conference on Natural Language Processing,* 5996-6000. 10.18653/v1/D19-1616

Pazos, R. A., Aguirre, A. G., Aguirre, M. A., & Martínez, J. A. (2015). Interface for composing queries for complex databases for inexperienced users. In E. Onieva, I. Santos, E. Osaba, H. Quintián, & E. Corchado (Eds.), *Hybrid Artificial Intelligent Systems. HAIS 2015* (pp. 61–72). Springer. doi:10.1007/978-3-319-19644-2_6

Pazos, R. A., Aguirre, M. A., González, J. J., Martínez, J. A., Pérez, J., & Verástegui, A. A. (2016). Comparative study on the customization of natural language interfaces to databases. *SpringePlus, 5*(553), 1–30. doi:10.118640064-016-2164-y

Pazos, R. A., González, J. J., Aguirre, M. A., Martínez, J. A., & Fraire, H. J. (2013). Natural Language Interfaces to Databases: An Analysis of the State of the Art. In *Recent Advances on Hybrid Intelligent Systems* (pp. 463–480). Springer-Verlag. doi:10.1007/978-3-642-33021-6_36

Pellegrini, T., Fontan, L., Mauclair, J., Farinas, J., & Robert, M. (2014). The goodness of pronunciation algorithm applied to disordered speech. In *Proceedings of the Annual Conference of the International Speech Communication Association, INTERSPEECH* (pp.1463–1467).

Peng, Y., Moh, M., & Moh, T. S. (2016). Efficient adverse drug event extraction using Twitter sentiment analysis. In *Proceedings of the 2016 IEEE/ACM International Conference on Advances in Social Networks Analysis and Mining, ASONAM 2016,* (pp. 1011–1018). 10.1109/ASONAM.2016.7752365

Penisi, R., & Kim, G. (2003). Customer Driven Innovation Process. *IEEE/CPMT/SEMI International Electronics Manufacturing Technology (IEMT) Symposium.*

Peral, J. (2003). Translation of Pronominal Anaphora between English and Spanish: Discrepancies and Evaluation. *Journal of Artiðcial Intelligence Research,* 117-147.

Pérez, J., Almanza, N. N., & Romero, D. (2018). Balancing effort and benefit of K-means clustering algorithms in Big Data realms. *PLoS One, 13*(9). PMID:30183705

Pérez, J., Almanza, N., Ruiz-Vanoye, J., Pazos, R., Sáenz, S., Rodríguez, J., & Martínez, A. (2018). A-means: Improving the cluster assignment phase of k-means for Big Data. *International Journal of Combinatorial Optimization Problems and Informatics, 9*(2), 3–10.

Pérez, J., Mexicano, A., Santaolaya, R., Hidalgo, M., Moreno, A., & Pazos, R. (2012). Improvement to the K-Means algorithm through a heuristics based on a bee honeycomb structure. In *2012 Fourth World Congress on Nature and Biologically Inspired Computing (NaBIC)* (pp. 175-180). IEEE. 10.1109/NaBIC.2012.6402258

Pérez, J., Pazos, R., Cruz, L., Reyes, G., Basave, R., & Fraire, H. (2007). Improving the efficiency and efficacy of the K-Means clustering algorithm through a new convergence condition. In *International Conference on Computational Science and Its Applications* (pp. 674-682). Springer. 10.1007/978-3-540-74484-9_58

Pérez, J., Pires, C. E., Balby, L., Mexicano, A., & Hidalgo, M. Á. (2013). Early classification: A new heuristic to improve the classification step of K-Means. *Journal of Information and Data Management, 4*(2), 94–103.

Pérez-Rosas, V., Banea, C., & Mihalcea, R. (2012). Learning Sentiment Lexicons in Spanish. In K. Jokinen, & S. Tenjes (eds.), *Proceedings of the Eighth International Conference on Language Resources and Evaluation (LREC'12)* (pp. 3077-3081). Istanbul, Turkey: European Language Resources Association (ELRA).

Pervaz, I., Ameer, I., Sittar, A., & Nawab, R. M. A. (2015). Identification of Author Personality Traits using Stylistic Features, In *CLEF 2015 Evaluation Labs and Workshop – Working Notes Papers.* Toulouse, France: CEUR-WS.org.

Pessina, F., Masseroli, M., & Canakoglu, A. (2013). Visual composition of complex queries on an integrative Genomic and Proteomic Data Warehouse. *Engineering (London), 5*(10, 10B), 94–98. doi:10.4236/eng.2013.510B019

Pilato, G., Augello, A., & Gaglio, S. (2011). AModular SystemOriented to the Design of Versatile Knowledge Bases for Chatbots. *ISRN Artificial Intelligence, 2012,* 1–10. doi:10.5402/2012/363840

Pilz, J., & Spöck, G. (2008). Why do we need and how should we implement Bayesian kriging methods. *Stochastic Environmental Research and Risk Assessment, 22*(5), 621–632. doi:10.100700477-007-0165-7

Pimas, O., Rexha, A., Kröll, M., & Kern, R. (2016). Profiling Microblog Authors Using Concreteness and Sentiment—Notebook for PAN at CLEF 2016. In K. Balog, L. Cappellato, N. Ferro, & C. Macdonald (Eds.), CLEF 2016 Evaluation Labs and Workshop – Working Notes Papers. Évora, Portugal: CEUR-WS.org.

Pitchayaviwat, T. (2016). A Study on Clustering Customer Suggestion on Online Social Media about Insurance Services by Using Text Mining Techniques. *Management and Innovation Technology International Conference, 1,* 148-151. 10.1109/MITICON.2016.8025228

Plu, J., Rizzo, G., & Troncy, R. (2016). Enhancing Entity Linking by Combining NER Models. In *Extended Semantic Web Conference (ESWC).* Springer.

Popescu, A. M., Armanasu, A., Etzioni, O., Ko, D., & Yates, A. (2004). Modern natural language interfaces to databases: Composing statistical parsing with semantic tractability. *Proceedings of the 20th international conference on Computational Linguistics.* 10.3115/1220355.1220376

Porras, J., Florencia-Juárez, R., Rivera, G., & García, V. (2018). Interfaz de lenguaje natural para consultar cubos multidimensionales utilizando procesamiento analítico en línea. *Research in Computing Science, 147*(6), 153–165. doi:10.13053/rcs-147-6-12

Portillo, J. (2019). *¿Cuáles son las mayores economías del mundo?* Retrieved from https://cincodias.elpais.com

Posadas-Durán, J., Sidorov, G., Batyrshin, I., & Mirasol-Meléndez, E. (2015). Author Verification Using Syntactic N-grams—Notebook for PAN at CLEF 2015. In L. Cappellato, N. Ferro, G. Jones, & E. San Juan (Eds.), *CLEF 2015 Evaluation Labs and Workshop – Working Notes Papers.* Toulouse, France: CEUR-WS.org.

Poteraş, C. M., Mihăescu, M. C., & Mocanu, M. (2014). An optimized version of the K-Means clustering algorithm. In *2014 Federated Conference on Computer Science and Information Systems* (pp. 695-699). IEEE. 10.15439/2014F258

Poulston, A., Stevenson, M., & Bontcheva, K. (2015). Topic Models and n-gram Language Models for Author Profiling—Notebook for PAN at CLEF 2015. In L. Cappellato, N.Ferro,G. Jones, & E. San Juan (Eds.), CLEF 2015 Evaluation Labs and Workshop – Working Notes Papers. Toulouse, France: CEUR-WS.org.

Povey, D., Ghoshal, A., Boulianne, G., Burget, L., Glembek, O., Goel, N., ...Vesely, K. (2011). The Kaldi Speech Recognition. *IEEE 2011 Workshop on Automatic Speech Recognition and Understanding.*

Pranay Mathur, A. G. (2017, April 5). *Text Summarization in Python: Extractive vs. Abstractive techniques revisited.* Retrieved from Rare Technologies: https://rare-technologies.com/text-summarization-in-python-extractive-vs-abstractive-techniques-revisited/

Prathima, M. R., & Divakar, H. R. (2018). Automatic Extractive Text Summarization Using K-Means Clustering. *International Journal on Computer Science and Engineering, 6*(6), 782–787.

Presutti, V., Nuzzolese, A. G., Consoli, S., Gangemi, A., & Reforgiato Recupero, D. (2016). From hyperlinks to Semantic Web properties using Open Knowledge Extraction. *Semantic Web, 7*(4), 351–378.

Prószéky, G. (1996). Morphological Analyzer as Syntactic Parser. In *Proceedings of the 16th conference on Computational linguistics* (pp. 1123-1226). Budapest: DBLP. 10.3115/993268.993381

Puneet Agarwal, P. K. (2020, January 16). *Google Patents.* Retrieved from Google Patents: https://patentimages.storage.googleapis.com/8c/5a/d9/8c6d5faeff865b/US20200019610A1.pdf

Qian, X., Meng, H., & Soong, F. (2012). The use of DBN-HMMs for mispronunciation detection and diagnosis in L2 english to support computer-aided pronunciation training. In *13th Annual Conference of the International Speech Communication Association 2012 INTERSPEECH*, (Vol. 1, pp.774–777).

Rahm, E., & Do, H. H. (2000). Data cleaning: Problems and current approaches. *A Quarterly Bulletin of the Computer Society of the IEEE Technical Committee on Data Engineering, 23*(4), 3–13.

Rajwani, H., Somvanshi, S., Upadhye, A., Vaidya, R., & Dange, T. (2015). Dynamic Traffic Analyzer Using Twitter. *International Journal of Scientific Research (Ahmedabad, India), 4*(10), 984–987.

Ramanand, J., Bhavsar, K., & Pedanekar, N. (2010). Wishful Thinking: Finding suggestions and 'buy' wishes from product reviews. *Workshop on Computational Approaches to Analysis and Generation of Emotion in Text.*

Randolph, J. J. (2005). Free-Marginal Multirater Kappa (multirater K [free]): An Alternative to Fleiss' Fixed-Marginal Multirater Kappa. *Joensuu Learning and Instruction Symposium.*

Ranganathan, S., Nakai, K., Gribskov, M., & Schonbach, C. (2019). *Encyclopedia of Bioinformatics and Computational Biology: ABC of Bioinformatics.* Elsevier.

Rathi, S., Shekhar, S., & Sharma, D. K. (2016). Opinion Mining Classification Based on Extension of Opinion Mining Phrases. In S. C. Satapathy, A. Joshi, N. Modi, & N. Pathak (Eds.), *Proceedings of international conference on ICT for sustainable development* (pp. 717–724). Springer Singapore. 10.1007/978-981-10-0129-1_74

Real Academia Española. (2019). *Banco de datos (CORDE).* Retrieved from Corpus diacrónico del español: http://www.rae.es

Real Academia Española. (2019). *Diccionario de la lengua española.* Retrieved 03 18, 2019, from Sugerencia: https://dle.rae.es/?id=YfTKl7q

Revuze. (2018). *Revuze Products.* Retrieved from http://revuze.it/product/

Riedel, S., Yao, L., & McCallum, A. (2010). *Modeling Relations and Their Mentions without Labeled Text. In Machine Learning and Knowledge Discovery in Databases.* Springer.

Rigney, J. (1978). Learning Strategies: A Theoretical Perspective. In Learning Strategies (pp. 165-205). Academic Press.

Riley, P. F., & Riley, G. F. (2003). Spades - A Distributed Agent Simulation Environment with Software-in-the-loop execution. In *Proceeding of the 2003 Winter Simulation Conference.* IEEE. 10.1109/WSC.2003.1261500

Rivero, I., Gómez, M., & Abrego, R. (2013). Tecnologías educativas y estrategias didácticas: Criterios de selección. *Educational Technology, 3,* 190–206.

Robertson, S. E., & Jones, K. S. (1988). *Document retrieval systems. chapter Relevance weighting of search terms.* Taylor Graham Publishing.

Roca, S., Sancho, J., García, J., & Alesanco, Á. (2019). Microservice chatbot architecture for chronic patient support. *Journal of Biomedical Informatics, 102,* 103305. doi:10.1016/j.jbi.2019.103305 PMID:31622802

Roitman, H., Mamou, J., Mehta, S., Satt, A., & Subramaniam, L. V. (2012). Harnessing the Crowds for Smart City Sensing. In *Proceedings of the 1st international workshop on Multimodal crowd sensing (CrowdSens '12).* New York: ACM. 10.1145/2390034.2390043

Roos, S. (2018). *Chatbots in education: A passing trend or a valuable pedagogical tool?* Retrieved from http://www.diva-portal.org/smash/record.jsf?pid=diva2%3A1223692&dswid=879

Rouces, J., de Melo, G., & Hose, K. (2015). Framebase: Representing n-ary relations using semantic frames. In *Extended Semantic Web Conference* (pp. 505-521). Springer.

Rozhkovsky, R., & Bil'chenko, A. (2014). *Live Universal Awareness Map.* Retrieved from https://liveuamap.com/

Ruiz Frutos, M. J. (2012, October 23). *Resolución de la anáfora correferencial con FunGramKB.* Retrieved from Resolución de la anáfora correferencial con FunGramKB: http://e-spacio.uned.es/fez/eserv/bibliuned:master-Filologia-TICETL-Mjfrutos/Frutos_mariajose_TFM.pdf

Rusu, D., Fortuna, B., & Mladenic, D. (2011). Automatically Annotating Text with Linked Open Data. In *Workshop on Linked Data on the Web.* CEUR.

Sabbagh, R., & Ameri, F. (2020). A Framework Based on K-Means Clustering and Topic Modeling for Analyzing Unstructured Manufacturing Capability Data. *Journal of Computing and Information Science in Engineering*, *20*(1), 1–13. doi:10.1115/1.4044506

Sabou, M., Arsal, I., & Braşoveanu, A. M. (2013). TourMISLOD: A tourism linked data set. *Semantic Web*, *4*(3), 271–276.

Sabra, S., Mahmood Malik, K., & Alobaidi, M. (2018). Prediction of venous thromboembolism using semantic and sentiment analyses of clinical narratives. *Computers in Biology and Medicine*, *94*, 1–10. doi:10.1016/j.compbiomed.2017.12.026 PMID:29353160

Safari, L., & Patrick, J. D. (2014). Restricted natural language based querying of clinical databases. *Journal of Biomedical Informatics*, *52*, 338–353. doi:10.1016/j.jbi.2014.07.012 PMID:25051402

Sagayam, R., Srinivasan, S., & Roshni, S. (2012). A survey of text mining: Retrieval, extraction and indexing techniques. *International Journal of Computational Engineering Research*, *2*(5), 1443–1446.

Saggion, H., & Lapalme, G. (2002). Generating indicative-informative summaries with sumUM. *Computational Linguistics*, *28*(4), 497–526. doi:10.1162/089120102762671963

Saini, A., Minocha, J., Ubriani, J., & Sharma, D. (2016). New approach for clustering of big data: DisK-Means. In *2016 International Conference on Computing, Communication and Automation (ICCCA)* (pp. 122-126). IEEE. 10.1109/CCAA.2016.7813702

Saiz, M. (2003). Procesamiento del lenguaje natural: Presente y perspectivas futuras. In *Proceedings of IX Jornadas Iberoamericanas de Informática, Ingeniería de Software en la Década del 2000* (pp. 191-226). Cartagena, Colombia: Academic Press.

Salas-Zárate, M. D. P., Medina-Moreira, J., Lagos-Ortiz, K., Luna-Aveiga, H., Rodríguez-García, M. Á., & Valencia-García, R. (2017). Sentiment Analysis on Tweets about Diabetes: An Aspect-Level Approach. *Computational and Mathematical Methods in Medicine*, *2017*, 1–9. Advance online publication. doi:10.1155/2017/5140631 PMID:28316638

Salton, G., & Buckley, C. (1988). Term-Weighting Approaches in Automatic Text Retrieval. *Information Processing and Management an International Journal*, *24*(5), 513–523. doi:10.1016/0306-4573(88)90021-0

Samsonova, V. P., Blagoveshchenskii, Y. N., & Meshalkina, Y. L. (2017). Use of empirical Bayesian Kriging for revealing heterogeneities in the distribution of organic carbon on agricultural lands. *Eurasian Soil Science*, *50*(3), 305–311. doi:10.1134/S1064229317030103

Sánchez-Cervantes, J. L., Colombo-Mendoza, L. O., Alor-Hernández, G., García-Alcaráz, J. L., Álvarez-Rodríguez, J. M., & Rodríguez-González, A. (2019). LINDASearch: A faceted search system for linked open datasets. *Wireless Networks*, 1–19.

SAP Conversational AI. (n.d.). *Automate Customer Service With AI Chatbots*. Retrieved January 26, 2020, from https://cai.tools.sap/

Saravanakumar, M., & SuganthaLakshmi, T. (2012). Social Media Marketing. *Life Science Journal*, *9*(4), 4444–4451.

Sarawagi, S. (2008). Information Extraction. *Foundations and Trends in Databases*, *1*(3), 261–377. doi:10.1561/1900000003

Sareen, S. (2018, Jul 4). *Text Summariser in Python*. Retrieved from Medium: https://medium.com/@shivangisareen/text-summariser-in-python-da5557d31aa0

Sareen, S. (2018, July 4). *Medium*. Retrieved November 18, 2019, from https://medium.com/@shivangisareen/text-summariser-in-python-da5557d31aa0

Sarkar, K. (2013). Automatic Single Document Text Summarization Using Key Concepts in Documents. *Journal of Information Processing Systems*.

Sasanuma, S. (1975). Kana and Kanji Processing in Japanese Aphasics. *Brain and Language*, 2, 369–383. doi:10.1016/S0093-934X(75)80077-0 PMID:1182502

Savington, S. J. (1991). Communicative Language Teaching: State of the Art. *TESOL Quarterly*, 25(2), 261–278. doi:10.2307/3587463

Sayyed, S.N., Aurangabad, B.A., & Mahender, C.N.(2020). Conceptual Dependency to Extract the important event from story to enhanced Summarization. *International Journal of Scientific & Technology Research, 9*(3), 6797-6801.

Schank, R. C. (1975). The primitive ACTs of conceptual dependency. Theoretical issues in natural language processing. doi:10.3115/980190.980205

Schank, R. C., & Abelson, R. P. (1977). *Scripts, plans, goals, and understanding: An inquiry into human knowledge structures*. Lawrence Erlbaum Associates.

Schler, J., Koppel, M., Argamon, S., & Pennebaker, J. (2006). Effects of age and gender on blogging. *AAAI Spring Symposium: Computational Approaches to Analyzing Weblogs, 6*, 199–205.

ScienceDirect. (2020). *Text Summarization - an overview*. Retrieved from ScienceDirect: https://www.sciencedirect.com/topics/computer-science/text-summarization

Seddik, K. M. (2014). Anaphora resolution. In I. Zitouni (Eds.), Natural language processing of semitic languages (pp. 247-277). doi:10.1007/978-3-642-45358-8_8

Seddik, K. M. (2014). *Natural Language Processing Applications*. Academic Press.

Seddik, K. M. (2014, March 1). *ResearchGate*. Retrieved from ResearchGate: https://www.researchgate.net/publication/300822578_Anaphora_Resolution

See, A. (2016). *Nearest Neighbors*. Retrieved from Stanford Computer Science: https://cs.stanford.edu/people/abisee/nn.pdf

Seema Mahato, A. T. (2020). Heuristic Algorithm for Resolving Pronominal Anaphora in Hindi Dialects. In A. T. Seema Mahato (Eds.), Advanced Computing and Intelligent Engineering (pp. 41-51). Springer Link.

Selim, S. Z., & Ismail, M. A. (1984). K-means-type algorithms: A generalized convergence theorem and characterization of local optimality. *IEEE Transactions on Pattern Analysis and Machine Intelligence*, PAMI-6(1), 81–87. doi:10.1109/TPAMI.1984.4767478 PMID:21869168

Seneff, S., Glass, J., Goddeau, D., Goodine, D., Hirschman, L., Leung, H., & Zue, V. (1991). Development and Preliminary Evaluation of the MIT ATIS System. *Speech and Natural Language: Proceedings of a Workshop Held at Pacific Grove*. 10.3115/112405.112417

Sengupta, S., Basak, S., Saikia, P., Paul, S., Tsalavoutis, V., Atiah, F., ... Peters, A. (2020). A review of deep learning with special emphasis on architectures, applications and recent trends. *Knowledge-Based Systems*, 1–100.

Sen, J., Ozcan, F., Quamar, A., Stager, G., Mittal, A., Jammi, M., ... Sankaranarayanan, K. (2019). Natural Language Querying of Complex Business Intelligence Queries. In *Proceedings of the 2019 International Conference on Management of Data, SIGMOD Conference* (pp. 1997-2000). 10.1145/3299869.3320248

Sergi Torner Castells, C. L. (2011). Problemas en el uso de las anáforas en producciones escritas de español como lengua extranjera. *Revista Española de Lingüística*, 147-174.

Sethi, C., & Mishra, G. (2013). A Linear PCA based hybrid K-Means PSO algorithm for clustering large dataset. *International Journal of Scientific and Engineering Research, 4*(6), 1559–1566.

Shabaz, K., O'Shea, J. D., Crockett, K. A., & Latham, A. (2015). Aneesah: A conversational natural language interface to databases. In *Proceedings of the World Congress on Engineering* (pp. 227-232). London, UK: Academic Press.

Shalom Lappin, H. J. (1994). *An Algorithm for Pronominal Anaphora Resolution.* Academic Press.

Sharma, M. (2018, September 15). *Text Summarization.* Retrieved from Medium: https://medium.com/incedge/text-summarization-96079bf23e83

Shawar, B. A. (2017). Integrating CALL Systems with Chatbots as Conversational Partners. *Computación y Sistemas, 21*(4), 615–626. doi:10.13053/CyS-21-4-2868

Sheth, A., Arpinar, I. B., & Kashyap, V. (2004). *Relationships at the heart of Semantic Web: Modeling, discovering, and exploiting complex semantic relationships. In Enhancing the Power of the Internet.* Springer.

Sheth, A., Yip, H. Y., Shekarpour, S., & Sheth, A. (2019). Extending Patient-Chatbot Experience with Internet-of-Things and Background Knowledge: Case Studies with Healthcare Applications. *IEEE Intelligent Systems, 34*(4), 24–30. doi:10.1109/MIS.2019.2905748

Shetty, K., & Kallimani, J. S. (2017). Automatic extractive text summarization using K-Means clustering. In *2017 International Conference on Electrical, Electronics, Communication, Computer, and Optimization Techniques (ICEECCOT)* (pp. 1-9). IEEE. 10.1109/ICEECCOT.2017.8284627

Siddiqui, M. H., Ameer, I., Gelbukh, A., & Sidorov, G. (2019). Bots and Gender Profiling on Twitter. In L. Cappellato, N. Ferro, D. Losada, & H. Müller (Eds.), *CLEF 2019 Labs and Workshops, Notebook Papers. CEUR-WS.org.*

Sidorov, G. (2019). *Syntactic n-grams in computational linguistics.* Springer. https://link.springer.com/book/10.1007%2F978-3-030-14771-6

Sidorov, G. (2013a). *Non-linear construction of n-grams in computational linguistics.* Sociedad Mexicana de Inteligencia Artificial.

Sidorov, G. (2013b). Syntactic dependency based n-grams in rule based automatic English as second language grammar correction. *International Journal of Computational Linguistics and Applications, 4*(2), 169–188.

Sidorov, G., Velasquez, F., Stamatatos, E., Gelbukh, A., & Chanona-Hernández, L. (2014). Syntactic n-grams as machine learning features for natural language processing. *Expert Systems with Applications, 41*(3), 853–860. doi:10.1016/j.eswa.2013.08.015

Sinclair, J. (1996). Preliminary Recommendations on Corpus Typology. *EAGLES (Expert Advisory Group on Language Engineering Standards) EAG-TCWG- CTYP/P, 4*–27. Retrieved from http://www.ilc.cnr.it/EAGLES96/corpustyp/node4.html

Sinha, A., Yadav, A., & Gahlot, A. (2018). *Extractive text summarization using neural networks.* arXiv preprint arXiv:1802.10137

Sittar, A., & Ameer, I. (2018). Multi-lingual Author Profiling Using Stylistic Features. In *Working Notes for MAPonSMS at FIRE'18 - Workshop Proceedings of the 10th International Forum for Information Retrieval Evaluation (FIRE'18).* CEUR-WS.org.

Slamet, C., Atmadja, A. R., Maylawati, D. S., Lestari, R. S., Darmalaksana, W., & Ramdhani, M. A. (2018). Automated text summarization for indonesian article using vector space model. IOP Conference Series: Materials Science and Engineering, 288(1). doi:10.1088/1757-899X/288/1/012037

Sleator, D. D. K., & Temperley, D. (1995). *Parsing English with a link grammar*. Retrieved from https://arxiv.org/pdf/cmp-lg/9508004v1.pdf

Smeureanu, I., & Bucur, C. (2012). Applying Supervised Opinion Mining Techniques on Online User Reviews. *Informações Econômicas, 16*(2), 81–91.

Software, E. L. F. (2002). *Demo Gallery*. Retrieved from http://www.elfsoft.com/help/accelf/Overview.htm

Software, E. L. F. (2009). *ELF Software Documentation Series*. Retrieved December 16, 2019, from http://www.elfsoft.com/help/accelf/Overview.htm

Solangi, Y. A., Solangi, Z. A., Aarain, S., Abro, A., Mallah, G. A., & Shah, A. (2019). Review on Natural Language Processing (NLP) and Its Toolkits for Opinion Mining and Sentiment Analysis. In *2018 IEEE 5th International Conference on Engineering Technologies and Applied Sciences, ICETAS 2018* (pp. 1–4). doi:10.1109/ICETAS.2018.8629198

Sompel, H., & Lagoze, C.(2000). The Santa Fe Convention of the Open Archives Initiative. *D-Lib Magazine, 6*(2).

Sourla, E., Paschou, M., Sakkopoulos, E., & Tsakalidis, A. (2013). Health Internet of Things: Metrics and methods for efficient data transfer. *Simulation Modelling Practice and Theory, 34*, 186–199. doi:10.1016/j.simpat.2012.08.002

Spacy. (2020). Retrieved from Spacy: https://spacy.io/usage/adding-languages#_title

Spacy. (2020, February 19). Retrieved from Spacy: https://spacy.io/

Spector, J. M. (2001). An Overview of Progress and Problems in Educational Technology. *IEM, 3*, 27–37.

Sreedhar, C., Kasiviswanath, N., & Reddy, P. C. (2017). Clustering large datasets using K-means modified inter and intra clustering (KM-I2C) in Hadoop. *Journal of Big Data, 4*(1), 27. doi:10.118640537-017-0087-2

Srivastava, A. N., & Sahami, M. (2009). *Text mining: Classification, clustering, and applications*. Chapman and Hall/CRC.

Stamatatos, E., Potthast, M., Rangel, F., Rosso, P., & Stein, B. (2015). Overview of the PAN/CLEF 2015 Evaluation Lab. In J. Mothe, J. Savoy, J. Kamps, K. Pinel-Sauvagnat, G. Jones, E. SanJuan, L. Cappellato, & N. Ferro (Eds.), *Experimental IR Meets Multilinguality, Multimodality, and Interaction. 6th International Conference of the CLEF Initiative (CLEF 15)*, (pp. 518–538). Springer. 10.1007/978-3-319-24027-5_49

Stanford N. L. P. Group. (2020, February 18). *Stanford NLP Group*. Retrieved from Stanford NLP Group: https://nlp.stanford.edu/

Stanford Natural Language Processing Group. (2019). *The Stanford parser: A statistical parser*. Retrieved from https://nlp.stanford.edu/software/lex-parser.shtml

Statista. (2019). *Los idiomas más hablados en el mundo (hablantes y hablantes nativos, en millones)*. Retrieved from https://es.statista.com

Steinhaus, H. (1956). Sur la division des corp materiels en parties. *Bull. Acad. Polon. Sci, 1*(804), 801–804.

Strand, P., Aono, T., Brown, J. E., Garnier-Laplace, J., Hosseini, A., Sazykina, T., ... Batlle, J. (2014). Assessment of Fukushima-Derived Radiation Doses and Effects on Wildlife in Japan. *Environmental Science & Technology Letters, 1*(3), 198–203. doi:10.1021/ez500019j

Stratica, N., Kosseim, L., & Desai, B. C. (2005). Using semantic templates for a natural language interface to the Cindi virtual library. *Data & Knowledge Engineering*, *55*(1), 4–19. doi:10.1016/j.datak.2004.12.002

Stricker, G. (2017, Diciembre 10). *The 2014 #YearOnTwitter*. Retrieved Julio 02, 2019, from https://blog.twitter.com/official/en_us/a/2014/the-2014-yearontwitter.html

Suanmali, L., Binwahlan, M. S., & Salim, N. (2009, August). Sentence features fusion for text summarization using fuzzy logic. In *2009 Ninth International Conference on Hybrid Intelligent Systems* (Vol. 1, pp. 142-146). IEEE. 10.1109/HIS.2009.36

Sujatha, B., & Raju, S. V. (2016). Ontology based natural language interface for relational databases. *Procedia Computer Science*, *92*, 487–492. doi:10.1016/j.procs.2016.07.372

Sujatha, B., Raju, S. V., & Shaziya, H. (2012). A Survey of Natural Language Interface to Database Management System. *International Journal of Science and Advanced Technology*, *2*(6), 56–60.

Su, K., Li, J., & Fu, H. (2011). Smart City and the Applications. *2011 International Conference on Electronics, Communications and Control (ICECC)*, 1028-1031. 10.1109/ICECC.2011.6066743

Sukthankar, N., Maharnawar, S., Deshmukh, P., Haribhakta, Y., & Kamble, V. (2017). nQuery - A natural language statement to SQL query generator. In *Proceedings of the 55th Annual Meeting of the Association for Computational Linguistics, Student Research Workshop* (pp. 17-23). 10.18653/v1/P17-3004

Sulea, O., & Dichiu, D. (2015). Automatic Profiling of Twitter Users Based on Their Tweets—Notebook for PAN at CLEF 2015. In L. Cappellato, N. Ferro, G. Jones, & E. San Juan (Eds.), CLEF 2015 Evaluation Labs and Workshop – Working Notes Papers. Toulouse, France: CEUR-WS.org.

Suleiman, D., A. A. (2019). Arabic Text Keywords Extraction using Word2vec. *2nd International Conference on new Trends in Computing Sciences (ICTCS)*, 1-7.

Su, P.-H., Wu, C.-H., & Lee, L.-S. (2015). A recursive dialogue game for personalized computer-aided pronunciation training. *IEEE/ACM Transactions on Audio, Speech, and Language Processing*, *23*(1), 127–141. doi:10.1109/TASLP.2014.2375572

Suykens, J. A., & Vandewalle, J. (1999). Least squares support vector machine classifiers. *Neural Processing Letters*, *9*(3), 293–300. doi:10.1023/A:1018628609742

Tamaoka, K., Leong, C. K., & Hatta, T. (1992). Effects of Vocal Interference on Identifying Kanji, Hiragana and Katakana Words by Skilled and Less Skilled Japanese Readers in Grades 4-6. [Matsuyama.]. *Psychologia*, *35*, 33–41.

Tan, J. J., Lane, H., & Rijanto, A. (2019). *Report on NLIDBs*. Retrieved from http://www.elfsoft.com/Resources/References.htm

Tanaka, H., Kinoshita, A., Kobayakawa, T., Kumano, T., & Kato, N. (2009, August). Syntax-driven sentence revision for broadcast news summarization. In *Proceedings of the 2009 Workshop on Language Generation and Summarisation* (pp. 39-47). Association for Computational Linguistics. 10.3115/1708155.1708163

Tandera, T., Suhartono, D., Wongso, R., Prasetio, Y. L., & ... (2017). Personality prediction system from facebook users. *Procedia Computer Science*, *116*, 604–611. doi:10.1016/j.procs.2017.10.016

Tang, L. R., & Mooney, R. J. (2001). Using multiple clause constructors in inductive logic programming for semantic parsing. In *European Conference on Machine Learning*, (pp. 466-477). Springer. 10.1007/3-540-44795-4_40

Tausczik, Y. R., & Pennebaker, J. W. (2010). The psychological meaning of words: LIWC and computerized text analysis methods. *Journal of Language and Social Psychology*, *29*(1), 24–54. doi:10.1177/0261927X09351676

Taylor, P. (2009). *Text-to-Speech Synthesys*. Cambridge University Press. doi:10.1017/CBO9780511816338

Technology, L. (1997). *English Wizard – Dictionary Administrator's Guide*. Linguistic Technology Corp.

tedboy. (2016). *gensim*. Retrieved from NLP APIs: https://tedboy.github.io/nlps/generated/generated/gensim.summarization.summarize.html

Thanaki, J. (2017). Feature Engineering and NLP Algorithms. In Python Natural Language Processing (p. 102). Academic Press.

Thomas, N. T. (2016). An e-business chatbot using AIML and LSA. In *2016 International Conference on Advances in Computing, Communications and Informatics (ICACCI)* (pp.2740–2742). 10.1109/ICACCI.2016.7732476

Thompson, C. (2003). Acquiring word-meaning mappings for natural language interfaces. *Journal of Artificial Intelligence Research*, *18*(1), 1–44. doi:10.1613/jair.1063

Toledo Gómez Israel, V. R. (2011). *Academia*. Retrieved from Academia: https://www.academia.edu/1588476/Construcci%C3%B3n_de_una_herramienta_para_la_identificaci%C3%B3n_y_resoluci%C3%B3n_de_pronombres_an%C3%A1foras_en_una_oraci%C3%B3n

Torres, M. D., Torres, A., Barajas, D., Campos, N., Ponce De León, E. E., & Velázquez, C. (2019). Suicidal tendency neural identifier in university students from aguascalientes, Mexico. In *2019- 14th Latin American Conference on Learning Technologies (LACLO)* (pp.387–392). doi:10.1109/LACLO49268.2019.00071

Trincado, B. (2019). *Evolución de las mayores economías del mundo*. Retrieved from https://www.cincodias.elpais.com

Tsarkov, D., & Horrocks, I. (2007). *FaCT++ resoner*. Retrieved from FaCT: http://owl.man.ac.uk/factplusplus/

Tudorache, T., Nyulas, C., Noy, N. F., & Musen, M. A. (2013). WebProtégé: A collaborative ontology editor and knowledge acquisition tool for the Web. *Semantic Web*, *4*(1), 89–99. PMID:23807872

Tu, M., Grabek, A., Liss, J., & Berisha, V. (2018). Investigating the role of L1 in automatic pronunciation evaluation of L2 speech. In *Proceedings of the Annual Conference of the International Speech Communication Association, INTERSPEECH* (pp.1636–1640). 10.21437/Interspeech.2018-1350

Tyagi, M. (2014). Natural Language Interface to Databases: A Survey. *International Journal of Scientific Research (Ahmedabad, India)*, *3*(5), 1443–1445.

Tzoukermann, E. (1991). The use of a commercial natural language interface in the ATIS task. *Speech and Natural Language: Proceedings of a Workshop Held at Pacific Grove*, 134-137. 10.3115/112405.112425

Umadevi, K. S., R. C. (2018). Text Summarization of Spanish Documents. *International Conference on Advances in Computing, Communications and Informatics (ICACCI)*, 1793-1797.

Umezawa, K. (2018). *Word2Vec: Obtain word embeddings*. Retrieved from https://medium.com/@keisukeumezawa/word2vec-obtain-word-embeddings-885716a56270

United Nations. (2018). *World Urbanization Prospects 2018*. Retrieved from https://population.un.org/wup/

Universidad Autonoma de Ciudad Juarez. (2019). *Universidad Autonoma de Ciudad Juarez*. Retrieved from https://www.uacj.mx/sa/ed/Paginas/default.aspx

Universidad Politécnica de Cataluña. (2020, March 9). *Computer science deparment*. Retrieved from https://www.cs.upc.edu/~nlp/tools/parole-sp.html#pronombres

Usbeck, R., Röder, M., Ngomo, A.-C. N., Baron, C., Both, A., Brümmer, M., ... Wesemann, L. (2015). GERBIL: General Entity Annotator Benchmarking Framework. In *Proceedings of the 24th International Conference on World Wide Web* (pp. 1133-1143). ACM.

Utama, P., Weir, N., Basık, F., Binnig, C., Cetintemel, U., Hättasch, B., . . . Usta, A. (2018). *DBPal: An end-to-end neural natural language interface for databases*. Retrieved from https://arxiv.org/abs/1804.00401

Valtierra Romero, E. (2014, February 1). *AnaPro, Tool for Identification and Resolution of Direct Anaphora inSpanish*. Retrieved from AnaPro, Tool for Identification and Resolution of Direct Anaphora inSpanish: https://www.academia.edu/10482656/201._AnaPro_Tool_for_Identification_and_Resolution_of_Direct_Anaphora_in_Spanish

Van den Berge, J., Schouten, H., Boomstra, S., van Drunen Littel, S., & Braakman, R. (1979). Interobserver agreement in assessment of ocular signs in coma. *Journal of Neurology, Neurosurgery, and Psychiatry, 42*(12), 1163–1168. PMID:533856

Van, T. P., & Thanh, T. M. (2017). Vietnamese news classification based on BoW with keywords extraction and neural network. In *2017 21st Asia Pacific Symposium on Intelligent and Evolutionary Systems (IES)* (pp. 43-48). Hanoi, Vientnam: IEEE. 10.1109/IESYS.2017.8233559

Vandenbussche, P.-Y., Atemezing, G., Poveda-Villalón, M., & Vatant, B. (2017). Linked Open Vocabularies (LOV): A gateway to reusable semantic vocabularies on the Web. *Semantic Web, 8*(3), 437–452. doi:10.3233/SW-160213

Vanderwende, L. (2015). *NLPwin – an introduction* (no. MSR-TR-2015-23). Retrieved from https://www.microsoft.com/en-us/research/publication/nlpwin-an-introduction/

Vijay, S., V. R. (2017). Extractive text summarisation in hindi. *International Conference on Asian Language Processing (IALP)*, 318-321. 10.1109/IALP.2017.8300607

Vladova, G., Haase, J., Rüdian, L. S., & Pinkwart, N. (2019). *Educational Chatbot with Learning Avatar for Personalization*. Association for Information Systems.

Vollenbroek, M. B., Carlotto, T., Kreutz, T., Medvedeva, M., Pool, C., Bjerva, J., & Nissim, M. (2016). GronUP: Groningen User Profiling—Notebook for PAN at CLEF 2016. In CLEF 2016 Evaluation Labs and Workshop – Working Notes Papers. Évora, Portugal: CEUR-WS.org.

W3C Community. (2014). *Vocabularies*. Retrieved from W3C: http://www.w3.org/standards/semanticweb/ontology

Wang, H., Xu, J., Ge, H., & Wang, Y. (2019). Design and implementation of an english pronunciation scoring system for pupils based on DNN-HMM. In *2019 10th International Conference on Information Technology in Medicine and Education (ITME)* (pp. 348–352). 10.1109/ITME.2019.00085

Wang, W. (2019). A cross-domain natural language interface to databases using adversarial text method. In *Proceedings of the Very Large Data Bases PhD Workshop*. Los Angeles, CA: Academic Press.

Wang, W., Tian, Y., Xiong, H., Wang, H., & Ku, W. (2018). *A transfer-learnable natural language interface for databases*. Retrieved from https://arxiv.org/abs/1809.02649

Wang, Y. (2008). *Designing Chatbot Interfaces for Language Learning: Ethnographic Research into Affect and Users' Experience* (Doctoral Dissertation). Vancouver.

Wang, C., Xiong, M., Zhou, Q., & Yu, Y. (2007). Panto: A portable natural language interface to ontologies. In *European Semantic Web Conference*, (pp. 473-487). Springer. 10.1007/978-3-540-72667-8_34

Wang, M., Wang, X., & Xu, C. (2005, October). An approach to concept-obtained text summarization. In *IEEE International Symposium on Communications and Information Technology, 2005. ISCIT 2005* (Vol. 2, pp. 1337-1340). IEEE.

Ward, W. (1991). Evaluation of the CMU ATIS System. *Speech and Natural Language: Proceedings of a Workshop*, 19-22.

Warren, D. H. (1981). Efficient processing of interactive relational data base queries expressed in logic. *Proceedings of the seventh international conference on Very Large Data Bases*, 272-281.

Washburn, D., Sindhu, U., Balaouras, S., Dines, R., Hayes, N., & Nelson, L. (2010). *Helping CIOs Understand "Smart City" Initiatives: Defining the Smart City, Its Drivers, and the Role of the CIO.* Forrester Research Inc.

Watanabe, K., & Goto, M. (2019). Query-by-Blending: a Music Exploration System Blending Latent Vector Representations of Lyric Word, Song Audio, and Artist. In *Proceedings of ISMIR* (pp. 144-151). Academic Press.

Webster, J. J., & Kit, C. (1992). Tokenization as the initial phase in NLP. In *COLING1992:The 15th International Conference on Computing Linguistics.* 10.3115/992424.992434

WEKA. (2020). *What is Weka.* Retrieved from University of Auckland School of Computer Science: https://www.cs.auckland.ac.nz/courses/compsci367s1c/tutorials/IntroductionToWeka.pdf

Wenden. (1985). Helping Language Learners Think about Learning. *ELT Journal, 40*, 3-12.

Weren, E. R. (2015). Information Retrieval Features for Personality Traits—Notebook for PAN at CLEF 2015. In L. Cappellato, N. Ferro, G. Jones, & E. San Juan (Eds.), CLEF 2015 Evaluation Labs and Workshop – Working Notes Papers. Toulouse, France: CEUR-WS.org.

Werlen, L. M. (2015). Statistical Learning Methods for Profiling Analysis—Notebook for PAN at CLEF 2015. In L. Cappellato, N. Ferro, G. Jones, & E. San Juan (Eds.), CLEF 2015 Evaluation Labs and Workshop – Working Notes Papers. Toulouse, France: CEUR-WS.org.

Williams, P. (2016). *What, Exactly, is a Smart City?* Retrieved from Meeting of the Minds: https://meetingoftheminds.org/exactly-smart-city-16098

Winograd, T. (1972). Understanding Natural Language. *Cognitive Psychology, 3*(1), 1–191. doi:10.1016/0010-0285(72)90002-3

Winterlich, A., Stevenson, I., Waldren, A., & Dawson, T. (2017). Diabetes Digital Coach: Developing an Infrastructure for e-Health Self-Management Tools. *2016 9th International Conference on Developments in ESystems Engineering, DeSE*, 68–73. doi:10.1109/DeSE.2016.56

Wit.ai. (n.d.). *Natural Language for developers.* Retrieved from https://wit.ai/

Witt, S. M., & Young, S. J. (2000). Phone-level pronunciation scoring and assessment for interactive language learning. *Speech Communication, 30*(2), 95–108. doi:10.1016/S0167-6393(99)00044-8

Wolpert, D. H., & Macready, W. G. (1997). No free lunch theorems for optimization. *IEEE Transactions on Evolutionary Computation, 1*(1), 67–82. doi:10.1109/4235.585893

Wong, S. K. M., Ziarko, W., & Wong, P. (1985). Generalized vector spaces model in information retrieval, In *Proceedings of the 8th annual international SIGIR ACM conference on Research and development in information retrieval* (pp 18-25). 10.1145/253495.253506

Wong, Y. W., & Mooney, R. J. (2006). Learning for semantic parsing with statistical machine translation. *Proceedings of the main conference on Human Language Technology Conference of the North American Chapter of the Association of Computational Linguistics*, 439-446. 10.3115/1220835.1220891

Woods, W. A., Kaplan, R. M., & Nash-Webber, B. (1972). T*he lunar sciences natural language information system.* BBN Report.

Woods, W. A., Kaplan, R. M., & Webber, B. N. (1972). The lunar sciences natural language information System (BBN Report 2378). Bolt Beranek and Newman Inc.

World Economic Forum. (2017). *Travel and Tourism Competitiveness Report 2017.* Retrieved from http://reports.we-forum.org

World Health Organization. (2014). *Prevención del suicidio un imperativo global.* Retrieved from https://apps.who.int/iris/bitstream/handle/10665/ 136083/9789275318508_spa.pdf;jsessionid=3449688B7BB864F3D4D35DCB65E13970 ?sequence=1

World Health Organization. (2015). *Pharmacovigilance.* Retrieved from https://www.who.int/medicines/areas/quality_safety/safety_efficacy/pharmvigi/en/

World Health Organization. (2020). *The top 10 causes of death.* Retrieved from www.who.int/news-room/fact-sheets/detail/the-top-10-causes-of-death

Wu, C., Liu, J., Wu, F., Huang, Y., Yuan, Z., & Xie, X. (2019). MSA: Jointly detecting drug name and adverse drug reaction mentioning tweets with multi-head self-attention.I n *WSDM 2019 - Proceedings of the 12th ACM International Conference on Web Search and Data Mining,* (pp.33–41). doi:10.1145/3289600.3290980

Wu, X., Kumar, V., Quinlan, J. R., Ghosh, J., Yang, Q., Motoda, H., ... Steinberg, D. (2008). Top 10 algorithms in data mining. *Knowledge and Information Systems, 14*(1), 1–37. doi:10.100710115-007-0114-2

Wu, Y., Wang, G., Li, W., & Li, Z. (2008). Automatic Chatbot Knowledge Acquisition from Online Forum via Rough Set and Ensemble Learning. In *2008 IFIP International Conference on Network and Parallel Computing* (pp. 242-246). Chongqing: IEEE. 10.1109/NPC.2008.24

Wu, Z., Eadon, G., Das, S., Inseok, E., Kolovski, V., Annamalai, M., & Srinivasan, J. (2008). Implementing an Inference Engine for RDFS/OWL Constructs and User-Defined Rules in Oracle. In *Proceedings of the 24th International Conference on Data Engineering* (pp. 1239-1248). Cancún, México: IEEE.

Wydell, T., Patterson, K. E., & Humphreys, G. W. (1993). Phonologically Mediated Access to Meaning for Kanji:Is a rows still a rose in Japanese Kanji? *Journal of Experimental Psychology. Learning, Memory, and Cognition, 19*(3), 491–514. doi:10.1037/0278-7393.19.3.491

Xu, B., Cai, R., Zhang, Z., Yang, X., Hao, Z., Li, Z., & Liang, Z. (2016). NADAQ: Natural language database querying based on deep learning. *IEEE Access: Practical Innovations, Open Solutions.* Advance online publication. doi:10.1109/access.2019.2904720

Xu, B., Guo, X., Ye, Y., & Cheng, J. (2012). An Improved Random Forest Classifier for Text Categorization. *JCP, 7*(12), 2913–2920. doi:10.4304/jcp.7.12.2913-2920

Xue, Q. (2010). Smart Healthcare: Applications of the Internet of Things in Medical Treatment and Health. *Informes de la Construcción, 5,* 56–58.

Yamagami, M., & Tollefson, J. (2011). Elite discourses of globalization in Japan: The role of Enflish. In *English in Japan in the Era of Globalization* (pp. 15–37). Palgrave Macmillan. doi:10.1057/9780230306196_2

Yao, M., Pi, D., & Cong, X. (2012). Chinese text clustering algorithm based k-means. *Physics Procedia, 33,* 301–307. doi:10.1016/j.phpro.2012.05.066

Yeasmin, S., Tumpa, P. B., Nitu, A. M., Uddin, M., Ali, E., & Afjal, M. (2017). Study of Abstractive Text Summarization Techniques. *American Journal of Engineering Research*, *6*(8), 253–260.

Yee Liau, B., & Pei Tan, P. (2014). Gaining customer knowledge in low cost airlines through text mining. *Industrial Management & Data Systems*, *114*(9), 1344–1359. doi:10.1108/IMDS-07-2014-0225

Yosef, M. A., Hoffart, J., Bordino, I., Spaniol, M., & Weikum, G. (2011). AIDA: An online tool for accurate disambiguation of named entities in text and tables. *PVLDB*, *4*(12).

Young, T., Hazarika, D., Poria, S., & Cambria, E. (2018). Recent trends in deep learning based natural language processing. *IEEE Computational Intelligence Magazine*, *13*(3), 55–75. doi:10.1109/MCI.2018.2840738

Yu, T., Zhang, R., Yang, K., Yasunaga, M., Wang, D., Li, Z., … Radev, D. R. (2018). *Spider: A large-scale human-labeled dataset for complex and cross-domain semantic parsing and text-to-SQL task*. Retrieved from https://arxiv.org/abs/1809.08887

Zamanifar, A., Minaei-Bidgoli, B., & Sharifi, M. (2008, August). A New Hybrid Farsi Text Summarization Technique Based on Term Co-Occurrence and Conceptual Property of the Text. In *2008 Ninth ACIS International Conference on Software Engineering, Artificial Intelligence, Networking, and Parallel/Distributed Computing* (pp. 635-639). IEEE Computer Society. 10.1109/SNPD.2008.57

Zaveri, A., Rula, A., Maurino, A., Pietrobon, R., Lehmann, J., & Auer, S. (2016). Quality assessment for Linked Data: A Survey. *Semantic Web*, *7*(1), 63–93.

Zelle, J. M., & Mooney, R. J. (1996). Learning to parse database queries using inductive logic programming. *Proceedings of the national conference on artificial intelligence*, 1050-1055.

Zemčík, T. (2018). A Brief History of Chatbots. *Perception, Control. Cognition.* Advance online publication. doi:10.12783/dtcse/aicae2019/31439

Zhang, C., & Zhang, P. (2010). Predicting gender from blog posts. Technical report. University of Massachusetts Amherst.

Zhang, P. Y., & Li, C. H. (2009, August). Automatic text summarization based on sentences clustering and extraction. In *2009 2nd IEEE international conference on computer science and information technology* (pp. 167-170). IEEE. 10.1109/ICCSIT.2009.5234971

Zhang, Y., & Vines, P. (2004, July). Using the web for automated translation extraction in cross-language information retrieval. In M. Sanderson, K. Järvelin, J. Allan, & P. Bruza (Eds.), *Proceedings of the 27th annual international ACM SIGIR conference on Research and development in information retrieval* (pp. 162-169). New York, NY: ACM. 10.1145/1008992.1009022

Zhang, Z., He, Q., Gao, J., & Ni, M. (2018). A deep learning approach for detecting traffic accidents from social media data. *Transportation Research Part C, Emerging Technologies*, *86*, 580–596. doi:10.1016/j.trc.2017.11.027

Zhao, L., Wu, L., & Huang, X. (2009). Using query expansion in graph-based approach for query-focused multi-document summarization. *Information Processing & Management*, *45*(1), 35–41. doi:10.1016/j.ipm.2008.07.001

Zheng, J., Howsmon, D., Zhang, B., Hahn, J., McGuinness, D. L., Hendler, J. A., & Ji, H. (2015). *Entity Linking for biomedical literature. In BMC Med. Inf. & Decision Making*. BMC Springer.

Zhong, V., Xiong, C., & Socher, R. (2017). *Seq2SQL: Generating structured queries from natural language using reinforcement learning*. Retrieved from https://arxiv.org/abs/1709.00103

Zhong, L. (2012). The Jena-Based Ontology Model Inference and Retrieval Application. *Intelligent Information Management*, *4*(4), 157–160.

Zhou, M. X., Wang, C., Mark, G., Yang, H., & Xu, K. (2019). *Building Real-World Chatbot Interviewers: Lessons from a Wizard-of-Oz Field Study*. IUI Workshops.

Zumstein, D., & Hundertmark, S. (2018). Chatbots : an interactive technology for personalized communication and transaction. *International Journal on WWW/Internet, 15*(1), 96–109.

Zwicklbauer, S., Seifert, C., & Granitzer, M. (2016). DoSeR - A Knowledge-Base-Agnostic Framework for Entity Disambiguation Using Semantic Embeddings. *Extended Semantic Web Conference*, 182-198.

About the Contributors

Mario Andrés Paredes Valverde received a Ph.D. degree in Computer Science from the University of Murcia with cum laude distinction and International mention in 2017. He holds a B.E. and MSc degrees in Computer Systems Engineering from the Instituto Tecnológico de Orizaba, Orizaba, México. His main research interests include the Semantic Web, Big Data, Internet of Things (IoT), and Human Language technologies such as Natural Language Processing (NLP), Information Retrieval, Information Extraction, opinion mining, and computational linguistics. He has extensive experience in the use and development of ontologies for domain conceptualization, NLP techniques to retrieve information from relational databases and distributed semantic knowledge bases, machine learning, and the development of Intelligent Systems based on the IoT. Mario Andrés has published over 20 articles in journals indexed in JCR, conferences, and book chapters. He is a member of the scientific committee of national and international conferences (CITI, INBAST, ISC, CIMPS, and CITAMA). Also, he has held stays in research centers in Spain and Norway, and he has collaborated with researchers' groups from Mexico, Spain, Ecuador, and Norway. Additionally, he has collaborated in the development of national and international research proposals financed by public and private entities such as the National Council of Science and Technology (CONACYT), Ministry of Economy and Competitiveness, Centre for Industrial Technological Development (CDTI) Government of Spain, Institute of Promotion of the Region of Murcia (INFO) and European Regional Development Fund (FEDER).

Gilberto Rivera received his Ph.D. in Computer Science (in 2015) from the Tecnológico Nacional de México (National Institute of Technology of Mexico). The Mexican Society for Artificial Intelligence (SMIA) recognized his doctoral research as the best one of the Ph.D. dissertations on Artificial Intelligence in 2015. He is currently a full-time professor of Computer Engineering at the Universidad Autónoma of Ciudad Juárez. Besides, he is a member of the Mexican National System of Researchers (SNI) since 2016. His primary interests are in the areas of multi-criteria optimization, applied soft computing, logistics, and swarm intelligence.

* * *

Marco Antonio Aguirre Lam received a Ph.D. degree in Computer Science from the Tijuana Institute of Technology, México. He is a full-time Professor of Computer Science at Madero Institute of Technology (National Mexican Institute of Technology). His research interests are in intelligent optimization techniques, algorithmics, autonomous agents, machine learning, and natural language processing.

Edwyn Aldana-Bobadilla was born in Bogotá, Colombia. He received the B. Eng. Laurea degree in computer engineering from the Universidad Distrital, Bogotá (Colombia), in 2003; the M.Sc. degree in Computer Engineering and the Ph.D.degree in Computer Science from the Universidad Nacional Autónoma de México (UNAM), in 2009 and 2015 respectively. He has worked in the software industry as a software engineer, software architect, and database designer and manager. In 2011, he joined UNAM as a professor in the Faculty of Applied Mathematics and Computer Science and the Faculty of Engineering at UNAM. Since 2015, he was commissioned by The National Council of Science and Technology of Mexico (CONACyT) as a researcher at Centro de Investigación y de Estudios Avanzados (CINVESTAV), Tamaulipas (Mexico). His research interests include machine learning, digital electronics, optimization, stochastic process, software engineering, and data analysis.

Nelva Nely Almanza-Ortega is a Computer Systems Engineer granted by the Instituto Tecnológico de Celaya (México), 2011. Master and Doctorate's Degrees in Computer Science granted by the National Center for Research and Technological Development (CENIDET) (México), 2014 and 2018, respectively. Since 2019, she is affiliated with the Department of Postgraduate Studies and Research of the Instituto Tecnológico de Tlalnepantla (México). She is a member of the National System of Researchers (SNI), Level C. Student Member number 92792570 of the IEEE Student Branch Morelos Section since July 2015. The areas of interest in research are data science, data mining, heuristic algorithms, and big data.

Giner Alor-Hernandez is a researcher of the Division of Research and Postgraduate Studies of the Instituto Tecnologico de Orizaba. He received an MSc and a PhD in Computer Science of the Center for Research and Advanced Studies of the National Polytechnic Institute (CINVESTAV), Mexico. He has headed ten Mexican research projects granted by CONACYT, DGEST and PROMEP. He is author/coauthor around 130 journal and conference papers in computer science. He has been a committee program member of around 30 international conferences sponsored by IEEE, ACM and Springer and editorial board member of five indexed journals. He has been guest editor of four JCR-indexed journals (CMMM, JMS, IJSEKE, JET&S). He is the principal author of the book entitled "Frameworks, Methodologies, and Tools for Developing Rich Internet Applications" by IGI Global Publishing. His research interests include Web services, e-commerce, Semantic Web, Web 2.0, service-oriented architectures and enterprise application integration. He is an IEEE and ACM member. He is a National Researcher recognized by the National Council of Science & Technology of Mexico (CONACYT). ORCID: 0000-0003-3296-0981, Scopus Author ID: 17433252100.

Iqra Ameer is a second year PhD. student. Her doctoral research classifies the emotions from text. She holds a Master from NLP Laboratory of Centro de Investigación en Computación, Instituto Politécnico Nacional, Mexico that classified author profiling on text.

Juan Carlos Bonilla Robles is a member of the Universidad Autónoma del Estado de Morelos.

Maritza Bustos-López received the M.Sc. degree and a Ph.D. degree in Engineering Sciences in the Instituto Tecnológico de Orizaba. Her research interests include machine learning, natural language processing, opinion mining, sentiment analysis, and recommender systems.

German Castillo graduated in Information Technology and acquired an interest for researching, which initially led him to collaborate in the IPN research centre (CICATA) in the oceanography area specifically in the image processing of the Lansad-7 satellite for the coast of the state of Tamaulipas. In 2014, he decided to follow the path of computer science in natural language area and with this, contribute to the improvement of systems with query composition interfaces. Currently, he is a project leader in a private company collaborating with the development of computer systems and optimization processes within warehouses.

Karina Castro-Pérez has a degree in Computer Systems Engineering (2017), is currently a student in the Master's program in Computer Systems at the Instituto Tecnológico de Orizaba, and she is an author in international congresses. His current research focuses on opinion mining, machine learning, natural language processing, and information retrieval using web scraping techniques.

Roberto Contreras is a Ph.D. student at the Universidad Autónoma de Ciudad Juarez. He is also a teacher at the National Institute of Technology of Mexico, teaching Computer Science. He holds two MS degrees, one in Administration and another in Computer Science. He has participated in many conferences across Latin America as a speaker of emerging technologies.

Jesus Fernandez-Avelino, who received his degree in Computer Systems Engineering in 2017, is currently a student in the Master's degree program in Computer Systems at the National Institute of Technology of Mexico. His current research focuses on Natural Language Processing for Spanish, and Automatic Code Generation of native apps for iOS and Android.

Rogelio Florencia-Juárez received the PhD degree in Computer Science from Tijuana Institute of Technology, Mexico, in 2016. He received the M.Sc. degree in Computer Science from Madero Institute of Technology, Mexico, in 2010. He is currently full-time Professor of the Software and Computer Systems Engineering at Universidad Autónoma de Ciudad Juárez, México and he is a member of the Mexican National System of Researchers (SNI) since 2019. His research interests are in the areas of natural language processing, knowledge representation machine learning and data analysis.

Juan Frausto Solís has a PhD in Electrotechnique from the Institute Nationale Polytechnique de Grenoble (INPG) & Ecole Centrale de Lyon. His master's studies are in two fields: Electrical Engineering (INPG) and Corporative Finance (UDALAP, Mexico). He was a Project Manager and Researcher at the National Institute of Electricity and Clean Energy (INEEL, before IIE) of the Hydrothermic Coordination Project. He was Head of a Graduate program at Monterrey Institute of Technology and Higher Education, and professor in several universities as the Fudan University (Shanghai, China). His main research areas are Mathematical and Optimization models for Artificial Intelligence, Energy, Forecasting, Decision Making Models, and Natural Language Processing. Now, he is a researcher at the Tecnológico National de México.

Vicente García Jiménez is a full-time professor since 2014 in the Department of Electrical and Computer Engineering at the Universidad Autónoma de Ciudad Juárez. He received the bachelor degree on Computer Systems from the Villahermosa Institute of Technology (Mexico) in 2000, the Master degree on Computer Science from the Toluca Institute of Technology (Mexico) in 2002, and, in 2010, the Ph.D. degree on Advanced Computer Systems from the Jaume I University of Castellón de la Plana, Spain. From 2010 to 2013, he worked at the Institute of New Imaging Technologies, Spain. He is a member of the IEEE, the ACM, and the Mexican Academy of Computing. Professor García Jiménez is the author or co-author of articles in prestigious journals, as well as publications at national and international conferences. His work has more than 2,00 citations. He has served as a guest editor for the International Journal of Combinatorial Optimization Problems and Informatics and Applied Sciences. He currently belongs to the (Mexican) National System of Researchers with level 1. His interests fall within the areas of pattern recognition, machine learning, data mining, data science, big data, including classification, data preprocessing, multiple classification systems, data complexity, unbalanced classes, as well, prediction and diagnosis techniques in quality control in the industry, credit rating, business bankruptcies, and DNA microarrays.

Alonso Garcia Del Rio is a computer engineer since 2018. He is currently studying for a master's degree in applied soft computing.

Juana Gaspar obtained her master's degree in computer science from the Tecnológico Nacional de México. Currently, she is pursuing a PhD Degree in Computer Science.

Alexander Gelbukh is a research professor and the Head of the Natural Language Processing Laboratory of the Center for Computing Research of the Instituto Politécnico Nacional, Mexico, Honorary Professor of the Amity University, India, and Invited Professor of the National University of Colombia. He has been a visiting researcher at the University of Wolverhampton, UK, invited researcher at the Waseda University, Japan, and distinguished visiting professor at the Chung-Ang University, Korea. He is a member of the Mexican Academy of Sciences and founding member of the Mexican Academy of Computing. He has been the president of the Mexican Society for Artificial Intelligence and founding president of the Mexican Association of Natural Language Processing. His main areas of interest include computational linguistics, natural language processing, and artificial intelligence, recently with a focus on sentiment analysis and opinion mining. He is an author or co-author of more than 500 publications, including eight books. He is an editor-in-chief, associate editor, or member of the editorial board for more than 20 international journals; he is the founder and chair of the CICLing series of international conferences. He was a Chair, Honorary Chair, or Program Committee Chair of over 40 international conferences. He has been advisor of more than 30 PhD students in universities of six countries.

Juan González obtained a PhD in Computer Science, major in Artificial Intelligence and NLP (Natural Language Processing) from the National Research and Technological Development Center, Mexico (2006). His research areas are Metaheuristics, Optimization and Machine Learning, and Artificial Intelligence. He works at the National Institute of Technology of Mexico where he started the LanTI research centre, where he leads the research line in Optimization and Artificial Intelligence.

Martha Victoria Gonzalez obtained a degree in Computer Engineering from Universidad Autónoma de Ciudad Juárez, and a Master of Science in Information and Communication Sciences from Ball State University (USA), she is a full time professor at Departamento de Ingenieria Electrica y Computacion at Universidad Autonoma de Ciudad Juarez (Mexico), her research interest include human computer interaction and user centered design.

José Guzmán Mendoza is a full-time professor in the Universidad Politécnica de Aguascalientes.

Rafael Jimenez is currently a master student at the Autonomous University of Ciudad Juárez. His interests include NLP, text mining, classification, and data visualization.

Namrata Kumari is a Ph.D. scholar in the Department of Computer Science and Engineering at the National Institute of Technology, Hamirpur. Her area of research is Natural Language Processing. She did her M.Tech. from Banasthali University, Jaipur.

Irvin López is a master's student in applied computing, in the area of artificial intelligence at the Autonomous University of Ciudad Juárez.

Abraham López Nájera is an engineer in computer systems, graduated from the Universidad Autónoma de Ciudad Juárez. He has a postgraduate degree in information technology management, graduated from ITESM. He is currently a full-time professor at the Universidad Autónoma de Ciudad Juárez.

Ivan Lopez-Arevalo received the Ph.D. degree in Artificial Intelligence from the Technical University of Catalonia (Barcelona) in 2006. Currently is Associate Professor at Cinvestav Tamaulipas (Mexico). His major research interests include different topics from Semantic Web, Data Analytics, and Cloud Computing.

Francisco López-Orozco is an associate professor in the software and computer systems engineering undergraduate programs at UACJ. He obtained his Ph.D. from the University of Grenoble, France, in 2013. He is a co-founder and permanent member of the Laboratory of Emerging Technologies in Computer Science (LABTEC2) at UACJ. His research focuses on cognitive computational and experimental psychology, human-computer interaction, and user-centered design.

Jaime I. Lopez-Veyna obtained a degree in Computer Sciences from the Instituto Tecnologico de Zacatecas (Mexico) in 1997. In 2001 received his M.S. degree from the Instituto Tecnologico de Toluca (Mexico) and the Ph.D. in Computer Sciences from the Laboratorio de Tecnologias de Informacion del Centro de Investigacion y Estudios Avanzados (CINVESTAV), in 2014. From 2015 to 2017 was a postdoctoral researcher at the Barcelona Supercomputing Center (Spain) in the Computer Sciences Department and Data Storage group. Currently, he is a Professor at the Instituto Tecnologico de Zacatecas (Mexico). His research interests include machine learning, big data, chatbots, and graph databases.

C. Mahender is an Assistant Professor, Department of CS and IT, Dr. Babasaheb Ambedkar Marathwada University, Aurangabad (India).

Ricardo Mar Cupido is a software engineering student from the Universidad Autónoma de Ciudad Juárez.

José Martínez F. graduated as a computer systems engineer in 1992 from the Instituto Tecnológico de Ciudad Madero (Tecnológico Nacional de México). Dr. Martínez concluded an MS program in Computer Science in 1996 at the Centro Nacional de Investigación y Desarrollo Tecnológico (Tecnológico

Nacional de México) and received the PhD in Computer Science from the Centro Nacional de Investigación y Desarrollo Tecnológico (Tecnológico Nacional de México) in 2006. He is currently working as researcher-professor at the Instituto Tecnológico de Ciudad Madero (Tecnológico Nacional de México). Dr. Martínez has published more than 10 articles in journals and over 22 papers in conference proceedings on natural language interfaces, distributed database systems and optimization algorithms.

Marcos Eduardo Martinez-Quezada is a graduate in computer engineering of the Universidad Autónoma de Ciudad Juárez. He is studying for a master's degree in applied computing. His research interests are NLP and automatic speech recognition.

Jose L. Martinez-Rodriguez received his Ph.D. in Computer Science from Cinvestav Tamaulipas in 2018. He is currently a full-time professor at the Autonomous University of Tamaulipas, Reynosa, Mexico. His research interests include The Semantic Web, Data Mining, and Information Extraction.

Jose Mejia received his MS and Ph.D. from the Universidad Autónoma de CiudadJuárez (México). He has worked for the consumer electronics and automotive industry as an electronic designer and as a consultant. He is currently a professor at Universidad Autónoma de Ciudad Juárez. His research interests include statistical image-signal processing and machine learning.

Alejandra Mendoza Carreón has a Master of Science degree in Computer Science by the University of Texas at Dallas, and a B. Eng. in Digital Systems and Communications by the Universidad Autónoma de Ciudad Juárez.

Martín Montes Rivera is a professor of artificial intelligence, bio-inspired control, process control, soft computing, pattern recognition, and expert systems in the Department of Research and Postgraduate Studies at the Universidad Politécnica de Aguascalientes (México).

Alberto Ochoa is a full-time professor in the Technology Doctorate program at UACJ; his research is involved in artificial intelligence applied to improve problems related to smart cities and Industry 4.0

Diego Oliva received a BS degree in Electronics and Computer Engineering from the Industrial Technical Education Centre (CETI) of Guadalajara, Mexico in 2007, the M.Sc. degree in Electronic Engineering and Computer Sciences from the University of Guadalajara, Mexico in 2010 and the Ph. D. degree with distinction in Informatics from the Complutense University of Madrid, Spain in 2015. Currently, he is a full-time professor at the University of Guadalajara. His current research interests include computer vision, image processing, artificial intelligence and metaheuristic optimization algorithms.

Karla Olmos-Sánchez completed her doctorate studies in engineering sciences at the Universidad Autónoma de Ciudad Juárez and a master's degree in Computer Sciences from CENIDET. His main line of research is Knowledge Engineering applied to requirements elicitation. She is currently working on developing cognitive solutions for the Health sector.

Javier Ortiz-Hernández is a Ph.D. in Automation and Computer Science, Automation Laboratory of Besançon, National School of Mechanics and Microtechnics, France (1995). Thesis: "Socio-technical

Approach of Automated Systems." Development of computer models for the automotive sector group GIE-Recherche PSA-Renault, explicitly incorporating various views of the processes of value aggregation of industrial activity. Master of Computer Science, National Polytechnic Institute, Mexico, D.F. (1991). Thesis: Expert System of Selection and Acquisition of Technical Information at the International Level." For the processing of information requests in the Information Unit of the Electrical Research Institute.

Joaquín Pérez Ortega has Master and Doctorate's Degrees by The Monterrey Institute of Technology and Higher Education (ITESM). Since 1989, he has been a professor at the National Center for Research and Technological Development (CENIDET). He previously worked at The Electric Research Institute (IIE), Cuernavaca, Morelos, Mexico (1985-2001). Also, Joaquin Perez is a member of the National System of Researchers (SNI), Level II, and Senior Member number 00832766 of IEEE since 2005. Research interests span many areas, including Data Science, Heuristic algorithms, Data Mining, Combinatorial Optimization, Databases, Big Data, and Software Engineering.

Julio Ponce Gallegos is a full-time professor to the Department of Computer Science, Autonomous University of Aguascalientes (UAA). Ph.D. in Computer Science from the UAA (Mexico). Currently, Head of the Department of Computer Science. Member of the Academic Corps of Intelligent Systems. Professor in UAA graduate programs, Doctorate in Applied Sciences and Technology, Master of Science with an option to Computation and Applied Mathematics. Author of books and articles on the lines of Artificial Intelligence, and Educational Technology.

Benito Alan Ponce Rodríguez is a professor at the Universidad Autónoma de Ciudad Juárez. Research interest: Artificial intelligence, Data Science, Machine and Deep Learning, and NLP.

Raúl Porras Alaniz is passionate about mathematical modeling and artificial intelligence (AI), to promote AI techniques in the country's agriculture. His first encounter with bio-inspired metaheuristics was during his undergraduate studies; here, he parallelized the operations of an ACO algorithm. Since then, Raúl began to have an increasing interest in learning more about this type of AI techniques. So, he decided to get a master's degree through the development of a PSO algorithm for the shipping industry, which seeks the best compromise solutions taking into account the decision-maker preferences in a case study of the scheduling problem.

Carlos Manuel Ramírez López, an electronic engineer, currently about to complete the master's degree in Engineering Sciences with a major in networks and systems, more than ten years of experience in the area of telecommunications and computer systems. He is working at the State Center for Telecommunications C-4, responsible for the 911 Emergency Service Telephony as well as administrative support in the State Radio Communication Network.

Alejandro Requejo is a software engineer based in Mexico working with web technologies.

Ana B. Rios-Alvarado obtained her Ph.D. degree in Computer Science from Cinvestav Tamaulipas in 2013. She is currently a full-time professor at the Autonomous University of Tamaulipas, Victoria (Mexico); her research interests include text mining and knowledge representation.

Jorge Rodas-Osollo is a researcher professor of the UACJ since 1998, working on several areas of Artificial Intelligence (AI), including knowledge acquisition for developing knowledge-based systems, machine learning, and intelligent data analysis. Jorge is working in the development and deployment of several intelligent systems and medical research protocols, in collaboration with the Sistema Estatal de Salud (SES) and the Unidad de Investigación de Salud (UIS) since 2003.

Lisbeth Rodríguez-Mazahua holds a B.Sc. degree in Informatics and an M.Sc. degree in Computer Science from the Instituto Tecnológico de Orizaba, in 2004 and 2007, respectively. In 2012 she got a Ph.D. in Computer Science from the Center for Research and Advanced Studies of the CINVESTAV. Her recent research interests include distributed database design, database theory, autonomic database systems, multimedia databases, data mining, and big data.

Alejandro Ruiz is a computer science student from the Universidad Autónoma de Ciudad Juárez.

María del Pilar Salas-Zárate received her Ph.D. degree in Computer Science from the University of Murcia, Spain. She holds B.E. and M.Sc. degrees in Computer System Engineering from the Instituto Tecnológico de Orizaba (México). Her recent research is focused on sentiment analysis, natural language processing, and figurative language detection. She has published several articles in journals indexed in JCR and book chapters and taken part in several conferences. She has participated in nine research projects. She is a member of the (Mexican) National System of Researches (SNI-I) and the Computing Mexican Academy. SCOPUS ID: 56326000900.

José Luis Sánchez-Cervantes has a Ph.D. in Computer Science and Technology from the Carlos III University of Madrid, Spain. As of October 2016, he is a CONACYT (National Council of Science & Technology of Mexico) professor commissioned as a full-time researcher at the Technological Institute of Orizaba, an institution in which he made a postdoctoral stay. He graduated from the Master in Computer Systems and is received as an Engineer in Computer Systems at the Technological Institute of Orizaba. He is the author/co-author of several research papers in computer science published in journals indexed in the JCR, as well as in peer-reviewed journals and reports of national and international congresses. His research interests include the Semantic Web, Linked Data (Linked Open Data), Social Media, Big Data, and the Internet of Things. He is an ACM member and Computing Mexican Academy adherent member, and he is a National Researcher recognized by the CONACYT. ORCID: http://orcid.org/0000-0001-5194-1263.

Juan Paulo Sánchez-Hernández obtained a PhD in computer science from the Monterrey Institute of Technology and Higher Education. He also has a Master's Degree in Computer Science. His main research area is artificial intelligence, particularly, optimization, computer vision, and machine learning. He has published papers in journals with international indexes and rigorous review.

Laura Nely Sánchez-Morales is a PhD student of the Division of Research and Postgraduate Studies at the Instituto Tecnológico de Orizaba. She received an MSc degree in Computer Systems from the Instituto Tecnológico de Orizaba (Mexico). Her research interests include image processing, neuronal networks, UI design patterns, automatic software generation and mobile applications.

Julia Patricia Sanchez-Solis received the PhD degree in Computer Science (in 2017) from the Mexican National Institute of Technology. She is currently a full-time professor at the Universidad Autónoma de Ciudad Juárez (Mexico). Besides, she is a Member of the (Mexican) National System of Researchers. Her research interests are in the areas of evolutionary multi-objective optimization, multi-criteria decision making, applied soft computing, and project portfolio selection.

Sanah Sayyed is a Research Scholar, Dept of CS and IT, Dr. Babasaheb Ambedkar Marathwada University, Aurangabad.

Grigori Sidorov is a full-time professor and researcher at Natural Language and Text Processing Laboratory, Centro de Investigación en Computación, Instituto Politécnico Nacional Mexico City (Mexico). His research interests are text processing techniques and systems, automatic dictionary processing, automatic morphological analysis of different languages, automatic syntactic analysis, anaphora resolution, word sense disambiguation, corpus linguistics, parallel texts, and linguistic software development.

Pardeep Singh is currently working as an Assistant Professor in the Department of Computer Science and Engineering at the National Institute of Technology, Hamirpur, and he did his Ph.D. in the area of Natural Language Processing (NLP). He also obtained a B. Tech. in Computer Science & Engineering from the Guru Nanak Dev University, Amritsar, Punjab (India). He has been in the faculty of the National Institute of Technology, Hamirpur, since Aug 2006. He has guided sixteen graduate theses and published about 48 papers at National and International levels. His research interests are in the domains of NLP, empirical linguistic, and machine learning. He is a member of ISTE, the International Association of Computer Science & Information Technology (IACSIT), and the International Association of Engineers (IAENG). In his leisure, he engages in photography. He is fluent in Hindi, English and Punjabi languages.

Maritza Varela Alvarez is a graduate of the Computer Engineering Program from the Universidad Autónoma de Ciudad Juárez. She worked as a high school teacher and later worked in the Jonhson Controls company, where the files of the car seat patterns were digitized. She has a Master in Free Software from the Universidad Autónoma de Chihuahua. She has been teaching computer science for seven years at universities. She is an expert in Web development, and she has expertise in programming languages like C, C ++, C #, Java, PHP, as well as SQL Server and MySQL database managers.

Andrea Vega-Villalobos is a Ph.D. student at the National Institute of Technology of Mexico / CENIDET.

Andres Verastegui is a PhD candidate at the Instituto Tecnológico de Cd. Madero. Area of interest: Artificial intelligence.

Ossiel Villanueva-Mendoza is a Computer Systems Engineer, graduated from the Universidad Autónoma de Ciudad Juárez in 2019.

Lucero Zamora Merino is a teacher at the Universidad Autónoma de Ciudad Juárez for the Computer Engineering Program. She has a master´s degree in Free Software from the Universidad Autónoma de Chihuahua.

Crispín Zavala-Díaz has a Ph.D. in Computer Sciences from the Monterrey Institute of Technology and Higher Studies, Professor-researcher at the Autonomous University of the State of Morelos for 20 years. Research lines: construction of solutions to combinatorial optimization problems, and development and improvement of clustering algorithms.

Index

A

Abstractive 46, 48-50, 52-54, 63, 67-69, 368-372, 374-378, 380, 382-384, 390-391

Abstractive Approaches 368

Anaphora Resolution 46, 48, 56-59, 66, 309-311, 313, 316-318, 321, 323-325

Automatic Personality Classification 266

Automatic Text Summarization 63, 67, 310, 368, 377-379, 381

Avatar Representation 180

B

Bag of Words 34, 86, 227, 232, 237-238, 240, 242, 248, 455, 457, 459, 470, 477-479

Bagging Classifier 438-440, 481, 493

Big Data 43, 67, 147, 289-290, 293-294, 296, 299, 303-308, 351, 423, 442, 450

C

Characters n-gram 245

Chatbots 32, 37-39, 42-45, 102-104, 117, 130, 133, 135-137, 139-146, 148-150, 153, 155

Chronic-Degenerative Diseases 445, 447, 454, 456, 458, 466, 471, 473

Classification 33, 90-91, 93, 143-145, 161, 183, 188, 227-229, 231-235, 237-238, 240, 243-244, 247-248, 251, 256-258, 261-263, 266, 276, 285, 292-293, 295, 299, 306-307, 348-350, 367, 371, 404, 425, 427, 429-430, 436-440, 442-443, 446-448, 451-453, 455, 459, 462-463, 467, 470, 475-476, 482-483, 485-486, 492, 494

Clustering 50, 53, 67, 242-243, 289-291, 294-296, 303-308, 348, 366, 378, 425, 429, 485, 498

Coherent 7, 55, 107, 214, 352, 378, 382

Completeness 322, 378, 419, 449

D

Data Mining 194-195, 243, 289, 307-308, 331, 344, 366, 411, 437, 474-476, 483

Data Science 289, 391

Decision Support System 195

Domain Independence 5, 12, 20, 196-198, 224

Domain-Independent Interface 70

Drugs Opinion 445

E

Eagle Standard 309-310, 312, 319-320, 323

Empirical Bayesian Kriging 327, 330-331, 338, 344-346

Exhaustive Algorithm 157, 166

Extractive 46-50, 52, 63, 67-68, 304, 306-307, 368-371, 374-375, 377-380, 382-385, 390-391

Extractive Approaches 379

Extractive Methods 50, 368, 382-383

Extrinsic 374, 378

F

Filtering 86, 91, 148, 183, 228, 232, 308, 351, 364, 451

G

Goodness of Pronunciation 31, 38-39, 43-44

Computational Linguistics

Computational Linguistics 1, 28-30, 67-68, 97-100, 154, 158, 161, 175, 262, 264-265, 311, 325, 366, 377-378, 422, 424-425, 463, 497

Conversational Agent(s) 14, 101, 107, 109, 111, 116-117, 119-121, 130, 135-136, 149

Conversational Skills 101, 104

Corpus to Tests 70

Purchase Print, E-Book, or Print + E-Book

IGI Global's reference books are available in three unique pricing formats:
Print Only, E-Book Only, or Print + E-Book.
Shipping fees may apply.

www.igi-global.com

Recommended Reference Books

ISBN: 978-1-5225-5912-2
© 2019; 349 pp.
List Price: $215

ISBN: 978-1-5225-8176-5
© 2019; 2,218 pp.
List Price: $2,950

ISBN: 978-1-5225-7811-6
© 2019; 317 pp.
List Price: $225

ISBN: 978-1-5225-7268-8
© 2019; 316 pp.
List Price: $215

ISBN: 978-1-5225-7455-2
© 2019; 288 pp.
List Price: $205

ISBN: 978-1-5225-8973-0
© 2019; 200 pp.
List Price: $195

Do you want to stay current on the latest research trends, product announcements, news and special offers?
Join IGI Global's mailing list today and start enjoying exclusive perks sent only to IGI Global members.
Add your name to the list at **www.igi-global.com/newsletters**.

Publisher of Peer-Reviewed, Timely, and Innovative Academic Research

IGI Global
DISSEMINATOR OF KNOWLEDGE

www.igi-global.com ✉ Sign up at www.igi-global.com/newsletters f facebook.com/igiglobal t twitter.com/igiglobal in linkedin.com/igiglobal

Ensure Quality Research is Introduced to the Academic Community

Become an IGI Global Reviewer for Authored Book Projects

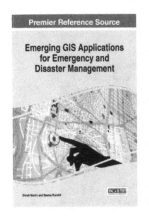
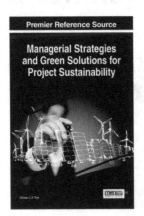

The overall success of an authored book project is dependent on quality and timely reviews.

In this competitive age of scholarly publishing, constructive and timely feedback significantly expedites the turnaround time of manuscripts from submission to acceptance, allowing the publication and discovery of forward-thinking research at a much more expeditious rate. Several IGI Global authored book projects are currently seeking highly-qualified experts in the field to fill vacancies on their respective editorial review boards:

Applications and Inquiries may be sent to:
development@igi-global.com

Applicants must have a doctorate (or an equivalent degree) as well as publishing and reviewing experience. Reviewers are asked to complete the open-ended evaluation questions with as much detail as possible in a timely, collegial, and constructive manner. All reviewers' tenures run for one-year terms on the editorial review boards and are expected to complete at least three reviews per term. Upon successful completion of this term, reviewers can be considered for an additional term.

If you have a colleague that may be interested in this opportunity, we encourage you to share this information with them.

IGI Global Proudly Partners With eContent Pro International

Receive a 25% Discount on all Editorial Services

Editorial Services

IGI Global expects all final manuscripts submitted for publication to be in their final form. This means they must be reviewed, revised, and professionally copy edited prior to their final submission. Not only does this support with accelerating the publication process, but it also ensures that the highest quality scholarly work can be disseminated.

English Language Copy Editing

Let eContent Pro International's expert copy editors perform edits on your manuscript to resolve spelling, punctuaion, grammar, syntax, flow, formatting issues and more.

Scientific and Scholarly Editing

Allow colleagues in your research area to examine the content of your manuscript and provide you with valuable feedback and suggestions before submission.

Figure, Table, Chart & Equation Conversions

Do you have poor quality figures? Do you need visual elements in your manuscript created or converted? A design expert can help!

Translation

Need your documjent translated into English? eContent Pro International's expert translators are fluent in English and more than 40 different languages.

Hear What Your Colleagues are Saying About Editorial Services Supported by IGI Global

"The service was very fast, very thorough, and very helpful in ensuring our chapter meets the criteria and requirements of the book's editors. I was quite impressed and happy with your service."

– Prof. Tom Brinthaupt,
Middle Tennessee State University, USA

"I found the work actually spectacular. The editing, formatting, and other checks were very thorough. The turnaround time was great as well. I will definitely use eContent Pro in the future."

– Nickanor Amwata, Lecturer,
University of Kurdistan Hawler, Iraq

"I was impressed that it was done timely, and wherever the content was not clear for the reader, the paper was improved with better readability for the audience."

– Prof. James Chilembwe,
Mzuzu University, Malawi

Email: customerservice@econtentpro.com   www.igi-global.com/editorial-service-partners

www.igi-global.com

Celebrating Over 30 Years of Scholarly
Knowledge Creation & Dissemination

InfoSci®-Books

A Database of Over 5,300+ Reference Books Containing Over 100,000+ Chapters Focusing on Emerging Research

GAIN ACCESS TO **THOUSANDS** OF REFERENCE BOOKS AT **A FRACTION** OF THEIR INDIVIDUAL LIST **PRICE**.

InfoSci®-Books Database

The **InfoSci®-Books** database is a collection of over 5,300+ IGI Global single and multi-volume reference books, handbooks of research, and encyclopedias, encompassing groundbreaking research from prominent experts worldwide that span over 350+ topics in 11 core subject areas including business, computer science, education, science and engineering, social sciences and more.

Open Access Fee Waiver (Offset Model) Initiative

For any library that invests in IGI Global's InfoSci-Journals and/or InfoSci-Books databases, IGI Global will match the library's investment with a fund of equal value to go toward **subsidizing the OA article processing charges (APCs) for their students, faculty, and staff** at that institution when their work is submitted and accepted under OA into an IGI Global journal.*

INFOSCI® PLATFORM FEATURES

- No DRM
- No Set-Up or Maintenance Fees
- A Guarantee of No More Than a 5% Annual Increase
- Full-Text HTML and PDF Viewing Options
- Downloadable MARC Records
- Unlimited Simultaneous Access
- COUNTER 5 Compliant Reports
- Formatted Citations With Ability to Export to RefWorks and EasyBib
- No Embargo of Content (Research is Available Months in Advance of the Print Release)

*The fund will be offered on an annual basis and expire at the end of the subscription period. The fund would renew as the subscription is renewed for each year thereafter. The open access fees will be waived after the student, faculty, or staff's paper has been vetted and accepted into an IGI Global journal and the fund can only be used toward publishing OA in an IGI Global journal. Libraries in developing countries will have the match on their investment doubled.

To Learn More or To Purchase This Database:
www.igi-global.com/infosci-books

www.igi-global.com

eresources@igi-global.com • Toll Free: 1-866-342-6657 ext. 100 • Phone: 717-533-8845 x100

www.igi-global.com

Publisher of Peer-Reviewed, Timely, and
Innovative Academic Research Since 1988

IGI Global's Transformative Open Access (OA) Model:
How to Turn Your University Library's Database Acquisitions Into a Source of OA Funding

In response to the OA movement and well in advance of Plan S, IGI Global, early last year, unveiled their OA Fee Waiver (Read & Publish) Initiative.

Under this initiative, librarians who invest in IGI Global's InfoSci-Books (5,300+ reference books) and/or InfoSci-Journals (185+ scholarly journals) databases will be able to subsidize their patron's OA article processing charges (APC) when their work is submitted and accepted (after the peer review process) into an IGI Global journal. *See website for details.

How Does it Work?

1. When a library subscribes or perpetually purchases IGI Global's InfoSci-Databases and/or their discipline/subject-focused subsets, IGI Global will match the library's investment with a fund of equal value to go toward subsidizing the OA article processing charges (APCs) for their patrons.

   Researchers: **Be sure to recommend the InfoSci-Books and InfoSci-Journals to take advantage of this initiative.**

2. When a student, faculty, or staff member submits a paper and it is accepted (following the peer review) into one of IGI Global's 185+ scholarly journals, the author will have the option to have their paper published under a traditional publishing model or as OA.

3. When the author chooses to have their paper published under OA, IGI Global will notify them of the OA Fee Waiver (Read and Publish) Initiative. If the author decides they would like to take advantage of this initiative, IGI Global will deduct the US$ 2,000 APC from the created fund.

4. This fund will be offered on an annual basis and will renew as the subscription is renewed for each year thereafter. IGI Global will manage the fund and award the APC waivers unless the librarian has a preference as to how the funds should be managed.

Hear From the Experts on This Initiative:

"I'm very happy to have been able to make one of my recent research contributions, "Visualizing the Social Media Conversations of a National Information Technology Professional Association" featured in the *International Journal of Human Capital and Information Technology Professionals*, freely available along with having access to the valuable resources found within IGI Global's InfoSci-Journals database."

– Prof. Stuart Palmer,
Deakin University, Australia

For More Information, Visit: www.igi-global.com/publish/contributor-resources/open-access/read-publish-model
or contact IGI Global's Database Team at eresources@igi-global.com.